SPORT SOCIOLOGY

SPORT SOCIOLOGY

Contemporary Themes

Andrew Yiannakis

Thomas D. McIntyre

Merrill J. Melnick

Dale P. Hart

SUNY at Brockport

KENDALL/HUNT PUBLISHING COMPANY
Dubuque, Iowa

Contents

Preface

Since the publication in 1969 of John Loy and Gerald Kenyon's reader *Sport, Culture, and Society*, several other anthologies have followed. One may well ask, therefore, "why another reader?" The fact is, the study of sport from a socio-cultural perspective has generated a substantial amount of literature in recent years. New themes and areas of interest have emerged, and the discipline of Sport Sociology has undergone substantial systematization. The editors believe that there is now a need for an anthology which captures and articulates the excitement of the contemporary literature, and, which attempts to present it in as lucid and intelligible manner as possible.

The articles in this book, while retaining the integrity of the discipline, reflect careful selection and screening. The majority have been "tried and tested" in the classroom with most favorable results. Recently published articles which have not been used in the classroom were evaluated by the editors for suitability with the needs and interests of the student in mind.

While the book is intended for beginning and intermediate level students of sport and society, some prior exposure to course work in the social sciences is advisable. However, in the absence of such a background, we have attempted to remedy the situation and assist students by including unit introductions. It is recommended that they be read prior to embarking on a specific unit since they highlight some of the major concepts and ideas contained in specific selections. In order to further assist the reader, both general and specific discussion questions are included at the end of each unit. These complement the unit introductions and are intended to guide both student and instructor in terms of "what to look for" in reading a particular article. The answers to these questions should also provide the student with a helpful review of the article for reference in small group discussion, and in writing papers and essays.

This anthology consists of forty-three articles organized into twelve teaching units. Seven of these units are unique in the sense that they present concepts or themes which, heretofore, have received only minimal attention in published form. Units such as *The American Sports Hero* (edited by Melnick), *Violence in Sport* (edited by Hart), *Adult-Sponsored Activities for Children* (edited by McIntyre), and *Sport Subcultures* (edited by Yiannakis) reflect some of the special interests and expertise of the editors; others, such as *Sport, Politics and Economics, An Assessment of the Value of Competition* and *The Future of American Sport* attempt to capture contemporary themes and/or problems. While it is recommended that the units be read in the order in which they are presented, to preserve topic continuity, each unit is sufficiently self-contained to be dealt with as a separate entity or to supplement other related readings.

A book such as this owes a debt of gratitude to many. In particular, we wish to thank all those contributors and publishers whose works appear in this edition.

The Editors
Brockport, New York

Unit I

The Sociological Study of Sport

This perspective, in its broadest sense, employs theoretical frameworks and the empirical tools of the social sciences to aid man in better understanding human behavior in sport contexts. All the research tools available to the sociologist, social psychologist, and anthropologist can and have been used in an effort to ascertain the manifest and latent functions of sport in modern society. As in any other scientific effort, scholars with an interest in sport have also attempted to describe, discover, and explain this phenomenon with the eventual goal being the prediction of sport-related human social behavior. The student of human social behavior must be constantly aware of the fact that prediction of behavior is not absolute but is necessarily stated in probabilistic terms.

In the initial selection, sociologists Eldon Snyder and Elmer Spreitzer address their remarks primarily to the sport sociologist. The major thrust of this article is their critique of the strengths and weaknesses of the sociological study of sport. Whereas the authors are advocating adoption of sport sociology by the discipline of sociology, there are many scholars in the field who would argue that sport sociology has already achieved an independent status as a discipline with its own focus of attention (sport), modes of inquiry (methods of the social sciences) and a unique body of knowledge (sport studies).

In the second selection, sport social psychologist, Rainer Martens, outlines a number of fundamental topics associated with the social psychology of physical activity. He also makes it quite clear that a social analysis approach is necessary if an integrated body of knowledge is to be forthcoming.

SOCIOLOGY OF SPORT: AN OVERVIEW

Eldon E. Snyder—Elmer Spreitzer

This review sketches some strengths and weaknesses in the subfield and its potential for generating and testing theoretical frameworks. The analysis includes research on sport from the following perspectives: interinstitutional relationships, social stratification, small groups, and social psychology. In recent years, the sociology of sport has become more sophisticated in terms of research questions posed, research design, quantitative analysis, and cross-cultural comparisons. As one dimension of leisure, sports represent a serious topic for scholarly research to round out our understanding of the human person as a social being.

The sociology of sport has yet to become a mainline specialty within the discipline, and some might question whether it should ever become one. Given the proliferation of specializations within sociology, we might ask to what end is such elaboration of descriptive content directed? In other words, does a discipline grow by spinning off more and more content areas, or does it develop through the creation of paradigms that are generic in nature. The "hard" sciences did not develop by continually carving out new content areas; rather, they developed through the creation of theoretical frameworks that transcended specific content. Why, then, should we legitimate an area such as the sociology of sport by instituting journals and convention sessions on that topic, textbooks and courses, and state-of-the-field articles?

We suggest that sport as a substantive topic has as much claim on the sociologist's attention as the more conventional specialties of family, religion, political, and industrial sociology. Sports and games are cultural universals and basic institutions in societies, and are some of the most pervasive aspects of culture in in-

Reprinted from *The Sociological Quarterly*, Vol. 15, No. 4 (Fall), 1974, pp. 467-487.

dustrialized societies. Moreover, all of the traditional content areas are, in principle, equal—unless we impose a value judgment of some type to assert that some institutional spheres are more important. Empirically, we could impose a hierarchy on the content areas in terms of their lineage (religion via Weber would be high here) or in terms of their explanatory power (economic sociology would be high here).

Basically, we argue that a sociologist studies sports for the same reasons as any other topic—for intrinsic interest and to impose sociological frameworks as a means of constructing and refining concepts, propositions, and theories from the larger discipline.[1] A scholar's claim, however, on institutional and societal resources to pursue one's intrinsic interests does not carry much weight these days. We suggest that the sociology of sport is of value to the larger discipline primarily in terms of its capacity to serve as a fertile testing ground for the generating and testing of theoretical frameworks. Sociology will not grow by filling in dots on the canvas of social life; rather, it grows by imposing order on clusters of dots. Substantive specialties such as the sociology of sport can feed back to the larger discipline in terms of concept formation, theory construction, and theory verification. Glaser and Straus (1967) recommend the inductive approach to theory building through wrestling with empirical content and ultimately deriving generic frameworks that are applicable to a variety of subject areas. From a theory verification perspective, substantive areas such as the sociology of sport represent a testing ground to explore the generality and explanatory power of theories in a variety of social settings.

One might suggest that the sociology of sport is a species of the sociology of leisure. Clearly, sport could be subsumed under leisure studies as simply another way in which people spend their discretionary time. Since both the sociology of leisure and sport focus on the non-instrumental facets of social life, they probably will merge into a more generic specialization such as the sociology of expressive behavior. Presently, however, the two content specialties are very distinct in the sense of having their own associations, conventions, professional registers, journals, and sessions within the conventions of general sociology. Given the separate evolution of the two specialties of leisure and sports, the present analysis focuses solely on sports.[2]

The phenomenon of sport represents one of the most pervasive social institutions in the United States. Sports permeate all levels of social reality from the societal down to the social psychological levels. The salience of sports can be documented in terms of news coverage, financial expenditures, number of participants and spectators, hours consumed, and time samplings of conversations. Given the salience of sports as a social institution, a sociology of sport has emerged that attempts to go beyond the descriptive level by providing theoretically informed analyses and explanations of sports activity.

One might speculate as to why sport is a recent entry to the substantive specialties within sociology. If, in fact,

sociology is a residual field that assimilates topics unclaimed by more established fields, why is it that sports (also, leisure and recreation) were not an early part of the sociological package? Perhaps one answer to this question lies in the increased salience of these spheres as concomitants of economic development and affluence. Another explanation may be that sports previously were viewed as primarily physical, rather than social interaction, and thus devoid of sociological significance. Still another explanation may be that the world of sports is often perceived as illusionary, fantasy, and a sphere apart from the "real" world (Huizinga, 1955). Perhaps Americans are uneasy with play and this ambivalence may explain the relative lack of interest in sports on the part of sociologists (Stone, 1971:48). In a similar vein, Dunning (1967) argues that sociologists who have defined play and sport in terms of fantasy, and who are thus ambivalent about seriously studying the topic, may be reflecting a Protestant Ethic orientation toward work and leisure. In fact, an element of snobbery is probably involved: "The serious analysis of popular sport is construed to be beneath the dignity of many academics" (Stone, 1971:62). In response to such sentiments, Dunning (1971:37) emphasizes that "sports and games are 'real' in the sense they are observable, whether directly through overt behavior of people or indirectly through the reports which players and spectators give of what they think and feel while playing and 'spectating'." There is increasing realization that sport as an institution permeates and articulates with other institutions. Consequently, a substantial literature is developing in the sociology of sport, some of which is cumulative, and much of which goes beyond description toward explanation.[3] Disciplines other than sociology contribute to this literature; physical educators are particularly visible in this specialty. Moreover, some prominent physical educators researching in this area are, in effect, sociologists, either through formal or informal training.

Definition of Sport

The meaning of sport, like time, is self-evident until one is asked to define it. There is little disagreement in classifying physical activities such as basketball, football, handball, tennis, and track as sports. Hunting, fishing, and camping are often considered sports, but do they contain the same elements as, say, football and basketball? Can mountain climbing, bridge, and poker be classified as sports? Edwards (1973) presents a typology to clarify the concepts of play, recreation, contest, game, and sport. He arrays these activities on a continuum in the above order with play and sport as the polar activities. As one moves from play toward sport the following occurs (Edwards, 1973:59):

Activity becomes less subject to individual prerogative, with spontaneity severely diminished.

Formal rules and structural role and position relationships

and responsibilities within the activity assume predominance.

Separation from the rigors and pressures of daily life becomes less prevalent.

Individual liability and responsibility for the quality and character of his behavior during the course of the activity is heightened.

The relevance of the outcome of the activity and the individual's role in it extends to groups and collectivities that do not participate directly in the act.

Goals become diverse, complex, and more related to values emanating from outside of the context of the activity.

The activity consumes a greater proportion of the individual's time and attention due to the need for preparation and the degree of seriousness involved in the act.

In summary, Edwards (1973:57-58) defines sport as "involving activities having formally recorded histories and traditions, stressing physical exertion through competition within limits set in explicit and formal rules governing role and position relationships, and carried out by actors who represent or who are part of formally organized associations having the goal of achieving valued tangibles or intangibles through defeating opposing groups." Lüschen (1967:127; 1970:6; 1972:119) defines sport as an institutionalized type of competitive physical activity located on a continuum between play and work. Sport contains intrinsic and extrinsic rewards; but the more it is rewarded extrinsically (including socially), the more it tends to become work in the sense of being instrumental rather than consummatory (also see Loy, 1968). These attempts to define sport are admittedly imprecise. Sport may be defined in terms of the participants' motivation or by the nature of the activity itself. Sport is a playful activity for some participants, while others participate in the context of work or an occupation. Moreover, the boundaries of sport as an activity blend into the more general sphere of recreation or leisure. In the present paper, we shall not attempt to carve out boundaries for the topic; rather, we delineate the specialty in operational terms of what sociologists actually do with the content of sport. We attempt to synthesize and interpret the work done in this area while organizing the literature in terms of the unit of analysis. We begin by analyzing sociological research concerning sport at the macro level.

Societal Perspectives

One research tradition within the sociology of sport focuses on the relationship between sports and the larger society. The analysis involves the following basic questions (Lüschen, 1970:8): What is the nature of sport as a social institution, and how does it relate to other institutions? What is the structure and function of sport, and what social values does it promote?

This macro level of analysis is probably the most well-developed area in the sociology of sport. Sport as a microcosm of society is a *leitmotiv* that permeates much of the literature. Particular emphasis involves the social values, beliefs, and ideologies that are expressed and transmitted through the institutional configuration of sport. This theme is discussed by Boyle (1963) in *Sport: Mirror of American Life*; he analyzes sport as a mirror of society involving elements of social life such as stratification, race relations, commerce, automotive design, clothing style, concepts of law, language, and ethical values. In this context, a recent study by Snyder (1972a) classifies slogans placed in dressing rooms by high school coaches into motifs that are used to transmit beliefs, values, and norms to athletes. These slogans emphasize the development of qualities such as mental and physical fitness, aggressiveness, competitiveness, perseverance, self-discipline, and subordination of self to the group. Many of these characteristics are supported by values inherent in the Protestant Ethic. In this sense, sport is a "value receptacle" for the dominant social values (Edwards, 1973:355). Furthermore, cross-cultural data concerning sports and games show that they tend to be representative of a particular society's values and norms (Roberts and Sutton-Smith, 1962).

Numerous researchers have documented the interrelationship between sport and society by analyzing specific sports. Riesman and Denny (1954) describe how rugby changed to become the game of football that was congruent with the American ethos. Similarly, cultural themes in major league baseball reflect American values of specialization, division of labor, individual success, and the importance of teamwork (Voigt, 1971; Haerle, 1973).

The prevalence of writings on the social functions of sport are supported from several disciplines—sociology, history, philosophy, and physical education. Methodologically, this literature relies on historical accounts, autobiographies, content analysis, and other qualitative techniques. These studies explicitly or implicitly embrace the theoretical posture of functionalism. In this regard the study of sports provides ample evidence of pattern maintenance, tension management, integration, and systemic linkages with other social institutions.

Many observers have pointed to the safety value function that sport serves for society. On a structural level of analysis, a vulgar Marxism is sometimes invoked in viewing sports as an opiate and as producing unreality, mystification, and false consciousness. Similarly, many scholars have commented on the psychodynamic function of sports. Gerth and Mills (1954:63), for example, suggest that "Many mass audience situations, with their 'vicarious' enjoyments, serve psychologically the unintended function of channeling and releasing otherwise unplaceable emotions. Thus, great values of aggression are 'cathartically' released by crowds of spectators cheering their favorite stars of sport—and jeering the umpire."

In related context, several empirical studies have attempted to document political concomitants of participation in sports. For instance, several surveys found that athletes tend to be more conservative, conventional, and conformist than their nonathletic counterparts (Phillips and Schafer, 1970; Rehberg, 1971; Schafer, 1971; and Scott, 1971). According to these observers, sport has a "conservatizing" effect on youth through its emphasis on hard work, persistence, diligence, and individual control over social mobility. Clearly, the transmission of societal values is an important function of schools anywhere. Schafer (1971) suggests, however, that the value mystique surrounding high school sports might be dangerous in the sense of producing conformist, authoritarian, cheerful robots who lack the autonomy and inner direction to accept innovation, contrasting value systems, and alternative life-styles. This provocative hypothesis is worthy of testing with a longitudinal design.

Although the above observations are intuitively persuasive, Petrie (1973) reports no significant political differences between athletes and nonathletes among Canadian college students in Ontario. Perhaps there are subcultural differences between the intercollegiate athletic programs in Canada and the United States that would account for his findings. Many questions in this area await further research. If sport promotes a conservative ideology, how pervasive is its influence, and what is the *process* by which it has this effect? Furthermore, how much transfer effect is there into adult life? And, if sport induces this type of politicoeconomic mentality, are the consequences primarily for athletes, or are other segments of the population likewise affected?

The economic, commercial, and occupational facets of sport also have been analyzed. Furst (1971:165) attributes the rise of commercialism in sport to the increasing number of people "with time, money, and energy to engage in and embrace the world of sports." Kenyon (1972) cites the change in American society toward mass consumption and professionalism as having ramifications within sport. The economic aspects of sport are evident in conflicts in several cities over the securing of professional sports franchises, the location of new stadia and arenas because of the multiplier effect on restaurants, hotels, parking lots, theatres, bars, etc. The fact that general scheduling of television programs is partly determined by the timing of prominent sports events bespeaks the economic salience of sports in the United States. We will discuss occupational and career aspects of sports later.

The articulation of sport with the religious institution is also of interest. As the ancient Olympic games were grand festivals with much religious and political significance, contemporary sports events can be seen as America's "civil religion" (Rogers, 1972:393). Athletic events often open with prayer as well as the national anthem, teams frequently have a chaplain, and many teams have prayer sessions prior to the contest. In a survey of high school basketball coaches and players, Snyder (1972a:91) reports that the majority of the teams sampled invoke prayer before or during games. Football coaches generally welcome reinforcement from the religious sector. "Louisiana State University's

coach . . . credits a Graham campus crusade in the Fall of 1970 with helping his football team win a victory over Auburn University. Dallas Cowboy's head football coach . . . presided over a Billy Graham Crusade For Christ held on the Cowboy's home field, the Cotton Bowl, in 1971" (Edwards, 1973:124). Rogers (1972:394) suggests that "sports are rapidly becoming the dominant ritualistic expression of the reification of established religion in America." In this context, a number of writers have suggested that religion and sport interact to reinforce the status quo and to reaffirm the conventional wisdom.

Similarly, the linkage between sport and the educational institution has been explored by sociologists. The United States differs from most nations in that amateur athletes are almost totally dominated by high schools and colleges; very little is carried on under the aegis of clubs or the government. The incorporation of amateur athletics into educational institutions has important consequences. As early as 1929 the Lynds noted the position of honor attributed to athletics and the low esteem accorded to academic pursuits in the high school status hierarchy of *Middletown*. Waller (1932) viewed the high school as a social organism and suggested that interscholastic athletics are justified because they promote the competitive spirit, act as a means of social control and system integration, and prepare students for adult life. The various sports themselves constitute a status hierarchy in schools and colleges; generally there is more interest in football and basketball than all the other sports and extracurricular activities combined (Hollingshead, 1949:193; Gordon, 1957; Coleman, 1961). These studies provide quantitative and qualitative documentation of the value orientations among youth and the relative importance of sports in the spectrum of high school activities.

A cumulative research tradition in the sociology of sport focuses on the relationship between participation in sport and academic performance and aspirations. Coleman's (1961) study of students in ten midwestern high schools suggests that the nature of interscholastic athletic competition focuses an inordinate amount of attention of sport which results in a depreciation of academic pursuits. His data, however, do not consistently support his hypothesis. For example, in six of the ten high schools, the grade averages of the top athletes were higher than their nonathletic peers. Additional studies generally show that, with qualifications, athletes tend to have as high or higher educational achievement and expectations than their nonathletic counterparts (Bend, 1968; Rehberg and Schafer, 1968; Schafer and Armer, 1968; Schafer and Rehberg, 1970; Spreitzer and Pugh, 1973). Additional analysis of the psychological and social concomitants of participation in interscholastic athletics is presented below in the section on social psychological aspects.

It is interesting to note that although conflict has long been defined as an essential element of most sports, nevertheless a functional model is inherent in most social scientific research on sport. In other words, the ways in which sport facilitates social integration and equilibrium have been of more interest than social conflict over scarce resources in the world of sport. The paradox of viewing explicit, structured conflict in the world of sport through the lens of an equilibrium framework is indicative of a root orientation toward harmony that spilled over from the larger discipline. It is curious that contemporary research on sport almost completely neglects current structural conflicts in the world of sport—exemption from anti-trust laws inter-league raiding of players, player drafts, the reserve clause, league expansions and mergers, strikes, and working conditions. The players themselves have not been unaware of economic antagonism in sport as evidenced by the players' ready reception of competing leagues, strikes, formation of players' associations (unions), expose books, and use of the judicial system for redress of economic grievances.

It is only in the last five years that the back regions and infrastructure of organized sports have been brought to light, and most of this writing appears in semipopular outlets such as the *Intellectual Digest, Psychology Today,* and the *New York Times Sunday Magazine.* Serious observers in this tradition (Edwards, 1969, 1973; and Scott, 1971) show how the youth movement of the late 1960s had reverberations in the world of sport. Perceived injustices in the sports establishment came under blistering attack. One segment of this "revolution" involved the black athlete and traces its roots to the civil rights movement. The threatened boycott of the XIX Olympiad and the clenched fist demonstration by black sprinters on the victory stand exemplify this reaction. Another facet of the conflict trend centers around the objections by athletes to imposition of a monolithic life-style (short hair, clean shaven, etc.). More recently, women's liberation appeared in the world of sport to seek more equitable distribution of the resources and rewards as well as to emancipate women from arbitrary sex role definitions regarding appropriate physical activities.

In sum, we argue that sport contains many of the sources of conflict inherent in the larger society. The contours of conflict in the world of sport are evident in bold relief as compared to the veiled manipulation of power in society at large. Therefore, the arena of sport represents a potentially rich area for the testing of generic theoretic frameworks concerning conflict:

> It seems not unreasonable to suggest that football and other similar sports can serve as a kind of "natural laboratory" for studying the dynamics of group conflicts in a more detached manner than has often proved possible in the past with respect, for example, to the study of union-management conflict, class, international and other types of group conflicts where the strength of the involvements on one side or the other has acted as a hindrance to the achievement of full objectivity (Dunning, 1971:43).

Stratification Aspects

When one considers the pervasiveness of social stratification, it is not surprising that processes of social differentiation operate within the world of sport. As early as Veblen (1899), social scientists have noted the pattern-

ing of leisure behavior along social class lines. Veblen suggested that a new era was emerging in which leisure for the few was yielding to leisure for the masses. Sport as a species of leisure is no exception to the pattern of differential participation across class lines. Lüschen (1969), for example, reports a positive relationship between socioeconomic status and sports involvement in Germany. Differences by class also have been reported in the preference, meaning, and salience of sports (Stone, 1969; Lüschen, 1972). Kenyon (1966) studied patterns of indirect and direct involvement in sports among adults in Wisconsin; he found no consistent relationship between social status and the degree of sports participation. Burdge (1966) analyzed involvement in sport according to level of occupation; he found that both active participation and spectatorship were more common at the higher occupational levels. Although the above research documents the expected variations in sports activities by social class, recent research indicates additional complexity. For example, recent data collected in the Midwest using a refined measure of sports involvement found a positive relationship between socioeconomic status and *cognitive* involvement (knowledge about sports), but no consistent relationship was observed on the *behavioral* and *affective* dimensions of involvement (Snyder and Spreitzer, 1973a). This study suggests that sports involvement tends to cut across social categories. Sport is so much a part of the cultural air through mass media and conversation that one cannot be totally insulated from its influence.

Within the sociology of sport, athletic achievement is frequently cited as an avenue for social mobility, particularly for minority groups, and there are a sufficient number of superstar celebrities to sustain this perception. Clearly, such cases are a tiny fraction of professional athletes; however, there are other ways in which sport can facilitate social mobility. Loy (1969) suggests that participation in athletics can stimulate higher levels of educational aspirations in order to extend one's athletic career, and thus indirectly result in higher educational achievement and the acquisition of secular skills that are functional in the nonathletic sphere. Youth who excel in athletics frequently receive educational and occupational sponsorship by influential persons which gives them leverage in the secular world. In this connection, a recent study shows that high school athletes rank their coach second only to parents in terms of influencing their educational and occupational plans (Snyder, 1972b). Moreover, coaches often gratuitously advise their players on educational and occupational matters. In addition, ever since the English gentleman proclaimed that the Battle of Waterloo was won on the playing fields of Eton, it has been argued that participation in sport generates character traits that transfer to other areas of life. There is limited evidence for this contention; we shall analyze the pertinent studies below in the section on social psychological aspects of sport.

Contrasting research findings suggest, however, that sport may also have a negative effect on the social mobility of participants. Spady (1970) interprets his findings as showing that athletic involvement is sometimes counter-productive in the sense of raising educational aspirations without providing the necessary cognitive skills for educational achievement. With respect to blacks, sports may function as a magnet attracting youth to one specialized channel of mobility which tends to cut down the number of mobility options perceived as available for minority youth. Edwards (1973:201-202) argues that the success of black athletes tends to have a boomerang effect of attracting black youth away from higher level occupations as an avenue for mobility. Of course, the actual number of individuals of any race who achieve eminence in sports is very small.[4]

Most of the literature concerning sports and social mobility is conjectural, anecdotal, or at best descriptive. Most studies are based on cross-sectional data, and thus the inferences drawn are tentative and exploratory. One study, however, provides a follow-up analysis of former high school and collegiate athletes (Bend, 1968). This research indicates that athletic participation is associated with postgraduate occupational mobility. This is an area ripe for systematic research particularly with longitudinal designs. Recently some interesting research has emerged concerning the career patterns and mobility processes of athletic coaches (Loy and Sage, 1972; Snyder, 1972c). This line of research contributes to the literature on the sociology of occupations.

Sociologists have also focused considerable attention on race as a dimension of stratification within sport. Since coaches are likely to recruit and play the most capable athletes regardless of race in order to enhance their own reputation as successful (winning) coaches, sport is often seen as a sphere of pure achievement and racial integration. Several research efforts challenge this assumption. Rosenblatt (1967) analyzes the batting averages of baseball players from 1953 to 1965 and concludes that discrimination is not directed at the superior black players; rather, he sees discrimination being directed at black players of the journeymen level. Pascal and Rapping (1970) extend this line of research and conclude that black pitchers must be superior to white pitchers in order to play in the big leagues. Yetman and Eitzen (1971, 1972) reach a similar conclusion from their findings that black players are disproportionately distributed in starting (star) roles. Johnson and Marple (1973) provide evidence to suggest that journeymen black players are dropped from professional basketball faster than comparable whites, a fact that would have dire economic consequences because pension plans are based on the number of years played.

There are several explanations for the apparent discrimination against medium-grade black players. One interpretation is that some coaches are prejudiced against blacks, but they must recruit the best minority players to remain competitive; yet they informally use a quota system to limit the number of blacks on the team. Thus, black players are more likely to be on the starting team (Yetman and Eitzen, 1972). Brower (1973:27) reports two reasons cited by owners of professional football teams for preferring white players: " . . . white players are desirable because white fans identify with them more readily than blacks, and most paying customers are white"; and "there are fewer problems with whites since blacks today have chips on their shoulders."

Another form of apparent discrimination in sports involves the practice of "stacking" wherein black athletes are allegedly assigned only to certain positions on the team (Edwards, 1973:205). In an interesting, theoretically informed study based on propositions derived from Grusky's (1963a:346) theory of the structure of formal organizations and Blalock's (1962) theory of occupational discrimination, Loy and McElvogue (1970:7) hypothesized that "There will be less discrimination where performance of independent tasks are largely involved, because such do not have to be coordinated with the activities of other persons, and therefore do not hinder the performance of others, nor require a great deal of skill in interpersonal relations." Loy and McElvogue found support in the data for their hypothesis that blacks are less likely to occupy central positions on professional baseball and football teams.

These studies are interesting contributions to the sociology of minority group relations. The work by Loy and McElvogue (1970) in this area is noteworthy since it synthesizes two theoretical frameworks from the larger discipline—Grusky's propositions on the formal structure of organizations and Blalock's (1962) propositions on racial discrimination. Such research efforts illustrate fruitful reciprocity between the sociology of sport and the larger discipline.

Recent research also focuses on discrimination in sport with respect to females. A girl actively involved in sport is likely to have her "femininity" called into question (Harris, 1973:15). Traditional sex role definitions either do not legitimate athletic pursuits for females or they narrowly define the range of appropriate physical activities (Griffin, 1973; Harris, 1971, 1973; Hart, 1972). In this regard, women are clearly at a disadvantage in terms of opportunities and resources available for physical expression of the self in the form of sport. Metheny (1965) traces the historical antecedents of the feminine image and the degree of acceptance for females in competitive sports. It is generally considered inappropriate for women to engage in sports where there is bodily contact, throwing of heavy objects, aggressive face-to-face competition, and long distance running or jumping. A recent survey by the authors of this article asked the respondents: "In your opinion, would participation in any of the following sports enhance a woman's feminine qualities?" The frequency distribution of affirmative responses was as follows: swimming 67 percent, tennis 57 percent, gymnastics 54 percent, softball 14 percent, basketball 14 percent, and track and field 13 percent.[5] The impact of the women's liberation movement on female involvement in sport represents a topic for additional research, and it is a research area that can feed back to the larger discipline in areas such as socialization, sex roles, and social movements.

Small Group Perspectives

The sociology of sport is a natural testing ground for theoretical frameworks in areas such as small group processes, collective behavior, personal influence, leadership, morale, and socialization. In sport the roles are clearly defined; performance measures are comparatively straightforward; and the contamination involved with artificiality and obtrusiveness of the investigator is less problematic than most areas of sociological research. Nevertheless, the sociology of sport includes relatively little experimental or even field studies. Sport teams represent an *in vivo* laboratory for the study of communication networks, cooperation, competition, conflict, division of labor, leadership, prestige, cohesion, and other structural properties of small groups. Several small group studies have focused on the effect of interpersonal relations among team members on team performance. One of the first studies (Fiedler, 1954) in this area analyzed the relationship between team effectiveness and the personal perceptions that team members have of one another. His findings suggest that winning teams are characterized by players who prefer to relate to one another in a task-oriented manner as contrasted with affective relations. Klein and Christiansen (1969), on the other hand, report a positive relationship between cohesiveness (interpersonal attractiveness) and performance of basketball teams. Their study also suggests that focused leadership (consensus concerning the peer leader) is conducive to team success. Heinicke and Bales (1953) likewise find an association between focused leadership and achieving task-oriented group goals. In a recent study, Eitzen (1973) shows that homogeneity in background characteristics of team members is related to team success. The relationship is interpreted in terms of heterogeneity increasing the likelihood of cliques within the team, which reduce cohesion and ultimately cause poor team performance.

Other studies, however, fail to replicate the finding of a relationship between cohesion and team success (Fielder, 1960; Lenk, 1969; Martens and Peterson, 1971). Nevertheless, these studies indicate the fruitfulness of research on sport teams using small group theoretical frameworks. The ambiguity of the findings shows the need for additional research to clarify our understanding of team structural characteristics, cohesiveness, and conflict according to the type of sport. For example, the role relations among a rowing crew require a synchronization of effort with each member performing a similar task, whereas most team sports involve individualization, specialization, and division of labor. Clearly, the dependent variable of team success is an applied perspective and approaches a market research orientation; however, we suggest that theoretically informed propositions that are derived from this type of research ultimately can be generalized to intergroup relations in general.

The utility of the sport context to test sociological propositions is illustrated in a further extension of Grusky's (1963a) concept of organizational *centrality* to the study of professional baseball team managers. Grusky analyzed differential recruitment of baseball players into managerial positions in terms of the centrality of the player's position. He found support for the hypothesis that centrality of position (e.g., infielders, catcher) is associated with higher rates of recruitment into managerial positions. Loy and Sage (1968) extend the centrality framework to explain the emergence of informal leaders on baseball teams. They found support for Grusky's hypothesis; infielders and catchers were more likely to be chosen as team captains, best liked, and perceived as highly valuable members of the team.

Grusky (1963b) also studied managerial succession (firing the manager) and team performance in major league baseball. He found that changing managers was negatively associated with team performance; however, he rejected the intuitive notion that managers are fired because of the team's poor performance. Rather, he suggested that the causal direction is two-way since managerial succession can also produce poor team performance. In a stimulating exchange, Gamson and Scotch (1964:70) argue that "the effect of the field manager on team performance is relatively unimportant." They suggest that Grusky's findings should be interpreted in terms of ritual scapegoating. Grusky's (1964) response included a specification of the relationship in terms of "inside" successors to the managerial position being less disruptive than "outside" successors (cf., Gouldner, 1954). Eitzen and Yetman (1971) also used Grusky's propositions concerning managerial succession in their study of coaching changes and performance of college basketball teams. They found support for Grusky's hypothesis, but basically they concluded that teams with poor performance records are likely to improve their records with or without a coaching change. Thus, the critical variable is the degree of team success before the arrival of the new coach—not the performance of the new coach.

Social Psychological Aspects

When viewed from the standpoint of the collectivity, socialization refers to the process of transmitting social values and norms to the individual members. Viewed from the perspective of the individual, socialization refers to the resulting changes that occur within the individual. Numerous observers have pointed to the potential of sport as an agency for socialization.[6] The theoretical rationale for examining socialization within the world of sport is implicit in the classic works of symbolic interaction (Cooley, 1922; Mead, 1934), where play and games are analyzed as part of the socialization process. More recently, psychologists have analyzed games and sport in the context of socialization (Piaget, 1962; Erickson, 1965; and Sutton-Smith, 1971). Ingham et al. (1973:243) observe that "the processes involved in the social construction of life-worlds are also in evidence in the social construction of play worlds. Similarly, the processes by which we come to know the life-world are the processes by which we come to know the play-world."

Basically, it is suggested that the athlete undergoes a socialization process when interacting with coaches and fellow athletes in the subculture of sport (Phillips and Schafer, 1970). If this line of reasoning is extended, we would expect the potency of the socialization process to vary according to the individual's degree of involvement in sport. Kenyon (1969) provided a theoretical discussion of this process, and Snyder (1972b) offers empirical support for this hypothesis of differential consequences according to degree of sport involvement. In the latter study, interestingly, the interaction patterns between the coach and outstanding athletes were markedly different from the coach's relations with marginal players.

Kenyon (1969:81) proposes that the socialization consequences of sports involvement be considered from a temporal perspective—particularly in terms of the stages of becoming involved, being involved, and becoming uninvolved. He suggests that research from this perspective could be informed by role theory and reference group frameworks. An intriguing study would be to trace the social psychological dynamics that trigger changes in the individual's progression from one stage of involvement to another.[7] In a similar vein, Page (1969:20) suggests the possibility of an identity crisis emerging after a successful athlete has completed his/her active playing days. A study of prominent soccer players in Yugoslavia reveals some negative psychological concomitants of the players' disengagement from athletic careers (Mihovilovic, 1968). The study indicates the importance of gradual withdrawal from the active role, especially when the athletic role is the individual's sole identity anchor. Taking on the role of coach, referee, or similar official has been one way in which the transition process is softened for former athletes (Snyder, 1972d).

Perhaps the topic that has received the most cumulative, quantitative research in the sociology of sport concerns the social psychological consequences of active participation in athletics by youth. A series of studies focus on the question of whether athletes differ from nonathletes on personality dimensions such as extraversion, conformism, conventionality, aspirations, conservatism, and rigidity (Schendel, 1965; Schafer and Armer, 1968; Phillips and Schafer, 1970). Earlier in this paper we discussed the positive relationship between participation in athletics and academic performance and aspirations among high school boys. Rehberg and Schafer (1968) report that participation in sport has the most effect on boys least disposed to attend college by raising their educational expectations to attend college. We alluded above to the possible two-edged sword effect of sport serving as a channel for mobility while also raising levels of aspiration without providing the corresponding instrumental skills (Spady, 1970). Similar studies on college level athletes yield inconsistent findings (Pilapil et al., 1970; Sage, 1967; and Spady, 1970). Additional research at the college level is needed.

A relatively underdeveloped area in this subfield is the social psychology of consciousness states, intrinsic satisfaction, body perceptions, and affective con-

comitants of sport. Some journalistic reports argue that commercialized sports desensitize, exploit, and manipulate players to achieve the ultimate goal of winning and profits (Meggyesy, 1971; Hoch, 1972; Shaw, 1972). On the other hand, several studies point to positive affective consequences of sport involvement (Layman, 1968, 1972). There is empirical evidence to suggest, for example, that sports participation is associated with life satisfaction (Washburne, 1941; Snyder and Spreitzer, 1973b). This finding is consistent with many studies documenting a positive relationship between social participation and psychological well-being (Wilson, 1967). Further explanation may rest with the intrinsic satisfaction that flows from involvement in sport. Dunning (1967:148) reasons that sport participation generates a "tension-excitement" that forms a pleasurable contrast to routinized aspects of everyday life.

A pertinent study by Snyder and Kivlin (1974) studied the self-perceptions of outstanding female athletes with the expectation that female athletes would evidence low scores on measures of psychological well-being and body image on the basis of role conflict reasoning. The findings did not support the hypothesis, and the authors concluded that the intrinsic satisfaction flowing from sports participation tended to counteract any negative impact from sex role stereotyping. Additional research is needed on this topic.

The "athletic revolution" described above involves protests against authoritarian practices within sport, particularly among coaches (Scott, 1971). A popular explanation is that the coaching profession either attracts persons with an authoritarian personality or, alternatively, coaches are socialized into this personality type. This explanation ignores the structural interpretation of authoritarian behavior developed in recent years.[8] In the latter context, Edwards (1973) reasons that the coach is *fully responsible* for the team's victories and defeats; yet he has *limited control* in determining the outcomes. Under these circumstances, then, Edwards (1973:139) points out that coaches insist upon running a tight ship and, consequently, a democratic leadership style would not enable the coach to maintain compliance under the tense conditions of a match where unquestioning obedience is required. The analysis of the coach's role shows that the authoritarian aspects of coaching behavior are structurally induced. Although the behavior of athletic coaches is not a particularly significant problem, it is a context in which the interpenetration of social structure and the personality is readily apparent.

Conclusion

Basically we have argued that sport is a social institution that interfaces with, and reflects, many dimensions of social life. Despite the pervasiveness of sport in society, the sociological study of sport is still not completely legitimated within the larger discipline. We suggest that research in this area will enter the mainstream when it reaches the level of theoretical and methodological self-consciousness characteristic of the better works in the larger discipline. In other words, it is vain to argue in the abstract that the world of sport is worthy of social scientific study. A more fruitful approach to legitimacy for a new specialty is simply for the practitioners in that area to produce research that will be interesting to social scientists at large. Research that is of interest only to persons who are already intrinsically interested in sports will necessarily be of dubious value from a social scientific perspective.

It is clear that most researchers in the sociology of sport have a strong intrinsic interest and existential involvement in the subject matter of the subfield that is not characteristic of most other specialties within sociology. We suggest that this intrinsic interest needs to be tempered by a generalizing orientation if the sociology of sport is to contribute to the large discipline. A basically content-oriented strategy will not result in a body of systematic knowledge about social life. In other words, when content from the world of sport is analyzed by the sociologist, it should be selected because it is informative about the nature, antecedents, and consequences of basic social processes, and not simply because of intrinsic interest on the part of the investigator. The content of the world of sport must at times be viewed in instrumental terms if the subfield is to be truly in a reciprocal relationship with the larger discipline. General sociologists are likely to be interested in contributions from the sociology of sport only if some generalizing thrust is contained therein: "The purpose of a generalizing investigation is to test, reformulate, refine, or extend an abstract, general theory. A large number of concretely quite different settings serve equally well as instances of the process, for no particular one of them has any special importance for the investigation" (Berger et al., 1972: xi).

In analyzing the sociology of sport, we were struck by the "loyalty" of the scholars in this area. That is, many of the researchers in the specialty have published regularly in the area over the years. This is apparent because of the fact that most of the literature in this specialty is contained in comparatively few outlets. Moreover, judging from the congregation of the scholars in the sociology of sport at conventions, there is a strong affinity among social scientists in this specialty. There is always a danger that a given specialty will become too insulated from the larger discipline; this is particularly a problem with the sociology of sport because of the multidisciplinary composition of the specialty.

This argument is based on the assumption that a strong identification with, and immersion in, the larger discipline is necessary to keep the taproot of the sociological imagination alive. If this assumption is valid, the most enduring contributions to the sociology of sport are likely to come from research efforts informed by intellectual concerns derived from the larger discipline.

In this context, it is interesting to note that more developed specialties such as medical sociology involve more practitioners who are just passing through and happen to touch down for an episodic research effort on the content of a given specialty. For example, prominent general sociologists have contributed important studies to medical sociology (e.g., Parsons, Merton, Srole, Becker, Hollingshead). This is not to suggest, however, that individual scholars should be only occasional or episodic contributors to an academic specialty. Rather, we argue that from an aggregate or macro level, it is desirable that a circulation of practitioners occur within a specialty. The circulation of practitioners assures a steady flow of theoretical and methodological nutrition from the larger discipline and, most importantly, will function to keep the resident practitioners sensitive to significant research questions of generic sociological interest.

We predict that the field will continue to be strengthened by increased theoretical and methodological sophistication. The present state of development reveals less barefooted empiricism and more theoretically informed hypothesis testing. The research designs and interpretations of data show increasing sensitivity to alternative explanations and spurious relationships.[9] We observe a greater use of multivariate statistical techniques, but most importantly, the sociological imagination is increasingly evident by research that is going beyond the surface manifestations of sports to pose generic theoretical questions stemming from the larger discipline. Consequently, we conclude that the sociology of sport is shedding its *lumpen* heritage and is gaining respectability. Sociologists in general can look forward to some interesting contributions from this fledgling subfield in the years to come.

REFERENCES

1. Bend, Emil. 1968. The Impact of Athletic Participation on Academic and Career Aspiration and Achievement. Pittsburgh: American Institutes for Research.
2. Berger, Joseph, Morris Zelditch, and Bo Anderson. 1972. Sociological Theories in Progress. New York: Houghton Mifflin.
3. Blalock, H.M. 1962. "Occupational discrimination: some theoretical propositions." Social Problems (Winter) :247-249.
4. Boyles, Robert H. 1963. Sport: Mirror of American Life. Boston: Little, Brown.
5. Brower, J.J. 1973. "Whitey's sport." Human Behavior 2 (November :22-27).
6. Burdge, R.J. 1966. "Levels of occupational prestige and leisure activity." Journal of Leisure Research (Summer) :262-274.
7. Coleman, James S. 1961. The Adolescent Society. New York: Free Press.
8. Cooley, Charles H. 1922. Human Nature and the Social Order. New York: Scribner's.
9. Dunning, E. 1971. "Some conceptual dilemmas in the sociology of sport." Pp. 34-37 in Magglinger Symposium, Sociology of Sport. Basel, Switzerland: Birkhauser Verlag. 1967. "Notes on some conceptual and theoretical problems in the sociology of sports." International Review of Sport Sociology 2:143-153.
10. Edwards, Harry. 1973. Sociology of Sport. Homewood, Illinois: Dorsey Press. 1969. The Revolt of the Black Athlete. New York: The Free Press.
11. Eitzen, D.S. 1973. "The effect of group structure on the success of athletic teams." International Review of Sport Sociology 8:7-17.

12. Eitzen, D. Stanley and Norman R. Yetman. 1971. "Managerial change and organizational effectiveness." Paper presented at the Ohio Valley Sociological Society, Cleveland, Ohio.

13. Erickson, Erik H. 1965. Childhood and Society. New York: W.W. Norton Company.

14. Fiedler, F.E. 1960. "The leader's psychological distance and group effectiveness." Pp. 526-606 in Dorwin Cartwright and Alvin Zander (eds.), Group Dynamics. Evanston: Northwestern. 1954. "Assumed similarity measures as predictors of team effectiveness." Journal of Abnormal Social Psychology 49 (July) :381-388.

15. Furst, R.T. 1971. "Social change and the commercialization of professional sports." International Review of Sport Sociology 6:153-173.

16. Gamson, W.A. and N.A. Scotch. 1964. "Scapegoating in baseball." American Journal of Sociology 70 (July) :69-72.

17. Gerth, Hans H. and C. Wright Mills. 1954. Character and Social Structure. New York: Harcourt, Brace and World.

18. Glaser, Barney G. and Anselm L. Strauss. 1967. The Discovery of Grounded Theory. Chicago: Aldine Publishing Company.

19. Gordon, C. Wayne. 1957. The Social System of the High School. New York: The Free Press.

20. Gouldner, Alvin W. 1954. Patterns of Industrial Bureaucracy. Glencoe, Illinois: The Free Press.

21. Griffin, P.S. 1973. "What's a nice girl like you doing in a profession like this?" Quest 19 (January) :96-101.

22. Grusky, O. 1964. "Reply to Gamson and Scotch." American Journal of Sociology 70 (July) :72-76. 1963a. "The effects of formal structure on managerial recruitment: a study of baseball organization." Sociometry 26 (September) :345-353. 1963b. "Managerial succession and organizational effectiveness." American Journal of Sociology 69 (July) :21-23.

23. Haerle, Rudolf K., Jr. 1973. "Heroes, success themes, and basic cultural values in baseball autobiographies: 1900-1970." Paper presented at the Third National Meeting of the Popular Culture Association, Indianapolis, Indiana.

24. Harris, D.V. 1973. "Dimensions of physical activity." Pp. 3-15 in Dorothy V. Harris (ed.), Women and Sport: A National Research Conference. University Park: The Pennsylvania State University. 1971. "The sportswoman in our society." Pp. 1-4 in Dorothy V. Harris (ed.), Women in Sports. Washington, D.C.: American Association for Health and Physical Education, and Recreation.

25. Hart, M.M. 1972. "On being female in sport." Pp. 291-302 in M. Marie Hart (ed.), Sport in the Socio-Cultural Process. Dubuque, Iowa: Wm. C. Brown, Company.

26. Heinicke, C. and R.F. Bales. 1953. "Developmental trends in the structure of groups." Sociometry, 16 (February) :7-38.

27. Hoch, Paul. 1972. Rip Off the Big Game. Garden City, New York: Doubleday and Company.

28. Hollingshead, August B. 1949. Elmtown's Youth. New York: John Wiley and Sons.

29. Huizinga, Jan. 1955. Homo Ludens: A Study of the Play Element in Culture. Boston: Beacon Press.

30. Ingham, A.G., J.W. Loy, Jr., and J.W. Berryman. 1973. "Socialization, dialects, and sport." Pp. 235-276 in Dorothy V. Harris (ed.), Women and Sport: A National Research Conference. University Park: The Pennsylvania State University.

31. Johnson, N.R. and D.F. Marple. 1973. "Racial discrimination in professional basketball: an empirical test." Paper presented at the North Central Sociological Association Meetings, Cincinnati, Ohio.

32. Kenyon, G.S. 1972. "Sport and society: at odds or in concert." Pp. 33-41 in Arnold Flath, Athletics in America. Corvallis, Oregon: Oregon State University Press. 1969 "Sport involvement: a conceptual go and some consequences thereof." Pp. 77-87 in Gerald S. Kenyon (ed.), Aspects of Contemporary Sport Sociology. Chicago: The Athletic Institute. 1966. "The significance of physical activity as a function of age, sex, education, and socioeconomic status of northern United States adults." International Review of Sport Sociology 1:41-57.

33. Killian, L.M. 1952. "The effects of southern white workers on race relations in northern plants." American Sociological Review 17 (June) :327-331.

34. Klein, M. and G. Christiansen. 1969. "Group composition, group structure, and group effectiveness of basketball teams." Pp. 397-408 in John W. Loy, Jr. and Gerald S. Kenyon (eds.), Sport, Culture and Society. London: Macmillan Company.

35. Kohn, M.L. and R.M. Williams, Jr. 1956. "Situational patterning in intergroup relations." American Sociological Review 21 (April) :164-174.

36. Layman, E.M. 1972. "The contribution of play and sports to emotional health." Pp. 163-185 in John E. Kane (ed.), Psychological Aspects of Physical Education and Sport. London: Routledge and Kegan Paul. 1968. "The role of play and sport in healthy emotional development: a reappraisal." Pp. 249-257 in Gerald S. Kenyon and Tom M. Grogg (eds.), Contemporary Psychology of Sport: Proceedings of the Second International Congress of Sport Psychology. Chicago: The Athletic Institute.

37. Lenk, H. 1969. "Top performance despite internal conflict: an antithesis to a functional propostion." Pp. 392-397 in John W. Loy, Jr. and Gerald S. Kenyon (eds.), Sport, Culture and Society. London: Macmillan Company.

38. Lohman, J. and D. Reitzes. 1952. "Note on race relations in mass society." The American Journal of Sociology 53 (November) :240-246.

39. Loy, J.W., Jr. 1969. "The study of sport and social mobility." Pp. 101-119 in Gerald S. Kenyon (ed.), Aspects of Contemporary Sport Sociology. Chicago: The Athletic Institute. 1968. "The nature of sport: a definitional effort." Quest 10 (May) :1-15.

40. Loy, J.W., and J.F. McElvogue. 1970. "Racial segregation in American sport." International Review of Sport Sociology 5:5-24.

41. Loy, J.W., Jr. and G.H. Sage. 1972. "Social origins, academic achievement, athletic achievement, and career mobility patterns of college coaches." Paper presented at the American Sociological Association, New Orleans, Louisiana.

42. Loy, J.W., Jr. and J.N. Sage. 1968. "The effects of formal structure on organizational leadership: an investigation of interscholastic baseball teams." Paper presented at Second International Congress of Sport Psychology. Washington, D.C.

43. Luschen, Gunther. 1972. "On sociology of sport—general orientation and its trends in the literature." Pp. 119-154 in Ommo Grupe et al. (eds.), The Scientific View of Sport. Heidelberg: Springer-Verlag Berlin. 1970. "Sociology of sport and the cross-cultural analysis of sport and games." Pp. 6-13 in Gunther Luschen (ed.), The Cross-Cultural Analysis of Sport and Games. Champaign, Illinois: Stripes Publishing Company. 1969. "Social stratification and social mobility among young sportsmen." Pp. 258-276 in John W. Loy, Jr. and Gerald S. Kenyon (eds.), Sport, Culture and Society. London: Macmillan Company. 1968. The Sociology of Sport. Paris: Mouton and Company. 1967. "The interdependence of sport and culture." International Review of Sport Sociology 2:127-141.

44. Lynd, Robert S. and Helen M. Lynd. 1929. Middletown, New York: Harcourt, Brace and Company.

45. Martens, R. and J.A. Peterson. 1971. "Group cohesiveness as a determinant of success and member satisfaction in team performance." International Review of Sport Sociology 6:49-61.

46. Mead, George H. 1934. Mind, Self, and Society. Chicago: University of Chicago Press.

47. Meggyesy, Dave. 1971. Out of Their League. New York: Paperback Library.

48. Metheny, E. 1965. "Symbolic forms of movement: the female image in sports." Pp. 43-56 in E. Metheny (ed.), Connotations of Movement in Sport and Dance. Dubuque, Iowa: Wm. C. Brown Company.

49. Meyersohn, R. 1969. "The sociology of leisure in the United States: introduction and bibliography, 1945-1965," Journal of Leisure Research 1 (Winter) :53-68.

50. Mihovilovic, M.A. 1968. "The status of former sportsmen." International Review of Sport Sociology 3:73-96.

51. Miller, Arthur. 1958. Death of a Salesman. New York: Viking Press.

52. Page, C.H. 1969. "Symposium summary, with reflections upon the sociology of sport as a research field." Pp. 189-202 in Gerald S. Kenyon (ed.), Aspects of Contemporary Sport Sociology. Chicago:The Athletic Institute.

53. Pascal, Anthony H. and Leonard A. Rapping. 1970. Racial Discrimination in Organized Baseball. Santa Monica, California: Rand Corporation.

54. Petrie, Brian M. 1973. "The political attitudes of Canadian university students: a comparison between athletes and nonathletes." Paper presented at the National Convention of the American Association of Health, Physical Education, and Recreation, Minneapolis, Minnesota.

55. Phillips, John C. and Walter E. Schafer. 1970. "The athletic subculture: a preliminary study." Paper presented at the American Sociological Association.

56. Piaget, Jean. 1962. Play, Dreams and Imitation in Childhood. New York: W.W. Norton Company.

57. Pilapil, Bonifacio, John E. Stecklein, and Han C. Liu. 1970. Intercollegiate Athletics and Academic Progress: A Comparison of Academic Characteristics of Athletes and Nonathletes at the University of Minnesota. Minneapolis: Bureau of Institutional Research.

58. Rehberg, Richard A. 1971. "Sport and political activism." Paper presented at the Conference on Sport and Social Deviancy, SUNY, Brockport, New York.

59. Rehberg, R.A. and W.E. Schafer. 1968. "Participation in interscholastic athletics and college expectations." American Journal of Sociology 73 (May) :732-740.

60. Reitzes, D.C. 1959 "Institutional structure and race relations." Phylon (Spring) :48-66.

61. Riesman, D. and R. Denny. 1954. "Football in America." Pp. 242-257 in David Riesman (ed.), Individualism Reconsidered. Glencoe, Ill.: The Free Press.

62. Roberts, J.M. and B. Sutton-Smith. 1962. "Child training and game involvement." Ethnology 1 (April) :166-185.

63. Rogers, C. 1972. "Sports, religion and politics: the renewal of an alliance." The Christian Century (April 5) :392-394.

64. Rosenblatt, A. 1967. "Negroes in baseball: the failure of success." Trans-action 4 (September) :51-53.

65. Sage, John N. 1967. "Adolescent values and the non-participating college athlete." Paper presented at the Southern Section California Health, Physical Education and Recreation Conference, San Fernando Valley State College.

66. Schafer, Walter E. 1971. "Sport, socialization and the school: toward maturity or enculturation?" Paper presented at the Third International Symposium on the Sociology of Sport, Waterloo, Ontario.

67. Schafer, W.E. and J.M. Armer. 1968. "Athletes are not inferior students." Trans-action 5 (November) :21-26, 61-62.

68. Schafer, W. and R. Rehberg. 1970. "Athletic participation, college aspirations and college encouragement." Pacific Sociological Review 13 (Summer) :182-186.

69. Schendel, J.S. 1965. "Psychological differences between athletes and non-participants at three educational levels." Research Quarterly 36 (March) :52-67.

70. Scott, Jack. 1971. The Athletic Revolution. New York: The Free Press.

71. Shaw, Gary. 1972. Meat On the Hoof. New York: Dell Publishing Company.

72. Snyder, E.E. 1972a. "Athletic dressingroom slogans as folklore: a means of socialization." International Review of Sport Sociology 7:89-102.

73. Snyder, Eldon E. 1972b. "Athletes' careers: the role of the coach in the athletes' future educational attainment." Paper presented at the Scientific Congress in conjunction with the XXth Olympic Games, Munich.

74. Snyder, E.E. 1972c. "High school athletes and their coaches: educational plans and advice." Sociology of Education 45 (Summer) :313-325. 1972d. "Social characteristics and motivations of basketball officials and aspects of sports involvement." The Ohio High School Athlete 32 (November) :66-67, 83.

75. Snyder, E.E. and J.E. Kivlin. 1974. "Women athletes and aspects of psychological well-being and body image." Paper read at the Popular Culture Association, Milwaukee.

76. Snyder, E.E. and E.A. Spreitzer. 1973a. "Family influence and involvement in sports." Research Quarterly 44 (October) :249-255. 1973b. "Involvement in sports and psychological well-being." International Journal of Sport Psychology 5 (1) :28-39.

77. Spady, W.G. 1970. "Lament for the letterman: effects of peer status and extracurricular activities on goals and achievement." American Journal of Sociology 75 (January) :680-702.

78. Spreitzer, E.A. and M.D. Pugh. 1973. "Interscholastic athletics and educational expectations." Sociology of Education 46 (Spring) :171-182.

79. Stone, G.P. 1969. "Some meanings of American sport: an extended view." Pp. 5-16 in G.S. Kenyon (ed.), Aspects of Contemporary Sport Sociology. Chicago: The Athletic Institute. 1971. "American sports: play and display." Pp. 47-65 in Eric Dunning (ed.), Sport: Readings from a Sociological Perspective. London: Frank Cass and Company.

80. Sutton-Smith, Brian. 1971. "A developmental approach to play, games and sport." Paper presented at the Second World Symposium on the History of Sport and Physical Education, Bannf, Alberta, Canada.

81. U.S. Department of Labor, Bureau of Labor Statistics. 1973. "Careers in professional sports." Occupational Outlook Quarterly 17 (Summer) :2-5.

82. Veblen, Thorstein. 1899. Theory of the Leisure Class. New York: Random House.

83. Voigt, David Q. 1971. America's Leisure Revolution. Reading, Pennsylvania: Albright College Book Store.

84. Waller, Willard. 1932. The Sociology of Teaching. New York: John Wiley and Sons.

85. Washburne, J.N. 1941. "Factors related to the social adjustment of college girls." Journal of Social Psychology 13 (May) :281-289.

86. Wilson, W. 1967. "Correlates of avowed happiness." Psychological Bulletin 67 (April) :294-306.

87. Yetman, N.R.and D.S. Eitzen. 1972. "Black Americans in sports: unequal opportunity for equal ability." Civil Rights Digest 5 (August) :21-34. 1971. "Black athletes on intercollegiate basketball teams: an empirical test of discrimination." Paper presented at the American Sociological Association, Denver, Colorado.

88. Yinger, J. Milton. 1965. Toward a Field Theory of Behavior. New York: McGraw-Hill Co.

NOTES

1. The term sociology of sport is simply a shorthand expression referring to "social scientific research in the area of sports."

2. For an overview of the sociology of leisure as an academic specialty, see R. Meyersohn (1969).

3. See Luschen (1968) for an extensive bibliography on the sociology of sport.

4. A newsletter dated June 21, 1973, from the U.S. Department of Labor reports "that about 400,000 young men played on high school baseball teams in 1970, another 25,000 were on college teams, and about 3,000 were in the minor leagues. However, only about 100 rookies made the 24 squads in the major leagues that year."

5. See Snyder and Spreitzer (1973a) for a description of the research procedures of this survey.

6. It is interesting to observe in this context that totalitarian governments invariably place a high priority on sport activities for youth.

7. Arthur Miller (1958) poignantly illustrates this type of process in his literary masterpiece, *The Death of a Salesman* (1958).

8. See Killian (1952), Lohman and Reitzes (1952), Kohn and Williams (1956), and Reitzes (1959), and Yinger (1965).

9. Parenthetically, we have found that research from the sociology of sport, particularly the analysis of the commonly held assumptions, are helpful and vivid aids in *teaching* general sociology and research methodology courses.

A SOCIAL PSYCHOLOGY OF
PHYSICAL ACTIVITY

Rainer Martens

Within this century, physical educators have begun to search for the complex physiological, psychological, and social factors that interrelate and act as antecedents and consequences of involvement in physical activity. Such areas as exercise physiology and kinesiology have made initial contributions to the understanding of these antecedents and consequences. More recently, psychology and sociology of sport have emerged as subdisciplines of considerable importance. Just beginning to emerge as an area in its own right is social psychology. This paper* delineates the relationship of social psychology with physical activity, and distinguishes between social psychology and its parent sciences—psychology and sociology. In addition, some of the concerns of a social psychology of physical activity are outlined.

Social Psychology and the Other Sciences

The sciences are commonly categorized into three main bodies: the physical sciences, the biological sciences, and the social sciences. Within this scheme, psychology is a hybrid being partly a biological and partly a social science. This paper is concerned with the social science aspect. Where psychology is concerned with the behavior of human beings in relationship to their environments, social psychology is concerned with human behavior in relationship to the social parts of those environments. Social psychology as a behavioral science may be defined as the "study of how human behavior is influenced by the presence, behavior, and products of other human beings, individually and collectively, past, present, and future."[1]

Social psychology has been viewed as a special field within sociology. In fact, some behavioral scientists consider social psychology to be "microsociology." Regardless of the terminology, the relationship between sociology and social psychology is important. General sociology is concerned with the forms and processes of collective behavior. Social psychology, however, deals with the articulation between the individual as an actor and as a target of effects, and with larger social entities as they affect and are affected by individuals. Thus, social psychology may be considered an interdisciplinary field of study analogous to biophysics and biochemistry. Similarly, social psychology has attained some maturity and independence from its parent disciplines and is considered as a distinctive field. This distinctiveness rests in two major factors: (1) its interest in the *individual* as a participant in social relationships, and (2) its emphasis on *understanding* the "social-influence processes" underlying these relationships.

Social psychology is primarily concerned with the process of social influence. Social influence occurs whenever one individual responds to the actual or implied presence of one or more other individuals. It may

occur in the reciprocal effect of one person upon another in social interaction, or between a group and an individual, or in the relationship between two or more groups. The goal of the social psychologist is to understand these social-influence processes and to predict the behavior of individuals on the basis of these understandings. Consequently, the social psychologist assumes that social behavior is not capricious but has some recurring order—or cause and effect. Obviously, every individual has some social experiences that are unique, associated with particular moments; whereas, other experiences recur again and again in much the same order or with much the same cause or effect. Social psychology attempts to understand the influences producing regularities and diversities in human social behavior through objective study and the use of scientific methods.

A Social Psychology of Physical Activity

A social psychology of physical activity may be defined simply as the application of social psychological theory and methods to the study of human social behavior while involved in physical activity. Physical activity, in this definition, is a somewhat more general term encompassing a large variety of vigorous activities ranging from highly competitive sports to more simple forms of human movement as found in games and calisthenics. Involvement refers to the relationship an individual has with physical activity. As Kenyon[2] notes, involvement may refer to actual participation or *primary involvement,* and also to such forms as the observance of sporting events or *secondary involvement.*

Most readers will quickly recognize that the study of human social behavior while involved in physical activity is not really any new development. Physical education literature has examples of social psychological research appearing as early as the 1940's.** The purpose of this paper therefore is not to propose that physical educators

Rainer Martens. "A Social Psychology of Physical Activity," in *Quest,* XIV June, 1970, pp. 8-17.

About the Author

Dr. Rainer Martens is presently on the staff of the Department of Kinesiology University of Waterloo, Canada. He has a number of published articles in the *Research Quarterly, Journal of Motor Behavior, Journal of Personality and Social Psychology.* His research interests are concerned with the Social Psychology of physical activity.

*This paper was written while the author was supported in part by a research grant to the Motor Performance and Play Research Laboratory via the Adler Zone Center by the Department of Mental Health of the State of Illinois and by United States Public Health Service Research Grant MH-07346 from the National Institute of Mental Health.

**It is interesting to note that the first social psychological study ever completed (Triplett, 1898) was concerned with the facilitating effects of competition and co-actors on bicycle riding and fishing-reel winding.

begin investigating a new field. Physical educators have long been aware that social psychology has considerable application to physical education. What is proposed here as "new" is the *approach* to investigating social psychological phenomena as related to physical activity.

Approaches to Social Psychology

Historically, three distinct approaches for studying social behavior have influenced modern social psychology. The oldest is *social philosophy* characterized by conjecture and speculation, usually in the absence of any systematic gathering of factual information. The next stage known as *social empiricism* arose in rebellion against the social philosophy approach. A nineteenth century development, social empiricism is characterized by systematic data-gathering not related to theory. This stage, while going beyond conjecture, is often guided by it. The third and most advanced stage, a twentieth century development, is known as *social analysis* and focuses on theory development in conjunction with the controlled testing of theoretically derived hypotheses. The major feature of this approach is to go beyond simple descriptive data to the level of verifying relationships between variables.

Research by physical educators pertaining to social psychological phenomena can best be described as exemplifying the social empiricism approach. Most has been oriented toward the investigation of practical problems rather than the resolution of broader theoretical problems. Unfortunately, most of this empirical research has not evolved from any systematic research program or from theory. This unsystematic testing of relationships between variables has been termed the "shot gun" approach. This term describes not only social psychological research related to physical activity but much of the research conducted by physical educators in general. Consequently, the social psychological research related to physical activity has derived few, if any significant generalizations.

One other deficiency in previous social psychological research is noteworthy. Many investigations were conducted oblivious to existing theory and empirical observations formulated by social psychologists. Upon careful examination of the social psychological literature, considerable research can be found that is quite relevant to physical activity. Physical educators can certainly draw upon these findings to increase their understanding of social-influence processes occurring during physical activity. These social psychological investigations provide valuable information by suggesting alternative hypotheses and procedural refinements. Fortunately, this shortcoming has come to the attention of some dedicated researchers. As a result, physical educators today have a greater awareness of the research developments in the behavioral sciences. Hopefully, the time is past for near-replication of experiments completed 20 years previously without utilizing the refinements suggested by these studies.

The Social Analysis Approach

The "new" approach advocated here is the development of a social psychology of physical activity which abandons both the social philosophy and the social empiricism approaches. Rather than research guided by conjecture and speculation and aimed solely at the description of social phenomena, "new" research should be directed at understanding the relationships underlying these social phenomena. Previously, the social empiricism approach provided a description of human characteristics and attributes associated with physical activity. Social analysis represents an extension of social empiricism toward establishing a scientifically valid foundation for what is described. The new social psychology of physical activity needs to probe beneath the descriptive data to understand the nature of causal relationships. Social psychology of physical activity research needs to strive for the development of theory and the testing of relevant hypotheses derived from these theories.

To alleviate the possibility of confusion, the term "theory" needs precise definition. For present purposes, theory is defined according to Kerlinger as:

> . . . a set of interrelated constructs (concepts), definitions, and propositions that presents a systematic view of phenomena by specifying relations among variables, with the purpose of explaining and predicting the phenomena.[3]

In these terms, theory may be considered the ultimate aim of science. Also, it is visibly evident that theory development in most subdisciplines of concern to physical educators has progressed very little. This failure is perhaps attributed to the applied nature of these fields and their heavy reliance upon the parent discipline. Because a social psychology of physical activity has no theories of its own, it is suggested that it is appropriate and parsimonious to borrow social psychological theories and determine their applicability to physical activity. Systematic testing to determine the appropriateness of these theories can lead in one of two directions: (1) Support may be found for these theories, or (2) They may be found inappropriate for physical activity. If the latter is the case, the theory can either be abandoned and a search made for another, or it may be modified based on theory-testing research. If no social psychological theories are found to be adequate, physical educators must attempt to construct their own.

The diversity and complexity of behavioral science research is nowhere manifested to any greater extent than in social psychological research. The complex social processes occurring between individuals, individuals and groups, and between groups themselves form much of the substance of physical activity. The final section of this paper discusses some of these social processes and attempts to show the relationship between them and physical activity.

Some Concerns of "A Social Psychology of Physical Activity"

In studying social-influence processes, social psychologists commonly refer to the constructs that they investigate as variables. A variable is an attribute or condition which can vary in one or more ways and which can be systematically shown to affect or be affected by other attributes or conditions. Many social psychological variables can be either "dependent" or "independent" and are not permanently fixed as one or the other with regard to the direction of effect when applied to the study of human behavior involved in physical activity. In other words, interest may be either in the effects that social psychological variables have on various aspects of physical activity, or in the effects that physical activity have on social psychological variables. In experiments using the former paradigm, the social psychological variable would be the independent variable and that aspect of physical activity measured would be the dependent variable. In the latter experimental arrangement, the independent variable becomes some aspect of physical activity and the dependent variable is some social psychological variable.

Social Influences on Motor Performance

A primary concern of a social psychology of physical activity is with an individual's behavior as influenced by other individuals when involved in physical activity. This problem is an example of the social psychological variable as the independent variable and some aspect of physical activity as the dependent variable. Several recent studies have investigated the effects of passive and active audiences as well as co-actors on one component of physical activity—motor behavior. For example, the presence of a passive audience has been shown to impair motor skill acquisition but to facilitate the performance of a well-learned motor skill.[4] Co-actors (other individuals performing the same task at the same time) have also been shown to facilitate performance on a simple muscular endurance task.[5] The influence of an active audience providing praise and reproof (social reinforcement) on motor skill acquisition is another social process not yet clearly understood.[6] Observational learning or imitation, cooperation, and competition are other basic social influence processes requiring further investigation.

Influence of Physical Activity on Social Performance

In contrast with the above research, a social psychology of physical activity is also concerned with how various facets of physical activity influence social performance. Problems in this area are exemplified by such questions as:

What are the effects of involvement in physical activities on social performance?

What are the consequences of successful competitive experiences on social performance?

What, if any, social skills are acquired during participation in physical activities?

Are certain social skills more effectively acquired while engaging in intensive physical activity?

What is the effect of physique on personal perception and how does body image influence social performance?

Answers to these questions would bring physical educators much closer to realizing and functionally assessing the attainment of the social objective so often claimed.

Paradoxically, this line of research probably has been less explored than any other. It is not difficult, however, to understand why. Manipulation of the independent variable has been difficult enough, but the dependent variable—i.e., social performance or social skills—has often seemed beyond measurement. Recently, however, social psychologists have made substantial progress in measuring social performance.[7] Therefore, with the operational measurement of social performance being more feasible and with the methodological advances in the behavioral sciences, the effects of participation in physical activities on social performance should in the near future receive more experimental attention.

Attitudes

Among the important social-influence processes with which a social psychology of physical activity is concerned are such variables as attitudes, personality, and culture. Probably, the most widely studied social-influence process in physical education research has been the construct of attitude. The study of attitudes is most useful in accounting for individual differences in reacting to a given situation. In large measure, attitudes conveniently sum up the past history of the individual's social experience to allow differential prediction of individual social behavior.

Attitude research in physical education probably offers the best example of using the social empiricism rather than the social analysis approach. This research has typically assessed attitudes toward various sports, athletes, physical education programs at every level, and competition. As a whole, these studies have not been theory oriented, but directed toward practical ends. The variety of methods employed and the diversity of attitudes assessed have made it virtually impossible to reach any generalizations. The value of these studies lies in a cataloguing of attitudes for a small sample of the population at one particular point in time. They do not probe beneath the surface to discover how the attitudes are formed or why they change.

A recent exception to the strictly empirical approach in the study of attitudes toward physical activity, however, is noteworthy. Kenyon[8] has used the social analysis approach by constructing a model to characterize physical activity as a social psychological phenomenon. His proposed model is based upon empirical data from which hypotheses may be derived for the study of attitudes toward physical activity. Even though, as Kenyon suggests, his model is only a crude beginning, it should be recognized as a big step in the right direction. Future attitude research in physical education needs to investigate the underlying reasons for the formation of attitudes toward physical activity and how and why these attitudes change. Anecdotally, a most fascinating problem is to discover why such a discrepancy exists between positively expressed attitudes toward physical activity and actual behavior!

Personality

Deeply entrenched in the sciences is a desire for parsimonious explanation of behavior. This desire is commonly bought at the price of grossly imprecise general statements about social behavior. It is apparent that persons differ markedly in their orientations to the social environment. General statements about the reaction of persons to a particular situation must all too often be modified. Therefore, adequate development of a social psychology of physical activity will ultimately depend on the integration of personality constructs into the explanation of social behavior of individuals engaged in physical activity.

Personality constructs refer to an individual's unique characteristics. The contemporary view of personality focuses on dispositions that lead individuals to typical responses rather than focusing on the responses alone. Dispositions are considered to function within the individual's psychological field and to intervene between experience and responses to social stimuli. A social psychology of physical activity is concerned with personality in two ways. First, it is concerned with the interaction of personality dispositions and situational variables on individual behavior while involved in physical activity. Second, it is concerned with the impact of the social environment surrounding physical activity on personality development.

Physical educators have been interested in personality dispositions for some time, but the research to date typifies the "shot gun" approach. Investigation of such dispositions as anxiety, need achievement, risk taking, authoritarianism, and internal and external locus of control by physical educators suffers from the same weaknesses identified in attitude research. Again, personality research offers a good example of the social empiricism approach. Any generalizations reached are extremely tenuous as a result of the diversity of methods used and samples studied. These descriptive data are not without use, but only by employing the social analysis approach can the nature of causal relationships between personality dispositions and components of physical activity be understood. Finally, it is apparent that the consideration of situational variables alone, without respect to the interaction of situation and personality, is a fruitless quest.

Culture

Another important influence on physical activity and sport is culture. A society's culture consists of the relationships and social arrangements passed on and institutionalized to routinely handle the characteristic problems of that society.[9] By providing social reality, the basic psychological effect of culture is to influence a society's members toward distinctive ways of thinking and acting. It should be important for physical educators to understand the effects of cultural norms on individual participation in physical activity. In social psychological terms, norms and roles are in the nature of social expectancies which individuals share in their psychological fields. Roles refer especially to those particular expectancies regarding appropriate behavior for a person occupying a position in a given situation.

From a social psychological point of view, physical educators need to be concerned about the cultural influences on individual behavior while involved in physical activity and the role of sport as a transmitter of cultural expectancies. The importance of physical activities as a medium for such transmissions is becoming increasingly recognized as an integral part of the socialization process.

Although some researchers in the area of sociology of sport have demonstrated interest in culture as a variable of study, few have explored cultural effects on physical activity from a social psychological or individual point of view. Answers to such questions as the following will increase our understanding of the relationship between culture and physical activity:

What effect does role variation have on individual motor performance?

What behavior is expected from individuals occupying various roles in sports?

Is the establishment of roles into a hierarchical order detrimental to certain individuals occupying lower roles?

What is the relationship between sport participation and such culturally affected variables as social class, social mobility, and ethnic affiliation?

Many more questions can be asked, but the point is that little is known about the array of cultural influences affecting involvement in physical activity.

The subcultural influences affecting individual involvement in physical activity are also of vital concern to the physical educator. Subcultures are divisions of society represented in social class, community, and ethnic differences. They are important in social psychology because of their influence on the values and behaviors of individuals identified with them in a reference group sense. Social class, for example, is a major subculture variation based on the qualities valued in a society such as family standing, income, and education. Physical educators can find the importance of subcultural influences on physical activity in such questions as:

What is the influence of the peer group, the family, a sibling, and the school on participation in and involvement with physical activity?

Do these early experiences affect an individual's disposition toward involvement in physical activity?

How does social class influence individual involvement in physical activity?

What influences do ethnic distinctions based on racial, religious, and national origins have on individual involvement in physical activity?

Group Dynamics

Social psychology of physical activity is also deeply concerned with the structure and processes of groups involved in physical activity. The study of groups, commonly referred to as group dynamics, is dedicated to increasing knowledge about the nature of groups, the laws of their development, and their interrelationships with individuals, other groups, and larger institutions. The affiliations individuals have in groups formed for purposes of involvement in physical activity possess the potential for affecting the individual's actions and psychological states. Even though considerable research has appeared in the field of group dynamics, physical educators as well as social psychologists know very little about the dynamics of sport groups and the effects they may produce.

Some of the variables included in the study of the structure and processes of groups formed for the purpose of involvement in physical activity are: group productivity, group cohesiveness, cooperation and competition, communication, leadership, and the power structure within the group. Another important variable is the relationships that exist between groups. For example, what effect does competition have on intergroup relations? What is the basis for intergroup conflict and how can it be managed? If direct conflict does not occur, intergroup tension usually takes the form of hostility and prejudice. What methods then can be employed to relieve such tensions? These and many other questions indicate some of the variables and problems of concern in the study of the structure and processes of groups involved in physical activity.

Extensive reference to the completed social psychological research related to physical activity has not been made in this paper. It should be noted, however, that a few physical educators have employed the social analysis approach to investigate social psychological phenomena related to physical activity. This research is noteworthy, but unfortunately has not been very extensive and is overshadowed by the strictly empirical investigations. Today, as never before, physical educators and coaches alike are seeking greater understanding of man's relationship with his social environment. Thus, the need for a concerted social analysis research program investigating the social psychology of physical activity on a much larger scale is warranted.

Conclusion

Thus far, the field of social psychology has been defined, distinguished from its parent disciplines, and the concerns of a subdiscipline called social psychology

of physical activity outlined. Social psychology was defined in terms of both its content and its method. Simply stated, its content deals with the individual's relationships with his social environment. Its method is that of modern psychology as an empirical science. A social psychology of physical activity is concerned with how human behavior is influenced by the presence, behavior, and products of other human beings individually and collectively, while involved in physical activity. A social analysis approach rather than a social empiricism approach was advocated for this field of study. The social analysis approach is a three-step process which involves: (a) the collection of carefully made observations, (b) the ordered integration of these observations to permit the statement of general principles describing the logical patterns into which they fall, and (c) the utilization of these general principles to predict future observations.

Physical educators have long claimed a social objective in their programs. Over the years, however, little tangible evidence has been found to support the achievement of this objective. Failure to rigorously study the social nature of man while involved in physical activity has been partially due to the complexity and limitations of behavioral science research techniques. With improvements in these techniques and the development of high speed computers, the ability to experimentally investigate the social concomitants associated with physical activity has greatly increased.

Today, more than ever, research in the behavioral sciences seems particularly challenging. It is now generally recognized that physical activity plays no small role in the social life of man. Therefore, the need to understand social behavior while involved in physical activity increases as we spend ever-increasing amounts of time in such pursuits. For the creative and dedicated scholar, the world of social phenomena is waiting to be explained.

NOTES

1. McGrath, J.E. *Social Psychology: A Brief Introduction.* New York:Holt, Rinehart and Winston, 1965, p. 1.
2. Kenyon, G.S. "Sport Involvement: A Conceptual Go and Some Consequences Thereof." Paper presented at Sociology of Sport Symposium, University of Wisconsin, November, 1968.
3. Kerlinger, F.N. *Foundation of Behavioral Research.* New York: Holt, Rinehart and Winston, 1967, p. 11.
4. Martens, R. "Effect of an Audience on Learning and Performance of a Complex Motor Skill." *Journal of Personality and Social Psychology,* 12, 252-260, 1969.
5. Martens, R., and Landers, D.M. "Coaction Effects on Muscular Endurance." *Research Quarterly,* 40, 733-737, 1969.
6. Roberts, G.C., and Martens, R. "Social Reinforcement and Complex Motor Performance." *Research Quarterly,* in press.
7. Argyle, M., and Kendon, A. "The Experimental Analysis of Social Performance." *Advances in Experimental Psychology,* Vol. 3. Edited by L. Berkowitz. New York: Academic Press, 1967.
8. Kenyon, G.S. "A Conceptual Model for Characterizing Physical Activity." *Research Quarterly,* 39, 96-105; "Six Scales for Assessing Attitude Toward Physical Acitivity." *Research Quarterly,* 39, 566-574, 1968.
9. Hollander, E.P. *Principles and Methods of Social Psychology,* New York: Oxford University Press, 1967, p. 239.

DISCUSSION QUESTIONS

A. *Eldon Snyder and Elmer Spreitzer*

1. What is the present academic relationship between Sociology of Sport and (its parent discipline) Sociology?

2. List and discuss some reasons why Sociology of Sport has yet to become a formal subfield within Sociology.

3. Which thematic areas have proved most popular for researches in Sociology of Sport?

4. Do gaps exist in the Sociology of Sport literature? Explain your answer.

5. Why is the small sport group such a fertile area for the small group researcher?

6. What future do the authors see for the subfield, Sociology of Sport?

7. Do you think the future of Sport Sociology would be best served if it becomes a sub-field of Sociology or, if it remains an area of specialization within Sport Studies?

B. *Rainer Martens*

1. According to the author, what is the academic relationship between Sociology and Social Psychology?

2. What is the primary concern of Social Psychology?

3. Briefly describe the three approaches for studying social behavior which have influenced modern Social Psychology.

4. List some research concerns in the social psychology of physical activity and provide sport-related examples for each.

Unit II

Sport and American Society

Those who would argue that sport is a non-serious, frivolous activity, removed from the vicissitudes of everyday life, may be guilty of having a rather myopic view of the world around them. Indeed, the pervasiveness of sport in practically every sector of American life, be it social, political or economic, suggests that it permeates the social fabric more deeply than was previously thought.

Since the publication of Robert Boyle's *Sport: Mirror of American Life* over a decade ago, many journalists, novelists, and researchers have elaborated further on this theme. In fact, the "list" of "interdependences," and "relationships" between sport and society has grown considerably. An in-depth analysis of the literature suggests that sport is functionally related to religion, the military, the polity, business and industry, education, and everyday language. Furthermore, it has been argued that sport is a means for the transmission of cultural values, the maintenance of the status quo, and for rallying and unifying loosely knit social groups and communities. It has also been suggested that many politicians identify with sport to enhance their political image before the voting public.

In the three selections which follow, the authors focus on the interdependence between sport and society, for the purpose of demonstrating the function of sport in society. In the first selection, sociologist Harry Edwards discusses sport as a social institution, and identifies a number of socially significant values which are thought to be transmitted through sport participation. The author also describes how American ideology is embedded in the sport institution, and explains why critics of sport are often perceived as attacking American society itself.

In the next selection, Michael Real, professor of communications, analyzes the manifest and latent functions of the Super Bowl. He suggests that the game "functions in a manner similar to traditional mythic activities" in which symbolic forms provide the opportunity for personal identification, a sense of community, heroic archetypes, and others. The author further suggests that the Super Bowl serves as a symbolic arena where dominant cultural value orientations are expressed and celebrated. The function of "big business" in both collegiate and professional sports, and its relationship to various corporate establishments is also discussed.

In the final selection, sociologists Thomas Martin and Kenneth Berry offer several explanations for the emergence of the phenomenon of motorcross in post-industrial American society. In their conclusions, they suggest that the activity may be a manifestation of a particular social class's response to societal "strain, conflict, and change."

SPORT AS A SOCIAL INSTITUTION

Harry Edwards

Throughout the discussion thus far references have been made to the "institution of sport" in American society. But "sport" consists of many complex and varied activities, values, positions, and role relationships. Is it justifiable to talk of sports as an institution?

We will use the definition of an "institution," offered by Williams, as

a set of institutional norms that cohere around a relatively distinct and socially important complex of values. The central core of an institution is a set of obligatory norms. In the fully developed case, institutional norms are: (1) widely known, accepted, and applied; (2) widely

Harry Edwards, "Sport and Social Change," in H. Edwards *Sociology of Sport* (Homewood, Illinois: The Dorsey Press, 1973), pp. 84-92.

enforced by strong sanctions continuously applied; (3) based upon revered sources of authority; (4) internalized in individual personalities, (5) inculcated and strongly reinforced early in life; and (6) objects of consistent and prevalent conformity.[1]

It follows from the substance of these definitions that institutions "define problems and approved solutions" and thereby "channelize" human experiences along certain lines while ignoring or prohibiting other possibilities.[2]

Now in a complex society such as the United States, publicly expressed and supported institutional values frequently fall far short of accounting for actual behavior. Therefore an analysis of these values de facto renders a highly selective and incomplete picture of society. However, discrepancies between ideal norms or values and actual patterns of behavior do not negate the fact that institutional structures do emerge and are perpetuated which regulate much human behavior in specific areas of social interaction.

Before applying these conceptions to sports, we need to ask who it is that is affected by the values centered upon sports activities. According to Kenyon "The cognitive world of most people includes sports. The amount of sport information made available to persons in most countries makes it almost impossible to avoid learning something about it."[3]

But obviously Williams' concept of the "channelizing" effect of institutions implies more than mere cognizance of sports endeavors, since many informational inputs may in fact be matters of indifference—affectively neutral in impact. Thus, some element of "involvement" must be taken into account, that is, the relative centrality of sport-related values to the outcomes of the various persons who are aware of sports activities. The notion of "relative centrality" refers to the significance of sports activities in relation to one's in-terests, life concerns, and outcomes. As relative centrality decreases, overt behavioral responses to the value demands and consequences of sports likewise decrease—ultimately, of course, diminishing to zero in the case of an individual totally unaware of sport.

Clearly, a description of each specific individual's involvement in sports would be both impossible and unnecessary. A more useful approach is to specify involvement by social role and position. Such specification can be aided by an adaptation of Kenyon's classification of types of involvement. He subdivides involvement as "overt behavior" into "primary involvement," referring to actual participation, and "secondary involvement," referring to all other forms of participation including participation by way of consumption (coaches, team leaders, fans, etc.) and via production (manufacturers, retailers, promoters). For our purposes, however, Kenyon's delineations require further specification. Using his concepts of primary and secondary involvement as foundations, Table 5-1 presents a more refined analysis.

Within the context of Table 5-1, a sizable portion—if not a majority—of American society's members would be found under one heading or another indicative of substantial involvement in sport.

The Function of Sport

Apart from the question of who is affected, what "needs" or functions are served by sport? If sport in fact constitutes an institution, what are the consequences or functions of its "channeling"? And, toward what values or goals does its channelizing of activity lead?

The answers to these questions depend both upon the content of the sports creed and upon the relationship between this content and other parts of America's cultural heritage. In a direct sense, sports activities produce no material commodities analogous, say, to the automobile

TABLE 5-1
Centrality of Sports-Related Values by Role, Position, and Degree of Involvement

Primary Involvement				Secondary Involvement			
Direct	Indirect			Direct		Indirect	
				Producer			
Participant (A)	Instrumental Leader (B)	Regulator or Administrator (C)	Expressive Leader (D)	Fiscal (A)	Entrepreneural (B)	Consumer (C)	Uninvolved
1. Superstar 2. Captain 3. First string 4. Substitute 5. Athlete incapacitated by sports injury	1. Coach or manager 2. Doctor 3. Trainer 4. Water boy	1. Sports governing bodies 2. Rules committees 3. Athletic director 4. Referee, umpire, field judge, etc.	1. Public relations personnel 2. Cheerleader 3. Band 4. Former outstanding team members, alumni	A. *Professional sports* 1. Owner 2. Promoter B. *Amateur sports* 1. Educational institutions 2. Alumni 3. Philanthropic "sportsmen"	1. Sports equipment wholesalers 2. Retailers 3. Salesmen 4. Concessionaires	1. Relatives and close friends of primary level actors 2. Fans ("fanatics") 3. Occasional spectators	1. The cognizant but nonaffected (some newly arrived foreigners who are unfamiliar with American sports; Americans who simply pay little or no attention to sports, etc.) 2. The noncognizant (The new born, the mentally incapacitated, the extremely alienated or isolated, etc.)

production of General Motors. It may be said that sports activities produce entertainment for the spectator and income for coaches and for athletes at the professional level. But motion pictures also provide entertainment as do phonograph records, live theater, and art shows. However, only rarely does one of these other components of the "entertainment industry" surpass sport in terms of the sustained "fanatical" devotion and loyalty that it commands from many of society's members. Thus, Beisser points to a striking characteristic of sport fans:

> One may explain the willingness of fans to pay for their sports events—and they pay handsomely—on the basis of entertainment. But does entertainment alone account for spectators who willingly endure inclement weather and personal sacrifice for the sake of a sport, for example, the loyal New York Mets fan who steadfastly supported their team in baseball's most miserable showing? Or the rioting that accompanies Stanley Cup competition in ice hockey? Clearly, one must look deeper than casual amusement to understand the fan's loyalty, commitment, and willingness to sacrifice. . . . 4

And though some coaches and outstanding athletes often receive very large salaries, in any realm other than sport all but a few of the very highest salaries would be regarded generally as inadequate—given that occupational security is virtually nonexistent and that high risk of serious injury are involved. Yet the fans continue to fill athletic facilities, sometimes paying fantastic prices, to see highly regarded teams or individuals confront each other. And there is no shortage of willing participants. In fact, over a million and a half amateur athletes each year—from the little leagues up through collegiate and semiprofessional sports—literally risk life and limb for nominal or no financial remuneration whatever. There must be something more involved here than mere "entertainment"—or even the creation of additional occupational positions or of opportunities for educational advancement.

In searching for this "something more"—this additional qualitative characteristic of sports, let us recall an earlier reference to a statement by Loy and Kenyon:

> . . . sociologists [in the Soviet Union] working within a Marxist context . . . assume certain end products [of sport] to be implicitly established, namely, the shaping of various social institutions to facilitate the ultimate achievement of a communist society. 5

Similarly, the observations below from the *Peking Review* indicate that the Russians are not alone in their belief in the socially and politically supportive potentialities of sports:

> Holding high the great red banner of Mao Tsetung thought, Ni Chihchin has trained painstakingly for many years with unmatched perseverance, displaying the revolutionary spirit. . . . His training plan was drawn under the guidance of Mao Tsetung Thought . . . then the moment for tempering the revolutionary will . . . up and over the 2.22 meter mark—a new national record. . . . The evening of the day he broke [the record], he again opened his book of the *Selected Works of Mao Tsetung* and read aloud: "To win country-wide victory is only the first step in a long march of ten thousand miles. . . ."6

In America, of course, the meaning of sports is interpreted within the context of a particular social and political heritage. Hence, the late General Douglas MacArthur echoes a familiar sentiment when he says of sport

> It is a vital character builder. It molds the youth of our country for their roles as custodians of the republic. It teaches them to be strong enough to know they are weak, and brave enough to face themselves when they are afraid. It teaches them to be proud and unbending in honest defeat, but humble and gentle in victory. . . . It gives them a predominance of courage over timidity, of appetite for adventure over love of ease. Fathers and mothers who would make their sons into men should have them participate in [sports]. 7

Given the explicit and implied potentials of sports as viewed from each of the three sociopolitical perspectives above—Russian-style Marxist-Leninism, Maoism, and, for want of a more precise concept, Americanism—it may be assumed (1) that most sports activities have few, if any, intrinsic and invariant socially or politically significant qualities (2) and that those qualities which such activities do possess are sufficiently "liquid" to fit comfortably within many diverse and even conflicting value and cultural traditions.

Now, while the range of possible human physical activity may be quite broad, there are nonetheless boundaries or limits in this regard which are determined by mankind's anatomical and physiological structure as a species and by the limiting influences of his environment, for instance, gravity. Thus, any particular movement is relatively quick or slow, any individual is relatively strong or weak, and so forth. All physical endeavors involve, in a substantive sense, merely the coordination and/or use of body movement, strength, speed, and endurance toward the end of accomplishing a particular goal; these actual substantive features are in and of themselves neutral. They simply fall within or outside of the physical capabilities of each individual. In sports, a premium is put upon pressing toward the upper limits of man's physical capability. For this reason, sports activities usually exact a price from the athlete in terms of physical exertion far beyond the "intrinsic worth" of the immediate goal accomplished (e.g., jumping over a bar seven feet high is itself of no direct concrete value—and may, in fact, result in some form of injury). Accomplishment in sports then is de facto exceptional in terms of both its quality and its goals relative to the "normal" physical efforts required of people in most societies in meeting their day-to-day role responsibilities. *It is this, the relatively extraordinary quality of the physical requirements involved in sports activities that is the first key to the functions of sport as an institution.*

All societies must solve the basic problem of regulating human behavior and directing efforts. In every society, "cultural blueprints" are developed that express axiomatic and unconditional ideal norms which are typically very plastic and nonspecific in terms of detailed application. Especially in highly heterogeneous societies, where dependence has shifted increasingly from primary to secondary forms of social control, the pressure to regulate and coordinate the values and perspectives operant in human interaction and day-to-day problem solving is imperative. Such cultural blueprints typically involve some definition of the "good" citizen and thus set boundaries upon acceptable behavior and goals.

By infusing exceptional, but "intrinsically" neutral, physical activity with socially significant values, societies reinforce prevalent sentiments regarding acceptable perspectives and behavior. They thus establish avenues of communicating to the populace those values focusing upon solutions to critical problems, most notably those involving needs for societal integration and goal attainment.

It will be recalled that sports activities are, in a *direct* sense, nonutilitarian in product but utilitarian in process. Hence, social concern is, officially or ideally, focused on the *quality of performance* by those involved in sports as primary participants. This focus upon the presentation of a "high-quality performance," the "exceptional" character of the physical demands involved in the achievement of any consequent success in sports, and the existence of a system of shared value orientations common to both the institution of sport and the larger society combine to attract widespread public attention and interest.

Sport thus is strongly marked by nonutilitarian loyalties and commitments, by much ritualized or ceremonial behavior, by expressive symbolism, and by ideological creeds justified in terms of "ultimate" values or ultimate conceptions of the good life.

In sum, sport is essentially a secular, quasi-religious institution. It does not however, constitute an alternative to or substitute for formal sacred religious involvement.

Nor does it typically espouse values which are in conflict with the general prescriptions of such religious bodies. Rather, since the socially significant secular values infused into sports activities typically have their roots in large part in the religious and moral heritages of the societies in which these activities are pursued, values disseminated through the institution of sport are (1) more supplemental and complementary than contradictory to established religious doctrines, and (2) they apply more directly to day-to-day secular concerns of a society's members.

If this characterization is correct, one would expect that any attack upon the institution of sport in a particular society would be widely interpreted (intuitively, if not explicitly) as an attack upon the fundamental way of life of that society as manifest in the value orientations it emphasizes through sport. Hence, an attack upon sport constitutes an attack upon the society itself. As we shall see later, this interpretation is affirmed by persons both supportive and critical of the functioning of sport in America. At this point, however, suffice it to say that there exists more than a minimal degree of plausibility in an assertion I have often made: "If there is a universal popular religion in America it is to be found within the institution of sport."

To reiterate then, sport is a social institution which has primary functions in disseminating and reinforcing the values regulating behavior and goal attainment and determining acceptable solutions to problems in the secular sphere of life. The channeling functions carried out in a general fashion through the religious institution (or through the dissemination of political ideology in atheistic societies) are thus extended and supported. This channeling affects not only perspectives on sport, but, it is commonly assumed, affects and aids in regulating perceptions of life in general. And herein lies the primary significance of sport as an institution.

Other observers have agreed with this general characterization of sport. For instance, Boyle states:

> Sport permeates any number of levels of contemporary society and it touches upon and deeply influences such disparate elements as status, race relations, business life, automotive design, clothing styles, the concept of the hero, language, and ethical values. For better or for worse, it gives form and substance to much in American life. . . .[8]

Within the context of the discussion of sport as an institution, we find some evidence supportive of the frequent claim that sports is "political" in nature, though this label typically is denied by persons responsible for the control and regulation of sports activities. If, in fact, our own diagnosis of the functions of sport is correct, then the institution of sport and the political institution in America do share to some degree a common focus. While, unlike the political institution, sport is not directly involved in political implementation, it does share with the polity the function of disseminating and reinforcing values that are influential in defining societal means and in determining acceptable solutions to problems, that is, goals to be attained. The fact, however, that sport as an institution is involved only with value dissemination rather than implementation means that its pronouncements need not stray from ideal values. For it is only within those institutions concerned with the actualization of political values in the general society that responsible persons of necessity must show flexibility in terms of their guiding ideology. While this characteristic of the institution of sport renders it ideal as a vehicle for value dissemination, it also renders the institution susceptible to criticisms that it operates consistently in ideological concert with the political right. To the degree that the political leanings of significant persons holding positions of control in sport can be assumed to be indicative of the political demeanor of the institution as a whole, there is some empirical basis for the assertion that sport is both political in character and basically conservative. For instance, Walter Bayers, director of the National Collegiate Athletic Association, in the April, 1970 *NCAA News Letter* wrote an editorial endorsing the political stance of Vice-President Spiro Agnew and denouncing those who criticized Agnew's conservative political position. There is also some evidence that the more conservative political figures tend to more strongly indorse the claimed benefits of sports activities. Max Rafferty, former California State Superintendent of

Public Instruction and generally considered to be on the political far right, has stated

> Critics of collegiate football are kooks, crumbums, and commies . . . hairy, loud-mouthed, beatniks. Football is war—without killing. Athletes possess the clear, bright, fighting spirit which is America itself.[9]

Similarly, in Robert Lipsyte's by-lined column, "Sports of the Times," in the *New York Times* of June 7, 1971, Vice-President Spiro Agnew stated:

> I believe that sport, all sport, is one of the few bits of glue that holds our society together, one of the few activities where young people can proceed along traditional lines . . . where he can learn how to win . . . and how to lose. . . .

A correlation between conservatism and fan enthusiasm for sport as suggested by the findings of a Gallup Poll (reported by William A. Seevert in the *Chronicle of Higher Education,* January 25, 1971, p. 1) indicates that the more politically conservative a region of the nation is, overall, the greater the perceived interest in sport. Of the college students polled in the relatively cosmopolitan western and eastern parts of the United States, 57 percent in the East felt interest in sport to be declining as did 44 percent in the Far West. By contrast, only 39 percent of students in the Midwest, and, in the traditionally more conservative South, only 35 percent felt sports interest to be on the wane.

This fragmentary evidence gives some plausibility to the idea that sport as an institution is conservative in its political affinities. The contention here is that both the apparently intrinsic political character of sport in America and the conservativeness of its appeal are mainly due to its characteristics as an in-

stitution—although the political conservatism of people holding certain key sports-related positions certainly might contribute to and highlight the overall political demeanor of the institution. An additional speculative hypothesis is, of course, that, due to the conservative political character of sport as determined by its functions in society, there is a tendency for those drawn into sports and filling instrumental and regulatory positions to adhere to conservative political philosophies. Though this supposition is certainly plausible, conclusive evidence in support of this idea is not now available.

NOTES

1. Robin M. Williams, Jr., *American Society* (New York: Alfred Knopf, 1970), p. 37. Williams' basic approach to the analysis of institutions is to classify norms according to the major "needs" or value centers they are most closely associated with, e.g., economic, political, religious, educational, etc.
2. Ibid, p. 38.
3. Gerald S. Kenyon, "Sport Involvement: A Conceptual Go and Some Consequences Thereof," in *Sociology of Sport,* ed. Gerald S. Kenyon (Athletic Institute, 1969), pp. 79-80.
4. Arnold Beisser, *The Madness in Sports* (New York: Appleton, Century, Crofts Publishing Co., 1966), pp. 6-7.
5. John W. Loy and Gerald S. Kenyon, *Sport, Culture and Society* (New York, Macmillan Co., 1969), pp. 9-10.
6. "Ni Chih-chin—The Man Who Set the World Record in Men's High Jump," *The Peking Review,* no. 7 (February 12, 1971), pp. 18-19.
7. Cited in "Education in America" (prepared by the staff), *Saturday Review,* October 16, 1971, p. 38.
8. Robert H. Boyle, *Sport: Mirror of American Life* (Boston: Little, Brown and Co., 1963), pp. 3-4. See also Loy and Kenyon, pp. 67-70.
9. N. Von Hoffman, "College Sports," *Washington Post,* November 25, 1970, p. B1.

SUPER BOWL: MYTHIC SPECTACLE
Michael R. Real

*Analysis of a telecast finds
in it expressions of values
and functions of the
larger social structure.*

What makes the Super Bowl the most lucrative annual spectacle in American mass culture? To answer that question I have used the 1974 Super Bowl VIII telecast on videotape as a para-literary text for exegesis, and emerged with this thesis: the Super Bowl (i) combines electronic media and spectator sports in a ritualized mass activity, (ii) reveals specific cultural values proper to American institutions and ideology, and (iii) is best explained as a contemporary form of mythic spectacle.

By successfully blending electronic media and spectator sports, the Super Bowl has become the capstone of

an empire. In its first eight years, the Super Bowl surpassed the 100-year-old Kentucky Derby and the 70-year-old World Series as the number one sports spectacle in the United States (1). Commercial time on the Super Bowl telecast is the most expensive of the television year, surpassing even the Academy Awards presentation. These are figures on Super Bowl VIII:

From *Journal of Communication.* Vol. 25, pp. 31-43, Winter, 1975.

Michael R. Real is Assistant Professor of Communications at the University of California at San Diego and a former quarterback (offense) and middle linebacker (defense) at a "*very* small school."

Live attendance: 71,882

Television audience: 70 to 95 million

CBS payment to NFLfor television rights: $2,750,000

CBS charge for advertising per minute: $200,000 to $240,000

Total CBS advertising income from game: over $4,000,000

Estimated expenditures in Houston by Super Bowl crowd: $12,000,000

Newsmen covering: over 1600

Words of copy sent out from newsmen: over 3,000,000[1]

Curiously, this mass cultural impact revolved around a telecast which was composed of the following distribution of elements:

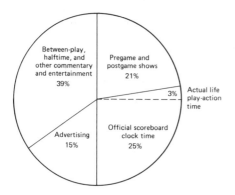

The excitement seemed to be about a football game, but the total play-action devoted in the telecast to live football was perhaps less than ten minutes.

Super Bowl VIII was only a recent climax in the sacred union of electronic media and spectator athletics. The courtship began with Edison's film of the Fitzsimmons-Corbett fight in 1897 and was consummated nationally in 1925 when the first radio network broadcast Graham McNamee's description of the World Series and in 1927 when the first cross-country radio hookup carried the Rose Bowl.

The Super Bowl VIII telecast was careful to convey a feeling of larger-than-life drama. Before the game, announcers proclaimed: "We fully believe that this game will live up to its title Super Bowl. . . . We expect this to be the greatest Super Bowl ever." The screen was filled with images of vast crowds, hulking superheroes, great plays from the past, even shots from and of the huge Goodyear blimp hovering over the field. During the game all-time records were set: Tarkenton completed 18 passes to break Namath's record for Super Bowls; Csonka broke Matt Snell's Super Bowl record by gaining 145 yards in his 33 rushing attempts. The actual game was one-sided and boring. *Sports Illustrated* led its coverage with "Super Bowl VIII had all the excitement and suspense of a master butcher quartering a steer" (21). But after the game the one-sidedness itself became the occasion for historic superlatives: "Are the Dolphins the greatest team ever?"

Why Do People Watch the Super Bowl?

Of 100 persons I questioned, two-thirds of the males and one-third of the females had watched Super Bowl VIII. The conscious motivation expressed varied from fanatic enthusiasm to bored escapism. Of those who watched: 40 percent said they watch football regularly; 18 percent said there was nothing else to do; 16 percent said this one is the big game; 12 percent said they were fans; 10 percent said they had bets on the game; 2 percent said it was the in thing; and 2 percent said their boy or girl friend would be watching. If the game were to be cancelled, 4 percent reported that they would be happy, while 25 percent reported that they would be very upset.[2]

Deeper reflection suggests that the game functions in a manner similar to traditional mythic activities. The symbolic forms of myth provide personal identification, heroic archetypes, communal focus, spatial and temporal frames of reference, and ecological regulatory mechanisms.

Personal identification. As viewers are drawn into the role of vicarious participant, they become partisan by choosing one team and putting their feelings and maybe some money on the line. A Purdue graduate picks Miami because Griese is his fellow alumnus; a Baltimore fan picks Miami because he liked Shula as Colts head coach—or picks Minnesota because he resents Shula's abandoning *his* team. Those who favor underdogs side with the Vikings. The seekers of perfection and "history's greatest" bless Miami with their support. Even "trapped" viewers (predominantly females) who watch only by default select a favorite team early in the telecast. The epic and its outcome then take on meaning to each individual. As Jacques Ellul argues, face-to-face relations are substantially displaced by the technological society: the individual, as well as the state, comes to *need* the modes of participation, identification, and meaning given to individual and collective life by what Ellul calls mass propaganda (9).

Heroic archetypes. The prototypical role of the sports hero is the most frequently found mythic function of American athletics. Holy places are established to which pilgrimages can be made. The football Hall of Fame in Canton, Ohio, commemorates the location where George Halas sat with others on the running board of a car and planned professional football almost half a century ago. Levi-Stauss notes how such contemporary historic sites function like primitive mythic foci: "Nothing in our civilization more closely resembles the periodic pilgrimages made by the initiated Australians, escorted by their sages, than our conducted tours to Goethe's or Victor Hugo's house, the furniture of which inspires emotions as strong as they are arbitrary" (13).

Communal focus. The feeling of collective participation in the Super Bowl is obvious in interviews with viewers and studies of viewer conversations and traffic patterns.[3] The majority of viewers saw the game in a group setting, used it as a social occasion, talked and moved at prescribed times during the telecast, and discussed the Super Bowl with acquaintances before and after the game. Especially for the more than half of the adult males in American who watched the game, it was a source of conversation at work, in the neighborhood, at shops, wherever regular or accidental interaction occurs.

By game time the viewer-participant knows he is joined with people in the room, in the stands, all over the country. As Cassirer and others point out, the essence of mythical belief and ritual activity lies in the feeling of collective participation and sharing of concerns and powers beyond the potential of the individual human (3).

Marking time and space are functions which sports have partially taken over from nature itself. Cummings observes:

> Nature has disappeared from most contemporary lives, shut out by gigantic buildings, train and walkway tunnels, a densely populated atmosphere. We have restructured our environment and our relations to it, and the artificial turf and Astrodome are physical symbols in the sport realm, a realm which has historically been associated with the "outdoorsman"(6).

"Football season," "basketball season," and "baseball season" are now commonly spoken of as much as summer, fall, winter, and spring. Far more newspaper space and broadcast time is given to sports than to weather, even in rural areas of the United States. Many males, isolated from weather all week by an office or plant, spend Saturday and Sunday afternoons not enjoying the elements but watching ball games. The seasons are orchestrated to provide overlaps, not gaps. As early spring grass begins to stir to life under the last film of snow, denatured American attention turns slowly toward baseball spring training while basketball season peaks toward its NCAA and NBA conclusion. National holidays are as closely identified with sports as with religious or historical meaning. Thanksgiving and New Year mean football; Memorial Day, auto racing; Christmas season, basketball tournaments; and so on. Sports overlie the sacred cycle of mythic time to provide a needed psychic relief from the tedium of western linear time.

In a similar vein, regional markings traditionally associated with family and neighborhood can, in the atomistic absence of such traditions, be regrouped around city and regional athletic teams. The Chicagoan may identify more with the Cubs, Sox, Bears, Hawks, or Bulls *in* a neighborhood bar, a place of work, the Daley fiefdom than he does with those institutions themselves. In these terms, Oakland did not exist prior to 1967, but now, with professional teams in football, baseball, basketball, and hockey, it is clearly on the big-league map.

The fact that all major professional sports are basically American national sports, even when playoffs are called the "World" Series or the "Super" Bowl, may account for more than a small part of the national cohesion and identity. The cycle of games and seasons, culminating in the annual Super Bowl, provides crucial "sacred" markers breaking the "profane" monopoly of secular time and space in our advanced industrial, technological society.

Ecologically regulatory mechanisms. Myth-ritual patterns may function as central control systems of the total ecological environment.

One of the directly regulatory functions of the Super Bowl is to move goods. The 1974 telecast, including the pre-game and post-game shows, contained 65 advertisements, of which 52 were 30- and 60-second commercials and the remainder were brief program or sponsor notices. Advertisements occupied slightly more than 15 percent of the Super Bowl VIII air time and were sponsored by 30 different companies. The product categories advertised were automobiles (7 advertisements), automobile tires (7), automobile batteries (4), beers (4), wines (3), television sets (3), insurance companies, credit cards, railroads, banks, NFL (2), and hotels, retail stores, airplanes, locks, movies, copiers, foods (1).

The advertisements for New York Life Insurance and Boeing were constructed on sports themes, as were notices for upcoming CBS sports programs. Tire and battery advertisements emphasized strength and dependability, virtues helpful in both winter and football. Liquor appeals included traditional glamor, gusto, and fun. The fuel shortage was evident in the emphasis of automobile advertisements on economy and efficiency. Consumer unrest was reflected by promotion of general corporate images as well as specific products. "Don't be fuelish" public service notices were included, in keeping with the Nixon administration's approach to fuel shortages, and a plug was inserted for NFL players going on a trip for the Department of Defense.

Myths Reflect and Sacralize the Dominant Tendencies of a Culture, Thereby Sustaining Social Institutions and Life Styles

In the classical manner of mythical beliefs and ritual activities, the Super Bowl is a communal celebration of and indoctrination into specific socially dominant emotions, life styles, and values. Further analysis of the structural and symbolic basis of the Super Bowl as a football game suggests a particular use of territoriality and property, time, labor, management, physical contact, motivation, infrastructure, packaging, game, and spectacle—all functional to the larger society.

Territoriality and property. Miami completed six of seven passes and gained 196 yards on the ground; Minnesota completed 18 of 28 passes for 166 yards but were penalized 65 yards to Miami's four. Other figures on total yardage gained, time of possession, kicking games, and third-down conversions were on the air and in the newspapers. But the *essential* datum was Miami 24, Minnesota 7. What those figures meant was that Miami had been able to occupy progressively enough of the 100 yards of the Rice Stadium playing field to move the ball on the ground, in the air, or by foot into the Minnesota end zone for three touchdowns, three conversions, and one field goal, against only one touchdown and one conversion in return.

Football centers around winning property by competition. Moreover, in football the winning of property means nothing unless one wins all the property—that is, backs one's opponent into his own valueless end zone. Points go up on the electronic scoreboard only when the opposition is driven off the field.

Time. The scoring drive by Miami in the opening minutes of Super Bowl VIII took ten plays to cover 62 yards. The series used up five minutes and 27 seconds on the official clock but took nine minutes of real time and only 42 seconds of actual play action. Football consists of very brief bursts of physical activity interspersed with much longer periods of cognitive planning and physical recuperation. It is strictly regulated by an official clock and ends, not organically when the last batter is retired as in baseball, but through external imposition when the clock runs out. Professional football is as segmented temporally, and almost as technological, as the firings of a piston engine or the sequential readouts of a computer. The periods of action have an intensity appropriate to a hyped-up, super-consumerist society, far removed from leisurely sun-filled afternoons at an early twentieth-century baseball park. In a society where virtually everyone wears a timer on his arm, one is a clock-watcher not in order to dally through work hours but because one knows that only a limited amount of time is available to achieve and accomplish.

Labor. Male domination of the Super Bowl is total. Of the hundreds of players, coaches, announcers, personalities in commercials, half-time entertainers, and celebrities in the crowd transmitted into millions of homes across the nation by Super Bowl VIII, only two halftime entertainers—Miss Texas and Miss Canada—and a small handful of anonymous actresses in commercials and faces in the crowd were female. The Super Bowl is covered by newspapers whose sports and business pages are both about as predominantly male as women's pages are female.

Racially, dozens of black players and several black announcers (although no black anchormen) were visible during Super Bowl VIII. But, more significantly, no head coaches, no team owners, and few of the super-wealthy Rice Stadium crowd were black. The Super Bowl telecast tended to support the claims of sociologist Harry Edwards of parallels between black athletes and Roman gladiators. From 1957 to 1971 black football players increased from 14 to 34 percent among the professional leagues (7). But the managerial levels remained largely closed to blacks.

Management. The organization of personnel in professional football is almost a caricature of the discipline of modern corporate-military society. Teams developed by years of training and planning, composed of 48 men, each performing highly specialized tasks, compete in the Super Bowl. Books by former players stress, whether approvingly or disapprovingly, the organizational discipline on and off the field (2, 10, 11, 14, 16, 19, 20). Meggyesy came to resent his authoritarian coaches; Jerry Kramer idolized his mentor Lombardi; and Pete Gent described his coach, Tom Landry, as a cold technician. Gent emphasized the role of professional football as a metaphor of American society even to the point of

employers moving employees—that is, teams trading players—around the country for the good of the corporations without regard for personal preference or welfare.[4] Super Bowl coaches like Shula and Grant appear on television like cool corporate executives or field marshals directing troops trained in boot camp, aided by scouts, prepared for complex attack and defense maneuvers with the aid of sophisticated telephone, film, and other modern technology. In an enterprise in which strict disciplinarians like Vince Lombardi and Don Shula have created the powerful empires, the primers for coaches might be military manuals and for players *The Organization Man.*

According to detailed accounts in *The New Yorker* and *Rolling Stone* (1, 12), top corporate executives from Ford, Shell, Xerox, and other giants of industry inundated Houston for Super Bowl VIII. The Alan R. Nelson Research firm of New York reports that 66 percent of executives earning $20,000 or more like pro football "quite a lot," while only 42 percent say the same of major-league baseball. The vice president of NBC Sports, Carl Lindemann, Jr., says, "I'd be hard-pressed to name a top executive who doesn't follow football avidly" (12). Chief Executives Nixon and Ford have typified the affinity corporate managers feel for professional football.

If One Wanted to Create from Scratch a Sport That Reflected the Sexual, Racial, and Organizational Priorities of American Social Structure, It Is Doubtful That One Could Improve on Football

In both time and space, the action of football is more compressed and boxed-in than that of the former national pastime, baseball. Both sports are sequenced around a single ball, require large teams, and are regulated by numerous rules and rule-enforcers. But, as even the simplest play diagram reveals, football's temporal and spatial confinement demands the most regimented and intricately coordinated forms of activity.

Action. Many sports provide no physical contact between participants. Some sports, like baseball, allow occasional contact. A few sports, like boxing and football, have physical contact as their base. In the Super Bowl, two opposing teams with members averaging roughly six feet two inches and 225 pounds repeatedly line up facing each other to engage in various kinds of body-to-body combat.

The television coverage of a typical Super Bowl VIII play showed an average of roughly 7.5 physical encounters between players per play. The extremes for any one play were a minimum of four and a maximum of 14 of what ranged from short-range physical contact to head-on full-speed collisions. On an extra point conversion, 20 of the 22 players on the field participate in such physical contact, normally exempting only the kicker and his holder. When Jake Scott fumbled a Mike Eischeid punt in Super Bowl VIII, at least 14 separate physical encounters took place on screen before all the blocking, downfield coverage, and scrambling for the ball were completed.

Participant observations of and about injuries reveal more of the physical nature of the game. Jim Mandich's broken thumb and Paul Warfield's pulled hamstring did not prevent their playing in Super Bowl VIII, although Milt Sunde's injuries prevented his participation at the last minute. Bob Kuechenberg, Miami offensive guard, broke his left arm four weeks before Super Bowl VII. A steel pin was inserted inside the bone for protection and he played, as did four other Dolphins with metal pins holding various limbs together. For the 1970 Super Bowl, the rib cage of Kansas City defensive back Johnny Robinson was "swollen and mushy" and he was in "misery." His roommate, Len Dawson, reported:

Wednesday of that week, I was sitting there thinking there's no way he can get out on a football field. . . . He got a local anesthetic just to see what it felt like and it made him woozy. So then they got a thoracic surgeon to go in and shoot him a different way. I don't know how they shot him or where, but they were able to deaden it and leave his mind clear (4, p. 9).

Jerry Stovall reported, when he retired after nine seasons as a St. Louis Cardinal safetyman:

In my years in football I've suffered a broken nose, fractured a right cheekbone, lost five teeth, broken my right clavicle, ripped my sternum, broken seven ribs, and have a calcium deposit in my right arm that prevents me from straightening it. I've also had 11 broken fingers. And I hurt my right foot so bad I almost lost it, injured my right arch and broke my right big toe three times. . . . The injuries hurt on rainy days—sometimes even on sunny days (4, p. 8).

Pete Gent, formerly of the Dallas Cowboys and author of *North Dallas Forty*, says: "My back is so sore I can't sit still for long. I've got arthritis in my neck from butting people with my head, and if I walk too far my knees swell. But I know plenty of guys who are hurt worse" (4, p. 10). Merlin Olsen, defensive tackle for the Los Angeles Rams, described the experience of getting injured:

I played 12 games in 1970 with a bad knee and I kept aggravating it. I knew it required an operation—both for torn ligaments and cartilage.

[Then, in the 1961 Pro Bowl] I was hit directly on the kneecap and my knee bent the wrong way about 15 degrees. The minute that contact was made I could feel things starting to tear.

I tried to get the foot out of the ground and couldn't. I couldn't stop my momentum, either. I was like slow motion. I could feel each muscle and ligament popping. Once I was on the ground the pain was about as intense as anything I've ever felt. But the pain was with me only about 30 seconds. Then it was gone—totally.

When I went in at halftime the doctors examined me. They'd pick up my foot and the knee would stay right on the table. I got off the table and went into the shower and the knee collapsed backward on its own. A couple of coaches were standing there and they turned white and almost passed out (4, p. 1).

Other professional football knees make equally grisly stories. After four operations on Joe Namath's knees, one doctor estimates. "He'll barely be able to walk by the time he's forty" (4, p. 8). When Dick Butkus, the Chicago Bears's middle linebacker, developed a bad right knee in the 1973 season, he continued to play. In September, he went to one of the nation's most prominent orthopedic surgons. The surgeon reportedly called it "the worst-looking knee I have ever seen," and told Butkus, "I don't know how a man in your shape can play football or why you would even want to." The doctor advised Butkus that, if he must play, he should spend all of his time from the end of one game until ten minutes before the kickoff of the next either in bed or on crutches. The surgeon thought there was no danger of ruining the knee further by playing, because there wasn't that much left to ruin. Butkus, needless to say, finished the season and was reportedly considering the installation of a metal knee after his playing days were over (18).

Such descriptions of injuries bring out, despite immensely sophisticated and thorough padding, how physically brutal football is. Only the low number of actual fatalities preserve it against public outcry and distinguish it from outright warfare.

Motivation. In some settings, football is played for fun. But the Super Bowl is far removed from such motivation. Members of the winning team in Super Bowl VIII each received $15,000; the losers, $7,500 (15). There may be a surface "thrill of combat," "test of masculinity," "search for glory and fame," and even "love of the game," but underneath there is one motive—money. When Duke Snider, center-fielder for the Brooklyn Dodgers, published an article in the *Saturday Evening Post* in the middle 1950s admitting "I Play Baseball for Money," there was a tremor of scandal that ran through the American public, as if a clergyman had said he did not much care for God but he liked the amenities of clerical life. But when Mercury Morris was asked on national television after the Dolphins' one-sided Super Bowl VIII victory, "Was it fun?" he replied, "It was work," and no one batted an eye.

Even nonprofessional football has a heavily commercial base. Penn State collected one million dollars from televised football in the 1973 season—$650,000 from the Orange Bowl and $350,000 from regional and national appearances during the regular season. Oklahoma's NCAA probation that same season cost them $500,000 in television revenue (5). Ohio State University led the nation with an average of 87,228 paying customers in each of its expensive seats at six home games in 1973. The 630 football-playing four year colleges in the United States attracted 31,282,540 spectators in 1973, averaging over 10,000 for each game played in the nation (1, 12). An unsuccessful coach is more than a spiritual liability to his school. A college player, even if his scholarship and employment "ride" does not make all the sacrifice and pain worthwhile, can hope for a return on his investment by making it financially in the pros. In fact, the feeder system which culminates in the Super Bowl, reaches down to any mobile, oversized high school or junior high player, drawing him on with the dream of fame and the crinkle of dollars.

Infrastructure. The institutional organization of professional football is not like American business; it is American business. Each team is normally a privately owned company or corporation with shareholders and top executive officers, including a president who is frequently the principal owner. Each corporation employs hundreds, including secretaries, public relations personnel, doctors, and scouts, of whom the public seldom hears. Employees, including players, receive salaries and bonuses and are hired and fired. Team corporations enter into multi-million-dollar television contracts and rent stadiums, which may have been financed by publicly voted bonds but leased at moderate fees to the privately-owned football enterprise. A franchise in the National Football League sells for many millions of dollars. The coordinated management of the teams under the superstructure of the League and its Commissioner Pete Rozelle is matched by an increasingly powerful player's union.

The Super Bowl itself becomes a "corporate orgy," with individual companies like Ford, Chrysler, and American Express each spending up to $150,000 hosting salesmen and customers through the weekend. A two-page article by Frank Lalli in *Rolling Stone* described Super Bowl VIII's "$12,000,000 Businessman's Special" in awesome detail (12). Lalli quoted Jimmy the Greek, who says that for corporate executives, the Super Bowl "is bigger than a political convention. Everybody tries to be here." Super Bowl tickets are allocated, and NFL broadcast coordinator Robert Cochran estimates that 80 percent wind up in corporate hands.

Packaging. The Super Bowl, as a commodity to be consumed from the television "box," receives careful packaging via the 21 percent of the broadcast devoted to pre- and post-game shows and the 39 percent between kick-off and final gun devoted to commentary and entertainment. The 1974 telecast opened with a pregame half-hour show featuring Bart Starr's analyses of filmed strengths, weaknesses, and strategies of each team, and it concluded with a panel of 15 CBS sportcasters interviewing heroes of the day's game. In between, there were the striking multicolor visuals with rapid, dramatic score opening each section of the telecast, the grandiose adjectives and historical allusions by announcers, the endless reciting or superimposing on screen of statistics and records, the pregame pageantry, the halftime extravaganzas and "Playbook," and, of course, the 52 advertisements.

The nationalism of American sports is made explicit by the playing of the national anthem at the beginning of virtually every competition from Little League baseball to the Super Bowl. Super Bowl VIII offered the ideal middle America popular singer, Charley Pride, who is both black and country-western—working-class America from Archie Bunker to Fred Sanford all rolled into one.

Halftime entertainment is replete with martial music, precision drills, uniforms, and massive formations. Super Bowl VIII featured the University of Texas marching band with Miss Texas playing a hoedown-style fiddle. They were followed by a three-ring circus with Miss Canada as ringmistress. The telecast then cut to the American Express "Playbook," followed by the live, on-field finals of the Ford Punt and Pass Competition for boys from across the country.

Spectacle. Mass culture functions at once as a celebration of dominant aspects of a society and as a diversion. Despite all the Super Bowl's overt and latent cultural significance, it is popular as a *game;* the formal competition itself has no overt functional utility. It is apart from the viewer's work, from bills, from family anxieties, from conflicts in the community, from national and international politics. Total involvement becomes desirable because the game is enjoyed for its own sake, unlike most activities in the deferred-reward world of laboring for salaries, home and self improvement, or eternal salvation. Unlike wars or family problems, the viewer is aware that he can enjoy or even opt out of the Super Bowl with the same free choice that he entered into it because "it's only a game."

The structural values of the Super Bowl can be summarized succinctly: *North American professional football is an aggressive, strictly regulated team game fought between males who use both violence and technology to gain control of property for the economic gain of individuals within a nationalistic entertainment context.* The Super Bowl propagates these values by elevating one game to the level of a spectacle of American ideology collectively celebrated. Rather than mere diversionary entertainment, it can be seen to function as a "propaganda" vehicle strengthening and developing the larger social structure.

REFERENCES

1. Angell, Roger. "Super." *New Yorker*, February 11, 1974, pp. 42-43.
2. Brown, Jimmy, with Myron Cope. *Off My Chest*. New York: Doubleday and Company, 1964.
3. Cassirer, Ernst. *Essay on Man*. New Haven: Yale University Press, 1944. (See also Cassirer's *The Myth of the State*. New Haven: Yale University Press, 1946.)
4. Chapin, Dwight. "Playing in Pain." *Los Angeles Times*, February 10, 1974, III.
5. *Chicago Tribune*. "TV Giveth and TV Taketh Away." "Ohio State Tops Nation in Football Attendance." December 23, 1973.
6. Cummings, Ronald. "The Superbowl Society." In Browne, Fishwick, and Marsden (Eds.) *Heroes of Popular Culture*. Bowling Green, Oh.: Bowling Green University Popular Press, 1972, p. 104.
7. Debord, Guy. *Society of the Spectacle*. Unauthorized translation. Detroit: Black and Red, Inc., 1970, paragraphs 1 and 6.
8. Edwards, Harry. "The Black Athletes: Twentieth Century Gladiators for White America." *Psychology Today*, VIII: 6, November, 1973, p. 44. (See also Edward's *Sociology of Sport*. Homewood, IL.: Dorsey Press, 1973.)
9. Ellul, Jacques. *Propaganda: The Formation of Men's Attitudes*, translated by Konrad Kellen and Jean Lerner. New York: Alfred A. Knopf, 1966, ch. 3. (See also Jacques Ellul, *Technological Society*, translated by John Wilkinson. New York: Alfred A. Knopf, 1964.)
10. Gent, Peter. *North Dallas Forty*. New York: William Morrow and Company, 1973.
11. Kramer, Jerry, and Dick Schaap. *Instant Replay*. New York: William W. Norton and Compnay, 1968.
12. Lalli, Frank. "And Now for the Pre-Game Scores." *Rolling Stone*, February 28, 1974, p. 40.

13. Levi-Strauss, Claude. The Savage Mind. Chicago, IL.: The University of Chicago Press, 1966, p. 244.
14. Lombardi, Vince. Run to Daylight. New York: Prentice-Hall, 1963.
15. Los Angeles Times. "Facts and Figures on Super Bowl VIII." January 13, 1974, III, p. 6.
16. Meggyesy, David M. Out of Their League. Berkeley: Ramparts Press, 1970.
17. Myerer, Anton. "The Giant in the Tube," Harper's, November 1972, p. 40.
18. Nightingale, Dave. "Butkus May Get Metal Knee." Los Angeles Times, February 10, 1974, III, pp. 8-9.
19. Oliver, Chip. High for the Game. Ron Rapoport (Ed.). New York: William Morrow and Company, 1971.
20. Plimpton, George. Paper Lion. New York: Harper and Row, 1965.
21. Sports Illustrated. January 21, 1974, p. 14.

NOTES

1. Data summarized and rounded off from figures cited in (1), (12), and (17) and in Variety and Broadcasting.
2. Survey by author and assistants during week of January 13, 1974, at University of California at San Diego.
3. The use of technology and managerial techniques is similar to that described in Ellul's Technological Society.
4. Ibid.

COMPETITIVE SPORT IN POST-INDUSTRIAL SOCIETY: THE CASE OF THE MOTOCROSS RACER

Thomas W. Martin and Kenneth J. Berry

Since World War II, American society has been marked by numerous radical transformations.[1] Rapid change, with its strains and dislocations, have been so pervasive that the behavioral sciences have become literally overwhelmed with social problems, issues and anomalies for study and solution. Amidst such an embarrassment of riches, it is not surprising that inquiry in the social sciences has increasingly become "problem" and "action" oriented.[2] One consequence of this general drift, however, is that sociologists sometimes are distracted from inquiring into some less dramatic, but equally theoretically important, aspects of contemporary life. One such area largely by-passed by sociology today concerns the role of recreation, leisure and sport in post-industrial society. While the general impression may be that inquiry into contemporary sport and recreation patterns is essentially peripheral or marginal to the mainstream of events and processes currently shaping our society, the position taken here is that the sociology of sport and recreation does in fact address certain fundamental sociological issues which are basic to an understanding of change processes in modern society.

Sport in Modern Society

In the course of the past two or so decades a small but growing body of sociological literature has developed in an area identifiable as The Sociology of Post-Industrial Leisure, Recreation and Sport.[3] Though at present coverage in this area is still sketchy and thin, with many residual areas still unexplored, some theoretical propositions have emerged to provide interpretive structure and direction to much of the work so far accomplished.[4] Two particular theoretical assumptions concerning the relationship of sport and recreation to the larger social order are of fundamental significance. They are:

I. That patterns of leisure, sport and recreation do not constitute unrelated and autonomous events occurring only in a make-believe "world of play" totally removed from the instrumental mainstream of life;[5]

II. That patterns of leisure, sport and recreation are reflective and resonant of, as well as functionally related to, deeper cultural values and institutional commitments which structure and lend meaning to life in the larger social order.[6] Thus they form an integral part of contemporary social structure producing specific and strategic contributions to other social processes.[7]

Against the backdrop of these two emergent and complementary assumptions, one of the continuing problems in Sport Sociology has been that of delineating precisely *how* recreation and sport reflect and relate to the overarching cultural values and institutional structures of given societies. The current perspective of sports sociologists suggests that complex and varied networks of *reciprocal functional relationships* exist between given types of sports and recreational patterns and the culture and social structure of the particular society in which they are found.[8] Therefore, in an attempt to shed some additional light on the nature of these relationships, this analysis will seek to make explicit how the sudden advent of *Motocrossing,* as an increasingly popular working-class sport, can be interpreted as an *innovative class-specific coping response* to stresses and strains endemic in the post-industrial tranformation of our society. To a large extent, this interpretation is linked to broader recent developments in American sport and recreation patterns.

Emerging Patterns

Broadly speaking, there are three current trends underway in post-industrial sport and recreation. They are: (1) an enormous growth in absolute numbers of sport and recreational enthusiasts; (2) an increase in the proportion of enthusiasts who actively participate in sport and recreational activities; and (3) a burgeoning in the number of forms of sport and recreation being pursued.

At first blush it would seem elemental that, given in-

From Journal of Popular Culture, VIII (1), pp. 107-120, Summer, 1974.

Dr. Martin is with the Department of Sociology and Anthropology at Colorado State University.

creasing affluence, expanding automation and advanced technology, recreation and sport would necessarily have to become a "big business" in the United States.[9] It also seems apparent that, given the increasing coverage of sports events by mass media, much of this expansion continues to take the form of passive vicarious involvement by the majority of the masses.[10] As expected, the most common statistic of sports, other than "scores," continues to be the thousands or millions of spectators or viewers who "came to watch." Such statistics may indeed index an increasing public need for distraction and entertainment, and many sports may very well still serve the time-honored expressive and integrative functions of a "Roman Circus" for post-industrial masses.

Complementing this basic pattern of passive involvement, recent trends indicate a growing proportion of enthusiasts who are physically active in their participation. This shift is marked by the large, if selective, popularity of such sports as bowling among the working classes, and by golf, sailing and skiing among the more well-to-do.[11] Moreover, active involvement of the public in a *variety* of recreational activities is widespread, and occasionally reaches "craze" proportions. Take camping as a case in point. Some two short decades ago camping was the esoteric pastime of a small group of purists who used the practice both to escape the noisome friction of urban assemblies, and to join in a simple and revivifying communion with nature.[12] The name of the game was enjoyment through roughing it. But the term has become relative, and today millions of Americans "rough it" each summer by crowding our parks and highways with their mobile campers, each crammed with the accoutrements of a modern civilization that has ostensibly been left behind. The irony of "leaving it all behind" while bringing most of "it" with you does not however, overshadow the fact that millions are in fact "doing it." As a matter of fact, so many are now participating in this form of recreation that annual campers' conventions are held, drawing thousands of enthusiasts from all parts of the country.

Another example of growing activism can be seen in the more recent snowmobile craze that has swept the northern latitudes and mountain regions of our country. Since its introduction in the mid-60's, thousands of these vehicles have been sold, and nearly all are being used in a recreational capacity. In some parts of the country the point has been reached where the possession and display of the snowmobile has become a badge of distinction proclaiming that the owner has "made it" and knows "where it's at." The function is similar to the display of power or sailboats, etc., on the front lawn or alongside the house.[13] But again muting the "conspicuous consumption" aspect, there remains a seriousness among many snowmobile buffs that has become expressed in the establishment of snowmobiling as a new and serious official sport involving scheduled events and drawing thousands of spectators.

This same basic observation carries through also with water sports. Boating and water skiing have become ex-

tremely popular, as well as expensive, pastimes for a large segment of the public. Moreover, observations could easily include the growing popularity of sailing, soaring, flying, snow skiing, parachute jumping, and so on, by now the point should be clear: there appears at every hand to be a correlation between post-industrial advancement and active individualistic involvement in recreational and sports activities.[14]

It is said that the fundamental role of the Sociologist is to discover and explain correlations between social events. In this case, many would perhaps be tempted to dismiss this correlation as the obvious consequence of the "unfolding" of post-industrial society: that increased popularity and active involvement in recreational and sports activities simply implies a logical and natural result of greater affluency, more leisure, and a mass need for diversion from the pressing exigencies of corporate life. Though all the data are not in, it is probably true that some of this correlation may indeed be accounted for by the logical power of this explanation: but certainly not all!

To view this shift towards increasing active involvement in sports and recreation as merely a residual effect of post-industrial development—frosting, as it were, on the cake of a hard-working efficient economy—ignores certain intriguing aspects which suggest the operation of yet other factors. One such puzzler is the observation that Motocrossing predominantly recruits enthusiasts from a working-class background. To assert that this anomaly is a manifest function of post-industrial development merely begs the question, and does not explain the phenomenon. Moreover, it specifically discourages the analysis of certain contemporary patterns in sport and recreation as the result of possible latent responses to strain, conflict and change in our society.

Motocrossing

In certain cases, particularly that of Motocrossing, increased participation in sports and recreation activities serves a major latent function for particular groups in post-industrial society. It does so in that such activities provide an effective framework for the expression of particular shared and basic values held by large segments our society; fundamental values, however, which are becoming increasingly anachronistic and dysfunctional relative to the basic instrumental processes of everyday life.

This thesis is primarily based on observations of a Motocross Racing Club during three seasons of operations (1970-71).[15] Among the several distinctive features of this club's membership,[16] one characteristic is outstanding. The members of the club are almost without exception *working class*. Occupationally, the membership (excluding the wives or girlfriends often attending club meetings) is employed at such jobs as heavy equipment operator, motocycle and auto mechanics, autoparts counterman, chain man on a surveying team, factory worker, carpet layer, and a local motocycles sales operator. Of the two clear exceptions to the rule, namely the writer and a graduate student from a local university, one comes from a working class background. Some upwardly mobile members of the club are currently occupied in such jobs as public school teacher, and assistant manager of a small theater, and a few members are unemployed either because of their youth or because of a locally depressed job market.

In terms of purpose, the club is singularly devoted to motocycle riding, and particularly to the organization of, and competition in, motocross races. To accomplish this goal, the club has obtained a long-term lease on a large section of nearby land desolated by strip-mining, and has constructed a tortuous one mile dirt track which only a motocycle can manuever. [17] In the course of a year, the club may sponsor anywhere from 8 to 16 events, conducted on Sundays, and consisting of 15 or more individual class races or "heats." For the racers in the club, the monetary investment in racing machine and equipment generally ranges from $600 to over $1600.

The bulk of the club's membership consists of racers. Other members in the club are wives of racers, ex-racers, and a few individuals otherwise interested in the sport. It is the racers who dominate the spirit of the club and give direction to its activities.

From a socio-psychological point of view, the racer is a distinguished breed. In ideal-typical terms, he is almost singularly consumed by the art, craft technics and challenge of motocross racing. To him, work is something that he has to do between Sunday races in order to race! In a very real sense, his job is something he does, and has to do, to fill in the void between races. The race, competition, winning and trophies constitute the main ingredients of his conversation and thought. The particular delight of the racer is to come in 1st against a hard-pushing competitor. Victory to him is a conclusive, visible, concrete thing. And it is for such a form of conquest and achievement that the motocrosser will invest most of his available time and resources.

The quest for competition and victory is dominant in the value system of the racer. He will go through inordinate pain and expense to prepare himself and his machine for weekend combat. No matter how poor his technique, or obsolescent his machine, he will go out there to win! In numerous conversations with club members and regional riders this central theme chronically emerges in a variety of forms, each exposing the psychological payoff of racing to victory for the rider. Basic to this theme is the sheer excitement of competition. [18] To many racers, the only time they "really live" is at the Sunday races: the rest of the week is viewed with detachment as they play out the other roles demanded of them by circumstance and society.

The need to compete and to win produce, in the motocross racer, a fundamental "instrumental" orientation toward his membership in the club, and especially toward the machine that he drives. It is particularly this pragmatic, functional view that distinguishes the motocrosser from other major types of riders, and

highlights his involvement with motocross racing as a main mechanism for the satisfaction of core values.

The Motocrosser

Almost any form of motocycle riding involves a man-machine relationship. The extent and form of this relationship is particularly reflected in the attitudes that a rider takes toward his machine. Many of these attitudes range along an "expressive-instrumental" continuum.

The Expressive Rider

Most cycle riders either consciously or unconsciously relate to their machines as extensions of their own personalities. Not infrequently this investment of self takes on such proportions that the cycle is attributed such anthropomorphic qualities as a name, a "personality," and even "feelings" of its own. The union, therefore, between man and machine is personalized into a friendship relationship, where neither lets the other down. Riding then becomes a cooperative effort where man and machine work together to create a smooth or pretty ride as an art form. The ultimate goal in performance is that of achieving, on the part of the rider, a psychological state of "michigoss," a feeling of euphoria that results from accomplishing a nicely styled fast ride over a challenging stretch of road.

For many of these riders, the machine also constitutes a platform for self-expression. Frequently they adorn their bikes, modestly or heavily, with a variety of bolt-on products, chroming plain parts, applying special or "custom" painting treatments, chopping and raking, mounting high "ape hanger" handlebars, and so on through a long gamut of accessories and modifications. In this way the expressive rider attempts to create in his motocycle a work of art that is at the same time an expression of his own unique aesthetic self. This transference sometimes reaches absurd proportions where the rider literally becomes enslaved by his machine; spending all available time and monies on its maintenance and "improvement," usually at the expense of his own physical and social welfare; avoiding unnecessary and excessive use of his machine as insurance against wear or accidental damage; and associating exclusively with like-minded others to the extent that his social circles contain only duplicates of himself. This pattern can be seen particularly among the membership of some large urban "outlaw" clubs, and in a few all-Black cycle clubs. At a much more muted level this syndrome also is reflected by most "loners" and/or long-distance road riders.

The Instrumental Motocrosser

The man-machine relationship of the motocross rider stands in extreme contrast to that of the "expressive" rider. To the motocrosser, his machine is an instrument pure and simple. If a motocrosser can be said to have an aesthetic appreciation of his machine, it is that the "beauty" of his machine lies not in its custom appearance or configuration, its dazzling chromework, its lean and racy look, in short its glamorous "presentation of self." Instead, the "beauty" of the machine lies in its stark utilitarian simplicity and in its Spartan structural integrity. Simply put, the motocrosser doesn't give a hoot what his machine *looks* like, just as long as it goes *fast* and *handles well* in the rough!

This utilitarian stance colors the whole of the motocrosser man-machine relationship. In contrast to the care often lavished by the expressive rider, in the heat of competition the motocross racer will delight in absolutely brutalizing his machine in order to squeeze out its last ounce of performance. Dents, bangs, broken parts are irrelevant; except in the latter case when a lost race or difficulty of replacement is involved. Secondly, in contrast to the personalized man-machine relationship projected by the expressive rider, to the motocrosser the machine is always a "thing." Two factors vitiate against the development of a close bond between the racer and his machine. On the one hand, the violent demands of racing give frequent opportunity for the machine to "let its rider down" through malfunction or breakage, thus evoking the fury and frustration of the rider on these not infrequent occasions. On the other hand, technological advances in new models, combined with rapid wear of the old, make it almost imperative that the serious racer obtain a new mount each season.

A third factor differentiating the instrumental rider concerns the social context of his cycling experience. For the expressive rider this context usually takes the form of riding with others on "trips" long or short. Often these others are fellow members of a local club or gang. Within this group the cycling experience is shared both in action and conversation. A trading-off of experiences, know-how in customization or riding styles creates a social atmosphere among expressive riders of a mutual support and admiration society. In contrast, the social relations among motocrossers are generally steeped with technological data and new advances concerning machine performance. In most get-togethers, however, one element is noticeably avoided: namely, conversation always skirts comparisons and explications of personal riding styles or techniques. Other than such cliches as "I push hard," "I go fast," "I brake early," and so on, it is a rare racer who enters into a detailed discussion or analysis of the "tricks" he uses in competition. There is, of course, an ill-perceived purpose for this mutually understood area of secrecy. Roughly, because technological advances have produced a variety of machines of more or less equal durability and performance, in competition the race often goes to the rider possessing luck (a considerable factor in the mind of the motocrosser) and superior riding skill. Riders possessing such skill thus attempt to conceal it both on the track and off. Particularly, they do not discuss exactly how they brake on certain corners, how they "track" a curve, or ride a "burm." Nor will they discuss in detail how they control their machines over jumps and dropoffs, through mud or water, or over ruts and breaks in the track. These are considered matters of personal taste and individual style, and can only be got at through close observation of actual performance. Thus among motocrossers, the specter of eventually having to compete even against fellow club members fosters a "professionally competitive" reserve which serves to diminish off-the-track social contact as a medium or context for the socialization and training of expertise among riders.

Finally, the off-the-road/on-the-road differences between the machines that these two classes of riders ride, the purposes to which they are put, are also reflected in the context of club gatherings or meetings. Among expressive riders, meetings of the group are generally social "get-togethers"; their *raison d'etre* being the enjoyment and camaraderie of each other's company. Among motocrossers, however, meetings are attended primarily to conduct business: scheduling, organizing, and conducting races. As a rule, a limited amount of socializing does usually occur, but only after meetings when sub-sets of friends may perhaps split off for beer and conversation. During the official meeting, however, attention is riveted to parliamentary procedure, the collection of dues, the problems of scheduling races, marshalling club manpower for race duties, admitting new club members, and the like. In part, this formalism is a function of the competitive club's being associated with a parent national motorcycle organization,[19] and because such involvement with pure business matters is necessary in staging the club's competitive events—the *raison d'etre* of the racer.

To sum up, then, in a very basic way the motocrosser is deeply engaged in and committed to a violent sport; a sport which provides him the opportunity to test his physical strength and tactical skills against competent opponents in an arena where total effort is required and success is both elusive and blatantly evident. To the racer, the trophy is more than a badge of courage. It is a symbol of excellence, of manhood, of a clearcut achievement of victory against heavy odds. His machine, his involvement with his club, are all instrumental to his entering the Sunday arena.

Social Sources of the Motocross-Working Class Syndrome

Given this sketch of the motocrosser and the mix of values and interests that give him motive force, the interesting sociological question remains as to *why* the apparent correlation between this sport and its selective recruitment among working class males. As a guide to further inquiry; the following rationale is offered:

1. One of the basic consequences of post-industrial development in our society has been its radical transformation of the working class "world of work."[20] Historically, the world of work has usually provided working class males with a major area of activity in which they were able to act out, express and reaffirm core identity values and a sense of self

respect and worth. Rivalry, competition, ribaldry, tests of skill and pride of work, camaraderie and reinforcement of identity was the common stuff produced in peer interaction and engagement with the work situation.

2. The American socialization process continues to selectively invest and instill among young working class males a deep appreciation of such values as "rugged individualism," "aggressive activism," "competition," "achievement" and "success."

3. However, at our present stage of post-industrial development, the world of work for working class males has become so corporatized, specialized, automated, assembly-lined, and in other ways so altered and changed as to depreciate and constrict opportunity structures for the expression and exercise of these basic values in their traditional form. In simple terms, technological and industrial growth has, in the last couple of decades, transformed the working man's world of work into a psychological wasteland.[21]

4. Hence, as a consequence, a segment of working class American males, increasingly estranged and alienated from the world of work as an opportunity structure or setting in which core values may be expressed and realized, turn to competitive forms of sport and recreation (in this case motocrossing) as an effective alternative or functional substitute.

The core of contention here is admittedly speculative in the sense that the theoretical linkages outlined in the preceding four paragraphs have not been empirically "proven" through a set of decisive critical experiments. But the rationale here presented is supported by the following observations:

The *first* proposition concerning the transformation of the working class's world of work is a basic focal point of much current work in industrial sociology; it stands without argument.

The *second* proposition, contending selective socialization processes among American males with an emphasis on competition, aggressive achievement and rugged individualism at the level of the working class takes into account that at lower class levels, where broken homes, unemployment, poverty and ghetto environments often color existence, the basic psychological stance inculcated by youth seems to be one of either "resignation," or institutionalized deviance.[22] On the other hand, among middle and upper-middle class youth, their socialization experiences both at home and at school are designed to effect a basic internalization of cooperative other-directedness instrumental to success in corporate professional careers. Among the offspring of our upper classes, to the extent that they constitute a significant class stratum in American society, class tradition and culture de-emphasize the crudities of the "frontier ethic," and substitute in its stead the polished veneer of the "Gentleman's C" as a basic attitudinal stance toward life. In juxtaposition then, it appears that only among the working or "blue collar" class elements in our society do the core values implied in standing on one's own two feet,

being a man, toughness and being able to take it, in short those values which are directed at taking the measure of a man in terms of physical competitiveness, go to making up the basic elements moulding what might be called a hard-minded "rugged individualism." Simply put then, differential placement in our social structure creates differences in perceived reality and socialization experiences which results in different types of attitudinal sets among the classes. In our society, social and historical changes have unfolded in such a manner as to make the working classes the sole bearers of a value legacy that in earlier times characterized most of our society.

To the extent that the argument so far is valid, then the *third* proposition, that our transition to a post industrial social order has constricted the opportunity structure for living out the frontier ethic of "rugged individualism," focusses on certain problems and contradictions in the life space of the working class male. If it is accurate to say that the psychology of the working class male is structured after the rugged individual model, and that historically its major arena for expression has been in the world of work, then certain changes have occurred in the world which frustrate the acting out of that stance. First, there has been a general escalation of occupations along a manual-to-brain power continuum resulting in status, recognition and rewards increasingly going to the smart (educated) and not the strong. Advances in machine technology have made some occupations obsolescent, and have reduced others to simple machine attendance. Advances in management science and organization have reduced other tasks to mere redundant assembly-line automatism. The monopoly of large-scale diversified industry has severely encroached upon the world of the small entrepreneur until "competition" no longer implies the possibility of eventual "success," but rather describes a prolonged battle of desperate survival. Further, among the blue-collar workers, the growth of unionism into monolithic bureaucracies sufficiently powerful to do battle with "ownership and management," has also brought on severe internal organization and regimentation of work life. The establishment and specification of job descriptions and controls have in effect standardized and delimited the freedom and autonomy of the worker to "prove himself" on the job. It does so to the extent that any worker trying to "show his stuff" either to his fellow workers or to management becomes labeled as a curve-breaker and gets a one-way ticket to Coventry. The point is this: in our contemporary highly organized system of division of labor based upon functional interdependence and strategic coordination, the "rugged individual" type is dysfunctional and is rapidly being displaced.

Which brings us to the *fourth* proposition, which is essentially that the rugged individualist, in some numbers, has turned to competitive sport and recreation as an arena in which he can act out and express the core values and motives structuring his ego. This is perhaps the most tenuous proposition of the lot. However, some argument can be marshalled in its support. First, from an institutional standpoint, the life-space of the working class male, divided as it is among such various spheres of activity as work, family life, religious activity, etc., offers little opportunity in any of these areas for the expression of core values of the sort with which we have been concerned. Neither the typical authoritarian stance of the husband role, nor that of the religious believer, nor any other institutionally related role which he typically plays, offers a clear-cut opportunity for playing the part of the rugged individualist.[23] Only in such recreational activities as, for example, playing poker or bowling with the boys, is it permissible to measure off one's own "mensch" against that of a significant other worthy of the challenge.

Secondly, although leisure and sport activities have historically been monopolized by the wealthy and ruling classes in the course of this century many have, as it were, "filtered down," through the class structure. A late impetus accelerating this percolator effect has been the increasing relative affluency of the working class coupled with a general society-wide displacement of "productive" values by an increasingly "consumptive" orientation.[24] Thus both greater relative wealth and a general value context changing in the direction of consumptive living has presented the working classes with a situation where recreational and sport activities have become more accessible and significant than at any time in the past.

Summary and Conclusion

The conditions outlined in this paper are taken to be indicative of certain change processes endemic to current stages of post-industrial development. The specific argument pressed here is that the selective recruitment of working class males into the sport of motocross racing is, in significant part, a latent function of certain "push-pull" factors generated by historical changes in their world of work. Such variables as the dehumanization of the work experience coupled with the continued socialization of such values as "rugged individualism" and the proving of manhood have, with a concommitant increase in relative affluence and leisure, made participation in certain forms of rugged sport (particularly motocrossing) an increasingly accessible and popular mechanism of relief and satisfaction for many otherwise alienated working class males in our society. To the extent that such involvement defuses, displaces or mutes alienation due to changes in the economic and class structures of our society, participation in the sport provides a latent contribution both to the stability of individual life and to the larger social processes with which it is connected.

NOTES

1. For example, during the past three decades our population has expanded by over a third, from 131 million in 1940 to over 200 million in 1970; our economy increased ten-fold during this same period; now nine out of ten Americans live in urban or suburban settings covering roughly 10% of our land; over half of our high school grads now try college; the thirty-five hour work week is now in effect in some branches of industry; government increasingly intervenes in public life, and in so doing has grown monolithic; our cities are chronically pressed by racial, financial and social problems; our youth now institutionalize their own counter-culture; and we are all affected by increasing alienation and fragmentation produced by the pressures and stresses endemic to our burgeoning post-industrial mass society. In the face of all this, however, most of us also enjoy a quality of life heretofor unequaled in history.
2. For a critique of the "problems" approach and its prominance in the social sciences see Herman R. Lantz, *The People of Coaltown* (Carbondale, Ill.: Southern Illinois University Press) 1971, pp. viii-xi.
3. Chief among the works which may be cited are Eric Larrabee and Rolf Meyersohn, *Mass Leisure* (Glencoe, Ill.: Free Press) 1958: 389-419; John Loy and Gerald Kenyon, *Sport, Culture and Society* (New York: Macmillan) 1969: 457-464; *International Review of Sport Sociology* (UNESCO) (Warsaw: Polish Scientific Publications) 1966-1970: Volumes 1-4 and *The Pacific Sociological Review* (July 1971) Volume 14, No. 3. In overview, the literature, originating from several disciplines in the behavioral sciences, is varied in levels of analysis and theoretical significance, and diverse in substance and scope. For more extensive listings, the reader may wish to consult the numerous bibliographies contained in the works cited here.
4. See particularly the works of Johan Huizinga, *Homo Ludens* (Boston: Beacon Press) 1950; Simon de Grazia, *Of Time, Work and Leisure* (Garden City, N.Y.: Doubleday); R. Callois, "The Structure and Classification of Games," in Loy and Kenyon, *op cit.*, 44-45; John W. Loy, "The Nature of Sport: A Definitional Effort," in *QUEST,* Monograph X (May 1968), 1-15; D. Riesman, "Work and Leisure in Post-Industrial Society," in Larrabee and Meyersohn, *op. cit.*, 383-385; John M. Roberts and Brian Sutton-Smith, "Child Training and Game Involvement," *Ethnology* (1962) I: 166-185; Sutton-Smith, Roberts and R. Kozelka, "Game Involvement in Adults," *Journal of Social Psychology* 60, 1963: 15-39. Of these works, the latter two are of particular interest in that, among other concerns, the authors utilize an interinstitutional "systemic" approach in their combined analysis of socialization and the social functions of games. The development and testing of their "Conflict-Enculturation Hypothesis" has particular relevance for the analysis conducted on these pages.
5. In contrast, see the contention of Huizinga that the distinguishing element of leisure, sport and recreation is the element of *play,* hence such activities stand "quite consciously outside 'ordinary' life as not being 'serious.' " *Homo Ludens,* p. 13.
6. See, for example, G. Stone and M. Taves, "Camping in the Wilderness," in Larrabee and Meyersohn, *op. cit.,* 290-305; D. Riesman and R. Denney, "Football in America: A Study in Cultural Diffusion," *American Quarterly* 3 (1951): 309-325; Florence Frederickson, "Sports and Cultures of Man," *Science and Medicine of Exercise and Sports,* Warren Johnson ed., (New York: Harper) 1960; John R. Betts, "The Technological Revolution and the Rise of Sports," *The Mississippi Valley Historical Review* XL (1953): 231-256; and Helen Dunlap, "Games, Sports, Dancing and Other Vigorous Recreational Activities and Their Function in Samoan Society," *Research Quarterly* 22 (1951): 298-311.
7. Here consult the works of G. Stone, "American Sports: Play and Display," *Chicago Review* 9 (1955): 83-100; J. Piaget, *Play, Dreams and Imitation in Childhood* (New York: Norton) 1951: 147-150; A. Natan, *Sports and Society* (London: Bowes and Bowes) 1958: Chapter V; M. Jackson, "College Football has become a Losing Business," *Fortune* (December 1962): 119-121; and Roberts, Sutton-Smith and Kozelka, *op. cit.* For a brief overview of the larger theoretical framework structuring these emergent propositions the reader is referred to: T. Parsons, "General Theory in Sociology," in R. Merton, *et al., Sociology Today* (New York: Basic Books) 1959: 3-38; R. Merton, *Social Theory and Social Structure* (Glencoe, Ill.: Free Press) 1949: 19-84; M. Levy, Jr., "Functional Analysis: Structural-Functional Analysis," pp. 21-29, and F. Cancian, "Functional Analysis: Varieties of Functional Analysis," in David Sills ed., *International Encyclopedia of the Social Sciences,* Volume 6 (New York: Macmillan) 1968. For more detailed review, see *Functionalism in the Social Sciences,* Monograph No. 5 of the American Academy of Political and Social Science (February 1965); and Walter Buckley, *Sociology and Modern Systems Theory* (New Jersey: Prentice-Hall) 1967.
8. By this is meant that sport and recreation constitute more than mere "escape mechanisms" or "time-outs" from the "real world"; that in fact they produce important feedback having significant impact on other more "practical" areas of human conduct. Hence, at a grander level it is assumed that not only does a society influence the kinds and types of sport and recreational activities

practiced by its citizenry, but also that such activities have a reciprocal influence on the character of the society itself in various obvious and subtle ways. For example, at a micro-sociological level, the ghetto dweller's penchant for games of chance (e.g., lottery, numbers, craps, boxing, etc.) complements, reflects and supports a basic mode of (mal)adaption to life in the ghetto; one in which pervasive resignation in the face of unyielding inopportunity is relieved only by the hope of escape through the unpredictable operations of luck and "the big chance." At a more macro-level, another "connection" between sports and other institutional areas of activity can be seen in the 1971 invitation and visit of the U.S. Table Tennis Team to Mainland China, and the political and international reverberations of this visit in terms of subsequent alterations in Sino-American foreign policy and trade. In this regard, see Natan, *op. cit.* And, of course, the tragic use of the 1972 Olympics as a stage for international political issues and violence re-emphasizes the same basic point.

9. One particularly pungent, though dated, inquiry into the new economics of sport and leisure is by the editors of *Fortune,* "$30 Billion for Fun," *The Changing American Market* (New York: Times) 1955: Chapter 10. Undoubtedly the thrust of the article is still valid, but in the course of the past 17 years the sum involved has increased enormously.

10. While active involvement in sport and recreational activities has grown, it still seems accurate to say that most "sport enthusiasts" are nonparticipants. For most, the major involvement with sports is through the sports page, the television set or, for the more "involved," a seat in the bleachers.

11. The Marxian specter of class-stratified sports, and the possible functions of sport and recreation, in addition to religion, as an "opiate of the masses" raises some interesting theoretical questions that have yet to be fully explored in the sociology of sports. cf. Andrzej Wohl, "The Problem of Leisure in Our Times," *International Review of Sport Sociology,* Volume 2, 1967.

12. Stone and Taves, *op cit.*

13. For an interesting and insightful foray into this side of Americana, see A.C. Spectorski, *The Exurbanites* (New York: Berkley) 1955.

14. One interesting feature of this is the relative absence of organized group structures in the form of "teams" as compared, say, to the development of sport in Europe. The emerging U.S. pattern of sports participation seems to be proceeding mainly on the line of *individual* or *family* involvement.

15. Although the writer has been engaged in one form of motocycling or another for the past 16 years, the period covers only his years of membership in this particular club.

16. During this time period, the club membership has ranged from 20 to 30 members, but contains a hard core of about a dozen.

17. The construction of the track in fact involved very little in the way of "land improvement." The design takes advantage of the ruggedest aspects of the terrain, contains many jumps, hairpin curves, mudholes, dropoffs, and other obstacles to test the strength and endurance of both machine and rider.

18. An interesting physiological study of the motocrosser indicates that extraordinary physical states of strength, excitement, heart rate and blood sugar are attained by the racer shortly before the start of a race, maintained throughout the race, to fall off gradually after the completion of a race. See "The Physiology of Various Sport Activities" in *The Textbook of Work Physiology,* pp. 554-57.

19. Usually the AMA (American Motorcycling Association), the dominant national organization in American motorcycling.

20. Robert Dubin, "Industrial Worker's World," *Social Problems 3* (January 1956): 131-142.

21. Although a considerable body of literature has developed in the area of work, alienation and leisure, the following may be of particular interest: Robert Dubin, *The World of Work* (New York: Prentice-Hall) 1958; Stanley Parker, *The Future of Work and Leisure* (New York: Praeger) 1971; and an interesting article concerned with a syndrome identified as the Blue Collar Blues, in "Collar Color Doesn't Count," *Psychology Today,* August 1972: p. 53.

22. *cf.* E. Alix and H. Lantz, "Socioeconomic Status and Low Occupational Aspirations: Resignation as an Orientational Variable." *Social Science Quarterly* (December 1973) Vol. 54, No. 3: 596-607.

23. *cf.* S.M. Lipset, *Political Man* (New York: Doubleday) 1960: Chapter IV.

24. Among the earliest, and still perhaps most pungent, observations concerning this value shift from productivity to consumption are to be found in Thorstein Veblen, *The Theory of the Leisure Class* (New York: Modern Library) 1934.

DISCUSSION QUESTIONS

A. *Harry Edwards*

1. Define the term in *institution* and show how this definition applies to sport in the United States.

2. "Societies, in order to reinforce prevalent sentiments" and acceptable standards of behavior tend to infuse physical activities with socially significant values, e.g., sport builds character. Discuss this statement and identify other values which are attributed to sport participation.

3. Edwards contends that "an attack upon sport constitutes an attack upon society itself." In your opinion, is there any justification for such a statement?

4. "Sport is basically political in character and basically conservative." React to this statement and explain your reasons. How does Edwards justify his position?

B. *Michael Real*

1. What functions (purpose, needs) does the Super Bowl serve to qualify the use of the term "mythic," as in mythic spectacle?

2. What similarities and symbolism can you identify between the Super Bowl and American Society?

3. Identify and discuss some of the ways in which business and industry are related to "big time" sports. Discuss the possible advantages/disadvantages of such a relationship to (a) the sport, (b) the players, (c) the community.

4. Real describes the Super Bowl as a "corporate orgy." Is there any justification for making such a statement?

C. *Thomas Martin and Kenneth Berry*

1. In what way is motocross a manifestation of a particular social class's response to "strain, conflict and change" in post-industrial society?

2. Speculate as to why motocross tends to attract mostly males from the lower social classes.

3. Motocross is seen as a mechanism for the satisfaction of "core values" of members of the working class. Identify some core values and explain how they may be satisfied in motocross.

4. Speculate how other social classes deal with the problems of "strain, conflict and change" through sport.

Unit III

The Interdependence of
Sport, Politics
and Economics

In society's arenas, where decisions affecting all of us are made by powerful interest groups, government bodies, and others, it is often the case that political decisions are motivated by self-interest for economic gain and/or for the acquisition of power. The results of such actions may not always be in the best interest of the public. Likewise, in the sport arena, where the sources (e.g., players, franchises) and means (stadia, mass media) of production are owned or controlled by millionaires or powerful conglomerates, influential decisions are frequently made which are not always in the best interest of the sport, the players, or the community. This problematic state has led to the development of a number of conflict situations. The struggle between Players' Associations and franchise owners over control of the sources and means of sport production can be considered one facet of this state of affairs. Another aspect of this conflict centers on a question of priorities. The spending of millions of dollars to produce a grandiose spectacle, such as the Olympic Games, "in the face of squalor, pollution and bad health" (McMurtry, 1973) to further national prestige is, at best, morally questionable; but when it becomes apparent that monetary and economic profit for a small cadre of financiers and politicians, underly considerations of national interest, then the situation becomes much more invidious.

The preceding observations set the tone, in this unit, for an in-depth analysis of the functional interdependence of sport, politics and economics.

Sport sociologists John Pooley and Arthur Webster introduce the topic, in the first selection, by discussing the relationship between sport and politics. In the articles which then follow, authors Paul Hoch (a theoretical physicist and a lecturer in political sociology) and John McMurtry (a social philosopher) develop the concept of power in relationship to the ownership of the sources and means of sport production. Hoch discusses the problem as it applies to professional sports in the United States, and McMurtry addresses himself specifically to the Olympic Games.

SPORT AND POLITICS: POWER PLAY

John C. Pooley and Arthur V. Webster

A paper presented at a symposium on "Sport, Man, and Contemporary Society" held at Queens College of the City University of New York on March 10 and 11, 1972.

"Do you ever play touch football?" Bob Hope claims to have asked one promising athlete during the Kennedy era. "No," came the reply, "I'm not interested in politics."[1]

Hope's wit should not conceal the more serious truth contained in the type of story only he can tell, since sport in the modern world has a prestige and an influence comparable to that of the church in medieval times.[2]

Sport has numerous connotations. Originally, it was designated in French to mean any diversion from the sad or serious side of life. As McIntosh has said, "it covers activities ranging from mountaineering to making love,

from motor racing to playing practical jokes."[3] The word does not have such clearly defined limits of application as "idrott" in Sweden, "spiel" in Germany or "athletics" in the United States.

Difficult as it may appear to define sport, its significance is quite apparent. From an anthropological approach, Hendrickson has stated

Reprinted by permission of the Canadian Association for Health, Physical Education and Recreation from *Cahper* Journal, Vol. 41, No. 3, Jan.-Feb. 1975.

"Research has shown that sport always plays a complex role in cultures, from the simplest to the most highly developed. Underlying their obvious identification as amusements and pleasurable tests of physical supremacy are often unstated but implicit functions in the culture. As old as the history of sport itself is the story of the use of sport as an instrumentality for accomplishing something else. . . . Whether at any given time in history man plays for fun and self-expression, for prestige, power, and glory, for financial gain or political advantage, his motivations are to a large degree culturally determined."[4]

This attribute of sport can be justified in terms of individual and group meaning. Slusher in his book *Man, Sport And Existence* has analyzed and described the meaning in sport from the point of view of existential philosophy. For example, those actively involved in sport may find empathy with the words of Roger Bannister, the great British miler: "Running has given me a glimpse of the greatest freedom a man can ever know."

Historically, four broad categories of sport are distinguishable: sport as exercise; sport as gambling; sport as a spectacle; and representative sport. The latter has largely developed as a twentieth century phenomenon, being primarily of interest to spectators.[5] The spectator participates in a vicarious way and also can derive meaning from the activity. Many of us can identify with the athlete in a manner aptly expressed by the late Soviet Premier Nikita Khruschev, an ardent soccer fan: "Whenever a player kicks the ball, it is Khruschev who kicks it, and whenever a player gets kicked in the shins, it is Khruschev who gets kicked."[6]

The significance of sport can be defended from historical, cultural and philosophical dimensions and thus can account for its ubiquitous development.

"Sport has, of course, developed on an extraordinarily wide scale. It is probably the aspect of modern life which is most widely encountered throughout the world—the only one, perhaps, which is common to both industrial societies and developing countries. It is also, in a steadily increasing degree, one of the most lively factors in international relations. There are few international exchanges, encounters or contracts which arouse so much mass feeling as sports events."[7]

In short, it can be asserted that sport has replaced religion as the 'opiate of the masses'.

Politics, in contrast to sport, is relatively more definitive. Webster interprets politics as the act of government or the administration of affairs.[8] Morgenthau, a political scientist, asserts that "politics is power" and elaborates:

"All politics, domestic and international, reveals three basic patterns: that is, all political phenomena can be reduced to one of three basic types. A political policy seeks either to keep power, to increase power, or to demonstrate power."[9]

The term power has rather nebulous meaning. Its inference is clear when perceived in terms of authority or control as with state governments. In international politics, "the concept of power denotes the general ability of one state to force another state to perform a particular act."[10] Power is "the ability to control the minds and actions of men."[11] Power has applicability for sport. That is, the acknowledged significance of sport enables it to be used to exert influence and thus it has power potential. However, since sport will continue to interest the people of the world what-ever governments want or want not to do, it possesses inherent power.

Mindful of the characteristics of power perceived in relation to sport and politics, it is quite conceivable that either one may exert influence or control over the other depending on the political context and the nature of sport in any given situation. Thus, a two-way relationship can be established:

SPORT ⟷ POLITICS

The purpose of this paper is to reveal and to examine this reciprocal relationship.

Municipal Level

At the municipal or local level, the political structure is defined and composed by the citizens of the area, the same citizens who partake in sport and its administration. At the municipal level, there is a balance of power between sport and politics.

SPORT ⟷ POLITICS

For example, local politics regulates the provision of sport facilities and financial assistance for amateur and minor league sports. Conversely, sport influences politics. If the demands of the citizens for new facilities or greater financial aid to support local leagues and recreation classes are strongly voiced, politicians must take heed and respond in proportion to the degree and intensity of these demands, that is, if they have any aspirations for re-election.

Similarly, this relationship exists in professional sport. A professional franchise will establish itself in a city regardless of that city's political inclination. On the other hand, politicians will use sport and advocate measures to encourage or promote the team in the realization that they are helping the political development of their cities. This can be realized in a number of ways; either as an added source of income in the form of taxes and from tourists, or as a means to unify various ethnic groups as in the case of professional soccer in Toronto.[12] Recently, the city of Halifax acquired a professional hockey franchise which undoubtedly has added prestige to Halifax and has promoted both the city and Nova Scotia. The mayor of Halifax, fully aware of the team's influence, has identified with the Nova Scotia Voyageurs to benefit from the exposure that it affords him.[13]

In summary, it can be said that at the municipal level, a balance of power between sport and politics prevails, for, in general, neither affects or influences the other to an appreciable degree.[14]

National Level

At the national level, the influence of politics on sport predominates.

POLITICS ⇄ SPORT

The majority of national governments have recognized the importance of sport and have set out to use sport as a means to achieve various political ends. For developing or emerging countries such as Uganda and Ghana that have only recently been granted independence, politicians recognize the role sport can play in contributing to the development of nationalism or 'national identity' and to the promotion of the general welfare and thus use it accordingly. As Wohl has stated:

Sport constitutes an exceptionally strong, most vital factor of social integration, and is an instrument for the successful breaking through national and religious, racial and political barriers, and all the various prejudices connected with them. That is why it is becoming a more and more recognized factor promoting progress.[15]

In Canada, where some of the problems inherent to emerging nations still prevail, the government's goal to be realized through sport is expressed differently.

The fact that we are all proud of our country regardless of what province we live in, or what language we speak, or what our political views are—shows another reason for strong federal effort in the sports field: National Unity.[16]

This is not to denigrate the role of the individual provinces in developing sport in a 'local' sense. Since institutional sport largely developed through education, the major historical antecedent which led to a provincial approach rather than a national one was the British North America Act of 1867. Since that time each province has had full authority to dictate educational policy—a right which has had important ramifications for the development of provincial sport. For example Quebec and Nova Scotia have implemented formal governmental organizations in their respective provinces to promote sport. Moreover, in the case of Quebec there is no doubt of the effect of the forthcoming Olympic Games in 1976 in Montreal in releasing monies for sport.

Sport in communist countries is used by the government as a lever of social control, attained through channeling activity towards State inspired goals. In the Soviet Union the sports program has carried a political tag since 1925, when the Party resolution was:

Physical culture must be considered not only from the point of view of physical training and health but should also be utilized as a means to rally the broad working masses around various Parties, Government and trade union organizations through which the masses of workers and peasants are drawn into social and political life. . . . Physical culture must play an integral part in the general political and cultural training and education of the masses.[17]

Stavislav Yananis, head of the Department of Sports Theory and History of the Lesgaft Institute in Leningrad, was reputed to say that sport is not an end in itself but is used to create a new man physically, mentally and morally.[18]

Similarly, Communist China uses sport to perpetrate its political ideology and as a means to achieve its revolutionary ends.

[our purpose is] to ensure that literature and art (and sport) fit well into the whole revolutionary machine as a component part, that they operate as powerful weapons for uniting and educating the people and for attacking and destroying the enemy, and that they help the people fight the enemy with one heart and one mind (and a sound body).[19]

A final example of a somewhat different nature again illustrates politics' dominance over sport at the domestic level. In the Union of South Africa, the government has vehemently denied blacks the right to compete in sport against whites, thereby enforcing their policy of apartheid through sport.[20] Recently the government has become more lenient but, by imposing special conditions for visiting black athletes, it continues to wield power over and through sport.[21]

Undoubtedly, a most prevalent aim of governments is to produce superior athletes for international competition. The reasons are numerous. For one, nations view success in international sport as a measure of the vitality and effectiveness of national character.

The 'elementary force and persistence' of the Russians, the individual initiative and inventiveness of the Americans, the undogmatic common sense of the British, the discipline and thoroughness of the Germans are some of the qualities which will manifest themselves, for better or for worse, in all the individual and collective activities in which the members of a nation can engage.[22]

The "individual and collective activities" of sport at the international level are excellent means for providing this opportunity.

Victories can also be equated in terms of success of the national political systems of life-style and in this sense sport is used as an instrument of nationalistic propaganda. In the Soviet Union, sport is viewed as an important reflection of the Marxist state so that a victory for an individual or a team is considered to be a victory for Marxism. As Natan reports:

It is no secret that the Soviet Union will try all she can to use her successes in the Olympic Games as a propaganda weapon in the Communist sport ideology. States such as Hungary, Poland and Czechoslovakia have also announced similar intentions.[23]

It is ironic that, although little money is given to British teams and although British teams are not charged with political gunpowder, more British athletes travel abroad than all the communist countries combined. [24] Likewise, the 'individual gains through individual achievement' principle, characteristic of the United States, is said to be mirrored through sport.

For these reasons, the following proposition seems warranted: The intent of government politics is to demonstrate power through international sport.

Even emerging countries and others who are minimally involved in international politics attach political importance to sporting victories. For example, in the Olympic games of 1960, there were eighty-four competing nations, many of which had an annual per capita income of less than one hundred dollars. [25]

It is universally conceded that triumphs in sport win recognition and prestige for a country. John Munro, Canada's Minister of National Health and Welfare, believes that emphasis on a pursuit of excellence in sport will not only provide youth with the incentive and perspective to participate, but will enhance Canada's world sport image.[26] Furthermore, some governments send their athletes to other countries as ambassadors to improve relations and to spread goodwill. It therefore seems likely that real political dividends are to be gathered from pouring government funds into the development of successful international teams. [27]

If sport is to be manipulated, government control and financing of sport is inevitable. By these measures, national governments seek to increase their power through sport in order to achieve their goals.

Following the report of the Sports Task Force (Task Force On Sports For Canadians) which truly reacted as a catalyst, the federal government has attempted to do everything possible to strengthen its position in sport . . . this role is one of support rather than control.

It is not our position to dictate. But neither are we without opinions—nor the will to put these opinions forward. [28]

As a result, a government department has been constituted, or is in existence, which has a responsibility for sport as part of its brief. Canada has appointed a directorate named the Fitness and Amateur Sport Branch within the Department of National Health and Welfare. At the time of this writing, the Directorate has two divisions; Recreation Canada with the purpose of achieving the expressed goal of national unity; and Sports Canada, which is primarily concerned with "improving Canada's image."

We (the Directorate of Sports Canada) must improve training programs and coaching talent, to see that our athletes are as ready as possible—both physically and mentally, to face the ever-increasing rigors of competition with the tough, well-organized teams from nations using sport as a vehicle of national policy. [29]

The Soviet Union has its USSO Central Council, Britain its Sports Council, and in East Germany the State Committee for Sport and Physical Culture act as the controlling sport body. Regardless of the difference in nomenclature, each may ostensibly be termed—Ministry of Sport. It is through this "Ministry of Sport" that governments finance sport. Molyneaux's report of central government aid disclosed the extent of direct financial assistance of Western European countries to sport and physical recreation. [30]

Lipsyte reports that the Soviet sport system spends more than $2.2 billion annually to fulfill an axiom attributed to Lenin—that a nation cannot be strong unless it is strong in sports. [31] As Natan[32] has suggested, the nations of the world can be placed on a scale according to the degree of involvement that the government takes in the organization and guidance of sport activities. On one end of the scale would be the nations where sport has become an integral part of the political system and a tool for the use of the state. On the other end would be the nations in which the government takes no active control in the regulation of sport activities. Certainly the communist countries would be located at the end having a high degree of involvement, while Britain, until recently, would occupy a position at the opposite end. In 1963, McIntosh interpreted Britain's approach to sport in this light:

Where sport is educational, and broadly speaking, is being taught or learned rather than played for its own sake, the Ministry of Education already exercises the functions of the Minister of Sport by permitting, assisting, controlling, inspecting, and some would say by interfering. When sport is educational it is considered worthy of political direction and some measure of control, but when sport becomes an end in itself it has so far ceased in Britain, to be an activity which is appropriate for political support. [33]

About the time of McIntosh's statement, which was an apt interpretation of the prevailing philosophy towards non-political intervention, a change has occurred which points the way to increased government intervention, thereby altering Britain's position on the scale identified above. This began with the Wolfenden Committee's Report on Sport and the Community[34] published in 1960, which recommended the formation of a Sports Council. This was established in January, 1965, being attached to the Department of Education and Science and was an "advisory and consultative committee" only.[35] It was not until 1971 that the Sports Council acquired executive powers, thereby forging closer links between sport and government.[36] In the light of this, Britain would now occupy a position similar to that of Canada—somewhere near the mid-point of Natan's scale.

The position of the United States could be said to rest at the lower end of the scale. There, sport at the international level is organized by independent bodies and is itself free of any overt political intervention. The Amateur Athletic Union presides as a governing body for international competitions and does not grant financial aid to amateur athletes.

The influence of politics on sport at the national level, although paramount, does not negate a reciprocal relationship. For example, sport has the capacity to affect national morale,[37] either positively or negatively, thereby having political overtones. In Canada for instance, national morale[38] has been weakened in response to the government's policy of not entering the national hockey team in international competition. Frank J. Shaughnessy, Canadian Olympic Association vice-president, is of the opinion that

"For many Canadians our participation in the winter Olympic Games will not be a happy occasion in as much as this will be the first time Canada will not send a hockey team. I know I feel that way about it."[39]

He believes that the majority of Canadians favour re-establishment of participation status and he personally supports this demand in addition to the support given by the Canadian Olympic Association.

From another stand-point, the recent entry of the United Kingdom into the European Common Market may well have been affected by the acceleration of Britain's involvement in European soccer competition. Certainly the increased exposure of European countries through the sports pages and on the television screens is a reality which has contributed to European feeling never before observed.

Alternatively, it has been suggested that an absence of competition in sport between two countries can mitigate against the continuity of inter-country harmony. Goodhart and Chataway have pointed out that "the fact that Englishmen and Canadians share so few sporting memories may account in part for the comparative coolness in recent decades of Anglo-Canadian relations."[40] By contrast, shared experiences through sport link countries together. Historical ties in cricket, (which extend back into the 19th century), and more recently in rugby, continue to nourish Anglo-Australian relations. However, in general, political hostility is reflected by sporting achievements as in the cases of the United States and the Soviet Union; the Soviet Union and China; East Germany and West Germany; England and Scotland; and South Africa and the Rest of 'Black' Africa. Hostility is further emphasized when sporting contests are used by athletes to gain political asylum, usually from communist to non-communist countries. Even spectators flee occasionally.

The foregoing remarks suggest the following proposition: When sporting contests are between countries having divergent ideologies, the political aspects are heightened and sporting aspects recede.

Thus a complete model of interaction from politics to sport and from sport to politics at the National scene is as follows:

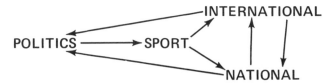

International Governing Bodies of Sport

The significant place of sport in present society invites its use by nations for different roles in international competition. Huxley claimed that sport is a "substitute for war" for it is both to prepare men for the militia, and to score points in political propaganda.[41] Military terminology pervades Natan's statement: "Sport and play in the Eastern bloc do not represent any voluntary and personal activity but rather a form of conscription for the sporting front line."[42] The Olympics, the epitome of international sport competition, has been regarded as merely a testing ground for two great political units. As Lipsyte puts it: "The Olympics which have always been subtly merchandized as a kind of moral equivalent to war, became an area for the muscle of ideology."[43] Some believe we are always at war, if not militarily, certainly in sport, which has been defined by the Nazi General Von Reichenau as "war with friendly arms."[44]

This view of sport as a substitute for war and for the purpose of preserving national prestige is gaining support. Natan warns against this trend when he asserts:

Nationalism is sport's deadliest enemy. It has given sport a political character and at the same time imposed on it a tag which is in direct contradiction to its original meaning of being a natural game for relaxation after the day's toil.[45]

Under the guise of 'nationalism', stress on 'winning or else' has increased. East and West sportsmen are in fact political emissaries under extreme pressure to vindicate not merely their own prowess but the ideology of their country. It has influenced some individuals to go to great lengths to win, thereby further damaging sport's name. The German weekly—*Der Speigel*, December 9, 1956, published a list of details occurring in the Melbourne Olympics which verify this point. In the waterpolo match between Russia and Hungary the game was fought with such a "sporting spirit" that the face of one of the Hungarians was "completely covered with blood." During the diving events the public demonstrated against a woman judge who deliberately "awarded points according to political convictions."[46] McIntosh reports that a game of ice hockey developed into an unregulated fist-fight in the 1960 Olympic Games at Squaw Valley.[47] Moreover, acts of cheating have been revealed, resulting in the establishment of mandatory tests for drugs of all athletes immediately following Olympic contests.

Despite these occurrences which suggest political undertones in international sport, the influence of international governing bodies of sport on politics predominates.

INTERNATIONAL
GOVERNING ────────────────▶
BODIES   POLITICS
OF SPORT ◀────────────────

The International Olympic Committee is the world's governing body for the Olympic Games. It delegates to each National Olympic Committee the function of coordinating the selection and certification of all competitors for the Games, and to international sport federations that of making international rules and standards for various sports. Neither the National Olympic Committees nor the international sport federations have a vote on the International Olympic Committee. The International Olympic Committee drafts the general program of the games, determines amateur standards, selects the competition sites, and its Executive Committee acts as a jury of appeals during the games.[48]

Its foremost function is to maintain the original intention of the games expressed by Baron de Coubertin.

Whereas the Greeks proclaimed peace in order to hold the (Olympic) Games, de Coubertin wanted to hold the games in order to foster peace. By bringing the youth of the world together for friendly rivalry on the field of sport, he hoped to encourage goodwill and understanding in the rising generations. "It will be a great date" he said, "not only in the history of the Games but in the history of the present age, when the young men from all nations enter the Stadium following their national flags and join in taking the Sacred Oath."[49]

The promotion of international understanding and goodwill is certainly a function of sport but perhaps de Coubertin was too idealistic in assuming that this would occur. There is much evidence to the contrary. Heinila in a paper entitled "Notes on the Inter-Group Conflicts in International Sport" presents certain facts to substantiate his argument and draws attention to the effect of sport on competing groups.[50] For example, he points out that "competition tends to reward exclusively but tends to frustrate inclusively" or as he says, "In competition there is only one winner but many losers," and later "competition, by its very nature, may sometimes be a sufficient cause for conflict but not invariably so."[51] As further reported by Heinila, Jones takes up the argument:

. . . the thousands of spectators, and sometimes the players as well, seem to behold a mighty contest between their country and the enemy. The national prestige is at stake; a victory is no longer the success of the team that could play better but becomes a national victory and is an occasion for national rejoicings, out of all proportion with reality. Such an at-titude is not favorable to international understanding.[52]

The words of Huxley best support this argument:

In a world that has no common religion or philosophy of life, but where every national group practices its own private idolatry, international football matches and athletic contests can do almost nothing but harm.[53]

Avery Brundage, the President of the International Olympic Committee, is perceived as the modern day de Coubertin and every bit as idealistic. He negates the validity of Huxley's argument and believes that in spite of the potentially disruptive nature of international competition, harmonious relations can be established. The success of the recent innovation of the Olympic Village for the competitors themselves, illustrates this fact. It is in this environment that national prejudices are reduced and national restrictions are overcome. He has incessantly argued that 'sport is completely free of politics' and that the enforcement of International Olympic Committee rules and policies ensure that political contamination does not and will not occur. As a result: The policies of the International Olympic Committee are contrived to maintain power.

Potentially, the power of the International Olympic Committee can force governments to abandon or modify their policy of discrimination and chauvinism. For example, its rules have forbidden the Union of South Africa to compete on the basis of its political policy of apartheid. Acceptance of the German Democratic Republic to the Games is contingent on the condition that she must be part of a combined all-German team. In 1962, the International Olympic Committee stated that The Olympic Games would be held only in countries which would guarantee free access for all recognized teams, thereby denying East Germany the privilege. Controversial decisions regarding amateur status have attempted to maintain some standard of 'amateurism' in the Games. By withstanding political pressures and enforcing traditional rules, the International Olympic Committee believes they are succeeding in providing a service towards the friendship of nations. This has caused Mr. Brundage at the completion of the Melbourne Olympic Games of 1956 to claim that "the Olympic Committee fully deserved the award of the Nobel Peace Prize."[54]

Sport in itself at the Olympics is an ideal vehicle for athletes to voice their political grievances, thus providing more evidence of sport's effect on politics. The fact that 'the whole world is watching' has embarrassed the hand-tied politicians of a country whose athletes rise in protest. An excellent example of this was John Carlos and Tommie Smith of the United States in the 1968 Olympics in Mexico. In 1956 over fifty Hungarians took advantage of the Olympic Games politically by seeking asylum in the West.[55]

The unique place of the International Olympic Committee in the hierarchy of international sport's governing bodies is partly due to the broad interest in the Olympics which exists throughout the world, and partly because the present committee continues to strain to perpetuate original philosophies, some of which would appear to jar with current societal mores. In short, decisions tend to be extremely controversial, yet defended by the Committee. There is no doubt that the International Olympic Committee still wields sufficient power to overcome national pressures.

Though, by degree, less powerful than the International Olympic Committee as international governing bodies, are those controlling soccer, tennis, rugby and cricket. FIFA[56] which controls soccer, dealt effectively with criticisms and conflicts which arose during or as a preamble to the last two World Cups held in Mexico (1970) and England (1966). The MCC,[57] controlling body of cricket, has stood its ground in the recent past when denying the right of South Africa to dictate its own rule preventing mixed racial teams from competing in international matches within the country. A similar stand has been made by the international rugby association.

Summary

In summary, we have unveiled and examined various interplays between sports and politics in their reciprocal relationship at the municipal, national and international levels. We have formulated propositions, most of which concern these interplays, and have designed simple models to illustrate this.

NOTES

1. Philip Goodhart and Christopher Chataway, *War Without Weapons* (London: W.H. Allen, 1968), p. 104.
2. Sir Arnold Lunn, "Politics and Sports," in *Sport in the Socio-Cultural Process*, edited by M. Marie Hart (Dubuque, Iowa: Wm. C. Brown Company Publishers, 1972), p. 484.
3. Peter McIntosh, *Sport in Society* (London: C.A. Watts, 1963), p. 11.
4. Florence S. Hendrickson, "Sport and the Cultures of Man," in *Sport, Culture and Society*, edited by John Loy and Gerald Kenyon (London: The Macmillan Company, 1969), pp. 89, 92.
5. Philip Goodhart and Christopher Chataway, *War Without Weapons*, pp. 2-3.
6. New York Times, October 28, 1959, quoted in Morton, "Soviet Sport in the 1960's," *Sport, Culture, and Society*, p. 192.
7. Rene Maheu, "Baron Pierre de Coubertin and the Sports Movement of Modern Times," Report of the ICSPE Conference in Paris, 1963, p. 8.
8. *Webster's Seventh New Collegiate Dictionary* (Toronto: Thomas Allen Ltd., 1963), p. 657.
9. Hans J. Morgenthau, *Politics among Nations* (New York: Borzoi Books, 1966), p. 36.
10. William D. Coplin, *Introduction to International Politics: A Theoretical Overview* (Chicago: Markham Publishing Company, 1971), p. 120.
11. Hans J. Morgenthau, *Politics Among Nations*, p. 26.
12. The effect of sport on ethnic group unity may be viewed in two contexts: (1) positively, in the case of a professional team representing a city; or (2) negatively, in the case of amateur teams representing ethnic enclaves. For an example of the latter, see John C. Pooley, "Ethnic Soccer Clubs in Milwaukee: A Study in Assimilation," in *Sport in the Socio-Cultural Process*, pp. 328-345.
13. Recorded in a private interview, February 17, 1972.
14. Peter McIntosh, *Sport in Society*, p. 189.
15. A. Wohl, "Conception and Range of Sport Sociology," in *International Review of Sport Sociology*, edited by A. Wohl. (Warsaw Ars. Polona, 1966), pp. 13-14.
16. John Munro, from the paper, "A Proposed Sports Policy for Canadians," presented by the Canadian Minister of National Health and Welfare, March 20, 1970, p. 1.
17. Henry Morton, "Soviet Sport in the 1960's," *Sport, Culture and Society*, p. 196, quoted from a Resolution of the Central Committee of the Russian Communist Party, July 13, 1925, reprinted in Kalendar Spravochnik Pizkedturnika na 1939 God (Moscow: Fuzkultura: Sport, 1939), pp. 5-7.
18. Robert Lipsyte, "The Soviet Life," in *The Soviet Union: The Fifty Years*, edited by Harrison Salisbury (New York: Harcourt, Brace and World, Inc., 1967), p. 387.
19. *Quotations from Chairman Mao Tse-Tung*. (Peking: Foreign Languages Press, 1967), p. 301.
20. Robert Conley. "Apartheid in Sports," *New York Times*, October 15, 1963.
R. Thompson, *Race and Sport* (London: Oxford University Press, 1964).
21. Reported in the Halifax Mail-Star, March 7, 1972.
22. Hans Morgenthau, *Politics among Nations*, p. 127.
23. Alex Natan, "Sport and Politics," *Sport, Culture, and Society*. p. 208.
24. Philip Goodhart and Christopher Chataway, *War Without Weapons*, p. 133.
25. Peter McIntosh, *Sport in Society*, p. 196.
26. John Munro, from the paper, "Sport Canada, Recreation Canada," presented to the National Advisory Council on Fitness and Amateur Sport, May 7, 1971, p. 24.
27. Philip Goodhart and Christopher Chataway, *War Without Weapons*, p. 97.
28. John Munro, from a paper presented at the National Conference on Olympics '76 Development, Ottawa, October 7, 1971, p. 1.
29. Ibid., p. 4.
30. D.D. Molyneux, *Central Government Aid to Sport and Physical Recreation in Countries of Western Europe*. (University of Birmingham, 1962).
31. Robert Lipsyte, "The Sporting Life," *The Soviet Union: The Fifty Years*, p. 387.
32. A. Natan, *Sport and Society* (London: Bowes and Bowes, 1958).
33. P. McIntosh, *Sport in Society*, p. 195.
34. Sir John Wolfenden, *Sport and the Community* (London: Central Council of Physical Education, 1960).
35. Walter Winterbottom, "The Pattern of Sport in the United Kingdom," in The Central Council of Physical Recreation, *Sport in Education and Recreation*. London, 1968, p. 27.
36. The Central Council of Physical Recreation, *Sports Development Bulletin*, No. 17, October, 1971.
37. H. Morgenthau. *Politics among Nations*, p. 129.
38. Frank J. Shaughnessy. "Brundage and Ahearne Praised by Shaughnessy," *Record*, Vol. 2, 4, December, 1971, p. 13.
39. Ibid., p. 13.
40. Philip Goodhart and Christopher Chataway, *War Without Weapons*, p. 154.
41. Aldous Huxley, *Ends and Means* (London: Chatto and Windus, 1937), p. 188.
42. A. Natan, "Sport and Politics," *Sport, Culture and Society*, p. 208.
43. R. Lipsyte, "The Sporting Life," The Soviet Union: The Fifty Years, p. 388.
44. A. Natan, "Sport and Politics," *Sport, Culture and Society*, p. 204.
45. Ibid., p. 205.
46. Ibid., p. 204.
47. P. McIntosh, *Sport in Society*, p. 199.

48. Lynn Vendien and John Nixon, *The World Today in Health, Physical Education, and Recreation* (Englewood Cliffs, New Jersey: Prentice-Hall, Inc., 1968), p. 380.
49. G. Sondhi, "New Forms of International Cooperation," Report of the ICSPE Conference in Paris, 1963, p. 33.
50. K. Heinila, "Notes on the Inter-Group Conflicts in International Sport," in *International Review of Sport Sociology*, edited by A. Wohl (Warsaw: Ais Polona, 1966).
51. Ibid., p. 32.

52. R.W. Jones, "Sport and International Understanding," Report of the UNESCO Congress "Sport—Work—Culture," Helsinki, 1959, p. 163.
53. A. Huxley, *Ends and Means*, p. 188.
54. A. Natan, "Sport and Politics," *Sport, Culture and Society*, p 205.
55. Ibid., p. 204.
56. Federation Internationale de Football Association.
57. Marylebone Cricket Club.

WHO OWNS SPORTS?
Paul Hoch

Around the simplicity which most of us want out of sports has grown a monster, a sprawling five-billion-dollar-a-year industry which pretends to cater to our love of games but instead has evolved into that one great American institution: big business. Winning, losing, playing the game, all count far less than counting the money.

Leonard Shecter, *The Jocks*

We have already noted that the first professional baseball team was "owned" by the players themselves, and embodied a kind of players' control over when, where, and how they should play, as well as how profits should be shared. At the time, most other baseball players also liked the idea of this arrangement. It took more than a third of a century to convince most of them that anyone else should "own" their labor or their contracts. (The basketball players took even longer.) And even in our enlightened era, many are still not convinced.

Prior to 1876, when the National League was formed, professional baseball players often moved around between whichever teams would pay them the most money, or they formed their own teams. But the capitalists who formed the new league had other ideas. They had the money for sports fields, promotion, and players' salaries, but they insisted that players sign contracts containing what was known as a "reserve clause," giving their "owners" the right to reserve their services, and exclude them from playing for other league teams. This infuriated the players, but since these owners seemed to be the only ones around able to borrow the money to bank roll such a large-scale operation (and since a good many players earned big money "fringe benefits" by fixing games) most grudgingly took their pay packets and played the game.

In 1882, however, the American Association was formed. Although the new league also had what the players called a "slave system"—whereby owners doled out amongst themselves monopolistic rights for contracting certain players—at least now players could choose between the two leagues. This meant owners had to compete for them. But this free competition lasted only one year. The owners of the two leagues finally decided among themselves that monopoly was best for all of them, and they agreed not to hire each others' players. So the players were right back where they started.

In 1884, just eight years after the National League was founded, its monopolistic ways of doing business were put to a stern test. Realtor Henry V. Lucas declared that the reserve rule "reserves all that is good for the owners." Since it was time to do something about the player's "bondage," he formed a new Union League. Naturally, the threat of free competition did not endear itself to the monopolists or their friends in the press. It was all-out war. But, as its finances plunged deeper and deeper into the red, the Union League collapsed after only one year. As part of the price of peace and profit, Lucas himself was admitted to the National League as owner of the St. Louis franchise. Monopoly was still intact.

The owners had a good thing going, until they started pushing the players too hard. As the 1880s ended they were trying to establish a sort of productivity scale for players, whereby each man would be graded on his playing from A to E, with salaries ranging in five grades from $2,500 down to $1,500. In effect, this would have taken away the player's right to negotiate his salary with the only boss he was allowed to work for. Full-scale rebellion broke out. Under the leadership of their union, the National Brotherhood of Professional Players, the athletes set up their own league. The National League was decimated. Even by paying huge salaries, it could hold so few of its players that it had to fill almost every position with rookies. It became known as the sand-lot league. The American Association found itself in a similar position. The Players' League promptly managed to attract more fans than either of the old leagues. Not surprisingly, other capitalists, including those who owned the newspapers, did not like the idea of workers deserting a business and setting up their own. So the new league found it impossible to raise money. It could not get bank loans. More often than not, its games received no press coverage. What news there was of the Players' League amounted to a new scandal "uncovered" every week. (In his book *Baseball: The Early Years,* Harold Seymour quotes a newspaper account of a players' meeting; they are reported as dressed in fur-lined overcoats, patent-leather shoes, silk hats, with $5,000 diamond stick-pins, gaudy rings, gold-headed canes, and smoking expensive cigars.) Without financial backing from the banks, the players found it hard to stand up to cutthroat competition. In a year this most popular of the three leagues, comprised of almost all the top players, had folded. The American Association (which used to refer to the NL as "the rich man's league") went down shortly thereafter. The players had been beaten back. The rule of monopoly continued.

The situation in other sports had been a bit better. High school and college sports, of which football was rapidly becoming the most popular, were for many years entirely under the control of the players themselves. Intramural and even intercollegiate games were simply organized by the students interested in such things, without much interest or interference from school administrations. For example, in his book *The Athletic Revolution* (New York: The Free Press, 1971, p. 161) Jack Scott notes that in the 1860s high school football matches between public and private schools became popular around Boston, and 1869 saw the first major American college football game, between Princeton and Rutgers. "American schools and colleges," he says, "followed the pattern of Oxford and Cambridge during the beginning years of interscholastic and intercollegiate competition, and the responsibility for organizing athletic programs remained in the hands of the undergraduates." It should be added, however, that these athletic activities developed for the most part at highly elite prep schools and universities where no one would have dreamed of ordering about and controlling the gentleman-players in the authoritarian manner that has become so common today.

In the 1880s, however, two things happened. First, college sports started spreading far beyond the elite colleges of the Ivy League and the Northeast to places, including especially the church-run schools like Notre Dame, which had no tradition of student-organized activities. More important, as the popularity of college football grew, the opportunity was seized to turn it into a big business. It was not long before the undergraduate sports programs were taken out of the hands of the undergraduates, and placed in the hands of a small elite clique of alumni, usually from the wealthiest families, who could be expected to exercise the same disproportionate influence on the college as a whole as they did on its sports program. In fact, in a very real sense the sports program *became* the college.

Frederick Rudolph, in his book *The American College and University* (New York: Vintage, 1962, p. 385) points out that in the 1890s at schools like Notre Dame sports became, in effect, the main agency for student recruitment. Even where this did not happen to such a great extent, college sports were to the outside world still the most visible—usually the *only* visible—part of college life, and functioned almost as a public relations program, helping to perpetuate the image of the well-rounded college man. "By 1900," says Rudolph, "the relationship between football and public relations had been firmly established and almost everywhere acknowledged as one of the sport's major justifications."

This mythical connection between the college sports program and the fiction of the "well-rounded college man" was particularly ironic, because the college sports programs came into vogue at precisely the same time as well-roundedness was being destroyed by the increasing demands for specialization. With the possible exception of the elite Ivy League schools, the college regimen became increasingly the factorylike one of greater fragmentation of disciplines, proliferating bureaucracies, and greater specialization. Instead of "well-rounded" men, the grads began increasingly to resemble mass-produced products. "Progressive" educators decided not to attack this proliferating specialization, but instead to add into the high school and college curricula a "liberal" sample of "extra-curricular" frills, including athletic teams and intramural programs, student governments, societies, and whatnot. Then the high schools and colleges could still produce the specialized robots required by the new mass-production monopolies and yet claim to be giving everyone a "well-rounded" education. It was precisely the solution that the factory owners themselves had opted for when they introduced factory sports programs to "broaden" the interests of their workers. High school and college sports were drafted to serve as the Emperor's clothes for an increasingly empty and dehumanizing style of education. They were good public relations, and brought in money, too.

Until the 1960s the money-making side of college sports was still important. College football at major schools could be depended upon to provide support for every other sport, and probably a good part of the academic program as well (either directly or through the contributions a winning team attracted from wealthy alumni). And the emphasis was mainly on "winning" almost as an end in itself. However, in the '60s, in the era of expensive athletic scholarships and slush funds, multiple-platoon teams, and declining student interest, football at a great many places was no longer even self-supporting, and had to be justified, to an increasing extent, as basically a public-relations expense.

In basketball there was much more flexibility. Not only was the sport not invented until around 1891, but it was to be dominated by player-controlled teams throughout most of its history. This came to a decisive end after World War II, when owners of sports arenas in the big cities decided there was big money to be made from professional basketball. So they formed their own league (soon to become the National Basketball Association). In competing with players' teams and non-league owners' teams, their one major advantage was control of the arenas (i.e., the means of sports production). They did not have to be so heavy-handed as to exclude the other teams entirely, although this sometimes happened.[1] All they had to do was raise the rental price of the arena to the point where almost no one could afford it. (The arena owners, of course, could afford it, since in booking their facilities for their own teams, they were paying themselves!) Thereafter, pro basketball, too, was monopolized and controlled by just a handful of "owners."

So throughout the sports industry, as in every other industry under capitalism, control is exercised, not by the consumers (fans), nor by the producers (players), but by the owners of capital. It is they who decide whether or not to stage their spectacles and when, where, and how to do so. Ownership gives them the power to dictate the complete development or nondevelopment of the industry, the very life and working conditions of those (players) whose labor they buy, and the nature of the product they produce. And the basis of their decisions is, first and foremost, personal profit. In this, sports owners are just like other capitalists (although some of them may, incidentally, be big sports fans on the side). However their loyalty to their capital will always surpass their loyalty to the team. If it did not they might quickly find themselves out of business. And there is a lot of money involved.

Indeed, the first thing we notice about the sports industry is that it is very expensive to become an owner. When the first professional baseball league was formed in 1871 the entrance fee for a team was just ten dollars. Five years later, when the National League was formed, the price of a franchise was just one hundred dollars plus players' salaries. By the mid-1960s, CBS had bought the New York Yankees for $15 million and later the Vancouver Canucks hockey team was purchased for $6 million. At these prices a situation is rapidly being created in which only corporations of substantial size, or syndicates of their executives, can raise the capital to buy a team. Under these conditions, a professional sports operation becomes little more than a cog in a giant corporate empire (or syndicate of interlocking directorates) and is run in the same way as the rest of the enterprise. "There's not much need, really, to document football's place in the great American free-enterprise system," wrote a columnist in the Toronto *Telegram's Weekend Magazine*. "All pro sports are run as efficiently, cold-bloodedly and greedily as any other big business with a lust for a buck." As elsewhere in the "game" of capitalist big business, we find boards of directors dictating from the top to their production managers who dictate to supervisors (coaches) dictating to workers (players). And the latter have been reduced to little more than pawns in a giant corporate machine concerned much more with profit than "play."

It is instructive to gauge the size of the American sports business. Every year about 300,000,000 admission tickets are bought for major sports events. An average take of at least $6 a head for admissions, confectionary, and parking gives an estimate of gross revenues of around $1.8 billion. Adding in revenues derived from the sale of TV rights brings the total to around $2.5 billion. In addition, a 1959 report from the First Federal Reserve Bank of Philadelphia estimated that such direct participation sports as boating, swimming, fishing, bicycling, roller skating, bowling, hunting, baseball and softball, pool, golf, tennis and skiing involved at least 286 million Americans and resulted in expenditures (mainly for equipment and travel) of over $10 billion. (The present figure is about double that.) In 1966 the U.S. Department of Commerce estimated the country's annual recreational expenditure (including sports and related entertainment and travel) at around $30 billion. We must also include the billions annually invested in such facilities as stadiums, practice fields, arenas, field houses, sports advertising, media equipment to cover sports events, costs of processing and distributing sports news ad infinitum. Although there is considerable overlap in these various figures, it seems apparent that total sports and sports-related expenditures in the United States cannot be less than around $25 billion annually. (And this says nothing whatever about the tens of billions made off products marketed via sports machismo.)

And it's not just the proceeds from the games, or the advertising, that makes sports such a lucrative enterprise. A 1963 article in the *Financial Post* noted that preparations for the Tokyo Olympics had sparked a rebuilding job costing a tidy $1.5 billion (including a $550-million rail line between Tokyo and Osaka, twenty-three new arteries and eight expressways into the city [mostly from the airport], nine miles of new subway, additions to the Tokyo police force and an $18-million television center capable of providing round-the-world coverage).

In preparation for the smaller 1968 Winter Olympics, Grenoble built a new city hall, post office, hospital, police station, school, exhibition hall, airport, railway station, cultural center, and various multi-lane highways. All told, it came to a $200-million investment. The *Financial Post* described it as "Grenoble's hopes of becoming a leading European city, an international convention center, a city trying to establish a reputation as France's 'City of Tomorrow' or 'Atlantic City'. . . . " (Nancy Greene, who won a skiing gold medal at Grenoble points out in her autobiography that, with this kind of money at stake, it was necessary to appeal to a gigantic audience to pay for it all: "The result inevitably is that the Olympic Games descend to the level of spectacle and begin to resemble some kind of circus.")

As I write this book the New York Yankees' bosses are negotiating to get the city to rebuild Yankee Stadium for them at a cost of around $30 million. The Detroit Lions' and the Detroit Tigers' brass are reportedly dickering to have the taxpayers build them a new stadium (possibly two) at a cost variously estimated as running around $150 million. The Yankees, it will be remembered, are owned by CBS, a corporation worth billions of dollars. The Lions are owned by William Clay Ford, vice-president and part owner of the Ford Motor Company, and reportedly worth around $140 million. Multimillionaire John Fetzer, who owns the Tigers, also owns the "Tiger Network" of eight radio stations as well as various television interests. And these are the sports magnates the taxpayers are supposed to be subsidizing to the tune of hundreds of millions for their stadiums! Meanwhile the Detroit Board of Health has termed some sixty thousand of that city's houses as substandard or unfit for human habitation.

In hockey, it's been a similar story. Without a big enough arena it was implied that Vancouver could not get a National Hockey League franchise. So Canadian taxpayers were encouraged to build the $6-million Pacific Coliseum. The government in Ottawa and the British Columbia provincial treasury each put up $2 million. The city of Vancouver added $1 3/4 million, and the Pacific National Exhibition (which owns the Coliseum building) added the final quarter million. The Vancouver Canucks were 87 per cent American-owned. So, what you had was three levels of Canadian government forking out about $6 million so that American millionaires could sell a Canadian game to Canadians.

One reason an aspiring sports magnate is willing to pay millions of dollars for a team is that the possession of a league franchise puts him in a monopolistic position in marketing his product in a particular city and hiring the players who will produce the product. The toleration by the dominant elements in society of such monopolistic agreements in restraint of a free-player market, as the reserve and option clauses written into all major league contracts, reflects the usefulness of the sports industry in providing a profitable investment channel for their surplus capital, and even more importantly, for furthering the sort of competitive, work-hard, be-disciplined, produce-more, consume-more ideology our capitalists find so attractive. The laws governing sports, including especially the 1922 Supreme Court decision exempting baseball from the anti-trust laws, arise out of both the economics of this capitalist industry and the place of sports production, including ideological indoctrination, in this society generally. Thus, the sports industry provides a graphic illustration of how, when the economic situation in a major industry violates the laws of capitalist society (in this case, the anti-trust laws), the laws are re-interpreted to agree with the economic "realities" and not the other way around. The ready acceptance of monopolistic practices in the sports industry goes hand in hand with the more covert acceptance of such practices throughout industry generally.

Under monopoly capitalism, owners are allowed not only full control over markets and players, but also tremendous tax loopholes. Since they have always considered players as "property" it was only a matter of

time before they started claiming the same sort of depreciation allowances as the oil industry. The way this "game" is played has been described by former Chicago White Sox owner Bill Veeck in his aptly titled book, *The Hustler's Handbook*. When buying a major league team, says Veeck, you can imagine that you are buying their whole operation—team plus franchise—or you can claim to be buying a franchise plus a series of players. In the first case, the players would be considered an "existing asset, which the previous ownership had already written off at the time of their original purchase" and you would not be eligible for any further tax write-offs to cover further depreciation. On the other hand, if you bought "the players from the old company before you liquidated, in distinct and separate transactions," they can be listed as an expense item. "It said so right in your books." You can then depreciate the cost of each player over a period ranging from about three to ten years, which you estimate to be his useful playing life. "If you expect to make a lot of money fast, you're better off being able to write them off as quickly as possible." If not, you choose the longer period.

The key is the amount of the purchase price of the team you assign to the players, and how much you claim as the cost of the franchise. In the early sixties, it was customary in baseball to estimate the worth of the franchise (i.e., the part that cannot be depreciated) as a mere $50,000. This left the new owners free to list around 98 per cent of the purchase price as an expense item—i.e., player costs—which they could then use for tax write-offs. (In fact, during baseball's expansion in the mid-sixties, there was no charge at all for the franchises; everything was supposedly being spent for tired, old, cast-off players.)

Veeck gives the example of the sale of the Milwaukee Braves just before they moved to Atlanta. After deducting the $50,000 franchise fee, the "cost of players" came to about $6 million. Depreciation over ten years would then give the new owners an annual tax write-off of about $600,000. Or, put slightly differently, they would pay *no taxes at all* on their first $600,000 of profit (and since the corporate tax runs about 50 per cent, they would be saving themselves around $300,000 a year for ten years, or $3 million). "If you want to be cynical, you might even say the Government was paying half of their purchase price for them."

You might think that the owners would still have to pay taxes on any profits above $600,000. Wrong again. They can spend them on new players, and then start depreciating them. After ten years they sell, and then somebody else starts the tax-write-off game all over again. It is important to see that they are not selling just a franchise and a team: they are selling, says Veeck, *"the right to depreciate."* This is the real reason the price of a major league team has been increasing steadily, since the more the price rises the larger the depreciation write-off becomes. But at these prices a situation is being created in which only corporations can afford to bid. CBS and the Yankees is the obvious example, but the Montreal

Expos, Los Angeles Angels, Detroit Tigers, and St. Louis Cards were all bought on behalf of substantial corporate empires (a whiskey company, various television and radio interests, and a brewery, respectively). "A corporation," says Veeck, "not only has the money, *but it can use the depreciation write-off on its total corporate profits even if the ball club itself hasn't made enough profit to cover it.*" He adds that, of the ten American League clubs in existence when he wrote his book, only two were not tied in some way to established profit-making corporations that could absorb either the operating losses or the player depreciation and, happily, "pass 50 per cent of the price on to the government." No wonder Veeck says our national pastime is not baseball but "how to make sure profits can be claimed as a capital gain rather than as income."

And sports may be leading the way. An article in the *Financial Post* headed

Tax Break for Mental Athletes?

notes that while there have been a lot of complaints that sports have become big business, "it seems entirely possible that big business may look more and more like big league sport." What with sports teams being allowed to depreciate their athletes, "why shouldn't fledgling firms in other industries be allowed to depreciate their new mental athletes?" And, competition between companies being what it is, the day might come when one of them might have to pay $1 million to sign up a valuable computer whiz kid. "The company will certainly want to find a way to spread that cost over the estimated useful life of the asset." Apparently, "all that has to be done is to form a new 'team'. "

All this may not even be the biggest part of the business. A few years ago the McClellan Senate subcommittee on organized crime gave estimates ranging from $7 billion to $50 billion as the amount bet on football every year in America. Per capita, the mania may be even greater in England. There are also close connections between sports owners and the bookmakers. For example, in his book *They Call It a Game* (New York: Dial, 1971, p. 187) Bernie Parrish writes, "National Football League franchise owners have backgrounds as bookies, racetrack owners, high-rolling sports bettors, and even tote-machine manufacturers." (It is also quite common for sports or arena owners to be big shots in jockey clubs.) A good part of the billions of dollars put down every year in the name of "sports" of course goes right into the coffers of organized crime.

But this multi-billion-dollar connection between sport and crime is not the worst of the betting mania. Much more damaging are the sociopsychological effects that go hand in hand with betting. Several generations ago in his *Theory of the Leisure Class* Thorstein Veblen pointed out that this widespread gambling on sports acts to promote acausal and animistic thinking in society generally, and to keep much of the citizenry in a state of drugged inability even to think logically. For example, there are few sportsmen who are not in the habit of wearing some kind of charm or talisman to which some winning magic or another is attributed. And, similarly, many fans will go through certain ritualized gestures while watching a game, or are afraid to leave their seats, or whatever, for fear of "hoodooing" the contestants on which they may have laid a wager. Many feel that by backing one side in the contest they have somehow strengthened it. Others attribute magical powers to a team "mascot" or crossing themselves at particular crucial moments or bringing along their rosary beads or what have you. (Actually, the belief in a sort of supernatural intervention in these contests dates from the medieval "wager of battle" and "the ordeal" in which the contestant staked his life on the outcome.) But Veblen notes that ultimately the gambling propensity is "of more ancient date than the predatory culture. It is one form of the animistic apprehension of things" and its outgrowth—the belief in a preternatural agency which might intervene in human affairs such as in the wager of battle where "the preternatural agent was conceived to act on request as umpire," and to shape the outcome according to natural justice. He says that this animism tends to lower industrial efficiency, probably disastrously, by interfering with workers' ability to comprehend causal sequences. However, it also induces and conserves "a certain habitual recognition of the relation to a superior . . . , so stiffening the current sense of status and allegiance" (i.e., the hierarchy of God, coach, team, and bettor, each having less and less power to shape the result). "Those modern representatives of the predacious barbarian temper that make up the sporting element," he says, ". . . commonly attach themselves to one of the naively and consistently anthropomorphic creeds [i.e., Christianity or Judaism, rather than say Unitarianism, agnosticism, etc.] . . . which act to conserve, if not to initiate, habits of mind favorable to a regime of status . . . the predatory habit of life." The point is that without stakes and competition, and the divinely ordained system of winners and losers they imply, there could be no stable, divinely sanctioned social-status system. Furthermore, the anthropomorphic cults, betting, and the predatory sporting temperament are good ways of keeping everyone drugged with animism and preternaturalism, thus ensuring that they will be no threat to the existing social dictatorship. This is more or less a refinement of Marx's religion-is-the-opiate-of-the-masses argument. Veblen seems to be saying that religion, sports, and betting form an interpenetrating complex of three opiates working in tandem. The stakes are enormously high—the perpetuation of the present system. As with the rest of sports, there's also a lot of easy money in it. Who's getting it?

There has always been a fair bit of centralization in the ownership of teams and facilities in different sports. In hockey and basketball, for example, the big-city American teams have typically been controlled by the owners of the major arenas in each city. James Norris at one time owned the "rival" Detroit Red Wings, New York Rangers, and Chicago Black Hawks of the National

Hockey League. He also owned the three pro basketball teams in those cities, and the arenas in those and other cities. For good measure, he controlled professional boxing through his International Boxing Club, which had its main exhibition headquarters at his Madison Square Garden. When the anti-trust laws belatedly caught up with him about a decade ago, he sold off the Rangers and the Red Wings (to his half-brother) and broke up his boxing empire.

His present successor as chairman of Madison Square Garden is Irving Mitchell Felt, who is also chairman of the New York Rangers, the New York Knickerbockers, Madison Square Garden Boxing, Holiday on Ice, Roosevelt Raceway, Cinema City, the HCA Food Corporation, and the huge Graham-Paige Corporation. In his spare time Felt has also been on the executive committee of the Hotel Corporation of America, and a director of Sonesta International Hotels, the Mayflower Hotel Corporation, Fred Fear and Company, Recipe Foods, H and B America Corporation, and Columbia Pictures. He is also national vice-president and a director of the Navy League, and a member of the Wall Street, Bankers, Lotus, and Harmonie clubs. James Norris' successor in Detroit is Bruce Norris, who, in addition to owning the Red Wings, is president of the Norris Cattle Company and Canadian-American Agys. He is also a director of the famous West Indian Sugar Company, Dominion Foundries and Steel, the Midland National Bank (Milwaukee) and Maple Leaf Mills.

The successor in Chicago is Arthur Wirtz. In addition to controlling the Black Hawks, he is director of the Consolidated Broadcasting Company, Consolidated Enterprises, Forman Realty Co., American Furniture Mart, Rathjen Brothers (San Francisco), the First National Bank of South Miami, and Chicago Stadium, Inc. (Recently Comiskey Park has been having trouble attracting fans from Chicago's all-white suburban areas. It seems that the blacks in the surrounding ghetto have been less than hospitable.)

Another big hockey baron is Jack Kent Cooke. He owns the Los Angeles Kings, the Los Angeles Forum, Cable TV (which broadcast the first Ali-Frazier fight), and a big stake in the Washington Redskins (of which he is vice-president). He has also owned the Los Angeles Lakers and the old Toronto baseball team in the International League. He is also president of a radio features company, an industrial crafts company, an investment company, and has heavy investments in publishing and newspapers as well.

Montreal's top hockey fan was until recently Canadian Senator Hartland Molson, who in addition to owning the Montreal Canadiens, the arena and the Molson Brewery, served as vice-president and director of the Bank of Montreal, is a director of Canadian Industries, Ltd., the Sun Life Assurance Company of Canada, Canadian Corporate Management, Jamaica Public Service, Ltd., and Stone & Webster (Can.), Ltd. His successor as owner is Sam Bronfman, who also owns the Montreal Expos baseball team, and is chairman of Seagrams whiskey.

In Toronto, the men most interested in hockey were, until recently, John Bassett, who is chairman of Maple Leaf Gardens, and Conn and Stafford Smythe who owned the team. Bassett doubles as publisher of the recently defunct Toronto *Telegram,* and is chairman of CFTO television and the Toronto Argonauts Canadian Football League club. Conn Smythe is the owner and operator of Racing & Breeding Stables, a director of the Jockey Club in Ontario, and president of C. Smythe Sands, Ltd. Stafford Smythe is president and managing director of Maple Leaf Gardens, president of a trucking firm, chairman of Viceroy Manufacturing, a director of Commonwealth Savings and Loan, and of C. Smythe Sands. (In 1970 Stafford Smythe was accused by the Canadian government of having evaded tax payment on some $289,000 between 1965 and 1968. In June of 1971 he was arrested with another Maple Leaf Gardens director, Harold Ballard, and jointly charged with the theft of $146,000 in cash and securities from the Gardens between 1964 and 1969. He was also charged with defrauding the arena of $249,000 in the same period.) Two weeks before his trial he suddenly died. Ballard succeeded Bassett as Maple Leaf Gardens boss, and, as this book went to press, his trial was still in progress.

Typically, the hockey owners are multimillionaires who own other large corporations, have close links in the media and banking businesses, own the arenas they play in, and also have big interests in other sports (basketball and boxing in New York, baseball in Chicago and Oakland, football and racing in Toronto, and so on).

In the case of baseball, the Yankees are, as we have seen, owned by CBS. The Los Angeles Angels and the Detroit Tigers are owned by Gene Autry and John Fetzer, both of whom have close television connections with CBS. Autry owns television stations KOOL in Phoenix and KOLD in Tucson, as well as radio stations in Hollywood, San Francisco, Seattle, and Portland. He is also president of Challenge Records and Flying A Productions. Fetzer is president of his own broadcasting company, TV company, music company, the Cornhusker Television Corporation, Wolverine Cablevision, and Amalgamated Properties. He is also a director of the American National Bank and Trust Company of Michigan.

Chicago's biggest baseball baron, at the time of writing this, is Art Allyn, the chairman of a major investment company, an oil survey company, a precision tool company, and Mono Containers. He is also president of Artnell Exploration, Ltd., a trustee of the National College of Education, director of Francis I Dupont, Hart Carter Corporation, Appleton Coated Paper, Vantress Farms, and the Allyn Foundation. His clubs are Executives, Economics (Chicago) and Mid-America. In Boston the Red Sox big man is Tom Yawkey, whose biography lists "management and control of mines, mineral interests, timber lands, lumber and paper mills in various states and Canada." Oakland's Charles O. Finley doubles as owner of the Seals hockey team and has his own big insurance brokers firm in Chicago. Cleveland's recent president Gabe Paul doubled as a director of the South Ohio Bank in Cincinnati. The new prospective owner, Nick Mileti, also owns the Cleveland Cavaliers of the NBA, the Cleveland Barons of the AHL, and the Cleveland arena. Jerry Hoffberger of the Baltimore Orioles is chairman of the National Brewing Company in Baltimore, Divex, Inc., and the Laco Corporation. He is on the executive committee of Baltimore Trotting Races, Inc., and of the Fairchild Hiller Corporation, and is also a director of a bank, a mortgage company, and a real estate holding company. The pattern, then, with the exception of CBS, is ownership by middle-range millionaires, with close connections in finance and media.

It is more or less the same in all other professional sports, though occasionally we find sports teams under the control of some of the "big boys"—men like Texas oilmen Lamar Hunt (who owns the Kansas City Chiefs and World Championship Tennis); Clint Murchison (who owns the Dallas Cowboys); Bud Adams (the Houston Oilers); and John Mecom, Jr. (the New Orleans Saints); as well as the previously mentioned William Clay Ford. The interlocking directorates of sports and the mass media are hardly surprising. One sells the other. They form part of a single complex. As for the connections with finance, it would be hard to find any big business these days without them.

Of course the claims of sports barons to their own feudalistic fiefdoms have never been entirely accepted. Other owners have repeatedly tried to cut in on them. And players, whether as individuals or through their associations, have continued the struggle as well. In 1901 the baseball brass of the National League were challenged by the founding of the rival American League. For two years there was a little free competition, but thereafter the two sets of owners agreed that there was more in it for them if they just respected one another's monopolies and exploited the players and fans together. In 1914 the Federal League was formed and promptly sued to have the whole monopolistic structure of the old leagues invalidated on the ground that it violated the anti-trust laws. The old owners were scared. But they managed to tie up the suit in the courts for over two years. Finally, in 1916, with the new league in debt to the tune of about $10 million, it was forced to accept a settlement. The Baltimore team was still unsatisfied and pressed on with the suit in the federal courts. It claimed, among other things, that the established leagues' coercive player regulations—in effect threatening blacklisting and banishment for any player who associated himself with the new league—had made it extremely difficult for the new clubs to secure trained players, and this was a violation in restraint of trade of the Sherman Anti-Trust Act. A lower court agreed and awarded the Federal League club treble damages of $240,000. A big lobbying and press campaign on behalf of the old leagues followed, and in 1922 the Supreme Court overruled the lower court and gave the established baseball owners their famous exemption from the anti-trust laws on the grounds that the "sports" is not engaged in interstate commerce.

In 1946 a good many of baseball's non-commercial players were offered higher salaries in the Mexican League, and they headed off south of the border. Baseball commissioner A.B. Chandler promptly announced that any player who "deserted" to Mexico would be banned from the major leagues for five years. A player named Gardella returned before the end of the ban, and was refused reinstatement. He took his case to the courts, claiming that organized baseball was run as an illegal monopoly that was depriving him of his livelihood. The Circuit Court of Appeals agreed. Furthermore, Judge Jerome N. Frank noted of baseball's reserve system, "If the players are regarded as quasi-peons, it is of no moment that they are well paid. Only the totalitarian-minded will believe that high pay excuses virtual slavery." (Actually, considering the years and years of training, and the fact that an average major league lifetime is about five years in baseball and only three years in football, the pay is certainly not excessive.) Gardella won a handsome settlement. Much more serious, from the viewpoint of all sports brass, the case cast strong doubts on their continued exemption from the anti-trust laws. Senator E.C. Johnson (then president of the Western League) and Congressman A.S. Herlong (a former president of the Florida State League) sponsored bills in Congress that would have granted anti-trust exemptions to all professional sports. But the lobbying was a bit too heavy-handed, and the bills ended up buried in committee.

In 1953, in the case of the United States versus National Football League, the Supreme Court handed down a decision that seemed to show that it regarded pro football as *not* being exempt from the anti-trust laws. The government had pressed for an injunction against the NFL's practice of blacking out telecasts of NFL games within a 75-mile radius. The effect of this practice, it was stated, was to preserve a geographic monopoly over all aspects of pro football for each home club on its home territory. The NFL had opposed the suit on the grounds that it, supposedly like baseball, was not engaged in trade or commerce. The Court replied, "It is immaterial whether professional football by itself is commerce or interstate commerce . . . radio and television [coverage of games] clearly are in interstate commerce." The Court granted an injunction against various NFL practices found to be unreasonable restraints of trade, but not against the TV black-outs themselves.

Shortly thereafter the St. Louis Cardinals were purchased by beer baron A.A. Busch, Jr., owner of the Anheuser-Busch Brewery, and a new anti-trust furor broke out in Congress. Inasmuch as the Cardinals were a wholly-owned subsidiary of the brewery, it was alleged that Busch was using baseball as an advertising vehicle for his beer. Senator E.C. Johnson demanded passage of a bill that would have made clubs owned by beer and whiskey interests subject to the anti-trust laws. (He claimed that in the past Colonel Jacob Ruppert, who had owned the Yankees, had at least kept the club separate from the Ruppert Brewery.) What the argument boiled down to was the fear on Johnson's part that unless baseball was kept separate from obviously commercial interests, it would be impossible to claim it was not commercial and the game would necessarily lose its anti-trust exemption. (Here he underestimated monopoly capital's ability to reconcile itself to violations of the law when there are big profits at stake. The Cardinals' take-over proved to be one of the first of a long series of take-overs of sports clubs by commercial interests, culminating with the take-over of the Yankees by CBS.) When the Justice Department opposed Johnson's bill as discriminatory toward alcohol interests, he offered to broaden it to include all commercial interests. The head of the Justice Department's Anti-Trust Division, Judge Stanley N. Barnes, stated that all of organized baseball, not just those clubs owned by businesses, should be made subject to the anti-trust laws. Under heavy lobbying, and a press barrage claiming that this would "ruin" baseball, the furor was allowed to die down, and nothing was done.

In 1955 the Supreme Court ruled that boxing was not exempt from the anti-trust laws, apparently because it derived approximately 25 per cent of its revenues from radio and television telecasts which are clearly interstate commerce. (By now both baseball and football were also deriving huge chunks of revenue from radio and TV.) Judge Felix Frankfurter seemed to be aware of the con-tradictory treatment his colleagues were giving baseball and boxing when he noted, "It would baffle the subtlest ingenuity to find a single differentiating factor between other sporting exhibitions . . . and baseball." In 1957 the Supreme Court again declared that the business of professional football was subject to the anti-trust laws. It ruled for the plaintiff in a case brought by Bill Radovich, a former pro footballer who charged the National Foot-ball League with monopolistic practices including coer-cive player restrictions and blacklisting.

Prior to the 1960s baseball owners had always op-posed expansion. (After all, why cut up the cake more ways?) However, when Branch Rickey began to gather support to form a new Continental League, the old owners moved some clubs to the West Coast and quickly doled out new franchises in order to pre-empt the market. Around this time Senator Kefauver had a bill pending to bring baseball under the anti-trust laws, but under heavy lobbying from the owners, the whole thing was pigeonholed. The bill favored by the owners was one drawn up by Senator Philip Hart of Michigan (who is married to one of the daughters of William O. Briggs, the late owner of the Detroit Tigers). This bill would nominally have put all professional sports under the anti-trust laws, but it also would have exempted all rules pertaining to player contracts and territorial rights. In short, pro sports were to be exempted from the anti-trust laws by the very bill that purported to control them. For a while it seemed that they would get away with it. In August 1964 the bill seemed certain to pass. It was at this point that CBS purchased the Yankees, and a new furor broke out over whether a station that was dealing with a team for its broadcast rights could also own the team (though this situation had existed with other teams long before that and has, in fact, become common of late). The Hart bill was then sent back to committee "for fur-ther study," and has not been heard of since (though the senator from Michigan is still scrambling about after a substitute).

In the late '60s, players in almost all major sports began to band together in real associations (in contrast to the "sweetheart" associations of earlier periods), and began to attack the monopolistic reserve and option clauses. The best-known case was probably that of St. Louis Cardinals outfielder Curt Flood. At the end of the 1969 season the Cards shipped him to the Phillies. Trades are common, and provisions are made for them in contracts. If the owners "own" a player, they can trade him off, fire him, or ship him off to the minors. This time, however, Flood said NO. He wrote to baseball's commissioner Bowie Kuhn to tell him that, as a human being, he could not accept being traded like cattle, without any say in the matter. He asked Kuhn to declare him a free agent with the option of selling his ser-vices to whatever team he chose. Kuhn conceded that Flood was a human being, but not much more. He refus-ed the request. So Flood filed suit against the baseball owners, charging them with violation of ballplayers' con-stitutional rights and of the anti-trust laws. He secured Arthur Goldberg as his lawyer and won the backing of the Major League Players' Association. But he had to sit out the 1970 season to avoid prejudicing his case. In August 1970, a lower court judge ruled against Flood on the grounds that "unless and until the Supreme Court or Congress" nullifies baseball's anti-trust exemption, "we have no basis for proceeding to the underlying question of whether baseball's reserve system would or would not be deemed reasonable if it were in fact subject to anti-trust legislation." The decision seemed to be an invita-tion to Flood and the other ballplayers to take the case to the Supreme Court, and they announced that they would do exactly that. In the meantime Flood wrote a very unusual baseball book called *The Way It Is,* documen-ting the mispractices of baseball's reigning establish-ment. Washington Senators owner, Bob Short, who seems to have made a career of signing on good players whom other owners consider too uppity, was able to coax Flood back for the start of the 1971 season. But the long lay-off, the sharp barbs of rival coaches, and establish-ment sports-writers, as well as unspecified personal troubles, had all taken their toll. With everything closing in on him, Curt Flood suddenly ducked off to Spain. Baseball's owners were not sorry to see him go. But his suit remained to be decided. He eventually lost it. The Supreme Court ruled that any change in baseball's anti-trust status would have to be made by Congress (though Congress never gave baseball an anti-trust exemption in the first place). The Justices again emphasized that the other sports—excluding baseball—are *not* exempt from the anti-trust laws.

In hockey, the NHL's reserve clause[2] came under

fairly weak attack from the Canadian government's Task Force on Sports. The Task Force members thought the reserve clause too unreasonable in terms, and suggested it would look less messy if it were replaced by the same sort of option clause that appears in pro football contracts (i.e., theoretically giving players the right to become free agents if they play out their options for one year at slightly reduced salaries). "An employer, of course," said the Task Force, "should have the right to restrict his employee from performing for anybody other than himself, but such restrictions should be reasonable in terms." Evidently, what was being recommended was "reasonable" slavery.

Football's option clause, a model in Canada, was being blasted by American players who had to adhere to it. "It doesn't work," charged former All-NFL defensive back Johnny Sample (after coming out of a hearing of a federal grand jury investigating pro football), because the owners "have an agreement among themselves" and enjoy "complete strangulation over the players." Sample also talked about the "blackballing" that forced him out of the (then) National Football League in 1966, and about racial quotas which he said are used to limit the number of blacks on any given team.

Jim Bouton and Bernie Parrish have pointed out that there is a National Football League rule whereby whenever a player who has played out his option is signed by another club, it must give full value for him. This amounts to a trade. If the new club refuses, Article XII, Section 12.1 (H) of the NFL Constitution provides, "the Commissioner may name and then award to the former club one or more players from the Active, Reserve, or Selection List (including future selection choices) of the acquiring club as the Commissioner in his sole discretion deems fair and equitable." It is obvious that no team is going to give a substantial pay increase to such a "free agent" who has played out his option if they also have to pay for him with players. Here, too, the vaunted option has been short-circuited by monopoly.

Meanwhile, one of the Canadian Football League's own star players was having troubles with the option clause. Vic Washington, the Ottawa halfback who had been voted the outstanding player of the 1968 Canadian pro championship game, tried to switch to the San Francisco Forty-Niners of the National Football League without playing out an option year. He failed. The Canadian Football League refused to waive him out of the League, and, as the CFL and the NFL frown on "raiding" (i.e., free competition) across the border, Washington was left in limbo. Ottawa suspended him, and then shipped his contract to British Columbia "for future considerations." "Football," said Vic Washington, "just wants to make an example of me." (He is now with San Francisco.)

Basketball player Spencer Haywood did considerably better. Signed after his sophomore year in college by the Denver Rockets of the American Basketball Association ("The school is making a lot of money out of me, so why shouldn't I be making some," he said at the time),

Haywood later "jumped" to the Seattle Sonics of the NBA. The Denver ownership brought suit against Haywood, the Sonics, and All-Pro Management, seeking to prove that he was still "Denver property." Meanwhile, the NBA sought to bar Haywood from playing in their league because their rules (i.e., their deal with the colleges) do not permit collegians to be signed until after their class has graduated. (This rule avoids the necessity of paying college stars big money to jump to the pros a year or two early, and for the NCAA it avoids the need to pay the athletes competitive wages while they are still being educated.) Haywood promptly initiated suit against the NBA, challenging, among other things, their draft laws for manipulating college players. The situation was clearly becoming dangerous for the monopolists. The NBA went to court and won a temporary order blocking Haywood from playing in their league. But this was overruled by U.S. District Court Judge Warren J. Ferguson, who ruled that Haywood could play for the Sonics through the 1971 season, pending the Court's decision on the Rockets' case. The Judge further added that professional athletes "cannot be used and cannot be treated as merchandise." This must have come as quite a shock to all sports magnates. Within two weeks of the Judge's provisional decision the NBA had come to a settlement with Haywood and Seattle. The league would interpose no further objection to Haywood playing on the Seattle club. In return Haywood would drop his suit against the NBA, and the club would pay the NBA $200,000 in fines for violating the league by-laws. At the time of this writing it seems quite likely that Haywood will win his other case with Denver as well, which would confirm a basketball player's right to sell his labor to teams in either league.

Not surprisingly, considering the possibility of some real free competition, the two pro basketball leagues are rapidly moving toward a merger that would keep the monopoly intact. The players don't like it one bit. According to Oscar Robertson, the militant black backcourt man who is president of the NBA Players' Association, the players are fully prepared to take whatever legal steps may be necessary to block the merger. A players' strike is also possible. There is also some opposition to the merger in Congress, led by Senator Sam Ervin, the chairman of the Senate Anti-Trust and Monopoly Subcommittee, and Congressman Emanuel Celler. "With the exception of the United States Government," Ervin told the president of the American Basketball Association, "which can draft people to serve in the services, there is no other business that can draft employees except professional sports. Now a man can get two bids, one from each league (NBA and ABA respectively). You want him to only be able to get one bid. You say you're doing this for the entertainment of the public. That's exactly what they said in Rome at the Coliseum." (New York *Daily News*, November 16, 1971.)

Another interesting case in which a player faced up to the power of the monopolists and forced them to back down was that of Jim Ninowski, the former Cleveland

Browns and Detroit Lions quarterback. In May 1966, when the American and National Football Leagues were supposedly in heated competition for players, Nino was offered about four hundred thousand dollars by the Oakland Raiders to play out his option with the Cleveland Browns and then play three seasons with the Raiders. Why an AFL team felt it had to respect the NFL's option clause is not entirely clear. Ninowski told his NFL owner about the offer, and then after a little time had passed, according to Bernie Parrish (*They Call It a Game*, p. 226 ff.), "He was told that a temporary truce had been arranged between the leagues and that the deal they had agreed on was off." Nino decided to file an anti-trust action against the two leagues. At first he was threatened, but the NFL was anxious not to have its collusion with the "rival" AFL dragged through the courts and press, he was eventually *paid off in full*, with one hundred thousand dollars a year for four years. After that, Parrish says, Nino was blacklisted by the owners. "Players have been blacklisted for a lot less than taking four hundred thousand dollars out of their tight fists," he adds.

Parrish has offered his own alternative to private monopolistic ownership of teams and players:

> The franchises should be owned by municipal corporations legally tied to the stadium authorities, having public common-stock ownership, with stock being offered to season-ticket holders on the basis of first refusal . . . a formula could be worked out to pay the players a percentage of the total income. Then the profits after expenses could be earmarked for the revitalization of the inner cities—improved wages for police, firemen, teachers, and other civil servants; upgrading of city and county hos-

pitals, and care for the aged; to name a few recipients. (Ibid., p. 290.)

And there would be no "option clause." Under the present system there is not the remotest chance that even this limited plan will be adopted. On the other hand, there is at present no good reason why the players' associations in all of the professional sports could not simply take *control* of their sports—rent stadiums, sell tickets, and divide up the profits among themselves. The present owners perform no worthwhile or necessary function whatever. (And the only injuries they get from the game are the arm strains accumulated raking in the profits.) Instead of the vulture's share of the take, these owners should be paid what they deserve for the amount of work they do—absolutely nothing. If the players' associations in the different sports were able to get together with each other in a professional athletes' union, and then approach other progressive labor unions for support, they would immensely strengthen their ability to win total players' control of sports. Which would, of course, serve as an excellent example for workers' control in industry generally.

NOTES

1. Similarly, in professional baseball, when there was talk of a New York team in the proposed Continental League in the early sixties, the Yankees let it be known that it would not be welcome to play in Yankee Stadium. The latter had been built in the '20s, because, when the Yanks' popularity began to rival that of the Giants, the Giant brass booted them out of the Polo Grounds.
2. "The player hereby undertakes that he will at the request of the club enter into a contract for the following playing season on the same terms and conditions as this contract, save as to salary . . ."

A CASE FOR KILLING THE OLYMPICS
John McMurtry

As with all institutions, the Olympic Games have a rhetoric of self-praise. So we hear a great deal about the games embodying in action the human quest for excellence and perfect form. About their bringing together the nations of the earth in peace, harmony and common pursuit. And about their holding up to us all global models of dedication, courage and skill.

These words can certainly grip the heart. The ideals they flourish seem so self-evidently fine that the body tends to shiver a little at the feeling of them. So much so that one *wants* to move from the deep chords they stir to the opinion that the Olympic Games we have actually exemplify such ideals—like some precious flash of light every four years in a generally darkening world.

The problem is so many vicious realities about the games keep intruding into one's illusions about them. I think, for example, of the hundreds of demonstrators gunned down by police during the Olympic preparations

in Mexico City in 1968; with little but lying counts of the dead and homilies on law and order emanating from the Olympic-opiated scene. ("We have been assured," said the International Olympic Committee during the slaughter, "that nothing will interfere with the peaceful entry of the Olympic flame nor with the competitions that follow.") I've been told, too, by Canadian runner Abby Hoffman that the response of a number of athletes to the Israel-Palestine tragedy at Munich was, in fact, *relief*: it meant they had a little more time before their events. "Forget the blood, everybody," the idea seems to be, "the Roman Circus is in town."

Then, of course, it's difficult to miss the stench of jingoism excited by the Olympics. Nationalistic gesture permeates just about every phase of the games; flags, anthems, uniforms and nation scores measure and punc-

From *Maclean's* January, 1973, p. 34.

tuate the action like a military exercise. If any athlete breaks national rank—as the black winners in the 400 meters have in both 1969 and 1972 by not assuming soldier postures during the post-race American victory anthems—he is almost certain to be persecuted as a national pariah. (In 1968, the fist-raising black runners Tommie Smith and John Carlos were immediately kicked off the American team, expelled from the Olympic Village as well as from all further Olympic competition, and given 48 hours by the Mexican state to leave the country.) For their part, the news media of every country broaden and deepen the whole nation-state regimen with a selective attention and solicitude for their country's athletes that would excite snorts of laughter were they not so reminiscent of the propaganda that precedes wars. As for the official Canadian attitude toward such media chauvinism, it's indicated by the remark of Bill Cox, a vice-president of the Canadian Olympic Association and chairman of its Communications Services: "Short of a world war, there is no bigger forum for our country than the Olympics." Typically this attitude mimics that of big brother America: the American Broadcasting Company, for example, sent 250 people to cover the 1968 winter games at Grenoble—more than the entire American team—on the grounds that the "only time all nations get in uniform is for war or the Olympics."

Acting as a sort of microcosm of this nationalistic glory tournament is the struggle for spotlight among the athletes themselves. Here too the grammar of the situation is imposed by Olympic regulation—formal king-of-the-castle podiums and ceremonies after every final event, recognition of top-finishing competitors only, and medal mania. And here too the media—not to mention the fans, both in the stands and back home—dramatically reinforce the formal mechanics of the victory-for-self imperative with words of pity for the great majority, the losers, and worshipping praise for a tiny minority, the winners.

This approach seemed reduced to absurdity in the 1972 Olympics when seven-gold-medalist Mark Spitz, who was really only best at two strokes of swimming, alone received more recognition and applause from the U.S. media than all the thousands of other athletes who had come from every reach of the human race. The message was pointed—being top dog is pretty much all that matters. Or, to use the more specific words of Mark Spitz's father to Mark Spitz, "Swimming isn't everything, winning is."

Possibly the most distressing aspect of all this is how the *athletes themselves* get into it. They seem to conceive of their very identities as depending on where they end up in this ego-trip machinery. They appear to really believe that their success as people, let alone as sportsmen, stands or falls with what they do inside the isolated and official Olympic frame.

Even when one takes a deliberately naive stance and considers the Olympics from the perspective of athletic performance alone, the reality is mean spirited. On the surface, there is undeniably beautiful and inspiring

human action—the courageous grace and explosive effort that has fixed me, for one, in a trance before the TV set for hours. But beneath the surface, one can't miss the anti-athletic phenomena. There's the grotesquely one-sided development of physique which accompanies the increasing specialization and fragmentation of events (imagine how well a shot-putter could run the mile). There's the universal commitment to dreary drill and routine that usurps the very nature of "sport" which, as its etymology makes clear, is properly a spontaneous rejoicing in bodily expression (one Olympic swimmer once told me that his experience had actually taught him to hate swimming—a not surprising result given the common Olympic-athlete schedule of training seven hours a day at one event for years on end). There's the preoccupation with winning that often so successfully distracts athletes from the performance itself that they are too tied up to let go (recall the reported "choke-ups" of great athletes like Jim Ryun); the same preoccupation can also make athletes so antagonistic toward their fellow competitors that they are happy to discover any means they can to beat them (for example, the groin kneeing and body grabbing that go on in Olympic water polo contests). Then there's the elitism that manages in one way or another to discourage the vast majority of people from any sport activity except watching others from a seat (consider the shockingly poor fitness ratings—Canada's 30-year-old males have the same rating as 60-year-old Swedes—of spectatorist countries like Canada and the U.S.). And there's the command relationship between coach and athlete, which so destroys fun and autonomy that continuing to call what happens "sport" seems obscene (the Japanese girl volleyball team, for instance, seems admired for the way its coach maintains discipline by making offending players weep with humiliation and pain in practice: he instructs the other girls to shout and drill volleyballs at anyone who fails to perform his orders correctly).

Lest anyone respond to all this with romantic invocations of the past and the "classical" notions of sport, remember that the founders of the Olympics, the ancient Greeks, were not much more enlightened. The Olympic events were originally founded on war skills—spear throwing, running, hand-to-hand fighting and so on—and they were approved most of all for the training they encouraged in this respect. Indeed, Plato and Aristotle more or less rejected such athletics, not because they were warlike but because they did not drill for war *well enough*. As for the jingoistic dimension of the Olympics, the ancient Hellenic states are said to have regarded a victory by one of their citizens as of similar status to a state victory by the sword. As today, this national glory seeking had its individual counterpart: only free Greeks (not women or slaves) were allowed to compete and victory or loss was regarded even more intensely as great honor or great disgrace. As for lavish rewards for the winners, they may have been even more spectacular than today with such things as income-for-life grants to those who emerged on top. In fact, the ancient Olympics were eventually banned by the Romans for being too professionalized.

None of this will surprise those who know much about the ancient and bellicose roots of our Western culture. Much like contemporary society, things then, too, tended to be run along the lines of antagonistic contest for personal status—drama festivals and philosophical intercourse as well as dirty politics and imperialism. Much like now, too, this fury to distinguish the self in conflict gave rise to considerable fear and hate, as the term *agon*—the Greek word for "contest" and the root of our word "agony"—suggests. The Olympic Games themselves merely reflected this general culture pattern—appropriately in honor of Zeus, the absolute power whose single principle of life was glorification of himself.

The Munich Olympics cost $30,000 a minute, for two weeks—and we're next.

Well, given all the inhumanities of the Olympic enterprise snarling beneath the gloss of spectacular entertainment and official rhetoric, what uplifts can we hope for? When I first started writing this piece my head spun with possibility. I thought of the noble principle of amateurism—giving freely of one's talents—being universalized across the Olympic event. With everyone from stadium workers to hotel owners, from television companies to the athletes themselves uniting in voluntary gift of their abilities to a global audience. I thought of the surplus wealth that would be set free by such a great effort of communal grace being dedicated to ever more play areas, greening the face of our cement-and-steel cities. With the greening beginning in the places I think we really owe—like Hanoi and Calcutta—and spreading across the globe with each Olympics like a gathering summer day. I thought of the king-of-the-castle podiums, flag waving, anthems and nation scores being dropped from the games altogether in favor of a real world "meet." With all the competitors rejoicing together after the events as a human community in celebrative harmony undivided by egotistic or nationalistic barriers. And I thought of all the events themselves as embodying a new kind of competition where the goal ceased to be victory of the self or of the nation state and became instead a human effort to overcome past limits of physical expression. With contestants vying together to achieve the greatest performance ever of human speed, endurance, daring and strength. In short, I imagined an Olympics lifting us out of the rat race of our everyday life and clasping hands above the fight as a new and visible world symbol of what the human soul truly yearns to be.

Such were my hopes.

But then I looked into the nitty-gritty of the Olympics. The scratch, the money. How much it costs, who benefits and who loses. After that, any illusions I had left were dissolved by the clang and snatch of silver.

In the Munich Olympics, the estimated cost of the games started off at $150 million. Then began the familiar pattern of escalation—cost after cost being added onto the backs of taxpayers to the music of politicians, sports barons and building developers giving justification and excuses. By the time the Munich games ended, the most conservative estimate of total cost was $600 million. To be borne by the German people, paying off federal, state and municipal governments. When calculated on a per-Olympic-minute basis, the Germans ended up having to pay *almost $30,000 a minute* for the privilege of hosting the two-week spectacle.

The same sort of thing happened in Mexico and Tokyo, and the same sort of thing is happening now in Canada for the scheduled '76 Olympics in Montreal. In all these places, too, the big con that "we'll get it all back from tourists and the future use of facilities" spun out from the promoters. In fact, no such thing happened. For example, the Mexican Olympics got only a little more than a third of the tourists the promoters predicted. What's more, the Olympic Village apartments, which were supposed to be sold after the games to big companies for tourist accommodations, just didn't sell. The Mexican government tried to get rid of them at $25,000 a shot to the Mexican privileged, but didn't have much luck (there aren't that many Mexican privileged). Further, the predicted tourist boom to *follow* the Olympics ended up as a tourist slump for two months (the same phenomenon occurred in Rome and Tokyo and after Montreal's Expo). As for Munich, the mayor of this city began by justifying the hosting of the games as a massive public works project to alleviate some of his worst municipal problems. But he ended up with new problems: bloody police-guerilla shoot-outs and German army patrols in the streets.

The public works projects planned for Montreal are pretty massive, too, even though Mayor Jean Drapeau—whose city still owes the federal government $123 million for Expo—started off in 1968 with a cost prediction for the Olympics of $10 to $15 million. Drapeau now seems at best incompetent when his projected 1976 figure turns out to have been *one-fortieth* the amount spent by Munich in 1972. He has since increased his estimate (to $126 million, one report said), but, as of this writing, has been systematically ambivalent about overall costs. The Quebec government, for its part, has estimated that Drapeau's Olympics will cost $300 million, *excluding* the cost of the Olympic Village which it places at $120 million. Since the Quebec government's total estimate, $420 million, does not allow for inflation in building costs, one can *conservatively* figure the final price to be about $600 million.

Now the Bourassa government has agreed to support the Montreal Olympics—but has never said *how much* this support will amount to. The federal government, at this writing, has made no significant commitment in the fact of an expenditure best indicated by *The Financial Post's* calculation of the interest charges on the Olympic Village alone: $309 million (at 8 1/4% over 25 years).

As far as the social worth of this enormous outlay of money is concerned, Drapeau's most plausible defense seems to be that one project, the Olympic Village, will eventually provide 4,000 housing units for Montreal's poor. Yet he must know that even here his justification lacks credibility. For he must know that his plan to scatter the Olympic Village units throughout Montreal will not meet the International Olympic Committee's requirements for a single unified village—Lord Killanin, the IOC's new president, has as much as said so. And if Drapeau doesn't scatter those units he'll have difficulty getting the financing he's reportedly counting on to build the village in the first place. He's expecting to get the money from the federal government's Central Mortgage and Housing Corporation and CMHC is not interested in a single unified development in urban Montreal. So either the CMHC will have to lower its standards of housing the poor or Drapeau is going to be without the funds he counts on for the Olympic Village. In either case, the prospects are not promising for the 12,000 to 15,000 people who are supposed to be getting a decent place to live.

What is even more vexing in this whole situation is that the problems already diseasing Montreal, poverty and pollution, are receiving brutally inadequate attention. For example, a recent study for the Montreal City Health Department of 3,400 urban core schoolchildren found that more than half of them were physically ill, most suffering from upper respiratory and skin diseases. Ten percent of these children required hospital treatment. In one school, 21% of the students were undernourished, 41% emotionally disturbed and 51% lived in houses with inadequate sanitation facilities. For further example, the Quebec government's Health and Welfare Commission, in its 1971 report, said that of 42,939 houses in six sectors of Montreal, 6,981 were found to be "uninhabitable" and 20,612 "substandard." For even further instance, Montreal's air is "past danger limits" (according to the commission), the city dumps 300 million gallons of raw sewage into the St. Lawrence every day and scores of Quebec municipalities have polluted drinking water. Yet the amount being spent on these problems—remember now that the Montreal Olympic costs are already estimated at $600 million—is typified by Quebec province's entire 1971-72 budget for the environment: $12.3 million. Or, comparatively, Montreal spent less than one quarter as much as Metro Toronto for sewage treatment and the removal of solid waste during the fiscal year 1969.

The real winners: A few athletes, politicians and big business builders

As one becomes aware of all these things, it gets more and more difficult to still in oneself a rise of savage indignation. But the story isn't finished. One has to ask how this grotesque inversion of priorities could possibly happen, ask who could possibly *want* it to happen. It would be a mistake to think that it springs from some mere social perversity of our citizens. After all, the games enterprise was not initiated by Canadians generally. No, it's been brought to Canada by an interested few, though

all Canadians through their federal taxes are going to have to pay a good part of its more than $600-million tab; nothing indicates that Montreal is in anything like the financial position to raise that kind of money (an amount, one suddenly realizes, that would cover our notorious Unemployment Insurance deficit for the first six months of '72 more than twice over). Since the games seem so obviously against the interests of the general population, who stand to lose a great deal from them and gain almost nothing, one must press the question. Who *does* stand to benefit from the Montreal Olympics of 1976? Who owns the real interest in having them here?

On the surface, there's the simple glory that is captured by the politicians who promote and figurehead a great world event. Recall how—before the bills came in—Drapeau was being touted as a national hero and possible future prime minister for his role in bringing Expo to Montreal.

Then there's the different sort of glory of the few athletes who come out on top. Not to mention the future pocket-filling they may secure by their performances, such as the $500,000 Ice Follies contract offered skater Peggy Fleming, the Mars bars and auto ad rewards of Nancy Greene Raine and the lucrative Hollywood offers for Mark Spitz.

Then, of course, there's the first-class free rides for thousands of people who control, coach, officiate and ballyhoo the games. The Canadian Olympic Association, for example, is pressing for a massive infusion of federal government money for its $10-million-a-year plan to train about 300 athletes over the next four years (at a time when 85% of our adult population has been classified as sedentary by a 1971 Department of Health and Welfare survey).

And then, too, there's the wonderful advertising context the games provide for the mass marketing of merchandise: in the last Olympics, it was fast and powerful cars—and deodorants—that were made out to look like gold medal surrogates for consumer television watchers.

But only a part of the hundreds of millions of dollars to be spent on the Montreal Olympics will go to these people. The real bulk expenditures of the games are earmarked for others, namely, big business builders. Consider the construction costs: $50 to $70 million for the stadium alone, another $120 million for the Olympic Village, and hundreds of millions more for such things as better transportation routes to and from the games and a lavish media centre to house the expected 4,000 newsmen from around the world. As we all know, these building enterprises—worthwhile or not—will make money for, most of all, building enterprisers. Perhaps this is the reason why civic politicians everywhere seem so anxious to get the Olympic Games into their cities. Not only can they ingratiate themselves thereby with hometown building magnates but with powerful merchants, too, who stand to make a good deal from stepped-up sales at stepped-up prices. It's enough to cause the big-business members of the city's Chamber of Commerce to come to their feet in excitement. And, as politicians recognize well, local big businessmen are valuable allies in paying for elections.

Of course, it's not hard to figure out that, given the chance, ambitious builders and merchants—who are among our society's most powerful and influential members—are going to press hard to encourage a tax-supported project that can bring them millions in windfall contracts and sales. It's a local pork barrel beyond parallel. (However, one profession within the building industry, the architects, are not going to get their fair share out of it; Drapeau bypassed all the talent in the country and hired Roger Taillebert, from France, to design the stadium complex.)

Builders and merchants, though, will not be the only special benefactors from a tax-supported Olympics. One must note that Montreal's privately owned Expos are presently required to provide a stadium seating more than 40,000 as a condition of their National Baseball League franchise. The Olympics will provide, by coincidence, just such a stadium, 80,000 seats at an estimated cost of $50 to $70 million. (Montreal's ordinary sports budget, it's worth mentioning, usually fluctuates between five and eight million dollars.) Perhaps, merely by further coincidence, Jerry Snyder, an ex-city councillor who was the main mover in bringing the Expos to Montreal, is in charge of Montreal's Olympic preparations. Snyder, furthermore, talks a lot about a National Football League team for his city. So even apparently neutral multimillion-dollar expenditures for Montreal's projected Olympics—such as the improved subways and roads which will go to and from the new stadium—seem to have a place in the scheme of it all.

At an Ottawa press conference last April, Prime Minister Trudeau remarked while answering questions about Montreal's '76 Olympics, "You smell a rat and so do I." Some time earlier, a confidential memorandum to then Urban Affairs Minister Robert Andras from a special assistant in his department said: "Although strategies might be devised to minimize adverse reaction in the rest of the country, it would seem unavoidable that significant political costs [from federal support to a '76 Olympics in Montreal] would be incurred. Within Quebec and Montreal, another Expo-type false boom would seem likely along with further distortion of social priorities and a further alienation of socially aware elements."

Perhaps predictably, the memorandum, as disclosed in the Toronto *Globe and Mail*, goes on to say: "Our relationship with Drapeau and Bourassa would be reinforced," a nice "image" could be generated and "significant employment" (here the earlier recognition of "false boom" disappears) would be created. Given that such political advantages as these are "imaginatively handled," the memorandum concludes, the scheme is okay.

So it's unclear, at this writing, whether the Liberals are going to ride along with the Olympic plan (or, for that matter, whether the opposition is going to let them). But if they do, those who matter will be happy—building businessmen, merchants, the Olympic hierarchy, sports barons, "progress" politicians and so on—*except* for the "socially aware" elements. But since the latter are likely to remain a small minority that can probably be brushed aside in the usual way as agitated misfits, and since it can be more or less counted on that most Canadian people will go along with almost anything (after all, they stood for the legal deprivation of their civil liberties by the War Measures Act after two political kidnappings), it's reasonable to expect that there won't be any trouble that can't be handled. Even if there is trouble, Mexico and Munich have shown that the police and army can step in and "pacify" the situation with most people's support. Modern citizens, Canadians as much as anybody, love sport spectacles and dislike rebels. So what have the established interests in the Montreal Olympics got to lose?

Let's take an overview of it all. In an important sense, the projected '76 Olympics represent, for me anyway, most of the problems of contemporary society in a pure-type form. Enormous rip-offs, personal and national glory hunger, luxury expenditure of hundreds of millions of dollars in the face of squalor, pollution and bad health, and an apathetic citizenry that has learned to spectate rather than express. In an important sense then, too, what Canadians *do* about these projected Olympics will represent whether or not we are going to continue to give in to all this, or are ready to do something about it. Inasmuch as all the world's eyes will be on us—the Olympics may be the only visible global event there is—our response must indicate in some way where we human beings are at now. In the covering social game, the ball is here in our hands.

Perhaps the most valuable tradition Canada has is a cool horse sense. A cool horse sense that we are appropriately beginning to be proud of as we recognize the ravages of excess in our big brother to the south. Even there, Colorado voters, in a state referendum, cut off public funds to the 1976 winter games which had been awarded to Denver, and Denver had to give them up. There were, obviously, much more important things to do with the money.

I suggest, then, that we take the ball, the ball we've now got as the next Olympic promoters, and fire it into the air. And as it sits up there like a torch for all the world to see, let the voices grow from us that we've had enough. That we care more about the air and the water and the land we live in, about the poor and oppressed who live among us, and about the concord of the earth's peoples than we do about glory-and-money circuses for the benefit of the few. Let us roll across our cities and prairies and northland and seacoasts a sound of common sense that blows a whistle on this greed contest for all the world to hear.

If we don't, maybe no one ever will.

DISCUSSION QUESTIONS

A. *John Pooley and Arthur Webster*

1. The authors assert that sport has "power potential." Explain what this means and illustrate your answer with examples.

2. Do you agree with the statement that "at the municipal level a balance of power between sport and politics prevails"? Support your answer by drawing upon your personal experiences.

3. In what ways has sport been used at the national level to achieve political ends? Discuss and provide some examples from your own personal experiences.

4. Identify and discuss the "political pay-offs" for a country which competes successfully in sport at the international level.

5. Should sport be used to attain political ends? Justify your answer.

6. Do you agree with the statement that "shared experiences through sport link countries together"? Give examples to support your answer.

7. One of the goals of the Olympic Games is to promote international understanding and goodwill. Do you think that the Games contribute to this goal? Explain your answer.

B. *Paul Hoch*

1. Discuss the advantages and disadvantages of having player-owned sports teams.

2. Identify and discuss some of the problems which were encountered by the Players' League. Explain why the league was unsuccessful.

3. What types of changes in the sports industry is Hoch advocating? Are these changes realistic in a capitalist society?

4. According to Hoch, in what way do the "Power Elite" exploit sports?

5. Many sports owners are "multimillionaires who own other large corporations, have close links in the media and banking business, own the arenas they play in, and also have big interests in other sports. . . ." What are some of the implications of this state of affairs for (a) the sport, (b) the players, (c) the community? What are your personal feelings on the matter?

6. Briefly describe the politico-economic structure of professional sports in the United States.

C. *John McMurtry*

1. Discuss the possible advantages and/or disadvantages to a country and/or city which hosts the Olympic Games.

2. According to McMurtry, "The real winners (in the Olympics) are a few athletes, politicians, and big business builders." How does he justify making such a statement? Do you agree with him?

3. McMurtry states that the Olympics represent "enormous rip-offs, personal and national glory hunger," and the spending of millions of dollars in the face of "squalor, pollution, and bad health." What arguments does McMurtry offer in support of these statements? Do you agree with his reasoning?

4. In class, debate the issue of whether the Olympic Games should be discontinued.

Unit IV

The American Sports Hero: Past, Present and Future

The sports hero is as much a part of Americana as "motherhood, the flag and apple pie." The legendary feats of sports heroes such as Babe Ruth, Jack Dempsey, Joe Louis, Red Grange, and Jim Thorpe, to name just a few, are well known to most sports fans and nonfans alike. Although long an object of public adulation, it wasn't until recently that the sports hero became a subject of scholarly investigation. Evidence to date strongly suggests that the importance of the sports hero transcends his particular athletic accomplishments, that to understand the relationship between a sports hero and his sociocultural milieu is to acquire valuable insight into cultural values, social processes, and social issues. As both an instrument and mirror reflection of society, the contemporary sports hero offers us a view of society's present stage of development and, perhaps, an inkling of what the future holds.

In the first selection, sociologist Orrin Klapp analyzes hero worship as a social process. Using a variety of heroic examples, the author describes how hero worship occurs, the function it performs in society and the ways in which it reveals the hero worshipper's values, traits, and interests. The author challenges the classical notion of hero worship as an upholder and reinforcer of societal values by pointing out that it can also be, and often is, excessive, irrational, trivial, and disturbing to the status quo.

Historian Randy Roberts takes us beyond the Dempsey myth and legend in the second reading and discusses how one of America's most revered heroes both reflected the collective psychology of the people during the period 1919-1927 as well as reinforced fundamental societal values. We learn that several of Dempsey's fights (*e.g.,* Jess Willard, 1919; Georges Carpentier, 1921; Luis Angel Firpo, 1923; and Gene Tunney, 1926) symbolized something much larger than an athletic contest between two men. Threading their way through these ring battles were the social themes most central to the 1920's, namely, war issues, race questions, cultural schisms, and nationalistic impulses. Against the background of World War I, race riots, and the Communist menace, Dempsey emerged to give the American people something stable upon which they could depend.

In the last selection, sport sociologist Garry Smith offers the provocative view that the sports hero may have had his day in the American sociocultural system and is now in the process of joining the grizzly bear, the blue whale, the whooping crane, and the timber wolf as an "endangered species." Smith believes that the "reinforcing" socially approved sports hero of the past has now given way to a modern day version who is brash, arrogant, haughty, overbearing, and who invites the bending of rules and resisting the established order. Whether this "anti-hero" merely parallels changes taking place in the American value system to later emerge in a new and vital role, or, whether he is the last in the lineage of American sports heroes is left for the reader to decide.

HERO WORSHIP IN AMERICA*

Orrin E. Klapp

In America the "great man" appears frequently to be an athlete, an entertainer, or a person of relatively trivial accomplishment, whose pre-eminence in our scale of values causes unfavorable comment concerning the "materialism" or "vulgarity" of the American style of life.

Reprinted from *American Sociological Review* Volume XIV, No. 1, February, 1949.

*Manuscript received September 8, 1948.

We have had in past years a number of such popular heroes, contrasting with the stainless integrity of our official national heroes and martyrs. In addition to this problem of values, the emergence of popular heroes has frequently constituted a disturbing political and social force. Mass hero worship leads naturally to excesses, to blind devotion to leaders. When it does not have these consequences, it leads often to the irrationality and triviality of fads and cults. In any case, a social force is loosed which acts in a disturbing way upon the *status quo*. The unpredictability of popular heroes and the apparent mystery[1] of what makes them lead us to attempt to formulate some of the general characteristics of hero worship as a social process in America.

While hero worship in America ranges from the adulation of entertainers and other celebrities to such diverse things as the celebration of legendary heroes, the decoration of military heroes, and the cult of saints, we believe that it represents a generic process which expresses itself in many aspects of life as the tendency to select certain individuals as collective ideals, to accord them special status, and to surround them with behavior characterized as "hero worship." The hero worshipper in America has become characterized as the "fan." Yet there is no reason to believe that similar behavior is not to be found in all societies.[2]

It is the description of hero worship with which the present paper is concerned, based largely upon data derived from a study of American hero worship.[3] Our problem is twofold: to describe hero worship as it occurs in America and secondly to attempt to visualize the generic character of hero worship as a social process.

At the point of origin of hero worship, the emergence of a hero may be noted by certain signs. One of these is sudden or unusual fame. Another is a marked shift in status. A third is the beginning of behavior characteristic of hero worship.[4] In the career of a public figure, for instance, a point may be reached at which the public acquires a special sentimentality toward him. It may be noted that he has gained in "stature," that he has become apotheosized.[5] The special sentimentality of the public toward a popular hero includes a certain endearment, a tremendous loyalty, a reluctance to admit critical reflection, and a faith and veneration which verge upon superstition. Once a public figure acquires the status of a popular hero, he is to be specially reckoned with as a social force.[6] If an entertainer, he becomes "box office."[7] If a political leader, he acquires generic appeal: he draws crowds, fills stadiums, makes money, gets votes, and gathers his following from all walks of life. His name and image act as an inspiration to organize large masses of people. Later in his career, particularly after death, he may be commemorated or canonised, his tomb becomes a place of pilgrimage, his fame becomes legendary, and a full-fledged hero cult may grow up as an institution.

We find hero worship to have a genetic sequence, going through a sort of cycle beginning with the emergence of a popular hero. The main phases of this process we shall designate as follows: (1) spontaneous or unorganized popular homage, (2) formal recognition and honor, (3) the building up of an idealized image or legend of the hero, (4) commemoration of the hero, and (5) established cult. While all heroes do not complete this cycle, there is a tendency for them to become legendary and to pass into the tradition of the group as cult symbols.

We shall consider in following sections the emergence of a typical popular hero, the social behavior of hero worship, the idealized image of the hero, and the status of the hero.

Emergence of a Typical Popular Hero

The emergence of Lindbergh during the nineteen-twenties provides one of the most complete case studies of a popular hero available. This case has a number of features which our study has shown to be typical of many popular heroes. First, the hero is often a person of relatively obscure social status prior to his elevation to the rank of a hero. Second, his fame was achieved by a spectacular demonstration which impressed the public and caused him to be recognized as a hero. Third, a spontaneous popular response of hero worship occurred before official recognition of his achievement, revealing many of the mechanisms of hero worship. Fourth, almost immediately a mythical interpretation began to grow up, in which various features were attributed to him in popular imagination through eulogy, art, story, song, and verse.[8] The case of Lindbergh illustrates what might be found to be true of many popular heroes, such as Jack Dempsey or Babe Ruth: how they are selected by colorful feats which draw attention to them and excite admiration, how hero worship elevates them in status, and how they are subject to a popular interpretation which constitutes the forming legend of the hero. We wish now to consider the nature of the popular reaction which defines the hero.

Social Behavior of Hero Worship

Contemporary America provides us with a multitude of examples of hero worship behavior, ranging from spontaneous popular homage to formal honor, commemoration, and cult. Much hero worship behavior is unorganized, naive, and spontaneous. It is extremely curious. The people themselves do not know why they do it. The unorganized behavior of hero worship includes certain distinctive forms which we shall here describe: popular homage, familiarity, possessiveness, curiosity, identification, and imitation.

Perhaps the most understandable form is the popular homage which greets heroes. Spontaneous acts, such as applause, cheers, raising upon shoulders, throwing of kisses, and the like, express the intense admiration of the people. The following example of the homage which greeted Lindbergh at his landing is a good one:[9]

The entire field . . . was covered with thousands of people all running towards my ship. . . . I started to climb out of the cockpit, but as soon as one foot appeared was dragged the rest of the way without assistance on my part. For nearly half an hour I was unable to touch the ground, during which time I was ardently carried around in what seemed to be a very small area and in every position it is possible to be in. Everyone had the best of intentions but no one seemed to know just what they were.

Along with physical gestures of homage goes spontaneous eulogy through songs, poems, anecdotes, popular drama, and other works of art. [10] Mass homage also includes fan mail containing expressions of admiration and appreciation. Numerous gifts and tributes are spontaneously given to the hero. [11]

Somewhat embarrassing to many heroes is the familiarity and possessiveness which the public displays toward them. It feels it "owns" the hero and endeavors to appropriate the hero in every type of relationship. We shall enumerate some of the ways in which the public invades the hero's privacy. Persons tried to reach Valentino's dressing room by every possible ruse. The hero is always being manhandled, pawed, and caressed, evidencing a desire to touch the hero and otherwise to become familiar with him. [12] People boasted of having gotten "that close" to Lindbergh. A man offered one thousand dollars simply for the chance to shake his hand. People try to crowd into photographs with the hero. Attempts at close relationship also include offers of marriage, business proposals, and claims of kinship. So many strangers claimed relationship with Jack Dempsey that he was called the "cousin of all the Dempseys." Not the least of the public possessiveness is its sense of appropriation in souvenir-hunting. [13] The sense of familiarity with the hero is expressed in popular affection: the public refers to him by nick-names and other terms of endearment. [14] Men shake his hand; women embrace him: [15]

When he (Lindbergh) entered the Times Building one girl was quite unable to restrain herself. She leaped from the stairway leading to the second floor and flung her arms around the flier's neck. The police dislodged her. Colonel Lindbergh blushed and shook his head as if to say, "No, no; you mustn't do that."

The public is, moreover, extremely proud and loyal with regard to its heroes, rallying to their defense when criticized or attacked. Finally, unusual demands are made on the hero by persons having no relationship to him. [16]

How are we to interpret this behavior? While homage represents the effort to raise the hero in status by honoring him, familiarity and possessiveness indicate a sense of identification with the hero, a collective effort to come into as close a relationship as possible with him, to apprehend him into a familiar category. This combination of distance with closeness represents a paradoxical element in hero worship: vertical distance is maintained through homage and admiration, and at the same time

social closeness is expressed through familiarity and possessiveness. There is an effort to become familiar with the hero and at the same time to put him upon a pedestal. [17]

The distance in hero worship is further seen in the curiosity with which the public regards its heroes. Despite its personal interest in the hero, it knows little of him. The public seems hungry for information concerning the life of the hero; his career is followed intently in news, magazines, and biography; crowds follow him wherever he goes. [18] Jack Dempsey expresses his attitude toward fans who forced their way into his dressing room as follows: [19]

They want to look at your eyes and your ears to see how badly you may have been injured. They want to pick up a word here or a gesture there which, later on, they can relay, magnified, to their own little public. I have always regarded these curious fans in a tolerant, even friendly way.

Since curiosity is premised upon lack of information, we may say that the distance with which the public is separated from its hero and its general ignorance of him contribute to the character of hero worship as a relationship. The hero is subject to constant talk and gossip as the public tries to interpret him. This leads to the formation of legends. A further inference from the curiosity toward heroes is that the intensity of the interest attests to the psychological importance of the hero as a symbol in the personalities of hero-worshippers.

Two more aspects of mass behavior distinctive of hero worship will be mentioned. These are identification and imitation. The behavior previously discussed under familiarity and possessiveness indicates a popular sense of identification with heroes. Imitation is also expressive of this identification. Imitation of heroes is seen in two particular forms: fads and the behavior of fans. Valentino, for instance, was responsible for a fad of side-burns and vaselined hair. His love-making technique was copied. A similar observation might be made with regard to Sinatra bow-ties and vocal mannerisms. Boys emulate Jack Dempsey and Babe Ruth. This may amount to literal impersonation, as in the case of hero-worshippers who even take the name and character of their heroes. [20] It is often possible to recognize a fan by his resemblance to some popular hero. Whether in the general diffusion of fashions or in the intense emulation of fans, we find imitation to be one of the characteristic types of behavior of hero worship. Identification with heroes helps to explain their extraordinary effectiveness in two fields: education [21] and leadership. In the latter case, because of the admiration of heroes and the strong sense of identification with them, heroes have a tendency to become powerful leaders. It is impossible, for instance, to explain the success of a leader such as Huey Long entirely by his leadership talents and techniques, without recourse to the fact that he was symbolically a hero to his followers. [22]

The more organized forms of hero worship in America include formal honor, commemoration, and cult. We see formal honor of heroes in the following familiar processes: ceremonies of recognition, special distinctions and privileges accorded to heroes, formal tributes and celebrations, and honorary adoption. All of these are methods of according status to heroes.[23] Recognition of heroes in America is seen in the decoration of military heroes,[24] the selection of athletic champions,[25] and the canonization of saints.[26] Special distinctions and privileges confer on the hero a unique status. The traffic rules of New York were reversed for Lindbergh's car.[27] He was honored by innumerable formal tributes and celebrations.[28] Another type of formal honor extended to heroes is seen in honorary adoption.[29] Funerals are a particular occasion for tributes and panegyrics to heroes. The magnitude of funeral honors reflects the hero's social value and status.[30]

Commemoration includes, beyond honor of heroes, the effort to perpetuate the memory of heroes in tradition. While honor creates status, commemoration expresses the peculiar value of the hero as a symbol. Monuments, likenesses, relics, legends, and periodic celebrations may be taken as mnemonic devices to preserve the collective image of a hero. The spontaneous representation of heroes in art attests to an unconscious effort to preserve them in memory.[31] The monuments and memorials to a hero are usually larger and more magnificent than those to ordinary persons.[32] Large edifices, funds, or institutions may be dedicated to a hero.[33] A plaque was unveiled at the Gare Maritime commemorating the spot where Lindbergh first flew over France on his way to Le Bourget field. The relics and historic sites connected with the hero's career become centers for legend.[34] The legend may be said to be perhaps the most durable and important part of the fame of a hero. Finally, namesakes help to preserve the memory of the hero.[35]

Hero cult grows out of these activities of hero worship. There is no definite line which demarcates the mass behavior of hero worship from cult, except in so far as it becomes periodic or regular.[36] Hero cult may be said to exist when there is regular devotion to or celebration of a hero by a group. Hero worship behavior tends to become regularized as an institution usually on some anniversary of the hero. The death of the hero is often taken as the occasion to institute a cult in his memory. For a hero cult to exist the fame of the hero must be a sufficient reality to the people to inspire continuous activity over a period of time.[37]

Thus we come to a difficulty in the study of American popular heroes. Many of them are not of sufficient antiquity to determine fully the outlines of their potential cult. "Babe Ruth Day," for instance, was celebrated in baseball parks all over America even before his death.[38] Other popular heroes in America have shrines to which pilgrimages are made, including Will Rogers, Buffalo Bill, Wild Bill Hickock, and Jesse James. An interesting example of hero cult is provided by the late Rudolph Valentino. Valentino Clubs sprang up all over the world, composed largely of women. Periodic observances of these groups included memorial services, dedication of monuments, plays, poems, songs, and revivals of Valentino films. Pilgrimages to his tomb were made by men as well as women. Shrines were maintained containing his relics and images.[39] The martyrs Sacco and Vanzetti were the objects of a nascent hero cult following their deaths. Heroic funeral honors were accorded them, their ashes and death masks were preserved, and the anniversary of their death was celebrated by groups in various parts of the world for at least ten years. Periodic celebrations are also dedicated in America to entirely legendary heroes.[40]

We distinguish two main forms of hero cult in America: (1) a general activity in honor of a hero participated in by the entire community or society;[41] and (2) a special group devoted to the hero, such as a fan club, honorary fraternity, or the like.[42]

If we might describe the principal features of a fully developed hero cult, these would include the following: (1) an institution or group exists for the purpose of honoring and commemorating a hero; (2) the image, relics, and monuments of the hero are preserved as cult objects; (3) the tomb or shrines of the hero constitute centers for pilgrimages and honorific or commemorative observances; (4) the observances include recounting or re-enactment of the career of the hero through story, drama, impersonation, pageant, dance, panegyric, ritual, or other symbolic medium, the purpose of these being to make the hero "live again" in the memory of the group; and (5) there are devotion to and emulation of the hero by members of the group.

The Idealized Image of the Hero

From the excessive adulation and eulogy characteristic of hero worship, it seems inevitable that an exaggerated popular conception of the hero should grow up. This has been designated by various students of hero worship as legend-building.[43] Our present concern is to show that in the case of many American popular heroes, despite an age of publicity and information, an exaggerated conception of the personalities, powers, or prowess of these heroes, that is to say a legend, was prevalent.

One of the features of the Lindbergh case which is of particular importance is the almost immediate formation of legend. Curiously, despite the regard of the public for him, Lindbergh remained personally an "unknown," aloof, and the reporters had difficulty penetrating to the "true" personality of this hero so admired by the people.[44] The popular conception was, therefore, built upon superficial interpretation of his feat, his looks, and his gestures. All features which might be given a heroic interpretation were seized upon by the public. His slimness and youth were really a sign of superior talent; his reticence was modesty. Without having had to do much on his own part, a conception of him grew rapidly as a fair-haired boy, the perfect hero. Almost as soon as he had landed, legends began to accumulate about his boyhood, his ancestry, what he said when he got out of his plane, how he flew the air mail, and so forth. An incident was circulated in which he had supposedly rescued a little girl from the whirling propeller blades of a plane.[45] Similar anecdotes might be itemized about any of the other heroes we have studied; for instance: how Pershing licked the bullies, his rise as a self-made man; the orphanage of Babe Ruth, his batting feats, his visits to sick boys; the power of Dempsey's fists, his "iron jaw," the time when he hit a fighter so hard on the jaw that he broke his leg; the sharp-shooting feats of Sergeant York in his home hills in Tennessee; the Santa-Claus-like benefactions of Al Capone, his invulnerability and power to evade any law.[46] A further indication of the idealized conception of the hero is seen in the failure of heroes occasionally to live up to the expectations of the public.[47] The tenacity of legends, however, is well known.

These exaggerations and interpretations as recounted in stories and supplied by art, literature, and eulogy, make up the myth of the hero. A picture is built up of an invincible, invulnerable, benevolent, superhuman personage: the ideal folk hero.[48] Illusion and myth, we conclude, are inherent to hero worship and belief in such helps to explain it.

Status of the Hero

The hero is thus seen to be a personage of idealized virtues, intensely admired and honored by the people. The processes of honor, commemoration, and cult devotion show most clearly the status of the hero, homage being the collective effort to accord status and commemoration the effort to preserve the image of the hero in tradition. The cult of the hero is essentially the institution of devotion to this honored image. It seems clear from his legendary status that the hero is properly conceived as a symbol rather than as a real person. He tends to be preserved in tradition and to function in the group as an idealized image, almost as an ikon. All things point to the conclusion that the hero is one of the most important symbols and occupies one of the highest statuses in social life.

Although the hero is set apart from ordinary men by deference, precedence, decorations, and the like, and is regarded as superhuman,[49] we must note that though standing out from other men the hero is not essentially a leader.[50] While the hero may be a leader, he is essentially a symbol, solitary and set apart. The existence of hero cults should not obscure this fact.[51] Where the hero is disposed to leadership, however, as in the case of Huey Long, Franklin Delano Roosevelt, or Hitler, we find that popular appeal, that is to say the force of leadership, is enormously enhanced by virtue of heroic symbolism, for the hero-worshipper is the perfect follower. On the other hand, leaders who lack the status of popular heroes show the essential distinctness of the roles. Leaders who are not heroes[52] are notably lacking in popular appeal and

are vulnerable to rivals who happen to combine these roles.

We might characterize the status of the hero, then, by the following features: (1) distance from group members, both vertical and horizontal, in that he has no necessary personal relationship with his followers and hero worship tends to set him apart; (2) nevertheless, strong identification of members of the group with the hero; (3) symbolic status, as the hero tends to be an image or legend rather than a real person, and is typically not a living member of the group; and (4) sacred or ritual status, as the devotion of cult places the hero within the realm of social values commonly ascribed to religion.

Because heroes are preserved and occupy such high status, it may be presumed that their functions are extremely important. We may suppose that the hero represents social roles or traits of unusual value to the group: acts commonly considered heroic include extraordinary achievement, defense and deliverance in time of need, contributions to culture, self-sacrifice and martyrdom, and other roles important for group survival and welfare. Not the least of the functions of heroes, it may be supposed, is the inspiration they offer for rise in status.[53] The hero thus functions as a symbol of enormous importance in personality development, education, and social control.[54] Moreover, in addition to presenting desirable roles for group members, they no doubt organize groups by providing common symbols for identification, either as leaders or as personages with whom the group feels a special pride and unity.

Conclusion

We have endeavored to describe hero worship and find in it a collective process for selecting, honoring, and preserving certain persons as group symbols. Hero worship in America expresses our characteristic values. It reveals not only the traits we admire most but also our fields of interest. While one age may emphasize strenuous piety,[55] another emphasizes war or athletics. Through the heroism of all societies, no doubt, run certain common threads: great achievement, heroism in war, martyrdom, and the like. The hero worship of American society reveals the run of our interests and consequently the fields in which heroes emerge.

An observation concerning American hero worship which seems pertinent is that in a secular era, when faith seems to be declining, the belief in heroes continues to thrive. The legend-making process and creation of folk heroes, in spite of modern communications, continues as a social and political force. Although hero worship is a democratic process in the sense that it selects heroes from all ranks of the social structure, it generates excessive veneration. It enthrones heroes in an irrational status which criticism is often powerless to qualify.

We have not examined a number of aspects of American hero worship, notably the relation of popular heroes to social movements and crises. Nor have we analyzed the impact of heroes on individual hero-worshippers. But enough has been said to suggest the importance of hero worship for further study.

NOTES

1. This mystery has been stated by Gerald Johnson in *American Heroes and Hero Worship* (New York, Harper & Bros., 1943).

2. It has been suggested that the Germans are pre-eminently a race of hero-worshippers and that this serves to explain the excesses associated with Hitler. See H.J.C. Grierson, *Carlyle and Hitler* (Cambridge, At the Univ. Press, 1933). The best survey of American hero worship is provided by Dixon Wecter, *The Hero in America* (New York, Chas. Scribner's Sons, 1941). See the following works for diverse aspects of hero worship: Stefan Czarnowski, *Le Culte des heros et les conditiones sociales* (Paris, Alcan, 1919); L.R. Farnell, *Greek Hero Cults* (Oxford, Clarendon Press, 1921); H. Delehaye, *Sanctus: essai sur le culte des saints dans l'antiquite* (Bruxells, Societe des Bollandistes, 1927); C.D. Gower, "The Supernatural Patron in Sicilian Life." (Chicago, Ph.D. thesis, Univ. of Chicago, 1928); F.R.S. Raglan, *The Hero, a Study in Tradition, Myth, and Drama* (London, Methuen & Co., Ltd., 1936); and Robert Redfield, *Tepoztlan, a Mexican Village* (Chicago, Univ. of Chicago Press, 1930).

3. Orrin E. Klapp, "The Hero as a Social Type," (Chicago, Unpubl. Ph.D. Thesis, Univ. of Chicago, 1948).

4. We have used the following criteria to define a popular hero: (1) a person of fame, as indicated by news-space devoted to him, rumor and legend concerning him, or the fact that everybody knows him; (2) a person who is commonly called a hero (or some equivalent or marginal term such as idol, champion, favorite son, patron saint, martyr); and (3) a person who is the object of hero worship. The criteria for hero worship are as follows: (a) the hero is admired, euolgized, acclaimed, or otherwise honored by his society; (b) he is formally recognized or canonised; (c) he is commemorated; or (d) he has a following of devotees, "fans," or hero-worshippers. "Fans" are distinguished from the general public by the intensity and self-consciousness of their enthusiasm, emulation, and devotion. Persons especially devoted to a hero frequently constitute a club or "cult" in his name, honoring or emulating him in various ways. According to these criteria, Charles Lindbergh, Babe Ruth, and Jack Dempsey would be outstanding among persons who became popular heroes in America during the nineteen-twenties. Other persons of this period having characteristics of popular heroes include: General J.J. Pershing, Sergeant York, Will Rogers, Rudolph Valentino, Sacco and Vanzetti, Huey Long, and Al Capone.

5. A study of this process has been provided by Lloyd Lewis in *Myths After Lincoln* (1929). See also R.P. Basler, *The Lincoln Legend* (Boston, Houghton Mifflin, 1935).

6. W.F. Ogburn, "The Great Man vs. Social Forces," *Social Forces* (1926), 5: 229-31. See also the concept of charismatic leadership as developed by Max Weber.

7. Babe Ruth noted that when he stood beside prominent statesmen, engineers, and other servants of humanity, it was he who got the cheers.

8. At the time of his flight in 1927, Lindbergh was an "unknown." On the day prior to his flight, he ate unrecognized in a restaurant. Almost overnight, by his exploit of flying the ocean alone in a small plane, he became the most eulogized hero in America, outranking in importance by far all other persons. This feat so struck the popular imagination that it provoked a flood of hysterical eulogy and mass adulation which lasted for several years. Lindbergh was literally jerked upward in status and in his vertical ascent became almost a demigod. From the moment of his landing in Paris a popular reaction began to grow which reached its height before, and must be considered apart from, his formal recognition as a national hero by Congress. Ten million medals were struck and a postage stamp was issued in his honor.

9. Charles Lindbergh, *We* (New York, Grosset & Dunlap, 1927), pp. 224-7. Note also the homage which greeted Al Capone: "The curious fact about Scarface Al is that Americans . . . used to go out of their way to shake hands with him, and when he and his eighteen bodyguards appeared in public at the races or a football game, there was not only a thrilled murmur in the stands, there were sometimes cheers. What were they cheering about?" "Capone Era," *Life*, February 10, 1947, v. 22, p. 24.

10. Several thousand poems were dedicated to Lindbergh; also dances, sculpture, paintings, cantatas, and popular songs. A heroic size statue of Babe Ruth swatting a ball was exhibited at Rockefeller Center.

11. A museum in St. Louis contains the thousands of gifts and trophies given to Lindbergh.

12. Note the well-known joke about small boys who boast: "Shake the hand that shook the hand of Babe Ruth."

13. Lindbergh's plane was almost destroyed by souvenir-hunters. He rarely got a shirt back from the laundry; and dared not lay down a hat, coat, or even a piece of paper. For some reason this is considered as a right of hero-worshippers rather than as theft.

14. It calls him "our boy," "favorite son," and so forth.

15. New York *Times*, June 16, 1927.

16. "My public" is no joke to a popular hero. Dempsey and Babe Ruth were constantly making donations to strangers.

17. The distance in hero worship is also expressed in the common phrases, "distance builds the great man," and "no man is a hero to his valet."

18. A respectable-looking woman of middle age came up to Lindbergh, at dinner in a New York hotel, and tried to look into his mouth to see whether he was eating "green beans or green peas."

19. C.F. Coe, "In This Corner," *Saturday Evening Post*, August 8, 1931, v. 204, p. 38.

20. A devotee of Robert Browning, for instance, has assumed the character of the poet, spent his life studying his career, become an authority on Browning, collected a museum of his relics, and wears his ring. *Time*, May 17, 1947.

21. Identification with heroes means that the public will be equipped with a number of approved roles, assuming the militant attitudes of war heroes in time of war, the sacrificial attitudes of martyrs, the industrious behavior of Poor Richards and Horatio Alger heroes, etc., in appropriate situations.

22. The martyr status of Huey Long became evident after his death.

23. Honor raises status, creating and maintaining hierarchical distinctions. See Hans Speier, "Honor and Social Structure," *Social Research* (1935), 2:74-97.

24. See A.T. Wilson, *Gallantry, its Public Recognition in Peace and War* (London, Oxford Univ. Press, 1939); T.S. Arbuthnot, *Heroes of Peace* (Hero Fund Commission, 1935); P.A. Wilkins, *History of the Victoria Cross* (London, A. Constable & Co., 1904).

25. Competitions or tournaments are typical institutions for the selection of champions. The hero is given a belt, cup, or other trophy, significant of his status, which is often transferable to another hero when the status is transferred.

26. As, for instance, Mother Cabrini. Canonization is perhaps the most completely developed institution for the selection and recognition of heroes. It is a complex judicial process, involving investigation of the life of the hero, examination of witnesses and evidence by a series of courts, and statutory delays, taking normally over fifty years before glorification of the saint.

27. A special air mail stamp was issued, the first time a stamp was issued for a man still living. Similarly, Pershing in France was accorded the unique honor of touching and kissing the hilt of the sword and cross of the Legion of Honor. "This was the most signal honor France ever bestowed on any man. Before this occasion, not even a Frenchman was permitted to hold the historic relics in his hands. Kings and Princes have been taken to the crypt . . . but they only viewed the sword and cross through the plate glass of the case in which they rest. The relics had not been touched since the time of Louis Philippe." "General Pershing in France," *Current History*, July 1917, v. 6, p. 8.

28. "The receptions . . . long ago have begun to be meaninglessly alike. First, the rush of people over the field . . . then the stepping out and shaking of hands, followed by the . . . flight to safety on the folded top of an official automobile; and at last the dinner where all the talk is of the air he has just come roaring through,

and of the further air he will go roaring through." "Loneliest Man," *Nation*, February 29, 1928, v. 126, p. 230.

29. It is common for groups to claim heroes as members or patrons. After Lindbergh's flight, various groups began to claim him. His "Irish" and "Norse" ancestries were discovered. His home town, Little Falls, Minnesota, proposed renaming itself after him. He was made an Honorary Boy Scout. Similarly, Babe Ruth while on a tour of the West was initiated into an Indian tribe and christened "Chief Big Bat." The adoption of saints as patrons by local groups is a familiar form of this tendency. The honorary adoption of heroes may be considered as a transmission of honor both ways, since the group acquires prestige through its relation to the hero just as it feels that it is honoring him by membership.

30. The size of gangsters' funerals in America during the nineteen-twenties has been noted. See John Landesco, *Organized Crime in Chicago*, Part III, Ill. Crime Survey (Chicago, Illinois, Assn. for Criminal Justice, 1929).

31. The essence of commemoration is expressed in the phrase, "Lest we forget."

32. Excepting, of course, the self-monuments of philanthropists and the pyramids.

33. A memorial fund, hotel, museum, library, and statute in the Capitol were dedicated to Will Rogers at his death. Note the Ruth Foundation. The Valentino Roof Garden of the Italian Hospital in London was contributed in memory of Rudolph Valentino.

34. As, for instance, the chairs in which George Washington sat or the bats used by Babe Ruth in his historic swats. Any part of his body, his clothes, or object which has been associated with the hero will serve to recall episodes connected with his career. The places he has lived become shrines. One gets a vivid sense of the reality of the hero by thus coming into contact with his relics. Note the preservation of the blood-stained clothes of Gandhi.

35. As, for instance, the christening of babies after saints. Scores of babies were christened after Lindbergh, as well as a St. Louis building, a Pullman car, a flying field, a street in Quimperle, Brittany, a dance, a sandwich, and a cocktail.

36. Thus, one of the criteria for the cult of saints has been popular devotion or pilgrimages at his tomb for some years. Canonization officially confirms regular cult by placing the saint upon the calendar of periodic celebrations.

37. Thus, the age of saint cults is measured in hundreds of years. Compare also our Washington and Lincoln cults.

38. On April 27, 1947. In a special ceremony at Yankee Stadium, also, his old uniform "Number 3," was dedicated as a relic to a museum, "never again to identify a Yankee." *Time*, June 21, 1948.

39. One of his old shirts was preserved in a gold-embroidered casket. The motto of the Valentino Memorial Guild of London is "Toujours Fidele." See "Women Who Enshrine Valentino," *Literary Digest*, February 7, 1931, 108: 19; and R. C. Peterson, *Valentino the Unforgotten* (L.A. Wetzel Co., 1937).

40. Annual community festivities in northern Minnesota are dedicated to Paul Bunyan. An enormous statue of him has been erected at Bemidji. In some towns the young men grow beards, wear red-checkered shirts, and impersonate the hero in parades, carrying huge saws, axes, playing cards, and jugs of whiskey. There is, of course, also a commercial element in this. Compare the annual reenactment of the death of Wild Bill at Deadwood, South Dakota, and "Jesse James Day" at Northfield, Minnesota.

41. Regular holidays, feasts, games, memorial services, pageants, dramas, rituals, and the like, on some anniversary of the hero, as in the case of our national heroes Washington and Lincoln.

42. The sodalities of saints are a good example. Also the boys' clubs devoted to Babe Ruth. An example of the fan club is provided by the Segovia Society of Washington, D.C. This group is composed of musical enthusiasts devoted to the renowned guitarist, Andres Segovia. Admirers of the virtuoso gather to listen to his phonograph recordings and emulate his technique. A "Segovia Room" is maintained as a shrine, containing his picture and a chair in which he once sat.

43. Basler, *op. cit.*; Lewis, *op. cit.*; H. Delehaye, *Legends of the Saints* (London, Longmans, Green & Co., 1907); E.G. Waas, *The Legendary Character of Kaiser Maximilian* (New York, Columbia Univ. Press, 1941); S.G. Fisher, *Legendary and Myth-Making Processes in Histories of the American Revolution* (Phila., S.G. Fisher, 1912); A.L. Guerard, *Reflections on the Napoleonic Legend* (New York, C. Scribner's Sons, 1924); R.J. Walsh and M.S. Salsbury, *The Making of Buffalo Bill* (Indianapolis, Bobbs-Merrill Co., 1928); Hamilton Basso, "The Huey Long Legend," *Life*, December 9, 1946, vol. 21, pp. 106ff.

44. It seems characteristic of popular heroes that they are unknown by their followers. The hero is paradoxically both well-known and unknown.

45. Another story told how his plane at one landing field "easily out-distanced" an escort of military planes, although the latter had much higher speeds than his plane.

46. See Fred Pasley, *Al Capone* (Garden City, Publ. Co., 1930).

47. The famous "feud" of Lindbergh with reporters helped to dispel some of the illusions about him. He was found to be unfriendly, even discourteous. According to one report he splashed mud on the public when landing his plane. The Lindbergh legend took a further decline at the time of his apparent sympathy for Germany in 1940. Another failure of a hero to live up to expectations is seen in the incredulity of followers of Jack Dempsey at his defeat by Tunney. A myth had grown up of his invincibility.

48. We have tried in another article to indicate the nature of this folk ideal. Orrin E. Klapp, "The Folk Hero," *Journal of American Folklore*, January, 1949.

49. Among the evidences of the exalted character of heroes we may note their rank in mythology as demigods, taking precedence over kings (the Greeks, thus, in the Iliad, honored Ajax by giving him first place at a feast, even before the king); and also the semi-divine status of saints in Christian hagiography.

50. Among the popular heroes we have studied, it may be noted that many were not leaders in the usual sense. While Huey Long, Pershing, and Capone were leaders of groups, Ruth, Dempsey, Lindbergh, Rogers, Sgt. York, and Sacco and Vanzetti were individualized heroes. That is to say, they lacked a number of characteristics of popular leaders, among these being the following: (1) they played no active role in appealing to the public through oratory, proselytism, etc., in the manner of popular leaders; (2) they lacked cults of personal disciples similar to those of charismatic leaders such as Father Divine or Mary Baker Eddy; (3) they occupied no formal positions of leadership in groups; and (4) their roles were solitary achievements, individualized performances, rather than group roles. For contrast with popular or charismatic leadership, see Joachim Wach, *Sociology of Religion* (Chicago, Univ. of Chicago Press, 1944), pp. 133-8, 334ff, 370; and Hadley Cantril, *Psychology of Social Movements* (New York, J. Wiley & Sons, 1941), pp. 123-43, 186.

51. It may be noted that the hero is characteristically absent as a person from hero cult. Instead of exercising personal leadership or ascendancy, he is *represented* rather than present.

52. Note, for instance, many American Presidents.

53. Heroism is an extreme example of what Linton would call status by achievement. To the extent that a society emphasizes competition and status-climbing, heroes would have a most important function as models for group members.

54. See D.W. Riddle, *The Martyrs, a Study in Social Control* (Chicago, University of Chicago Press, 1932).

55. See J.M. Mecklin, *Passing of the Saint, a Study of a Cultural Type* (Chicago, University of Chicago Press, 1941).

JACK DEMPSEY:
AN AMERICAN HERO IN THE 1920's
Randy Roberts

On the Fourth of July, 1919, as the temperature climbed to 114°, a nation said to be "surfeited with fighting and bloodshed" mustered 20,000 sanguinary spectators to the shores of Maumee Bay, just outside Toledo, Ohio, to witness what they hoped would be more fighting and bloodshed. They were not to be disappointed. For under that blazing sun, a brine-hardened, tan Jack Dempsey beat a flabby and aging Jess Willard into submission in three rounds. A New York *Times* reporter asserted that the crowd could find no enjoyment in watching a man receive cuts around both eyes, have six teeth forcibly removed, and absorb blows which swelled the right side of his face to twice its normal size. [1] Yet, the wild cheering and the excitement which pulsed through the capacity crowd refuted the reporter's claim. [2] The timeless axiom that nothing arouses public interest as quickly as a good fight was demonstrated in full. And for the next eight years, the aphorism would hold again and again for Dempsey's bouts.

From 1919 to 1927, Jack Dempsey was a celebrated figure. Newspapers mapped his varied movements, and magazines ranging from the middle-class *Saturday Evening Post* and *Collier's* to the more highbrow *New Republic* and the *American Mercury* carried articles on him. Crowds totaling over 500,000 saw his title fights, while millions more heard those bouts which were broadcasted over radio. [3] In eight years, Dempsey earned more than ten million dollars. [4] Certainly a man who could become as popular as Dempsey and earn as much money as he did deserves scholarly attention. Yet, Dempsey's impact on America has been all but ignored by historians. [5] Like most sports topics, the history of Dempsey's career has fallen by default into the hands of mythmakers. The following pages attempt to go beyond mere mythology to view Dempsey as a facet of a complex society rather than as a part of a circumscribed legend.

Discussing the impact of Muhammad Ali on American life in the 1960's, Eldridge Cleaver gave a cogent glimpse into the relationship between boxing and society when he wrote that "the boxing ring is the ultimate focus of masculinity in America, the two-fisted testing ground of manhood, and the heavyweight champion, as a symbol, is the real Mr. America." [6] Cleaver's view of the heavyweight champion as a national symbolic hero was not original with him. A 1921 editorial in the *New Republic* noted that Dempsey represented the ideal hero image to youths who had "a small verbal repertory but a large stock of scowls and blows." [7] Eleven years earlier, the heavyweight crown was viewed as the symbol of racial dominance. Discussing the upcoming title bout between black champion Jack Johnson and white ex-champion Jim Jeffries, columnist Max Balthazar wrote:

Can the huge white man, the California grizzly . . . beat down the wonderful black and restore to the Caucasians the crown of elemental greatness as measured by strength

of blow, power of heart and being, and, withal, that cunning or keenness that denotes mental as well as physical superiority. [8]

And even before 1910, as John Higham illustrated, the "heavyweight champions loomed large among American folk heroes." [9]

The dynamic impact of boxing champions and other popular folk heroes upon American life has been given serious attention by a number of psychologists, sociologists, and folklorists. Paul Meadows has noted that "the [popular] hero . . . may be utilized to typify the whole culture or perhaps some aspects of it. He may be thought of as an index to the national mind or spirit." [10] Representing the ethnocentric attitudes of a culture, national heroes are "what they always have been, the measure of the range of our values." [11] Like Meadows, Orrin E. Klapp emphasizes that the popular hero in America "expresses our characteristic values. [He] reveals not only the traits we admire but also our field of interest." [12] But the function of a hero such as Dempsey does more than simply characterize a social milieu. As a popular hero, he helps to perpetuate certain collective values and to nourish and maintain certain socially necessary sentiments. [13] Thus the popular hero serves a dual function: he both reflects the collective psychology of a society at a given time and acts to reinforce necessary social values. [14]

In an age of mass communications, heroes can be arbitrarily produced and widely diffused in a short time. [15] Sidney Hook has accurately observed that whoever controls the microphones and printing presses of a society can create a synthetic hero overnight. [16] In the case of an athletic personality, the sports section of newspapers and magazines is the instrumental tool in forming a hero. And more often than not, the image of a sports hero that a periodical forms is the one which is most compatible with its readers. As Harry Edwards has noted, public opinion studies continually demonstrate that people will neither buy nor read that with which they disagree. Americans, Edwards observes "tend to read only what reinforces their own attitudes." [17] Thus, if a newspaper or magazine continually emphasizes that a hero is kind, gentle, and truthful, it is safe to assume that this is what the readers want to believe about the hero.

As with most popular heroes, Dempsey the man was less important than Dempsey the image. The Dempsey image was dynamic, for at no time between 1919 and 1926 was it static. Forces and issues of the 1920's affected it and, as will be illustrated, his image underwent a considerable metamorphosis between his victory over Willard in 1919 and his defeat at the hands of Gene Tunney in 1926. But always the image would reflect the social and intellectual milieu which gave rise to it.

Journal of Popular Culture, VIII (2), pp. 411-426, Fall, 1974. Reprinted with the permission of the editor.

As early as 1921, it was noted that Americans' attitude toward Jack Dempsey lacked a "sense of proportion."[18] Boxing, a sport previously discredited in America, was by 1921 legalized and accepted as entertainment for all classes and both sexes. Why did a deplored sport become a national passion? Furthermore, why did Jack Dempsey become a national hero when the former world's heavyweight champion, Jess Willard, had barely been known?

Part of the "lack of proportion" toward boxing stemmed from the nation's World War I experience. The martial spirit of wartime carried over into the sports world and caused a renaissance of boxing in the United States.[19] The U.S. Army taught boxing to the World War I doughboy. According to the army's rationale, boxing served a dual function: it was excellent training for learning how to use a bayonet, and it relieved the tensions of camp life. In one camp alone 30,000 men received boxing lessons, and inter-camp competition spurred interest from the generals down to the privates.[20]

When the war ended the interest in boxing did not decline. In fact, boxing gained even more popularity in the post-war decade, and legislation was passed to legalize the sport in most of the states.[21] The man most directly responsible for the amazing rise in post-World War I boxing was Jack Dempsey. It was his career, his quick knockouts, which attracted the public's attention to boxing in the 1920's.

Dempsey's status as hero was built on only a handful of matches. An examination of Dempsey's fighting record prior to his winning the heavyweight crown in 1919 hardly reveals the unbeatable superman of popular fantasy. Only two years before Dempsey made his reputation by defeating Willard, he had been knocked out by "Fireman" Jim Flynn in less than one round, and less than a year before he won the title he had been humiliated by a fat little sailor named Willie Meehan.[22] Dempsey's knockout average, a popular yardstick for measuring relative punching ability, is only .613, well below that of such horrendous performers as Floyd Patterson and Primo Carnera and only a few points above Tommy Burns, the man considered by most ring historians as the worst heavyweight champion.[23] Therefore, considerably more went into the making of the Dempsey legend than just a fighting record.

To understand the nature of Dempsey's reputation as the "Manassa Mauler," one must return to the shores of Maumee Bay on that stifling hot July the Fourth, 1919. Dempsey entered the ring that day as the unquestionable underdog. His 6 ft. 1 in. and 189 pound frame was dwarfed by Jess Willard, the "Pattawatomie Giant" who stood 6 ft. 3 in. and weighed 250 pounds. Yet, Dempsey won, and in winning he punished his opponent to a degree he would never again equal.[24] After the fight, it was reasoned that any boxer who could inflict such damage must be in some way superhuman. The Dempsey legend was launched. Public acceptance was complete; in one bout Dempsey gained the fighting reputation which would remain virtually unaltered for the remainder of his career.[25]

Dempsey's emergence as a popular hero follows exactly the pattern of the typical "conquering hero" which Klapp has outlined.[26] All the major characteristics are present: Dempsey moved from relatively obscure social status to the rank of a hero by one spectacular demonstration of inordinate ability, and immediately a mythical interpretation of him arose.[27] Yet, as Klapp illustrates, a hero cannot emerge from a social vacuum; he is created to meet real emotional needs of a society.[28] So too, Dempsey acted as a point of social reorientation during the turbulent years of 1919-1920. With race riots erupting in cities throughout the United States and the Red Scare claiming victims by the hundreds, Dempsey seemed like something stable, something people could depend on.

The news media was quick to portray Dempsey as a person who represented all which America had long esteemed. His mere physical description exuded traditional values. To the New York *Times,* Dempsey was "modest, with boyish simplicity" and "refuses to indulge in broggadocia"; he was also seen as a "model of clean living . . . a gentleman from head to toes," and a person who loves children.[29] Further proof of Dempsey's adherence to the traditional American virtues can be seen in his first reported action after the Willard bout. He quickly sent off the following telegram: "Dear Mother: Won in third round. Received your wire. Will be home soon as possible. Love and Kisses. Jack."[30]

Labor Day, 1920, saw the Dempsey myth buttressed by another quick knockout and more all-American deeds. In his first title defense, he defeated Billy Miske in a bout held at Benton Harbor, Michigan. While it is entirely possible that Miske may have been a worthy contender had he not been dying of Bright's disease, Dempsey was depicted as reaching his humanitarian zenith when he sent his friend into a state of unconsciousness in the third round.[31] Not only was Dempsey portrayed as a humanitarian inside the ring, he was also seen as a kind-hearted soul outside the ropes. Again, it was the New York *Times* which furnished the best example of the ingredients which went into the making of the Dempsey myth. They printed a heart-warming story of how before the fight a cute little girl had presented Dempsey with a kiss and a four-leaf clover, which he kept in his glove.[32] This type of story could only add to the growing adulation of Dempsey.

The printing press was not the only mass media force which molded the popular image of Dempsey. The visual arts—painting, drama, and the cinema—were also active in its formulation. For the first time in America, painters in the twenties began to find boxing a suitable subject for their canvasses. George Bellows could find "no more dramatic clash in nature than the fury and the ruthlessness of combat within the ropes."[33] In his painting *Dempsey and Firpo,* Bellows graphically captures the importance Dempsey had to the lives of people in the 1920's. Commenting on the pictures of Dempsey by such artists as Bellows and Alonzo Victor Lewis, a New York *World* writer applauded their effort, stating that since Dempsey had the "native grace, physical beauty, and prowess which has fired the imagination of the world," he should by all means be preserved on a canvas. [34]

While painting captured and preserved the drama of Dempsey's life, it influenced the actual molding of the Dempsey myth only indirectly. After all, few of Dempsey's most ardent followers either saw or understood the paintings. However, the cinema did play a direct role. Millions of people went to movies, and the melodramas which Dempsey starred in were highly profitable. By the art of the make-up man, Dempsey was transformed from the "foremost demonstrator of modified murder" into a "somewhat sheepish and harmless-looking young man who makes moon faces at the heroines and pats the hand of a tubercular stage mother." [35] In all ways, Dempsey was cast in a role to epitomize the traditional values which the news media emphasized. W.O. McGeehan, the leading New York *Herald Tribune* sports columnist, wrote that a Dempsey movie was always of a high moral quality:

> There is nothing in them to bring the blush of shame to the most sensitive cheek. . . . Of course there is a hint of what they call "sex" in these films. But it is handled with a delicacy that would even get by the judge who maintained that all literature should be denatured to suit a seminary girl of the mid-Victorian period. Mr. Jack Dempsey does not make love with the brazeness of a Valentino. His love-making is repressed. Mr. Dempsey merely looks at the "goil." He does not manhandle her. There are no shameless petting parties in this clean and wholesome Dempsey film. The Dempsey "movies" are safe and sane, and will get by any censor. [36]

Thus the motion picture industry reinforced the image of Dempsey that was presented in the news media. In a time of change and flux, Dempsey was portrayed as a stable force. Whether he was composing a telegram to his mother, kissing cute little girls, or making his "mooncalf expression" at older "goils," Dempsey was always seen in the light of past values and time-honored traditions.

The only serious obstacle which threatened to block his hero-making process was Dempsey's fight with Georges Carpentier, or, as his name was anglicized, "Georgeous Car-painter." [37] Few ring battles have more dramatically symbolized the conflict of the values and issues of a given time. That the bout held a symbolic importance was clearly recognized at the time of the fight. A *New Republic* editorial warned specifically against forcing a boxer into becoming a representative symbol. [38] The public, the editorial observed, "took the fight as an orgy of sentimentality, and twisted Carpentier into a figure which the realities of this attractive prize-fighter do not support." [39] On the international level, the *Neue Zurcher Zeitung,* a liberal Swiss daily, said the bout symbolized the fact that "the young democratic giant—as dramatically incorporated in Dempsey's powerful, bru-

tal, natural strength, born of the American West . . . has become the master of the world." [40]

The central issue which animated the contest was each fighter's war record. Throughout World War I, Dempsey had done his fighting in the rings of the West Coast rather than in the trenches of France. Jack "Doc" Kearns, Dempsey's manager, offered the explanation that Dempsey, under "work or fight" orders, had decided he could best serve his country by working in the shipyards of Seattle. [41] In justifying his action, Dempsey said that since government had not instructed him to join the army, he was just following orders. [42] However, the issue could not be easily evaded. A New York *Times* editorial clearly dramatized the larger moral issue at stake:

> Dempsey says that he is not a draft dodger. Technical facts sustain him. His adherents assert that his negative patriotism, negative action, brings him forth from the slacker shadows and puts him, head up and dauntless, in the clear light of noble duty, nobly done. . . . Dempsey, whose profession is fighting, whose living is combat, whose fame is battle; Dempsey six feet one of strength, in the glowing splendor of youth, a man fashioned by nature as an athlete and a warrior—Dempsey did not go to the war, while weak-armed, strong-hearted clerks reeled under pack and rifle; while middle-aged men with families volunteered; while America asked for its manhood. Dempsey did not go to France to do battle for forty-eight states, but is ready now to go for four hundred thousand dollars. Our greatest fighter sidestepped our greatest fight. There rests the reason for the Dempsey chorus of dispraise. [43]

Dempsey's war record was brought into a sharper focus when compared to the record of Georges Carpentier, his French opponent. When the war started in August, 1914, Carpentier joined the French Air Force as a pilot. [44] During the war, he was twice wounded by shrapnel, once in the right foot and once in the head, and he was twice decorated, with the Croix de Guerre and the *Medaille Militaire.* [45] Thus the fight pitted the "slacker" against the military hero. Emphasizing this theme, a *Literary Digest* story observed that "one of the two men . . . has a war-record made in the trenches; the other has a war-record which was made far in the rear of the fighting-line. Georges Carpentier pulled off the gloves, picked up the bayonet, faced the German shells, and won the war-cross of gallantry in action; Jack Dempsey dropt his mitts to handle tools in a shipyard." [46]

Yet as central as the war question was, there were other issues which further complicated matters. Dempsey, for the most part, was a known quantity. Except for his amorphous stand on the war, he seemed quintessentially American. The Dempsey myth was certainly established and widely understood by the summer of 1921. Carpentier, on the other hand, was both physically and symbolically foreign. He came from France and neither spoke nor wanted to speak English. [47] Everything about him seemed somehow too flashy, too foreign. In shades of Valentino, he was described as being a "tall, slender, urban, and debonair young exquisite."[48] His tastes were portrayed as being strictly aristocratic. Owning over 200 suits and changing clothes six or eight times a day, Carpentier was always the height of fashion.[49] In his leisure time, he enjoyed fast cars, billiards, bridge, serious plays, highbrow literature, opera, and dancing.[50] Thus although he liked movies and Charlie Chaplin—illustrating that he was "not too bright or good for human nature's daily food"—Carpentier was most assuredly not the representative of traditional values that Dempsey was.[51]

Viewing the two boxers, the American public was faced with a perplexing dilemma: Carpentier was a war hero but he also was a foreigner, while the American, Dempsey, was a draft dodger. Obviously, this was no easy choice to make. Intellectuals on both sides of the Atlantic came out overwhelmingly for Carpentier.[52] But the support the masses had to offer was split. The American Legion adopted a resolution condemning Dempsey as a draft dodger and appropriated money to bet on Carpentier.[53] Reacting to the American Legion's stand, the Veterans of Foreign Wars of Atlantic City pledged their support of Dempsey. Justifying their stand, a leader said, "We look on Dempsey as the American champion going into the ring to uphold America's title of supremacy in a game at which it has excelled for generations."[54]

After he had chosen his favorite, the American fan could only sit back and watch the pre-fight build-up, which was, in fact, spectacular. Newspapers and magazines in both the United States and Europe printed daily articles about the fight. The inordinate amount of press space devoted to the fight went neither unnoticed nor unquestioned in foreign countries. Both the London *Times* and the *Manchester Guardian* noted that the American people had lost all "sense of proportion" regarding the bout.[55] In tiny, neutral Switzerland, the *Neue Zurche Zeitung* wrote that "one tenth of this interest and of the press-power concentrated upon this event would have easily put the United States into the League of Nations. . . . America is more engaged by this event than by the Versailles peace or by the greatest European revolution."[56] Even in the Far East, the fight gained newspaper coverage. The *Japan Times* claimed that American fight promoters were insensitive to Eastern feeling because they scheduled the Dempsey-Carpentier match for Saturday, July 2, which meant the fight would be held on Sunday, Japanese time.[57] Furthermore, the paper was incensed that the bout monopolized "the telegraph and cable lines to the exclusion of debates and decisions that will influence the sections of the larger part of mankind for years to come."[58]

If foreign papers mapped every undulation of the fighters' lives, the American press detailed every sweat pore Dempsey and Carpentier opened while training. This was no mere flirtation with the combatants; the press was quite serious in their coverage of the pre-fight

events. For weeks before the bout, the New York *Times*, St. Louis *Post-Dispatch*, New Orleans *Times-Picayune*, and New York *Tribune* carried front-page stories about the fighters. In the newspapers, the match was also used as a catalyst for selling consumer goods. For example, the New Orleans *Times-Picayune* ran a full-page advertisement entitled, "The 'Fight of the Century' Will End in Round??" Each of twelve stores picked a round; if the bout ended in round one, the Delta Lumber Company would give five dollars reduction on the first purchase made on July 4, 1921; or, if the fight ended in round two, A.V.S. Falling Hair and Dandruff Remedy would sell thirty 60c bottles at one-half price.[59] Nor were the newspapers the only mass media platform which showed excessive interest in the affair. Magazines of every nature, from the highbrow to the lowbrow, also demonstrated an inordinate interest in the two men. Magazines made the bout subject to psychological interpretation, literary speculation, and religious controversy.[60] Indeed, by the time of the fight, it is hard to imagine a single sector of American life which had not in one way or another expressed an interest in the outcome.

The stage was thus set for the fight. On July 2, 1921, the attention of millions of people around the world focused on a ring built at Boyle's Thirty Acres in Jersey City, New Jersey. As a financial experiment, the fight was an unqualified success: 80,183 people paid $1,789,238 to see the fight in person.[61] As an outstanding sports event, the fight left much to be desired; Dempsey weathered a mild attack in the second round and knocked Carpentier out in the fourth round. But as uneventful as the actual fighting was, the press reported it as if it were the only news fit to print. Even a newspaper as traditionally conservative in its treatment of sports as the New York *Times* announced the result of the bout in three streamer headlines running all the way across its first page.[62] Nothing but information about the fight covered most of the first thirteen pages of the *Times*. An exception to this was a small article entitled, "Harding Ends War." The war was the same one Dempsey had sidestepped, but in the carnival mood which prevailed after the fight no one seemed interested in the war issue anymore. Dempsey had won. The American champion, albeit one with certain defects, had triumphed over the European champion. Public opinion, as reflected in the press, seemed satisfied.

In the wake of the Carpentier fray, Dempsey was once again placed in a pantheon reserved only for unblemished idols. The *Japan Times* wrote that Dempsey's name was far better known than Lloyd George's, and thousands of boys would "rather be Dempsey . . . than be the President of the United States or the greatest force in the world of finance, art or letters."[63] Francis Hackett, writer for the *New Republic,* noted that Dempsey was not cruel, humiliating, or brutal: "He was simply superior."[64] Many writers echoed the same views, while still other journalists continued the adulation on a higher, symbolic level. P.W. Wilson, for example, wrote that too often men think only in terms of politics, theologies, and economic systems; yet Dempsey's victory declared to everyone that "it is, ultimately, the man who counts. His food, his muscles, his habit, his frame of mind, his morale, matter infinitely to the whole world." [65]

Of more interest than the praise for Dempsey was what the fight's result represented to American society. On one level, the ministers of America saw the fight, as Dr. John Roach Straton said, as clear proof that "we have relapsed into paganism." [66] A cross section of surveyed ministers generally agreed with Straton. But to others, the affair represented less a shift toward barbarism than an indication of the weakening of the power of the pulpit. According to the New Haven *Journal-Courier,* the masses were no longer content to follow blindly the moral precepts of the "intemperate guardians of other people's business," whose methods were "intemperate and insolent, overbearing and dictatorial." [67]

If the fight highlighted a conflict in the moral predilections of society, it certainly demonstrated a growing rift between the "highbrows" and "lowbrows." It has been illustrated that the rich and more educated people interested in boxing had been for Carpentier. From Heywood Broun in America to George Bernard Shaw in Europe, writers for the more selective magazines had gone to their thesauruses searching for better adjectives to describe Carpentier. Also, from the readiness of the public to forget the war issue, one suspects that among the literary inarticulate Dempsey always had strong support. By 1921, many people were beginning to question American involvement in the Great War. War idealism had been diminished by the Red Scare and race riots of 1919, and the Wilsonian rationale for war had been undermined by the League fight in America. Nowhere was the disillusionment by the masses more clearly portrayed than in the following editorial in the St. Louis *Post-Dispatch:*

> The highbrows have had their day. They have wrangled over world peace and protection against future war for nearly three years, and they have accomplished neither. They have left no brain cell unagitated to resume the turning of the economic wheels, but in vain. Now, let us see what the lowbrows have done. In gate receipts alone they have shaken into circulation $1,600,000 from the pockets of people who have been holding back on the monopoly game. Of this, $400,000 is going into the Federal Treasury, where it will pay for a coat of paint and possibly a big gun or two on one of our sorely needed new battleships. . . . A Dempsey-Carpentier fight in every state . . . would put old doldrums on the blink. [68]

Thus the Dempsey-Carpentier bout was more than an athletic contest between two men. It also became a platform for debates over grave moral, social, and political issues, debates which were central to the 1920's.

Dempsey's victory over Carpentier ended the debate over his war record. Free from this albatross, his popularity took a sharp turn upward. Twice in 1923 he defended his title, and both fights received banner treatment by the major American newspapers. [69] As a public hero, Dempsey became a lucrative commodity. One Florida land firm paid him $10,000 a day for shaking hands with prospective buyers. Falling into the land craze himself, Dempsey claimed he was in on the "ground floor" of a five million dollar land deal. [70] Yet if the 1923 bouts increased his value as a public commodity, they also highlight different social themes which span the 1920's.

Tommy Gibbons became the first of Dempsey's 1923 opponents. In an actionless bout which lasted fifteen dreary rounds, Dempsey edged out a victory. Dull though the actual fighting was, the match generated a storm of controversy. The issue which precipitated the conflict was money. Before the 1920's athletes had not been paid what the public considered outrageous amounts of money for performing their particular skill. For instance, when John L. Sullivan became the first heavyweight champion by virtue of his 1892 defeat of Paddy Ryan, he was paid only five thousand dollars. [71] In the 1920's, however, the price went up. Sports became "big business," and no sport more so than boxing. Throughout the 1920's, the large purses Dempsey won caused discussion. According to a San Francisco *Chronicle* editorialist, the money involved in the Dempsey-Gibbons bout indicated that professional boxing had lost "all sense of proportion." [72] To the New Haven *Journal-Courier,* the money paid the champion was "a study of national degeneracy." [73] Even the *Christian Science Monitor*, a newspaper which rarely devoted space to sports coverage, noted that war veterans must "wonder at the national temperament that leaves them to shift as best they may for a livelihood, while giving $500,000 and unbounded adulation to a pugilist who carefully avoided the trenches." [74]

While the money issue dominated the Gibbons affair, Dempsey's second fight of 1923 raised the topic of nationalism. Once again, as in the Carpentier fight, Dempsey was challenged by a foreigner; this time it was the Argentinian, Luis Angel Firpo. After two rounds of furious action, which saw Firpo knocked down eight times and Dempsey beaten out of the ring, the champion saved his title by knocking his adversary out. But to the news media, the fight was more than just a sensational display of punching power. They transformed Dempsey's fistic victory into a victory for Americanism. Bruce Bliven, a writer for the *New Republic,* went to the fight to see the "Nordic race defend itself against the Latin. . . ." [75] More to the point was an editorial in the *Brooklyn Eagle.* "One shudders," the editorialist wrote, "to think of what might have happened to the Monroe Doctrine if Firpo had won. Today it is safe to say that South America has more respect for us than ever before. If Europe would only send over a first-class challenger, Mr. Dempsey might do something to restore American prestige abroad." [76] The Dempsey corollary to the Monroe Doctrine may come as a surprise to diplomatic historians, but to an American concerned over its own image, Dempsey, both as a moral reflection and an international interpreter, was seen as a bold reaffirmation of Americanism.

After the Firpo bout of September 14, 1923, Dempsey rested. Not until three years later, September 23, 1926, would he defend his title again. In part, these were years of ballyhoo, meant for the titillation of the public. Newspapers, serious and sensational alike, were caught up in the process. The New York *Times* printed a challenge to Dempsey from Prince Mohammed Ali Ibrahim of Egypt. Ali's trainer, Blink McClosky, said the prince had a blow called the "Pyramid punch" that "lands with the force of a falling pyramid and knocks a rival stiffer than a sphinx." [77] But these were also serious years, for a profound atmosphere of racism hung over the surface ballyhoo excitement. Harry Wills, the major heavyweight contender, constantly clamored for a title match, but because he was black he was refused the fight. Indeed, Dempsey's first public statement after he had destroyed Willard in 1919 was that he would not under any circumstances pay attention to a "Negro challenger." [78] True to his word, he never did. And, for the most part, the press and New York Boxing Commission never seriously tried to stage the fight. [79]

When official and public pressure did force Dempsey to fight again, he chose Gene Tunney. Literally and symbolically, this was a match of contrasts. Dempsey, the crude, wild-swinging mauler inside the ring lived a life of action outside the ring. But always, he maintained his attachments with his followers. He joked and talked with them; he always seemed one of the "boys." [80] While he had his troubles—the draft issue, divorces, moral improprieties—the public always seemed to forgive him. Like the proverbial "bad little boy," Dempsey was viewed as basically good, no matter what wrong he did.

By contrast, Tunney was smooth inside the ring and socially polished outside the ropes. No draft issue clouded his past. An ex-marine, Tunney had not waited to be drafted to serve his country during the war. [81] And no personal scandals shaded his career. One observer wrote: "Tunney looks and acts clean. His private life. . . .has been above reproach. . . . Socially, Tunney is a charming, cultured gentleman. . . ." [82] To the press as a whole, no single person in sports better illustrated the virtue in American society than Tunney. As a New York *Times* editorialist wrote:

> Tunney should make an ideal heavyweight champion. He has a flawless record; he did his first fighting for his country, then he fought for himself. Of unblemished character, representing the highest ideals in American manhood, an example for the younger generation, modest, retiring, unassessing, well read and educated—he combines every desirable characteristic. [83]

Surely, then, the public would be delighted if Tunney defeated Dempsey.

Yet lines are seldom this clearly drawn. Even in sports, which by their very nature lend themselves to black and white issues, the conflicts are not so tightly constructed. While on the surface Tunney seemed per-fect to succeed Dempsey in capturing the public's imagination, the process was by no means that simple. For however ideal Tunney seemed, there was in his character a tragic flaw: he just did not seem truly American. To the masses, Tunney represented something as foreign as Carpentier. Tunney, who had lectured on Shakespeare before Professor Wendell Phelp's class at Yale, who went on walking trips in Europe with Thornton Wilder, who married a socially prominent woman, and who regarded the public with a lofty indifference, was certainly viewed as anti-athletic, if not downright anti-American, by the masses. [84]

Tunney's tragic flaw was seen during the 1920's. Heywood Broun, writing for the *Nation,* noted that while Tunney was enormously popular with the "wise public which came to boxing matches on passes," he had "not touched the heart of America." [85] James J. Corbett, an ex-heavyweight champion who was unpopular in his own time as titleholder, warned Tunney that if he did not show he was part of the "common people" he would never be popular. [86] But Tunney ignored all advice. He continued to speak in metaphors which only further alienated the public. Unlike Dempsey, whose crude manners and aggressive fighting style people could easily identify with, Tunney always remained above the public's love.

The actual fight was never in doubt. Tunney, full of grace and polish, outpointed Dempsey with little trouble. [87] Dempsey's career as heavyweight champion had ended. Yet even in defeat, he continued to express the sentiments which had made him a popular hero. Striking a humbly nationalistic pose, Dempsey said, "I have no alibis to offer. I lost to a good man, an American—a man who speaks the English language. I have no alibis." [88] This was the style of language the public loved to hear, and when it was gone boxing as a sport lost the fantastic popularity it had enjoyed from 1919 to 1926.

Dempsey's loss to Tunney signified an end to the Golden Age of boxing. It also marked the symbolic death of one of the greatest heroes of the 1920's. Neither Babe Ruth nor Bobby Jones commanded the press space that Dempsey did. But the question remains: What did Dempsey mean to or represent about the 1920's? It has been shown that the career of Jack Dempsey encompassed more than just his fights. Each fight became symbolically something larger. Each became a platform from which to debate issues central to the 1920's. War issues, race questions, cultural schisms, and nationalistic impulses all found their way into Dempsey's fights. No newspaper or magazine was above using some aspect of Dempsey's career to demonstrate symbolically some facet of a social, political, or economic issue.

More importantly, Dempsey, the hero, tells us something about the temperament of the 1920's. Roderick Nash, in *The Nervous Generation: American Thought 1917-1930,* wrote that "Ideas change with glacial slowness. A new attitude may appear and gain strength, but the older one does not automatically disappear."[89] This concept is of paramount importance in understanding the influence of Dempsey. While the 1920's may have seen something of what Frederick Lewis Allen called "the revolution in manners and morals," the old virtues were not stifled. When the masses wanted a hero, they chose a fighter who had been characterized as a possessor of the traditional mores, and not a fighter who symbolized the "lost generation." Just as the public showed support for the timeless American virtues by making Gene Stratton-Porter the preeminent popular novelist of the 1920's, they voiced their acceptance of the old American ways by their adherence to the Dempsey myth.[90]

NOTES

1. New York *Times*, July 5, 1919, p. 1.
2. John Lardner, *White Hopes and Other Tigers* (New York, 1951), pp. 58-59.
3. Nat Loubet, et al., *The 1973 Ring Boxing Encyclopedia and Record* (New York, 1973), pp. 86-87; Frederick Lewis Allen, *Only Yesterday: An Informal History of the 1920's* (New York, 1964), pp. 174-75. In the second Dempsey-Tunney bout alone some 145,000 people paid over $2,600,000 to see the match and over 40,000,000 heard the fight over the radio.
4. Loubet, *Ring Record Book*, pp. 81-82.
5. One finds occasional references such as that by Robert K. Murray, *Red Scare: A Study of National Hysteria, 1919-1920* (New York, 1964), p. 241, that "A growing public interest in post war sports . . . helped take the nation's mind off bolshevism as attention shifted from the antics of Lusk and Palmer to those of Jack Dempsey and Babe Ruth."
6. Eldridge Cleaver, *Soul on Ice* (New York, 1968), p. 85.
7. "Carpentier: A Symbol," *The New Republic*, July 20, 1921, p. 206.
8. Omaha *Evening World-Herald*, July 1, 1910, p. 11.
9. John Higham, *Writing American History: Essays on Modern Scholarship* (Bloomington, 1972), p. 80.
10. Paul Meadows, "Some Notes on the Social Psychology of the Hero," *Southwestern Social Science Quarterly*, XXVI (1945), 239.
11. *Ibid.*, 239.
12. Orrin E. Klapp, "Hero Worship in America," *American Sociological Review*, XIV (1949), 62. Klapp has written a great deal on this subject. The reader might consult other works by him which include *Heroes, Villains and Fools: The Changing American Character* (Englewood Cliffs, N.J., 1962), pp. 95-124; *Symbolic Leaders: Public Dramas and Public Men* (Chicago, 1964), pp. 211-64; "Creation of Popular Heroes," *American Journal of Sociology*, LIV (1948), 135-41; "Heroes, Villains, and Fools, as Agent of Social Control," *American Sociological Review*, XIX (1954), 56-62; and "The Folk Hero," *Journal of American Folklore*, LVII (1949), 17-25.
13. Klapp, "Heroes, Villains, and Fools, as Agents of Social Control," p. 62.
14. Klapp, "Creation of Popular Heroes," p. 141.
15. Sidney Hook, *The Hero in History: A Study in Limitations and Possibility* (New York, 1943), Chapter 1; Klapp, "Creation of Popular Heroes," p. 139; Harry Edwards, "Sports and the Mass Media," in Marie M. Hart (ed.), *Sport in the Socio-Cultural Process* (Dubuque, Iowa, 1972), pp. 363-368; and Leonard Shecter, *The Jocks* (New York, 1969), p. 131.
16. Hook, *The Hero in History*, p. 10.
17. Edwards, "Sports and the Mass Media," *Sport in the Socio-Cultural Process*, p. 365.
18. *The Times* (London), July 2, 1921, p. 13.
19. It is interesting to note that the previous high point of boxing in the United States had occurred during the middle to late 1890's. Its zenith was reached at approximately the same time as the Spanish-American War, when Jim Jeffries won the title in 1899.
20. Thomas Foster, "Why Our Soldiers Learn to Box," *Outing*, May, 1918, pp. 114-16.
21. The single most important piece of boxing legislation was the Walker Law which went into effect on May 24, 1920. Under this New York State law, boxing was permitted. Bouts could be scheduled for up to fifteen rounds, and decisions could be given. The law also provided for a commission to be established to supervise the sport. The Walker Law has served as the pattern for world wide boxing since it was passed. For a history of New York boxing laws, see Loubet, *Ring Record Book*, p. 129.
22. "Dempsey and the Fat Sailor," *Boxing Illustrated and Wrestling News*, July, 1962, pp. 32-33.
23. Nat Fleischer, *The 1964 Ring Record Book and Boxing Encyclopedia* (New York: Ring Book Shop, 1964), p. 614.
24. The Dempsey-Willard bout has been clouded by controversy ever since the day of the fight. It was rumored shortly after the fight that Dempsey's gloves were "loaded." Dempsey's manager, Jack "Doc" Kearns, substantiated these claims in an article entitled "He Didn't Know the Gloves were Loaded," *Sports Illustrated*, January 13, 1964, pp. 48-56. According to Kearns, he had bet $10,000 at ten to one odds that Dempsey would win the title fight in less than one round. In order to guarantee a victory, he had Dempsey's hands soaked in plaster of paris. The mere fact that Dempsey never again inflicted such a devastating battering to an opponent lends validity to Kearn's assertion. However, an article by John Hollis, "Were Dempsey's Fists Loaded in Toledo?," *Boxing Illustrated and Wrestling News*, May, 1964, pp. 10-24, reaches the opposite conclusion. Hollis applied the plaster of paris as Kearns allegedly had and found it simply would not dry.
25. New York *Times*, September 14, 1919, p. 6.
26. Klapp, "Creation of Popular Heroes," p. 136; Klapp, "Hero Worship in America," p. 55.
27. *Ibid.*
28. Klapp, "Creation of Popular Heroes," p. 135.
29. New York *Times*, July 5, 1919, p. 5.
30. *Ibid.*, p. 2.
31. Miske died shortly after the bout but supposedly always thought well of Dempsey for giving him one last big payday. On his deathbed, Miske was reported to have gasped: "Tell Jack thanks. Tell him thanks from Bill." It is stories like this, read by thousands, which help to keep the Dempsey myth alive today. See Michael A. Glick, "Boxing's Tender Side," *Boxing Illustrated and Wrestling News*, December, 1958, pp. 34-35.
32. New York *Times*, September 7, 1920, p. 13.
33. John Betts, "Organized Sports in Industrial America," (unpublished Ph.D. dissertation, 1951), pp. 398-399. When Bellows died in 1925, he had already established himself as the greatest American artist of the ring. *Introducing Georges Carpentier* (1921) and *Dempsey-Firpo* (1923) successfully capture the dynamic impact of Dempsey and boxing.
34. "Jack Dempsey in Oil," *The Literary Digest*, August 18, 1923, p. 34.
35. New York *Herald Tribune*, June 5, 1924, p. 17; "Dempsey as a Movie Actor," *The Literary Digest*, June 21, 1924, pp. 61-63.
36. New York *Herald Tribune*, June 5, 1924, p. 17. For a review of Dempsey on the stage, see G.J. Nathan, "Dempsey as an Actor," *The American Mercury*, November 1928, pp. 377-78. Stressing the effeminacy of most of the professional actors, Nathan wrote that "Mr. Dempsey may not be much of an actor, but his worst enemy certainly cannot accuse him of belonging to the court of Titania."
37. "Carpentier, From Pit-boy to Esthete of the 'Boxer,'" *The Literary Digest*, June 11, 1922, p. 34.
38. "Carpentier: A Symbol," *The New Republic*, pp. 206-07.
39. *Ibid.*, p. 207.
40. "First Civilization vs. Sword Civilization," *The Living Age*, September 24, 1921, p. 774.
41. New York *Times*, February 28, 1920, p. 6.
42. *Ibid.*, January 23, 1920, p. 14.
43. *Ibid.*, January 26, 1920, p. 8.
44. "Did 'Psychic' Power Aid Brown When Carpentier Licked Beckett?," *The Literary Digest*, January 17, 1920, p. 127.

45. "Georges Carpentier—Gentleman, Athlete, and Connoisseur of the 'Boxe,' " *ibid.,* April 17, 1920, p. 130; New York *Times,* June 10, 1921, p. 15.
46. "War-Record of Dempsey," *The Literary Digest,* February 14, 1920, p. 122.
47. "Georges Carpentier—Gentleman, Athlete, and Connoisseur of the 'Boxe,' " *The Literary Digest,* pp. 130-36.
48. *Ibid.,* p. 130.
49. *Ibid.,* pp. 33-34.
50. *Ibid.,* pp. 130-36; "Carpentier, From Pit-boy to Esthete of the 'Boxe,' " *ibid.,* p. 39. As a dancer Carpentier was said to be unsurpassed.
51. "Georges Carpentier—Gentleman, Athlete, and Connoisseur of the 'Boxe,' " *ibid.,* p. 133.
52. For the views of the intellectuals who were interested in boxing, see Arnold Bennett, "The Great Prize Fight." *The Living Age,* January 24, 1920, pp. 124-27; Francis Hackett, "The Carpentier Fight: Bennett vs. Shaw," *The New Republic,* January 14, 1920, pp. 198-200; Francis Hackett, "Dempsey-Carpentier," *ibid.,* July 13, 1921, pp. 185-87; Heywood Broun, "Mr. Dempsey's Five Foot Shelf," *The Bookman,* August 1921, pp. 521-24; "Boswell Takes Dr. Samuel Johnson to the Beckett-Carpentier Fight," *The Literary Digest,* January 17, 1920, pp. 127-28; and "Shaw called a 'Colossal Joke' as a Prize-Fight Reporter," *ibid.,* April 17, 1920, pp. 146-48.
53. New York *Times,* January 14, 1920, p. 24; "War Record of Dempsey," *The Literary Digest,* p. 124.
54. New York *Times,* May 18, 1921, p. 14.
55. The *Times* (London), July 2, 1921, p. 13; *The Manchester Guardian,* July 2, 1921, p. 8.
56. "First Civilization vs. Sword Civilization," *The Living Age,* pp. 773-74. The daily went on to say, "People greedily read every scrap of information, every prophecy and speculation, published regarding the coming fight, every detail of the biography of the contestants, their weight, physical condition, health, and programme of daily acts." From all indications this seems fairly accurate.
57. The Japan *Times,* July 2, 1921, p. 2.
58. *Ibid.,* July 4, 1921, p. 4.
59. New Orleans *Times Picayune,* July 1, 1921, p. 13.
60. P.W. Wilson, "The Big Prize-Fight Psychologically Considered," *Current Opinion,* August 1921, pp. 172-75. Heywood Broun, "Mr. Dempsey's Five Foot Shelf." *The Bookman,* pp. 512-24; " 'Carbuncle' of Boyle's Thirty Acres," *The Literary Digest,* July 30, 1921, pp. 31-32.
61. Loubet, *Ring Record Book,* p. 86.
62. New York *Times,* July 3, 1921, p. 1; Allen, *Only Yesterday,* p. 174. The *Times* is by no means unique in this respect.
63. The Japan *Times,* July 4, 1921, p. 4.
64. Francis Hackett, *The New Republic,* p. 187.
65. P.W. Wilson, "The Big Prize-Fight Psychologically Considered," *Current Opinion,* p. 175.
66. " 'Carbuncle' of Boyle's Thirty Acres," *The Literary Digest,* p. 31.
67. *Ibid.,* pp. 31-32.
68. St. Louis *Post-Dispatch,* July 2, 1921, p. 14.
69. See the July 5, 1923, and September 15, 1923, issues of the New York *Times,* San Francisco *Chronicle,* New Orleans *Times-Picayune,* St. Louis *Post-Dispatch,* and New York *Herald Tribune.*
70. New York *Times,* January 29, 1926, p. 24.
71. Loubet, *Ring Record Book,* p. 81.
72. San Francisco *Chronicle,* July 6, 1923, p. 22.
73. "Moralizing on the Million-Dollar Fight," *The Literary Digest,* October 6, 1923, p. 36.
74. *Ibid.,* p. 35. These disputes over the sum of money an athlete should or should not receive illustrates an interesting paradox at work in the 1920's. Clearly, the increased amount of public attention and mass media coverage devoted to sporting events created a situation where athletes could gain exorbitant sums of money. By gaining so much money, the athlete then came under public and media attack because he seemed to threaten the moral posture (i.e., "sports sake") of sports. This paradox is certainly seen in Dempsey's career. See New York *Times* editorial "The Welfare of Boxing," September 8, 1922, p. 12; and "From Homer to Hearst," *The Outlook,* July 18, 1923, pp. 401-02.
75. Bruce Bliven, "Arc Lights and Blood: Ringside Notes at the Dempsey-Firpo Fight," *The New Republic,* September 26, 1923, p. 125.
76. " 'Big Business' of Prize-Fighting," *The Literary Digest,* October 13, 1923, p. 62.
77. New York *Times,* March 4, 1924, p. 14.
78. *Ibid.,* July 6, 1919, p. 17.
79. The issue of racism in boxing in the 1920's is a constant one; Wills from 1919 to 1926 was always the number one contender. But a full discussion of it is out of the range of the present paper. Suffice it to say, "they [Dempsey and Wills] never fought because Tex Richard refused to promote it." (Correspondence with Nat Fleischer, November 3, 1972).
80. Fleischer, *Jack Dempsey,* pp. 149-60.
81. "Lieutenant Tunney, The Pride of the Marines," *The Literary Digest,* October 16, 1926, pp. 42-46.
82. *Ibid.,* p. 44
83. New York *Times,* Sept. 27, 1926, p. 18.
84. Allen, *Only Yesterday,* p. 175.
85. Heywood Broun, "It Seems to Heywood Broun," *The Nation,* August 8, 1928, p. 125.
86. "Corbett to Tunney on 'How to Win the Mob,' " *The Literary Digest,* January 14, 1928, pp. 54-60.
87. New York *Times,* September 24, 1926, p. 1.
88. *Ibid.*
89. Roderick Nash, *The Nervous Generation: American Thought, 1917-1930* (Chicago: Rand McNally and Company, 1970), pp. 41-42.
90. *Ibid.,* p. 137.

THE SPORT HERO: AN ENDANGERED SPECIES

Garry Smith

What Are Heroes?

In antiquity a hero was a mythical or legendary person who was strong, noble and brave. Often the hero was thought to be favored by the gods, and in some cases the hero himself was deified. The mythical hero served a valuable function as a medium through which culture was transmitted from generation to generation. Usually, stories about the hero were related to an historical event and attempted to explain some of the basic beliefs, values and traditions of the society.

A story involving a mythical hero frequently had a basis in fact, but as the story was told and re-told the heroic aspects of the person were magnified. Carlyle (1840), was aware of this penchant for hyperbole where heroes were concerned when he noted: "If a man was great while living he becomes ten-fold greater when dead [p. 26]."

Carlyle's major premise was that "society is founded on hero worship [p. 12]," and he believed the hero was "like lightning out of heaven; the rest of men waited for him like fuel, then they too would flame [p. 77]." In this context the hero is regarded as an innovator and a catalyst. The hero is distinct from the ordinary man in that he is more sincere, has greater vision and insight, and has "fully met his obligation of self-development [Lehman, 1928, p. 26]."

To illustrate his theory, Carlyle employed six categories of heroes: the hero as divinity, the hero as prophet, the hero as poet, the hero as priest, the hero as a man of letters, and the hero as king. In this sense the hero truly was a great man as opposed to a merely famous man. Carlyle's heroes were: "the modellers, patterns, and in a wide sense creators of whatsoever the general mass of men contrived to do or to attain [Lehman, 1928, p. 56]."

Contemporary scholars who have studied the hero have added to Carlyle's great man theory. Lerner (1957) speaks of two kinds of heroes; the history book hero and the vernacular or archetypal hero. The history book hero is roughly the equivalent of Carlyle's idea of the hero as someone who epitomizes the best in cultural and moral values. The vernacular or archetypal hero is more contemporary, and usually is a larger than life figure through which people can escape. The vernacular hero has fewer traditional heroic qualities than the history book hero and his fame is much more ephemeral.

Hook (1957) also has a useful way of distinguishing between hero types. He compares the "event-making" to the "eventful" man. In essence, the event-making man is someone who has an effect on significant developments, but who is merely in the right place at the right time. The eventful man is one whose actions are based on his outstanding capabilities rather than on the accident of time or position.

The most penetrating study of heroes is that by Klapp (1962, 1969) in his two books; *Heroes, Villains and Fools*

and *Collective Search for Identity*. Klapp divides heroes into five main categories each with several sub-categories. The skeleton of this classification system is presented below.

Category	Theme

1. *Winners*
  (a) strong man
  (b) the brain
  (c) the smart operator
  (d) the great lover
	Getting what you want, beating everyone, being a champ.

2. *Splendid Performers*
  (a) showmen
  (b) heroes of play
  (c) playboy
	Shining before an audience, making a hit.

3. *Heroes of Social Acceptability*
  (a) the pin-up
  (b) the charmer
  (c) the good fellow
  (d) conforming heroes
	Being liked, attractive, good, or otherwise personally acceptable to groups and epitomizing the pleasures of belonging.

4. *Independent Spirits*
  (a) bohemian
  (b) jester
  (c) angry commentator
	Standing alone, making one's way by oneself.

5. *Group Servants*
  (a) defenders
  (b) martyrs
  (c) benefactors
	Helping people, cooperation, self-sacrifice, group service and solidarity.

Klapp's classification scheme is comprehensive, perhaps too much so. Can the great lover, the charmer and the jester really be heroic in the accepted sense of the word? A second taxonometric problem involves the possibility of a single individual fitting into more than one category. For example, Klapp consigns athletes to the sub-category "heroes of play." It may be equally fruitful to view some athletic heroes as the strong man, showman, martyr or as a member of several categories at the same time.

The Functions of Heroes

The hero is a primary social model used by society to help maintain the social structure. Fishwick (1954) con-

Garry Smith, "The Sport Hero: An Endangered Species," *Quest*, Monograph XIX, January, 1973, pp. 59-70.

About the Author

Garry Smith is an Assistant Professor on the Faculty of Physical Education at the University of Alberta. Presently completing his doctorate, Mr. Smith has had extensive coaching experience both in his present position and in his previous appointment at the University of Western Ontario. His area of specialization is sport sociology with particular interest in the relationship between sport and the mass media.

curs with this viewpoint, although he may overstate the case when he says, "just as a pier holds up the bridge, so does the hero support society [p. 226]." Supposedly, societal models will best represent the major norms, values and beliefs of the society. When societal models are successful, there should be a close relationship between the models and the rest of the society. A society usually will support its models and it will "recruit, train, and control members of the society in accordance with these models [Klapp, 1962, p. 18]."

The hero as a social model should be consistent in his behavior, and should be considerably better in a positive sense than most of the other members of the society. One of the hero's main functions is to raise the aspiration levels of the people in the society. Klapp (1962) argues that the hero lifts people above where they would be without the model. The essential feature of the hero from the societal vantage point is that the hero should behave in such a way as to perpetuate collective values, affirm social norms, and contribute to the solidarity of the society.

Why People Worship Heroes

Klapp (1969) defines hero worship as "a yearning relationship in which a person, in a sense, gets away from himself by wishing or imagining himself to be like someone whom he admires [p. 211]." Fishwick (1954) feels that hero worship is inherent in human nature. If his assessment is correct, then everyone has the need to worship heroes as a form of escape. According to Fishwick the hero "helps us to transcend our drab back yards, apartment terraces, and tenements, and to regain a sense of the world's bigness [p. 226]." This need to escape via the hero has been described variously by Klapp (1962) as: an identity voyage, psychic mobility and dream realization. These terms are nearly synonymous and refer to the capacity of an individual to live vicariously through his hero. Assumably by worshipping a hero, the individual adds meaning and fulfillment to what otherwise would be a boring, stultifying existence.

Klapp (1969) suggests that there are three main directions hero worship can take; reinforcement, seduction and transcendence. Reinforcement keeps the individual within the social structure and directs him toward socially approved goals. Seduction keeps the individual within societal bounds, but tempts him to break rules. Transcendence takes the individual outside of the societal structure, and provides him with a new identity, new experiences and new norms.

A hero that reinforces would be someone who embodies the major social values (John F. Kennedy for example). The seductive hero would be someone like the fictional James Bond. He lives largely within the social structure, but he tempts us to gamble, to be violent and to be immoral. The transcendent hero leads us out of this society and forms a new society (Timothy Leary or Charles Manson would be candidates for transcendent heroes).

A person's identity voyage through a hero can be helpful as in a budding athlete learning and imitating the professional's particular skills. Hero worship also may serve a compensatory role in that the adulation may not provide tangible benefit for the person, but he feels good about the experience. Hero worship may serve as an important mechanism in adolescents for whom parents no longer serve as primary models. The heroes chosen by the adolescent may have a significant, positive influence on decisions about careers and life styles. Alternately, the individual may choose a negative model or the individual may become locked into a fantasy world of vicarious heroism and eventually have difficulty coping with reality. The hero worshipper who aspires too unreservedly to follow in his hero's footsteps can suffer psychological trauma if he is thwarted.

The Cult of the Hero

A cultic response to a hero refers to mass hero worship. Mass communication facilities have allowed images to be projected to large numbers of people simultaneously. This in turn has enabled the masses to use media celebrities for their identity voyages. Mass hero worship gives a feeling of fellowship and belonging to the individual worshipper. Mass hero worship seems to sanction the act, with so many people doing it, it must be all right.

A cult is formed when people become devoted to a particular ideal or value and engage in ritual to achieve it. The activity becomes truly cultic when it is the central focus of people's lives. A cult thus differs from a fad in the degree of seriousness and commitment involved. For many, the hero cult is a search for a life style, it fills a spiritual void. Correspondingly, Klapp (1969) feels that cultism is a response to the strain imposed by such factors as emotional impoverishment, banality and stylelessness. Essentially, then, a cultic reaction to a hero gives meaning and fulfillment to empty lives through the celebration of shared ritual.

How Hero Worship Develops

A child's social learning takes place primarily through social models. The child's first model usually is one of his parents. As he grows older, he is more influenced by models from his peer group and by the multiplicity of models proffered by the mass media. Before the child acquires an identity he will have been confronted with a vast array of model types.

Bandura's (1969) studies on social learning provide a key to understanding how hero worship develops. A person will identify with a model if that model is rewarded in front of observers. The reward has essentially the same effect on the observer as on the model. Heroes are rewarded repeatedly through applause, mass media coverage and special awards. This has the effect of reinforcing the identification process between fan and hero.

Although a reward may improve the model, punishment may or may not devalue it. If a hero is punished, his followers have one of two choices: (a) drop the hero or (b) vent their anger on the authority who imposes the sanction. When Denny McLain was suspended from the American League for four months in 1970, he lost a great deal of his lustre. On the other hand, Maurice Richard's fans reacted to his suspension in 1955 by pelting Commissioner Clarence Campbell with eggs and by rioting and looting in the streets.

Bandura (1969) has further suggested that modelling is more likely to occur if observers feel they have something in common with the model. A person is more likely to be used as a model if, in addition to being socially powerful, highly competent, a purported expert, a celebrity and a symbol of socioeconomic success, he is of the same sex, ethnic group and age as the observer.

The Sports Hero

The sports hero has long been an object of adulation. There were encomiums for early Olympic winners, Roman gladiators were given special privileges, and Sir Lancelot usually rode off with the fairest maiden. The sports hero has been popular because people can readily identify with him. It is natural to appreciate the best in any endeavor and the sporting hero is a relatively unrefined model. Athletic hero worship has been accepted and even encouraged because sport represents major cultural values.

As a child grows up he sees his older male models attending sporting events, watching games on television and reading about sports in magazines and newspapers. With so much attention devoted to sport the child soon learns that sport is important and worthwhile. This idea is further reinforced in school, as certain times are set aside for sports competition, and sport often becomes the focal point for student activity. The better athletes in the school are glorified and receive many rewards as a result of this status. Although only a few students actually can garner the rewards of heroic status, the rest receive vicarious pleasure through watching their athletic counterparts perform.

Coleman (1961) has observed that in the American high school, the athlete is at the top of the status hierarchy.[1] There are numerous case studies which support Coleman's findings, indeed the attention given some high school athletes borders on subservience and obsequity. A variety of contemporary accounts (Johnson, 1971; Linderman, 1971; Ricke, 1971) demonstrate how high school athletes can control a community.

Schafer (1971) sees the dominance of the high school athlete as an insidious way of inculcating the societal values of competition and goal-orientation.

> With their stress above all on winning as a team and becoming a champion as an individual athlete (thereby becoming a hero in the eyes of one's peers and community), school sports are a significant means by which an instrumental or goal orientation is developed in youth—not only in participants, but in student fans who idolize them as well [p. 6].

The end product of this socialization process is a person who believes that sport is significant and worthwhile,

and this belief in the importance of sport frequently is demonstrated by worshipping athletic heroes.

Manifestations of Sports Hero Worship

There is much evidence to indicate that people worship sports heroes, either collectively (as in teams) or as individuals. Fans clamor for autographs and engage in fist-fights over a baseball that has gone into the stands (Wecter, 1963). Attendance at most sporting events is up and sport on television is very close to the saturation level.

Bubble gum cards [2] of sports heroes are still popular with children, and magazines containing profiles of sports heroes abound. Newspapers publish obscure sports statistics and books on sporting teams and individuals have made a dent on the best seller charts.[3]

Athletic stars receive mountains of fan mail, are feted publicly at benefits and make television appearances on talk shows and in advertisements. The movies even are soliciting sports heroes in an effort to shore up the sagging box office. Joe Namath and Jim Brown are two of the most famous athletes who have succumbed to the lure of Hollywood.

Halls of Fame, where former athletes are immortalized, are numerous as are various fan clubs for teams and players (Kirshenbaum, 1971). These fan clubs hold regular meetings, publish monthly news letters and on occasion travel en masse to a game to view and meet the object of their desires.

The Changing Role of the Sports Hero

One of the most famous athletic heroes in North American history is a fictional character. His name was Frank Merriwell and he was featured in a series of dime store novels which appeared in print between 1896 and 1914. Frank was a master of all the sports he played (and indeed he played most of them). Typical of his athletic prowess was his "double shoot" pitch which curved in both directions to strike out a batter in the clutch.

> Frank Merriwell in the words of his creator, Gilbert Patten, stood for truth, faith, justice, the triumph of right, mother, home, friendship, loyalty, patriotism, the love of *alma mater*, duty, sacrifice, retribution, and strength of soul as well as body [Boyle, 1963, p. 242].

Frank Merriwell undoubtedly influenced many youngsters' lives. There has never been anyone to really take his place. His disappearance is lamented by many for the reason that his stories taught a sense of values that are missing today. In recent years there have been efforts to revive Frank Merriwell. In some cases through the medium of republication, and in others through the founding of Frank Merriwell clubs, who meet in the name of fair play and sportsmanship and whose motto is "no toadies or bullies allowed."

Frank Merriwell represented the all-around athlete, his counterpart in society was the pioneer, the person who had to be adept in a variety of skills to survive.

When Merriwell was at the peak of his popularity there was an emphasis on athletic heroes with strength. People like John L. Sullivan, James J. Corbett and Louis Cyr were idolized. At the turn of the century strength was still a valuable commodity in North American society.

Gurko (1953), aware that early heroes were noted for their strength, is critical of this superficial role model.

> The idealized American male has leaned strongly in the direction of brawn and egotism. . . . The accent has been on muscle over mind, instinct instead of brain, impulsiveness at the expense of reflectiveness, producing a series of exaggeratedly one-sided, immature personalities [p. 168].

The rise of technology placed an emphasis on new skills. The importance of physical strength was waning as characteristics such as persistence, finesse and guile became the required assets to rise in the new society. The athletic heroes of the 1920's and 30's seem to reflect this shift in societal values as Jesse Owens, Red Grange, Babe Ruth and Johnny Weismueller became the new idols.

The war years were accompanied by a diminution in athletic interest. The few sport heroes who did exist were those who had a military connection. Ted Williams, the ex-marine fighter pilot, was the most popular baseball player and Blanchard and Davis of Army were the two most heralded college football players. Maurice Richard was a Canadian sports hero in the 1940's, but he was heavily criticized for his decision not to join the army.

In the 1950's and 60's football emerged as the most popular sport. It was a sport for the times, the highly complex organization, specialization and division of labor in the game coincided exactly with the key characteristics of a highly industrialized society. The sports heroes were the equivalent of business executives, Bart Starr and Johnny Unitas were typical of this breed. Coaches like Vince Lombardi achieved hero status, and teams which were reminiscent of staid, conservative, efficient business corporations were glamorized. The New York Yankees, Green Bay Packers, Montreal Canadiens and Boston Celtics were heroic because of their efficient domination over competitors in the same marketplace.

The late 1960's and early 70's have given rise to a counter culture, the chief values of which are: an aversion to war, and a distaste for the corporate state and all that it represents. Advocates of the counter culture espouse coming together, sharing, a return to nature and a variety of antithetical values. Instead of competing, they want to cooperate, instead of fighting they want to make love and instead of conforming they want to express their individuality. In accord with this philosophy, athletic heroes are beginning to make public their anti-war views and are speaking out against violence, racism and dehumanization in sport. Athletes also are letting their personalities show through their white shoes, mod clothes and long hair.

The point to be made is that the sports hero is an accurate barometer of the times. Approximately every twenty years over the past century the type of sports hero in vogue has changed and these changes have roughly paralleled changes in societal values.

Categories of Sports Heroes

In Klapp's (1962) typology of heroes, athletes are listed under the category entitled "heroes of play." Klapp treats the athletic hero quite superficially in that he presents him as being only a uni-dimensional model. For Klapp, the athletic hero simply is one who performs well in front of an audience. This description really does not differentiate between athletes and entertainers, nor does it take into account the variety of ways in which an athletic hero establishes rapport with his audience. There are many subtleties and nuances in an adequate social model of the athletic hero, and a much more refined system of classification is necessary.

To be a sports hero the athlete must have a high level of physical ability. Sometimes this ability in itself is enough to make the athlete a hero. In other instances the athlete must have particular attributes in addition to his physical skill before he acquires the title of hero. Deford (1969) alludes to this point when he states that "Talent is only the first part of being a superstar. Beyond that, to deserve the title a player must establish a notoriety and an impact that can be turned into box office [p. 33]."

At the basic level many athletes have been decent, honorable, unassuming individuals. They have served as acceptable role models, especially for children and adolescents, the people most prone to emulate their behavior. This type of hero fits into Klapp's (1969) reinforcement category, in that they usually are quiet, respectable, family men who personify middle class values. Athletic heroes of this ilk emerge because of outstanding performances over a number of years. These athletes possess awesome skill, they are dedicated and they reliably produce a quality effort game by game, season by season. The type of athlete who fits this category would be: Gordie Howe, Bart Starr, Stan Musial and Billy Casper.

Another way for the athletic hero to emerge is to be the man of the hour. This refers either to an athlete who makes an outstanding play in the last seconds to win an important game; or to an athlete who makes a spectacular performance over a relatively short time span. An example of the former would be: Bobby Thompson hitting a game winning home run with two out in the bottom of the ninth to win a play-off game for the New York Giants in 1951. Examples of the latter instance would be: Don Schollander winning four gold medals in the 1964 Olympics; or Ken Dryden almost single-handedly winning a Stanley Cup for Montreal in 1971.

The underdog is another type of athletic hero. This label applies to players who perform at a high level despite some particular disadvantage. The underdog according to Sagarin (1970) is one who is "not favored or expected to win, by virtue of size, strength, experience or even birth [p.430]." Sports history is replete with examples of heroes who have overcome severe odds. Golfer Ben Hogan recovered from a near fatal automobile accident to come back within a year to win the United States Open. Jackie Robinson became one of the best players in baseball despite the degradation he suffered as the first black player in the major leagues.

Some athletes became heroes because of their individual flair or charisma. Arnold Palmer was chosen an athlete of the decade in 1970 primarily because of the tenacity and aggressiveness he showed when fighting to come from behind. Joe DiMaggio played the outfield effortlessly with a special kind of classic grace. Willie Mays has an inimitable style, fans like his exuberance, his casual basket catches and the way his hat flies off when he runs. Mays has so much panache that fans have even said he looks good striking out. Perhaps the best example of a unique style in contemporary sport is Bobby Orr. Dowling (1971) claims that Orr's style as a defenseman is revolutionary, it has permanently changed the game.

The aforementioned athletic hero types are in line with Klapp's socially approved, reinforcing hero. There has been a trend in recent years, however, for athletic heroes to fit more comfortably into the seductive category. Some modern sports heroes are brash and arrogant, they are people who have supreme confidence in their ability and often can back it up. Muhammed Ali's inane though accurate poems telling when his opponent would fall and Joe Namath guaranteeing a Super Bowl victory are examples of this type of sports hero. Deford (1969) aptly describes this new trend in athletic heroes.

> . . . all of the most recently ordained Impact Champions have required off-the-field controversy to complement their athletic exploits. Muhammed Ali and Namath had the facility of being heard at an extraordinary distance [p. 34].

In many cases these athletes are not taken to the public's heart. Admired for their ability, they also are despised because they are too haughty and over-bearing. Although seductive heroes don't inspire universal love, they often remain heroes because of their box office magnetism.

The anti-hero is popular in books and movies and in sport as well.

> The day of the establishment player is rapidly passing away in favor of sports performers who now live it up more, talk more, think more, and raise more hell with management than their predecessors ever considered attempting in the benign old days of boss-dominated sports [Batten, 1971, p. 2].

The anti-hero is someone who eschews traditional heroic qualities, yet is heroic either in spite of or because of this. The anti-hero is particularly popular with the youth because of their predilection for rankling the silent majority. Joe Namath and Derek Sanderson are the prototypes of the anti-hero in sport. Both are bachelor swingers, who frequent night clubs, sport long hair and mustaches, wear mod clothes, and who flaunt team rules. Both have penchant for the limelight and the more

they irk the older generation, the more they are lionized by the young. Neither of these two athletes portrays the public virtures of the traditional hero: honesty, dedication and strength of character. Namath is famous for his answer to the stock question inquiring about what he did the night before the big game, "I took a broad and a bottle of scotch to bed [Batten, 1971, p. 2]." [4]

Anti-hero athletes have the seductive quality that Klapp (1969) underscored, a quality which may induce young fans to bend the rules and resist the established order. Since Namath appeared with a Fu Manchu beard and white playing shoes this equipment has become de rigueur for many football players. This is not to say that such influences necessarily are bad, only that seductive heroes inevitably invite changes in established patterns of behavior.

It would be rare for an athlete to fit Klapp's (1969) transcendent category. An athletic hero normally does not have the power to take his followers outside the bounds of the social structure to produce a person with a new identity. Athletics represent stability and conservatism, the antithesis of what the transcendent hero stands for.

The Demise of the Sports Hero

"Where have you gone Joe DiMaggio, a nation turns its lonely eyes to you." [5] This lament from a recent popular song seems to say it all about the disappearance of the traditional hero. What we seem to have left is a collection of incomplete or tarnished quasi-heroes. We still have the need to worship heroes, but the models that are available are becoming less and less exemplary. Klapp (1969) has noticed this trend and has reappraised his definition of a celebrity hero. "A celebrity hero is not someone who is especially good, but only someone who realizes dreams for people that they cannot do for themselves [p. 214]."

Hook (1957) claims that there is little opportunity for genuine heroism in a democratic society. The hallmark of heroism is singularity, and in a democracy it is difficult for one individual to have significant effect on matters. In this connection, the editors of *Time* (1966) noted that heroes now are emerging as composite figures rather than as individuals. The astronauts are used to illustrate this point, very few people remember all of them individually, but they do have the status of a collective hero. Deford (1969) bemoans the fact that this lack of interest in the individual hero has carried over into sport.

> Sport offers too much tribute to the peripheral contributions of the super-numeraries at the expense of the great stars who really make it. Writers and commentators (must they be "color men?") wallow in mechanical expertise. It is always shrewd planning, gears meshing, wonderful organization. Perhaps it only reflects our anonymous lives, but it is forever the battle plan that is celebrated not the classic individual achievement [p. 34].

One hundred years ago when there was a paucity of mass communication, myth making was easy, for it was difficult to refute stories about athletic heroes. When mass communications started to cover sporting events they continued to preserve the sanctity of the athletic hero. Comments either written or spoken about athletes seldom were objective, they served only to patronize and glorify the athlete. Often the mass media created heroes out of athletes who were less than deserving. Babe Ruth, for example, was one of the most celebrated sports heroes of all time, but as Schecter (1970) observes, "Ruth had an undisciplined appetite for food, whiskey and women [p. 119]." Schecter goes on to say that "little of this was available to the contemporary public. The Babe was thoroughly protected by the news media [p. 119]." Hook (1957) concurs with the latter judgment when he notes the pervasive control of mass media over the process of hero making.

Today, more than ever before belief in "the hero" is a synthetic product. Whoever controls the microphones and printing presses can make or unmake beliefs overnight [p. 10].

Sport Magazine (1970) in an introspective editorial actually apologized for its lack of objectivity in covering athletic heroes.

It is true that for many years "Sport" along with the rest of the world treated the big-name athlete in a Frank Merriwell fashion. We were all content to dote on his statistics, on what he ate for breakfast, on his serene home life, on his virtues as a man. And we over-laid the portrait with a heavy helping of pancake makeup, lest any blemishes peek through [p. 84].

This uncritical attitude on the part of the mass media has changed somewhat in recent years. Irreverent books such as: Schecter's *The Jocks,* Meggyesy's *Out of Their League* (1970), Bouton's *Ball Four* (1971), Conacher's *Hockey in Canada: The Way It Is* (1970) and Barnes' *The Plastic Orgasm* (1971) have ripped the halos from modern sports heroes. This type of book is an antidote to cloying trade books like Robertson's *Rusty Staub of the Expos* (1971). Jennings (1971), when reviewing the latter, found that after wading through paeans of repetitious praise he "expected an announcement of mass canonization with every page [p. 14]."

In the electronic media the move away from sugar coating has been slower, but at least one United States network has attempted a small gesture in that direction. The American Broadcasting Company employs the acerbic Howard Cosell as a color man on their Monday night football telecasts. Cosell's central claim to fame is that he tells it like it is (Lisker, 1971). It seems that the mass media which once pandered to athletic heroes now is contributing to their decanonization, if not their decline.

Another reason for the loss of interest in sports heroes is that there are just too many sports and too many teams for people to follow. The overall growth of sport has had a benumbing effect on fans. Who can keep the perpet- ually expanding and reorganizing leagues straight, let alone the athletes and the tidal wave of related statistics? A further consequence of sport expansion is that there are too many good performers. It is difficult to distinguish between the great player, the record holder and the good player. Perhaps Deford's (1969) term "impact champion" is useful here, the only true heroes being those athletes whose mere presence makes a sizeable increase in the box office take.

Athletic heroes are losing their credibility and thus their utility for many fans. More and more it is player holdouts and potential strikes that fill the sports pages. Fans seek sports heroes to escape, not to be burdened with the economic problems of the professional athlete. It becomes difficult to sympathize or even identify with the six figure athlete if you are an eight thousand dollar-a-year man yourself.

The athlete also loses credibility when he is seen in less than flattering advertisements. Joe Namath getting $10,000 to shave his beard for a TV commercial is seen as a rip-off by many fans. Famous athletes seen crying for their Maypo and lathering up with Rise are degraded by the banal dialogue placed in their mouths. Ross (1971) declared recently that the testimonial was not a particularly effective method of selling. If the sport testimonial doesn't do much for the product, it may achieve even less for the hero athlete who is doing the shilling.

The public is becoming increasingly wary of being used by their sports heroes. Athletes who have lately tried to use their names as spring boards into politics and business have been rebuffed. In recent Canadian and American elections only those former athletes who were eminently qualified were elected (Ryan, 1970). In business many well known athletes have found that their name was not enough. Last year a number of athletes with floundering businesses were forced to file for bankruptcy.

The decline of the athletic hero may also be linked to the fact that many of them represent counter culture values. The counter culture is only a sub-culture and the majority simply do not relate to this system of values (Agnew and Johnson, 1971).

Summary

The hero is an ancient and honorable role of great cultural utility. Heroes are created in many guises and perform many functions. As a special object of adulation, the sports hero is both the instrument of and the mirror for a variety of social processes. Consequently, changes in cultural value systems evoke parallel changes in the archetype elected to heroic status in sport. It is not unexpected, therefore, to find that the relationship between sports heroes and their audience has altered in the fast pace of recent years. Whether the traditional sport hero simply is undergoing a metamorphosis, to later emerge in a new and vital cultural role, or indeed has reached the end of his usefulness and is doomed to extinction, only the unwinding of the century can reveal.

REFERENCES

1. Agnew, S. and Johnson, W. Not infected with the conceit of infallibility. *Sports Illustrated.* June 21, 1971, pp. 61-75.
2. Bandura, A. Social-learning theory of identificatory processes, in D.A. Goslin. *Handbook of socialization theory and research.* Chicago: Rand McNally and Co., 1969, pp. 213-262.
3. Barnes, L. *The plastic orgasm.* Toronto: McLelland and Stewart, 1971.
4. Batten, J. Whatever happened to the clean-living athletes who were a credit to the game? *Canadian Magazine.* March 13, 1971, pp. 2-6.
5. Bouton, J. *Ball four.* New York: Dell Publishing Co., 1971.
6. Boyle, R.H. *Sport—mirror of American life.* Boston: Little Brown and Co., 1963.
7. Carlyle, T. *On heroes and hero worship.* London: Oxford University Press, 1840.
8. Coleman, J. *The adolescent society.* New York: Free Press, 1961.
9. Conacher, B. *Hockey in Canada: the way it is.* Toronto: Gateway Press, 1970.
10. Deford, F. What price heroes? *Sports Illustrated,* June 9, 1969, pp. 33-40.
11. Dowling, T. The Orr effect. *Atlantic,* April, 1971, Vol. 227.
12. Fishwick, M. *American heroes, myth and reality.* Washington, D.C.: Public Affairs Press, 1954.
13. Friesen, D. Academic-athletic-popularity syndrome in Canadian high school society (1967). *Adolescence.* Vol. III, No. 9, Spring, 1968.
14. Gurko, L. *Heroes, highbrows and the popular mind.* Indianapolis: Charter Books, 1953.
15. Hook, S. *The hero in history: a study in limitation and possibility.* Boston: Beacon Press, 1957.
16. Jennings, C. Semi-canonization of a sports hero. *Toronto Globe and Mail Magazine.* September 4, 1971, p. 14.
17. Johnson, W. The greatest athlete in Yates Center, Kansas. *Sports Illustrated,* August 9, 1971, pp. 27-31.
18. Kirshenbaum, J. Bats and busts, size-15 sneakers and a dead bird. *Sports Illustrated,* June 28, 1971, pp. 63-74.
19. Klapp, O.E. *Heroes, villains and fools.* Englewood Cliffs: Prentice-Hall Inc., 1962.
20. Klapp, O.E. *Collective search for identity.* New York: Holt Rinehart and Winston Inc., 1969.
21. Lehman, B.H. *Carlyle's theory of the hero.* Durham, N.C.: Duke University Press, 1928.
22. Lerner, M. *America as a civilization.* Vol. 2, New York: Simon and Schuster, 1957.
23. Linderman, L. The Tom McMillen affair. *Playboy,* Nov., 1971, p. 148.
24. Lisker, J. Cosell explains his success: a man has to take a stand. *Detroit Free Press.* May 2, 1971, Sec. D, p. 6.
25. Meggyesy, D. *Out of their league.* Berkeley: Ramparts Press Inc., 1970.
26. Ricke, T. A town where boys are kings and the court business is basketball. *Detroit Free Press Magazine,* March 14, 1971, pp. 6-11.
27. Ross, N. Hitch your product to a star. *Washington Post,* August 31, 1971, pp. 1-2.
28. Russell, W.F. Success is a journey. *Sports Illustrated,* June 8, 1970, pp. 81-93.
29. Ryan, P. The making of a quarterback 1970. *Sports Illustrated,* December 7, 1970, p. 83.
30. Sagarin, E. Who roots for the underdog? *Journal of Popular Culture,* Fall, 1970, Vol. IV, No. 2, pp. 425-431.
31. Schafer, W. *Sport socialization and the school.* Paper presented at the Third International Symposium on the Sociology of Sport. Waterloo, Ontario, August 22-28, 1971.
32. Schecter, L. *The jocks.* New York: Paperback Library, 1970.
33. Schwartz, J.M. *Causes and effects of spectator sports.* Paper presented at the Third International Symposium on the Sociology of Sport. Waterloo, Ontario, August 22-28, 1971.
34. Scott, J. Sauer power. Monthly column from the Institute for the Study of Sport in Society. October, 1971.
35. *Sport.* Frank Merriwell is dead. (In Time out with the editors.) *Sport,* April, 1970, p. 84.
36. *Time Essay.* On the difficulty of being a contemporary hero. *Time,* June 24, 1966, p. 24.
37. Wecter, D. *The hero in America.* Ann Arbor: University of Michigan Press, 1963.

NOTES

1. Friesen (1968) claims that this is not the case in Canada where academics outrank athletics in the high school value system.
2. A quote by J.M. Schwartz (1971) is relevant here:
   . . . baseball cards don't just sell bubble gum. They are a small cog in an elaborate socialization system which aids in the process of molding youngsters to fit the American way of life.
3. For example *Paper Lion* and *Bogey Man* by George Plimpton, *Instant Replay* by Jerry Kramer and *Ball Four* by Jim Bouton.
4. Bill Russell (1970) trenchantly summarizes the establishment's point of view when speaking of Joe Namath. Russell says that he likes Namath personally, but that he doesn't admire or respect him because Namath stands for nothing except having a good time.
5. From the song "Mrs. Robinson" by P. Simon and A. Garfunkel.

DISCUSSION QUESTIONS

A. *Orrin E. Klapp*

1. List and briefly discuss the major phases of hero worship as a social process.
2. What is so paradoxical about the combination of *distance* with *closeness* in hero worship?
3. How do heroes contribute to such important societal functions as personality development, education, and social control?
4. Are there any negative aspects to hero worship? Explain your answer.
5. How do you explain the seemingly high incidence of hero worship in the United States?

B. *Randy Roberts*

1. How did Dempsey's emergence as a hero in 1919 follow the pattern that Klapp outlined in his article, "Hero Worship in America"?
2. Dempsey's emergence as a popular hero following his destruction of Jess Willard on July 4, 1919 helped satisfy what important emotional need of the American people?
3. How did the printing press, painting, drama, and the cinema help to mold the popular Dempsey image?
4. In what ways was the heavyweight championship fight between Dempsey and Georges Carpentier on July 2, 1921 more than just a ring battle between two men? How did the outcome of the fight contribute to Dempsey's heroic image?
5. What aspects of Dempsey's life and boxing career were *less* than heroic?
6. In order to know what Dempsey meant to, or, represented about the 1920's, one must know what about the American temperament during this decade?

C. *Garry Smith*

1. Why do people worship heroes?
2. Why has the sport hero been such a popular object of adulation in American society and not the politician, scientist, doctor, or teacher?

3. If Smith is correct in his assertion that "the sports hero is an accurate barometer of the times," what changes, if any, in societal values do each of the following contemporary sports heroes represent: Billie Jean King, Bobbie Clarke, Johnny Miller, O.J. Simpson, Walt Frazier, Muhammed Ali, Johnny Bench, and Evel Knievel?

4. Would you classify the majority of today's sports heroes as "reinforcing," "seductive," or "transcendent"? Explain your answer.

5. What factors have contributed to the apparent demise of the traditional, idealized, reinforcing, sports hero? Do you think that we have seen the last of such legendary sports heroes as Babe Ruth, Jack Dempsey, Red Grange, Joe Louis, and Willie Mays? Explain your answer.

6. In what ways can an understanding of the sports hero help us acquire insight into the relationship between sport and the American sociocultural system?

Unit V

An Assessment of the Value of Competition

Call it the "competitive urge," the "competitive spirit," or, the "competitive ethic," the fact is, competition is synonymous with the American way of life. Whether it be "sibling rivalry" in the family, Democrats versus Republicans in the political arena, organized religions bidding against one another for followers, or, the Army outlobbying the Navy for military appropriations, institutional competition is the rule of thumb in the United States and winning is the name of the game. The presence of "hot" competition and the inordinate importance placed on winning is perhaps no better observed than in the world of sport. The famous quote attributed to the late Vince Lombardi that "Winning isn't everything, it's the only thing," reflects the feelings of many who identify with sport, including most players, coaches, and fans. For example, after a recent Bluebonnet Bowl football game that wound up in a 31-31 tie, players from both teams generally considered it a *loss* even though the game was one of the most exciting, well-played contests in recent memory. In the last few years, however, the competitive way of life has come under considerable scrutiny and criticism. Not only are the excesses of competition under attack, but competition as a cultural value is being seriously questioned. That this reassessment of competition may have profound implications for the sport institution and its future is strongly suggested in the three selections which follow.

In the first selection, educator Arthur Combs discusses three popular beliefs about competition, namely, the very competitive nature of American society, the motivational force of competition, and the use of competition for quality control. The implications of this article for sport are obvious since it is beliefs such as these that provide the support and justification for the importance placed on competition and winning in sports today.

Author and lecturer George Leonard continues Combs' critical analysis of competition in the second selection. In short order, Leonard labels the late Vince Lombardi's dictum that "Winning isn't everything, it's the only thing" our society's neurosis, refutes the popular notion that human evolution is the product of competition, questions the commonly held belief that "competition motivates behavior" and, charges that "hot" competition makes losers of us all. Leonard argues that our glorification of competition and winning in sports reflects our society's neurotic and corrosive social structure and a way of life that is eventually doomed if peaceful, humane changes are not forthcoming.

In the final selection, President Gerald R. Ford, and sports writer John Underwood, present a point of view that is shared by millions but not frequently stated in the public forum. In response to a lot of "home-cooked psychology in recent years that winning isn't all that important anymore," the authors take the offensive and argue that competition and winning on the athletic field are more important than ever and directly related to achieving personal excellence, healthful living, all-round character, and leadership on the individual level, and, national prestige, power, and morale on the societal level. In this far-ranging article in which the President offers his opinions on a variety of sport-related topics, he makes the point in no uncertain terms that he is unalterably opposed to any efforts that would "water down" America's competitive urge.

THE MYTH OF COMPETITION

Arthur W. Combs

Every age has been the victim of its myths. Ours is no exception. When people believed the world was flat, they stayed from the edge for fear of falling over. When people believed in witches, innocent people were put to death. When it was thought that illness was the result of "bad blood," many a defenseless sick man was "cured" of his malady by bleeding him to death. Myths can have disastrous consequences vitally affecting our ability to deal with pressing problems.

Guided by Beliefs

All this would not be so bad if it were not for the unfortunate effects a myth can have upon our success in dealing with our pressing human problems. What a man believes is important. If he believes the Democrats have the right answers to government, he votes the Democratic ticket. If he believes the Republicans would do a better job, he votes for the GOP. He can only behave in terms of what seems to him to be so. This will be true whether the beliefs he holds are *really* so or not. As individuals or as nations, our beliefs guide our every act. Myths, false beliefs, have the same effects as true ones.

Imprisoned by Misconceptions

Horrible as it seems to us today, the snake pit treatment of the insane in the last century seemed sane and sensible to our forefathers who believed in the myth of men possessed of devils. Myths always seem right and proper to those who hold them. They always have. They still do. We, too, can be prisoners of our misconceptions, dupes of our false beliefs. Among the worse offenders in our time is the myth of competition.

Misled by Fables

"Competition," we have told ourselves, "is a powerful motivating force!" "We live in a competitive society!" "Competition makes us efficient and improves the quality of the product!" These are fables with which we delude ourselves in this generation. These are principles we have often chosen to guide us in industry, government, athletics—even in education. If these principles are not true, we run a great risk.

We cannot afford to become victims of our myths any longer than absolutely necessary. Modern myths can be just as frustrating and inaccurate as those of years ago. Confusion in our beliefs leads to confusion in our acts. Beliefs based upon false assumptions lead to behavior that is likewise false and ineffective. It is particularly important in time of world crises that the fundamental assumptions on which we base behavior be as clear and precise as we can make them. Above all, we cannot afford to base our educational system upon fallacies lest

we saddle the next generation with our own misperceptions. If our beliefs about competition are myths, we need to re-examine some of our most cherished fundamental assumptions.

Myths are insidious things. They provide us with comfort and lull us to sleep. The great danger of myths is not that they are wrong. Rather the danger lies in the fact that myths are likely to be partly right. Unfortunately, there is nothing more dangerous than a half-right idea. A half truth is worse than a falsehood. Falsehood is easy to reject, but half truths have just enough of the genuine to give us a feeling of contentment. They encourage us to go on in the ways we have started in the vain hope that, if we can but do it a little better or try a little harder, surely sooner or later we shall achieve perfection. Sometimes this does happen. But sometimes it is better to give up the old ideas and search for better ones.

Let us examine the three most common beliefs about competition.

Myth #1. *We live in a competitive society.* **The Fact:** *We live in the most cooperative interdependent society the world has ever known!* Two great trends in history have made cooperation an absolute must for our way of life—the ever increasing dependence of people on one another and the tremendous increase of power in the hands of individuals. The world has become a very small place where we live, almost literally, in each other's laps. People of whom we have never heard produce and control our food, clothing and shelter. Thousands of people are involved in the delivery of a quart of milk to our door each morning! Milk would never reach us without the smooth cooperation of all friends on whom we depend for its production, processing, and transportation from the cow to our doorstep. Thousands more are or have been engaged in producing machinery for handling crops to feed cows, for pasteurizing and bottling the milk or in building roads and vehicles which make its transportation possible.

We are impressed by the competitive features of our society and like to think of ourselves as essentially a competitive people. Yet we are thoroughly and completely dependent upon the goodwill and cooperation of millions of our fellow men. From the engineer who keeps the electric turbines running through the night to the garbage men who keep our cities livable, each of us must rely on others to carry out the tasks we cannot perform ourselves. Few of us could live for more than a very short

"The Myth of Competition" in *Childhood Education* Vol. 33, pp. 264-68, February 1957 by Arthur W. Combs. Reprinted by permission of Arthur W. Combs and the Association for Childhood Education International, 3615 Wisconsin Avenue, N.W., Washington, D.C. Copyright © 1957 by the Association.

Arthur W. Combs is professor of education, College of Education, University of Florida, Gainesville.

time apart from others. Whether we like it or not, we are thoroughly and completely dependent upon the goodwill and cooperation of others at every moment of our lives. In turn, thousands of other people are dependent on us. We are indeed "our brothers' keepers" as never before in history.

Although it is true that we occasionally compete with others, competition is not the rule of life but the exception. Competition makes the news, while cooperation supplies the progress. One needs but to reflect on his own past twenty-four hours to discover how overwhelmingly his behavior has been cooperative and how seldom competitive.

The great industrial and scientific advances of the last century have made individual people more important than ever. The net effect of our great technological advances has been to place ever-increasing amounts of power in the hands of ordinary people. Even the least of us has control over the welfare of others. The average man has hundreds of horsepower at his fingertips at the nearest light switch. When he sits behind the wheel of his car, he has a fearful projectile at his command. He could not drive unless he could count on others to cooperate with him by staying on his own side of the road. The welfare and safety of each of us in a cooperative society depends upon the cooperation of each of our fellow citizens. We may live for days without competing with others, but we cooperate from morning to night.

The very history of our country has been one of increasing cooperation. Our nation was founded when a group of separate colonies agreed to join in a cooperative republic. Our great Civil War was fought to assure continued cooperation between North and South. Our legislatures, courts, government bureaus and agencies are institutions for cooperative effort. Who can forget the tremendous cooperative effort carried on by our armed forces in World War II? At the very moment we pat ourselves on the back as a great competitive people, we stand in awe of the release of atomic energy, the greatest cooperative scientific effort of all time.

Even our great industries which we often point out with pride as samples of our competitive way of life turn out, on closer analysis, to be outstanding examples of cooperation. Although they loudly proclaim the virtues of competition, our great industrial organizations are thoroughly dependent upon the smooth integration of thousands of interdependent workers. We are likely to forget that the great contribution of Henry Ford to modern industry was the development of the assembly line—a highly organized method of getting people to work together in the manufacture of a product. Our great "competitive" industries are marvels of cooperative effort.

Despite the fact that we live in the most cooperative, interdependent society the world has ever known, we persist in the fallacy that our way of life is based on competition. Even worse, some would have us teach our children, who must live in a cooperative world, that competition is the way to successful living! This is training children to live in a world that does not exist! Fortunately, children themselves resist this process with great vigor. We are lucky indeed that they never quite fall for this deception. They quickly learn for themselves the value of working together and cooperate just like the grownups they see around them.

Myth #2. *Competition is a powerful motivating force.* **The Fact:** *Only those compete who feel they have a chance of winning. The rest ignore the competition.*

Psychologists, sociologists and educators who have been doing research on competition for several decades tell us that the people who work for prizes—who enter into competition with other people—are only those who feel they have a chance of winning. Competition is of limited value as a means of motivation since it motivates few. We do not work for things we feel we cannot achieve. We work only for things that seem within our grasp. It makes little difference how the situation looks to an outsider. We are motivated by competition only *when we feel we have a chance of winning.* It may seem to others we have a splendid chance for success; if it doesn't seem so to us it might just as well not be so. No one has yet figured out a way of making people feel what does not seem to them to be so. Our feelings are still our private property.

People who do not see much chance of success cannot be inveigled into making an effort. They ignore the competition whenever they are able. Any teacher knows that children who work for scholastic honors are only the few who feel a possibility of winning. The rest of the children sit back and let the competitors work like crazy while the noncompetitors go about more important business of their own choosing. Those who feel they cannot achieve are quite content to let others do it. This is very frustrating in children, but adults behave so too. On any fall Saturday afternoon one can find in any football stadium thousands of adults who need exercise gathered to watch twenty-two men who don't need it get it. Competition exists only among those who feel able. The rest of us sit back as spectators and watch them beat their brains out. Competition as a means of motivation has been vastly over-rated.

Forcing people to compete may even have serious negative consequences, for *competition is threatening and discouraging to those who feel they cannot compete.* Competition is often used as a means of getting people to extend themselves. Although it is thought to be a means of "challenging" people, it may actually be severely threatening. Whether or not competition is challenging or threatening will depend upon how the situation seems to the competitor, not how it seems to an outsider. The difference between threat and challenge is something inside of one. People feel challenged when confronted with a situation they feel able to deal with successfully. They feel threatened and discouraged by situations that seem to them beyond their capacities. What seems like a challenge to an outsider may seem to an individual to be deeply threatening and discouraging. How things seem to people is an internal affair that goes on inside their own skins and is only indirectly open to external manipulation.

Left to themselves people will compete only rarely, and then only when they feel a chance of success. Forcing people to compete in spite of themselves can only result in discouragement or rebellion. That is what people are like. When the cards are stacked against us, we give up playing or start a fight with the people responsible for the stacking. Forced to compete against his will, a child may simply "go through the motions" of his job in a dispirited listless manner or break out in some form of opposition to his oppressors. It is only those who have been fairly successful who value competition so highly. *People do not learn to feel able by repeated experience of failure.*

A democratic society is dependent upon our ability to produce people who see themselves as adequate and able. People who feel inadequate to deal with life are, at best, a drag upon society and, at worst, an outright danger. An interdependent way of life like ours requires people who feel adequate and able and who are dependable. One of the great tragedies of our time is that millions of people feel far less able than they really are. What is more, because they feel so they behave so. This in turn leads to a deadly vicious circle. Believing themselves inadequate, people behave inadequately. The rest of us, seeing them behave inadequately, judge them to be inadequate, which proves what they thought in the first place! This kind of merry-go-round can be dangerous to our way of life. People without faith in themselves are fair game for the Communist lure of salvation. We cannot afford a threatened and discouraged population. Too much is at stake.

The aim of competition is to win and the temptation is to win at any cost. Although it begins with the laudable aim of encouraging production, competition quickly breaks down to a struggle to win at any price. Competition is a powerful motivating force—for those who think they have a chance of winning. Winning, itself, is a "heady" business which can become an end in itself, trapping the competitor in a net of his own making. Many schools can observe this in their own varsity sports where the game and the players are often lost in the desperate need for victory.

The means we use to achieve our ends are always bought at a price. The price of winning may be more than we want to pay. Price tags must be read not only in dollars and cents; they must be read as well in terms of human values, of broken bodies, broken spirits and disheartened and disillusioned people who do not appear in the winner's circle, on the sports pages or as guests of honor at the testimonial banquet.

Competition encourages lone-wolf endeavors, and lone-wolves can be dangerous to a cooperative society. We need to be able to count on other people to seek our best interests along with their own. In the headlong rush to win, competition too easily loses sight of responsibility. It values aggression, hostility and scorn. "Dog eat dog" becomes its philosophy. Too often the degree of glory involved for the victor is only in direct proportion to the abasement and degradation of the loser.

Myth #3. *Competition is a useful device for controlling and improving quality.* **The Fact:** *Competition is inefficient and outmoded as a means for quality production.*

Progress of society is dependent upon success in producing the best possible products at the least possible cost. This is true whether we are talking about things or people. Furthermore, to assure improvement, we need to engage in a continual process of evaluation of our products and ourselves. We need to be forever engaged in a process of quality testing. Quality testing, however, should not be confused with competition.

Through a kind of "survival of the fittest," competition has historically served as a rough device for screening out quality. There can be no doubt that contrast is an effective means of emphasizing the respective qualities of objects being compared. There can be no doubt either that this sort of elimination process does provide us with a kind of quality testing. But at what a price! With all the means of quality testing which modern science has placed at our disposal, must we still be tied to horse and buggy methods? While competition may result in better products over a period of time, it is an inefficient and fumbling means of improving quality at best. Like going from New York to Chicago, you can make it on foot if you like, but it takes a lot longer that way.

Although competition may sometimes serve as a primitive approach to quality testing, these two are by no means the same. Quality testing seeks to discover the facts, to determine quality on the basis of disinterested examination. Competition is not concerned with production of quality, but with winning acceptance. One seeks facts, the other seeks to convince. One seeks the truth as an end in itself, the other uses the truth for its own extrinsic purposes.

Encourages Deception

The aim of competition often becomes one of winning the market rather than producing a better product. The salesman competing for my business is not so much interested in producing a good product as in *selling* his product regardless of its defects. He does not display its weaknesses; he hides them. Competition seeks to prove superiority, even if it does not exist. It places the emphasis upon capturing the buyer rather than producing a better product. As a result it encourages deception and places a premium upon dishonesty. Quality testing, on the other hand, examines the product and rests its case on quality. It is a scientific approach to the improvement of people or things. Competition as a means of assuring us of quality has been almost entirely supplanted by the much better, more efficient means supplied by modern science. So accurate is much of this testing that with modern methods we can even predict the quality of an airplane wing before it is made!

Controls Prices

The major value of competition in our modern industrial structure seems to lie in its control of prices. By placing two products in competition we sometimes encourage producers to cut costs and lower prices. Interestingly enough, even then they can only cut costs by improved cooperation for more efficient production. In recent years businessmen themselves have turned their backs on competition. Fair trade laws are needed, they claim, to prevent their being forced out of business by cut-throat competition!

Competition and Democracy

The kind of interdependent cooperative society we live in requires people upon whom we can depend. Competition destroys feeling of trust in ourselves and other people. By glorifying winning even at the cost of human values, competition produces a fear of other people. This is in direct contradiction to the kind of attitude required for a successful cooperating organization. A cooperative society like ours must be based upon faith in other people. One cannot cooperate effectively with people he fears.

The success of a democracy depends upon the production of independent people of dignity and integrity provided with accurate and realistic information about themselves and their surroundings. What undermines respect for ourselves or other people is dangerous to all of us. Whether we like it or not, we are completely dependent on the goodwill of our fellows at every moment of modern complex existence. What destroys trust in ourselves or others makes communication difficult and cripples cooperative effort.

When our beliefs have been clear and accurate, we have made progress. As each age has succeeded in casting off the shackles of its peculiar myths and misperceptions, it has found new ways to deal with old problems, more effective means of achieving a better life for all. When we gave up thinking that weather was solely the whim of the gods, its prediction became possible. The science of medicine became possible with development of the germ theory of disease. Whenever we have succeeded in throwing off the shackles of our current myths and fables we have found it possible to make new strides toward greater understanding and a better life. This has been true in every age, and it's just as true in ours.

The greatest problems of our times are problems of human interrelationships. We cannot afford to be guided in these relationships by misconceptions about how these human relations can best be achieved. We cannot afford to base educational practices on ideas of doubtful value. Education cannot be satisfied with part truths. The stakes are too great. Unless we can learn to live together, we may not live at all. The myth of competition has been with us long enough.

WINNING ISN'T EVERYTHING. IT'S NOTHING.

George B. Leonard

In less than a generation, the prevailing sports ethos in America has shifted from, "It's not whether you win or lose, it's how you play the game," to "Winning isn't everything. It's the only thing." The current public glorification of winning at all costs came to the fore during a war we did not win. Sermons by top corporate executives on hot competition as the American way were being directed at the younger generation during a period when many of these same executives were making every effort to get around the federal regulations against price-fixing and illegal cooperation among corporate "competitors." The use of sports terminology by our national administration became commonplace just before the nation learned how misleading and disastrous "game plans" and "enemy lists" can be.

If winning has become our national religion, the Super Bowl is its apotheosis. But the ceremony, in spite of the huge crowd, the music, the flags, the pom-pom girls, the special coin struck off in memory of the late Vince Lombardi, is somehow unconvincing. We are embarrassed when the three Apollo 17 astronauts, paraded out to lead the Pledge of Allegiance, become confused, make several false starts and look at each other to see if the right hand should be placed over the heart. And we are perhaps relieved when their ordeal ends and a disembodied voice floats out over the stadium: "Now, to honor America, let's join The Little Angels for the singing of the national anthem."

Contradictions, anomalies and grotesqueries in the current sports scene should not surprise us. A neurosis asserts itself most painfully and insistently just as it is being uprooted and cast out. The final period in any

From *Intellectual Digest*, October 1973, pp. 45-47. Published by Ziff-Davis Publishing Company.

evolutionary line of development—of a biological species, an artistic movement or a society—is often marked by convolution, overspecialization and other bizarre extremes. If, as many scholars have pointed out, a society's sports and games mirror its basic structure, then what we may be seeing in the current worship of hot competition and winning at all costs is the end of a particular line of social development. The Super Bowl may ultimately stand as a symbol of a culture in transformation.

Because our own sports are so highly competitive, we may tend to believe that all human beings, especially males, are born competitors, driven by their genetic nature to the proposition that winning is "the only thing." The games of many cultures, however, have no competitive element whatever. For example, the Tangu people of New Guinea play a popular game known as *taketak,* which involves throwing a spinning top into massed lots of stakes driven into the ground. There are two teams. Players of each team try to touch as many stakes with their tops as possible. In the end, however, the participants play not to win but to draw. The game must go on until an exact draw is reached. This requires great skill, since players sometimes must throw their tops into the massed stakes without touching a single one. *Taketak* expresses a prime value in Tangu culture, that is, the concept of moral equivalency, which is reflected in the precise sharing of foodstuffs among the people.

"The notion that humans evolved through relentless competition with nature and each other is false."

Indeed, the notion that humans evolved only through relentless, grinding competition with nature and each other is a false one. The familiar cartoon showing the caveman as a brutish creature carrying a club with one hand and dragging a woman by the other tells us nothing about primitive life. The Stone Age peoples that survive in remote corners of the world are, until we meddle with them, usually gentle and sensitive, with a fine ecological sense. The recently discovered Tasaday tribe of Mindanao in the Philippines, true Stone Age cave dwellers, have no words for "hate" or "fight." They are cooperative and loving. The brute in the cartoon is our secret image of ourselves.

Darwin's theory—natural selection, the "survival of the fittest"—is sometimes cited as justification for hot competition. Social philosophers of the propertied, industrial classes in the late nineteenth and early twentieth centuries promoted a brutal, jungle philosophy, but it was based on Darwin's account of the predatory rather than the social animals. This social Darwinism was long ago discredited. Charles Darwin is clear on the point that, for the human race, the highest survival value lies in intelligence, a moral sense and social cooperation, not competition.

Among the English-speaking peoples, the close and inevitable relationship between sport and competition is of fairly recent origin. According to *Webster's New Inter-*national Dictionary (second edition), the word "sport" comes from "disport," which originally meant "to carry away from work." The first definition applied to the word is, "that which diverts and makes mirth; pastime; amusement." In a series of definitions 40 lines long, there is no mention whatever of competition and only one brief reference to sport as a "contest."

The attempt to justify hot competition as an essential aspect of human existence goes on in the face of all the evidence. There exists, for example, a common assumption that competition is needed to "motivate behavior." Yet no study has shown that competition necessarily motivates behavior any more effectively than other means—extrinsic reinforcement, for instance, or even the sheer joy of doing something well. To see the real function of competition in our society, we must look deeper.

In 1967, I collaborated with Marshall McLuhan on an article entitled, "The Future of Education." Our idea sessions ranged over a number of topics but kept coming back to the question of competition and why it is so tirelessly proclaimed, not only by coaches, but by educators and all those traditionalists who concern themselves with shaping the lives of our young people. At last, McLuhan came forth with one of his "probes"—a sudden thought from an unexpected direction.

"I know," he said. "Competition creates resemblance."

To compete with someone, in other words, you must agree to run on the same track, to do what he is doing, to follow the same set of rules. The only way you'll differentiate yourself is by doing precisely the same thing, slightly faster or better. Thus, though performance may improve, the chances are you will become increasingly like the person with whom you compete.

In this light, it is easy to see that a culture dedicated to creating standardized, specialized, predictable human components could find no better way of grinding them out than by making every possible aspect of life a matter of competition. "Winning out" in this respect does not make rugged individualists. It shapes conformist robots. Keep your eyes open during the football season. The defensive ends begin to look more and more alike. The cornerbacks become ever more interchangeable.

The final argument for hot competition all the way down to nursery school is that competition makes winners. The argument is, at best, half true. It makes nonwinners, too—generally more nonwinners than winners. And a number of studies indicate that losing can become a lifelong habit. What is more, when competition reaches the present level, the argument becomes altogether false. As proclaimed by the more extreme coaches and sportswriters today, competition makes us—all of us—losers.

Between 1958 and 1971, the San Francisco Giants had the best overall won-lost record in the National League. For five straight years, from 1965 through 1969, they finished in second place. To do so, you would think, they must have "won out" over many other teams. Increasingly during this period of second-place finishes, however, they came to be characterized by fan and sportswriter alike as born losers.

"Winning isn't everything. It's the only thing." And in our present-day sports culture, that means being Number One, Numero Uno, the one and only.

Take the Dallas Cowboys. For five straight years, from 1966 through 1970, the Cowboys won their division championships, then were eliminated, either in the play-offs or finally, in January of 1971, in the Super Bowl itself. And what was said of this fine professional football team during this period of unprecedented winning? They "couldn't win the big ones." They were, you see, just losers.

"Competition makes more nonwinners than winners. Studies indicate that losing can become a habit."

When the Cowboys did at last win the Super Bowl, in January 1972, it became apparent that the players themselves had been swept up in the Numero Uno mystique. One by one they came to the TV cameras after the game to affirm that nothing had really meant anything except this victory. The champagne flowed. The players were probably happy for a moment, but their faces were not entirely unclouded. And the mask of fear that coach Tom Landry wears along the sidelines during every game when his winning record is threatened was not entirely erased. The problem is this: even after you've just won the Super Bowl—*especially* after you've just won the Super Bowl—*there's always next year*.

If "Winning isn't everything. It's the only thing," then "the only thing" is nothing—emptiness, the nightmare of life without ultimate meaning. This emptiness pursues us wherever "winning out" is proclaimed as God. I once spoke to a group of top-ranking industrialists in a seminar session and argued that hot competition is far from inevitable in the future. As my argument developed, I noticed a look of real anxiety on some of the faces around me. One industrialist finally spoke up, "If there is to be no competition, then what will life be all about?" We would probably be appalled to discover how many people in this culture have no notion of accomplishment for its own sake and define their own existence solely in terms of how many other people they can beat out.

Only through this viewpoint can we understand how a talented young athlete can let himself become what Gary Shaw in his new book has called *Meat on the Hoof*, a commodity to be manipulated, hazed, drugged, used, traded and discarded. And we may be able, by imagining the emptiness that accompanies "winning," to comprehend why (as David Meggyesy has revealed in his book, *Out of Their League*) a prototype of super-masculinity would allow himself to be treated in the

manner of a eunuch, prevented at times from having sexual relations with his own wife.

There is nothing wrong with competition in the proper proportion. Like a little salt, it adds zest to the game and to life itself. But when the seasoning is mistaken for the substance, only sickness can follow. Similarly, when winning becomes "the only thing," it can lead only to eventual emptiness and anomie.

The time has come, I feel, to blow the whistle on this madness. We may not be able to turn the American sports juggernaut around overnight, but we can suggest that sports are possible without beating the brains out of the opposing team, and that it may be possible for players and fans alike to take great pleasure in a beautiful play, even if it's executed by the opposition. We can start working out new sports that are noncompetitive or less competitive or in which competition is placed in the proper perspective, as a matter of good sport and good humor. We can start looking for the larger potentialities that actually already exist in the realm of sports and games.

Our present way of life, based upon endless, ever-increasing expansion of the production and consumption of energy, is eventually doomed. And so much else is based upon that expansion—our definition of job and full employment, our inculcation and suppression of aggression, our attempts to fix consciousness at a single point, our whole neurosis structure, our glorification of what we call "competition" and "winning." The present rate of expansion in the United States can go on for a few more decades, but then it comes up against the most fundamental law of thermodynamics. Even with perfectly clean nuclear energy, the final result of all our burning and wasteful consumption will be the overheating of this small planet. We must seek alternate modes of life, other ways of being on this earth.

"There is nothing wrong with competition in the proper proportion. Like a little salt, it adds zest to life."

Changes are coming. Sports represent a key joint in any society. To turn this society toward peaceful, humane change, we can begin with reform of sports. Some intellectuals have ignored this aspect of our life, believing somehow that sports are beyond serious consideration. They are quite mistaken. There is nothing trivial about the flight of a ball, for it traces for us the course of the planet. Through the movement of the human body, we can come to know what the philosopher Pythagoras called *kosmos,* a word containing the idea of both perfect order and intense beauty. Sports are too beautiful and profound for simplistic slogans. How we play the game may turn out to be more important than we imagine, for it signifies nothing less than our way of being in the world.

IN DEFENSE OF THE COMPETITIVE URGE

Gerald R. Ford
with John Underwood
(written during Mr. Ford's vice-presidency)

The Vice-President reflects fondly on his "halcyon days" as a Michigan football star and Yale coach, and ponders the current state of sport, arguing that winning is a necessary goal; that international athletic victories serve nations well; and that the preoccupation with money may end up alienating the fan.

One lesson to be learned in reaching an age where you are both a viable politician and a washed-up lineman is that past glories are not negotiable in the open market. When you stop winning they not only start booing, they start forgetting.

I used to think of myself as a pretty dashing figure on the ski slopes of the East and in northern Michigan, and could at least count on outstripping my children on the various runs we tried. Nowadays, when the family gets together at Vail for our annual Christmas ski reunion, my sons and my daughter go zooming by, usually with just the encouragement to make me boil. Such as: "Hurry up, Dad." They see themselves getting faster and faster as I get slower and slower. They forget all the times I picked them out of the snowbank.

When I was House Minority Leader and a regular adversary of Lyndon Johnson's, he once said—with minimum affection—"There's nothing wrong with Jerry Ford except that he played football too long without his helmet." Lyndon got a lot of mileage out of that quote, and I used it myself one year when I addressed the Gridiron Club in Washington. I said he was wrong, that I always wore my helmet on any gridiron, and I picked up my old leather bonnet and put it on, right on top of my white tie and tails. It had been a while, though. I had a hard time getting it down over my ears. Of course, heads do have a tendency to swell here in Washington.

My playing days at Michigan are now a standard introduction in magazine stories such as this, usually accompanied by a picture of a rugged-looking hairy young man (me) hunched over a ball in the center's position, and the notation that Ford was "the most valuable player on a losing Michigan team." I always feel damned with faint praise when I read that. I'd much rather have been the "least valuable player on a winning Michigan team," the kind we had my sophomore and junior years when we were undefeated and won national championships.

Those were what sportswriters up on their cliches would call my "halcyon days." Certainly they offer brighter memories than my efforts to stay competitive—and fit—since. Today I am a habitual exerciser—a 15-minute swim twice a day in the backyard pool, slower-and-slower skiing near our place in Vail, and an occasional round of golf with fellow hackers around Washington.

The reason I make reference to those winning seasons at Michigan is that we have been asked to swallow a lot of home-cooked psychology in recent years that winning isn't all that important anymore, whether on the athletic field or in any other field, national and international. I don't buy that for a minute. It is not enough to just compete. Winning is very important. Maybe more important than ever.

Don't misunderstand. I am not low-rating the value of informal participation. Competing is always preferable to not competing, whether you win or not, and one reason is as good as another for getting involved. Swimming laps, for example, is preferable to doubling your waistline. As a young man I took up skiing in order to get to know a certain young lady better. She happened to be a devotee, and I an eager beginner. I lost the girl but I learned to ski. The subject used to be a sensitive one with my wife, who came along afterward, but I have reminded her that that was instructive athletics, not competitive athletics. The important thing was I learned to ski.

If you don't win elections you don't play, so the importance of winning is more drastic in that field. In athletics and in most other worthwhile pursuits first place is the manifestation of the desire to excel, and how else can you achieve anything? I certainly do not feel we achieved very much as a Michigan football team in 1934. And I can assure you we had more fun on those championship teams in 1932-33.

Broadly speaking, outside of a national character and an educated society, there are few things more important to a country's growth and well-being than competitive athletics. If it is a cliché to say athletics build character as well as muscle, then I subscribe to the cliché. It has been said, too, that we are losing our competitive spirit in this country, the thing that made us great, the guts of the free-enterprise system. I don't agree with that; the competitive urge is deep-rooted in the American character. I do wonder sometimes if we are adjusting to the times, or if we have been spoiled by them.

For one, do we realize how important it is to compete successfully with other nations? Not just the Russians, but many nations that are growing and challenging. Being a leader, the U.S. has an obligation to set high standards. I don't know of a better advertisement for a nation's good health than a healthy athletic representation. Athletics happens to be an extraordinarily swift avenue of communication. The broader the achievement the greater the impact. There is much to be said for Ping-Pong diplomacy.

With communications what they are, a sports triumph can be as uplifting to a nation's spirit as, well, a battlefield victory. And surely no one will argue that it is not more healthful. The Africans were terrific in the last two Olympics, and their stars have become national heroes. These countries were tasting the first fruits of internationl achievement, and their pride was justified. In a wink of the eye they caught us in some areas, passed us in others.

When I was in China a few years ago I was astounded by the number of basketball courts. They were everywhere—in school yards, outside factories and farms. Boys and girls were playing basketball at age three and four, with miniature balls and undersized baskets. The sizes and heights were graded to coincide with the age group, something we might consider here, even up to the professional level. The agricultural and factory communes were alive with competition, in conjunction with their mandatory calisthenics.

In 1972, when I received the college Football Hall of Fame award at the Waldorf in New York, I remarked on this new Chinese passion for the old American game, and I said that one day soon we would have to cope with a seven-foot Chinese Wilt Chamberlain. Sure enough, last year the Chinese had a touring team that featured some real giants, and they did all right. In five years they will be competitive. Of course, the Chinese do things we would never find acceptable in a free society. Completely regimented, state-supported, state-manipulated athletic programs are not for us. It is a matter of style as well as philosophy. But if we want to remain competitive, and I think we do, we owe it to ourselves to reassess our priorities, to broaden our base of achievement so that we again present our best in the world's arenas. From a purely political viewpoint, I don't know of anything more beneficial in diplomacy and prestige. I don't think we really want to be booed or forgotten.

For that reason I am in favor of doing all we can, as quickly as we can, to resolve the jurisdictional differences which hurt our Olympic effort, which hinder at the grass-roots level the development of athletes. It is a disgrace in this country for anyone not to realize his or her potential in any sport. The petty conflict between the NCAA and the AAU is, as Mike Harrigan of the President's Council on Physical Fitness outlined recently, just the most visible symptom of an overall organizational problem.

I leave the details to Congressman Bob Mathias, the former decathlon champion, and those more acquainted with the specific difficulties, but certain things proposed in the recent flurry of congressional activity have my support. No one will deny that the United States Olympic Committee, a federally chartered organization and therefore a legitimate area of federal concern, needs to be restructured. The Administration has under advisement a plan—Mr. Harrigan's—to accomplish this with minimal federal involvement and control, and therefore at minimal cost to the taxpayer. This would include the creation of a President's Commission on Olympic Sports, composed of prominent interested Americans who are not partisan to either of the conflicting organizations. Two members of the Senate and two of the House would serve on the commission and it would have a fixed life of 15 months—eight to examine the USOC and report, and seven to make proposals and iron out the problems in time for the 1976 Olympics, and beyond.

The Amateur Athletic Act of 1974, sponsored by Senator Jim Pearson, is anathema to most governing athletic bodies because it implies too much federal control, including the formation of a permanent sanctioning federal amateur sports body. Congressman Mathias' amendment to the federal Olympic charter would remove some of the onus by providing that the American Arbitration Association act as a binding arbiter in settling disputes. But regardless of how it is achieved, something should be achieved—and soon—to improve the systems for developing our athletes.

Even if there were no other nations to impress, even if there were no international events to prepare for, the value of competitive athletics in this country would still be boundless. Consider what an athletic field does for a depressed neighborhood, or a successful sports program for a college—the spirit it breeds on campus and the moneys it generates to provide a broader intramural base. The whole school benefits. I don't know anything that gave a greater boost to Michigan than our football teams in 1932 and 1933 (but not necessarily 1934).

A winning pro football team like the Dolphins can galvanize an entire metropolitan area. Washington rallied around the Redskins. I found myself identifying with their success. George Allen's principles are consistent with mine (his dedication to hard work, his personal habits), and the Redskins were extraordinarily unified. The man holding an end-zone season ticket—or, if he is like me, the three-game-a-Sunday armchair quarterback watching at home while trying to get some work done (at about 50% capacity)—not only identifies, he feels a part of the effort.

I am beginning to wonder, however, if that vital relationship might not have taken a turn for the worse in recent months. Or been given a shove in the wrong direction. I refer to what seems to be a growing appetite—an apparently insatiable one—for money in sports, a preoccupation with "how much" instead of "how good," with cost instead of value. If I read my sports pages correctly, and I read them every day, the age of benevolent ownership is over. The emerging super figures of the '70s are the dollar-oriented athlete and the profit-oriented owner, usually in conflict. Neither side trusts the other. And neither is particularly attractive. The sports news is glutted with salary disputes and threats of strike, of demands and contractual harangues, of players jumping from one league to another, or owners threatening to pull their franchises out of this or that city unless demands are met or profits improve.

I have mixed emotions about much of this. On the one hand I would not deny an athlete his opportunity for maximum compensation. A professional athletic career is short-lived at best, and in the free enterprise system a man should be able to realize his worth. By the same token, management can handle just so much. Professional sport has a history of failing ownerships, of bankrupt franchises. The balance is often delicate and Congress has, in the past, been very sympathetic with its anti-trust legislation.

I take neither side. But I do pose a few questions on behalf of the man in the middle: the fan. I'm one myself, and what scares me is that the fan may ultimately be abused, if he has not been already. The money has to come from somewhere. Traditionally, the somewhere is the fan's pocketbook—and in the electronic age in which we live, the advertiser's. At what point will the fan become disillusioned? When he comes to the conclusion that the team he is supporting has no reciprocal interest in his affection, I think there will be a withdrawal of support. It might not come today, or this season, but it will surely come.

It will be interesting to see how the fans react to the players who are now jumping to the new World Football League. It will be interesting to see how the Miami fans react this season to Csonka, Kiick and Warfield, who are committed to the Memphis franchise in 1975. I personally wish them well, because they are fine athletes who are fun to watch. From the rival Redskins' point of view, goodby will no doubt be good riddance.

I wonder, too, what the preoccupation with money is doing to the athletes themselves. When a pitcher throws a no-hitter and is quoted that from the fifth inning on he was thinking about the bonus he would get, how does this affect the young athlete reading the story? When a college basketball senior drafted by the NBA in the first round talks about being worth "at least three million," what clicks in the mind of the freshman on that team?

There must be some serious clicking going on because I am told that the colleges are experiencing the worst run of recruiting violations since World War II. Whether or not the super-paid athlete begets the super-paid-under-the-table athlete I would not venture to say, but I was shocked when I heard that. I was under the impression the colleges were in a saner period, were better controlled, with safeguards at both conference and national levels.

When honesty and integrity suffer nationally, they no doubt suffer in athletics. And vice versa. It would be difficult to measure what effect scandalous behavior in sport has on the nation as a whole, but I do not doubt there is one. The last thing we need is to be cynical about it.

I don't think the fan is unaware. In their rush to get his money promoters have often tried to sell him labels rather than contents, figures rather than pedigrees, and as often as not he turns up his nose. It will be interesting to see how the World Football League fares in that re-spect. It will not be the NFL's equal for some time, but it is going to ask the fan to consider it major league. If it *is* major league, the fan will recognize it as such and support it.

I have my doubts about the advisability of the WFL telecasting games on week nights, in effect invading the time and territory of the high schools. We already have legislation preventing Friday night NFL telecasts. I don't know if the Congress will sit still for Thursday night telecasts that might cut the revenue of high school sports.

I have to admit to a certain empathetic thrill in reading about all the money being tossed around today in sports. It takes me back to the time I was offered a big-money deal to play for the Green Bay Packers: $200 a game, with a 14-game schedule and a 10-day contract cancellation provision.

There was a lot happening to me then to turn my head. In 1931, when I was being recruited out of South High in Grand Rapids, Harry Kipke himself, the famous Michigan coach, brought me to Ann Arbor for a visit. I had made two All-State teams—one of which I captained—and must have been worth rushing because Michigan State, Northwestern and Harvard also expressed interest, and in those days recruiting wasn't as widespread as it is today.

The Kipkes took me to their home for the weekend, and to several sports events, and then to the bus on Sunday night. I had to be impressed by the personal attention.

So the hotshot center from Grand Rapids came to live at Michigan, in a third-floor 10-by-10 room way in the back of the cheapest rooming house I could find. I shared the rent ($4 a week) with a basketball player from my hometown. We each had a desk and a bed, which pretty much exhausted the floor space, and there was one small window between us.

The Big Ten did not give athletic scholarships then. My tuition was paid by a scholarship from South High, and Coach Kipke got me a job waiting on tables in the interns' dining room at University Hospital and cleaning up in the nurses' cafeteria. My aunt and uncle sent me $2 a week for Depression-day extravagances. My father's paint factory was going through a depression of its own, and since there were three other Fords to raise he couldn't send anything.

When I pledged Delta Kappa Epsilon my sophomore year, I moved into the fraternity house and got a job washing dishes. There were four of us at the sink; including Herman Everhardus, an outstanding Michigan football player. As dishwashers I would say we showed good early foot but uncertain technique. I doubt we would pass today's sanitation codes.

I know I am guilty of leaning heavily on football jargon in speeches and off-the-cuff remarks, but for two reasons I think this is understandable. First, there is obviously a deep American involvement in and a great social significance to the game. No game is like football in that respect. It has so many special qualities, among them the combination of teamwork involving a large number of people, with precise strategies and coordination that are essential if anyone is going to benefit. The athletes are highly skilled, but subservient to the team. Yet if they do their job, they give an individual an opportunity for stardom. I know of no other sport that demands so much, and returns so much.

The experience of playing the game can be applied to the rest of your life, and drawn from freely. I know it is easy to find similarities in politics. How you can't make it in either field without teamwork and great leadership. How you attract grandstand quarterbacks by the droves. In football you hear them during and after the game. In politics we hear them 30 seconds after our last speech. Or during it. Most grandstand quarterbacks have never played either game, yet are the loudest and most knowledgeable critics. The thick skin developed in football pays off.

The second reason is that I truly enjoyed my football experience, and just don't want to forget it. Under Harry Kipke, Michigan used the short-punt formation, which was popular then, and as the center I fancied myself the second-best passer in the lineup. If I'm dating you, the center in the short punt or single wing is not just a guy who sticks the ball in the quarterback's hands. Every center snap must truly be a pass (between the legs), often leading the tailback who is in motion and in full stride when he takes the ball. I don't mean to be critical, but I think that is why you now see so many bad passes from center on punts and field goals. They don't have to do it enough. I must have centered the ball 500,000 times in high school and college.

Football was probably more enjoyable for us then because the pressures were not as great as they seem to be now. What made it *less* enjoyable was that we labored under limited-substitution rules, which reads out as total exhaustion after every game. In a close one no more than 15 or 16 men would play. If you left the game at any point during either half you couldn't go back during that half. The rule was modified my senior year to allow you to return to play in the next period. It didn't help much.

I averaged about a fourth of a game my first two years. Kipke had superb teams, so a lot of guys played. I got the "best prospect" award after the 1932 season, but the next fall I hurt a knee and was out of the running early. Chuck Bernard not only kept the job at center but made All-America.

My senior year, when I played regularly and was voted Most Valuable, the team, as I've mentioned, was not as good, and we didn't run up any scores. We were too busy trying to keep them from being run up on us. The starters were usually the finishers. We held Minnesota, the Big Ten champion that year with such stars as Pug Lund, Phil Bengtson and Bud Wilkinson, scoreless in the first half, and missed two good scoring opportunities ourselves. Then we ran down and were overwhelmed 34-0. (Having been worn out once too often, I would say that today's unlimited substitution is better.

More people get to play, and the game is less a test of stamina and more of skill.)

But though we weren't very good, we weren't very exciting, either. Kipke's style was written up in *The Saturday Evening Post* under the headline "A Punt, A Pass and A Prayer." As far as I know that was the origin of the phrase, and it bespoke the Michigan system: Play tough defense. Punt when in doubt. Force the other guy into mistakes. Then score on a pass. And pray for deliverance. We *always* kicked off. We *always* punted on third down inside our own 25, unless we had about a yard to go. We played tough defense—a straight 6-2-2-1, with none of the sliding and stunting you see today. We ran the short punt to death. We were dull.

That last year we had an excellent passer named Bill Renner, who broke his leg before the season started. Our punter was the best I ever saw in pro or college, John Regeczi, and he got hurt in the third game. If your system depends on a punt, a pass and a prayer, and all you have left is a prayer—well, that might put you in good hands, but you better not count on any favors. We lost seven out of eight.

Despite our humble record I was invited to play in the East-West Shrine Game in San Francisco on Jan. 1, 1935, primarily on the recommendation of Dick Hanley, the Northwestern coach. I had had a pretty good day against his star guard, Rip Whalen. According to Hanley, when he asked Whalen why Michigan made so much ground up the middle that day, Whalen said, "Ford was the best blocking center I ever played against." I still cherish that remark.

The Shrine signed two centers for the East, a boy from Colgate named George Akerstrom, and me. On the train ride from Chicago to California, Curly Lambeau, the coach of the Packers, went from player to player, plying the good ones about their pro football interest. He ignored me. Then in the first two minutes of the game Akerstrom got hurt. I played the rest of the way—58 minutes, offense and defense. After the game a group of us were given the option of a train ride home or a free trip to Los Angeles to see the movie studios. Being a conservative Midwesterner unacquainted with glamour, I naturally chose Hollywood.

On the train from San Francisco to Los Angeles, Curly Lambeau sat with me the whole way. He suddenly knew my name. And he asked me to sign with the Packers. I told him I'd think about it.

That August I played in the All-Star game in Chicago, the second in which the college stars played a pro team. We had Don Hutson and a number of outstanding players, but the Bears beat us 5-0. Shortly after that I got Curly's offer in writing: $200 a game for the 14 games. Potsy Clark of the Lions matched the bid.

But pro football did not have the allure it has now, and though my interest was piqued I didn't lose any sleep over my decision. When Ducky Pond, the Yale coach, came to Ann Arbor at Kipke's bidding to ask me to be on his staff at New Haven, I saw the chance to realize two dreams at once—to stay in football and to pursue a long-nurtured aspiration for law school. Pond's offer was $2,400 for the full 12 months, as his assistant line coach, jayvee coach and scout—and to coach the boxing team in the winter. Of boxing I knew next to nothing. No, that's not right. I knew absolutely nothing.

So that summer while working in my father's paint factory I slipped off to the YMCA three times a week to get punched around by the Y's boxing coach. I didn't get good, but I got good enough to fool the Yale freshmen, one of whom was Bill Proxmire.

I coached at Yale for six football seasons, from 1935 through 1940. My scholastic advisers were convinced I couldn't handle law school and a full-time job, so they wouldn't let me try until 1938 when, with reluctance, they relented for two courses. I was warned that of the 125 students entering law school that year, 98 were Phi Beta Kappa, and that was clearly another league from the one I had been in. Somehow I got by, and that spring, without telling Ducky Pond, I began a full load of law courses.

In the fall of 1938 Pond made me head jayvee coach in charge of scouting and raised my pay to a fabulous $3,600 a year. One of the teams I scouted that year was my alma mater, Michigan, starring the great Tom Harmon. Michigan beat Yale, but barely—15-13.

The Yale staff was excellent. Greasy Neale was on it, and Ivy Williamson, who had played at Michigan before me and was my roommate one summer when I took a couple of law courses there. He was going for his master's in education. Williamson later became a winning head coach at Wisconsin.

By January of 1941 I had completed my law requirements and I received my degree in June. World War II ended my football career. I was in Tom Hamilton's V-5 program for two years, working as athletic officer with responsibilities as an assistant ship's navigator on an aircraft carrier in the Pacific, but I never went back to coaching, except vicariously on Sunday afternoons at RFK Stadium. I doubt George Allen notices.

I spoke earlier of the lessons to be learned from football. The reverse is also true: football learns. Or at least its practitioners do. Of all our sports I think football best reflects the nation's tastes, and is constantly adjusting to meet them. I know of none that changes as often, or as radically.

I don't think anyone—except the coaches and the place-kickers—would argue that the changes in the pro game that were adopted this winter were not in answer to public taste. There had been a growing conservatism in pro football, and by nature Americans are not conservative—at least not in sports. The last several Super Bowl games were played by highly competent teams, maybe the best ever, but they were so competent within the framework of their own restrictions that the Super Bowl lost the spontaneity and the sparkle the public likes. They were almost too good for their own good, if that's possible. The fan likes to see an error as a very real

threat, as a possible sudden turn to rev up a game. Right or wrong he likes his heroes to take gambles now and then, to make mistakes. Interestingly enough, the impact of the new rules brings the pro game closer to the college game, and as far as I'm concerned that's for the better. The colleges have had that spontaneity. Their coaches have been more daring. Two or three of the most recent college bowl games were far more interesting than the Super Bowl.

As I think back on my own football days, I find myself marveling at today's athletes—in all sports. They are better in every respect; bigger, stronger, faster and better cared for. I think it is true that they have had much to divert their attention from the drive to excel—affluence can be disconcerting, and there was the war in Vietnam. But these are hardly insurmountable handicaps. Affluence should be an asset. It helps provide the facilities that broaden the base we need now. And, of course, all wars end.

The fact remains that these athletes *do* excel. And together with our international programs, I would like to see our national institutions reflect that excellence. I would prefer, to mention one example, that the service academies be in the forefront of college football instead of in the rear. Or at least be above average.

The reason for their current slump is obvious and forgivable: the five-year service commitment a cadet or midshipman has after graduation. Proposals have been made to get around that commitment, to balance the need for good intercollegiate representation by the academies against the requirements of the services. One idea is to allow academy graduates who have a chance for a professional athletic career to postpone their military duty for X number of years. The argument is that they will wind up being more valuable to the service at an older, more settled age, when they will be looking for the post-athletic career so many pros fail to establish. And, of course, they would still be young men.

My surface judgment is that it might be workable for an athlete to spend, say, five years after his academy class graduates in a reservist's role, meeting once a week for training and two weeks a year on active duty, and then fulfill his service obligation. There well may be an Arnold Tucker or a Doc Blanchard or a Pete Dawkins out there waiting for such a chance. All three were All-Americans, and all became outstanding career military men.

I think this, too: that our better athletes today, despite the times and all the terrible crises, are really the vanguard of our young leadership. I know that in terms of spiritual awareness they are way out in front.

A friend of mine from my old Congressional District, Billy Zeoli, does a lot of ministerial work for the Dallas Cowboys, and over the years—at various group meetings and breakfasts and banquets—I have come to know men like Norm Evans, Bobby Richardson, Stan Smith and Bill Glass, and each time I meet another one like them I am reassured.

Three years ago Billy took me to his services for the Cowboys when they were in Washington to play the Redskins. I can't tell you how impressed I was. But my son Jack was really impressed. Jack got to sit next to Jethro Pugh. He didn't tell his old man to hurry up that day.

DISCUSSION QUESTIONS

A. *Arthur R. Combs*

1. In what sense are myths and false beliefs dangerous?
2. List some sport-related myths that you are personally aware of.
3. What is Combs' reply to those who argue that "hot" competition in sports is desirable because it helps prepare the participant to live in our very competitive society?
4. What is Combs' position with respect to the popular belief that competition is a powerful motivating force?
5. Although Combs' discussion of the myth of competition as a device for controlling and improving quality is directed toward the economic sector of American life, it has implications for sport as well. Can you think of some sport-related examples where competition, rather than producing a "better product," *e.g.*, an educationally justifiable intercollegiate athletic program, encourages the production of just the opposite?

B. *George B. Leonard*

1. Do you agree with Leonard that the current worship of "hot" competition and winning at all costs in American sports represents "the *end* of a particular line of social development" to eventually be replaced by a new sports ethos? Explain your answer.
2. What is Leonard's reply to those who argue that competition is an essential aspect of human existence and "deep-rooted in the American character" (President Ford, 1973)?

3. In what sense does competition create sameness and conformity?
4. What role would Leonard like to see competition play in American sports?

C. *Gerald R. Ford*

1. Why does Mr. Ford feel that competition and winning on the athletic field are important to a country's growth and well-being? Do you agree with his reasoning?
2. What is your reaction to Mr. Ford's statement that he would much rather have been "the least valuable player on a winning Michigan team than the most valuable player on a losing Michigan team"?
3. All of our recent presidents have been either active sports participants or enthusiastic sports fans. Is this apparent marriage between the presidency and sport a coincidence or, is there a logical explanation for this close articulation between the political and sport institutions?
4. In discussing the value of competitive athletics in the United States, Mr. Ford challenges the reader to "consider what an athletic field does for a depressed neighborhood, or a successful sports program for a college. . . ." What do *you* think an athletic field or a successful sports program can do?
5. What factors in Mr. Ford's early life as well as the times in which he grew up, could have contributed to the great love he had and still has for the game of football?
6. Are the authors of the articles included in this unit criticizing (supporting in Mr. Ford's case) *competition*, *winning*, or both? Do you feel that it is important to differentiate between the two? Can the two be separated? Should they be?
7. Is there an alternative to the competitive way of life in general and "hot" competition in sports in particular? If there is, what would be gained and what would be sacrificed if this alternative life style was adopted?

Unit VI

Adult-Sponsored Sports Activities for Children

Since the founding of Little League Baseball at Williamsport, Pennsylvania in 1939, North America has experienced an escalating growth of adult-sponsored sports programs for children. As so often happens in periods of rapid social change, the attendant growth of "kid sports" programs was not guided by scientific research which attempted to measure the benefits children received from organized sports competition. In fact, until the early seventies the scholarly investigation of these highly structured programs suffered from benign neglect. More recently, although results are far from conclusive, several research studies have attempted to answer the question—"How good are highly organized sports for children?" The four selections which follow strongly indicate that basic changes are needed in the structure of adult-sponsored sports activities for children.

The initial selection, an editorial from *U.S. News and World Report* provides some basic demographic data documenting the scope of "kids sports" programs in the United States. Literally millions of young boys and girls are involved in adult-sponsored sports. Unfortunately, these children are participating in programs where the dominant ethos is often to "win at all cost." Not infrequently this ethos is fostered by overzealous adults.

Edward Devereux, a developmental psychologist, focuses upon what participation in highly competitive, adult-organized athletic programs *does not* do for young children. He argues that "Little Leaguism" is threatening to wipe out the spontaneous culture of free play and games among American children, thus robbing them of their childish fun and also of some valuable learning experiences. Devereux develops a strong case that the culture of children's games in America is sadly impoverished. He suggests less structure and a general return to spontaneity in children's play and games.

In the third selection, Hank Burchard, a journalist, documents the "win at all cost" syndrome for young boys in football. The author points out that if having *fun* is an objective of kid sports programs, then why are the participants often so serious? Why are there rarely any displays of laughter or frivolity? Burchard also criticizes the inordinately high profile of administrators, coaches, and parents involved in some youth sports programs. The question may well be asked whether over-zealous adults are on an ego-trip at the expense of our children.

Sport psychologist, Terry Orlick, draws attention to one of the most critical problems indigenous to youth sports, i.e., the problem of exclusion. In order to determine why children drop out of sports programs at an early age, the writer interviewed eight- and nine-year-old sports participants and dropouts. He found that, all too often, children drop out because of a perceived failure to meet adult standards of performance.

IS THE BOOM IN "KID SPORTS" GOOD FOR THE KIDS?

"Burned-out, turned-off" athletes, age 14 . . . hockey players, 3 1/2. . . . Increasingly, experts ask if adult-run sports for youngsters are overdone.

Across the U.S. this winter, millions of youngsters are turning the nation's boom in kids' sports into a year-round phenomenon—not without controversy.

From Massachusetts to California, grade-school boys are arising before 4 a.m. to play ice-hockey matches. Basketball is attracting thousands into "pee-wee"

Reprinted from February 4, 1974 *U.S. News & World Report.*

leagues. Gymnastics is becoming a winter and summer passion for girls. Construction of new indoor swimming pools allows boys and girls to compete most of the year.

As a result, a debate is growing over the long-held maxim that organized sports are automatically a good thing for children.

Adult pressures. Critics cite increasing evidence of youngsters' "burning out" as athletes before they even enter high school. Emotional damage is becoming more of a problem to competitors, in many instances, than is physical injury.

The main culprits according to many experts: win-at-any-cost adults who put make-or-break pressure on child athletes.

Because of such doubts plus costs and other reasons, many schools bar interscholastic competition below high school.

In Illinois, for instance, the Illinois Elementary School Association says only 20,000 youngsters in its 475 member schools participate in interscholastic sports, and then only in baseball, basketball and track for boys, and track for girls.

Still, the boom in organized sports for children 14 and under shows few signs of abating, as reported by staff members of "U.S. News & World Report" across the nation.

Basketball is on the rise at this time of year. League elimination contests involving some 5,000 youngsters all under 5 feet 6 inches from a dozen States will put teams into the Biddy Basketball tournament in Louisiana this spring, for example.

This summer, thousands of boys from Bainbridge Island, Wash., to Arlington, Va., will attend basketball "clinics" to brush up on their skills.

Many other sports are booming, too. All in all, the surge in kids' athletics involves at least 27 sports, including baseball, football, soccer, wrestling, boxing, bowling, golf, swimming, tennis and track and field.

Millions involved. Estimates of the total number of participants run to 4 million or more out of approximately 36.6 million boys and girls 5 to 14 years old in the U.S.

As an indicator of the boom, about 2 million boys, aged 8 to 14, play Little League baseball or its community equivalent each summer. Little League Baseball, Inc., with headquarters in Williamsport, Pa., lists 40,000 teams and 1 million players on its rolls.

About 1 million boys play tackle football in organized leagues, according to an "educated guess" by J. Maxson Cunningham, commissioner of the Capital Beltway League, Inc., in the Washington, D.C., area. The Ford Motor Company's "Punt, Pass & Kick" contest had 1.2 million entrants aged 8 to 13 years old in 1973.

Some football leagues capped their seasons last autumn with their own "superbowls" complete with marching bands, cheerleaders and TV coverage.

Organized golf and bowling associations each list about 1.2 million junior members, including high-schoolers.

Many teams are organized by such groups as the Boys' Clubs of America, which lists 1,100 affiliates with more than 1 million members, a large share of whom participate in pre-high-school team sports.

In New York City, the Police Athletic League (PAL) has activities in 22 sports. Roughly half the 80,000 members are 12 or younger.

Conrad Ford, PAL's executive director, says the sports program "gets the youngsters off the street and gives them a constructive outlet for their energies."

Cities in other areas find similar values, leading municipal recreation departments to sponsor teams and leagues.

Enthusiastic kids. In Atlanta more than 30,000 under-14 youngsters participate in city-sponsored sports. Another 6,000 belong to the Boys' Club. Thousands more play in some 30 independent sports leagues in and around Atlanta.

To illustrate the enthusiasm the programs generate, Jack L. Roebuck, director of a Boys' Club in Atlanta, tells the story of an 11-year-old football player who walked 4 miles to play in a "bowl" game against a Mississippi team because his brothers had left him without carfare. He arrived 3 1/2 hours before game time and, during play, scored two touchdowns.

After the game, the coaches discovered he had a 102-degree temperature.

Now, ice hockey. The sport that may be blossoming the most dramatically at the moment is ice hockey.

In Evanston, Ill., city employes ice over tennis courts in parks, and Northwestern University permits use of its outdoor rink. Even so, the demand for playing time is so great that games are scheduled at midnight.

The construction of new ice rinks nationwide is making what is true in Evanston the rule in many urban areas.

Meryl Baxter, manager of a San Jose, Calif., rink, says, "Parents know ice hockey is a good healthy sport and keeps their youngster out of trouble while he is on the ice."

Some families, according to Mr. Baxter, arise at 3 a.m. so their sons can make a 4 to 6 a.m. practice session. The early hours are the only time peewee players can find time on the ice.

In Los Angeles, ice-hockey teams take players as young as 3 1/2.

Though many teams are sponsored and guided by schools, churches and neighborhood groups, others are organized on an even broader scale.

The costs. In a Houston suburb, for instance, the Spring Branch Memorial Sports Association sponsors 100 football teams, 250 baseball teams and 100 girls' softball teams.

The price isn't cheap. The Spring Branch association has an annual budget of $200,000. On the average nationally, it costs teams $35 to $50 to outfit one small football player, and teams often carry 35 to 40 players each on their rosters. To field a four-team baseball league costs a minimum of $1,000. Many participants in ice hockey put up $50 each for skates and uniforms plus another $50 a season for rink time.

Girls are getting more attention, after decades in which athletic competition was regarded as primarily for boys.

"We just had our first girls' touch-football competition," says John Nihill of the San Francisco recreation department. In that city's junior high schools, girls have also recently begun interschool competition in volleyball.

Girls' basketball is an important sport in some parts of the country. And softball has long been played in a number of cities.

Parents are increasingly drawn into child sports activities.

A whole life. A Citrus Heights family in the suburbs of Sacramento, Calif., points this up: Jeffrey Obenland, 14, son of Mr. and Mrs. Richard Obenland, has been playing Little League baseball for five years. Mr. and Mrs. Obenland participate actively in team affairs, giving the annual baseball party for families with sons on the team with Jeffrey. Mrs. Obenland notes that "for many men, their whole life revolves around their son's team."

For all the good that many parents find in the organized sports programs, though, there are dangers, too. It is the combination of these physical and emotional hazards that is stirring fresh debate over the spread of competition for kids.

Physical injuries. On the physical side, injuries are a constant concern. A computer survey of emergency rooms in 119 hospitals between July 1 and Sept. 30, 1973, made by the U.S. Consumer Products Safety Commission, shows that these hospitals treated 10,010 injuries resulting from team sports. Of the total, 40.7 per cent were in the 5-to-14 age group.

An injury is defined as a hurt that restricts activity for a day. Most of the recorded injuries were described as minor, involving at the most simple fractures.

By way of comparison, more than 1.2 million high-school boys played football in 1973, and, according to an American Medical Association estimate, about half sustained some form of injury.

There were 16 high-school football fatalities in 1973.

One of the controversies swirling around kid sports involves what has come to be known in medical circles as "little league" elbows and shoulders. Both relate to muscle and joint damage from excessive throwing. The technical term is epiphyseal injury. It can also crop up in tennis players.

A study by Little League Baseball, Inc., of injuries among 5 million players showed 1.96 per cent suffered some form of injury requiring medical attention. Many of these injuries were associated with batting or sliding. Only .016 per cent of the pitchers sustained an epiphyseal injury, the survey says.

Emotional damage. Whatever the physical dangers for the 5 to 14-year-olds engaged in team sports, they stir up less controversy than what some critics see as possibilities of emotional damage.

Darrell Tully, athletic director of the Spring Branch independent school district in Texas, notes:

"I see some youngsters who drop out of sports in high school because they got burned out too young. Others go on to become outstanding high-school and college athletes. I think the biggest problem is parent involvement. The kids are frustrated and the coaches are frustrated. There is too much emphasis on winning at the third and fourth-grade levels when the games should be fun. It turns many kids off sports."

Mr. Tully's observations were echoed by William Russell, commissioner of the California Interscholastic Federation, Santa Barbara:

"Coaches report conflicting findings. Some feel if youngsters in highly competitive sports are pushed by parents or the community then by the time they reach high school they rebel and turn to something else. But others feel the knowledge and skills learned in competition make them better and more skilled competitors in high school."

These observations reflect questions being raised more and more by sociologists and psychologists. Some sociologists maintain that sports are a means through which a child becomes "acculturized," that is, learns that success depends on discipline and hard work.

Myths and egos. But Dr. Lee Vander Velden, a sport sociologist at the University of Maryland in College Park, had this observation: "There are numerous myths about sports—sports build character, for example—and we can't substantiate any of them."

Dr. Vander Velden and Richard C. Mantel, a sociologist, football coach and physical-education teacher at Oleny, Md., studied 133 boys, aged 10 and 11, from middle-income families. They found that among those who had played organized sports for at least two years, more than half ranked achievement ahead of fair play.

Dr. Vander Velden says he is convinced there is considerable "ego extension" involved by adults who urge on children.

As the debate widens, organizations in some cities are beginning to play down sports in their programs.

Daniel Swope, associate director of the Chicago Boys Clubs, says that sports have been a selling point for years for social workers seeking contributions from businessmen. But now, he reports:

"More people are realizing sports are only a vehicle for reaching a kid and giving him counseling and guidance. It is no longer enough for us to teach a boy to shoot basketballs and say we've done our job."

Yet, despite such concerns over the role of sports for children, the increasing swirl of activities across the nation seems to indicate that the trend toward more and more participation is not likely to end soon.

BACKYARD VERSUS LITTLE LEAGUE BASEBALL: SOME OBSERVATIONS ON THE IMPOVERISHMENT OF CHILDREN'S GAMES IN CONTEMPORARY AMERICA

Edward C. Devereux

In this presentation, I plan to focus on a few more general issues. Most generally, my critique of Little League Baseball, and other such major sports programs for children, will be based not so much upon what participation in such activities does for the child-participants as upon what it does *not* do for them. I will argue that "Little Leaguism" is threatening to wipe out the spontaneous culture of free play and games among American children, and thus that it is robbing our children not just of their childish fun but also of some of their most valuable learning experiences.

On the impoverishment of children's games in America. One way to gain insight about what is happening in contemporary America is to look at ourselves in cross-cultural and historical perspective. Earlier this year, I spent two months in Japan, carrying out a survey among Japanese school children. While there, I spent as much time as I could observing children in informal play settings, such as parks, neighborhood playgrounds, school yards, apartment court yards and city streets. What struck me most forcefully was the observation that Japanese children seem to spend very little time just "hanging around"; whenever two or more children found themselves together, they seemed to move very quickly into some kind of self-organized but rule-oriented play. Though I made no formal inventory, I was impressed with the great variety and richness of the games I observed. Although the Japanese also have Little League Baseball, most of the games I observed were carried out wholly without adult instigation or supervision.

On one occasion my wife and I observed a group of some dozen kindergarten children playing ring games in a public park. I have no doubt that these children were brought to the park by some teacher or adult supervisor, and I kept waiting for some adult to appear to structure the next game for them. But during the forty-five minutes we remained in the vicinity no adult ever approached or spoke to the children. Evidently the game repertory, the motivation to play, and the ability to organize and pace their own activities were well rooted in the children's own heads.

Later in the year, I went to Israel on another research project, and again I spent as much time as I could observing the informal play activities of the Israeli children. Here also I was impressed with the enormous variety of spontaneous games and play activities I observed. On this, we also have some impressive research documentation in the work of the Israeli psychologist Rivka Eifermann (1971a). In her study, a team of some 150 observers recorded the play activities of some fourteen thousand Israeli school children, in Kibbutzim, Moshavim and cities, in school yards, playgrounds and streets, over a two year period. One result of this research was the compilation of an encyclopedia of over 2000 games the children were observed to be playing, including many bewildering variants on such well-known games as soccer, tag and hop-scotch, as well as hundreds of less well known games, also in endless variations (Eifermann, 1971b). Most of these games, moreover, were being played wholly without adult instigation or supervision.

All this challenges us to raise the question: What has happened to the culture of children's games in America? Looking back to my own childhood, some fifty years ago, I can recall literally dozens of games we played regularly and with enthusiasm—puss in the corner, red rover, capture the flag, one-o-cat, statues, stealing sticks, blind man's buff, croquet, leap frog, duck on the rock, prisoner's base, and many, many more. No doubt some of these are still around, in vestigial form; but my impression is that I rarely see these, or other games like them, being played spontaneously by children. Those which are played seem to be adult-instigated and supervised, in schools, camps or other organized play settings, or in party settings in homes. And even here, our game culture has become sadly impoverished. Ask any group of children what they did at a birthday party and nine out of ten will say they pinned the tail on the donkey. Halloween? Bob for apples and tricks or treats! What ever happened to the tricks, incidentally? We have institutionalized and sterilized Halloween, and thereby killed most of its creativity and fun. Most generally, it appears that our game culture has become sadly impoverished from lack of use and from an excess of adult supervision and control. "Come on, children, we're all going to play a game now!" "Do we *have* to?" You can almost hear the groans.

On these trends, there is also some research evidence in a fascinating study by Sutton-Smith and Rosenberg (1971). In their monograph, these authors compare game preferences of American children as documented in four different research studies spanning a sixty-year period from the late 1890's to the late 1950's. Even though these four studies are not strictly comparable, nevertheless certain general trends are impressively clear. The great variety of once-popular indoor and backyard skill games, such as croquet and quoits, have all declined in interest, to be replaced by the ubiquitous ping-pong. Leader games, such as Simon Says, statues, and follow the leader, are now of little interest for boys.

Paper presented by Edward C. Devereux (Dept. of Human Development and Family Studies, Cornell University) to the *Conference on Sport and Social Deviancy,* sponsored by the State University of New York College at Brockport, December 9-11, 1971. This paper also published in Daniel Landers, ed. *Social Problems in Athletics,* University of Illinois Press, Urbana, Ill., 1976.

Chasing games, like tag, are now acceptable only to very little children. Central person parlor games, such as hide the thimble, forfeits and twenty questions, have mostly disappeared, as have the endless varieties of ring games, such as drop the handkerchief and London Bridge, and the team guessing and acting games, like charades. Individual games of skill—remember mumble-de-peg?—are withering away. Virtually all of the undifferentiated team games, such as hare and hound, prisoner's base, etc., have either disappeared or declined in interest, as boys have devoted more of their attention to a few major sports. And even here, the authors conclude, the range of choice has narrowed significantly: ". . . trends would indicate that boys are spending more and more time on fewer sports. Bowling, Basketball, and Football improve in rank positions, but all other sports decline. . . . This would appear to be further evidence of the increasing circumscription of the boy's play role." (p. 47)

How can we account for this apparently very real constriction in the game culture of American children? How do American children really spend their spare time? In the presence of this audience, I am tempted to say that they are all out there on the baseball and football fields, or on the hockey rinks, participating according to season in the sports programs organized for them by schools and other adult sponsoring agencies. In fact, as we all know, several hundred thousand of them are doing just that, for example, as members of the now more than forty thousand Little League Baseball teams. For these children, there can be no doubt that such team activities capture a very large share of their time and attention. In one study reported by Skubic (1956), for example, 81 out of 96 Little League players in the Santa Maria area "reported that half to most of their leisure time during the whole year is spent on baseball." (p. 102)

But even conceding that a very large absolute number of children are now involved in such organized sports, the fact remains that the vast majority of children in the 8 to 12 age range are not. What do they do instead? A great deal of unstructured, non-rule-oriented play: bike riding, for example, still ranks very high with both boys and girls. In American homes, toys, hobby kits and various proprietary games such as Monopoly still find wide acceptance among children. Just hanging around and talking, or very informal horseplay with friends, now occupies a very large share of the typical preadolescent's time. Finally, and by far the most important, there is television watching, to which this age group now devotes some twenty hours per week.

On this, I would speculate that the availability of a mass television audience has had a lot to do with the extraordinary ascendency of Big Leaguism in America, and perhaps indirectly, of Little Leaguism as well. By focusing the attention of millions of viewers on a handful of major sports, and on the heroic teams and individual stars within them, we have converted ourselves to a nation of spectators. For most of us, sports are something to be watched, not played—or at least not by amateurs.

Personally, I doubt that very many children in the 8-

12 range are television sports addicts, though some undoubtedly are. But children surely perceive where their father's interests are focused, and by 10 or 12 are well aware of the extraordinary pay-off value of success in major sports in America. They see how the star athletes are rewarded in college and high school sports, and how pleased their fathers are at any athletic achievements of their own. I suspect that Little Leaguism for elementary school children is fostered more by the parents than by the children themselves, though for some it falls on well-cultivated ground. Here is a chance to "play" at something really important that parents and adults generally seem to take very seriously.

But even for the children who have no special interest or competence in any major sport, probably a majority of all children, or who are actually alienated by the whole sub-culture of organized, competitive sports, the model is still there and highly salient. Against the heroic, if perhaps somewhat myopic, standards of Big League or Little League sports, who would dare propose a simple game of puss in the corner, capture the flag or red rover? Kid stuff, unworthy of the time and attention of any red-blooded American boy past the age of seven or eight!

On the educational functions of play and games. Why should we care about what has been happening to the recreational and spare time activities of our children? In approaching an answer to this question, I would like to say just a bit about the functions of games and informal play activities in childhood and comment specifically about the kinds of learning which may occur in spontaneous, self-organized children's games. I will then go on to assess how organized, adult sponsored competitive sports stack up against this model.

It has long been recognized that children's games and play activities represent miniature and playful models of a wide variety of cultural and social activities and concerns. To take a familiar example, the activities of little girls revolving about dolls and playing house undoubtedly serve some function in the process of anticipatory socialization to future roles as mothers and housekeepers. Similarly, in the games of boys, such elemental social themes as leading and following, of capturing and rescuing, of attacking and defending, of concealing and searching, are endlessly recombined in games of varying complexity in what Sutton-Smith (1971) has called a syntax of play. For example, the chase and elude themes of tag are combined with the capture and rescue elements of relievo in the more complex game of prisoner's base. When the chase and elude themes of tag are combined with the attack and defend themes of dodge ball, we have the more complex game type represented in football.

As Roberts and Sutton-Smith (1962) have pointed out, games of different types represent microcosmic social structures in which various different styles of competing, and of winning or losing, are subtly encoded. Through their participation in a wide variety of *different* game types, in which the various elements of skill, chance, and strategy are variously recombined in gradually increasing complexity, children find an opportunity to experiment with *different* success styles, and gain experience in a variety of cognitive and emotional processes which cannot yet be learned in full scale cultural participation.

I would stress in particular, at this point, that for game experiences to serve their socialization functions effectively, it is essential that children engage in a wide variety of different types of games, and at varying levels of complexity appropriate to their stage of development. If the American game culture is becoming overly constricted, will our coping styles and success strategies as adults also become constricted? Could it be, as journalists have speculated, that America's inability to cope with the realities of world politics stems in part from the fact that our president, a football addict, is committed to a narrow-gage game plan and success style which is grossly inadequate to deal with those of opponents who are skilled in such sophisticated games as chess and go?

There is another feature of spontaneous games which renders them especially effective in serving as "buffered learning experiences" for our children: The fact that the models they embody are miniaturized and rendered relatively safe by the "having fun" context in which they typically occur. As Lewin (1944) noted, games tend to occur on a "plane of unreality," a fact which renders them especially well suited as contexts in which to "toy" with potentially dangerous psychological and emotional problems. Thus Phillips (1960) has observed that many children's games provide a miniature and relatively safe context in which children may gain useful experience in the mastery of anxiety. Consider in this connection the titillating joys of peek-a-boo, the universally popular game in which infants toy with the anxieties associated with mother-absence, and the happy resolution achieved in the discovery that one can bring her back by uncovering one's eyes. In playful games, older children deliberately project themselves into situations involving risk, uncertainty and insecurity, and the tensions generated by the conflicting valences of hope and fear. Particularly where some element of chance is involved, as it is in many children's games, failure is less invidious and hence more easily bearable. Similarly, in games involving mock combat, aggression may be safely expressed because, as Menninger (1942, p. 175) pointed out, "one can hurt people without really hurting them"; and of course without too much danger of being really hurt yourself.

I must stress in particular the point that children's games are effective as expressive models for gaining experience in the mastery of dangerous emotions very largely because of their miniature scale and their playful context. They are rendered safe by remaining on a plane of unreality, in which "reality consequences" do not have to be faced.

I would like to go on to argue that "child's play," far from being a frivolous waste of time as it is so often pictured in our task-oriented, Puritan culture, may in fact represent an optimum setting for children's learning.

To gain some perspective on this matter, consider what psychologists are saying about the kinds of condi-

tions in which optimum learning may occur. In designing their famous computer-typewriter-teaching-machine, or "automatic reflexive environment," O.K. Moore and A.R. Anderson (1969) were careful to take into account what they believe to be the essential features of a really good learning environment: That it should permit free and safe exploration; that it should be self-pacing; that it should be "agent-responsive"; that it should provide immediate and directly relevant feedback; that it should be "productive," that is to say, so structured that a wide variety of ramifying principles and interconnections can be learned; that it should be "autotelic" or self-rewarding, that is to say, related directly to the child's own spontaneous interests and motivations; and finally, that it should be responsive to the child's own initiatives in a way which will permit him to take a "reflexive view of himself." Otherwise put, the environment should be such that the child may alternate in the roles of "active agent" and "patient," and at times may step back and view the whole setting from the viewpoint of an "umpire."

If we take these principles seriously, as I believe we must, it is easy to see why many children do not learn very much in traditionally-structured school settings. For in such traditional schools, the pupils are "patients" and the teacher is the active agent. The "principles" to be learned are explained, perhaps even demonstrated by the teacher, rather than being discovered by the children themselves. Learning is defined as "work," with all the implications that the children, left to follow their own motivations and interests freely, would rather be doing something else. The pacing of activities is rigidly controlled by the teacher, or by the school schedules, or by the tyranny of the lesson plan. And the evaluative feedback, coming from the teacher rather than from the materials themselves, is often delayed, irrelevant and peculiarly invidious.

I will try to show you that these principles, so widely violated in the regular educational settings in which children are supposed to be learning, are all admirably incorporated in a spontaneous, self-organized and self-paced game of backyard baseball, and in many other children's games and play activities. And I will argue that Little League Baseball—and other adult-organized and supervised sports—do a pretty good job of bankrupting most of the features of this, and other, learning models.

But first I would call your attention to the observations of another eminent child psychologist about the functions of spontaneous, self-organized children's games. In his classic study of the moral development of children, Jean Piaget (1932) noted that social rules, for the young child, originally appear as part of the external situation, defined and enforced by powerful adults. At an early stage of "moral realism," the child conforms because he must, to avoid punishment and to maintain the needed goodwill of his parents. But he feels no internalized moral commitment to these rules, because he had no share in defining them, because they often seem arbitrary or unnecessary, and because they are often imposed in an arbitrary and punitive fashion. Piaget argued that the experiences children have in informal games and play activities with their own age mates play an essential role in moving them beyond this stage of moral realism. In an informal game of marbles, for example, where there is no rule book and no adult rule-imposer or enforcer, and where the children know "the rules" only vaguely or have differences of opinion about what they really are, the children must finally face up to the realization that some kinds of rules really are necessary; they must decide for themselves what kinds of rules are "fair," to keep the game going, and interesting, and fun for all; they must participate in establishing the rules and must learn how to enforce them on themselves and others. Experiences like this, Piaget theorized, play a vital role in helping the child grow to a more mature stage of moral development based on the principles of cooperation and consent.

Along somewhat similar lines, Parsons and Bales (1955) have argued that the enormous power differentials between adults and children present serious obstacles to certain kinds of essential learning. For example, adult authority usually appears to young children to be heavily ascriptive in character; authority flows from the fact that one is a parent, a teacher, a coach, or simply an "adult," possessed of awesome powers to punish or reward. But the relevance of this power is not always obvious. Within the peer group, however, where differences in power are on a much smaller scale, leadership is much more likely to be based on relevant, universalistic criteria. A child leader is accepted and followed only to the extent that he effectively expresses the children's own values and helps them to work or play together in self-satisfying ways. It is largely within the framework of informally organized peer groups, these authors reason, that the child learns to conceive of social relationships as being patterned on relevant, universalistic principles in which people must get along in common subjection to general rules.

Kohlberg (1962) has pointed to yet another feature of unstructured children's play for the processes of moral development. If the "rules" are rigidly fixed once and for all by parents, teachers, coaches, or rule books, the child may learn them and perhaps accept them. But he will not gain much experience in the development of mature moral judgment. According to Kohlberg, it is only with some real experience with dissonance, as when the rules are ambiguous or when there is some cross-pressure or opinion difference about which rules should apply, that children learn to understand how certain more general moral principles must be formulated to help them decide for themselves what they should do. Much of my own recent research has tended to support the notion that informal peer group experiences and their accompanying dissonance contribute to the development of moral autonomy in children (Devereux, 1970) and that authoritarian control by adults has precisely the opposite effect (Devereux, 1972).

Backyard versus Little League Baseball, viewed as learning settings. In the light of what has been said thus far, I would now like to comment on what I see as some crucial differences between an informal and spontaneous version of backyard baseball and the organized and adult-controlled Little League version of the same game. Let me grant at once that the latter form of the game is obviously much better equipped, better coached and probably also a good deal safer. No doubt Little League children really do get better training in the official rules and strategies of our national sport, and better experience in the complex physical skills of ball handling, fielding, and so on. If the purpose of the game is to serve as an anticipatory socialization setting for developing future high school, college and professional ball players, the Little League sport is clearly the winner.

But if we look at the matter in a more general educational perspective, it appears that those gains are not achieved without serious cost. In educational terms, the crucial question must always be not what the child is doing to the ball, but what the ball is doing to the child. My most general point must be that in Little League baseball this is often not the case. Almost inevitably, in a highly organized, competitive sport, the focus is on winning and the eye is on the ball. How often does the well-intentioned volunteer coach from the phys-ed department really think about what kind of total experience his boys are having, including those who have warmed the bench all afternoon, or who were not selected for League competition?

Of that, more shortly. But first let me describe a typical variant of backyard baseball, as played in my own neighborhood some fifty years ago. We called it One-o-Cat. There were no teams. With a minimum of five kids you could start up a game, though it was better with seven or eight; once the game got started, usually a few more kids would wander over to join in, often kids of the wrong age or sex. But no matter: It was more fun with more kids, and the child population was a bit sparce back then. One base—usually a tree, or somebody's sweater or cap. Home plate usually a flat stone. Two batters, a catcher, a pitcher, a first baseman. If other kids were available, you had some fielders, too. If someone had a catcher's mit, we'd use a hard ball; otherwise a softball, or tennis ball or anything else. If someone had a face mask, the catcher would play right behind the batter; otherwise way back. There was no umpire to call balls and strikes, so the pitcher was disciplined mostly by shouts of "put it over!" Fouls were balls that went to the right of the tree marking first base or to the left of a shrub on the other side; in other yards or fields, other foul markers would have to be agreed upon.

The "rules" of the game, as we vaguely understood or invented them, were fairly simple. Pitched balls not swung at didn't count either as balls or strikes. Three swings without a hit and you were out. In principle you could go on hitting fouls indefinitely, but after a while the other kids would complain and make you go shack a wild one. A caught fly put you out. A good hit could get you to the tree and back for a home run; a lesser hit could leave you stranded at first, to be hit in, maybe, by the other batter. Or you could be put out either at first base or at the home plate in the usual fashion. Since there were no fixed base lines, when a runner was caught between the first baseman and the catcher, a wild chase all over the yard frequently ensued. When you went out, you retired to right field and everybody moved up one notch, catcher to batter, pitcher to catcher, first baseman to pitcher, left fielder to first, etc. There were no teams and nobody really bothered to keep score, since the personnel of the game usually changed during the session anyway, as some kids had to go do their chores or as other joined in. The object seemed to be to stay at bat as long as you could; but during the afternoon every kid would have plenty of opportunities to play in every position, and no one was ever on the bench. If a few more kids showed up, the game was magically transformed to Two-o-Cat, now with three rotating batters and a second base somewhere over there where third would have been; the runners now had to make the full triangular circuit before completing their run.

Maybe we didn't learn to be expert baseball players, but we did have a lot of fun; moreover, in an indirect and incidental way, we learned a lot of other kinds of things which are probably more important for children in the eight to twelve age range to learn. Precisely because there was no official rule book and no adult or even other child designated as rule enforcer, we somehow had to improvise the whole thing all by ourselves—endless hassles about whether a ball was fair or foul, whether a runner was safe or out, or more generally, simply about what was fair. On the anvil of experience we gradually learned to control our affect and to understand the invisible boundary conditions of our relationships to each other. Don't be a poor sport or the other kids won't want you to play with them. Don't push your point so hard that the kid with the only catcher's mit will quit the game. Pitch a bit more gently to the littler kids so they can have some fun too; and besides, you realize it's important to keep them in the game because numbers are important. How to get a game started and somehow keep it going, so long as the fun lasted. How to pace it. When to quit for a while to get a round of cokes or just to sit under a tree for a bit. How to recognize the subtle boundaries indicating that the game was really over—not an easy thing, since there were no innings, no winners or losers—and slide over into some other activity. "Let's play tag"—"Not it!" Perhaps after supper, a game of catch with your father, who might try to give you a few very non-professional pointers. Perhaps for a few, excited accounts to the family of your success at bat that day and momentary dreams of later glory in the big leagues. But mostly on to the endless variety of other games, pastimes and interests which could so engage a young boy on a summer afternoon or evening.

In terms of the learning models proposed by Roberts, Sutton-Smith, Moore, Piaget, Parsons, Kohlberg, and many others, it was all there. It was fun; the scale was small, and the risks were minimal; we felt free and

relatively safe (at least psychologically); it was spontaneous, autotelic, and agent responsive; it was self-pacing and the feedback was continuous and relevant; and the game was so structured that it required us to use our utmost ingenuity to discover and understand the hidden rules behind the rules—the general principles which make games fair, fun and interesting, and which had to govern our complex relationships with each other; the recognition of the subtle differences in skills, including social skills, which gave added respect and informal authority to some; the ability to handle poor sports, incompetents, cry-babies, little kids, and girls, when the easy out of excluding them from the game entirely was somehow impractical. How to handle it when your own anger or frustrations welled up dangerously close to the point of tears. Most generally, although the formal structure of the game was based on a model of competition and physical skill, many of its most important lessons were in the social-emotional sector—how to keep the group sufficiently cohesive to get on with the play, and how to handle the tensions which arose within us and between us.

All these are things which were happening to the boys when left to themselves in this informal game situation. And it seems to me that they are far more important than what was happening to the ball. By now the ball is lost, anyway, somewhere in the bushes over by left field. Perhaps someone will find it tomorrow. And besides, its too hot for baseball now, and the kids have all gone skinny-dipping in the little pond down the road a bit.

How does Little League Baseball stack up against this model? Rather badly, in my opinion. The scale is no longer miniature and safe, what with scoreboards, coaches, umpires, parents, and a grandstand full of spectators all looking at you and evaluating your every move with a single, myopic criterion: Perform! Win! The risks of failure are large and wounding. And in the pyramidal structure of league competition only a few can be winners and everybody else must be some kind of loser.

In Little League ball, the spontaneity is largely killed by schedules, rules, and adult supervision—a fixed time and place for each game, a set number of innings, a commitment to a whole season's schedule, at the expense of all alternative activities. Self pacing? Obviously not. Fun? Yes, in a hard sort of way; but please, no fooling around or goofing off out there in right field; keep your eyes on the ball. Instant feedback? Yes, loud and clear from all sides, if you make a mistake; but mostly from adults in terms of their criteria of proper baseball performance.

But the major problem with Little League Baseball, as I see it, is that the whole structure of the game is rigidly fixed once and for all. It's all there in the rule books and in the organization of the League and of the game itself. It is all handed to the children, ready-made, on a silver platter, together with the diamonds, the bats and the uniforms. It is all so carefully supervised by adults, who are the teachers, coaches, rule enforcers, decision makers, and principal rewarders and punishers, that there's almost nothing left for the children to do but "play" the game. Almost all of the opportunities for incidental learning which occur in spontaneous self-organized and self-governed children's games have somehow been sacrificed on the altar of safety (physical only) and competence (in baseball only).

Competition and Little Leaguism in Contemporary America. No doubt there are some who will argue that ours is a tough, competitive society and that somehow, during the educational process, children must be hardened up and readied for the rigorous competition of real life they will face later on. It is certainly true that competition has indeed played a central role in American society, and for generations there were many, like Theodore Roosevelt, who thought of it as the backbone of American character and achievement. But at what cost to other values? More than thirty years ago the great psychoanalyst, Karen Horney, in her classic analysis of *The Neurotic Personality of Our Time* (1937) saw fit to devote an entire chapter to "neurotic competitiveness." But while Horney saw the problem clearly enough, most psychologists and educators of that generation did not. It is interesting to note that among the 23 experimental studies of competition reported by Murphy, Murphy and Newcomb (1937), the focus is almost invariably upon the effects of competition on the performance of some task; not a single one of these studies dealt with any measures of the effects of competition upon the subjects themselves!

But effects there undoubtedly are, among them the apparent inability of American children, reared in a competitive style, to know when *not* to compete. This point was neatly demonstrated in an experiment by Madsen and Shapira (1970) in which an apparatus was so arranged that no child could get any reward at all without cooperating with the others. Mexican children, and in another study by Shapira and Madsen (1969), Israeli Kibbutz children, were quick to fall into a cooperative plan to everybody's mutual advantage, but the American children continued to compete even after it became quite obvious that no one could "win" anything at all.

The time has surely come to reassess the heavy stress we have placed on competition in our educational system, and in our culture generally. In this connection it is interesting to note that recent movements toward educational reform call for a drastic reduction in the role of competition. More generally, the new "counter culture" flourishing on our college campuses is strongly anti-competitive in basic orientation. Somehow a whole generation of fathers, still deeply involved in major sports and other facets of the old American dream, has managed to rear a generation of sons among which a very substantial segment will have no part of it.

What can we say, more specifically, of the effects of Little League competition for children? I shall not take space here to consider such measured physiological side-effects as the famous Little League elbow; or the evidences of measured Galvanic Skin Responses of young boys before and after competition (Skubic, 1955); or the reported losses of sleep and appetite before or following competition (Skubic, 1956). I have no reason to doubt that first rate child athletes, like the adult athletes studied by Ogilvie and Tutko (1971), are better built physically, better coordinated and have fairly well integrated, if somewhat aggressive, personalities, in comparison with less athletic peers.

But the crucial question must be whether participation in Little League sports helps make them that way, or whether the reported differences are a result of the selection processes involved. In the adult study cited above, the authors believe that most of observed differences result from the selection processes rather than from the character-molding experiences of athletic competition. Hale's (1956) finding that the Little League players who made it to the Williamsport national competition had more, darker and curlier pubic hair than non-playing age mates almost certainly reflects a selective factor rather than a consequence of ball playing.

Similarly, in Seymour's (1956) study, it is clear that all the major reported differences between the Little Leaguers and their classmates, all documenting the "superiority" of the League players, existed *before* the season began. On all the self-rating scales used in this study, moreover, the non-participants actually *improved more* than the participants, ending ahead of the participants in their post-season self-ratings of their feelings about "me and my school" and "me and my home." In this study, the non-participants also gained somewhat more than the participants in the teacher ratings on "social consciousness," "emotional adjustment," and "responsibility." On the sociometric ratings, as expected, the boy athletes were the sociometric stars in their classrooms both before and after the season. The author does note, however, that on the post-season sociometric test, the Little League boys were somewhat *less* accepting of their peers, as measured by ratings they extended to others, than they had been before the season started. Could these results represent a gentle forecast of the Ogilvie-Tutko description of adult athletes: "Most athletes indicate low interest in receiving support and concern from others, low need to take care of others and low need for affiliation. Such a personality seems necessary to achieve victory over others." (p. 61-62.)

If some processes of selection are at work in sifting out the children who get to play in League or interscholastic competition, as they quite obviously are; and if both the adult and peer culture shower these children with special attention and kudos, as they surely do, then responsible educators must have some concern about all the other children, who are losers or non-participants in this one-dimensional competition. How sure are we that the values and character traits selected and carefully reinforced in Little League sports are really the best for wholesome child development? In a culture as fanatically dedicated to excellence in competitive sports as we have become in modern America, are we needlessly and cruelly punishing the children who are physically smaller or less mature, or less well coordinated or aggressive, who can't compete successfully and perhaps don't even want to. Many will no doubt turn into fine and productive adults, but only following a childhood in which they were never able to live up to the myopic values of the peer culture or to the expectancies of their sport-addicted fathers.

Let me not be misunderstood. I am certainly not coming out against baseball as such, though for reasons indicated, I believe the informal, backyard variants have far more learning values for children than the formally organized, adult-supervised version. My most fundamental opposition to Little League Baseball, however, is based not so much to what it does by way of either harm or good to the player, as it is upon what Little Leaguism is doing to the whole culture of childhood, to participants and non-participants alike, and to the schools, families, neighborhoods and communities where Little Leaguism has taken root.

Look first at what has happened to organized sports in high schools, and the picture is perhaps clearer. In a high school of two thousand students, only a relative handful get to participate even on the squads of any of the major sports teams. All the rest are consigned to the role of frenzied spectators at interscholastic meets, or still worse, in many sport-minded communities, to non-participant-non-spectators, perceived by adults and peers alike as odd-balls, pariahs, or queers. As Coleman (1961) showed, this group may in fact include some of the best students, but they get precious little reward for their academic efforts. And the kids who do go out in earnest for a high school sport find that, to compete at all effectively against our fanatic standards of excellence, they have to make it almost a full time job both in season and out, at the expense of virtually *all* other extra-curricular and leisure time activities. In one way, you're damned if you don't participate; in another way, you're damned if you do. . . .

In Little League and other variations of organized interscholastic sport, we now see clear indications of the invasions of this sports culture into the much more precious and vulnerable world of little children. Like the bad currency in Gresham's famous law, it is an inferior product which ends by driving out the good. Because of its peculiar fascination, more for the parents than for the children themselves, it ends by nearly monopolizing the field and driving almost to bankruptcy the natural and spontaneous culture of play and games among American children.

REFERENCES

1. Coleman, J., *The Adolescent Society*, Glencoe, Ill: Free Press, 1961.

2. Devereux, E.C., "Authority and moral development among American and West German children," *Journal of Comparative Family Studies*, Vol. III, Spring, 1972. In press.
3. ———, "The role of peer-group experience in moral development," in J.P. Hill, ed., *Minnesota Symposia on Child Psychology*, Minneapolis: University of Minnesota Press. 1970. Vol. IV, pp. 94-140.
4. Eifermann, Rivka R., *Determinants of children's game styles*, Jerusalem: The Israel Academy of Sciences and Humanities, 1971b. In press.
5. ———, "Social play in childhood," in R.E. Herron & Brian Sutton-Smith, eds., *Child's Play*, New York: John Wiley & Sons, 1971a. pp. 270-297.
6. Hale, C.J., "Physiological maturity of Little League baseball players," *Research Quarterly*, 1956, 27, 276-282.
7. Herron, R.E., and Sutton-Smith, B., *Child's Play*, New York: Wiley & Son, 1971.
8. Horney, Karen, *The Neurotic Personality of Our Time*, New York: W.W. Norton & Co., 1937.
9. Kohlberg, L., "Development of moral character and moral ideology," in M.L. Hoffman and L.W. Hoffman, eds., *Review of Child Development Research*, New York: Russell Sage Foundation, 1964, Vol. I, pp. 383-431.
10. Lewin, Kurt, et al., "Level of Aspiration," in J.M. Hunt, ed., *Personality and Behavior Disorders*, New York: Ronald Press, 1944.
11. Madsen, M.C., and Shapira, A., "Cooperative and competitive behavior of urban Afro-American, Anglo-American, Mexican-American and Mexican village children," *Developmental Psychology*, 1970, 3(1), 16-20.
12. Menninger, Karl, *Love Against Hate*, New York: Harcourt, 1942.
13. Moore, Omar Khayyam & Anderson, A.R., "Some principles for the design of clarifying educational environments," in D. Goslin, ed., *Handbook of Socialization Theory and Research*, New York: Rand McNally, 1969, pp. 571-613.
14. Murphy, G., Murphy, L.B. & Newcomb, T.M., *Experimental Social Psychology*, New York: Harper Bros., rev. ed., 1937.
15. Ogilvie, B.C., and Tutko, T.A., "If you want to build character, try something else," *Psychology Today*, 1971, Vol. 5, pp. 60-63.
16. Parsons, T., and Bales, R.F., *Family, Socialization and Interaction Process*, Glencoe, Ill.: Free Press, 1955.
17. Piaget, J., *The Moral Judgment of the Child*, New York: Harcourt, 1932.
18. Phillips, R.H., "The nature and function of children's formal games," *Psychoanalytic Quarterly*, 1960, 29, 200-207.
19. Roberts, J.M., & Sutton-Smith, B., "Child training and game involvement," *Ethnology*, 1962, 1, 166-185.
20. Seymour, E.W., "Comparative study of certain behavior characteristics of participants and non-participants in Little League Baseball," *Research Quarterly*, 1956, 27, 338-346.
21. Shapira, A., and Madsen, M.C., "Cooperative and competitive behavior of Kibbutz and urban children in Israel," *Child Development*, 1969, 40, 609-617.
22. Skubic, E., "Emotional responses of boys to Little League and Middle League competitive baseball," *Research Quarterly*, 1955, 26, 342-352.
23. ———, "Studies of Little League and Middle League Baseball," *Research Quarterly*, 1956, 27, 97-110.
24. Sutton-Smith, B., "A syntax for play and games," in R.E. Herron and B. Sutton-Smith, eds., *Child's Play*, New York: John Wiley & Sons, 1971, pp. 298-307.
25. Sutton-Smith, B., and Rosenberg, R.G., "Sixty years of historical change in the game preferences of American children," in R.E. Herron and B. Sutton-Smith, eds., *Child's Play*, New York: John Wiley & Sons, 1971, pp. 18-50.

BOYS PLAY THE MEN'S GAME

Hank Burchard

A Sub-Teen Beltway League Football Showdown

The harvest moon rising over Our Lady of Mercy Catholic Church is even larger, oranger and more gorgeous than the sun that had flooded suburban Potomac with unseasonable warmth a few hours earlier.

None of the hundreds of boys and men on the football field is heard to remark upon the spectacle; no one seems even to have noticed. It is serious work they are engaged in. Do the Dolphins take time out to marvel at the moon over Miami?

There are six football squads on the field but room remains for as many more. The young boys don't take up much space—they run about two dozen to the ton—and their bulky shoulder pads and helmets for some reason make them seem even smaller.

Floating above the haze of dust over the nearly grassless field come the deep voices of men and the bird-song notes of boys, encouraging, cajoling, commanding, cursing. (In practice and at games, on the fields and on the sidelines, profanity is loud and constant, as though it were written into the rules.)

"No dammit, you dummy, the five hole! The five hole! Jesus, haven't you learned anything since August?"

"Way to get on it, Smith! Way to pop! Good hit!"

"Hey, man, you call that a pushup?"

There is an island of calm in the hubbub, centered around a short, heavy black-haired man standing alone at midfield. Of the score of coaches on the field only he is silent, and only he is smiling.

He is Gene Bovello, 45, executive director of the Bethesda Boys Club and coach of the BBC junior (100-pound) team, a powerhouse of the Beltway League, which, in turn, is regarded as the toughest in the area.

"This is the American way," Bovello said as he watched his assistant coaches and their assistants direct a light-contact scrimmage. "If these boys weren't out here tonight, God knows where they'd be. You don't see any hippies here, do you? I mean, some of the guys' hair may be a little long, but they're good boys. These are all-American boys, just like we were."

Their mothers know where these boys are, five or six nights a week during the football season. Practices run from about 5 p.m. to 8 p.m., Tuesday (and sometimes Monday) through Friday. The games are on Saturday, about half of them at night.

There are about 3,000 boys in the Beltway League, which has two divisions of 10 teams, each of which may have as many as six subdivisions of age and weight groups that range from 9 to 15 years old and from less than 75 to 135 pounds.

The league represents most of the Washington suburbs and is but a fraction of the nonacademic organized football establishment in the metropolitan area that Bovello estimates involves about 25,000 boys.

BBC fields five teams, totaling more than 200 boys. Bovello's division embraces the 11- to 13-year-olds, and he suits up about 40 boys, give or take a cold or sprain, on any given Saturday.

If Bovello's boys run true to his form this year, they are headed for the Marriott Super Bowl, which will be videotaped for broadcast Dec. 14.

They didn't make it last year because they were beaten in the crucial game by Maplewood Recreation Association. The same thing could happen this season. BBC and Maplewood have equivalent records: BBC has lost once and Maplewood has two ties. They will play each other Saturday, and the winner is all but assured of the division championship.

Bovello does not intend to lose. He has been coaching boys' football for 24 years and has won 22 championships, a number of them with the Silver Spring Boys Club. "This BBC used to be the patsy of the league," he said. "They brought me over here to turn it around. When I came, BBC was 4 for 46; since then, we're 54 and 8. We've got two teams in first place, two tied for first, and one in second. These boys are playing football, now.

"Once I went six seasons, 54 games, unbeaten and, get this, *unscored on*. I've lost 12 out of more than 250 games.

"I'm the No. 1 offensive coach in this league and the No. 12 defensive coach. We average about 38 points a game, even trying to hold the scores down. I don't want to sound like I'm bragging, but I'm just telling you facts so you'll understand."

For a man about to put his record on the line in yet another Big Game, Bovello seems rather relaxed. Only occasionally does he wander over to say something to an assistant or to a boy on the first- or second-string offensive or defensive squads or the several special teams.

"I did my work in the summer, training my boys and my coaches," he said. "They know my system, or if they don't, it's too late now to teach them."

Bovello's system is contained in a playbook that started out with 30 basic plays and built to 45. "We used a lot of sets," he said. "We've got a double wing, tight T, proset short T, wing T, wing double-T, the I and the wishbone. There are eight or 10 plays off each set, use about 200, maybe."

The sets and plays being practiced at the moment include none of the above. "This is some junk we're doing now," he said. "Maplewood's got some spies up in the woods there, so we're showing them junk, garbage we'd never use in a million years.

"Boys Play the Men's Game" by Hank Burchard, Washington Post Staff Writer. *The Washington Post*, November 8, 1974, pp. 1D-2D.

"The point of this practice is timing and quickness, that's what my teams win on. Anybody can tell a Bovello team, because we always beat everybody off the ball. The other kids are still listening to the count when we're gone."

Bovello moves closer, glancing over his shoulder at the woods, which come nearly to the sidelines and are utterly opaque from the lighted field. "Could be a hundred guys in those trees, you'd never see one of them," he said. He lowered his voice. "Tomorrow night we're going to move the practice to St. Bart's, over across the Beltway. Don't you pass it on to anybody.

"You see . . ." he broke off as the father of a boy on another BBC team walked up. They chatted for a few minutes about this and that and the father moved off. "His boy used to play for Maplewood, so I had to stop talking about our plans," he said. "I don't know, his boy plays for us now, but somehow everything we're doing gets back to them. You can't be too careful."

One of Bovello's boys goes down after taking a thump in the ribs. He is crying. Bovello kneels down and runs practiced fingers over the bony chest. "Take a deep breath," he says. "It hurts," the boy groans. "O.K.," Bovello says, "That's all for you tonight. If it doesn't feel better in the morning you tell your mother to get you X-rayed."

Moments later another boy goes down after catching a finger in the right eye. It pours tears that soak the shirttail he keeps wiping it with against everybody's instructions. Bevello looks at the eye, barely visible in the dim light. "It'll be all right in the morning," he says.

Even in light-contact scrimmage the collisions make hurtful noises, and it gets more wincy when the 100-pound defensive unit goes up against the 135 pounders for a 10-minute, full-speed drill. Bovello's boys give better than they get.

"Look at that," he said after a particularly vigorous clash. "Almost every one of them on the ground. Most little league football, you see everybody standing around after a play. These kids are where they're supposed to be, on the ground. That's real hitting; that's football."

Like many of those involved in youth football programs, Bovello is sensitive to criticism of pitting growing boys in dangerous sport. "We're very safety-conscious in this league," he said. "I've coached over 2,000 boys, and I've only had two serious injuries, what I call serious, broken bones.

"One was a broken collar bone and one was this year, a broken bone in the foot, and it happened when the boy was running free, nobody around him, I don't know, just a little bone popped.

"Did you see that (ABC-TV) special about spearing (tackling by driving one's head into the opponent)? We don't do any of that. We've even got a rule against it. These boys get a lot of conditioning before they ever even go into practice, and we put the best uniforms on them that you can get, good equipment. It takes a budget of $20,000 a year to supply these boys with equipment, all good fitted, full pads, no inserts or cheap stuff, and

we've got a doctor who travels with the team. And there's insurance and everything. My big problem is with our players getting hurt in gym classes at school. They really break 'em up."

Practice is nearly over. One of the assistants gathers the boys for a pep talk:

"Gentlemen, I don't think I have to tell you what we're facing Saturday. This is the Super Bowl game. You know what happened to us last year, what Maplewood did to us, you know some of the things that have been going on.

"You know how (their guy) got the Touchdown Club award last year when (our guy) was the one that earned it. I think it was just politics, there's an awful lot of politics in this league, but we're not going to let that stop us."

"You know we got some bad calls in our games, maybe that's because we're a big team, I don't know, but nobody can stop us if we try hard enough. And I mean everybody; you've got to talk it up, you've got to keep it up, you've got to take it to them.

"You subs, I know you didn't play last week, but you're important too. And we won. That should be the big thing for all of us. You've got to be ready."

Bovello walked slowly from the field. "I've sent four boys to the pros, won a lot of ball games. I don't care about championships or not; I want to teach them the right way to play. The big thing is for the boys to enjoy themselves. I don't care what the score is, every boy gets to play at least a full (10-minute) quarter of every game.

"I guess I put 50-60 hours a week into this, sometimes more. My wife used to mind it, a little at first anyway, but now she says, 'Gene, you couldn't be spending your time any better than helping boys.'

"At least she knows where I am, she knows I'm not with any other women or anything. I don't have any bad habits (here he ground out his umpteenth Kent of the evening), don't drink, I just work (as an electrician) and work with boys.

"Don't you let on about where we're practicing, remember."

Maplewood

There are no lights at Maplewood's field in Bethesda, and dusk already is gathering as a score of boys break away from a pickup game of touch and more or less assemble around assistant coach Fuzzy Myers, a salesman who admits to no other name. Head coach Mike Sommer, a doctor and former pro football player, will miss the practice because he cannot get away from his duties at Fairfax Hospital. Happens all the time.

"We pride ourselves on hitting," Myers said as the boys did calisthenics. "We like to think we can hit with anybody, even if we're just a neighborhood outfit. Most of the teams we play have squads that are twice as large, and heavier, but we just go on in there and hit."

Myers works the boys into a scrimmage somewhat complicated by the fact that he can't put 11 men on each side because only 18 (of 22) have showed up. The center, who seems to be the designated morale officer, leads a cheer between every play, but cuss as they can the squad sounds faint compared to Bovello's crowd.

"Most of our boys play both ways," said Myers, who was coaching both ways, running from one huddle to the other telling one group how to defeat the plans he was laying with the other bunch.

The scrimmage is made even more disjointed by the antics of the Maplewood 85-pound team, which is running wind sprints through the 100-pounders' formations.

"You see our No. 17 there?" Myers asks. "He's super. You know he won the Touchdown Club award last year. There were a lot of complaints about it from Bethesda, but the fact is they always lean toward the younger boys when they give that one out.

"He is not only fast and strong, but he thinks; he thinks about what's coming, studies strength and weakness on offense and defense, analyzes. . . .He has the maturity of a kid in junior high school."

Few as they are, the Maplewoods raise plenty of dust in a 15-minute no-contact scrimmage and Myers is coated with dust, the distinguishing feature of youth football coaches, to whom grass and Astro Turf are not known.

Dark comes after an hour and practice ends with sprints and a search for a lost football. "We aren't very big but we play pretty big," Myers said as the team trooped off. "I think we'll be ready Saturday. At least they'll know they were in a game."

A Long Week of Sweat, A 40-Minute Showdown

The Big Game

BBC and Maplewood arrive as an 85-pound team plays out a one-sided confrontation at Our Lady of Mercy, who has none for Peppermill Village, being thumped by Fairfax. Bovello has predicted a crowd of 1,500, and there seem to be at least that many kids playing unorganized football on and around the field while the official game is in progress. The final score is 18-0, to the best recollection of the referee ("Man, you got to catch me before I erase my scorecard; this is the fourth game I've done today.").

The Maplewoods chatter it up, with the exception of one boy in blue who is sitting apart. "Going to clean Bethesda's plow tonight?" a bystander asks him.

"They're going to run our ass out of town," the boy responds.

Coach Sommer, by some miracle of modern medicine, arrives before game time. "Don't write about all the screaming and yelling and all the other Little League stuff we're not supposed to do," he said. "We do it all."

A BBC assistant coach, at the other end of the field, has brief remarks for his gentlemen: "I want you to play nasty tonight. I want you to be mean. They don't like physical football, they like to play playground football. They don't want to get hit. So stick it to 'em early."

Coach Bovello is even briefer: "Don't take nothing off of it. Pour it on 'em."

Myers tells the Maplewoods: "We're going to start with a 5-4 (defense) and stunt to the strong side. You've got to play tough because they have to sweep. And their quarterback doesn't like to throw with people around him, so get in there.

"Last year we beat Bethesda and then needed help to get to the Super Bowl and we didn't get that help. This year we don't need help. We can do it ourselves. Tonight."

BBC receives the kickoff and makes a good return, aided by a late-hit penalty against Maplewood. BBC has penalty problems too, and has to punt. The ball goes into the end zone and Maplewood starts from its own 20-yard line, finishing in the same vicinity, and punts on fourth down.

BBC, after some short gains, makes bold to try to run the ball on fourth down with a yard to go at midfield and is stopped by Maplewood, which soon faces a similar situation at BBC's 43. Maplewood also goes for it and also is stopped.

It has been noticed on both benches and by the spectators that Maplewood's blocking lacks authority. "Your sister can block better than that, you sissy!" an adult female voice chastens one offender, admitting, under questioning, that the miscreant is her son.

BBC's drive from its own 43 moves in fits and starts until suddenly the boys in red have a first and goal to go on the Maplewood six-yard line. Then it is second and goal on the six-inch line. Maplewood stiffens and stops BBC on third and fourth down, taking over on the one-yard line in a glory of cheers.

The effort seems to have drained the Maplewoods, because after three tries they have to punt. The ball goes only to their own 30; two running plays and two passes later BBC scores. The extra point kick is good, something not often seen in youth football.

Maplewood's ensuing drive is dispirited, especially after their star has to be helped from the field after a hard lick. He is playing with a case of diarrhea.

It is halftime: BBC 7, Maplewood 0.

Lacking locker rooms, the coaches take the boys to secluded corners. The Maplewoods hear this:

From Sommer: "These guys are big, but you are tougher. Just don't quit. Some of you guys are crying, but you're not beat; seven-nothing doesn't beat you. There's a whole half to go yet. They're running up our right side like it was water. . . .We've got some guys (he names one) who don't seem to want to play football any more."

From Myers: "Let's just reach back and get it up."

From Sommer: "Get your heads out of your . . ."

The Bethesdans hear this: "They've found out they can't move the ball on us, so we've got to be ready for the big play. The long ball."

The second half is more of the same. Maplewood receives the kickoff, fails to move the ball and punts. It is a good punt, and the BBC receiver fumbles it. But another red shirt picks it up and runs it back for a touchdown. Again the kick is good, and it's BBC 14, Maplewood 0.

On the next series the Maplewood star is hurt again and leaves the field. On third and nine the referee finds himself in the middle of an attempted Maplewood sweep around right end and the play dissolves in a heap on the sideline.

Sommer, enraged, leaps cursing onto the pile, fists raised, then just as quickly recovers himself and walks away.

Maplewood gains one first down, its first of the game, and gets another on a penalty. A drive falls short on the BBC 10, a fumble is recovered but is followed immediately by a BBC interception, and so it goes. There is no more scoring, mainly because BBC has long gain after long gain called back on penalties.

The game is over. The Maplewoods do their best to give a good-sport cheer to BBC, get one back, and go home.

Bovello is back-patted around the field until he breaks away to address his assembled team members, whose expressions are only slightly less serious than they were before the game. It occurs to an onlooker that in a week of watching play and practice, he has seen only a few boys cry and has heard none laugh.

Bovello: "I knew you could do it. I'm proud of you. We have a day off Monday, and then you know we've got just one more game before the Super Bowl.

A BBC assistant: "Tuesday we start for Fairfax. They're out of it, but they'd love to put us out of it. . . . Tuesday, gentlemen, come for work."

WHY ELIMINATE KIDS?

Terry Orlick and Cal Botterill

Elimination is a critical problem, perhaps the most critical problem which exists in children's sport.

According to Canadian Amateur Hockey Association statistics, of the 600,000 players registered or affiliated with the C.A.H.A. in 1973, 53 percent were under the age of twelve, 35 percent were from twelve to fifteen, and 11 percent were over fifteen years of age. Hockey statistics over the past five years indicate that only about 10 percent of the players register to continue participating in organized hockey beyond their fifteenth birthday, and similar trends reportedly exist in other organized sports like little league baseball and minor league soccer (Orlick, 1974). This provides clear cut evidence that either kids are being eliminated or they are voluntarily dropping out. Perhaps even more staggering than these statistics is the fact that kids are beginning to drop out of organized sports as early as seven and eight years of age.

In some cases, the elimination of children is calculated and intentional, while in other cases it is completely unintentional. Whether elimination is intentional or unintentional, it has similar effects. Kids come to feel unworthy, unwanted, and unacceptable.

It is absurd that on the one hand we feel that sports are good for kids and on the other hand we set up a system which eliminates poorer performers, girls, late-maturing boys, kids who are not aggressive enough, and so on.

Although the elimination of kids is often unintentional, "cutting" is one form of intentional elimination which can have drastically negative effects on kids. They are "cut" not only physically but also psychologically. Setting limits on the kind and number of kids allowed to be involved is essentially what cutting is all about. This is an all too common occurrence in communities and schools across the nation. An example which comes to mind occurred when two little girls recently went to "try out" for the softball team. Shortly after they left for the field, one of the girls returned home without her girlfriend. Her father asked her what had happened. The little girl replied, "They already had enough people." So it goes. Similarly, we may have 100 boys try out for a basketball team, or 100 girls try out for a gymnastic team—but in each case, only about ten or fifteen *make the team*. Instead of cutting children, we should be personally encouraging them to come out for sport and making it a meaningful place for them.

We should field as many teams as there are interested kids to fill them. It is ridiculous to promote participation on the one hand, and then to cut interested individuals from the team, or to in any way limit their participation. This type of action provides the rejected child with massive negative reinforcement and counters our basic reason for existing (that is, to serve the children). To cut a child because he is not good enough negates our purpose and our responsibility to our children and to society. It is comparable to a doctor refusing to treat his sickest patients to insure that his win-loss record looks good. Those people seeking athletic participation who are cut-off may be the ones who could benefit most from this experience. Just as the least lovable child is the one who needs loving the most, the least athletic child may need athletics the most. The process of cutting is a vicious circle for the one who doesn't make it. He is cut because he is not good enough to make it and is consequently given no opportunity to practice on a regular basis so that he can become good enough to make it—so he is rejected again the following year. We not only are doing an injustice to the individual but also are cutting our own sporting throats. Twenty years later, these cut individuals do not support our programs, and they refuse to pay for new facilities. Through our negative conditioning program we have firmly entrenched in them a negative feeling about sport. The least that this negative feeling will do is to relegate these people to the role of spectators, which is bad enough in itself.

Elimination is a long term process. Although it may occur at an early age, it can last a lifetime. By eight or nine years of age, many children have already turned off sports. In one study, many young children who had opted out of sports indicated that they never wanted to go out again (see Orlick, 1973a). A seventeen-year-old female cross-country skier of national caliber revealed some possible reasons why many children may not want to go out again as well as why she dropped out herself:

Q. Why do you think you stopped skiing?
A. I liked it when I started but later it wasn't fun anymore.
Q. What didn't you like?
A. There was too much criticism . . . he [the coach] didn't act like he wanted me on the team . . . he never gave any positive suggestions . . . just criticism.
Q. Is there anything else that bothered you?
A. Yes, the coaches ignored the younger skiers . . . in order to get attention you have to be good . . . lots of kids gave it up because nobody took any interest in them.
Q. Is there anything you would like to see changed in the cross-country ski program?
A. Yes, there's no promotion for recreational skiing . . . it's only for the ones who want to compete. The program shouldn't be concerned only with producing racers. Kids may want to compete once they learn how to ski . . . or just ski later on. Now they never hear anything about it.

Her perceptive insights were borne out time and time again in interviews conducted with athletic drop-outs (young and old) in skiing as well as in many other sports.

The reward structure which now exists in organized sports does not appear to be consistent with what is in the best interest of the majority of children. There appears to be an over-emphasis on winning at the expense of fun involvement. This gives rise to an elitist atmosphere wherein many youngsters eliminate themselves before they start, while others begin to withdraw at seven and eight years of age.

In many cases, organized sport (team or individual) appears to operate as an extremely efficient screening process for the elimination of children.

The findings of a study by Orlick (1972a) indicate that a major change in emphasis is needed in children's sport in order to operate in the child's best interest with regard to motivation, program, and personnel. Extensive interviews conducted with eight- and nine-year-old organized sports participants, nonparticipants, and drop-outs showed that the children strongly felt that they had to be good enough to make the team or to play regularly. Seventy-five percent of the nonparticipant children, *all of whom thought they were not good enough to make the team,* indicated that they would go out for a team if they thought they would surely make it. *Fear of failure,* or the psychological *stress of disapproval, appeared to influence certain children to the extent that they were afraid to participate.* It has become evident that there are many nonparticipants who would like to participate in a variety of sports, and they would participate if they knew they would be acceptable in the sports setting and if they were assured of having a rewarding experience. However, they generally do not feel that this is the case. Rather, they feel that they do not have much to contribute or gain from a sporting system where acceptance is seen as being conditional upon performance (see Orlick, 1973b).

Children who drop out of sport at an early age appear to be merely reacting to negative situations which are largely due to the structure of the game or the emphasis of the coaches. The majority of the children drop out because they are not given an adequate opportunity to play, or they are not having a positive experience (e.g., it's not any fun). Sitting on the bench, being ignored, or being yelled at for making a mistake, certainly isn't much fun. Generally these kids are not getting positive reinforcement from the coach or from the competitive situation itself. If they are getting any positive feedback, it is outweighed by negative feedback which leads to their decision to drop out. Most negative experiences are related to an overconcern with perfection, particularly at an early age.

One seven-year-old child and two eight-year-old children, who dropped out of sport, bring out this point quite clearly in their responses to the following question: "How good would you like to be at sport?" Their responses were: "Really good . . . because if you're not the coach won't think very much about you." "Perfect . . . so when I wanted to play, I could play." "Good enough so I could play sports and I wouldn't get fired on anything I went on" (Orlick, 1973a).

The mother of an eight-year-old hockey player summed up the situation well when she said: "How can kids become enthused when they're not allowed to become involved?"

The following interview excerpts are presented in order to help you get a view from the perspective of two seven-year-old drop-outs and two eight-year-old drop-outs.

Case 1: eight-year-old soccer drop-out. (Started at eight, dropped out at eight, about three-fourths of the way through the season.)

Q. Are you going to go out [for soccer] again?
A. I was planning on it, but I don't think I will.
Q. Why not?
A. It's not that much fun anymore.
Q. Did you play for the whole season?
A. For the last three games I didn't play, but the other games I did.
Q. Why did you decide to stop?
A. 'Cause whenever we had a game I was usually an extra so I didn't get to play very much.
Q. So what did you do during the game?
A. Just stand around and let the mosquitoes eat me.
Q. Were there a lot of kids who didn't play?
A. Yes, there were a lot of extras . . . didn't get to play.
Q. Why didn't they get to play?
A. 'Cause there was already enough guys.
Q. What do you like least about sports?
A. Baseball.
Q. Why?
A. Well, most of the time you're in outfield anyway, and you hardly ever catch one . . . they hardly ever come out that far. I get too bored.
Q. Is there anything you'd like to see changed in sports to make them better?
A. Baseball maybe . . . make the field smaller and the bases a little shorter.
Q. Would you like to be an athlete or a member of a little league team?
A. No.
Q. Why not?
A. Well, you just waste time . . . like you could do some other good stuff . . . like build something or something like that.
Q. Would you like to be good at sports?
A. Yes.
Q. How good?
A. Perfect.
Q. Why would you want to be perfect?
A. So when I wanted to play I could play.
Q. What do you think it would be like for you this year if you went out for the team?
A. I wouldn't make it . . . I don't think I would.
Q. If you thought you would surely make the team, would you go out for it?
A. Yes.

Case 2: seven-year-old soccer drop-out. (Started soccer at seven, dropped out at seven [within a few weeks after starting].)

Q. How did you like it last year when you went out for soccer?
A. I didn't like it very much 'cause they never let me play. They just let the good guys play . . . the little guys just have to stand around . . . and watch.
Q. Are you going to go out again?
A. If they let me play I would.
Q. Were there a lot of kids who didn't play?

A. Yup, most of the team didn't get to play . . . just some guys did . . . just the big guys. Everybody else just stands around.
Q. Did you stay for the whole season?
A. I stayed a couple of weeks . . . then I quit because I never got to be what I wanted to.

Case 3: seven-year-old hockey drop-out. (Started hockey at five, dropped out at seven; started baseball at six, dropped out at seven.)

Q. Why did you stop playing hockey?
A. I started not to like it.
Q. What didn't you like?
A. Well, in hockey I quit because I didn't get the puck passed to me too many times.
Q. You didn't get the puck?
A. Oh . . . only once.
Q. Only once in all the time you played?
A. I think so but I'm not pretty sure . . . I might have got it a couple of more times than that.
Q. Is that the main reason you don't want to play?
A. Yeah . . . you know 'cause I got bored with it.
Q. You got bored? How come?
A. 'Cause every night you could be fooling around at your house instead of wasting your time playing hockey. All's I did was sit around. . . .
Q. What do you mean?
A. Well, like baseball . . . it's like hockey 'cause you. . . . I hardly even get a chance . . . 'cause I'm always at the end of the line in baseball.
Q. So you don't get a chance?
A. Well, I get up to bat but I wait such a long time, I forget what I'm doing and I struck out . . . that's what I did I struck out . . . every time I went up. Oh, I hit the ball and then I got out and then I struck out . . . and then I struck out again.
Q. Is that why you didn't go out for baseball again?
A. Yeah.
Q. How good would you like to be in sport?
A. Real good.
Q. Why do you think you'd want to be real good?
A. Because if you're not the coach won't think very much about you.
Q. Do you think you will ever want to go out for a sports team?
Q. What do you think is the real reason that you don't want to go out for a team any more?
A. It just kind of bothers me . . . it bores me. . . .
Q. If you were better do you think you'd want to go out?
A. Yeah. . . . Right now I don't have very much fun. In hockey, I didn't get very much chance to get the puck and in baseball I didn't hit the ball very much. Now I don't want to go out any more.

Case 4: eight-year-old baseball drop-out. (Started at seven, dropped out at eight after one season.)

Q. Have you ever played on any regular league teams?
A. No.

A. Yes. I played baseball last year but I don't think I want to play baseball anymore.

Q. What didn't you like about it?

A. Well, I didn't get to go up to bat any time. . . . I usually just stay on bases and everything and play shortstop. I got to go up to bat once every time we played. I didn't get to bat that much. They let me play outfielder . . . and shortstop. I wasn't that good an outfielder anyway.

Q. Is there anything else that bothers you about playing sports?

A. Yeah, if you play and you have a bad match and guys come up to you and say you're no good at playing baseball or anything like that . . . and you haven't had a chance to do anything.

Q. Would you like to be good at sports?

A. Yes.

Q. How good would you want to be?

A. Good enough so I could play sports and I wouldn't get fired on anything I went on.

Q. What do you think it would be like for you if you went out for a team this year?

A. I don't know . . . it might be sort of hard. . . . I don't know if I'd be any good or anything.

In conclusion, it can be said that many boys and girls are being robbed of an early positive sports experience. Little girls are forced to ask the question: "Why can't I play?" And we ask you, why is there nothing, or so little for the girls? Girls have the same need for activity, companionship, and fun-filled play experiences as do boys. However, what little girls do not need is to be faced with the same kinds of piercing questions that little boys constantly have hanging over their heads: "Am I good enough to play?" "If I go out how will others respond to my performance?" "Am I good enough to be acceptable?" And again we ask you, why does a little boy or girl have to be so tremendously overconcerned with his or her performance in order to play? Why are the rewards reserved only for the small percentage that excel? If sports have the potential to be beneficial to all, why eliminate kids?

Until there are some positive changes in regard to the limited opportunities which exist for girls and the reward structures which exist for boys, we will be robbing many kids of an important part of their childhood. Let's give them all a good fun-filled experience!

REFERENCES

1. Orlick, T.D. "A socio-psychological analysis of early sports participation." Unpublished Ph.D. thesis, University of Alberta, 1972a.

2. ———. "Children's sport—a revolution is coming." *Journal of the Canadian Association for Health, Physical Education and Recreation,* January/February, 1973a.

3. ———. "An analysis of expectancy as a motivational factor influencing sport participation." Paper presented at the Third World Congress on Sport Psychology, Madrid, Spain, June 1973b.

4. ———. "The athletic drop out—a high price for inefficiency." *CAHPER Journal,* September/October, 1974.

DISCUSSION QUESTIONS

A. *United States News and World Report Editorial*

1. How extensive are adult-sponsored sports programs for children in the United States?

2. According to this editorial, what is the major objective of these programs?

3. What was the major research finding in the Mantel and Vander Velden study referred to in this editorial?

B. *Edward Devereux*

1. According to the author, what has happened to the culture of children's games in America?

2. List some of the functions of informal children's games and play activities.

3. What are the essential features of a good learning environment?

4. Do you agree or disagree with Devereux's contention that children have more fun in unstructured play and game settings than in highly-structured adult-sponsored activities?

5. Observe young children in your community in both formal and informal play settings and relate your observations to the points raised in Devereux's paper.

C. *Hank Burchard*

1. List some examples which show how the Little Guy Football program discussed in this article is a mirror reflection of intercollegiate and professional sports programs.

2. In what ways is the executive director of the Boys Club program a hypocrite?

3. Is "having fun" a major objective of this particular program?

4. Can you suggest some changes that would create a more wholesome learning environment for these young boys?

D. *Terry Orlick*

1. List some reasons why children are intentionally or unintentionally eliminated from "kid sports" programs.

2. Can you suggest some changes in the structure of children's sports programs which would reduce the rate of drop-outs?

Unit VII

Social Correlates
of Interscholastic
Athletic Participation

The status of interscholastic sports in American education has increased over the years. Today, many Americans practically revere their interscholastic athletic teams. Even in times of teacher strikes and failing school bond issues, which often force schools to shut down for varying periods of time, interscholastic sports programs frequently remain intact. This suggests that many parents see great value in athletic programs or it may be just a simple case of parents refusing to do without the entertainment provided by an athletic contest.

The value of interscholastic athletic programs has frequently been questioned by educators and the public. Since James S. Coleman first criticized interscholastic athletic programs in the late 1950's many other researchers have shown an interest in the social dimensions of interscholastic athletic participation. The four readings in this unit draw together some of the most significant and recent research findings on the social implications of interscholastic sports participation.

In the first reading sociologists John Phillips and Walter Schafer review the related research prior to 1972. In addition, they allude to the possible existence of an athletic subculture as being one explanation for the social consequences of interscholastic athletic participation.

In the next reading sociologist Stanley Eitzen presents the findings of a study which essentially replicates Coleman's earlier work. His data generally support Coleman's conclusion that sports participation is a major determinant of social status among American adolescents.

In the third selection sociologists Elmer Spreitzer and Meredith Pugh investigate the effects of athletic participation, perceived status, and school value climate on educational goal setting. Their data indicate that perceived peer status and school value climate interact with athletic participation to affect educational aspirations.

In the final selection, physical educator Wendy Jerome and sociologist John Phillips compare academic achievement levels of American and Canadian interscholastic athletes. Their comparison reveals some striking differences. The authors attribute the observed differences to differential reward systems operating within the American and Canadian educational environments.

CONSEQUENCES OF PARTICIPATION
IN INTERSCHOLASTIC SPORTS: A REVIEW
AND PROSPECTUS

John C. Phillips and Walter E. Schafer

Very few sociological studies on the role of athletics in high schools appear to have been done prior to 1960. Since that time, a considerable amount of work has appeared, with generally consistent findings on certain aspects of high school athletics. The research the authors are presently doing involved an effort to explain one of those consistent findings—the fact that athletes tend to exceed comparable nonathletes in their achievement of educational goals. In this paper, we will review the evidence on the academic achievement of high school athletes, discuss our efforts to employ the concept of subculture to explain the advantage that athletes enjoy and, finally, speculate on possible broader applications of the kind of work we have been doing.

"Consequences of Participation in Interscholastic Sports: A Review and Prospectus," by John C. Phillips and Walter E. Schafer, is reprinted from *Pacific Sociological Review*, Volume 14, No. 3 (July 1971), pp. 328-338 by permission of the Publisher, Sage Publications, Inc.

Athletes and Academic Achievement

As information about high school athletes has grown more and more plentiful, a number of popular myths about the effects of athletic participation have been supplanted. Perhaps the best example of factual information replacing myth is the relationship between athletic participation and high school scholastic achievement. Athletics has been considered an anti-intellectual influence by some authors (Henry, 1963; Coleman, 1960, 1961, 1966), but there is compelling evidence that athletes get slightly better grades than do comparable nonathletes. Schafer and Armer (1968) found that high school athletes got slightly better grades than nonathletes in their matched sample. Athletes from blue-collar homes and boys who were not in a college-preparatory program got even better grades than their nonathlete counterparts. Bend (1968) found substantially the same pattern. Athletes got slightly better grades and the advantage of athletes was most pronounced among "low-endowment" (low-IQ, low-SES) boys.

The fact that "low endowment" athletes showed the most pronounced difference in achievement could be important to our interest in subculture as an explanation of these differences. Could it be that athletes are put under special pressure to perform well in the classroom? Perhaps the low-endowment athletes do better than low-endowment nonathletes because they experience pro-educational influences similar to those experienced by middle-class boys.

There is strong evidence to indicate that athletes aspire to and succeed in attending college more than do nonathletes. Bend found that 81.8% of his sample of superior athletes compared to 56.1% of the nonathletes aspired to at least some college education. The figures for low-endowment superior athletes and nonathletes was 39.8% and 13.3% respectively. Over 71% of the superior athletes actually attended college, while 50.0% of the nonathletes attended. Figures for low-endowment athletes and nonathletes were 14.8% and 6.9%. Bend's large sample, longitudinal design, and the fact that the relationship between athletic participation and educational achievement increased as degree of athletic involvement increased inspire confidence in his results. Rehberg and Schafer (1968) and Schafer and Rehberg (1970a, 1970b) found similar patterns in aspirations and expectations for college attendance.

Again, we see blue-collar athletes far exceeding comparable nonathletes in aspirations for college attendance and in the achievement of college attendance. We contend that this difference can be attributed, at least in part, to their experiences as athletes.

Schafer (1969) provides data that indicate that athletes are less likely to be deviant than comparable nonathletes. Again, blue-collar athletes were markedly less likely to be delinquent than blue-collar nonathletes, while the relationship is virtually eliminated among white-collar boys. Schafer argues that, unless some selection factor is working, there must be some influences in athletics that deter boys from engaging in delinquent behavior. We will argue that if potentially delinquent boys were being selected out of athletic participation, then white-collar as well as blue-collar delinquents would be selected. Thus, the negative relationship between athletic participation and delinquency would hold for boys from all socioeconomic backgrounds, not just for lower blue-collar boys.

With the association between athletic participation and educational success especially marked among blue-collar boys, one has firm grounds for expecting more upward social mobility among athletes than among comparable nonathletes. Schafer and Stehr (1968) suggest that, since blue-collar and white-collar athletes are more likely than are nonathletes to associate with the white-collar, college-bound "leading crowd" in high schools (Coleman, 1961: 35-50, 145-151), their mobility chances are enhanced. In a later paper, Schafer and Rehberg (1970a) found that athletes, compared with nonathletes, are more likely to report having been encouraged by teachers and counselors to go on to college. This relationship grows stronger as aspirations for going on to college diminish. Thus it appears that athletes not only attain higher educational achievement, but those who are not disposed toward furthering their education receive special encouragement or sponsorship to do so.

Phillips' (1965) study of college athletes has suggested another possible source of upward mobility among athletes. Phillips found that athletes tended to interact with one another much more than did nonathletes. He argued that this high interaction reduced what Hodges (1964) has termed "the psychic cost of mobility." By having a ready circle of middle-class friends, a blue-collar athlete might better develop the manners, mannerisms, attitudes, and social contacts that facilitate upward mobility. This tendency for athletes to choose other athletes as friends has also been found by Schafer and Rehberg (1970b).

Schafer and Rehberg (1970b:12) also found that athletes "tend to have close friends who are more positive in educational attitudes, aspirations, and behavior than the close friends of nonathletes." While the nature of their data prohibits firm conclusions, they do suggest the possibility that the differences between athletes and nonathletes can, at least in part, be attributed to their greater exposure to pro-educational peer influences.

We may summarize the evidence on differences between high school athletes and nonathletes as follows:

1. Athletes generally receive slightly better grades and are more likely to aspire to and attain more education than comparable nonathletes. This is especially marked among athletes from blue-collar homes.

2. There is some evidence to indicate that athletes are less likely than nonathletes to become delinquent. We do not know whether this relationship is due to selection factors or due to some deterrent effect of athletic participation.

3. Athletes from blue-collar backgrounds are more likely to be upwardly mobile than nonathletes. This can be explained to a great extent by their greater educational attainment, but other factors such as

sponsorship and association may also bear on this mobility.

What are the sources of these differences? Schafer and Armer (1968) suggest several possible explanations. First, athletes may receive special assistance in academic matters from teachers, peers, or coaches. Athletes might simply be graded more leniently. Second, there may be certain organizational requirements that might motivate athletes to perform better than nonathletes. Most high schools require a minimum grade-point average for participation. Athletes may work not only to achieve good enough grades for participation, but to qualify for entry into a college to continue their athletic careers. Third, athletes may be favored by "spillover" of certain qualities they have developed through sport. Higher peer status due to the generalization of their athletic status to other areas of social participation may enhance the athletes' self-esteem and, hence, their motivation to succeed in school work. Values of hard work, excellence, and persistence may be developed in sports activities and applied to academic and other activities. Practice and training regimens may influence athletes to use their study time more efficiently. Fourth, it is possible that conforming, ambitious, able boys tend to go out for sports more than do boys who are less "in tune" with the expectations of the school authorities. That is, athletics selects good students and tends to reject bad students (Schafer, 1969).

One recent article has examined the several possible sources of the educational advantages of athletes. Jerome and Phillips (1971) note the evidence of greater attainment of educational goals by athletes in American high schools. They point out the fact that sports programs in American and Canadian high schools are very similar, but that in Canada athletic participation does not receive the same status and esteem it does in American high schools. The authors argue that if good students, more than poor students, tend to go out for and be selected for athletic teams, the educational advantages of American athletes should exist among Canadian athletes as well. Likewise, if values and habits developed in athletics are applied to one's studies, the Canadian athletes should enjoy the same educational advantages that the American athletes enjoy.

Since the Canadian athletes do not appear to be better than their nonparticipating classmates in the achievement of educational objectives, Jerome and Phillips argue that the source of the American athletes' greater achievement lies not in "spillover" or selection but in one or more of the other explanations suggested by Schafer and Armer. These explanations (see above) center on *special experiences that are encountered by athletes* but not by nonathletes.

The Athletic Subculture

The evidence that athletes in American high schools appear to have certain special experiences, coupled with evidence of differences of behavior between athletes and nonathletes, has led us to the concept of subculture as a possible explanation of the processes intervening between athletic participation and various behavioral outcomes.

We should note here that two of the crucial conditions for the emergence of a subculture exist among athletes—special experiences and high rates of interaction (Phillips and Schafer, 1970). According to Cohen (1955) and Cohen and Short (1958), persons in like circumstances sharing like experiences should tend to develop values, norms, and beliefs (i.e., a subculture) favorable to those in the special circumstances. Our findings indicate that athletes, who experience special rewards in school, tend to develop a pro-school subculture (Phillips and Schafer, 1970).

In two recent papers, Phillips and Schafer (1971, 1970) have tried to develop a conceptual and methodological approach to the study of subcultures. We follow the thinking of Vander Zanden (1970) in conceiving of subculture as values, beliefs, symbols, and norms that are shared among some people but not by the general population. Thus, a subculture exists to the extent that a number of people differ in the norms, values, beliefs, and symbols that they share.

Wolfgang and Ferracuti (1967) point out the problems in measuring the elements of subcultures and point to the salient importance of measuring norms of conduct if we are to study subcultures at all. We contend that, since culture tends "to form a consistent and integrated whole" (Vander Zanden, 1970:35), we can gain an understanding of all the elements of a subculture by studying any single element—in this case, norms. The return potential model for the measurement of norms (Jackson, 1966, 1960) appears to provide a solution to many of the problems that Wolfgang and Ferracuti cite as impediments to the study of subcultures.

Our recent investigations have been concerned with determining the extent to which there exists a distinguishable subculture shared by interscholastic athletes, and the extent to which such a subculture might account for the differences between athletes and nonathletes reported earlier in this paper.

In a preliminary study of one high school, we found that athletes interact with other athletes much more than do nonathletes, and, while athletes appear to expect the same kinds of conduct from their friends, the norms shared by the athletes are much more intense and more likely to regulate behavior. That is, athletes appear to be under greater pressure to conform to conventional school standards than are nonathletes (Phillips and Schafer, 1970). This greater pressure to conform to conventional standards of behavior is reflected from time to time in newspaper stories depicting often sharp controversies regarding the misbehavior of athletes (albeit not high school athletes). Few college students need fear reprisals for wearing beards or mustaches, but one can read about athletes being removed from their team rosters for even so minor a transgression.

We are also interested in the role of the coach as a link between the official school culture and the athletic subculture, which, as we have discussed above, reflects the official school culture. We believe that coaches affect not only the norms shared among athletes but the individual athletes themselves. To the extent that we find the official school norms, values, and beliefs being transmitted through the coach to the athletes, and the norms, values and beliefs they share, we will be able to explain the tendency of athletes to conform to the official school goals of academic achievement and conventional conduct.

While we have emphasized the positive outcomes of interscholastic athletics, we are interested in some of the criticisms of highly competitive interscholastic athletics as well. Could it be that the more conventional athletes tend toward intergroup and interpersonal intolerance, uncritical acceptance of existing systems, and a disinterest in public affairs? Since they are rewarded by the "system," athletes may well resist change and reform. We know of one recent incident where high school athletes joined together to suppress an effort by certain other students to challenge a number of school rules.

Further Research

Until now, we have discussed only the possible existence of subcultural influences on American high school athletes and how those influences might produce the differences we have observed between athletes and nonathletes. We have paid little attention to collegiate athletes, club athletes, and professional athletes. Neither have we sought to investigate the possible impact of the game itself on the participant. These questions promise to be interesting and important if the existing literature is any indication. Weinberg and Arond (1952), Charnofsky (1968), and Scott (1968) respectively provide us with insights on the occupational culture of boxers, baseball players, and jockeys. They discuss the role of superstitions, norms regarding physical courage, beliefs about how one might best win, the athletes' image of themselves, and other matters that suggest the presence of an occupational subculture and, perhaps, certain shared norms, values, beliefs, and symbols that stem from the participants' common interest in the game, but extend to matters external to sports.

Another focus on subcultures in sport might involve participants' commitment to the official value system of a given sports organization or movement. Hans Lenk (1964) has investigated athletes' commitments to the traditional and official aims and values of the Olympic games. He has also examined the implications of the postwar tendency of German athletes to be committed to their clubs only in the realm of sport, not in other aspects of their lives (Lenk, 1966). We would expect the degree of athletes' commitment to sports organizations to strongly influence the degree to which the official organizational norms regulate the behavior of club athletes.

It is possible that a national sports movement might enhance certain government efforts toward social change. Wohl (1969a, 1969b) discusses how sports clubs have helped to reduce certain traditional hostilities based on social and geographical origins, as well as replacing certain backward peasant traditions with more open, modern modes of behavior. We would hope to someday examine the condition of peasant and worker sports club participants and nonparticipants to determine if patterns exist that are similar to those we have observed in American high school athletes.

A final aspect of sports that might play a role in the generation of subcultural influences is the meaning of the game to the participants. Webb (1969) discusses the way in which attitudes toward sport are "professionalized." While young children tend to just play at their games, older children appear to place an increasing emphasis on skill and winning. Heinila (1969) employs a similar notion of playing for the sake of a "good match" and playing to win. Whether a team emphasizes the game (good match) or the game outcome (winning) may determine the nature of the interpersonal and organizational relationships among members of the team. These relationships may, in turn, influence the development of subculture among the participants.

In summary, we have convincing evidence that American interscholastic athletes achieve educational goals more than do comparable nonathletes. We have some preliminary evidence that indicates that the athletes share norms that exert a strong pro-school influence on them, and that these norms appear to fit our concept of subculture. We are still investigating the sources and content of this apparent athletic subculture. In the future, we hope to investigate whether subcultures develop among athletes in certain sports, or among members of sports clubs or organizations. We also hope to employ the concepts of professionalization of and commitment to sports and determine their impact, if any, on the development of subcultures in sport. If athletes collectively or individually continue to exert the influence they have in the recent past, the nature of any athletic subculture could take on an increasing importance that extends beyond the world of sport.

REFERENCES

1. Bend, Emil, *The Impact of Athletic Participation on Academic and Career Aspiration and Achievement*, New Brunswick, N.J.: National Football Foundation and Hall of Fame, 1968.
2. Charnofsky, Harold, "The major league professional baseball player: self-conception versus the popular image," *International Rev. of Sport Sociology*, 3:39-55, 1968.
3. Cohen, Albert K., *Delinquent Boys: The Culture of the Gang*, Glencoe, Ill.: Free Press, 1955.
4. ———, and James F. Short, Jr., "Research in delinquent subcultures," *J. of Social Issues*, 14:20-37, 1958.
5. Coleman, James S., "Adolescent subculture and academic achievement," *Amer. J. of Sociology*, 65 (January): 337-347, 1960.
6. ———, *The Adolescent Society*, New York: Free Press, 1961.
7. ———, "Peer cultures and education in modern society," pp. 266-269 in T.M. Newcomb and E.K. Wilson (eds.), *College Peer Groups: Problems and Prospects for Research*, Chicago: Aldine, 1966.
8. Heinila, Kalevi, "Football at the crossroads," *International Rev. of Sport Sociology*, 4:5-30, 1969.
9. Henry, Jules, *Culture Against Man*, New York: John Wiley, 1963.
10. Hodges, Harold M., Jr., *Social Stratification: Class in America*, Cambridge: Schenkman, 1964.

11. Jackson, Jay, "Structural characteristics of norms," pp. 136-163 in *The Dynamics of Instructional Groups*, Yearbook of the National Society for the Study of Education, Chicago: Univ. of Chicago Press, 1960.

12. ———, "A conceptual and measurement model for norms and roles," *Pacific Soc. Rev.*, 9 (Spring): 63-72, 1966.

13. Jerome, Wendy C., and John C. Phillips, "The relationship between academic achievement and interscholastic participation: a comparison of Canadian and American high schools," *C.A.H.P.E.R.J.*, 37 (January/February): 18-21, 1971.

14. Lenk, Hans, *Werte, Ziele, Wirklichkeit der Modernen Olympischen Spiele* (*Values, Aims, Reality of the Modern Olympic Games*), Scharndorf bei Stuttgart: Karl Hoffmann, 1964.

15. ———, "Total or partial engagement? Changes regarding personal ties with the sports club," *International Rev. of Sport Sociology*, 1:85-108, 1966.

16. Phillips, John C., "Motivation for participation in athletics: an exploratory study," M.A. thesis, San Jose State College, 1965.

17. ———, and Walter E. Schafer, "The athletic subculture: a preliminary study," presented at the annual meetings of the American Sociological Association, Washington, D.C., 1970.

18. ———, "Subcultures in sport: a conceptual and methodological model," in Publication 2 of the Research Institute of the Swiss Federal School of Gymnastics and Sport, Basel: Birkhauser, 1971.

19. Rehberg, Richard A., and Walter E. Schafer, "Participation in interscholastic athletics and college expectations," *Amer. J. of Sociology*, 73 (May): 732-740, 1968.

20. Schafer, Walter E., "Participation in interscholastic athletics and delinquency: a preliminary study," *Social Problems*, 17 (Summer): 40-47, 1969.

21. ———, and J. Michael Armer, "Athletes are not inferior students," *Trans-Action* (November): 21-26, 61-62, 1968.

22. Schafer, Walter E., and Richard A. Rehberg, "Athletic participation, college aspirations, and college encouragement," University of Oregon (unpublished), 1970a.

23. ———, "Athletic participation, peer influences, and educational aspirations: toward a theory of the athletic subculture," University of Oregon (unpublished), 1970b.

24. Schafer, Walter E., and Nico Stehr, "Participation in competitive athletics and social mobility, some intervening social processes," presented at the meetings of the International Committee on Sociology of Sport, Vienna, Austria, 1968.

25. Scott, Marvin B., *The Racing Game*, Chicago: Aldine, 1968.

26. Vander Zanden, James W., *Sociology: A Systematic Analysis*, New York: Ronald Press, 1970.

27. Webb, Harry, "Professionalization of attitudes toward play among adolescents," pp. 161-178 in Gerald S. Kenyon (ed.), *Aspects of Contemporary Sport Sociology*, Chicago: Athletic Institute, 1969.

28. Weinberg, S. Kirson, and Henry Arond, "The occupational culture of the boxer," *Amer. J. of Sociology*, 57 (March): 460-469, 1952.

29. Wohl, Andrzej, "Integrational functions of sport," in Publication 2 of the Research Institute of the Swiss Federal School of Gymnastics and Sport, Basel: Birkhauser, 1969a.

30. ———, "Engagement in sports activity on the part of the workers of large industrial establishment in peoples Poland," *International Rev. of Sport Sociology*, r:83-127.

31. Wolfgang, Marvin E., and Franco Ferracuti, *The Subculture of Violence*, London: Tavistock, 1967.

ATHLETICS IN THE STATUS SYSTEM OF MALE ADOLESCENTS: A REPLICATION OF COLEMAN'S *THE ADOLESCENT SOCIETY**

D. Stanley Eitzen

James Coleman, after studying the adolescent status systems in ten Illinois high schools in 1957 and 1958, concluded that athletic prowess was the single most important criterion for high status (1). But is this still the case? Significant changes have occurred in American society in the intervening years such as the rise of the counterculture, increased drug usage by youth, heightened racial unrest in schools, and the ever greater tendency to question persons in authority roles (teachers, principals, coaches, ministers, parents, police, and government leaders). Quite possibly, these and other factors have led to the athlete being replaced as the "big man on campus" by student activists, rock musicians, scholars, or some other social category.

The evidence is unclear. Occasional articles appear in the popular press which suggest that boys still want desperately to be athletes because that remains the most highly rewarded activity in their school and community. This has been recently documented, for example, for Benton, Illinois (5), Yates Center, Kansas (3), Stockbridge, Michigan (7), and Tracy, California (2). At the same time, however, there is evidence that increasing numbers of high school youngsters are becoming disenchanted with sports. This was the conclusion of Frank Jones who made a survey for the Athletic Institute, an organization supported by the sporting goods industry (4, 6). The affluent youngster in the suburbs is also losing interest in sports, according to Talamini. Apathy or antagonism toward athletic programs by the affluent is the result of the regimentation demanded in sports and the denial of creativity and self-expression (8). While this increased questioning of sports appears to be an urban and suburban phenomenon, high school sports continue to flourish and go relatively unquestioned in rural

Stanley D. Eitzen, "Athletics in the Status System of Male Adolescents: A Replication of Coleman's *The Adolescent Society*," *Adolescence* Vol. X, No. 38, Summer, 1975, pp. 268-276.

*This is a revised version of a paper presented to the session on Sport and Leisure at the annual meetings of the Midwest Sociological Society, Milwaukee, Wisconsin, April 26-27, 1973. Funds for this study were provided by the General Research Fund of the University of Kansas. The author would like to give special thanks to James Crone and Calvin Broughton for their assistance in the coding and analysis of the data.

America, where they are the "only show in town" (2, 3, 4, 5, 6, 7).

This paper will present data that replicates and extends the landmark study by Coleman. Two questions guide this study: (a) Does sports participation remain as the primary determinant of adolescent male status? and (b) Under what conditions is sports participation the most important criterion for status among high school males? In the latter case, we will investigate if there are differences by community, school, and individual characteristics.

Methods. As was the case in Coleman's study, schools were selected for inclusion in the sample not because they were "representative" but because they differed on certain dimensions. The community characteristics considered important because of their potential for affecting the role of athletics in adolescent status systems were: community size, affluence of community, occupational structure, and rural/urban. These data were obtained from the 1970 census data. Relevant school characteristics were size, degree of success in major sports, authority structure, public or private, and proportion of graduates enrolling in college. These data were obtained from a questionnaire completed by school principals. The schools, with the pertinent community and school information, are listed in Table 1.

Questionnaires, including many items from Coleman's original, were completed by a sample of students in each of the nine schools. The questionnaires were distributed to a random sample of sophomores, juniors, and seniors in each school. The number in each class was intended to be 50 to 70 taken from required courses (omitting accelerated and slow classes). Although males and females were included, the study reported here is limited to males.

The Findings

The first consideration was to determine whether boys are any less interested in sports now than they were when Coleman conducted his study 16 years ago. Four items from Coleman's study were selected to tap the importance of sport now and compare this with the past. The first is probably the most often quoted: "If you could be remembered here at school for one of the three things below, which would you want it to be?" The comparison between Coleman's findings and those for the present study shows: "Athletic star"—Coleman (44 percent), Eitzen (47 percent); "brilliant student"—Coleman (31 percent), Eitzen (23 percent); and "most popular"—Coleman (25 percent), Eitzen (30 percent).

The second item used to determine the degree to which athletes are respected among adolescent boys was "Would you rather be friends with and be like . . ." Coleman's analysis did not include the overall percentages for each of his categories, but it is clear from his discussion that the most popular category was "athlete but not scholar" (1). The results from the present study were: athlete but not scholar (56.1 percent), scholar but not athlete (19.9 percent), and ladies' man but neither scholar nor athlete (24.0 percent). We added the category "member of the counter culture" since that may now be a meaningful criterion for status among some adolescents. With this included, the recalculated percentages were 46.3, 16.4, 19.8 and 17.5, respectively.

TABLE 1
Characteristics of the Schools and Communities in the Sample

School	State	Community Size	Median Income	% of families with Income <$3,000	% Prof & Managers	Community Type	School Size (3 classes)	Athletic Success	School Authority Structure	Public-Private	% College Bound
A	KS.	76,127	$14,172	1.9	33.8%	Suburb	2,160	Excellent	Middle	Public	65%
B	KS.	20,446	12,143	2.5	29.0	Suburb	290	Excellent	Tight	Catholic	50
C	KS.	10,851	9,363	5.0	24.4	Agriculture	690	Good	Middle	Public	54
D	ILL.	400 app.*	Low*	High*	Low*	Agriculture	92	Poor	Middle	Public	65
E	KS.	13,379	9,240	8.7	14.9	Agri./Ind.	780	Good	Tight	Public	78
F	KS.	11,036	7,717	12.2	22.0	Agri./Ind.	585	Excellent	Tight	Public	60
G	IND.	500 app.*	Low*	High*	Low*	Agriculture	132	Poor	Tight	Public	10
H	IND.	17,604	8,703	8.6	16.6	Business	1,365	Average	Middle	Public	32
I	KS.	132,135	9,585	8.0	25.0	State Capital	1,914	Average	Loose	Public	50

*Census data were not available for communities of less than 2,500 persons.

Clearly, the overall comparisons from the first two items show that adolescents today are just as enthusiastic about sports as they were in the late 1950s. But these first two items only indirectly get at the status system of male adolescents since they ask what the respondent would want to be. This is based on the assumption that teenage boys want to be whatever is highly rewarded by their peers. Thus, it is probably safe to assume that answers to these questions reflect the values of adolescents.

Two additional items from Coleman are more direct measures of the status system of adolescents because they ask the respondent to rank different activities on the basis of the importance of each in achieving status. The first involves the ranking of five possible criteria for status among boys. The second ranks criteria that "make a guy popular with girls around here." Table 2 presents what Coleman found compared to the present findings.

The comparisons in Table 2 show that the relative ranks of the criteria for status among boys and what boys believe it takes to be popular with girls have remained stable over time.

The overall comparison of the data from Coleman with the present study provides clear support that athletics remain *very* important in the status system of teenage males. If anything, the present data indicate a slightly greater enthusiasm for sports than Coleman found. These data may, however, hide the possibility that some categories of adolescents are disenchanted and apathetic about athletics. Thus, the remainder of this paper will focus on the way boys vary in the importance they attach to athletics by individual, school, and community characteristics. In each case we will assess the differences these characteristics make on only one of Coleman's items—how the individual would like to be remembered.

Individual factors. It could be assumed that boys differ in their enthusiasm for sport by their particular situation. To determine if this is a valid assumption, we selected four individual characteristics for analysis—familial social class, age, college prep or not, and placement in the school status hierarchy. Table 3 provides these data.

Table 3 shows that all of the variables but track in school make a difference in the desire to be an athlete. In general, the variables taken one at a time suggest that sons of under-educated fathers, sophomores, and those in the center of the status hierarchy of the school are more inclined toward sports than their counterparts.

School related factors. The nine schools were divided into large (1,300 to 2,200 students), medium (500-800) and small (less than 300). Since the proportion of boys participating in interscholastic sports is higher in small schools, one could assume a greater enthusiasm for sports by males there. The data in Table 4 show the highest enthusiasm for sport is in the smaller schools while the interest for sport in the largest schools is decidedly less.

An obvious consideration, but one omitted by Coleman, is the potential impact of a winning or losing tradition in the school on importance of sports. The principal in each school was asked to rate his school over the past five years in football, basketball, and minor sports. An overall composite score was used combining the two major sports to label a school as being successful in sports or not. As expected, students from winning schools had more favorable attitudes toward athletics than students from schools with average or poor athletic success.

The principal of each school in the sample was also asked to rate the formation and administration of rules at his school on a scale from 1 (tight) to 5 (permissive). This was included on the possibility that a rigid authoritarian structure in a school might be an indicator of a non-questioning tradition in which athletics might flourish. Whether this assumption is correct or not remains to be seen, but the data in Table 5 shows clearly that students in schools with a "tight" authority structure are much more inclined toward athletics than students in the more permissive schools. Another possibility may be that "tight" schools are more likely to have ex-coaches as administrators. It is well-known that successful coaches often become secondary school administrators. Presumably this is because they have not only been successful but perhaps more important to the school board is that they have demonstrated that they are strict. Ex-coaches turned administrators may, and this is speculation, not only be more likely to run a "tight ship" but also give extraordinary encouragement to the school athletic program.

TABLE 2

The comparison of Coleman's Findings with Those of the Present Study on the Ranking of Various Criteria for Status

A. Ranking of Criteria to be Popular with Boys

Average Ranking

Criteria for Status	Coleman[a]	Eitzen
Be an athlete	2.2	2.06
Be in leading crowd	2.6	2.10
Leader in activities	2.9	2.82
High grades, honor roll	3.5	3.73
Come from right family	4.5	3.98

B. Ranking of Criteria to be Popular with Girls

Average Ranking

Criteria for Status	Coleman	Eitzen
Be an athlete	2.2	1.94
Be in leading crowd	2.5	2.12
Have a nice car	3.2	2.81
High grades, honor roll	4.0	3.87
Come from right family	4.2	3.89

[a]These ranks are approximations extrapolated from a bar graph supplied by Coleman (1).

TABLE 3
Individual Factors Related to How One Wishes to be Remembered

| | How Remembered | | | | | | | |
Individual Factors	Brilliant Student		Athletic Star		Most Popular		Totals	
Father's education	%	N	%	N	%	N	%	N
Nonhigh school graduate	13.7	(28)	56.9	(116)	29.4	(60)	100.0	(204)
High school graduate	27.0	(74)	41.2	(113)	31.8	(87)	100.0	(274)
At least some college	23.7	(70)	47.5	(140)	28.8	(85)	100.0	(295)
Year in school								
Sophomores	21.2	(69)	55.5	(181)	23.2	(76)	100.0	(326)
Juniors	22.7	(64)	47.2	(133)	30.1	(85)	100.0	(282)
Seniors	25.4	(61)	36.3	(87)	38.3	(92)	100.0	(240)
Track in school								
College	31.8	(96)	47.0	(142)	21.2	(64)	100.0	(302)
Noncollege	17.8	(93)	47.2	(247)	35.0	(183)	100.0	(523)
Degree of centrality[a]								
Center	22.8	(18)	50.6	(40)	26.6	(21)	100.0	(79)
Above average	14.3	(25)	59.4	(104)	26.3	(46)	100.0	(175)
Average	20.7	(58)	51.4	(144)	27.9	(78)	100.0	(280)
Below average	29.2	(45)	37.7	(58)	33.1	(51)	100.0	(154)
Fringe	28.3	(47)	34.9	(58)	36.7	(61)	99.9	(166)

[a]Centrality refers to the perception of the individual to how close he is to the center of activities at his school. To get at this each respondent circled the appropriate circle from among four concentric circles on the questionnaire. The question (taken exactly from Coleman) reads: "Suppose the circle below represented the activities that go on here at school. How far out from the center are you?"

TABLE 4
School Related Factors and How One Wishes to be Remembered

School Factors	Brilliant Student		Athletic Star		Most Popular		Totals	
School size	%	N	%	N	%	N	%	N
Large (2,160-1,365) AHI[a]	28.8	(78)	35.8	(97)	35.4	(96)	100.0	(271)
Medium (800-500) CEF	22.3	(77)	49.3	(170)	28.4	(98)	100.0	(345)
Small (300) BDG	18.3	(46)	54.8	(138)	27.0	(68)	100.1	(252)
Success in sports								
Good schools ABCEF	21.3	(125)	47.8	(280)	30.9	(181)	100.0	(586)
Average or poor DGHI	27.0	(76)	44.3	(125)	28.7	(81)	100.0	(282)
Authority structure								
Tight schools BEFG	19.3	(93)	50.8	(245)	29.9	(144)	100.0	(482)
Permissive ACDHI	28.0	(108)	41.5	(160)	30.6	(118)	100.1	(386)

[a]These initials refer to the schools as labelled in Table 1.

Community related factors. It is widely believed that small rural communities are especially enthusiastic about their local high school teams. These local teams provide much of the entertainment and are a source of community pride and unity. The data from Table 5 substantiate this claim.

We also examined the proportion of professionals in the community, dividing the sample into those communities exceeding 22 percent and those with a smaller percentage. The data in Table 5 reveal that students from communities with fewer professionals were more inclined to wish to be remembered as an athletic star than students where there were more professional persons.

When the communities were separated by the extent of families living in poverty, the results show that students in the highest poverty communities were more likely than the other to want to be remembered as an "athletic star."

The final community characteristic, the percentage of wage earners in manufacturing, was included to indicate not only the extent of industry in the community but also as an indirect measure of the urban-rural dimension. The results show that boys from communities with relatively little manufacturing were more likely to choose "athletic star" than those who came from more industrialized communities.

Summary. This study was guided by two questions.

First, is sports participation as dominant a criterion for status among adolescent males now as it was in the 1950s? The data from students in the nine schools in our sample provide strong support that it continues to prevail.

Although there appears to be widespread acceptance of sports among teenage boys, our second question was: are there certain sectors where support may be breaking down? The data suggest that certain variables appear to affect one's perception of the importance of sport. Our data suggest that the strongest support for sport is found among sons of the undereducated, in small schools, in schools with a strict authority structure, and among students at the center of the schools activities. Conversely, sons of college educated fathers from large urban or suburban schools, affluent and permissive schools are the less enthused about sports (although it should be remembered that they, too, chose sports over the other possibilities but in lower percentages). Thus, several trends lead to the speculation that the enthusiasm for sports may wane in the future. School unification makes schools larger, a larger proportion of youngsters attend suburban schools each year, each generation is better educated, and schools are generally more permissive than in the past. If these conditions lead to somewhat less enthusiasm for sports as our data indicate, then sports participation as the dominant criterion for social status will diminish in the future.

TABLE 5

Community Related Factors and How One Wishes to be Remembered

Community Factors	Brilliant Student		Athletic Star		Most Popular		Totals	
	%	N	%	N	%	N	%	N
Community size								
Large (above 15,000) ABHI	24.0	(99)	41.4	(171)	34.6	(143)	100.0	(413)
Small (below 15,000) CDEFG	22.4	(102)	51.4	(234)	26.2	(119)	100.0	(455)
Percentage of professionals								
High (22% or above) ABCFI	23.5	(112)	44.7	(213)	31.9	(152)	100.1	(477)
Low (Less than 22%) DEGH	22.8	(89)	49.1	(192)	28.1	(110)	100.0	(391)
Percentage of families with incomes less than $3,000								
Low (<5%) ABC	23.4	(68)	44.1	(128)	32.4	(94)	99.9	(290)
Medium (8-9%) EHI	24.2	(86)	42.3	(150)	33.5	(119)	100.0	(355)
High (10% or more) DFG	23.3	(47)	52.5	(106)	24.2	(49)	100.0	(202)
Percentage of wage earners in manufacturing								
High (>18.2%) ABCFH	23.8	(119)	45.7	(228)	30.5	(152)	100.0	(499)
Low (<13.6%) DEGI	22.2	(82)	48.0	(177)	29.8	(110)	100.0	(369)

How Remembered

REFERENCES

1. Coleman, James S. *The Adolescent Society: The Social Life of the Teenager and Its Impact on Education.* New York: Free Press, 1961.
2. Divoky, Diane, and Peter Schrag. "Football and Cheers," *Saturday Review*, (November 11, 1972), pp. 59-65.
3. Johnson, William. "The Greatest Athlete in Yates Center, Kansas," *Sports Illustrated*, (August 9, 1971), pp. 27-31.
4. Jones, Frank B. "Intercollegiate and Interscholastic Athletic Programs in the 1970's," *Sportscope*, (June, 1970), pp. 1-20.
5. Klein, Frederick C. "Hoopster Hoopla: High School Basketball is a Serious Matter in a Small Illinois Town," *Wall Street Journal*, (March 1, 1970).
6. Loyd, F. Glen. "Jack Armstrong is Dead," *Today's Health*, (October, 1970), pp. 47-48; 84-86.
7. Ricke, Tom. "A Town Where Boys are Kings and the Court Business is Basketball," *Detroit Free Press*, (March 14, 1971).
8. Talamini, John T. "Occupational Ideologies and Behavioral Patterns in School Athletics," Ph.D. dissertation, Rutgers University, 1971.

INTERSCHOLASTIC ATHLETICS AND
EDUCATIONAL EXPECTATIONS*

Elmer Spreitzer and Meredith Pugh

This paper represents a replication and extension of a study reported by Rehberg and Schafer in 1968. Our findings reproduce the original study in showing that the relationship between athletic participation and higher educational goals is not eliminated when controlling for parental SES, parental academic encouragement, and student grade average. The extension of the original study involves introducing perceived peer status and school value climate as intervening variables between athletic involvement and educational expectations.

A growing body of literature has established a number of psychological and sociological differences between athletes and non-athletes. Athletes tend to be more extroverted, conventional in life-style, more positive in self-concepts, and have lower rates of juvenile delinquency than non-athletes (Schendel, 1965; Schafer, 1969). Moreover, survey research indicates that although there are no systematic differences in intelligence between the two comparison groups, high school and college athletes achieve higher grade point averages than non-athletes (Bowlin quoted in Schafer, 1968:7; Eidsmore, 1963; Schafer and Armer, 1968). Several studies also suggest that athletes tend to have higher educational expectations and higher rates of college attendance than their non-athletic counterparts (Bend, 1968; Buhrmann, 1969; Rehberg and Schafer, 1968; Schafer and Rehberg, 1970).

Although systematic evidence indicates that athletics are not necessarily detrimental to the educational enterprise, additional research is needed to specify the process mediating between athletic participation and academic performance. One can interpret observed differences between athletes and non-athletes in a number of ways (Schafer, 1968). First, athletes may receive special academic encouragement and assistance from teachers, counselors, coaches, and peers. Secondly, the physical conditioning and discipline accompanying athletics might transfer to educational endeavors. Thirdly, eligibility requirements and the hope of qualifying for college scholarships might motivate athletes to achieve higher grades than they would otherwise. Fourthly, the prestige resulting from athletic participation may produce a more positive self-concept and higher aspirations in other activities, including academic work. In addition, athletic participation facilitates membership in the "leading crowd" in high school which is disproportionately middle class in origin and typically is college oriented (Rehberg, 1969:77).

This paper attempts to clarify the relationship between athletic involvement and educational goals by replicating and extending a study reported by Rehberg and Schafer in 1968. The replication essentially consists of showing that the relationship between athletic participation and educational expectations is not accounted for by familial socio-economic status, parental academic encouragement, or student grade point average. The extension of the Rehberg and Schafer study focuses on the students' peer status as a mediating variable between involvement in athletics and educational expectations. In a recent study, Spady (1970: 691) argues that the high educational expectations of athletes are a consequence of their enhanced popularity which stimulates a desire for further recognition through college attendance. This process, however, may have the unfortunate consequence of inflating educational aspirations while not providing the skills required for later

Elmer Spreitzer and Meredith Pugh, "Interscholastic Athletics and Educational Expectations," *SOE*, Vol. 46, 1973 Spring, pp. 171-182.

*The authors express their appreciation to Professors Irving L. Allen, J. David Colfax, and Henry Stetler for making available the data analyzed in the present paper. Their research was performed pursuant to a contract with the United States Department of Health, Education and Welfare, Office of Education, under the provisions of the Cooperative Research Program (Contract No. OE-6-10-068; Project No. 3285). Additional support was received from the University of Connecticut Research Foundation. An earlier version of this paper was presented at the Annual Meeting of the Ohio Valley Sociological Society, Cleveland, April, 1971. The authors also express their gratitude to Professors Ronald Corwin and John Loy for their constructive comments on an earlier version of this paper.

academic success (Spady, 1970:700). Our objective is to relate athletic participation to educational goals while controlling for perceived status and school value climates. It is possible that the sequence described by Spady is limited to high schools in which athletics, rather than scholarship, leads to high status perceptions and heightened educational goals.

Nature of the Data

This paper is a secondary analysis of data that originally were collected at the University of Connecticut as part of the "Community Structure Research Project." The respondents in the survey represent a probability sample of the 5,236 high school seniors who were attending thirteen high schools in five Connecticut cities in the spring of 1966. The sample totaled 1,780 students, which represented 33 per cent of the high school seniors in these cities; the response rate was 92 per cent of the intended sample.

The sex composition of the next sample was 55 per cent female and 45 per cent males. The racial distribution was 84 per cent white and 14 per cent black. The demographic information supplied by the students indicate that the respondents were generally long-term residents of the metropolitan northeast; 85 per cent were born in a metropolitan area; 83 per cent had lived in Connecticut for at least ten years.

The data reported in this paper were collected by means of an anonymous, self-administered questionnaire. The "Student Opinion Survey" schedule consisted of 124 items and represented a revised version of the survey instrument constructed by Coleman et al. (1966) in their study of educational opportunity. The Connecticut survey also utilized the revised Henmon-Nelson test of mental ability.

Findings

A Replication

The first stage of our analysis involves a replication of the study by Rehberg and Schafer (1968) concerning the influence of interscholastic sports on the educational plans of high school boys. The independent variable, participation in interscholastic athletics, was measured in both studies by means of an item checklist of student extracurricular activities during the senior year.[1] Both studies operationalized the dependent variable, educational expectations, in terms of actual educational plans after graduation, as contrasted with ideal goals or aspiration.[2]

Table 1 presents the zero-order correlations between the independent and dependent variables as well as among the three control variables. The observed relationships among the five variables are very similar in both studies. For example, Rehberg and Schafer (1968:102) report a gamma of .28 for the association between athletic participation and educational expectations; we found a corresponding gamma value of .26 in our replication. Our data showed that 64 per cent of the male

high school athletes expect to complete four or more years of college as compared to 51 per cent of their non-athletic counterparts. It is interesting to note that the strength of this association is somewhat stronger (.41) when educational expectations are indexed by the relative proportion of athletes and non-athletes who had submitted applications for college admission at the time of the survey: 79 per cent of the athletes versus only 62 per cent of the non-athletes. The tendency for athletes to have higher educational expectations is suggested additionally by our finding that a higher proportion of athletes were enrolled in the college preparatory curriculum of their high schools (71 per cent as compared to 58 per cent of the non-athletes). Moreover, it is relevant to note that the same percentage (31 per cent) of athletes and non-athletes reported that they expect to continue their education beyond the bachelor's degree.

Table 2 reports a series of partial correlations between athletic involvement and educational expectations when holding constant three variables included in the Rehberg and Schafer study.[3] Table 2 replicates the original study in showing that the relationship between participation and expectations is reduced only slightly when controlling for parental socio-economic status—the zero-order gamma of .26 dropping to .22 in the first-order partial correlation.[4] Similarly, controlling for parental academic encouragement and student grade average only slightly weakens the original relationship between participation and expectations, findings which also replicate the Rehberg and Schafer study.[5] Our study also indicates that controlling for student IQ does not alter the relationship between participation and expectation; the zero-order and first-order gammas are identical (.26).

Table 2 also shows that the zero-order relationship between the independent and dependent variables is only slightly reduced in the third-order partial correlation. When simultaneously controlling for parental SES, parental academic encouragement, and student grade average, the zero-order gamma of .26 is reduced to .21 in the third-order partial correlation. In short, the observed partial correlations in both studies are very similar and suggest that athletic involvement during high school has an independent positive effect on educational expectations.

An Extension of the Analysis

Extracurricular activities in high school function as a context for interpersonal competition and status enhancement. Within the informal peer system, personal prestige can be achieved by outstanding performance in activities that are both conspicuous and bring honor to the school (Spady, 1970). Coleman's (1961) study of the adolescent society indicates that athletes often are prominent members of "the leading crowd" and that athletic involvement is an important source of peer group status. Spady (1970:688) found that students who perceive themselves to be near the top of the informal status hierarchy have higher educational aspirations than less

TABLE 1
Correlation Matrix Comparing Gamma Coefficients from the Original and
Replicational Studies (Zero-Order)

	(1)		(2)		(3)		(4)		(5)	
	Orig.	Rep.	Orig.	Rep.	Orig.	Rep.	Orig.	Rep.	Orig.	Rep.
(1) Athletic Participation	...	...	.28	.26	.28	.26	.02	.00	.04	.03
(2) Educational Expectations	...	...	...	...	.58	.55	.73	.65	.50	.58
(3) Parental Academic Encouragement	...	...	...	...	...	...	a	.14	a	.13
(4) Cumulative Grade Average	...	...	...	...	...	...	...	...	a	.24
(5) Parental Socio-Economic Position	...	...	...	...	...	...	...	...	...	...

[a] Gamma coefficient not reported in original study by Rehberg and Schafer (1968).

popular students even when controlling for father's occupation, father's civic activity, student's IQ, and student's grade average.

If, as Spady suggests, the higher educational aspirations of athletes are due to enhanced peer status, one would expect to find a strong correlation between involvement in interscholastic athletics and perceived popularity. Moreover, we would expect the association between participation and educational expectations to be strongly diminished among athletes who do not view themselves as highly popular. In the latter situation, low perceived peer status does not stimulate a desire for additional status increments through educational achievement.

Our data support Spady's argument. The relationship between athletic participation and perceived peer status is quite strong (gamma = .53). Thirty-four per cent of the athletes defined themselves as "one of the most popular" or as "very popular" compared with 14 per cent of the non-athletes. Table 3 presents the relationship between participation and expectations when controlling for self-evaluated popularity.[6] As anticipated, the relationship is strongest among students who see themselves as very popular (gamma = .28), and declines among students viewing themselves as moderately popular (gamma = .21), with the relationship washed out among those who reported low peer status (gamma = .00).

Assuming some degree of correspondence between perceived popularity and actual peer status, the data suggest that athletes who fail to achieve high peer status concomitantly do not inflate their educational expectations. This finding raises the question of whether the observed pattern of association between athletic participation and educational expectations is specific to

schools in which athletic accomplishments are valued highly and are likely to result in enhanced popularity, thus producing inflated aspirations. In *The Adolescent Society,* Coleman (1961) reported that high schools vary in terms of their value climates. The school value systems determine the extent to which achievement in various activities results in peer recognition and prestige. For example, some school value climates reward the "all-around boy" who is both an athlete and scholar, whereas other value climates reward the "athletic specialist" without a corresponding emphasis on scholarship. Still other school value climates are oriented around the "scholar specialist" with a deemphasis on athletic pursuits.

In schools where athletic achievement is rewarded in isolation from academic excellence, one would expect athletes to experience enhanced popularity which in turn stimulates higher educational goals. Similarly, in schools where academic excellence alone is rewarded, athletes would ostensibly not achieve greater popularity, and thus the relationship between athletic participation and educational expectations should be substantially weaker in this type of school. The data in Table 4 support these hypotheses. In schools where the athletic specialist is highly regarded, the relationship between participation and expectations is quite strong (gamma = .47), with 80 per cent of the athletes expecting to complete at least four years of college as compared to 57 of the non-athletes.[7] The correlation is somewhat weaker (.33) in schools where the value climate rewards the "all-around boy," and in schools where scholarship serves as the primary means of status acquisition the relationship between athletic participation and educational expectations virtually is washed out (gamma = .02). Thus, it appears that the higher educational expectations of high

TABLE 2
Comparison of Partial Correlations from the Original and Replicational Studies

First-Order Relationships	Gamma Value	
	Original Study	Replication
Educational expectations and athletic participation, controlling for parental socio-economic position.[a]	.28	.22
Educational expectations and athletic participation, controlling for parental academic encouragement.	.22	.24
Educational expectations and athletic participation, controlling for grade average.[a]	.29	.28
Third-Order Relationships		
Educational expectations and athletic participation, controlling for parental SES, parental encouragement, and grade average.	.24	.21

[a]Since neither parental SES or grade average is related to athletic participation, technically there was no need to control for these two variables when relating athletic participation to educational expectations. However, we controlled on these two factors in order to maintain comparability with the original study by Rehberg and Schafer (1968) where parental SES and grade average were controlled.

TABLE 3
Educational Expectations by Athletic Participation, Controlling for Perceived Peer Status

High Peer Status

Educational Expectations	Athletes (%)	Nonathletes (%)
16 or more years	69	56
13-15 years	16	22
12 years	15	22
	(N=94)	(N=59)
	Gamma=.28	

Medium Peer Status

Educational Expectations		
16 or more years	63	54
13-15 years	17	15
12 years	20	31
	(N=161)	(N=258)
	Gamma=.21	

Low Peer Status

Educational Expectations		
16 or more years	44	44
13-15 years	19	17
12 years	37	39
	(N=16)	(N=88)
	Gamma=.00	

school athletes are mediated by enhanced peer status; however, this process is specific to schools where interscholastic athletics are highly valued.

Coleman (1961, 1965) and Rehberg (1969) implicitly have suggested further explanation for the importance of popularity as an intermediary between athletic participation and educational plans which is not based on a stimulated psychological desire for future recognition and status increments. They reason that the higher educational goals of student athletes result from the fact that athletes usually are members of "the leading crowd" which is predominantly middle class in origin and is college-oriented. Our data revealed a definite association between athletic participation and number of close friends planning to attend college, even when simultaneously controlling for SES, IQ, and grade average (third-order gamma = .30). This pro-educational peer influence appears to be strongest among "low endowment" athletes. Our findings revealed that among boys in the low SES, low IQ, and poor grades category, only 6 per cent of the athletes reported *no* close friends planning on college as contrasted with 39 per cent of the non-athletes.[8]

A second social, rather than psychological, explanation for the importance of popularity might be based on the greater visibility of popular athletes which results in greater encouragement and attention from teachers and guidance counselors. Our findings support this interpretation. We found that the tendency for athletes to receive more academic encouragement from teachers and counselors remains even after simultaneously con-

TABLE 4
Educational Expectations by Athletic Participation, Controlling for School Value Climate

Athletic Specialist Value Climate

Educational Expectations	Athletes (%)	Nonathletes (%)
16 or more years	80	57
13-15 years	7	13
12 years	13	30
	(N=85)	(N=107)
(3 schools)		Gamma=.47

All-Around Boy Value Climate

Educational Expectations		
16 or more years	59	43
13-15 years	23	20
12 years	18	37
	(N=24)	(N=60)
(2 schools)		Gamma=.33

Scholar Specialist Value Climate

Educational Expectations		
16 or more years	52	53
13-15 years	23	23
12 years	25	24
	(N=31)	(N=53)
(2 schools)		Gamma=.02

Mixed-Type, Indeterminate Climate

Educational Expectations		
16 or more years	58	49
13-15 years	19	17
12 years	23	34
	(N=130)	(N=214)
(6 schools)		Gamma=.19

trolling for parental SES, IQ, and grade average (third-order gamma of .20).[9] For example, among the low endowment boys (i.e., low SES, low IQ, poor grades), 59 per cent of the athletes reported receiving encouragement from teachers and counselors to attend a four-year college as compared to 32 per cent of the non-athletes.[10] Furthermore, athletes were more likely to receive such encouragement regardless of their own level of educational expectations. Among those boys who had no plans for additional education after high school, 41 per cent of the athletes and 31 per cent of the nonathletes reported receiving encouragement from teachers and counselors to attend a four-year college. Similar findings concerning the association between athletic participation and academic encouragement from teachers recently were reported by Schafer and Rehberg (1970).

Conclusion

Our findings indicate that the association between athletic participation and higher educational goals is not eliminated when controlling for parental socio-economic status, parental academic encouragement, student grade average, and measured intelligence. Although this relationship is not strong enough to explain most of the variance in educational expectations, the findings from our study and previous research suggest that sports involvement is not necessarily detrimental to academic pursuits. More importantly, we found, as did Rehberg and Schafer (1968) that the influence of sports involvement was particularly strong for boys who were not otherwise predisposed to attend college. This interaction effect is largely attributable to a ceiling effect—since the proportion of boys in the "high endowment" category who plan on college is already very high, participation in sports can have little influence on their educational expectations.

Our findings also indicate that school value climate and perceived peer status are important variables intervening between participation and expectations. Our data support Spady's (1970) contention that sports involvement tends to engender high perceived peer status which in turn stimulates a desire for further status acquisition through college attendance. We found, however, that this process operates only in high schools where interscholastic achievement is valued highly relative to scholarly achievement. Our cross-sectional data prevent us from testing Spady's (1970) hypothesis that athletic involvement tends to generate false hopes in that athletes raise status perceptions and future goals without inculcating the skills and orientations requisite for their fulfillment. Further research utilizing a panel design well could be directed at this question.

REFERENCES

1. Bend, E. 1968. The Impact of Athletic Participation on Academic and Career Aspiration and Achievement. The National Football Foundation and Hall of Fame: New Brunswick, New Jersey.

2. Buhrmann, H. 1968. Longitudinal Study of the Relationship Between Athletic Participation, Various Social-Psychological Variables and Academic Achievement of Junior High School Boys. (Unpublished Doctoral Dissertation) University of Oregon.

3. Coleman, James S. 1961. The Adolescent Society. New York: Free Press. 1965. "Athletics in High School." Pp. 35-51 in his Adolescents and the Schools. New York: Basic Books.

4. ———, et al. 1966. Equality of Educational Opportunity. U.S. Department of Health, Education and Welfare. Washington, D.C.: Government Printing Office.

5. Eidsmore, R.M. 1963. "High school athletes are brighter." School Activities 35 (November):75-77.

6. Rehberg, R.A. 1969. "Behavioral and attitudinal consequences of high school interscholastic sports: A speculative consideration." Adolescence 4 (Spring):69-88.

7. ——— and W.E. Schafer. 1968. "Participation in interscholastic athletics and college expectations." American Journal of Sociology 63 (May):732-740.

8. Rosenberg, Morris. 1962. "Test factor standardization as a method of interpretation." Social Forces 41 (October):53-61.

9. Schafer, W.E. 1968. "Athletic success and social mobility." Paper presented at Annual Meetings of the American Association of Health, Physical Education and Recreation: St. Louis, Missouri. 1969. "Some social sources and consequences of interscholastic athletics: The case of participation and delinquency." International Review of Sport Sociology 4:63-79.

10. ——— and J.M. Armer. 1968. "Athletes are not inferior students." Transaction 5 (November):21-26, 61-62.

11. ——— and R.A. Rehberg. 1970. "Athletic participation, college aspirations and college encouragement." Pacific Sociological Review 13 (Summer):182-186.

12. Schendel, J. 1965. "Psychological differences between athletes and nonparticipants at three educational levels." Research Quarterly 36 (March):52-67.

13. Spady, William G. 1970. "Lament for the letterman: Effects of peer status and extracurricular activities on goals and achievement." American Journal of Sociology 75 (January):680-702.

NOTES

1. We operationally defined athletic participation as having participated in one or more interscholastic sport during the senior year. The questionnaire item was worded as follows:
   Have you participated in any of the following extracurricular activities this year? You may check more than one.
   _____ varsity athletics
   _____ debating
   _____ National Honor Society
   _____ band, orchestra, chorus
   _____ cheerleading
   _____ school paper or yearbook
   _____ student council
   _____ sorority or fraternity
   _____ dramatics, class play
   _____ foreign language club

2. The questionnaire item used to quantify educational expectations was worded as follows:
   What do you think you *really will* do after you leave high school?
   1. _____ Get a job and go to college part-time.
   2. _____ Go to college for one to three years.
   3. _____ Graduate from college.
   4. _____ Go to a business or vocational school.
   5. _____ Get a full-time job.
   6. _____ Get a part-time job.
   7. _____ Go into military service.
   8. _____ Take any job I can get.
   9. _____ Not be able to find a regular job.
   In an attempt to reproduce the breaking points used by Rehberg and Schafer (1968), response #3 was coded as 16 or more years of intended schooling; responses #1, 2, and 4, were coded as 13-15 years of intended schooling; and responses 5 through 9 were coded as 12 years of expected education.

3. Rosenberg's (1962) procedure for test factor standardization was used before calculating the Goodman-Kruskal gamma coefficients.

4. Rehberg and Schafer used Hollingshead's Two Factor Index of Social Position to measure parental SES. Our study used Duncan's Index of Occupational Status. In order to approximate the marginal distributions from the original study, we coded a score of 60 or higher on the Duncan Index as "high parental socioeconomic status," and a score under 60 was defined as "low parental status."

5. The following item was used as an indicator of parental academic encouragement; perhaps a less inferential name for this variable would be parental "involvement":
How often do you and your parents talk about your school work?
_____ Almost everyday.
_____ Once or twice a week.
_____ Once or twice a month.
_____ Less than once a month.
_____ Never or hardly ever.
Checking either of the first two response alternatives was defined as "high" parental academic encouragement. Rehberg and Schafer (1968:109-110) used a two-item index to measure parental academic involvement.

6. Perceived peer status was operationalized by the following questionnaire item:
About how popular do you think you are in this school?
_____ One of the most popular.
_____ Very popular.
_____ Popular enough.
_____ Not very popular.
In Table 3, "high" perceived peer status was defined as checking either the first or second response category; "medium" peer status was coded as checking the third response category, and "low" status as the fourth response category.

7. School value climates were differentiated in terms of the relative proportion of students in the various schools who checked "high grades, honor roll" and "being an athletic star" on the questionnaire item listed below. This item originally was used by Coleman in *The Adolescent Society* (1961:72). Empirical breaking points in school response rates on this item were used to classify the value climates of the various schools.
Among the things listed below, what does it take to get to be important and be looked up to by the other students here at school?
_____ Coming from the right family.
_____ Leader in activities.
_____ Having a nice car.
_____ High grades, honor roll.
_____ Being an athletic star.
_____ Being in the leading crowd.

8. There is a positive relationship between the number of close friends planning to attend college and the individual's educational expectations (Gamma=.50); however, this relationship is equally strong among the athletes and non-athletes.

9. The questionnaire item used to measure academic encouragement from teachers/counselors was worded as follows:
Has your teacher or counselor encouraged you to go farther in school after graduating from high school?
_____ Yes, to go to college
_____ Yes, for technical or advanced job training.
_____ Yes, for business or commercial training.
_____ Yes, other training.
_____ No.
Checking the first response alternative was defined as "high" academic encouragement from teachers and counselors.

10. There is a strong positive relationship between academic encouragement from teachers/counselors and educational expectations (Gamma=.81), but this relationship is equally strong among the athletes and non-athletes.

THE RELATIONSHIP BETWEEN ACADEMIC ACHIEVEMENT AND INTERSCHOLASTIC PARTICIPATION: A COMPARISON OF CANADIAN AND AMERICAN HIGH SCHOOLS

Wendy C. Jerome

and

John C. Phillips

Interscholastic athletics have been considered an anti-intellectual influence by some authors (Henry, 1963; Coleman, 1961, 1965) who argue that school athletic programs encourage a diversion of school resources, parental support, and student energies away from the mission of scholastic excellence. Recent studies of American high school athletic programs, however, provide compelling evidence that participation in athletics is associated with better grades, higher aspiration levels, and a more positive attitude towards school.

A variety of plausible explanations for this phenomenon have been suggested which center around three basic themes: (1) selection—the better, more pro-school students try out for, and are selected to membership on school teams; (2) "spill-over"—there is a transfer of positive work habits, attitudes, and values

from sports to school work; and (3) differential school experiences—athletes are more visible, acquire increased status, and receive more encouragement from school personnel than do non-athletes.

This paper will review some of the evidence concerning athletic participation and scholastic achievement in American and Canadian high schools and discuss certain cultural differences which may explain the variation noted in the relationships between sports and studies.

Schafer and Armer (1968) found that high school athletes achieved slightly better grades than their non-

Wendy C. Jerome and John C. Phillips, "The Relationship Between Academic Achievement and Interscholastic Participation: A Comparison of Canadian and American High Schools," *Journal of the Canadian Association for Health, Physical Education and Recreation,* January-February 1971, Volume 37, pp. 18-21.

athlete matches and that this advantage increased among boys from blue-collar homes and boys who were not in a college-preparatory program. Bend (1968), in a nationwide study of American high school athletes, found substantially the same pattern. Athletes got slightly better grades and the advantage of the athletes was most pronounced among "low endowment" (low IQ, blue-collar) boys. Buhrmann's (1968) study of junior high school boys in Oregon also found that participation seemed to encourage students from poor and disadvantaged groups to achieve scholastically at a much higher level than their non-participating peers.

There is strong evidence to indicate that athletes aspire to attend college and succeed in attending college more than do non-athletes. Bend (1968) found that 81.8% of his superior athletes aspired to at least some college work compared to 56.1% of his non-athletes. The figures for low-endowment superior athletes were 39.8% and 13.3% respectively. Of the superior athletes, 71.4% actually attended college while 50% of the non-athletes attended. Figures for the low-endowment athletes and non-athletes were 14.8% and 6.9%. Rehberg and Schafer (1968; 1970) found similar patterns in aspirations and expectations for college attendance.

In a recent study of one American high school, Phillips and Schafer (1970) found that athletes, when compared to non-athletes, shared attitudes which were somewhat more favourable toward the school and its traditions. They concluded that the better academic performance by athletes could be explained by the greater pressures toward conformity to school rules and traditions expected of athletes, as well as a more positive attitude toward the school among athletes. Since athletics, to a greater degree than scholarship, also provides entry to elite school status in American schools (Coleman, 1960; Clark, 1957; Horowitz, 1967), we should not be surprised at the athletes' relatively strong support for school rules and traditions.

It should be noted that there is some support for the concept of the "all-round" individual. Both Coleman and Horowitz found that the "athlete-scholar" rated highest on measures of interpersonal popularity. In comparisons between the "pure" athlete and the "pure" scholar, however, both found that the athlete was accorded much higher status. Explaining this phenomenon, Coleman presents the view that because members of the school and community identify strongly with the success and failure of "their" team, the athlete gains status because he is doing something for the community. Success in scholastic matters, on the other hand, is obtained at the expense of classmates and often results ridicule and rejection of the achiever, unless balanced by athletic contributions.

These, and other recent studies, have provided some insight into the relationship of high school athletic participation to scholastic achievement. However, the results of these studies conducted in American high schools are often applied to the Canadian high school, perhaps because of the apparent similarities between the two countries and the fact that little research has been conducted on the Canadian high school athlete.

It would appear from the results of the few studies that have been conducted that a difference does exist. Jerome, in a study currently underway in Sudbury, Ontario finds that while the majority of students would aspire to be "athlete-scholars," in comparisons between the "pure" athlete and the "pure" scholar, the athlete was far down the line. This attitude among Canadian students is further supported by Zentner and Parr (1968) whose study of social status among high school students in Calgary led them to conclude that high academic performance was a positive factor in the student status structure. In that study, students with high academic achievement were overrepresented in the leading crowds.

As for the relationship between academic achievement and athletic participation, Jerome found that when final grade averages obtained by students prior to opportunity for interscholastic competition were compared to those achieved after this opportunity was available, the non-participants' grades changed in an upward direction while those of the athletes became lower. The differences between the two groups were significant at the .05 level. Further, when socio-economic status and academic program were considered, it was found that non-participant's grades improved to a greater degree than did those of athletes of the same social class and academic program. Again the differences were significant.

A further study by King and Angi (1968) of the hockey playing student in Ontario found that in Grade 9 hockey playing students achieved similar marks to non-hockey playing students, were slightly lower on achievement and aptitude tests, and had higher academic and vocational goals. However, by the time these hockey players had reached Grade 12 they had significantly lower school marks than the non-players, significantly lower achievement and aptitude scores, and had lowered their academic and vocational goals. It should be noted that these hockey players were not involved in interscholastic hockey, but in highly organized Junior A, B, C, and D hockey programs in the community which are not conducted to fit around the students' academic responsibilities as are interscholastic sports.

Why these differences between school athletes in the two countries? On the surface it would appear that the interscholastic programs in Canada and the United States are similar. A wide range of activities, competitive leagues, school awards, state and provincial championships are common to both. Certified teachers coach the teams. The local news media cover the competitions and report on the results.

Returning to the three explanations posed earlier, if the better, more motivated students tend to go out for, and be selected to athletic teams, we would expect the positive relationship between athletic participation and academics to hold in both American and Canadian schools. Also, if, as Schafer and Armer (1968) have suggested, good habits and application to sports carry over to academic matters, we would expect athletes from both cultures to do better in school. If we accept this reasoning, we can expect students to do better in studies as a result of participation in athletics regardless of whether they receive special attention from the school. This does not appear to be so in Canadian schools. It would seem, then, that the third explanation offered, differential school experiences, would be the most plausible.

It is clear that in the American secondary school high recognition and accompanying status are achieved directly through athletic activities. Athletes are more likely to be members of the leading crowds than are scholars. Coleman (1960) showed that athletic success was clearly and consistently the most important means to achievement of status in every school he studied. Schafer and Armer (1968) feel that for the blue-collar boy the most certain means of entry into the "leading crowd" is athletics. This does not appear to be the case in the Canadian school. The athlete is visible, but not to the same degree, and his acceptance into the leading crowd appears to be dependent to a greater degree on his scholastic aptitude.

Downey's (1960) study of cultural differences between various regions of the United States and Canada sheds some light on why this situation may be present. He found that Canadians placed a greater emphasis on the pursuit of knowledge and scholarly attitudes as an outcome of schooling than did Americans. The American schools tended to emphasize physical development, citizenship, and social skills. The reward structures of the schools would tend to reflect these emphases. Spady (1970) has suggested that many students may view athletics as an alternative to, rather than complementary to, the academic mission of the school. Canadian schools, by increasing the rewards available to participants in academic areas may encourage the less interested students to use athletics as an alternative.

Schafer and Armer (1968) reason that another positive effect participation in athletics may have upon the grades of American students is the "lure" of a college career in sports provided through athletic scholarships. This financial assistance available in almost every post-high school institution in the United States is not common in Canadian institutions of higher learning. The availability of these scholarships to American students might well encourage them to maintain their grades at a level which would assure them of consideration by college coaches.

In addition, the degree of emphasis and support from the American community for the high school athletic program is much greater than that found in Canada. American communities identify with "their" team. It is not uncommon to see a large number of adults mixed with students at high school athletic contests. In most Canadian schools, it is uncommon to see a large number of students in attendance. Local news media in both countries provide coverage for high school sports; however, in the United States this coverage extends to national sports magazines. These periodicals carry results of high school competitions, they publicize all-stars, and carry articles on high school athletes of national calibre. Rarely does one see a Canadian high school athlete mentioned outside the high school column of the local newspaper.

The findings suggest that the positive relationship between athletic participation and academic achievement in American high schools can probably best be explained by special rewarding experiences in and from the school and community. Athletes, like all other creatures, appear to become positively attached to sources of rewarding experiences, in this case the school. Perhaps, too, as Schafer and Armer (1968) suggest, the high prestige that American students obtain from sports participation gives them a better self-concept resulting in a more positive attitude towards themselves and their abilities—both athletic and scholastic. In the absence of a differential reward structure favouring athletics, one cannot expect athletes, as a group, to excel in their school work to a greater degree than other students.

REFERENCES

1. Bend, Emil. *The Impact of Athletic Participation on Academic and Career Aspiration and Achievement.* (New Brunswick, New Jersey: The National Football Foundation and Hall of Fame, 1968).

2. Buhrmann, Hans G. "Longitudinal Study of the Relationship Between Athletic Participation, Various Social-Psychological Variables, and Academic Achievement of Junior High School Boys" (Microcarded Ph.D. dissertation, University of Oregon, 1968).

3. Clark, B.R. *Educating the Expert Society.* (San Francisco: Chandler, 1962), pp. 244-258.

4. Coleman, James S. "Adolescent Subculture and Academic Achievement," *American Journal of Sociology*, Vol. LXV (January, 1960), pp. 337-347.

5. ———. *The Adolescent Society.* (New York: The Free Press, 1961).

6. ———. "Peer Cultures and Education in Modern Society." In Theodore M. Newcomb and Everett K. Wilson (eds.), *College Peer Groups: Problems and Prospects for Research.* (Chicago: Aldine, 1966), pp. 244-269.

7. Downey, L.W. "Regional Variations in Educational Viewpoint," *Alberta Journal of Educational Research*, Vol. VI, No. 4 (December, 1960), pp. 195-199.

8. Hargreaves, David H. *Social Relation in a Secondary School.* (London: Routledge and Kegan Paul, 1967).

9. Henry, Jules. *Culture Against Man.* (New York: John Wiley and Sons, 1963).

10. Horowitz, Herbert. "Prediction of Adolescent Popularity and Rejection from Achievement and Interest Tests," *Journal of Educational Psychology*, Volume 58, No. 3 (1967), pp. 170-174.

11. Jerome, Wendy C. "A Study to Determine the Relationships Between Participation in Organized Interscholastic and Community Sports and Academic Achievement," (Unfinished Ph.D. dissertation, University of Oregon).

12. King, A.J.C., and Carol E. Angi. "The Hockey Playing Student," *CAHPER Journal*, Vol. 35, No. 1 (October-November, 1968), pp. 25-28.

13. Phillips, John C., and Walter E. Schafer. "The Athletic Subculture: A Preliminary Study." Paper presented at the annual meeting of the American Sociological Association, Washington, D.C. 1970.

14. Rehberg, Richard A., and Walter E. Schafer. "Participation in Interscholastic Athletics and College Expectations," *American Journal of Sociology*, 73 (May, 1968), pp. 732-740.

15. Schafer, Walter E., and J. Michael Armer. "Athletes are Not Inferior Students," *Trans-action*, (November, 1968), pp. 21-26, 61-62.

16. ——— and Richard A. Rehberg. "Athletic Participation, College Aspirations and College Encouragement," *Pacific Sociological Review*, 13 (Summer, 1970), pp. 182-186.

17. Spady, William G. "Lament for the Letterman: Effects of Peer Status and Extracurricular Activities on Goals and Achievement," *American Journal of Sociology*, 75 (January, 1970), pp. 680-702.

18. Zentner, Henry, and Arnold R. Parr. "Social Status in the High School: An Analysis of Some Related Variables," *Alberta Journal of Educational Research*, Vol. XIV, No. 4 (December, 1968).

DISCUSSION QUESTIONS

A. *John C. Phillips and Walter E. Schafer*

1. How does the athlete compare with the non-athlete in terms of grades, educational aspirations and attainment, delinquency and mobility?

2. Students from which socio-economic class are most likely to profit from interscholastic athletic participation? Explain your answer.

3. In what ways does membership in the athletic subculture encourage conformity to formal school goals?

B. *Stanley D. Eitzen*

1. What were Coleman's major findings in his study of high school adolescent status systems?

2. Based upon Eitzen's findings, is sport today of lesser importance in the adolescent status system than during the late 1950's? Explain your answer.

3. List and discuss several variables which often affect a student's perception of the importance of interscholastic sports.

C. *Elmer Spreitzer and Meredith Pugh*

1. What were the major findings of Rehberg and Schafer's 1968 study?

2. What extension did Spreitzer and Pugh make in their replication of Rehberg and Schafer's study?

3. Describe the research methods used by Spreitzer and Pugh.

4. Discuss and compare the results of the Spreitzer and Pugh study with those of the Rehberg and Schafer study.

5. How are educational expectations related to school value climate and perceived peer status?

D. *Wendy C. Jerome and John C. Phillips*

1. How do American and Canadian student-athletes compare in terms of academic achievement?

2. What accounts for the differences in academic achievement between American and Canadian student-athletes?

3. Do you feel that another type of reward system could successfully replace athletics in the American school system? Explain your answer.

Unit VIII

Sport Subcultures

The study of sport subcultures has, until recently, received little attention from social scientists. While sociologists and anthropologists have written extensively in such areas as primitive, occupational and deviant subcultures, the world of the sportsman has escaped rigorous and systematic investigation.

A sport subculture may be viewed as a subsystem of a larger society, and is characterized by a distinguishing pattern of values, norms, beliefs and material properties. These and other elements give the subculture cultural integrity. That is to say, those elements which go to make up the subculture provide it with a rather unique identity and character. Thus, we may speak of the subculture of boxers, skiers and hockey players. What differentiates one sport from another, however, is that the participants possess a common value system, have relatively similar backgrounds (e.g., most rock climbers tend to come from the higher socioeconomic strata), share a system of argot (jargon), and use equipment, clothing and facilities which reflect the requirements of the activity and the aspirations of the participants. Sport subcultures may be analyzed either as microsystems (e.g., a particular ski team), or, as macrosystems (skiers in general).

In the first selection, sociologists John Phillips and Walter Schafer provide the reader with a framework, or a conceptual map for analyzing sport subcultures, and offer a model for measuring group norms. Since norms constitute a major differentiating element among sport subcultures, this model enables the user to compare members' expected behaviors among different sport subcultures.

Glenn Jacobs, a sociologist, offers in the second selection an in-depth analysis of the subculture of karate players. Reference is made to such elements as the acquisition of status, the learning and enactment of appropriate roles, and the function of initiation rites. What emerges is a subculture whose members form an in-group, and whose internal mechanisms of social control reflect a quasi-martial and authoritarian system.

The growing sport of parachuting is analyzed in the next selection by sociologist David Arnold. Through participant-observation, the author provides the reader with some insights into the value system of the participant, and his attitude toward risk taking. He alludes to the function of the sport's accoutrements (e.g., badges on jump suits) and their possible contribution to group cohesiveness. The author also discusses how the subculture views women parachutists, and notes that blacks and orientals are significantly underrepresented. One may speculate that some of the reasons for the above include the absence of role models, socioeconomic factors and the possible existence of a "culture clash."

In the fourth selection, sociologist Harvey Hyman studied the subculture of a tennis court to determine the function of such elements as norms, cliques and informal role playing. In his analysis, he identifies the existence of a definite status hierarchy which serves both manifest and latent functions in the subculture. The reader is encouraged to speculate about these functions, and to compare them with the functions of hierarchies in other sports.

In the final selection, head football coach John Massengale offers the reader an insider's view of the stresses and organizational strain which many coaches experience. The author also discusses methods of social control and the consequences of failure to conform to the values and norms of the coaching subculture. In addition, the nature of the occupational reward system is analyzed in relationship to upward mobility.

SUBCULTURES IN SPORT—A CONCEPTUAL AND METHODOLOGICAL APPROACH

John C. Phillips and Walter E. Schafer

One intriguing question for the sociologist of sport involves the nature, agencies and outcomes of socialization resulting from an individual's participation in sports. We know that athletes have a variety of experiences related to their sport such as competition, training requirements, possible notoriety, victory and defeat, that non-athletes are unlikely to have. Further, athletes engage in interaction with a variety of people—coaches, press, other athletes—to a greater extent than do non-athletes.

It would seem likely that with their special patterns of interaction, sports related activities, and sports related role expectations, athletes in various sports might develop patterns of symbols, meanings, beliefs, norms and values shared among athletes but not with non-athletes. That is, athletes may have a subculture. We might also expect that these athletic subcultures might influence the participant's behavior in areas outside of sports, and his experience with an athletic subculture might influence his behavior even after he retires from active athletics.

In this paper we shall attempt to review the concept of subculture; propose a conceptual and methodological model for studying one component of subculture, norms; and finally to suggest a variety of sports related research questions for which this model might prove useful.

The Concept of Subculture

The term 'subculture' has been applied to a wide variety of phenomena since Gordon's formulation (1947). Gordon defined subculture as:

> . . . a subdivision of a national culture, composed of a combination of factorable social situations . . . *forming in their combination a functioning unity which has an integrated impact on the participating individual* (p. 40, Gordon's emphasis).

While the term has been applied to a variety of social situations including age groups, social classes, regional, ethnic or occupational groups, delinquent gangs and total institutions, little attention has been paid to whether such phenomena formed a functioning unit that had an impact on the individual. The term has, rather, simply been applied to any apparent variation from the general culture. No concept can be of much use unless it can be defined in terms that allow researchers to employ it with at least some degree of uniformity.

Since Gordon's article, a number of contributions have appeared that appear to have brought the concept of subculture and what might be termed subcultural theory to the threshold of much exciting and meaningful research and theorization. The key contributors we wish to review include Alfred R. Lindesmith and Anselm Strauss, Albert K. Cohen, Howard Becker, Marvin E. Wolfgang and Franco Ferracuti, and James Van Der Zanden.

In their chapter, 'Deviant Subsystems', Lindesmith and Strauss (1956) make some valuable points regarding the creation of subcultures as well as some of the characteristics of subcultures. The authors describe how diabetics in Hong Kong during World War II developed the beginnings of a subculture after they began to face a common problem—a scarcity of insulin. The authors point out that the American treatment of the problem of drug addiction has led to the rise of an 'addict subculture'. They continue:

> It is a significant sociological fact that the American drug user has developed a rich and varied argot whereas European addicts apparently have not. This, of course, is because there is what we might call an 'addict culture' in the United States—a subculture that . . . has a tradition, a philosophy, norms . . . and a means of renewing itself through the recruitment of new members . . . (p. 677-678).

Variations in language—argot—appear to be a good indicator of the presence and the content of subcultures.[1] The other key point made by Lindesmith and Strauss is their suggestion of the importance of some shared need or trait in the formation of a subculture. Cohen, in his book, *Delinquent Boys* (1953), presents a general theory of subcultures. While Cohen applies the term promiscuously to factory, neighborhood, family, clique or gang, this theory is probably the single most important contribution to the development of theories of subcultures.

Cohen begins his discussion by pointing out that 'culture is continually being created, recreated and modified whenever individuals sense in one another like needs, generated by like circumstances, not shared generally by the larger social system [p. 65]'. These like needs coupled with interaction result in new norms shared by those who stand to gain by adopting them.

In his chapter, 'Juvenile Delinquency' (1961), written with James F. Short, Cohen summarizes his own theory. He contends that working class boys desire to move into the middle class but lack the means—manners, parental support—and find themselves continually 'at the bottom of the heap'. This continual failure damages their self respect. But the boys find that there are others in the same situation, so 'those individuals, possessing similar problems of adjustment, tend to draw together and, through their sympathetic interaction, develop social systems of their own. . .[p. 108]'.

In another restatement of Cohen's theory, Cohen and Short (1958) make the point that subcultures consist of systems of beliefs and values, thus providing a theory of the process of the development of subcultures as well as a statement of what factors actually constitute a subculture.

Reprinted by permission of Birkhauser Verlag.

Howard S. Becker (1963) provides us with a rich body of descriptive data about the content of certain deviant subcultures and the process of socialization to a deviant subculture. We might adapt Becker's description of how one becomes a marijuana user to provide a general pattern of socialization into any subculture. Becker contends that a marijuana user must (1) learn to smoke the drug, (2) learn to perceive its effects, and (3) learn to enjoy the sensations he perceives (see Becker, 1963, p. 58). A more general model might read (1) learning subcultural techniques, (2) adopting subcultural meanings, and (3) adopting subcultural values.

Marvin E. Wolfgang and Franco Ferracuti (1967) provide a much needed, comprehensive discussion of subculture as a concept, as well as of problems related to methodology in the study of subcultures. We will restrict ourselves in this section to their treatment of the concept.

Wolfgang and Ferracuti choose to define subculture in terms of values and norms. They contend that in a subculture there is 'a central theme, a sub-ethos, or a cluster of values that is differentiated from those in the total culture [p. 100]'. The authors continue:

The values shared in a subculture are often made evident and can be identified phenomenologically in terms of the conduct that is expected, ranging from the permissible to the required, in certain kinds of like situation (p. 101).

Another important point made by Wolfgang and Ferracuti is the distinction between social groups and subcultures. Subcultural values and norms are shared among members of groups, but those who share in a subculture need not interact with one another as a group any more than those who share in the Japanese, Spanish or any other 'parent' culture. Indeed those who share in many subcultures—hippies, for example—are widely dispersed and could not possibly interact as a group. Paul Lerman (1967a) adds credence to this contention in his study of delinquent gangs. He found that while there appeared to be a general delinquent subculture, boys exhibiting subcultural traits interacted in pairs and triads, not as large gangs. Thus, Lerman suggested that 'subcultural boundaries and interaction boundaries are, in fact, distinct phenomena [p. 70, original in italics]'.

Wolfgang and Ferracuti make a further distinction between group and subcultural norms. They point out that while conduct may be a 'valid index of normatively induced values, latent and different values may be retained by some individuals who are members of the group . . .[p. 103]'. Thus, a soldier may fight bravely not because he holds the military value for bravery, but because he is loyal to his primary group. What appears to be a manifestation of subcultural norms may in fact be a manifestation of group norms, a distinct phenomenon.

In what may be the most significant portion of their book, Wolfgang and Ferracuti discuss some key problems of research in subcultures:

When we speak of the 'teenage culture' or . . . the 'delinquent' subculture we have not yet stated whether we are discussing quantitative variables or qualitative attributes or both. We have not isolated sufficiently the differentiating normative items. (Hypotheses about subcultures) cannot be tested until we have objective and independent measurements of the norms of conduct (p. 102).

Thus Wolfgang and Ferracuti contend that we cannot successfully study subcultures unless we have acceptable ways of measuring the elements that constitute subcultures. They later point to the need for a method of determining the degree to which the subcultural norms differ from the norms of the larger culture.

Wolfgang and Ferracuti (pp. 110-115) go on to propose four criteria that might enable us to designate a given system of values and norms as subcultural. We summarize here the criteria they suggest:

1. Classification of values—we will have to distinguish between tolerated, concordant values and untolerated, discordant values; that is, between subcultural values that are acceptable in the larger culture and values that are unacceptable in the larger culture.
2. Number of values that are different from the general cultural values—a prerequisite to counting the number of values would be construction of a scale of values of the dominant culture so that we might assign weights to various values in accordance with their importance.
3. Stability—values that are transient do not serve as indicators of subcultureness. Perhaps they are better conceived as fads.
4. Intensity or strength of values—normness. To what extent are variant values translated into expectations for behavior? Some allegiance to subcultural values and some impact on the participants' behavior will be expected in any subculture.

While Wolfgang and Ferracuti direct attention to several important distinctions in the use of the concept subculture, they fail to distinguish clearly between norms and values. A recent work by James Van Der Zanden (1965) not only pays heed to the important conceptual differences between norms and values, but provides a broader conceptualization of subcultures which we believe will prove useful in this study of subcultures and sport.

For Van Der Zanden (1965), a subculture is the set of cultural patterns that sets a group apart from larger society or a larger organization. When those patterns not only differ but conflict with the larger culture then a contraculture may be said to exist. According to Van Der Zanden, a culture consists of four parts:

1. Norms, or generally accepted, sanctioned prescriptions for, or prohibitions against, various types of behavior.
2. Values, or shared criteria or conceptions used in evaluating things (including objects, ideas, acts, feelings, and events) as to their relative desirability, merit or correctness.

3. Beliefs, or shared ideas concerning the nature of the universe or any of its component parts, including man.
4. Symbols, or any shared act or object that has to be accepted socially as standing for something else.

A subculture exists to the extent that members of any sub-group differ in their norms, values, beliefs, or symbols from a larger organization.

Van Der Zanden, following Yinger (1960), points out the utility of distinguishing between 'subculture', variations from the general culture, and 'contraculture', which Yinger describes as variations in which normative systems contain:

. . . as a primary element, a theme of conflict with the values of the total society, where personality variables are directly involved in the development and maintenance of the group's values, and wherever its norms can be understood only by reference to the relationships of the group to a surrounding dominant culture (Yinger, 1960, p. 629).

It should be noted that our notion of the meaning of subculture is close to Yinger's use of the term contraculture. Sportsmen, however, share generally *approved* or *desirable* characteristics, rather than a stigma such as drug addiction or homosexuality. While sportsmen may develop special norms, values, beliefs, and symbols which enable them to function more comfortably in their societies, they probably do not share norms or values which are in *conflict* with the dominant culture.

At this point, it should be clear that it is probably less fruitful to study total subcultures than it is to develop descriptions or causal generalizations about how their parts (i.e., norms, values, beliefs or symbols) relate either as a cause or effect to each other, to the behavior or attitudes of group members, or to the larger environment. Certainly, a systematic and careful study of any single component is a major theoretical and methodological task itself. Once this approach has been followed, findings will accumulate to increase our understanding of the total subculture.

In the next section, we present a model for measuring a key element of subcultures, norms, while in the last section we will identify problems in the sociology of sport to which the model might be applied.

A Model for Conceptualizing and Measuring Norms

The model of norms developed by Jay Jackson (1960, 1966) is at once a conceptual and methodological tool, and, as such, has substantial promise for studying norms within a subcultural framework. This model, which for reasons that will become clear has come to be known as the Return Potential Model (RPM), consists of two dimensions, a behavior dimension and an evaluation dimension. Referring to the behavior dimension, Jackson has noted that:

A norm is always about something; it has an object. Ordinarily its object is some behavior on the part of the person that is considered to be appropriate or inappropriate. A student is expected to wear certain articles of clothing and not others in the classroom. There are norms about coming to class on time, about being absent, about disagreeing with the instructor—in fact, about most aspects of behavior in an instructional situation. (1960, p. 137)

The behaviors which are evaluated always vary in degree along a dimension of quantity or quality. In measurement terms, then, this dimension consists of values ranging from zero to five, ten, or some other number.

The idea of a norm also implies evaluation—degrees of approval or disapproval by other persons—of each type of behavior the individual might engage in. Groups or sub-groups usually share tendencies to approve or disapprove a particular kind of behavior. Evaluation of behavior is almost always a matter of degree, ranging from high approval, to indifference, to high disapproval. In measurement terms, then, the evaluation dimension might be assigned values ranging, for example, from plus 5, through zero, to minus 5. When two dimensions are combined, the resulting model takes the form shown in Figure 1. Corresponding to the model is a simple approach to data collection consisting of questionnaire items taking the following illustrative form. It will be noted that the respondent is asked to indicate his degree of approval for each value on the behavior dimension (number of friends).

From such data, a number of characteristics of norms can be developed, each of which becomes useful in studying norms within a subcultural framework.

1. *Return Potential Curve.* For each actor or group of actors, a curve can be plotted depicting the distribution of potential group approval or disapproval for each behavior. An illustrative curve, shown in Figure 1, might be the average responses of a high school athletic team to an item about drinking beer.
2. *Point of Maximum Return.* The ideal behavior in the eyes of group members, or the point of maximum return, is that point along the behavior dimension associated with the highest degree of approval. In the case of having hippie friends, this would probably be close to the zero end of the behavior dimension.
3. *Range of Tolerable Behavior.* The behaviors which elicit some degree of approval fall within the range of tolerable behavior and may be referred to as *conformity*. Those which fall outside this range and elicit some degree of disapproval may be referred to as *deviancy*. In the case of beer drinking in an adult athletic club, the range of tolerable behavior may exclude too much or too little drinking, while for a Little League baseball team, the range of tolerance will only cover no drinking at all.
4. *Intensity.* This measure, obtained by summing the mean approval-disapproval scores for each behavior

Schematic Diagram of Return Potential Model

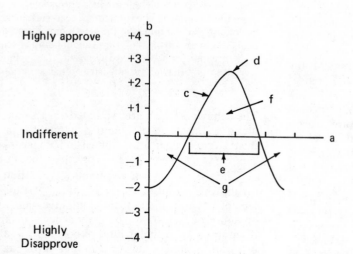

a. Behavior dimension
b. Return potential dimension
c. Return potential curve
d. Point of maximum return
e. Range of tolerable behavior
f. Area of conforming behavior
g. Area of deviant behavior

How would you feel about a teammate who had the following numbers of hippies as close friends?

Number of Hippie Friends	Degree of Approval or Disapproval													
	High Approval					Indifference		High Disapproval						
None	5	4	3	2	1		0		−1	−2	−3	−4	−5
1	5	4	3	2	1		0		−1	−2	−3	−4	−5
2	5	4	3	2	1		0		−1	−2	−3	−4	−5
3	5	4	3	2	1		0		−1	−2	−3	−4	−5
4	5	4	3	2	1		0		−1	−2	−3	−4	−5
5	5	4	3	2	1		0		−1	−2	−3	−4	−5

(Circle one number on each line)

refers to the overall-strength of feeling in the group. To the extent there is low feeling or intensity, the approval-disapproval scores will cluster toward the zero or indifference point. An example of low intensity might be norms in American high school teams about church attendance of members.

5. *Crystallization.* The degree of agreement among group members as to the degree of approval or disapproval for particular degrees or qualities of behavior may vary markedly. For some groups, there may be a high agreement (high crystallization), while for others, there may be high disagreement (low crystallization). A measurement of dispersion or variance is needed to determine crystallization scores for groups or sub-groups. A high degree of agreement or crystallization of norms regarding performance in training may be essential for team success in sport. Jackson uses the term *ambiguity* to refer to a bi-modal distribution in which two or more sub-groups differ markedly between

each other but have high crystallization within each one.

Each of the above properties refers to single norms. However, the RPM is also useful for studying the over-all normative structure of groups. The following properties refer to such structures, rather than to specific norms.

6. *Scope of Norms.* Groups differ in the degree to which their norms regulate a wide or narrow scope of members' behavior. In some sport situations, for example, the norms may pervade almost the entire life space of the team member, while in others the norms may regulate only limited areas of behavior.

7. *Integration.* A group's norms are integrated to the extent that conformity with one does not necessitate violation of another. As new norms are developed, they sometimes conflict with old ones, creating a circumstance of low integration. In sport, there is an ever-present potential of conflict between norms

calling for maximum individual effort and performance and those calling for contribution to a team effort.

8. *Mean Range of Tolerable Behavior.* This measure produces an over-all indicator of the degree to which a group's norms are restrictive (narrow range) or tolerant (broad range).
9. *Mean Intensity of Norms.* Another cross-norm measure, this refers to the over-all strength of approval-disapproval in the group confronting a group member.
10. *Mean Crystallization.* By measuring the average degree of agreement among a set of norms, it is possible to assess another important dimension of a group's internal climate.
11. *Normative Power.* By combining the intensity and crystallization scores for individual norms, it is possible to assess the degree of 'power' exerted on the individual group member in each area of behavior. The greater the feeling and agreement in the group, the greater the power.

Jackson has presented still other characteristics of norms and normative structure, but these are sufficient to illustrate their rich analysis which the model permits. It should be even more clear now that analysis of a single component of a subculture, such as norms, can be very complicated and intricate. While the analysis of a total subculture may be useful for description and other limited purposes, it is likely to be relatively superficial and unsystematic.

Illustrative Problems in Sport

There are numerous theoretical problems for which this model and its characteristics have relevance. Here, however, we will point to a few illustrative problems within the framework of subcultural analysis in sport.

First, the model is useful for comparing the norms shared by athletes with those shared by members of the larger school or community. In a previous study, Rehberg and Schafer (1968) suggested that one reason why high school athletes more often expect to go on to college than do non-athletes comparable in ability and background is that athletes share norms calling for achievement in general and college attendance in particular. Using the measure for point of maximum return, one could easily determine the validity of this suggestion. Similarly, one could test the suggestion by Schafer and Armer (1968) that one reason athletes obtain higher academic grades is that the sport subculture places greater emphasis than does the wider youth culture on effort, hard work, persistence, and achievement, which 'spill over' into non-athletic activities such as school work. More recently Schafer (1969) reported that working class, low IQ athletes were delinquent less often than non-athletes of comparable backgrounds and ability, and, as one interpretation, he suggested the influence of norms toward conforming, non-delinquent

behavior shared among athletes. Until now, the actual existence of such norms has never been studied. Other normative differences between the athletic sub-system and the larger sub-system of adolescence which need to be investigated include approval-disapproval of political involvement and political radicalism in particular, association with hippies and other marginal or deviant persons or groups, use of drugs, resistance or acceptance of fads in dress, hair and the like, and acquiescence to authority. In investigating all these issues, one should find several of the model's characteristics useful. Since the norms shared by athletes may well be important socializing influences, greater efforts should be made to see how they differ from those shared by members of other groups.

Second, the model can be used to analyze normative influence as an intervening variable between participation in sport and other individual outcomes, such as upward mobility and self-esteem. It may be, for example, that the reason athletes are more upwardly mobile is that they are more often exposed to communication and sanctions in the direction of approval for achievement, behavior and attitudes (Schafer, 1968). Similarly they may enjoy higher self-esteem because of their exposure to normative influences giving greater approval for physical performance or achievement in general.

Third, the model can be applied to the comparative study of the norms of different teams in the same sport, different sub-groups within the same team, and teams in different sports. For example, one might compare the extent to which high school football teams support norms which vary from their surrounding cultural environment as compared with college football teams. Or one might simply compare the teams of different schools or communities in terms of intensity, crystallization, or range of toleration. One also might compare the norms regarding drinking, smoking, obedience to training rules, and behavior before crowds among field event men, sprinters, and distance runners, or between members of individual and team sports. Analysis of differences in the crystallization, intensity, and range of tolerance of norms between individual and team sports would be especially interesting.

Fourth, the analysis of cross-national subcultures in different sports or even among sub-groups, such as distance runners, might be facilitated with the RPM. Not only do distance runners everywhere probably share symbols and meanings, but they probably also share norms pertaining to behavior during the race, training techniques, relations with others such as hippies and radicals, and appropriate ways of relating to each other.

Fifth, the model can be used to analyze the norms shared by coaches and physical education teachers and professors. This is a very important problem, since coaches and physical education teachers probably have a great deal of influence on the norms developed and shared by athletes, and physical education faculties in universities probably have a great deal of influence on the attitudes and expectations of coaches and physical education teachers. Does the political conservatism or indifference, intolerance of diverse life styles and civil liberties, and acquiescence to authority, which some have said characterize coaches and their athletes develop as a result of the professionalization process in universities and colleges? Studies are only now beginning to focus on this question.

These, then, are illustrative of the theoretical and empirical problems for which the RPM might be useful as a conceptual and methodological device. When findings based on its use begin to accumulate, we should be in a better position to understand the nature and effects of norms as one component of subcultures in sport and subcultures in general.

REFERENCES

1. Becker, H.S., Inference and Proof in Participant Observation, American Sociological Review 1958, 23, pp. 652-660.
2. ———, Outsiders: Studies in the Sociology of Deviance, Glencoe, The Free Press 1963.
3. Cohen, A.K., Delinquent Boys: The Culture of the Gang, Glencoe, The Free Press 1955.
4. Cohen, A.K. and J.F. Short, Jr., Research in Delinquent Subcultures, Journal of Social Issues 1961, 14 (3), pp. 20-37.
5. ———, Juvenile Delinquency, in: R.K. Merton and R.A. Nisbet (eds.), Contemporary Social Problems, New York, Harcourt, Brace and World 1961.
6. Gordon, M.M., The Concept of Sub-cultures and Its Application, Social Forces 1947, 260, pp. 40-42.
7. Jackson, J., Structural Characteristics of Norms, The Dynamics of Instructional Groups (The Fifty-ninth Yearbook of the National Society for the Study of Education, Part II), Chicago, The University of Chicago Press 1960, pp. 136-163.
8. ———, A Conceptual and Measurement Model for Norms and Roles, Pacific Sociological Review 1966, 9 (1), pp. 35-47.
9. Lerman, P., (a) Gangs, Networks and Subcultural Delinquency, American Journal of Sociology 1967, 73 (1), pp. 63-72.
10. ———, (b) Argot, Symbolic Deviance and Subcultural Delinquency, American Sociological Review 1967, 32 (2), pp. 209-224.
11. Lindesmith, A.R. and A.L. Strauss, Social Psychology (Rev. Ed.), New York, Holt, Rinehart and Winston 1956.
12. Rehberg, R.A. and W.E. Schafer, Participation in Interscholastic Athletics and College Expectations, American Journal of Sociology, 1968, LXIII (May), pp. 732-740.
13. Schafer, W.E. and J.M. Armer, Athletes Are Not Inferior Students, Trans-action 1968 (November), pp. 21-26, 61-62.
14. Schafer, W.E., Athletic Success and Social Mobility, paper presented at the annual meetings of the American Association of Health, Physical Education and Recreation, St. Louis, Missouri, 1968, April.
15. ———, Participation in Interscholastic Athletics and Delinquency: A Preliminary Study, Social Problems 1969, (Summer), pp. 40-47.
16. Van Der Zanden, J.W., Sociology: A Systematic Analysis, New York, The Ronald Press Company 1965.
17. Wolfgang, M.E. and F. Ferracuti, The Subculture of Violence, London, Travistock 1967.
18. Yinger, J.M., Contraculture and Subculture, American Sociological Review, 1960, 25 (5) (October), pp. 625-635.

URBAN SAMURAI: *THE "KARATE DOJO"**

Glenn Jacobs

The current interest in things Oriental embraces not only philosophy and religion, but also the Japanese martial arts such as judo, aikido, and karate. Schools have sprouted all over, and the arts are included in the athletic curricula of many high schools and colleges; most newsstands now carry a selection of magazines and paperbacks devoted to these subjects. Aside from their obvious exotic character, which seems to render them unique, the schools where these arts are taught exhibit traits which put them in the company of as diverse an assortment of groups as boys' gangs, men's fraternal organizations, religious cults, and high school athletic teams. Accordingly, this study examines a karate dojo (school) as a reality within a world of multiple realities. As the veils of mystery and secrecy are peeled away, the realities of group life are revealed.

The Setting

During the day, lower Manhattan's drug and cosmetic district is filled with the hustle of people moving through the many wholesale and retail stores. It resounds with the cacophony of truck and automobile horns, reflecting the irritation of truck drivers, commuters, and businessmen anxious to perform their rounds and seek refuge in comfortable offices and homes. The shabby offices and lofts above the stores house the outlets of a staggering diversity of goods and services, only barely cataloged in the yellow pages of the telephone directory of a vast metropolis.

For the human traffic, the area is just another annoy-ing bottleneck to be suffered while going somewhere else or while "picking up a few things"; not many are aware of the upstairs of these buildings. Sandwiched in among

George Braziller, Inc., from *The Participant Observer* by Glenn Jacobs (ed.), reprinted with the permission of the publisher. Copyright © 1970 by Glenn Jacobs.

Glenn Jacobs, instructor of sociology, University of Wisconsin, Rock County Campus, is a doctoral candidate at that university.

*This study was presented in an abbreviated form as a paper entitled "Communication and Mystification in the *Karate Dojo*'" at the 1969 Annual Meeting of the American Sociological Association in San Francisco, September 3, 1969.

these upstairs nooks is a converted loft containing the *Goju Karate Dojo* (*Goju* meaning "hard-soft," a style of karate; *dojo,* a place where the Japanese martial arts are studied).

The *dojo* is open to its membership evenings from 6:30 to 8:30, and on Sundays from 12:00 to 4:00 in the afternoon—the hours when the neighborhood changes into a deserted array of shabby buildings.

The decor of the *dojo* is designed in such a way as to convince the spectator that he has at once entered a place pregnant with the mysteries of the East, the austerity of a professional's office, the savoir-faire of a ballet school, and the "men only" atmosphere of a boys' hangout. The rows of observation benches and the training equipment, rice paper lamps, documents written in calligraphy, and mazelike partitions dividing the place are all orchestrated to conjure up the exotic and the bizarre. Coupled with this, one is struck by the rather unorthodox movements, gestures, and vocalizations associated with the practice of the art. The formalism of the various drilled techniques, the homogeneity of barefoot members in baggy white muslin uniforms combined with the quasi-oriental atmosphere, are attractive to tourists and prospective members.

Proficiency in karate calls for strength, stamina, and speed. This makes the sport uncongenial to older men, women, and young children. As a result, the membership consists largely of males ranging between the ages of fourteen and forty. Their occupational backgrounds are varied, with a skewness toward older high school and college males and young middle- and working-class men. In our *dojo* there was one minor celebrity, a cartoonist for *Playboy* magazine. There were also several policemen studying karate. Reminiscent of cheap western movies, they deposited their revolvers at the desk before exercises.

The Company Chart

The formal organization of the *dojo* consists of a scheme involving the student's progression through hierarchically ordered statuses, the ranks being indicated by the color of the cotton belts. Each status group also must learn the techniques appropriate to it. The specifications of skill and acquisition of particular techniques are partially determined by the customary standards of Japanese *dojos,* and partially idiosyncratic to a given school. The succession of statuses are: (1) white belt—*shirobi* (*obi* meaning "belt"); (2) green belt—*midori obi;* (3) brown belt—*chowbi;* (4) black belt (first through third levels)—*kurobi;* (5) black belt (fourth and fifth levels)—*renshi* (meaning "expert"); (6) black belt (sixth through eighth levels)—*kyoshi* (meaning "wizard"); (7) black belt (ninth level)—*hanshi* (meaning "chief"); and (8) black belt (tenth level)—*hanshi seiko-sheehan* (meaning "chief master"). Honorary belt colors for the fourth through fifth, sixth through eighth, and ninth and tenth degrees are, respectively, black-red-white, black-red, and solid red. (Both ninth

and tenth levels of black belt are solid red.) In the *dojo* of Mr. Urban, the master-proprietor, the highest rank attained was the third level black belt; Urban himself was a seventh level black belt. The wearing of belts obviously makes it easy for members to identify one another as status equals, superiors, and inferiors, and the entire structure of the cliques are predicated upon formal group levels.

Hypothetically, mobility proceeds up or down, but in actuality the latter seldom occurs. Advance requires a formal examination of skill; demotion can result from unprincipled activity involving indiscriminate use of karate in or out of the *dojo.* In Japan the delinquent member is required to fight the master without pulled punches; but in the United States such authority cannot be exercised and the offender is simply dismissed. The prerequisites for advancement are satisfactory completion of and adeptness in the techniques of one's status. These include skill in various appropriate hand and foot techniques, free-style fighting or sparring (*kumite*) and, most important, excellence in the performance of forms resembling choreographic or shadow boxing routines (*katas*). *Katas* are symbolic representations in dance form of stereotyped fighting situations and appropriate techniques integrated into organized routines; each belt level has its own *katas.* Judgment of skill in *kata* is based upon criteria including rhythm and grace. It is considered the most important index of the acquisition of skill and proficiency in the art, and all the martial arts and the various styles of karate have their own series of *katas.*

As shall be stressed later, the status symbols of the upper belt ranks are communicated by loose clique formations, and the caricaturing of the most prominent *dojo* denizens. The more concrete signs of status typically include, for example, the amount of wear shown in a member's uniform, indicated by the degree of whiteness, limpness, and shrinkage produced by repeated washing and bleaching. The whiter, limper, and more form-fitting one's uniform is, the greater amount of seniority the member has attributed to him, even within a particular belt level, and hence, the greater amount of skill and proficiency that is imputed to him. As Gregory Stone has pointed out:

> . . . the uniform is precisely any apparent representation of the self, at once reminding the wearer and others of an *appropriate* identity, a *real* identity. The team-player is uniformed; the play actor is costumed. When we asked our informants their earliest recollections of wanting to wear any particular item of clothing, they responded almost unanimously by recalling their earliest self-conscious appropriations of the dress of their peer groups. In a sense, the earliest items of clothing they wanted comprised the *uniforms* of the peer circle. [1]

With the gaining of status also come greater privileges, such as the black belt prerogative of crossing the threshold into the sacrosanct confines of the master's "office," the greater accessibility of esoteric karate knowledge (such as *katsu,* a highly mystified art of resuscitation), and the acquisition of weaponry techniques other than the empty hands and extremities. With these privileges also comes the responsibility of teaching. This too is a privilege, since the best black belts are given the title "drill master." Like staff sergeants, and with the same demeanor, they drill the new recruits. The other black and brown belts do remedial work with deficient members, generally below their rank. The upper belts, then, through the teaching obligation, are given the authority to lord it over the lower ranking members and to ape the master's mannerisms.

Rites of Passage

Competition for all levels above white belt is keen. Tryouts are usually held on Friday evenings, and there is always a great deal of gossip and rumor circulated about who will compete and what his chances of success are. A member who has tried out for the same rank and failed, or one who has spent an excessive length of time at a lower level, will often become discouraged and quit. This is understandable, since the dropout's first group of peers has long since progressed to other levels. Quitting saves him humiliation at the hands of peers who are now his superiors.

At the tryouts a procedure is followed which resembles the initiation rites of so-called primitive societies, wherein the aspirants to a particular status in the *dojo* ritually go through symbolic separation from the old status, encounter the new status (transition), and experience incorporation into it. [2]

The aspirant, for example, must perform before the master and an audience, the class, seated on the floor on the periphery of the training area. First, he demonstrates his ability in *kata*, then he enters into *kumite* (sparring) with his "brothers" of the same level, and finally, with those of the aspired level. In this ritualistic sparring, the new member is bade welcome by his new group of "brothers." He has been admitted publicly into the establishment, so to speak. Achievement of the black belt marks one's real maturity within the *dojo*. In Japan, all levels under black belt are considered to be of minor importance. In short, "making black belt" means becoming one of the men. By sparring with his new peers, he has officially renounced his past. He is now ready to learn more esoteric techniques and skills, and has formally acquired the privilege to teach as well as learn.

When a member advances to any level he is given a diploma bearing his name, birth date, accreditation date, karate registration number, and certification of the fact that he has satisfactorily completed the requirements prerequisite to his new status. The new status incumbent is also given a letter of congratulation including an epigram or two, encouraging hard work and perseverance in what is assumed optimistically to be the student's upward mobile career. [3]

Years ago, among judo students in Japan, black belt initiation was marked by a "strangulation ceremony,"

where the master, usually in his own home, would literally strangle new black belt initiates into unconsciousness and then revive them by administering *katsu*. According to one writer, this was done "both to steel the victim's nerves and round off his experience." [4] It is conceivable that the American emphasis on status achievement on levels below black belt is a reflection of the differing focal concerns of American culture. The death and rebirth theme of such a psychological cataclysm understandably is prone to dilution in a competitive context, so it is no surprise that the achievement of statuses below black belt has everywhere become emphasized as the martial arts gain in popularity.

The Class Routine

The training of the karate student is conducted with strict discipline, and classes are run in militaristic fashion. Usually the beginning exercises apply to all belt levels, with one of the drill masters leading the class; in the *dojo*, the drill masters lead the routine class exercises. In addition, they transmit notices to the class and handle all remedial work for the lower belts. Thus, as in the manner of the military, the "orders of the day" are transmitted through the drill masters to the membership.

When the class is assembled, commands are given in Japanese: these act as cues to perform certain habitualized preliminary routines. Various stances are taken which correspond to the familiar "ten hut!" and "at ease!" No extraneous body movement is permitted, not even an adjustment of a uniform. No gestures other than those congruent with the spirit of the class are allowed. A prolonged smile or a whisper is met with a loud reprimand by the drill master. With regard to discipline, Urban says: "Decorum and procedure are necessary because they are better than we are." While such reverence for discipline is supposed to yield spiritual transcendence, it results in an idolatry of procedure here as well as in the Orient—*nirvana* never comes cheap! As Urban points out, he knows of no one who has achieved enlightenment in the *dojo*. According to him, the students get caught up in "the dance"; that is, they have yet to achieve the freedom that comes with the conquest of technique—or so the ideology goes.

Predictably, most of the techniques are performed in unison. Each belt level performs in its turn before a seated audience comprising the other levels. In this respect training and formal competition for belt statuses are the same. The audience plays a major role, even though it can never show approval by whistling, shouting, or applause of any sort. The final judgment of a performance rests with the master or an appointed referee. The karate *dojo* audience ostensibly differs from other conventional audiences; there is a mutual acquaintance between the players and the audience, and the first consideration of the player is for the approval or scrutiny of the referee. The main function of the audience then is to exercise the social pressure of simple spectatorship—the consciousness of many eyes on the player, the judgment of the spectators presumably reflecting that of the referee. Since the audience is never given the opportunity to disagree with the referee's decision during a performance, it can only disagree when it is disassembled, and hence, when it is not properly an audience.

A typical class begins when the drill master appears on the training floor of the main gym. The members immediately line up in formation, with arms apart, at attention, awaiting command. The teacher bows from the waist, making a salutatory utterance that sounds like "eesh." The class bows in return, and the "at ease" position is commanded. The order is then given to "loosen out." This is the warm-up period in which various calisthenics, similar to those used by ballet dancers, are executed. They are strenuous, however, and include a succession of push-ups on the knuckles of the hands. Next, the whole class (all levels) goes through the *kihon*, referred to as the "bread and butter" techniques. *Kihon* is a standard drill series of techniques, constantly practiced and mastered in much the same fashion as a musician does his scales. Their mastery is considered necessary to the perfection of derivative techniques such as the *katas*. After the *kihon*, the teacher has each level go through specific procedures as dual preparation for *katas* and *kumite* (free-style sparring). Each level awaits its turn to perform and be instructed in the order of high levels to low. The same follows for the performance of *kata* and *kumite*, although in the latter, representatives from different levels may occasionally spar. Criticism by the teacher is frank but never abusive. Denigration is not necessary because of the tense atmosphere generated by the scrutiny of master and audience.

The main learning method is constant repetition of the teacher's example; the keyword is always *copy*. The teacher demonstrates before the class, sometimes with the assistance of another member, simultaneously explaining his actions throughout the performance. After the demonstration, the class is instructed to copy while the master and/or several drill masters inspect, observe, and criticize individual performances. If certain members have difficulty with something, groups may be formed of superior and inferior ability; after regular class the deficient members are sent to do remedial work with a drill master in the main or auxiliary gym, until they are able to keep up with the rest. To fall behind is considered an indication of laxity and neglectful home practice. The public division into two groups of different proficiencies acts as an impetus to catch up and maintain standards of acceptable performance. However, few are ever expelled as a result of deficient skills. As Urban puts it: "Those who can't make it fall by the wayside," not out of physical exhaustion, but out of embarrassment.

Thus far, the picture that has been formed of the *dojo* offers one the temptation to identify it as a microcosm of society. While the *dojo* does betray a sort of stratified organization, replete with statuses, roles, incentives, goals, rewards, and a quasi-judiciary authority, one must not draw hasty parallels. It is important to keep in mind

the fact that the *dojo* exists in the midst of a large American metropolis. Its members bring into the *dojo* certain experiences from their lives in other groups and subcultures, with the various contradictions that go along with those experiences. Yet one must also keep in mind that the *dojo*, in a sense, has an existence apart from these inconsistencies; it is both apart from them and of them. Participation in the *dojo*, as in other recreational forms, offers a constancy which is sought by its members as an antidote, a replacement, a suspension of their everyday lives.

What follows will be devoted to the *dojo* peer group as a reality within a world of multiple realities.[5] It will touch on relevant aspects of peer group organization and values in society as they relate to the *dojo* and the cliques within it.

Cliques

The periods before and after class are about a half hour in length. On arriving at the *dojo* one immediately changes into uniform, in order to utilize every bit of free time for practice. "Locker-room" talk, although casual, mostly concerns karate. Conversation tends to gravitate about the events of previous sessions, contests, meets with other schools, intra-*dojo* competition, also anecdotes about street fights, boasting, and gossip about other members, usually the upper belts. Preclass dressing-room talk is more abbreviated than after-class "bull sessions," since there is less time and everyone is anxious to get out onto the training floor to warm up.[6]

On the floor one exercises casually while chatting with someone nearby. Members may idle over toward acquaintances for small talk, which, again, revolves around karate, although with more specificity, since it usually focuses upon a particular technique or *kata* that is being practiced. A group of three or four might watch someone perform and comment on his ability and form. Sometimes this takes on a complimentary tone; at other times it may involve wisecracking, especially if the performer is too affected in his performance. Being too affected means that his facial gesticulations are exaggerated, that he pays inordinate attention to perfection, or that he uses ostentatious flourishes in executing a technique.

Individuals who are not working out will confine themselves to the periphery, some in casual aggregations, some solitary. Among those who stand by themselves are new members or, more distinctively, individuals of a type classed by the *dojo* membership as "*dojo* bums." The "*dojo* bum" is one who attends infrequently and goes from one karate *dojo* to another in the metropolitan area. Some may maintain multiple *dojo* memberships, or simply be visitors. They are often viewed with a folkloristic mistrust as "spies" who try to steal techniques or gather information useful to another *dojo* for a forthcoming competition. These "loners" will usually stay off by themselves; if by chance they begin to chat with a member, their manner is characteristically slick. One is tempted to liken them to the old displaced *samurai* or *ronin* of feudal Japan. Their social image corresponds to that of the strangers in other sports, such as skiing, tennis, and golf. Very often these "bums" have achieved a high rank in one *dojo* or another, and turn up on the Sunday when occasional exhibitions are held. They are often rough and are frequently disqualified during *kumite* (sparring).

Observation of the various aggregations on the gym floor reveals that the various clumps of people conversing wear the same colored belts or belts of adjacent levels (e.g., black belts conversing with brown belts). Members with seniority will tend to seek each other out to converse. The white belt groups are larger and give the impression of huddling together for security in the face of their inexperience in the *dojo*. In the course of several weeks, the more experienced white belt members will also break up into conversational groups among themselves, or a few will talk with an upper belt. The various conversation clusters, viewed together, begin gradually to give the appearance of a "pool" of social interaction. As members climb in the hierarchy, and as they become more experienced in learning karate argot and *dojo* norms, shifts occur; some are left behind in their original groups, and some make acquaintance with new recruits, their peers having passed them by. Because of continuous promotions, the membership of a particular conversation clique does not remain highly solidified. Often the fact of seniority has a leveling effect, and people who have "hung around" the *dojo* long enough will mingle with upper belt groups.

Although members of like or contiguous belt levels usually confine their attention to one another, one often finds single black or brown belts conversing with a white belt or a group of white belts. He is probably explaining something to the lower belt members. He may be carrying out his teaching responsibility, or, if the conversation is informal, is boasting about his experiences. The mien of an upper belt man is usually one of studied aloofness. He will, for example, amiably show a lower belt member a technique, but will rarely chat with him as an equal. After class, in the dressing area, there may be some casual talk between an upper belt member and several lower belts, but the tone is that of a superior recounting his exploits to fledgling admirers. He will usually take a know-it-all attitude and occasionally, if a personal question is asked, resume his formal, instructor's composure. This happened once in the dressing room when a white belt asked a black belt about the utility of karate in a street fight. The black belt began to recount an experience in which he took on three assailants. When the white belt asked him if he ever lost a fight, the black belt replied: "Don't start using karate unless you know what you are doing. Keep out of fights until you can handle yourself. When I was a white belt I was cocky and got into a lot of fights and lost some; but now I don't advertise that I know karate and only use it when I have to." That ended the conversation.

When black belts meet and converse among themselves, it is as if friends in a hobby club were getting to tell each other about some new experience or project. This holds true among cliques of all levels, but is more apparent among black belts because they have acquired a great deal more karate lore and are more proficient in handling the jargon. The conversation will usually concern a meet, a newly acquired technique or *kata*, or will be devoted to the faults of a member known in common. New books on karate will be discussed, and their merits or demerits will be analyzed according to how much of the spirit of the art has been captured by the author. The more common "how-to" books are usually frowned upon because they are "wrong," the author did not study in Japan or under a Japanese, there is not enough "philosophy" in it, or because the style of karate advocated is too crude, too effeminate, not "traditional" (i.e., too eclectic), and so forth. Heroes of other *dojos* are maligned because they are "phonies," "just use a lot of fancy technique with no *kime*" ("heart" or strength), emphasize "too much speed and no strength," "would get whipped in a street fight," "would never have gotten those points in a meet if the ref was from our school." If white belts are standing nearby they will usually chime in and agree with all of these comments, so that they can get into the conversation and inject the small store of their own tidbits. However, they are usually ignored when they try to break into a conversation, or typically acknowledged with a halfhearted "yeah," or "uh, huh."

Making Faces

In general, the haughtiness of an upper level member is designed to maintain social distance through the mystifying aura of superior status. Another aspect of the composure of some upper level members is the highly dramatized caricaturing and aping of the master. From the time a member begins his stint in the *dojo*, he soon learns to adopt a frozen expression of mystical seriousness, aloofness, and reticence. This is designed to convey the belief and conviction that karate is serious business, that it is religious, intellectual, and "cultural." The "karate poker face" is adopted from Urban's own composure and may be defined as a symbolization of leadership, enlightenment, and skill. During drill, for instance, all smiling, giggling, and extraneous movement are forbidden. If this command is broken, the member is sternly reprimanded. The absence of visible emotion provides the "blank" upon which later embellishments are made.

As the member becomes socialized, the poker face acquires new meanings. He begins to notice that whole *dojo* personalities or trait constellations form about the seriousness of the facial expression, and that these are more pronounced among several upper level members. The more extreme caricatures serve to inculcate the meanings of these social masks into the membership body, despite the fact that they are cynically construed by some.[7]

Even black belt members criticize their peers who are prone to "put on the dog." An example of one such situation occurred when one member was running through some calisthenics on the training floor. He seemed to be devoting a lot of effort to perfecting a superfluous movement. Two black belts were watching, and one said: "He must think he's hot shit the way he carries on." His neighbor smiled in agreement and then went on to relate how so-and-so acted when he was called upon to perform, or how ridiculous so-and-so looked during *kumite* last week. The idea is that one can palm the act off on someone less sophisticated (e.g., white belts), but this sort of behavior "doesn't bounce" with peers, although one's public face belies this attitude.

Some of the more colorful *dojo* personalities reflect the diffusion of the master's image among the members. One black belt member affects an air of great pomposity. Since he is approaching middle age, it is generally acknowledged that he has passed his prime and is too old to compete any longer. He is a comical sight, strutting through eccentric ballet-styled calisthenics and explaining the more "philosophical" aspects of karate to younger members. One black belt peer of his exclaimed: "The way that guy acts, you would think he had a stick up his ass." Often, he performs with a lot of dainty flourishes. He is much like an old barnyard rooster relying on symbols of a bygone prowess and potency to gain respect. Should he make a mistake in executing some maneuver, he will grimace and shrug his shoulders in affected disappointment. If, during free-style sparring, one of the participants is injured, at a glance from the master, he runs to the aid of the vanquished to administer *katsu* (first aid). It is questionable that his ministrations bring relief to the injured, but since very few members have acquired the arcane methods of *katsu*, he is awarded the distinction of being the *dojo* healer. His behavior provokes a great deal of snickering and ridicule, but a perverse kind of respect is still held for him by master and membership alike, as for the punctilios of an ante-bellum southern aristocrat gone seedy. Much of the cynicism about him derives from resentment of his polished ways and the possibility of a superior station in life outside the *dojo*.

Another black belt member is also the butt of *dojo* humor and criticism. Despite his exceptional skill, he does not give the appearance of having much intelligence. Contrary to the previous member who presents himself as the quintessence of urbanity and sophistication, he acts like a tough, "dumb," army sergeant. His manner is gruff and crude, and he has been known to lose control and fail to pull his punches while sparring with lower belt members. He is disliked by the lower belts, and even a few of his peers have remarked on his lack of polish. He is never, however, criticized for his skill in karate, for his *katas* are perfectly executed and his fighting skill is exemplary. He is a drill master, and often conducts the lower belt classes. When the master is teaching, he assists in supervising and correcting students. While other upper level members will sometimes stop to explain a technique to a lower belt member, he always falls back on demonstration and imitation as his method of teaching. His response, when requested for some information or instruction, is always "Copy!" Unfortunately, he has a penchant for reciting some of the master's didactic metaphors and quaint, stylized, Oriental anecdotes, and invariably twists the moral of the tale until it loses its intended meaning completely; his unsophisticated speech makes a mockery out of anything more complicated than an order. Both men characterize the extreme ends of a brains-brawn continuum of values, encapsulated in the *dojo* peer group culture.

The Master as Peer Group Leader

As I have mentioned, the poker face and the caricatures have as their source the image projected by the master. Urban exudes an aura of invincibility. He is of medium height, but well-muscled, and his hands, as a result of brutal conditioning, look like two sledge hammers. His reticence is flawless. If in the elevator he is encountered by a student, he will nod and without a smile utter a perfunctory "hello." He will rarely engage anyone in casual conversation, and when interviewed behaves like a dignitary being questioned by news reporters. He projects an image similar to that of a general who must always be a source of strength and morale for his men. The following dialogue elicited his views on discipline:

Q: Is it considered admirable to maintain strict discipline?
A: The master must be one hundred percent autocratic.
Q: Do the people with higher belt positions have more privileges than those with lower belts?
A: The higher belts have *less* privileges! The whites [i.e., white belts] have more privilege to make mistakes.
Q: I've heard that only black belts may enter your office; is this true?
A: Yes, some black belts can enter; the admission is excellence.
Q: Do you have any personal contact with any of your students outside of the *dojo*?
A: No, this has to be—it is natural. I am not their friend, I am their teacher.

By maintaining social distance, and by the cultivation of an air of enigmatic oriental wisdom along with brute strength and skill, Urban never reveals anything to the membership other than the symbolic features of a folk hero. As a result, the membership is provided with a somewhat apocryphal base from which to fill in any meanings or characteristics that they want to attribute to him.

Again, Urban portrayed himself as a father-figure:

> You're like a father. You represent the unattainable, and you're all alone. The students want to knock you down from where you are. They are always fighting the father, and when they get to the top they don't even thank you. Being a *sensei* [pronounced sen-say, meaning master] is a thankless job.

In short, he tends to characterize himself as a benevolent dictator "concerned for the welfare of his children," but often standing alone in the manner of the archetypal father.[8]

At this point one may be tempted to apply to Urban the Freudian interpretation of the father role, but given the facts of the "Americanization of the unconscious," to use John R. Seeley's expression, and Urban's own subscription to this rationale, a significant modification is in order. It is more appropriate, therefore, to visualize him as an adult peer group leader, a *mock* father; that is, a marginal composite, perhaps, of what the membership would like a father to be. In this respect, he resembles a coach or even the literary figures representing adult "friends" of children such as portrayed by Mark Twain, Dickens, and others. As Willard Waller put it:

> . . . the athletes stand in a very close and personal relationship to at least one faculty member, the coach, who has, if he is an intelligent man or a disciplinarian, an opportunity to exert a great deal of influence upon the members of the team. The coach has prestige, he has favors to give, and he is in intimate rapport with his players. Ordinarily he uses his opportunities well. As the system usually works out, the members of the major teams form a nucleus of natural leaders among the student body, and their influence is more or less conservative and more or less on the side of what the faculty would call decent school citizenship. The necessarily close correspondence between athletic prowess and so-called clean living is another factor which affects the influence of athletes upon nonathletes. . . . An antisocial coach, or a coach who allows his players to believe themselves to be indispensable, so that they wrest control of athletes from his hands, can vitiate the whole system. When the system does go wrong, athletes and athletics become an insufferable nuisance to teachers.[9]

Speak Softly But Carry a Big Fist

According to one scholar, the peer group offers a "defensive and offensive alliance in which they can experiment with ways to short-circuit the authority of parents, especially of mothers, and of parent substitutes." They test "social controls over the illicit,"[10] many times by behaving "aggressively."

Aggressiveness, while formally channeled in the *dojo*, is a prominent *dojo* value. During sparring, one's punches are supposed to stop short of contact; yet, the frequency of "accidents" and the absence of harsh reprimands for overaggressiveness testify to the fact that occasionally even violent behavior is considered a favorable attribute. Take, for example, Urban's own description of *kumite:*

> *Kumite* is ideally a realistic highly spirited practice of *"Shobu."* *Shobu* is the term for actual combat. It is the responsibility of each individual to defend himself while practicing sparring in the *dojo* with others to keep from unnecessarily hurting them. Both the stronger and the weaker opponents should benefit from sparring practice. . . . Undue hostility and dangerous aggression are never tolerated during sparring in a well controlled dojo. . . . The orthodox *Jiu-Kumite* bout begins with an introductory phase whereby the fighters usually try their feinting techniques and various opening moves to check the reactions of their opponent. This is to see where the skills are the strongest. It then goes into the expository or infighting. It is here that the fighters' speed and close hand work come out. The conclusion then follows by the first fighter to take the initiative of a full focused attack resulting in a definite overpowering conclusion of the fight such as a knocking down of an opponent by a sweep or any series of body and head blows.[11]

It seems to be almost impossible to exhibit such ferocity and at the same time squelch the satisfaction of making contact. Once, while sparring in the *dojo*, an opponent did not pull a kick and an excruciating blow was delivered to the solar plexus. After the match the assailant, queried about his carelessness, replied, "I don't know what happened, I just couldn't control myself." The reprimand he received took the form of a brief lecture to the class, by Urban, on the danger of "losing your head" in a match. If one is injured during sparring, he is encouraged to continue fighting if he can, and to try to keep his adversary from recognizing the weakness. This is supposed to act as preparation for actual combat conditions. Several examples will make this more apparent.

During a sparring session, one of the antagonists had failed to pull a punch and had injured his opponent. The man would not continue fighting. He started to walk off the floor, but the drill master, who was acting as referee, called him back and ordered him to bow to his opponent. He did as he was told, showed no evidence of anger or resentment, and then left. There was wry joking about this among the spectators, but it was clear that any of them would have acquiesced in the same circumstances.

Another time a member broke a bone in his hand during a sparring competition for green belt rank. He was aware of the injury but kept on fighting and won. He fought again immediately and won the second time as well. This same person, a month earlier, was dealt an unpulled blow to the temple near the ear which, he subsequently learned, resulted in a minor concussion. His opponent, a black belt, either out of fear of being reprimanded or out of blind idolatry for procedure, hissed: "Keep fighting, keep fighting!" The injured man was unable to move, numbed by the blow.

This aggressiveness is not merely accidental, as is indicated by the number of dressing-room anecdotes boasting of street fights actually provoked by members under the guise of self-defense. The alleged brutality of the sport was rationalized by Urban during an interview:

Q: Some people consider karate brutal. What are your feelings about this?

A: Karate is not brutal; it's safe. Karate becomes brutal without ethics. One must have respect for the art, and respect is an art; and one must have self-respect to have the respect of others.

The enigmatic contradiction between violence and control is thus not a contradiction. Outright hostility is prohibited only in its most extreme forms, as when a particular member who continuously inflicts injury on his opponents is disqualified from a meet or dismissed from the *dojo*.

Aggression is a positive peer group value. While *dojo* aggressiveness is at times crude and relatively undisguised, its nature is intrinsic to childhood peer activities which, later on, in successor groups, becomes shunted off into more subtly disguised and socially approved forms, such as enterprising activity. [12]

As Bloch and Niederhoffer hypothesize, adolescent gang activity offers a substitute for the relatively ambiguous and undefined rites of passage in our society. In consequence, "equivalent forms of behavior arise spontaneously among adolescents themselves, reinforced by their own group structures which seemingly provide the same psychological content and function of the more formalized rituals found in other societies." [13] The *dojo*, stripped of all its accouterments, performs the same role. For the adolescent and young adult members, the karate *dojo* is either an adjunct to or a primary source of this satisfaction; for the older men in their late twenties and thirties, it is possibly a compensation for a childhood deficit or a continuation of peer activities, taking its place alongside such groups as fraternal organizations and athletic clubs. As A. M. Lee comments:

> The strong appeal of men's social fraternities is to those who in childhood developed needs for the satisfactions possible in nonsibling peer groups. This appeal contrasts with the typical glorifications of sibling-type competitiveness by students who are "squares" (academic conformists) and by professors (frequently "squares" grown older). [14]

The hierarchy of belt status levels acts as a model for age-grading activity, which is so indistinct in our society. There one finds behavioral coordinates appropriate to his status. In this sense, the hierarchical grouping of statuses sustains social solidarity in the *dojo*, a solidarity inspirited with mystery. As Kenneth Burke has remarked, " 'order' is not just 'regularity.' It also involves a distribution of *authority*. And such mutuality . . . takes roughly a pyramidal or hierarchical form (or at least, it is like a ladder with 'up' and 'down')." [15] However, sometimes the reality of the world outside can intrude, as exemplified by the following exchange between two brown belt members after class:

> Mr. "A": Jesus, all this training every night of the week knocks me out. I don't know how the hell I'm gonna get up tomorrow to go to work.

> Mr. "B": Yeah, but it's great exercise—you can really sleep well after training.

> Mr. "A": Oh sure, what'll I do when I come in late tomorrow to work—show my boss a *kata*?

Groups, no matter how impermeable their boundaries may seem, no matter how solidary they are, exist within a larger social context (something which the students of "small groups" and "group dynamics" seem to have ignored), including other groups, which, in turn, play a part in shaping the contours of the in-group. In a society such as our own, with its industrial complexity, extensive geographical mobility, and ethnic, regional, social class, religious, community, and associational diversity, an individual's multiple group commitments sometimes make alternation from one context to another a hazardous affair, as Mr. "A" illustrates. [16] Groups cope with the threat of rivalry through the cultivation of the various forms and manifestations of ethnocentrism, to wit, the conglomeration of techniques, procedures, esoterica, and decor which all enhance the elements of mystery and secrecy in the *dojo*. In addition, the image of the master, and the caricaturing of him, contribute to a growing store of karate lore and myth. These aid in shielding the individual member from other groups' claims. In effect, he is socialized into particular roles and assumes an identity which may "stick" across group lines, an identity reinforced by the *dojo* hierarchy which provides an alternate status universe to others in the world of everyday life. The sociologist Frederick Thrasher in his classic study, *The Gang*, saw similar factors operating in the cumulative development of the culture of the adolescent gang. [17]

While children seldom have to pay for such peer group experience, the *dojo* member is charged a monthly fee for it, similar to the prostitute's fee for sexual experience (it is always emphasized how karate "will make a man out of you"), or even the fee paid to a psychiatrist for social contact. [18] What at first glance appears to be the natural course of a person's social development becomes an experiential commodity. But the *dojo* member gets a good deal for his money. His *dojo* peers and their proprietor-leader offer him the trappings of the secret society and the opportunities of group camaraderie. As the sociologist Simmel observed:

> . . . The total action and interest sphere of the secret becomes a well-rounded unity only through inclusion, in the secret, of a whole complex of external forms. Under its characteristic categories, the secret society must seek to create a sort of life totality. For this reason, it builds round its sharply emphasized purposive content a system of formulas, like a body round a soul. . . . The particular emphasis with which the secrecy of the external element is thereby stressed . . . is necessitated by the fact that this secrecy is not required so obviously and much by sheer, immediate interest as is the secrecy of the objective group purpose. It must be added that, through such formalism, as well as through the hierarchical organization itself, the secret society makes itself into a sort of counter-image of the official world, to which it places itself in contrast. [19]

I would hasten to add that the *dojo* can be interpreted as playing a quasi-therapeutic role in mass society where denominational religion, along with conventional psychotherapy, is being phased out by emergent group forms of a therapeutic-religious character.[20]

Thus, I have traced the forms and processes of interaction in the karate *dojo*. What at first seemed to be a school is now understood as a successor or substitute for childhood peer group experience. Viewed from this perspective, it no longer remains an oddity or small point of interest. In terms of human needs and experience, it is comparable to other groups in the world of everyday life. It stands for its members as a place where some aspect of their many-sided selves can become rooted, a place where a uniform and a colored belt become the criteria of who they are and what they do, in this time, in that place.[21]

NOTES

1. Gregory P. Stone, "Appearance and the Self," *Human Behavior and Social Processes: An Interactionist Approach,* ed. Arnold Rose (Boston: Houghton Mifflin Co., 1962), p. 113. See also Hugh Dalziel Duncan, *Communication and Social Order* (New York: Bedminster Press, 1962), pp. 190-94.

2. Arnold van Gennep, *The Rites of Passage* (Chicago: Phoenix Books, University of Chicago Press, 1960), pp. 10-11, 65-115. On this subject, also see Bruno Bettelheim, *Symbolic Wounds* (Glencoe, Illinois: The Free Press, 1954); Hutton Webster, *Primitive Secret Societies* (New York: The Macmillan Co., rev. ed., 1931); Theodore Reik, *Ritual* (New York: Grove Press, 1946, 1962), pp. 91-166; John M. Whiting, Richard Kluckhohn, and Albert Anthony, "The Function of Male Initiation Ceremonies at Puberty," *Readings in Social Psychology,* ed. Maccoby *et. al.* (New York: Holt, Rinehart and Winston, Inc., 1958), pp. 359-70; Alfred McClung Lee, *Fraternities Without Brotherhood* (Boston: Beacon Press, 1955); and Duncan, *op. cit.*, pp. 257-61.

3. On the subject of status passage and careers, see Everett C. Hughes, "Cycles, Turning Points and Careers," in his *Men and Their Work* (Glencoe, Illinois: The Free Press, 1958), pp. 11-12.

4. E. J. Harrison, *The Fighting Spirit of Japan* (London: W. Foulsham and Company, Ltd., n.d.), pp. 59-60.

5. For an interesting philosophical discussion of the phenomenology of the social world, see Alfred Schutz, *Collected Papers: The Problem of Social Reality* (The Hague: Martinus Nijhoff, 1962), I, pp. 207-59.

6. One writer, in commenting on the cultural differences prevailing in the Japanese and American martial arts, notes that Westerners indulge in conversation and intellectual explanation during practice, whereas the Japanese frown upon this, insisting that too much talk and explanation in teaching and practice result in intellectual conceit. See Robert Frager, "The Psychology of the Samurai," *Psychology Today,* Vol. 2 (January, 1969), p. 50.

7. The wearing of such visible "masks," if not intended to sustain social distance, by its obvious hauteur at least results in maintain-ing distance. Nor is the situation drastically changed in Japan; it is only more subtle. While one might be tempted to make invidious distinctions vis-a-vis the purity of the arts in Japan versus their adulteration in the Western world, notice how the following quote, albeit laudatory, reveals the same elements of "face-making": "Discipline in all Japanese arts is so demanding that it reshapes the student completely—mentally and physically. A man who has attained mastery of an art reveals it in his every action." Frager, *op. cit.*, p. 49. For some revealing discussions on "face," see Erving Goffman, *The Presentation of Self in Everyday Life* (Garden City, New York: Doubleday Anchor Books, 1959), pp. 57-70; Ernest Becker, *The Birth and Death of Meaning* (New York: The Free Press of Glencoe, 1962), pp. 95-101; and Erving Goffman, *Interaction Ritual* (Garden City, New York: Doubleday Anchor Books, 1967), pp. 5-45.

8. In several talks with Mr. Urban, he was careful to enunciate this characterization of himself. This same point was brought out in a recent interview for a karate magazine. See Herman Petras, "Peter Urban: Founder of American Style Goju," *Official Karate,* Vol. I (June, 1969), pp. 30-35.

9. Willard Waller, *The Sociology of Teaching* (New York: John Wiley and Sons, 1932, 1965), pp. 116-17. James Coleman follows through on Waller's ideas in his analysis of the role of athletics in maintaining the identity of the school and the community in, "Athletics in High School," *The Annals of the American Academy of Political and Social Science,* 338 (November, 1961), pp. 33-43. Terry Southern's short stories "Red Dirt Marijuana" and "Razor Fight" carry on Twain's apotheosis of egalitarian peer group values. See his *Red Dirt Marijuana and Other Tastes* (New York: Signet Books, New American Library, 1968), pp. 9-38. Also see Duncan, *op. cit.*, pp. 326-45.

10. Alfred McClung Lee, *Multivalent Man* (New York: George Braziller, 1966), p. 236.

11. Peter Urban, *The Karate Dojo* (New York: privately published, 1964), pp. 8, 9.

12. Lee, *Multivalent Man,* pp. 230-37.

13. Herbert Bloch and Arthur Niederhoffer, *The Gang* (New York: Philosophical Library, 1958), p. 17.

14. Lee, *Multivalent Man, p,* 154.

15. Kenneth Burke, *Permanence and Change* (2nd rev. ed., Indianapolis, Indiana: Bobbs-Merrill Co., Inc., 1954, 1965), p. 276.

16. For an interesting discussion of this problem see Peter L. Berger and Thomas Luckmann, *The Social Construction of Reality* (Garden City, New York: Doubleday and Co., 1966), pp. 119-68.

17. Frederic M. Thrasher, *The Gang* (Chicago: Phoenix Books, University of Chicago Press, rev. ed., 1963), p. 55.

18. See W. A. Schofield, *Psychotherapy: the Purchase of Friendship* (Englewood Cliffs, New Jersey: Prentice-Hall, 1964).

19. *Georg Simmel, The Sociology of Georg Simmel,* ed. Kurt Wolff (Glencoe, Illinois: The Free Press, 1950), pp. 359-60.

20. The hippie phenomenon in some sense is indicative of this, as are the Esalen and encounter type therapies which have borrowed culture traits from the former.

21. The sociologist Orrin E. Klapp has come to some similar conclusions insofar as he recognizes that leisure pursuits often constitute identity-seeking activities outside the organizational and institutional channels (i.e., the regularized status passages) under the aegis of "fun." See his *Collective Search for Identity* (New York: Holt, Rinehart and Winston, Inc., 1969).

A SOCIOLOGIST LOOKS AT SPORT PARACHUTING

David O. Arnold

Russ Gunby's book, *Sport Parachuting,* opens with the statement that "different people like different sports . . . this book is about a different sport." The general public shares this notion, as do the few social scientists who have written about sport parachuting. Thus I need to make it clear at the outset that my reason for studying this sport is its basic similarity to other activities, not its differences.

Many studies have documented that Americans are spending an increasing number of hours at leisure pursuits. Other studies have documented that they are spending an increasing number of dollars in the process. But in this search for quantitative shifts in leisure activity we have tended to overlook the *qualitative* shift that has accompanied them. Leisure activities are no longer merely recreation in the sense of "re-creating" us to better perform our work; they have come to replace work as the prime reason for being for millions of Americans. One such group of leisure-oriented Americans is sport parachutists.

Sociologist Erving Goffman views parachuting as a "recreational non-spectator sport that [is] full of risk," and lumps it together with big game hunting, bob-sledding, and mountain climbing.[1] Kepecs, a psychiatrist, argues (on the basis of a sample of only *five*!) that all parachutists have neurotic reactions to activity.[2] Fenz and Epstein studied sky divers to learn about stress.[3] Klausner, while he looked at other things as well, focused heavily on fear in his study.[4]

Only two writers appear to understand what the sport means to its participants. Farrell points out that "most parachutists jump because they like to jump," adding that "this seems quite obvious, yet it is a point that has been ignored or misunderstood by some nonparticipant observers."[5] And Toffler, in *Future Shock,* points out that "at least for some, a leisure-time commitment can also serve as the basis for an entire life style . . . Skydivers have their own little world, as do glider enthusiasts, scuba-divers, hot-rodders, drag-racers and motorcyclists. Each of these represents a leisure-based subcult organized around a technological device."[6]

Jumping out of airplanes is as natural to a skydiver as having money is to a member of the upper class, speaking with a drawl is to a Southerner, or citing Durkheim and computing chi-square is to a sociologist.

While I was spending an evening with a group of jumpers, the movie "Gypsy Moths," in which Burt Lancaster falls to his death, entered the conversation. One of the jumpers asked me what I thought "when the guy zinged in. Weren't you surprised?" I replied, "Not really; the whole movie seemed to be building up to it." In the ensuing discussion it became apparent that whereas a non-jumper views jumping mainly in terms of closeness to death, the experienced jumper expects the chute to open as a matter of course. The chute might open late, he might have what he euphemistically refers to as "a problem," but it still opens. Opening close to the ground is seen by a jumper merely as opening late, whereas the non-jumper views it as barely avoiding death. As a consequence the jumpers present had not perceived the string of late parachute openings in the movie as building up to a non-opening, and the death caught them by surprise.

Ernest Hemingway once commented that "it is one thing to be in the proximity of death, to know more or less what she is, and it is quite another thing to seek her."[7] Skydivers are not daredevils, whatever the general public may think. Basing his conclusions on questionnaires and the results of the standardized Minnesota Multiphasic Personality Inventory (MMPI) tests, Delk states that "concern with death [among sport parachutists] appears to be minimal and realistically consistent with the slight chance that some type of mishap could take place during a skydive."[8]

If fear doesn't explain this activity, what does? A number of factors are involved; however, they are similar to those involved in explaining any other leisure activity. Two of the most important are a desire for *escape* and a desire for *community*.

Like most other leisure activities, sport parachuting provides an escape from the everyday world with its wars, economic problems, etc. But additionally the activity itself removes the participant from this world. Although what goes up must come down, while in the air the subjective experience is one of floating, with the earth appearing to be a distant object which is coming no closer and which has no bearing on the skydiver.

Along with providing escape or freedom, sport parachuting provides community. While on the ground the jumper is with a group of colleagues who have shared similar experiences, and who also share a common argot, a common store of knowledge and stories, and common norms. For the typical skydiver, his sport is very central in his life. He makes an average of 60 or more jumps a year, and even when away from the drop zone, he spends much of his free time with other jumpers.

Anthropologist Nelson Graburn has suggested that Americans technologize and statisticalize their leisure. His generalization holds true for sport parachutists.

First, technologizing. Americans are hung up on "things." Motorcyclists spend hours debating the relative merits of Mikuni and Amal carburetors, runners spend miles quizzing each other about the relative merits of Puma, Tiger, and Adidas shoes. The pages of parachuting magazines are filled with ads for new and presumably better canopies, goggles, jump boots, etc., etc. Many of the articles discuss equipment, and a large portion of the talk heard at drop zones centers around

"A Sociologist Looks at Sport Parachuting" by David Arnold, Ph.D. in *Parachutist*, June 1974.

equipment. At home, jumpers pore over thick catalogs filled with prices and specifications. In recent years several radically different parachute designs have appeared, and a lot of discussion among jumpers concerns their relative merits.

Second, statisticalizing. Just as every runner knows his times and every bowler his average, so every skydiver knows precisely how many jumps he has made. While it is not polite to ask someone about it right off, when two skydivers meet, the subject comes up early in their conversation. When I asked sport parachutists how many jumps they had made they would usually reply with the precise number: "247" rather than "about 250." Jumpers usually do something special to mark certain numbers, and the United States Parachute Association awards a highly prized pair of gold wings for reaching 1,000 freefalls. The amount of time spent in freefall is also logged, and the USPA awards special badges to jumpers who have accumulated a total of 12 hours or 24 hours of freefall time.

A third characteristic of American leisure is competitiveness. It is hard to think of an activity to which we haven't managed to add competition. Everything from sex to stamp collecting is seen as an opportunity to prove our superiority. There is even a national frisbee competition.

In parachuting, competition takes three forms: accuracy, style, and relative work. In accuracy a small plastic disc is placed in the center of the landing area and the jumper steers so as to land as close to it as possible. Distances are measured to the nearest centimeter, and dead centers are quite common. In style the jumper goes through a series of maneuvers reminiscent of trampoliners, high divers, or aerobatic airplanes. The time required to complete the series is measured to the nearest tenth of a second, with penalties for errors such as stopping a turn short of the proper heading.

Until recently competition was limited to accuracy and style. But while these individual activities were going on, jumpers were also making group jumps, termed "relative work," where they would exit the plane moments apart, then maneuver in freefall and join hands to form a circle or "star." A few years ago relative work entered the competitive arena with 10-man star meets. Each team tries to get all 10 members into the star in the shortest time. Again, timing is to the nearest tenth of a second. Most recently, 4-man relative work competition has evolved. Here, as in style, a standard series of maneuvers is to be completed in the shortest possible time. The team members form a star, separate, and re-form in a straight line, etc.

Although a number of other aspects of sport parachuting are worthy of detailed examination, there is only space here to mention some of them briefly. Communication is one of these. When the surfing subculture was at its most cohesive point, the main means of communicating both techniques and norms beyond the face-to-face group was through surfing movies, which originated in 1954; only later, in 1960, were these supplemented by

magazines. Among jumpers "freefall movies" create a lot of interest, but are definitely secondary to printed communication. Every jumper I queried was familiar with Gunby's book *Sport Parachuting* and reads *Parachutist* magazine. While *Sky Diver* Magazine's circulation is lower, the majority of jumpers have read at least some issues of it. There are also a number of regional and club newsletters, mostly mimeographed.

While most jumpers have a home DZ, many visit others at least occasionally, and competitors do so more than occasionally. This serves as an additional and more informal communications mode. Thus while there are normative variations from DZ to DZ, this continual contact keeps them minor. Here is just one example: Most jumpers, though not all, wear special jump suits. However, whereas at some drop zones they cover them with every sew-on patch imaginable (flags, peace symbols, Snoopy, the zig-zag man, and even one that certified in Hebrew that the wearer was kosher), at other DZ's jump suits are either unembellished or bear only the jumper's name (on a military-style cloth tape over the pocket) or his USPA license number.

Virtually all leisure activities have participants who go in for that activity in a big way. There are people who play bridge seven nights a week, others who run 15 miles each day, and still others who spend hour after hour playing pinball machines. But there are even more who play bridge once every few weeks, jog around the block occasionally, or feed just a few dimes a year into the machines. In sport parachuting, by contrast, the typical participant is the enthusiast. While there are a lot of people who have gone through a quickie "hero course" and made one jump, never to show up again, those who stay with it tend to manifest high rather than only moderate involvement. As Klausner points out, "skydiving tends to be a consuming interest of its devotees." Turnover among beginners is high, but it can be assumed that most of these never intended to go beyond a single jump. It should be noted, however, that some with one-jump intentions get hooked and go on to become enthusiasts. Unfortunately, no precise data on turnover is available. One instructor estimated that nationally only one person in ten goes beyond his initial jump, while another told me he believes one in four does, and that at some club-operated drop zones it may be more like one in two. The USPA's annual renewal rate averages around 45 percent.

Because of their heavy involvement with parachuting, jumpers tend not to be simultaneously involved in other leisure activities to any great degree. However, their previous interests center around the activities Callois classifies as "vertigo," as contrasted to activities whose primary focus is chance, competition, or mimicry.[9] I found a large number of jumpers who have been involved with motorcycles, both street and dirt, several with racing experience. Scuba diving is also common, followed by skiing. Surfing and water skiing also turned up, though not as frequently. Many jumpers are pilots, though as often as not their interest in airplanes was precipitated by their involvement in parachuting.

While parachutists' leisure life lends itself to generalization, their non-leisure life does not. Among the several hundred people who enter the cross-country motorcycle races each weekend in the California desert, skilled blue collar workers are over-represented. Truck drivers are over-represented among pin-ball addicts. And among rock climbers, mathematicians and physicists turn up with striking frequency. But if there is any such regularity in the occupations of jumpers, I have been unable to uncover it.

Although the average jumper is in his middle to late twenties, the range is great, from late teens on up. There is an active organization named POPS (the Parachutists Over Phorty Society); and one veteran skydiver celebrated his 51st birthday by making 51 jumps on that day. (Another recently made 62 jumps on his 62nd birthday.)

Male hair length has become a characteristic dividing many Americans. The sport parachuting fraternity contains a greater proportion of short haircuts than the general population, but also a goodly number of longhairs. (Note that this investigation is over two years old.—Ed.) But among jumpers hair length creates no noticeable division.

Some social scientists have claimed other regularities, but while a few are significant, others appear spurious. Klausner, for example, makes much of parachuting as a "western" activity; his data show that whereas only 16 percent of the U.S. population resides in the western states, 27 percent of parachutists do. However, since parachuting requires good weather his data appear explainable by this variable alone.

On the other hand it is clear that parachuting is both heavily white and heavily male. There are very few black or Oriental jumpers, although in California there are a fair number of jumpers of Mexican descent. While there is little data to go on, I have detected no systematic racial or ethnic prejudice or discrimination. Women, however, are another matter. While their presence is not uncommon, and there is women's competition in accuracy and style as well as women on some of the relative work teams, there is a definite bias against them. A number of male jumpers and a couple of instructors have told me either that they don't trust women in the sport or that women are incapable of developing the same skill level as men. They point to statistics that seem to bear them out: While only 5 to 8 percent of jumpers are female, they account for 15 percent of the fatalities, and, turning to competition, the winning distances and times for women are higher. However given the male attitudes toward training, the former could be the result of a self-fulfilling prophecy, while the latter, as in many other sports, could be explained by the smaller pool from which competitors

are drawn. (Also, other data indicate that the percentage of females in the sport might be higher, more like 13 percent.) There has been some discussion of this issue in *Parachutist*, but not a lot. I imagine that as awareness of sexism in the society as a whole grows, the issue will draw more discussion, and also that the percentage of female jumpers will increase. I should point out that while there is clear evidence of sexism in sport parachuting, the sport is more equalitarian than most other sports in our society.

Jumpers are more likely to be single than are non-jumpers of similar age, and dropping out of the sport after marriage is not uncommon. However this is true of many other leisure activities as well. Also, there are many couples who jump, and a few instances of entire families.

I'll close with a brief mention of humor in sport parachuting. Perhaps because of government regulation, there has been little of the unorganized sort of activity existing in the early days of hot rodding and surfing which led to various sorts of practical joking aimed at outsiders. Another factor is the ever-present danger of the sport; no one messes with another's equipment. The danger is made light of by the humor, however. Driving to the drop zone the day I was to make my first jump, one of the experienced jumpers in the car commented that he was glad he was along that day to "see a beginner bounce." He said it in a casual, humorous way, and it seemed appropriate for me to reply, "I'm too thin to bounce; I'll just go splat."

Rock climbers have a saying, "It's not the long fall that hurts, it's the short stop at the bottom." Gunby's *Sport Parachuting* contains a similar remark: "Out of 10,000 feet of fall, always remember that the last half inch hurts the most."

REFERENCES

1. E. Goffman, "Where the Action Is," in E. Goffman, *Interaction Ritual*, Garden City: Doubleday Ancher (1967), p. 174.
2. J.G. Kepecs, "Neurotic Reactions in Parachutists," *Psychoanalytic Quarterly* 13 (1944), pp. 273-299.
3. W.D. Fenz and S. Epstein, "Stress: In the Air," *Psychology Today* 3, No. 4 (September, 1969), pp. 27-28, 58-59.
4. S.D. Klausner, "Sport Parachuting," in R. Slovenko and J.A. Knight, eds., *Motivations in Play, Games and Sports*, Springfield, Ill.: Charles C. Thomas (1967), pp. 670-694.
5. D. Farrel, "The Psychology of Parachuting," in R. Slovenko and J.A. Knight, *op. cit.*, p. 665.
6. A. Toffler, *Future Shock*, New York: Bantam Books (1970), pp. 288-9
7. E. Hemingway, "The Christmas Gift," in W. White, ed., *By-Line Ernest Hemingway*, London: Collins (1968), p. 428.
8. J.L. Delk, "Why They Jump: A Psychological Study of Skydivers," *Parachutist* 12, no. 5 (May, 1971), p. 15.
9. R. Caillois, *Man, Play, and Games*, New York: The Free Press (1961), pp. 11-36.

PRESENT DAY

A SOCIOLOGICAL ANALYSIS OF A TENNIS COURT

Harvey Hyman

Tennis and its progenitor, Royal or Court Tennis, was once played exclusively by the upper classes. Happily, as a result of increasing affluence, the sport was filtered down to the middle class and, through the advent of municipal courts, which merely require a permit at a nominal fee, virtually anyone from any socio-economic bracket can afford to play.

A typical facility is Kissena Park, located in the heart of Flushing not far from Queens College. It has 12 clay courts which are immaculately maintained. They are surrounded by a profusion of beautiful trees which act as wind-breakers. The area is quiet, idyllic and serene. Although they are City courts, their quality and atmosphere place them on a par with many private clubs. This has helped to produce their constantly over-crowded state and the ensuing interaction which makes it rich broth for sociological inspection.

Players at Kissena are of middle class and lower middle class background. Middle class people are attracted to the sport because of its identification with upper class life. Thus playing tennis becomes a status symbol. Players here can be classified as "Regulars" (those who play every day) and "Occasionals" (those who play sporadically). All the Regulars are acquainted with each other, but aside from "off the court" social amenities, all athletic interaction is restricted to the subgroups and cliques to which they all belong. Each clique consists of four to eight players who play rotating singles and doubles each day. Who plays whom is prearranged the previous day, on the court or by telephone.

For the purpose of this analysis, it would be helpful to view players and cliques as belonging to one of three categories based on proficiency—low, medium and high—although there is a more definitive ranking system within each category. Each individual knows his rank and that of the others (this is usually not discussed across clique boundaries). The ranking and clique structure has grown partly out of a need for players to joust with others of relatively equal ability. A "high status" player who has reduced his game to a science would be poorly matched if confronted with a player of erratic ability who muffs most of his shots.

At Kissena, as in everyday life, rank has its privilege. A player of higher status who is in want of a game because of a breakdown of pre-arrangements in his clique may ask a player of lower status from a different clique to play. However, the player of lower station may not make such an overture to a higher status player. Consistent violation of the code could give the lower status player a reputation of being a nuisance and he could even incur the contempt of his own clique. Thus it is not unusual to see a high status player and a low or middle status player sitting around the perimeter of the courts for a couple of hours, waiting for someone who is

relatively their equivalent to show up. They may even strike up a conversation about the weather or the latest professional match, but the delicate gesture to interact on the court is never broached.

Manifestly this standoff is rationalized by the technical disparity in their games. Can we realistically accept this logic? I think not. More often than not, the difference in ability is not that great. This suggests a latent function which might be understood by equating this situation to sociological observations in everyday life. For example, persons of the middle class will have no contact with those of the lower class except in very limited areas. In the employment milieu, their relationship may be quite cordial with a potential for a friendship off-the-job. But outside of the employment sphere this friendship never comes to fruition. The lower class individual might feel inhibited about making the gesture and the higher class individual, due to implicit pressure from his peer group and threat to his own status, will feel equally constrained.

On the tennis court similar social forces come into play. The difference, and a factor which makes the "standoffishness" even more rigid, is that tennis status is never ascribed but always achieved. At Kissena the Regulars are extremely conscious of their court status and oriented towards upward mobility on the court. Tennis is not only a marginal sphere of everyday life but a projection of goals and values. Tennis becomes not a game to be played in the outdoors, enjoying the sunshine, being with people and appreciating intrinsic values this recreation has to offer, but a stage upon which the goals of everyday life are abstracted and reified in the form of roles which reflect and compensate for the frustrations and disappointments in everyday life.

The devotees at Kissena are predominantly of middle class background, in part because of the physical location of the tennis courts in Flushing. Teachers and students comprise the major social categories. This can be attributed to their liberal summer vacations. It should be noted that the teaching profession has traditionally derived its membership from the lower-middle class where upward mobility and status are particularly emphasized. The students are of the more conservative variety; the hip crowd find the sport too straight. The patterns of behavior on the courts at Kissena reflect the folkways and institutions of its constituents. Individuals who initially come down to the courts to enjoy the sport for its own intrinsic value are immersed in its atmosphere and are in short order conforming to its values and expectations.

Waves are often made in the structured equilibrium by a Regular who is not imbued with a drive for upward

"A Sociological Analysis of a Tennis Court" by Harvey Hyman in *World Tennis*, February 1971, pp. 60-61.

mobility but who has the means of achieving it. For example, if a player of a specific rank who has been playing within his clique for the past two seasons finds that his ability has reached a point where his peers no longer offer him competition, he may feel sufficiently confident, if not compelled, to violate the norm "Thou shalt not ask a better player to play." He must be fairly aggressive, seizing every opportunity to play a better man in order to be adopted by a higher status clique. He may no doubt arouse the envy and ill-will of his own clique. If he meets with rejection at the higher level, he could find himself "A Man without a Clique." Generally, though, a transition does take place, he does find himself a niche at a more suitable level and the equilibrium is re-established.

The difficulty in transition appears to be due to the fact that the tennis clique, like any other clique, is not readily open to anyone. Its members identify with it and try to perpetuate it. The higher up you go, the more true this becomes. At Kissena there is an elite clique composed of the best players; the phenomenon is epitomized at this level.

The thrust of this analysis has been directed at the everyday player (the Regular). The role of the "Occasional," the player who comes down to Kissena every now and then, is different. Although there is a rivalry and a current of underlying hostility which belies the placidity of the atmosphere, there is an overriding cohesiveness among Regulars. The integrity of the clique is even more stringently maintained against the inroads of the Occasional, the outsider. It is "Tennis-centrism." This "Ism" appears to serve a latent functional purpose of restricting the number of participants at the courts, which the Regulars feel is already in excess.

If the Occasional is going to play at all, he must be particularly enterprising. His bearing must be confident and aggressive, with just the right amount of nonchalance to portray an image of a Master private-court player who has condescended to play at a city court just for kicks. As for the beginning player, his chances are nil. His best bet is to come with some friends and start his own clique.

To most of the Regulars, tennis is a stage; when they come down to Kissena, they are "on." This situation is engendered by the identification of tennis with the elite set life-style and the cultural values which the players themselves bring to the court.

Aside from the more obvious feature of wearing white apparel, which is traditional, and being impeccably groomed, there is a mode of speech peculiar to the Kissena Park tennis enthusiast and other members of the species obsessed with upward mobility. Special mannerisms accompany particular points. For example, it is acceptable and even customary when missing an important shot to go through the motion of hitting the racket violently on the ground (not with sufficient force to damage the racket) and exclaiming "Oh, blast!" or some other appropriate ejaculation. Other gestures are throwing the racket up in the air or standing transfixed as if struck by a bolt of lightning. The latent function of these histrionics is not so much to let out steam but to show your opponent that he is really not that good; you just missed a simple shot. These are, in effect, face-saving gestures.

In conclusion, one is likely to have the impression that playing tennis at Kissena Park is a "Gesellschaft" type of shtic. I think one can generalize and state with a fair degree of certainty that any tennis court which is burdened with an over-population of players is going to develop cliques. They serve as an institution which attempts to restrict the size of the regular membership, they place players on proper levels and they regulate who plays whom.

The attitudes and norms of the participants at Kissena are reflections of middle class strivings and exemplify the technocratic mentality so vividly depicted by Roszac in the "Making of a Counter Culture."

COACHING AS AN OCCUPATIONAL SUBCULTURE

John D. Massengale

Their special role and the unusual demands placed upon them isolate coaches from the rest of the academic bureaucracy, with some interesting results.

Coaches have been called many things—particularly by rival coaches—but rarely something as erudite, or as apt, as an occupational subculture. Yet the unique position occupied by coaches in the academic bureaucracy has isolated them from their peers and created for them a game with decidedly nonacademic rules.

A subculture displays distinctive ways of thinking, feeling, and acting that separate it from the larger culture.[1] Although coaches participate in a larger group—the total educational organization—and share

"Coaching as an Occupational Subculture" by John D. Massengale in *Phi Delta Kappan*, October 1974, pp. 140-142.

John D. Massengale is associate professor in the Division of Health, Physical Education, Recreation, and Athletics and head football coach at Eastern Washington State College, Cheney.

most of its culture, they remain in an occupational subculture. This subculture, perpetuated apart from subject matter teaching responsibilities—in many cases even apart from the teaching of physical education—is characterized by a particular set of behaviors, values, language, and life-style.

The teacher-coach usually perceives his main—and occasionally his only—responsibilities as coaching and winning.[2] Coaches count on support from fellow coaches who function under similar pressures far different from the standard academic pressure (at the college level) to publish or perish.

Recruitment, Socialization, Promotion

The members of a subculture are recruited from a larger group, socialized and/or educated, and then often promoted for their success within the subculture. Coaching is no exception to this process. Coaches are a product of the American athletic system.

Athletes entering the field of coaching are so thoroughly socialized that they bring with them certain personality traits characteristic of athletes and coaches and distinct from other members of the faculty.[3] Coaches as a group are aggressive and highly organized, seldom paying attention to what others say. They display unusually high psychological endurance, persistence, and inflexibility. Coaches appear to dislike change and tend to be very conservative politically, socially, and attitudinally.

In addition to the apparent socialization resulting from athletic participation, coaches are often formally educated in the field of physical education. Physical education majors tend to have little in common with other students in the field of education.[4] They have a more traditional philosophy of education and a slightly lower social class background. They tend to be more dogmatic and appear to have different social values from other prospective teachers.

Absorption of coaching's unique values and behaviors begins within the teacher preparation program. Aspiring coaches are themselves coached by representatives of the subculture, learning what is expected and accepted within their chosen occupation. Social sanctions, such as preferential grading, may be applied to prospective coaches when expected behaviors, values, and life-styles are not followed. These sanctions become very evident in the closed, preferential hiring practices associated with coaching positions. Young coaches soon discover that good coaching positions are seldom gained through placement bureaus, and that an open, competitive hiring situation is rare. The more prestigious coaching jobs may be gained with the support of other members of the occupational subculture. That support is earned by conforming to the expected values and behaviors of the subculture, both during the formal educational process and the early years of coaching and teaching. The subculture can become a referral system to

vested interest groups such as alumni organizations or athletic booster clubs, or it can become an acceptable sponsor and offer unsolicited firsthand personal recommendations. Members of the subculture can also use a "favored models" concept, emphasizing an applicant's similarities to successful coaches favored by subculture members. Thus many schools have attempted to hire proteges or assistants of Oklahoma's Bud Wilkinson, hoping that some of his winning ways will have been communicated to those well versed in his coaching techniques. That same "nothing succeeds like success" frame of mind has created a ready market for coaches in the identifiable style of a Bear Bryant or a Duffy Daugherty.

The all-important values and behaviors are taught by placing the student teacher-coach in practicum, internship, or practice teaching roles. One of his supervisory teachers will usually be an experienced teacher-coach and a member of the occupational subculture. Student teacher-coaches must learn to emulate these subculture representatives, or they may never make it professionally. The power of the academic letter grade, and the power of the professional recommendation, however subjective, become significant tools of social control within the subculture.

Allegiance to the subculture's values is reinforced by professional coaching organizations and coaching journals. Most teacher-coaches, regardless of their teaching field, tend to ignore teaching journals and become devoted readers of coaching journals. They also tend to ignore educational conferences, but regularly attend coaching conventions, clinics, and workshops.

Subculture Maintenance

Open opposition from the academic community strengthens the isolation caused by the uniqueness of coaching. That hostility reinforces the subculture by creating alienation and polarization; the separation is maintained by the complete or partial exclusion of the coach from the academic in-crowd.

The result of this extreme polarization between the coaching and the academic communities is the creation of an in-group/out-group relationship.[5] The two groups identify each other as opponents, and each group regards itself as the guardian of its members' virtues, values, and loyalties. The out-group becomes viewed as a threat to the cherished values of the in-group.

Clearly, such an antagonistic relationship develops solidarity in the coach's occupational subculture and tends to rally the membership around specific beliefs. To have an opponent is very important for subculture maintenance, particularly when the opponent can become a scapegoat.

This occupational isolation allows coaches to assume the role of professionals or "cosmopolitans."[6] They feel very little loyalty or commitment to their school, and become devoted to professional coaching careers that exceed all organizational boundaries. Coaches cannot develop loyalty to an organization when they view their position as temporary. If they are successful, they will attempt to move upward to a better position; if they are unsuccessful, they will expect to be fired.

The stereotypes of coaches often held by other members of the faculty contribute to subculture solidarity. The critics view coaches as dehumanizing, autocratic, and insensitive to the individuality of the athletes they coach.[7] Faculty members often view coach/faculty alienation as a direct result of the unusually stern, authoritarian leadership behavior of coaches, citing examples such as rigid rules and an overemphasis on discipline.

In contrast, coaches maintain that authoritarianism does not cause alienation, but that alienation is caused by the overreaction of an uninformed, anti-athletic faculty. Critics of authoritarian coaching methods often assume that such leadership is bad, forgetting that most coaches are concerned with the good of the team member as well as the good of the team.[8]

At the root of the problem of authoritarianism in coaching is the traditional role of the coach as father figure. Coaches are expected to fulfill many of the functions of the archetypal father: to be strong, virile, and tough.[9] Although fast disappearing from the home, firm discipline is still demanded in athletics. Coaches such as the late Vince Lombardi of the Green Bay Packers and Washington Redskins derive much of their authority and power from presenting the image of an extremely tough father figure. Lombardi ran his phenomenally successful teams like the overlord of a large family; his players played to their limits for his approval. The father role is seldom initiated by, or expected of, other members of the faculty; it is a must for the coach. However, coaches seldom receive extra credit merely for fulfilling this role; they must win to receive credit. Coaches view their authority as a prerequisite for molding a winning team. Any real or imagined attempt to strip them of their authority greatly increases the coach/faculty alienation.

The academic community often views the coach's authoritarian control of the athlete as a violation of individual rights and freedoms, an unnecessary restraint on the athlete's total educational development. Coaches seldom question their right of infringement, for they consider themselves faculty experts in coaching and assume the ultimate responsibility for the total performance of the team. They demand dedication, obedience, and loyalty, for they, not the team members, are held responsible for losing.

Coaches are seldom fired for their academic reputation. Winning often substitutes for academic inadequacies, if inadequacies exist. However, academic excellence and teaching expertise will seldom substitute for losing. Faculty outside the coaching subculture do not face this dilemma, and seldom understand the problem. This dilemma, as well as the failure of the academic community to appreciate the complexity of the coach's role

as decision-making executive, adds to the problem of alienation, often creates polarization, and results in the formation of a very homogeneous group of coaches, both locally and nationally.

Further coach/faculty alienation may be caused by the decision-making powers of the coach. An important aspect of coaching decisions is the method and manner in which they are made. Coaching decisions are characteristically practical, rational, and expedient; often they are made in the shortest possible time. This type of rapid-fire decision making comes easy to the coach, since it is the type he is forced to use in day-to-day and game-to-game situations. An example would be the instructions all coaches issue to their players during a time-out situation near the end of a game. The decision upon which victory may rest must come from one person—the coach. Continued success with this type of pressure decision making leads to its repeated, and increasingly sophisticated, use at critical times.

Success with instant decision making may also be the main reason that coaches constantly criticize the time-consuming decision-making process of the faculty and the administration. Most coaches' criticisms of faculty and administration decision making cite delay tactics and dependence on theory rather than down-to-earth reality. Coaches tend to view indecision as no decision at all, and usually maintain that even a bad decision is better than indecision. Many coaches view indecision as weakness, and weakness is seldom acceptable to coaches, since it is a trait that is not allowed in their occupation. Prominent coaches have condemned administrators for lack of knowledge and understanding of the coach/player relationship, fear of decision making, weakness under pressure, inability to understand coaching responsibilities, and various forms of gutlessness.[10] Such polarization aids in the creation and maintenance of the coaching subculture.

Coaches have attempted to use athletic governing bodies and professional organizations to bolster what they view as a diminishing authority structure within their occupation. While this trend increases coaching autonomy and subculture solidarity, it also increases coach/faculty alienation, especially when public policy statements are issued that attempt to reinforce the coach's position.

Coaches continually attempt to gain more control of their position, although they realize that complete control is impossible. The more control gained, the stronger their position. They willingly accept total responsibility for team performance, but also insist on no outside interference. Coaches ask for, and completely accept, responsibility for positions filled with uncertainty, in order to eliminate as much uncertainty as possible. Much of coaching's authoritarianism and inflexibility may be caused by the institutional demand that coaches assume total accountability for extremely uncertain situations.[11] When coaches are held accountable for the total performance of a team, they demand complete authority to make any decisions necessary for team success.

Failure, Demotion, and Dismissal

Subculture support is very important to coaches, since they realize they may be fired at the end of any losing season, even though the losing record may not have been their fault. An example of a built-in occupational coaching hazard would be a coach's position at West Point. There the coach has little control over the prowess of his raw material, but must instead hope that the Academy will attract suitable candidates. Occasionally, such as during the 1973 football season, those hopes are in vain. Through the subculture, coaches learn how they, as well as the school organization, are expected to manage failure, demotion, and dismissal. The situation causes organizational strain; management of that strain becomes a necessity.

The organization can manage the strain by making rather obscure demotions. Coaches can be demoted by placing them in assistant coaching positions, or by making them head coaches of what the organization has designated as less important sports. In some cases the school administration chooses to manage the strain by complete dismissal, making replacements as soon as possible.

Management of the strain may also take the form of promotion. Coaches can be promoted to positions with lesser responsibilities such as assistant athletic director, attendance counselor, or executive coordinator of something that does not need executive coordination. In a sense, they can be promoted out of the way, as explained so aptly by Laurence Peter in *The Peter Principle*. They can be assigned to a lower job status, then receive a raise in salary, or at least keep their same salary, which in many cases is higher than that of other faculty members.

Coaches must learn to manage failure, even though their own view and that of the subculture may be that they have not failed. Coaching failure is seldom determined by peer-group evaluation. It is usually determined by those who have no expertise for making such decisions; therefore, the decision is often ignored by the membership of the subculture. Coaches often depend on, and receive, the support of their subculture when they feel they have been unfairly evaluated.

Losing becomes the only measure of failure and the source of stigma. That stigma creates a process of downward mobility, with a corresponding loss of social prominence in the community.

In the end, coaches can personally manage failure by accepting one of three options. They can change jobs, which amounts to changing sports or changing specific responsibilities in the same sport; change careers, either within or outside their present organization; or change organizations and start all over again.

NOTES

1. James W. Vander Zanden, *Sociology: A Systematic Approach* (New York: Ronald Press, 1970).
2. Harry Edwards, *Sociology of Sport* (Homewood, Ill.: Dorsey Press, 1973).
3. Bruce C. Ogilvie and Thomas A. Tutko, "Sport: If You Want To Build Character, Try Something Else," *Psychology Today,* October, 1971, pp. 61-63.
4. Gerald S. Kenyon, "Certain Psychosocial and Cultural Characteristics Unique to Prospective Teachers of Physical Education," *Research Quarterly,* March, 1965, pp. 105-12.
5. Herbert Blumer, "Social Movements," in Alfred M. Lee, ed., *Principles of Sociology* (New York: Barnes & Noble, 1965).
6. Alvin W. Gouldner, "Cosmopolitans and Locals," in Barney G. Glaser, ed., *Organizational Careers* (Chicago: Aldine, 1968).
7. Jack Scott, *The Athletic Revolution* (New York: Free Press, 1970).
8. George H. Sage, "The Coach as Management: Organizational Leadership in American Sport," *Quest,* January, 1973, pp. 35-40.
9. Arnold Beisser, *The Madness in Sports* (New York: Appleton-Century-Crofts, 1966).
10. John Underwood, "The Desperate Coach," *Sports Illustrated,* September, 1969, pp. 63-70.
11. Edwards, op. cit.

DISCUSSION QUESTIONS

A. *John Phillips and Walter Schafer*

1. Identify and explain the function of the major elements, or components (e.g., values, norms, etc.) which are common to all subcultures.
2. Discuss and explain the process by which one is socialized into a subculture. What must a newcomer learn in order to achieve full membership status?
3. Describe the RPM model for measuring norms and discuss its strengths and weaknesses.
4. What are some practical implications of the RPM model?
5. There is a paucity of discussion in the literature of the material elements (e.g., facilities, clothing, instruments) of sport subcultures. What contribution, if any, can a consideration of these elements make toward a more complete understanding of the functioning of a sport subculture?

B. *Glenn Jacobs*

1. Identify and discuss some of the official (formal) and unofficial (informal) indicators of status in karate. How do these enhance the karate player's identity?
2. Discuss and explain the function of initiation rites (rites of passage) in karate. Can you identify similar rites in American society? What function do they serve?
3. What are some of the major values and norms in the karate subculture? How do they differ from the values and norms found in other combative sports?
4. Becoming an accepted karate member requires the learning and enactment of appropriate roles. Identify as many of these roles as possible (formal and informal) and explain the function, or purpose they serve.
5. Discuss and react to the "master's role" in the karate subculture.
6. Given the authoritarian structure and reward system of karate, speculate as to what types of persons are most likely to engage in this activity.

C. *David Arnold*

1. Can sport parachuting be viewed as a subculture? Justify your answer.

2. Identify and discuss some of the major values and norms found in sport parachuting. How do they differ from those found in your favorite sport?

3. Discuss and explain some of the ways in which technology (e.g., clothing, equipment, etc.) is used in this subculture.

4. Speculate and discuss (a) how parachuting literature contributes to group cohesiveness, and, (b) the purpose of badges on jump suits.

5. Discuss some of the reasons why blacks, orientals and women are underrepresented in sport parachuting.

D. *Harvey Hyman*

1. Identify and discuss the major norms found within the subculture of the tennis court. What function do they serve?

2. It appears that playing ability is a major determinant of status in this subculture. Can you list and explain any other factors which contribute to one's status in this activity?

3. Hyman refers to the tennis court as a stage, complete with actors and role playing. Identify some of these roles and explain their functions.

4. Discuss some functions of tennis cliques. Do cliques serve similar functions in your favorite sport?

E. *John Massengale*

1. In what ways do the role expectations found within the coaching subculture differ from those of the rest of the academic community?

2. Identify and discuss some of the major social and personality characteristics of coaches. Do these factors help explain the character of the coaching subculture?

3. Identify and discuss some of the mechanisms of social control in the coaching subculture and discuss how they ensure conformity to values and norms.

4. What kinds of behaviors, values, norms, etc., must the aspiring coach learn in order to (a) be accepted into the coaching subculture, and, (b) attain upward occupational mobility?

5. A coach who has a losing record oftentimes experiences "organizational strain." According to Massengale, how do losing coaches manage this organizational strain?

6. Apply the conceptual framework discussed by Phillips and Schafer and show how it can be used to study the coaching subculture.

Unit IX

Sport and Racism:
Fact or Fantasy?

Traditionally, sport has been viewed by most Americans as an arena of free and open competition in which ethnicity, political stance, or socioeconomic background are of little consequence. Further support for this belief is obtained upon examination of the dominant role that the black athlete plays in America's most celebrated sports, e.g., football, basketball, baseball, and track and field. But why should the institution of sport reflect values at variance with those held by the larger society? Why should sport not be a microcosm of society? If a color line exists in the polity, the economic sphere, and in covert and subtle discrimination at the personal level, it then follows that one should expect to find racism extant in the world of sport. In the four selections which follow, the question of racism in sport is documented and discussed in the light of recent research findings.

In the initial reading, Barry McPherson, a sport sociologist, presents an extensive synthesis of the literature pertaining to the involvement of the black athlete in both amateur and professional sport. He also discusses prominent factors which affect the socialization of black youths into sports. The author concludes by presenting a number of reasons why more studies of black athletes are needed, and offers some suggestions regarding design and substantive themes for future research.

Sociologist Harry Edwards, gives several poignant reasons why the institution of sport is an opiate of the black masses. He then critically analyzes a number of determinants which help explain the black athlete's superiority in certain sports. Edwards contends that white racism has limited the range of opportunity for black Americans to achieve success in professions other than sports and entertainment.

In the third selection, sociologist Jonathan Brower, employed observational techniques to study interaction patterns within a professional football team. His findings suggest the presence of a "culture clash" between the values of black athletes, and the predominantly white values of the professional football establishment. The author suggests that this clash leads to a subtle but pervasive form of racism.

In the final selection, McPherson suggests that there is not enough empirical evidence to unequivocally state that blacks are segregated into specific playing positions because of discrimination. He suggests, based on socialization theory, that quite possibly the inordinate number of blacks in certain positions may be self induced, e.g., they choose positions where visible role models are available. It should be pointed out, however, that this may not be a totally adequate explanation since the question can be asked, "how did blacks first come to assume noncentral playing positions?"

MINORITY GROUP INVOLVEMENT IN SPORT: THE BLACK ATHLETE

Barry D. McPherson

I. Introduction

Although ·members of ethnic groups have participated in institutionalized sport since early in the twentieth century (e.g., Riesman and Denny, 1951), no group has been as successful or as controversial as the black American. As a result, with few exceptions (Dunlap, 1951; Fox, 1961; Roberts and Sutton-Smith, 1962; Zurcher and Meadow, 1967; Lever, 1969; Glassford, 1970; Pooley, 1972; Smith, 1972), most of the literature pertaining to ethnic or racial involvement in sport has been concerned with the involvement of blacks in professional and amateur sport. For example, at various times sport has been praised for its role in integrating blacks into the mainstream of the dominant society, whereas at other times it has been vilified for fostering prejudice, discrimination, and segregation similar to that in other social institutions. More specifically, interest in the black athlete arose when it became apparent that although the involvement of blacks in many social institutions was severely restricted, the complexion of an athlete was of little consequence when success in sport was highly valued by members of the dominant society. That is, participation by blacks was differentially encouraged and sanctioned by those who controlled and supported sport teams associated with particular institutions, cities, or nations.

Within the same sport milieu, even though a black was encouraged and permitted to play the role of athlete, he often experienced subtle or overt acts of segregation, discrimination, or racism, similar to those he encountered in other social institutions (Davie, 1949; Davis, 1966). This differential interaction between members of the dominant and minority group has been examined by both black and white authors in recent years. Much of this literature has been journalistic and anecdotal, with few attempts to collect data and test

hypotheses. Recognizing this limitation, the present chapter reviews the literature pertaining to the historical involvement of blacks in amateur and professional sport, the amount and type of role enactment by blacks in the sport system, the impact of social processes on black sportsmen, and the incidence and causes of discrimination against black sportsmen in social institutions. The chapter concludes with some suggestions for future research efforts.

II. History of Black Involvement in Sport

The involvement of blacks in institutionalized sport has been characterized by alternating cycles of segregation and integration. Thus, prior to the Emancipation Proclamation all sport was segregated. Following emancipation, varying degrees of integration were present until the late 1890s when all professional sport except boxing became segregated once again. This section of the chapter reviews some of the historical highlights which chronicle black involvement in institutionalized sport.[1]

Prior to emancipation, blacks engaged in both formal and informal sport activities (Henderson, 1968; Govan, 1971). For example, not only were there intraplantation boxing matches to determine the most proficient boxer, but also matches (promoted by the plantation owner) with champions from other plantations. Success often led to preferential treatment, suggesting that sport was an early avenue for social mobility. In the 1800s blacks were active and successful participants in a variety of sports. For example, in 1805 a black won a "colored" American boxing championship; by the 1860s a number of black baseball stars were integrated into organized baseball (Boyle, 1963; Voight, 1966; Peterson, 1970); and in the late 1800s a black jockey rode three Kentucky Derby winners (Clement, 1954; Quaries, 1964, p. 247). Thus, throughout the 1800s, a few select blacks were involved in integrated sport. However, by the late 1800s overt discrimination against blacks in organized sport was increasing and by 1898 the last black was forced out of professional baseball (Peterson, 1970, p. 49). Soon thereafter black athletes were excluded from horse racing and most other sports. The one exception was boxing where they frequently had to consent to lose before they could obtain a match (Boyle, 1963, p. 103). Barred from organized baseball they formed their own league in 1920 (Peterson, 1970), and did likewise in basketball in the late 1920s. In horse racing they continued to be involved but occupied lesser roles such as that of stable boy.

On the amateur level, with the emergence of black colleges, many blacks were given the opportunity to engage in competitive sport both within their college and

"Minority Group Involvement in Sport: The Black Athlete" by Barry McPherson in *Exercise and Sport Sciences Reviews*, Volume 2, pp. 71-101. Published by Academic Press, New York, 1974.

against other black colleges. In addition, blacks attending Eastern schools such as Rutgers, Brown, Amherst, and Harvard were able to participate in football, baseball, and track and field (Henderson, 1949). Berryman (1972) reported that in addition to being on the team, some occupied leadership roles. For example, M.W. Bullock was appointed head coach at Massachusetts Agricultural College (University of Massachusetts) in 1904, and two others were elected as team captain in 1905 (Berryman, 1972, p. 1). The black amateur athlete also gained an opportunity to engage in competitive and recreational sport in the United States Army between 1890 and 1916 (Fletcher, 1972). Fletcher reported that the all-black cavalry and infantry units, usually coached by white officers, competed in baseball and boxing within their regiment, against other black regiments, and against white military and civilian teams. In the Olympic Games, a black athlete won a bronze medal in the 200-meter sprint for the first time in 1904, and in 1908, J. B. Taylor won the first gold medal as a member of the 1600-meter relay team. Since then, blacks have been highly successful in track and field but have frequently been the center of controversy (cf. Edwards, 1969; Mandell, 1971).

In summary, black athletes were excluded from most professional sports until the "color bar" was broken[2] by Jackie Robinson. From the early 1900s until 1947 the color line was prevalent in most professional sports just as it was in most other social institutions. Thus, except for the few amateur athletes who competed in track and field in the Olympics or who competed in college or the Army, integrated organized sport was not available to most blacks until the late 1940s.

III. Role Enactment by Blacks in Institutionalized Sport

The extent to which blacks are involved in sport as *active* participants (i.e., athletes) has been investigated almost annually since the color line was broken in 1947. In most cases, these descriptive studies have been interested in the *number* of blacks involved in professional sport. Because these statistics change annually, rather than redundantly cite statistics from the plethora of reports (Dodson, 1954; Davie, 1949; Baltimore, 1951; Abrahams, 1952; Boulding, 1957; Boyle, 1963; Davis, 1966; Blalock, 1967; Henderson, 1968; Maher, 1968; Olsen, 1968; Greendorfer, 1970; Loy and McElvogue, 1970; Smith and Grindstaff, 1970; Pascal and Rapping, 1972; Brown, 1973; *Black Sports, Sports Illustrated,* and many daily newspapers), a brief overview is presented.

Boulding (1957, p. 115) reported that the percentage of blacks participating in professional baseball, basketball, and football grew from 0% in 1935 to 10.9% in 1955. During this same period, the total black population only increased from 9.7 to 10.5%. Brown (1969) noted that since 1956 there have been 10 NBA black leading scorers, 15 NBA black rebounding leaders, and 10 NBA black assist leaders. Thus, basketball is statistically dominated by blacks in a number of performance categories. Greendorfer (1970), after examining the *Baseball Register: 1970,* indicated that 15% of the active major league baseball players were black, with another 11% being foreign born (including Latin Americans). More recently, Brown (1973) reported that approximately 35 to 40% of the players in professional baseball are black, approximately 30 to 35% of professional football players are black, and over 50% of the professional basketball players are black. It has also been noted (*Time,* 1970) that a black won the National Baseball League's Most Valuable Player award 16 times in a 20-year period; that the Most Valuable Player award in professional basketball was won by a black 12 times in 15 years; and, that all four Rookie of the Year awards in professional football in 1970 were won by blacks. They have also been highly successful in boxing. For example, prior to Marciano winning the heavyweight title in 1952, blacks had dominated this event for 15 years. Similarly, after the defeat of Marciano they have continued to dominate most weight divisions. Thus, not only are they involved to an increasing extent, they are also highly successful.[3]

Although there is no direct indication of the extent to which blacks are involved in college sport, a survey conducted in 1968 (*Sports Illus.* 1968) showed that for the fifty-nine schools in the sample, 10,698 grants-in-aid were awarded, of which only 634 (6%) went to black athletes. The survey also indicated that the number of scholarships that were given to blacks not only varied from conference to conference, but also from school to school within a conference. In a more recent report, Yetman and Eitzen (1972, p. 27) reported that the percentage of NCAA basketball teams with black players increased from 9.8 to 79.8% from 1948 to 1970. During this same period the percentage of black players increased from 1.4 to 27.1%. Finally, Edwards (1973, p. 191) noted that 165 of the first 250 athletes drafted by professional football teams in 1971 were blacks. As can be seen, blacks are now well represented in the major sports—baseball, basketball, football, and boxing. However, in the minor or so-called social sports (tennis, golf, swimming) they tend to be under-represented, although the situation is improving as more facilities and opportunities are opened to them, and as more blacks attain success in these areas.

The involvement of black youth in amateur sport has been studied indirectly by Short and Tennyson (1963) and directly by Kraus (1969). In an analysis of the behavior of adolescent gangs, Short and Tennyson reported that sport was a favorite activity for both white and black gangs. However, there were sport differences for each race. For example, black gangs were more involved in basketball, boxing, wrestling, and track and field; whereas white gangs were more involved in bowling and football. These differences may be related to the socializing situation and to the availability of visible role models and facilities. Kraus (1969) found that blacks in New York City and four suburban New York communities tended to participate both in activities and in age groupings that varied widely from those of white residents. Although data were not presented for the white residents, boxing, judo, karate, track and field, basketball, and weight-training were identified, in rank order, as being the activities in which blacks were most involved.

To date there have been no studies that indicate the number of black professional or college female athletes, nor the number of black athletes participating in sport in other countries. Nevertheless, the reader should be aware that the black female athlete is under-represented in most sports, with the possible exception of track and field. Cross-nationally, depending on the racial composition and racial policy of a country, the number involved can vary greatly. For example, despite a racial majority in Rhodesia and South Africa, teams are segregated so that blacks are excluded from many international competitions (Cheffers, 1972).

Finally, the opportunity to occupy roles other than athlete or spectator has been severely restricted. For example, there have been no black major league baseball managers, no head football coaches, only one general manager, and few black play-by-play announcers or commentators identified with any network or sport team.

In summary, it can be seen that blacks are somewhat over-represented in professional sport compared to society at large; that they have achieved a high level and degree of success in baseball, basketball, boxing, football, and track and field; that they are becoming more involved and more successful in the traditionally exclusive sports and, that they are under-represented at the management and executive levels. Similarly, black females, as well as white females, tend to be under-represented, and involvement varies cross-nationally according to the racial composition and racial policy of the specific country. At the descriptive level then, it would appear that participation in professional sport fosters social equality.

IV. Influence of Social Processes on Black Sportsmen

A. The Socialization Process

This section is concerned with how blacks learn to play a sport role, regardless of the success they may ultimately attain. The following three sections discuss the influence of significant others (role models), the social situation, and the personal attributes of the black on the early socialization experiences of black youth.

1. The Social Situation

The social environment in which the black lives exerts a profound influence on his life-style, including his recreational pursuits. Davis (1966) suggested that the majority of blacks are forced to develop their athletic skill in a kind of sports ghetto. He illustrated this statement by noting that in the past there were few available facilities within the economic reach of black boys and girls. Where facilities were available they were often substandard and characterized by the wider prejudicial trends of society (Clift, 1959; Kraus, 1969).

Although these facts would suggest that few, if any, elite black athletes would come from the ghetto, Bontemps (1964) indicated that Joe Louis, Sugar Ray Robinson, Jackie Robinson, Willie Mays, Jesse Owens, and Althen Gibson all spent their childhood and adolescent years in a ghetto. An explanation offered by Henderson (1968) suggests that black children are prohibited (financially and socially) from attending shows and hanging around restaurants, and that this leads to increased interest and proficiency in sports. Brown (1969), in drawing a parallel between the elite Jewish basketball players of the 1920s and 1930s and the elite black basketball players of today, stated that both came from a ghetto where basketball courts and nets were the most accessible sport facility. More specifically, Davie (1949) stated that the black has engaged in track because it is less expensive in terms of equipment, requires less intensive coaching, and historically has not discriminated against blacks. He further noted that racial prejudice has prevented the black from competing against or with whites in numerous types of athletic contests, especially those that involve physical contact or suggest social equality. In summary, it may be that the availability of facilities, leaders, and organized programs in the early social environment greatly influences the extent to which the black becomes involved in sport.

2. Personal Attributes

The personal attributes of black youth have also contributed to the learning of sport roles. Stoll, Inbar, and Fennessey (1968) investigated the role of play and games in the socialization process. They investigated four types of games (individual, sports, board-card, and party) and found that the frequent participation in sport and individual games exhibited by blacks is related to a feeling that one can learn and succeed. For example, they found that blacks who frequently participated in sport had higher scholastic achievement scores than infrequent players.

Rosenberg (1967, p. 24) hypothesized that individuals become differentially socialized as a function of their attitudes and values interacting within a given social context. For example, Rosenblatt (1967) found that compared to white adolescents, blacks assigned greater esteem to a sport career and thus a larger proportion had aspirations to become professional athletes. In addition, he suggested that blacks consider success in sport more within their grasp than careers that require years of academic training.

Closely allied with achievement is the attainment of status. Henderson (1968) stated that being an athlete gives black youth a status that they might not otherwise attain. In a study of black involvement in voluntary associations, Babchuk and Thompson (1962) indicated that participation in voluntary associations provides an avenue whereby an individual can gain prestige, hold office, exercise power and control, and win applause and acclaim. Since sport, especially for youth, can be considered a voluntary association, similar outcomes may motivate black youth to learn sport roles.

Kraus (1960, p. 34) reported that, regardless of race, there is evidence to suggest that lower-class males, especially those who are gang-affiliated, have a markedly different set of values with respect to athletic participation than do middle- or upper-class youth. He suggested that they are less disciplined and less well-organized; that they tend to emphasize individual performance rather than subordination of self to a team; and that they seek immediate gratification rather than the achievement of long-term goals. Therefore, since many black youth are members of the lower class, they may have different values and different achievement motivation with respect to involvement in sport. Thus, personal attributes may also account for socialization into sport involvement.

3. Significant Others

If a novice is to learn a sport role, significant others (i.e. family members, peers, or professional athletes) who enact these roles must be available. For example, Loy (1969) stated that there is much identification associated with sport by some economic or social classes and that generally the lower economic groups tend to indulge in hero worship and ethnic identification with athletes from their own group. Because black athletes have become symbols of black participation in a white world, black youths may be segregating themselves into specific sports and sport roles because they concentrate on positions in which black role models are available (Frazier, 1957; Davis, 1966; Pascal and Rapping, 1972). Weinberg and Arond (1952) also supported this view when they reported that successful amateur and professional boxers serve as highly visible role models for lower-class males, especially urban blacks. They found that most boxers were influenced to become "ring fighters" by either a boxer in the neighborhood or by a member of the family. A second explanation was supplied by Brown (1969) who suggested that teachers and coaches often discourage black youth from participating in such activities as golf, tennis, and swimming in order to prevent later frustration and embarrassment.

McPherson (1971) hypothesized that since success increases visibility, the greater the success achieved by an individual occupying a specific role (e.g., pitcher), the greater the exposure and the greater the imitation of this role by novices. Thus it was argued that black youth, in the early stages of sport role socialization, seek to enact the specific role played by black athletes. Although little empirical support for this hypothesis is available at the present time, retrospectively it is noted that the first black baseball players to enter the major leagues played at first base and in the outfield. At the present time, blacks are over-represented at these positions (Loy and McElvogue, 1970). Similarly, in football the first positions to be occupied by blacks were offensive and defensive halfbacks; today, blacks are over-represented in these positions (Loy and McElvogue, 1970; Smith and

Grindstaff, 1970; Ball, 1973). More recently, Brower (1972) interviewed 23 white and 20 black high school football players and found that 90% of the black athletes had one or more black role models and that over 70% had no white role model. He also learned that a majority of the black football players aspired to play traditionally black positions, whereas the white athletes aspired to attain specific positions, regardless of whether they were traditionally occupied by blacks or whites.

Some minimal support for the hypothesis that members of minority groups are differentially socialized into sport roles was recently reported by Kenyon and McPherson (1973). Questionnaires completed by 96 white athletes and 17 black athletes competing in the 1968 Olympic track and field trials at Lake Tahoe revealed some differences in the early socialization experiences. Recognizing the limitation of extrapolations based on a sample of 17 subjects, and considering the *social situation* first, it was found that compared to white athletes, black athletes were raised in larger families (4.5 children compared to 2.4 for white families); were from a lower socioeconomic background; and were raised in large urban centers to a greater extent (56 versus 29%). Moreover, they became involved in track at an earlier age; developed their first interest in the sport in the neighbourhood and home, rather than in the school as the white athletes did; and perceived track to be more highly valued by students at school and by members of the community. An examination of the influence of *significant others* suggests that the role models for blacks and whites are different, that the role models for the blacks differ at each stage of their sport career, and that economic rewards related to track (scholarships) are more important to the black athlete. Finally, when comparing the differences in the *personal attributes* of the two groups, it was noted that the black athletes were more successful in making a team on their first attempt; experienced success (won a race or event) at an earlier age, especially in the track events; and appeared willing to sacrifice more in the realm of cultural pursuits and part-time jobs in order to compete in sport.

In summary, the literature suggests that involvement in sport by members of a minority group may result from differential socialization experiences early in life. More specifically, the occupation of specific sport roles by blacks may result from self-induced and situationally determined factors such as the opportunity set; the apparent influence of stereotypes held by coaches (Brower, 1972; Williams and Youssef, 1973); the value orientations of the school, peer group, and family; and, the availability of specific role models during the impressionistic years of childhood and early adolescence.

B. Social Integration

Since 1947 it has often been suggested that sport facilitates the integration of blacks into the dominant society and thereby functions as a model for what could be attained in other societal institutions (White, 1951; Clement, 1954; Dodson, 1954; Young, 1963; Quaries,

1964; Simon and Carey, 1966; Olsen, 1968). Thus, from the point of view of many who are outside the sport system, it would appear that black athletes are readily integrated into the dominant society. In reality, however, although the black athlete has been partially integrated into a sport system, he has not always been totally integrated into white society. One of the frequent complaints of black athletes on college campuses, and in professional sport, is that once they leave the locker room they are subjected to the same prejudices and discrimination as a ghetto resident who ventures out into white society. For example, black collegiate and professional athletes reported that they were dehumanized and exploited, while others indicated that they were happier back in the ghetto (Olsen, 1968). Frequently this prejudice is demonstrated by their teammates. This is not surprising in view of the finding (Charnofsky, 1968; Ibrahim, 1968) that there are no differences between athletes and nonathletes in their attitudes toward minority group members (Jews and Negroes). Similarly, Brown (1969) suggested that the biggest disappointments experienced by the black athlete were those that occur off the field wherein their interactions with white society in nonsport situations were frequently similar to those experienced by other blacks who interacted within the dominant group (cf. Carter, 1970).

Fitzgerald (1960) and Boyle (1963), after examining black-white relations away from the sport environment, noted that blacks tended to segregate themselves from whites. For example, they reported that blacks declined invitations to parties, had their own hangouts in each city, had an argot which they guarded closely, and had leaders on each club to socialize newcomers into the major leagues with respect to acceptable social behavior. Similarly, Charnofsky (1968), in a study of 58 major league baseball players, concluded that most players (57 of 58) preferred to spend their leisure time with others of the same ethnic or racial background. Davis (1966, p. 808) observed that integration did not extend beyond the locker room and suggested that one reason why blacks have not been readily accepted in tennis and golf is that these sports involve social interaction with the opponent after the contest.

Although most interest has been centered upon the elite athlete in college or professional sport, a study by Kraus (1969) sought to determine whether recreational sport programs for the masses were fostering integration and improving race relations. He found that when blacks entered community recreation programs, whites tended to withdraw from the program, that most teams were segregated across all sports, and that this trend increased with the age of the participants. This finding is supported by Petroni and Hirsch (1970) who reported that most integration between Afro-American and white adolescents occurs in athletics. Yet at the same time they noted that athletic participation did not facilitate the integration of Mexican-American adolescents.

In summary, it appears that although the elite black athlete has been integrated into college and professional sport as a functioning member of a team, he has not been totally integrated into the dominant group with respect to his nonsport roles. Similarly, participation in sport does not guarantee integration for the masses. Thus the athlete, whether interacting in a recreational, college, or professional sport environment, may find himself in a position similar to that of an assembly-line worker who, although integrated into a large corporation for his work role, faces segregation in his nonwork or leisure roles.

C. Social Mobility

In addition to claims that sport facilitates the integration of blacks into white society, it has been suggested that participation in sport functions as a catalyst for upward social mobility. For example, Schafer (1968) suggested that there are at least four ways in which successful participation in athletics might bring later rewards that might not otherwise be attained. First, he suggested that participation in high school and college athletics may enhance educational attainment, which, in turn, increases the chances for later rewards in money, power, and prestige. Studies by Eggleston (1965), Loy (1969), and Webb (1969) suggest that it is difficult to make the case that members of a lower class will move upward because of participation in sport. The key question concerns whether it is participation in sport or a college degree which facilitates upward mobility. Because many black and white athletes do not receive a college degree, it may be possible to control for this variable in future longitudinal studies. Schafer also hypothesized that professional sport often serves as a direct immediate channel to money and prestige, without going through the usual educational or early occupational route. Again there is little empirical support for this hypothesis as it applies to black athletes. The extent to which this may apply likely varies for different sports, both in terms of prestige and income. For example, Weinberg and Arond (1952) in their study of black professional boxers found that even if upward mobility occurred, it was usually not sustained once the career was terminated.

The third proposal by Schafer indicated that "occupational sponsorship" may occur for athletes whereby they are sought out or given special consideration in hiring and in promotion. As the next section of this chapter indicates, blacks have had little opportunity in this area.

The fourth way in which sport participation may facilitate upward mobility is by developing or reinforcing values, skills, or attitudes that enhance one's attractiveness to an employer or improve one's job performance. Although many have claimed (cf. Kenyon, 1968) that these characteristics are developed in sport, we do not really know to what extent, if any, these traits are developed in black or white athletes.

The contention that athletes from lower-class or minority backgrounds are able to turn a successful career in athletics into subsequent upward mobility is based on case studies of a few elite athletes. To date, only Blalock (1962) has attempted to study this question. By analyzing the situation of the black in baseball, he concluded that a high level of performance could enable an individual to raise his status. This potential mobility was attributed to the following situational factors found within baseball: (*1*) there is no direct competition among teammates; (*2*) there is no control over teammates; (*3*) there are no educational requirements necessary for success; (*4*) there is only a slight dependence in the performance of the task on others; and (*5*) there is no interaction on the job with the opposite sex.

In summary, it appears that only a minority of blacks will experience upward mobility as a result of participation in college or professional sport. For most blacks, upward movement on the social scale may be of short duration and may vary directly with the success of their athletic career. For those who attain the "star" category and the associated income, upward mobility may be more permanent. Although they may lose the prestige and the occupational component of social status when their career is completed, they may retain their social position due to wise economic investments in their most productive years. For others in the "journeyman" category, upward movement may be followed by a regression toward their original social position. Again, however, investigators must ask whether this phenomenon is unique to the black athlete or whether it holds for all athletes.

V. Institutionalized Discrimination Against Black Athletes

An individual's racial background is a characteristic that has led to unequal treatment in social situations. For example, via the process of segregation, individuals are either totally excluded from social organizations or from specific positions within an organization. This section will analyze the extent to which segregation and discrimination are present for black athletes in the following social institutions: (*a*) the social structure of amateur and professional sport; (*b*) the educational domain; (*c*) the interpersonal domain away from the playing milieu; and (*d*) the economic sector.

A. Discrimination Within the Social Structure of Sport

Boyle (1963, p. 103) reported that discrimination against the black athlete began as early as the late 1800s. The prevailing attitude in society at that time was reflected in sport by accusations that the "feet-first" slide in baseball was innovated in order to injure blacks playing second base (Boyle, 1963, pp. 103-105). Similarly, Fleischer (1938:6) reported that editorials appearing in the late 1800s and early 1900s warned the public of a growing threat of black supremacy in athletics. In recent years, however, the forms and incidents of discrimination have become more subtle. As a result, a number of empirical studies have been completed related to the following themes: (*1*) unequal distribution of blacks by playing position and (*2*) unequal opportunity for equal ability.

In an early paper designed to study occupational discrimination, Blalock (1962) generated thirteen propositions suggesting that discrimination in professional baseball was low compared to that of other occupations. He believed that blacks possessed a positive skill advantage over white players and, hence, once the racial barrier was broken there was a rush to tap the reservoir of skilled manpower. Thus he concluded that the integration of blacks into baseball was a legitimate act and was not merely a token attempt to dispel charges of discrimination. More recently, however, the following studies have suggested that there is discrimination within sport and that the black athlete is faced with unequal opportunity for equal ability. For example, Rosenblatt (1967) studied the distribution of blacks in proportion to whites in professional baseball to determine whether blacks were as well represented among the journeyman players as among the stars. He found that the higher the batting average, the greater the proportion of blacks in that performance category, and that, as the batting average declined, fewer blacks were represented at each level. He concluded that there was discrimination against the "substar" black and that the journeyman black was less likely to play regularly than the equally undistinguished white player. Yetman and Eitzen (1972) reported that for the 1966-1970 period this performance difference persisted. In a critique of Rosenblatt's work, Whitehead (1967) claimed that other facets of the game must also be considered before drawing the conclusion that blacks must be superior to be treated equally. He noted that managers weigh the key baseball skills differently and, therefore, only if defensive skills and bunting ability were considered could one conclude that racial discrimination does or does not occur at the substar level.

Pascal and Rapping (1972), in a study completed in 1969, examined whether a black minor league baseball player must have more ability than a white minor leaguer in order to have an equal chance of being promoted to a major league. Based on a sample of 784 major league players divided into the veteran ($N = 453$) and nonveteran ($N = 331$) categories, they found that position by position the mean lifetime average of the blacks exceeded that of the whites by from 1 to 32 points, whereas black pitchers won a mean number of 10.2 games compared to 7.5 games for white pitchers. They concluded that on the average a black player must be better than a white player if he is to have an equal chance of moving into the major leagues.

Smith and Grindstaff (1970), on the basis of interviews with 5 black and 11 white players in the Canadian Football League, reported that 6 of the white players and all 5 of the black players unequivocally felt that the black player had to be better or exceptional to make the team. Scully (1971), in a comprehensive analysis of discrimination in baseball, concluded that entry barriers appear higher for black infielders and pitchers than for the outfield positions. Furthermore, he suggested that in addition to outperforming whites in order to enter the major leagues, the black ballplayers must outperform whites throughout their careers in order to remain in the major leagues. Johnson and Marple (1973) argued that if discrimination exists in professional basketball, a less productive black player would be dropped from the team earlier than a white player performing at the same level. To test this hypothesis the players were placed in one of three categories: rookies; those with 2 to 4 years experience; and, those with 5 or more years of experience. They found that there was a reduction in the percentage of white players on the teams from 46.5 ($N = 40$) to 37.7% ($N = 58$) between the rookie and the 2-4 year category, whereas for blacks there was an increase from 53.5 ($N = 46$) to 62.% ($N = 96$). They suggested that since more whites were dropped from the team after the "rookie" year, then more less-skilled whites than blacks were being given an opportunity to make the teams initially. They also reported that there was a decrease in the percentage of blacks in the fifth year (53.7%) and suggested that perhaps blacks are dropped from the team earlier than whites. To test this proposition they examined years of experience by race and by points per game and found that among the marginal players who score less than 10 points per game, but are in at least their fifth year, only 42.8% were black. They concluded that black marginal players are less likely to continue to play after 5 years than are white marginal players. This finding may provide some indirect support that a quota system is present and a faster turnover of blacks is required in order to admit black rookies. In addition to the empirical studies just cited, many authors (Boyle, 1963, p. 129; Boulding, 1957; Olsen, 1968; Edwards, 1969; Bouton, 1971; Sample, 1971) have claimed that blacks must be better to be given a chance to play in professional sport organizations.

Yetman and Eitzen (1971, 1972) investigated the extent to which black college basketball players are over-represented in the star category and under-represented in the journeyman category. In their first study (Yetman and Eitzen, 1971) they analyzed the performance of players on 246 integrated NCAA basketball teams in 1970. They found that two-thirds of all black players were members of the starting five as opposed to 44% for the white athletes. These results held regardless of region of the country or size and type of school. The investigators suggested that this finding might be explained in two ways. First, there may be discrimination in recruitment practices (cf. Edwards, 1969, pp. 9-10), and, second, as an alternative explanation, blacks may have different expectations than whites concerning their role in sport. They argued that these expectations may be learned as a result of differential socialization experiences early in life (cf. McPherson, 1971) wherein young black males consciously avoid those positions for which opportunities are (or are believed to be) low. In the second study by Yetman and Eitzen (1972), the historical trend from 1954 to 1970 was examined. They found that blacks were disproportionately under-represented on the second five. For the professional teams, the blacks were slightly over-represented in starting roles, but the dif-

ferences diminished from 1958 to 1970. Johnson and Marple (1973), in a similar analysis with professional basketball, considered the first eight players on the team and noted that approximately 60% of those in the top eight and 52.2% of those in the lower four positions were black.

A further aspect of discrimination which provides an entry barrier was suggested by Pascal and Rapping (1972, pp. 145-147) in their study of professional baseball. Although they did not find a significant within-league variation in the number of blacks on a team, they did find a significant between-league difference. They suggested that the American Baseball League have fewer blacks because they were initially slower to acquire black players, or that each team in the league may hire a minimal number of blacks, equal to the average proportion in the league, in order to remain competitive with the other teams.

Smith and Grindstaff (1970) in their study of the Canadian Football League found that the Eastern Conference teams historically (1954-1969) employed more black players than the Western Conference teams. On the basis of interviews, it was noted that the players felt that the management was a more critical factor than the city in influencing the number of black players on a given team. Nevertheless, the interviews revealed that the West was more conservative and that it was easier for blacks to be assimilated in the larger Eastern cities. The authors concluded that the reason for the differential distribution of blacks was not clear but may have been due to interaction of the attitude's of both the management and the community.

In summary, the anecdotal accounts and the empirical studies suggest that entrance into professional sport may be more difficult for the black athlete since he must be superior to the white athlete in order to make the team. This appears to hold for sport roles where some subjective rating on the part of a coach is involved. For example, in a sport such as track and field where an objective measure of performance is readily available, there may be less discrimination.

Another form of discrimination within the social structure of sport was first noted by Rosenblatt (1967). He observed that the distribution of positions on a team was different for blacks and whites. For example, he noted that despite the fact that there were twice as many pitchers on a team as there were outfielders, there were 3 times as many black outfielders as there were black pitchers. He hypothesized that it is difficult for a black to become a pitcher since it is a decision-making position and it also places him in a face-to-face confrontation (in which he has control) which may stimulate racial tension. On the other hand, when a black plays in the outfield, he is not involved in direct interaction with teammates or opposing white players (cf. Blalock, 1962). Thus, Rosenblatt concluded that blacks appear to be more readily accepted in follower roles than in leadership roles.

Pascal and Rapping (1972) surveyed the *Baseball*

Register for 1968 and found that a high percentage of blacks played in the outfield (53%) and at first base (40%), while a low percentage were pitchers (9%) and catchers (12%). The investigators offered two explanations and a prediction based on these observations. First, they attributed this segregation by playing position to the fact that blacks are excluded from the key positions of pitcher and catcher because they are important decision-making positions and blacks are not to be trusted with this responsibility. A second explanation proposed that the position of pitcher and catcher requires more coaching and minor league experience and, therefore, if white managers and coaches prefer not to interact with blacks, players attempting to play these positions are disadvantaged. This latter suggestion may be a plausible reason why more blacks do not make the major leagues in these positions. However, it cannot be validated until statistics are available indicating the percentage of black pitchers and catchers who play these roles in the youth and minor leagues. Finally, recognizing the importance of role models, they suggested that segregation by position is reinforced as black youths concentrate on positions in which black stars are most visible (cf. McPherson, 1971; Brower, 1972) and therefore blacks will continue to be concentrated in the outfield and at first base.

Scully (1971) hypothesized that skin color was associated with the distribution of blacks by position. He classified the 159 black players into one of five color classifications and found that very light and light-brown blacks were over-represented in the infield and pitching positions, whereas very dark-brown blacks were significantly under-represented. In the same study, Scully (1971) also hypothesized that the exclusion of blacks from coaching and managerial positions was related to geographic origin and playing position. He reported that from 1947 to 1967, 73.5% of the 88 baseball managers came from non-Southern states and nearly 80% were former infielders. However, only 10.3% of the available infield positions in 1969 were filled by blacks.

An alternative explanation for the frequent occupation of specific positions by blacks was offered by Worthy and Markle (1970). Their hypothesis that blacks tend to perform better in reactive activities (i.e., where the individual must respond appropriately to changes in the stimulus situation) than in self-paced activities (i.e., where the individual responds when he chooses to a relatively static or unchanging stimulus) was supported. More specifically, they found that more blacks than whites excelled as hitters (reactive) than as pitchers (self-paced) in baseball, and as field goal scorers than as foul shooters in basketball. The investigators also suggested that such social factors as father deprivation, experiences with coaches, racial differences in preferred activities, and ability to delay gratification (e.g., practicing self-paced activities by oneself) may be related to the type of activity selected for specialization.

Bloomberg (1972) examined the performance levels of professional baseball players in response to the Worthy and Markle (1970) study. He found support for the hypothesis that black hitters excel in the National League but did not find racial differences in the American League. For the self-paced activity, there were no significant differences between black and white pitchers within either league. In a recent study, Jones and Hochner (1973) questioned the assumption of Worthy and Markle (1970) that opportunity and interest is equally distributed across race and that any racial difference in position is due to ability. Because Worthy and Markle did not assess racial differences in performance among the athletes, Jones and Hochner examined statistics for hitting and pitching performance in professional baseball for 1971, and free throw and field goal shooting proficiency in professional basketball for the 1966-1969 seasons. They found that both black pitchers and black hitters showed consistently superior performance and concluded that the selection process for black pitchers is more rigorous than for white pitchers. For basketball there were no racial differences in field goal accuracy but there was a significantly greater free throw accuracy by white players. Thus, the findings are inconsistent. The authors suggested that the reactive, self-paced hypothesis is too simple to account for differences in performance and proposed that personality orientation is an important factor in determining choice of sport as well as the way in which the sport is performed.

In one of the few studies having a theoretical frame of reference, Loy and McElvogue (1970) examined racial segregation in professional baseball and football in 1967 and 1968, respectively. Drawing upon Grusky's (1963) theory of the formal structure of organizations they investigated the relationship between segregation and spatial location in a sport group. In their examination of baseball they defined catchers and infield positions as central positions, the outfield as noncentral. They found that 7 out of 10 white players occupied central positions, whereas only 1 out of 3 blacks were so located. Similar results were obtained when the offensive and defensive positions in the National Football League were dichotomized into central (center, offensive guard, quarterback, linebacker) and noncentral roles (all other positions). Hence, the hypothesis that racial segregation in professional sport is related to centrality was supported. Yetman and Eitzen (1972) indicated that the relationship between centrality and race continued through 1971 in professional football. In addition, they found that the greater the number of years in the league, the higher the proportion of white players in central positions (e.g., for 1 to 3 years, 82% were white; for 4 to 6 years, 90% were white; for 7 to 9 years, 96% were white, and for 10 years or more, 97% were white). Edwards (1973, pp. 209-211), however, argued that centrality is an "incidental factor in the explanation of positional segregation by race in sport." He suggested that central positions have leadership responsibilities and are high in outcome control and therefore blacks are excluded (cf. Blalock, 1962).

The centrality hypothesis may not be tenable for professional basketball or hockey, suggesting that the segregation by playing position hypothesis may be sport-specific. Furthermore, it can be argued that, although there may be clusters of positions that are structurally central, these same positions may not be functionally central with respect to the purpose of the game, namely success. For example, some baseball managers would argue that the key to a team's success is the level of ability "down the middle," that is, in the role of catcher, pitcher, second baseman, and centerfielder. Therefore, it might be fruitful to reanalyze the data in terms of functionally central roles.

In a related study concerning centrality, Smith and Grindstaff (1970) found that in the preceeding 15 years only 11% of the black athletes on Canadian football teams occupied central offensive positions. However, on defense, they found that the black players were not over- or under-represented at any position, central or non-central. This difference between the offensive and defensive teams was accounted for by the fact that each team is allowed 14 imports (non-Canadians) and most teams employ their imports, black and white, on offense. More recently, Ball (1973) compared the data from the Canadian League in 1971 with the Loy and McElvogue data and found that blacks were excluded from central positions in both football leagues. Finally, Yetman and Eitzen (1972) noted that playing in a noncentral position may shorten one's career. They examined the *Football Register* and found that only 5.8% of the black players in the three major black positions (defensive back, running back, and wide receiver) were in professional football for 10 years or more, whereas 10.4% of players listed in the three major white positions (quarterback, center, offensive guard) remained 10 years or more.

Brower (1972) suggested yet another explanation for racial representation in the division of labor in professional football. He argued that the division of labor according to race is based on stereotyped race-linked characteristics held by society with respect to athletic ability. That is, the institutionalized stereotype of blacks becomes a self-fulfilling prophecy whereby there is an absence of blacks in some positions and an over-representation in other positions. Based on a combination of psychological and physical requirements believed necessary for success in certain postions, Brower identified five categories of positions and examined the percentage of blacks and whites occupying each type. He found that "the believed requirements for the playing positions can account for a large part of the ascribed division of labor in professional football" (Brower, 1972, p. 30). In addition, he noted that these steoeotypes interact with the selective selection via role models to account for racial divisions of labor and that, as these change, the racial division of labor may diminish. In a similar study, Williams and Youssef (1973) reported that college football coaches stereotyped football positions and football players by race. Furthermore, they found that a disproportionately high percentage of blacks were assigned to positions that require characteristics considered by coaches to be dominant in black players.

In concluding this section on segregation by playing position, two additional charges of discrimination should be noted. Interviews with black athletes and white coaches (Charnofsky, 1968, p. 45; Olsen, 1968; Smith and Grindstaff, 1970) indicated that a *quota* system restricts the number of blacks on any one college or professional team. A second charge, related to the "be better" theme and the "centrality" hypothesis, is that through the process of "stacking" (blacks are forced to change positions so that they will be placed in competition with another black for one position) only one black gains a position. This policy, if it exists, insures that a white player will not have to compete with a black to win a position on a team and thereby racial conflict within a team will be avoided. To date very little empirical evidence is available to substantiate these charges.

Simon and Carey (1966) reported that they received the continuous "impression" that an athlete senses discrimination to the degree that he is unsuccessful in athletics. However, little empirical evidence is available to support this impression. One approach was the study by Smith and Grindstaff (1970). They reported that the 5 black football players felt that there definitely was a quota system whereby each team limited the number of black players to 4 or 5, especially in Western Canada. Similarly, 6 of the 11 white players felt there was a quota system, 4 felt there wasn't, and 1 said that the quota system applied only to certain teams. With respect to stacking, the perceptions of the black and white players differed. Whereas the majority of the black players reported that there definitely was stacking, especially at offensive back or receiver, only 3 of the 11 white players felt this was a problem for black athletes. Rather, they reported that this practice was more prevalent for American imports whether they were white or black. Smith and Grindstaff (1970) also investigated stacking by comparing training camp with midseason rosters, but they found little evidence to suggest that this phenomenon was a factor in team selection.

Ball (1973) introduced an alternative to the centrality model whereby he divided the tasks of the football organization into primary (doers) and supporting (helpers) positions. Controlling for race, he compared the distribution of Canadians and imports and found that only on defense did the proportion of Canadians exceed that of blacks in primary positions. When Ball utilized the primary-supporting model with the Loy and McElvogue data, the model did not produce the same results since blacks were over-represented in the primary positions on offense.

In summary, although many players perceive both a quota system and the practice of stacking, the evidence is based on limited samples in a few sports. Therefore, future studies should be concerned with a variety of sports and should elicit responses from both successful and unsuccessful black and white college and professional athletes. In addition, coaches and general managers should be interviewed, and samples should account for regional differences.

In view of the brevity of an athletic career, athletes must obtain post-retirement employment. Although a frequent source of employment for many ex-athletes is within the social structure of organized sport (e.g., coaches, managers, or general managers), discrimination has occurred with respect to the desire of blacks to pursue leader, official, and entrepreneurial roles. A number of articles (Fitzgerald, 1960; Boyle, 1963; Rosenblatt, 1967; Olsen, 1968; Brown, 1969) have cited statistics that indicate the relative absence of blacks at the managerial or executive level in college and professional sport. Pascal and Rapping (1972) reported that successful black baseball players are not yet considered qualified for major supervisory positions in organized baseball. This finding is in agreement with the results of a study by Baron (1968) in which it was demonstrated that blacks in nonsport institutions are under-represented in policy-making positions. He also noted that when they do get representation their power is restricted. Similarly, Kraus (1969) found that, although substantial numbers of blacks were employed in leadership positions in public recreation and park programs, few of them held supervisory or administrative positions. In high schools, however, the situation may be improving, especially in the larger urban centers where an increasing number of blacks are occupying the role of head coach for the first time (cf. Jordan, 1971).

In summary, it appears that blacks are over-represented in certain sport roles and that they do experience some discrimination in gaining entry to, and remaining a member of, organized sport systems. However, despite the presence of many explanatory concepts, a definitive explanation for the phenomenon of racial segregation in sport has yet to be presented.

B. Discrimination in the Educational Sector

In addition to statements that involvement in sport facilitates social integration for blacks, it has been claimed that success in sport at the high school level increases the chances of being awarded an athletic scholarship and receiving an "education." A closer analysis, however, reveals that, although athletic prowess may permit a black to receive an athletic scholarship and thereby move into an institution of higher education, it in no way insures that he will be educated or receive a degree. For example, Olsen (1968) cited statistics showing the number of black athletes who failed to graduate. He suggested that this occurs because they lack financial support once their athletic eligibility expires, because they lack credits, or because they do not have a required concentrated area of study.

These statistics indicate that black athletes are exploited within the educational domain. However, since the evidence is based on isolated case studies in the late 1960s, definitive conclusions cannot be drawn. For example, the deprived educational background of the black athlete and the problem of entering into a white middle-class environment (i.e., the university campus) must be considered as one alternative explanation.

Coleman (1966) demonstrated that the quality of elementary and secondary school education received by blacks is inferior to nonblacks. As a result a greater number of potential scholarship athletes may be marginal students and if they are recruited may experience academic problems. The impact of a deprived high school education may also indirectly influence the opportunity for black athletes to receive an athletic grant-in-aid. Yetman and Eitzen (1972) argued that, if academic ability is a significant variable influencing the recruitment of marginal black athletes, the GPA's of second-string black players would be higher than those of first-string blacks. They examined the Grade Point Average (GPA) of blacks on 110 integrated basketball teams, and, although the average of the second-stringers was 0.07 points higher, the difference was not statistically significant. Nevertheless, this is an interesting hypothesis, but a more convincing argument could be made if the high school GPA's were examined.

In addition to being educationally deprived, the black athlete who arrives on the white middle-class campus often experiences "cultural shock," both academically and socially. It has been suggested that having some identify with a team may facilitate the adaptation of black student athletes to a greater extent than black nonathletes who experience the same shock. Some tentative support for this statement can be found in the study by Simon and Carey (1966). They reported that black athletes did not share the same sense of alienation as other campus blacks since they were better integrated into the structure of the university because of their involvement in athletics. Thus, in future studies the academic ability and cultural background of an individual and the admission requirements of a particular institution should be considered prior to citing failure rates as an indication of exploitation and discrimination. For example, Brown (1969) revealed that the overemphasis on sport in some schools may be deleterious to the educational progress of blacks, especially at a segregated school. As an illustration he cited the strike in 1968 at a predominantly black college by athletes who demanded a greater emphasis on education and less emphasis on sport. Thus, future studies should be concerned with the quality of education that athletes, especially blacks, are receiving at both the high school and college level.

A second explanation as to why black athletes fail to graduate may be related to experiences common to all black students; that is, comparable data on black nonathletes is needed to determine whether the failure to graduate is unique to athletes or whether it is related to the early socialization experiences or to the place of education in the value hierarchy of all blacks. A third factor that must be considered is the extent to which white athletes are similarly exploited and fail to graduate. For example, Webb (1969), in an analysis of the relationship between sport and mobility, reported that only 56% of the white athletes and 38% of the black athletes received degrees. Finally, Pascal and Rapping

(1972) found that, although comparable proportions (48% of blacks, 47% of whites) of professional black and white baseball players attended college, only 5% of the black and only 14% of the white players eventually graduated.

A second type of discrimination within the educational sector is related to the right of athletes to select a program of studies. Olsen (1968) reported that this is one of the major grievances of contemporary black college athletes. For example, they are frequently enrolled in physical education programs, regardless of interest or intellectual capabilities, or are placed in classes that are scheduled by the coach in order to avoid conflicts with team practices. This scheduling is often completed with little regard for institutional regulations concerning required courses or the necessity of a major. Again, investigators must consider whether these acts are experienced by just the black athletes or whether it is a problem encountered by all athletes.

In summary, the popular literature suggests that the educational sector exploits the black athlete. However, until empirical studies have been completed controlling for factors such as a deprived high school education and the academic experiences of all black and white athletes and nonathletes, no definitive conclusions should be drawn.

C. Discrimination in the Interpersonal Domain

Although many incidents of discrimination involving black athletes are isolated cases, problems can be identified when recurrences begin to evolve around central themes. For example, Simon and Carey (1966), Charnofsky (1968), Olsen (1968), Alcindor (1969), Edwards (1969), and Smith and Grindstaff (1970) all reported that the social lives of black athletes were regulated by coaches. More specifically, black athletes reported that they were overtly or covertly discouraged from dating white girls on college campuses, that roommates were assigned on the basis of color, that they were prevented from joining fraternities, and that they had difficulty in finding suitable accommodations. However, since the late 1960s there have been relatively few charges of discrimination in the social realm. This does not indicate that discrimination is no longer present but, rather, that it may be less intense. For example, there is an increasing acceptance of inter-racial dating in most regions of the country, and civil rights legislation has resulted in some minimal benefits for blacks with respect to housing.

It has also been alleged that the introduction of black players into professional sport adversely influences attendance. Although there is very little concrete evidence to support or refute this hypothesis, Scully (1971, pp. 21-25) studied the relationship between the race of the starting pitchers and average home attendance in 1967. He found that 1,969 fewer fans attended games that were pitched by blacks and concluded, on the basis of his regression analysis, that fans appear to alter their attendance on the basis of the race of the pitchers. Scully

noted that since black pitchers have better records (2.7 more games won than white pitchers), differences in pitching performance do not account for differences in attendance.

Finally, the incidence and frequency of discrimination in interpersonal relations may be legitimated by institutionalized discrimination within a particular society. For example, the formal and informal norms regarding interpersonal relations with those of another race that are found in apartheid societies has been well documented (Thompson, 1969; Hain, 1971; Cheffers, 1972) and will not be repeated in this chapter. In short, the reader should be aware that the opportunities for social interaction in sport situations varies cross-nationally and regionally for the black athlete according to the prevailing norms within a given society.

D. Discrimination in the Economic Sector

Within sport, it has been alleged that the economic opportunities open to professional athletes are not only a function of ability, but also a function of race. However, an article in *Time* (1970) reported that black athletes, at least those who are highly successful, do not lag behind in salary. They noted that, in the 1970 season, 4 of the 6 baseball players earning over $100,000 were black. A recent empirical study (Pascal and Rapping, 1972) also supports this finding. They found that contrary to popular belief there was no salary discrimination (1968-1969), regardless of position, against black baseball players who had achieved major league status. This conclusion was based on a linear regression model in which the player's salary for the coming season was regressed on his expected ability (based on lifetime batting average, batting average for the previous year, and number of years of experience in the major leagues) and the alternative salary that the player could earn outside baseball. In addition, they reported that, on the average, black salaries were higher than white salaries in the major leagues. They suggested that this occurs for two reasons: (1) major league executives tend to pay players as a function of their demonstrated ability, and (2) baseball appears to restrict major league opportunities to those blacks who are superior to their white counterparts. Thus, they noted "that there seems to occur equal pay for equal work but unequal opportunity for equal ability" (Pascal and Rapping, 1972, p. 149).

Scully (1971) also examined this question. Employing the salary data from the Pascal and Rapping study, he found that blacks earn more, position by position, than whites. However, he also noted that whites earn significantly more than blacks for improving their hitting performance, whereas blacks gain larger salary increments over their playing careers than do white players. He indicated that the salary differentials favoring blacks are due to the equal pay for superior performance theme. For example, based on regression analyses, he stated that to earn $30,000 black outfielders must outperform whites by about 65 points in their slugging average. In summary, by holding performance levels constant, Scully found that there was salary discrimination against blacks since they earn less for equivalent performance. Since Pascal and Rapping and Scully studied only professional baseball, their studies should be duplicated for professional basketball and football and replicated for baseball over a longer temporal period. In addition, both studies should be expanded so that the regression model accounts for total income (salary, endorsements, off-season earnings), thereby clarifying if, and where, black athletes experience discrimination in the financial domain of professional sport.

Similar to contemporary white athletes, the black athlete also seeks to pursue entrepreneurial gains while he is an active player and can capitalize on his achieved prestige from the role of professional athlete. Two additional sources of income include a bonus for signing the initial contract with a team, and remuneration received for endorsing or promoting commercial products. Again, it has been claimed that access to these benefits is highly dependent on the race of the athlete. For example, Boyle (1963, pp. 129-130) reported that black major league baseball players complained about the lack of commercial endorsements and about receiving lower bonuses than whites when they signed their initial contract. Thus, it has been charged that only the few black athletes who are potential stars and are, therefore, highly visible will receive a bonus comparable to that which a white player might receive. Pascal and Rapping (1972, pp. 135-136) found that the difference in the percent of whites and blacks who received large bonuses was substantial and statistically significant prior to 1958 in professional baseball. However, this difference decreased so that by 1965-1967, it was almost totally eliminated. They interpreted the initial differential to be the result of "a combination of information lag and monopolistic practice rather than bigotry, per se" (Pascal and Rapping, 1972, p. 137). Again, this study should be replicated for other professional sports, especially basketball. Similarly, it is argued that only a minority of black athletes are associated with a commercial product, and that those offers they do receive are less lucrative than those received by their white teammates. For example, Pascal and Rapping (1972, p. 148), citing the Equal Employment Opportunity Commission Report of 1968, state that black athletes appeared in only 5% of 351 television commercials associated with New York sport events in the fall of 1966. In a similar analysis, Yetman and Eitzen (1972) found that of the starting players on one professional football team in 1971, 8 of 11 whites and only 2 of 13 blacks appeared in advertising and media program slots. They hypothesized that this difference may be related to the fact that blacks are relegated to noncentral positions. For example, for the seventeen professional football teams which returned data to the investigators in 1971, 75% of all advertising opportunities (television, radio, newspapers) were given to football players who occupied central positions.

Thus, the evidence indicates that some segregation and discrimination is found in sport, both on and off the field. At the present time, however, it is impossible to identify to what extent this is attributable to (1) a conscious or unconscious act by the white sporting establishment; (2) self-inflicted segregation by the black himself through the process of minority group socialization experiences in the early years; or (3) some combination of both of these factors.

VI. Summary and Conclusions

This overview of the popular and empirical literature concerning sport and the black athlete indicates the following:

1. Sport is salient for blacks, especially as participants.
2. Participation in sport does not guarantee access to or permanent membership in the higher strata of the dominant society.
3. Sport as a social institution is not devoid of prejudice, discrimination, and racism.
4. Sport has been utilized, at least for a minority of superior black athletes, to bring about social, economic, and academic gains that are not available in other social institutions.

To conclude, some suggestions are made as to what approaches might be taken in order to justify this phenomenon as a viable research area. First, in view of the fact that very little empirical work concerning the black athlete has appeared recently, social scientists must decide whether the phenomenon is a viable research area and, if so, must decide which issues and hypotheses should be examined. For example, (1) Has the social situation for black athletes, both within and outside sport, improved to the extent that it is no longer a social problem? and (2) Was the interest in this area in the late 1960s merely a passing fad as an area of study and concern for sport sociologists? If the problem is worthy of further study, then frames of reference or perspectives should be established.

The approaches for examining the phenomenon of the black athlete in a basically white institution might include the following: (1) as a social problem associated with a culturally and economically disadvantaged minority group interacting in a dominant culture; (2) as a study of intergroup relations (white "hope" vs. black "hope") or intragroup relations (black-white role relationships in a small group); (3) as a study of social change (the integration of "white" institutions); (4) as a study of social conflict (double standard, opposing interests, and values); (5) as a study of the socialization process of minority groups in their early years, and the desocialization and resocialization process in the later years (e.g., the adaptive patterns of retired black athletes); (6) as a study of the role of blacks within a social institution (varying expectations concerning enactment of roles by blacks and whites); (7) as a study of social disorganization (society's inability to cope with social change); and, (8) as a study of the inequality of economic or educational opportunity (cf. Pascal and Rapping, 1972).

Regardless of the frame of reference, studies should be based on models and theories, should be empirical rather than impressionistic in nature, and should include the construction and testing of theories. With respect to methodology, longitudinal and cross-sectional studies rather than isolated case studies should be initiated, and the multivariate approach should be employed. For example, in order to examine the extent to which the early life and present experiences of black athletes, white athletes, and coaches contribute to discriminatory or racist acts in a sport context, the multivariate path analysis technique (Land, 1969) might be employed. Furthermore, in addition to the problem areas discussed in the present paper, future efforts should be directed toward the consideration of related, but hitherto neglected problems such as (1) the black woman athlete (cf. Hart, 1971, p. 64; Edwards, 1973, pp. 227-234), (2) the participation in, and consumption of sport by blacks who are not elite athletes, and (3) the relationship between sport involvement and community identification by blacks (especially the question as to whether identification varies with the success achieved by community teams).

REFERENCES

1. Abrahams, A. (1952). Race and athletics. *Eugen. Rev.* **44**(Oct.), 143-145.
2. Alcindor, L. (1969). My story. *Sports Illus.* **31**(Oct. 27), 82-98.
3. Babchuk, N., and Thompson, R.V. (1962). The voluntary associations of Negroes. *Amer. Sociol. Rev.* **27**,647-655.
4. Ball, D.W. (1973). Ascription and position: A comparative analysis of "stacking" in professional football. *Can. Rev. Sociol. Anthropol.* **10**(May), 97-113.
5. Baltimore, C.H. (1951). Negro in basketball. *Negro Hist. Bull.* **25**,49-50.
6. Baron, H.M. (1968). Black powerlessness in Chicago. *Trans-Action* **6**(Nov.), 27-33.
7. Berryman, J. (1972). Early Black leadership in collegiate football. *Can. Symp. Hist. Sport Phys. Educ., 2nd, Windsor, Ont.*
8. *Black Sports* (1972). **2**(May/June).
9. Blalock, H.M. (1962). Occupational discrimination: Some empirical propositions. *Social Probl.* **9**,210-247.
10. Blalock, H.M. (1967). "Toward a Theory of Minority Group Relations." Wiley, New York.
11. Bloomberg, M. (1972). Achievement differences between Black and White professional baseball players in 1970. *Percept. Mot. Skills* **34**,269-270.
12. Bontemps, A. (1964). "Famous Negro Athletes." Dodd, Mead, New York.
13. Boulding, D.C. (1957). Participation of the Negro in selected amateur and professional athletics from 1935 to 1955. M.S. Thesis, 174 pp. Univ. of Wisconsin, Madison.
14. Bouton, J. (1971). "Ball Four." Dell, New York.
15. Boyle, R.H. (1963). A minority group—The Negro baseball player. *In* "Sports—Mirror of American Life" (R.H. Boyle, ed.), pp. 100-134. Little, Brown, Boston, Massachusetts.
16. Brower, J.J. (1972). The racial basis of the division of labor among players in the National Football League as a function of racial stereotypes. *Pac. Sociol. Ass. Meet., Portland, Ore.*
17. Brown, R.C. (1969). The Black athlete in perspective. *Annu. Meet. Amer. Coll. Sports Med., Atlanta, Ga.*
18. ———. (1973). The Black gladiator—The *major force* in modern American sport. *Annu. Conf. Nat. Coll. Phys. Educ. Ass. Conv.,* 76th, Pittsburgh, Pa.
19. Carter, M.A. (1970). Black fullback. *Christian Century* **87**(Jan.), 69.
20. Charnofsky, H. (1968). The Major League baseball player: Self-conception versus the popular image. *Int. Rev. Sport Sociol.* **3**,39-55.
21. Cheffers, J. (1972). "A Wilderness of Spite or Rhodesia Demand." Vantage Press. New York.
22. Clement, R.E. (1954). Racial integration in the field of sports. *J. Negro Educ.* **23**,222-230.
23. Clift, V.A. (1950). Recreational and leisure-time problems and needs of Negro children and youth. *J. Negro Educ.* **19**,333-340.
24. Coleman, J.S. (1966). "Equality of Educational Opportunity." U.S. Dep. Health, Educ., Welfare, Washington, D.C.
25. Davie, M.R. (1949). 'Negroes in American Society." McGraw-Hill, New York.
26. Davis, J.P. (1966). The Negro in American sports. *In* "The American Negro Reference Book" (J.P. Davis, ed.), pp. 775-825. Prentice-Hall, Englewood Cliffs, New Jersey.
27. Dodson, D.W. (1954). The integration of Negroes in baseball. *J. Educ. Sociol.* **28**(Oct.), 73-82.
28. Dunlap, H.L. (1951). Games, sports, dancing and other vigorous recreational activities and their function in Samoan culture. *Res. Quart.* **22**,208-311.
29. Edwards, H. (1969). "The Revolt of the Black Athlete." Free Press, New York.
30. ———. (1973). "Sociology of Sport." Dorsey Press, Homewood, Illinois.
31. Eggleston, J. (1965). Secondary schools and Oxbridge blues. *Brit. J. Sociol.* **16**,232-242.
32. Fitzgerald, E. (1960). The Negro in American sport. *Negro Hist. Bull.* **24**,27-31.
33. Fletcher, M.E. (1972). The Black soldier athlete in the United States Army, 1890-1916. *Can. J. Hist. Sport Phys. Educ.* **3**(Dec.), 16-26.
34. Fox, J.R. (1961). Pueblo baseball: A new use for old withcraft. *J. Amer. Folklore* **74**, 9-16.
35. Frazier, E.F. (1957). "Black Bourgeoisie." Free Press, Glencoe, Illinois.
36. Glassford, R.G. (1970). Organization of games and adaptive strategies of the Canadian Eskimo. **In** "The Cross-Cultural Analysis of Sport and Games" (G. Luschen, ed.), pp. 70-84, Stipes Publ., Champaign, Illinois.
37. Govan, M. (1971). The emergence of the Black athlete in America. *Black Scholar* **3**(Nov.), 16-28.
38. Greendorfer, S. (1970). Birthplace of baseball players: City size, state and region. Unpublished paper, Univ. of Wisconsin, Madison.
39. Grusky, O. (1963). The effects of formal structure on managerial recruitment: A study of baseball organization. *Sociometry* **26**, 345-353.
40. Hain, P. (1971). "Don't Play With Apartheid." Allen & Unwin, London.
41. Hart, M. (1971). Sport: Women sit in the back of the bus. *Psychol. Today* **5**(Oct.), 64, 66.
42. Henderson, E.B. (1949). "The Negro in Sports." Associated Publ., Washington, D.C.
43. Henderson, E.B. (1968). "The Black Athlete—Emergence Arrival." Publishers Co., New York.
44. Ibrahim, H. (1968). Prejudice among college athletes. *Res. Quart.* Oct., 556-559.
45. Johnson, N.R., and Marple, D.P. (1973). Racial discrimination in professional basketball: An empirical test. *Sociological Focus* **6**(Fall), 6-18.
46. Jones, J.M., and Hochner, A.R. (1973). Racial differences in sports activities: A look at the self-paced versus reactive hypothesis. *Journal of Personality and Social Psychology* **27**(July), 86-95.
47. Jordan, P. (1971). "Black Coach." Dodd, Mead, New York.

48. Kenyon, G.S. (1968). Sociological considerations. *J. Health, Phys. Educ. Recreation* **39**(Nov.-Dec.), 31-33.

49. Kenyon, G.S., and McPherson, B.D. (1973). Becoming involved in physical activity and sport: A process of socialization. In "Physical Activity: Human Growth and Development" (G.L. Rarick, ed.), Ch. 12, pp. 303-332. Academic Press, New York.

50. Kraus, R. (1969). Race and sports: The challenge to recreation. *J. Health, Phys. Educ. Recreation* **40**(Apr.), 32-34.

51. Land, K.C. (1969). Principles of path analysis. In "Sociological Methodology 1969" (E.F. Borgatta, ed.), Ch. 1, pp. 3-37. Jossey-Bass, San Francisco, California.

52. Lever, J. (1969). Soccer as a Brazilian way of life. *Trans-Action* **7**(Dec.), 36-43.

53. Loy, J.W. (1969). The study of sport and social mobility. In "Aspects of Contemporary Sport Sociology" (G.S. Kenyon, ed.), pp. 101-119. Athletic Inst., Chicago, Illinois.

54. Loy, J.W., and McElvogue, J.F. (1970). Racial segregation in American sport. *Int. Rev. Sport Sociol.* **5**,5-23.

55. McPherson, B.D. (1971). Minority group socialization: An alternative explanation for the segregation by playing position hypothesis. *Int. Symp. Sociol. Sport, 3rd, Waterloo, Ont.*

56. Maher, C. (1968). The Negro athlete in America. *Los Angeles Times* Mar. 24, 26, 27, 28, 29, Sport Sect., Part 3.

57. Mandell, R.D. (1971). "The Nazi Olympics." Macmillan, New York.

58. Olsen, J. (1968). "The Black Athlete—A Shameful Story." Time, New York.

59. Orr, J. (1969). "The Black Athlete: His Story in American History." Lion Press, New York.

60. Pascal, A.H., and Rapping, L.A. (1972). The economics of racial discrimination in organized baseball. In "Racial Discrimination in Economic Life" (A.H. Pascal, ed.), pp. 119-156. Heath, Lexington, Massachusetts.

61. Peterson, R.W. (1970). "Only the Ball Was White." Prentice-Hall, Englewood Cliffs, New Jersey.

62. Petroni, F.A., and Hirsch, E.A. (1970). "Two, Four, Six, Eight, When You Gonna Integrate?" Behavioral Publ., New York.

63. Pooley, J.C. (1972). Ethnic soccer clubs in Milwaukee: A study in assimilation. *In* "Sport in the Socio-Cultural Process" (M. Hart, ed.), pp. 328-345. Brown, Dubuque, Iowa.

64. Quaries, B. (1961). "The Negro in the Making of America." Collier, New York.

65. Riesman, D., and Denny, R. (1951). Football in America: A study in culture diffusion. *Amer. Quart.* **3**,309-319.

66. Roberts, J.M., and Sutton-Smith, B. (1962). Child training and game involvement. *Ethnology* **1**,166-185.

67. Rosenberg, M. (1967). "Occupations and Values." Free Press, Glencoe, Illinois.

68. Rosenblatt, A. (1967). Negroes in baseball: The failure of success. *Trans-Action* **5**(Sept.), 51-53.

69. Sample, J. (1971). "Confessions of a Dirty Ballplayer." Dell Publ., New York.

70. Schafer, W.E. (1968). Athletic success and social mobility. *Annu. Meet. Amer. Ass. Health, Phys. Educ. Recreation, St. Louis, Mo.*

71. Scully, G.W. (1971). The economics of discrimination in professional sports: The case of baseball. *Conf. Gov. Sports Bus., Brooking Inst., Washington, D.C.*

72. Short, J.F., and Tennyson, R.A. (1963). Behavior dimensions of gang delinquency. *Amer. Sociol. Rev.* **28**,411-428.

73. Simon, R.J., and Carey, J.W. (1966). The phantom racist. *Trans-Action* **4**(Nov.) 5-11.

74. Smith, G., and Grindstaff, C.F. (1970). Race and sport in Canada. *Can. Ass. Sport Sci. Meet., Quebec City.*

75. Smith, J.C.((1972). The native American ball games. *In* "Sport in the Socio-Cultural Process" (M. Hart, ed.), pp. 346-358. Brown, Dubuque, Iowa.

76. *Sports Illus.* (1968). In black and white. **28**(Feb. 19), 10.

77. Stoll, C.S., Inbar, M., and Fennessey, J.S. (1968). Socialization and games: An exploratory study of race differences. Rep. No. 31. Cent. for the Study of Social Org. of Sch., Johns Hopkins Univ., Baltimore, Maryland.

78. Thompson, R. (1969). "Race and Sport." Oxford Univ. Press, London, and New York.

79. *Time* (1970). Black America, 1970. Apr. 6, p. 79.

80. Voight, D.Q. (1966). "American Baseball: From Gentleman's Sport to the Commissioner System." Univ. of Oklahoma Press, Norman, Oklahoma.

81. Webb, H. (1969). Reaction to Loy presentation. In "Aspects of Contemporary Sport Sociology" (G.S. Kenyon, ed.), pp. 120-131. Athletic Inst., Chicago, Illinois.

82. Weinberg, S.K., and Arond, H. (1952). The occupational culture of the boxer. *Amer. J. Sociol.* **57**,460-469.

83. White, W. (1951). Time for a progress report. *Saturday Rev.* **34**(Sept. 22), 9-10, 38-41.

84. Whitehead, P.C. (1967). Letter on Rosenblatt's article: Negroes in baseball. *Trans-Action* **5**(Oct.). 63-64.

85. Williams, R.L., and Youssef, Z.I. (1973). Division of labor in college football along racial lines. *Annu. Meet. Amer. Coll. Sports Med., 20th, Seattle, Wash.*

86. Worthy, M., and Markle, A. (1970). Racial differences in reactive versus self-paced sports activities. *J. Pers. Social Psychol.* **16**,439-443.

87. Yetman, N.R., and Eitzen, D.S. (1971). Black athletes on intercollegiate basketball teams: An empirical test of discrimination. **In** "Majority and Minority: The Dynamics of Racial and Ethnic Relations" (N.R. Yetman, ed.), pp. 509-517. Allyn & Bacon, Massachusetts.

88. Yetman, N.R., and Eitzen, D.S. (1972). Black Americans in sports: Unequal opportunity for equal ability. *Civil Rights Dig.* **5** (Aug.), 20-34.

89. Young, A.S. (1963). "Negro Firsts in Sports." Johnson Publ., Chicago, Illinois.

90. Zurcher, L.A., and Meadow, A. (1967). On bullfights and baseball: An example of interaction of social institutions. *Int. J. Comp. Sociol.* **8**,99-117.

NOTES

1. For more specific historical information, see Boulding (1957), Davie (1949), Young (1963), Davis (1966), Henderson (1968), Orr (1969), Peterson (1970), Govan (1971), *Black Sports* (1972), and Brown (1973).

2. For a detailed discussion of how integration was achieved, see Dodson (1954).

3. Henderson (1968) documents the success of blacks in all sports, and *Black Sports* (1972), reports the track and field achievements of black athletes on the U.S. Olympic Team from 1904 to 1968.

THE BLACK ATHLETES
20TH CENTURY GLADIATORS
FOR WHITE AMERICA

Harry Edwards

We have long regarded sport as the perfect embodiment of American ideals. It is the very symbol of free and open competition, discipline, hard work, good character, patriotism, and the Protestant Ethic. In essence, sport in America constitutes a quasireligious institution that reinforces traditional values and perspectives in American life. Although sports have traditionally embodied all of those American ideals, they have been universally considered a realm apart, a component of American life isolated from and immune to, the stresses, strains and incongruities that lace our highly complex social system.

The black athlete's unmasking a few years ago of the problems endemic to sports, therefore, shocked many Americans. At the 1968 Olympics in Mexico City, Tommie Smith and John Carlos raised the clenched fists of black power in protest while on the victory stand. Wayne Collett and Vincent Matthews, at the 1972 Olympics in Munich, stood casually on the victory stand while the national anthem played on international TV, their actions symbolizing the casual attitude of whites towards the needs and desires of blacks in America.

The new turmoil in athletics caught social scientists, in particular, off guard. They had usually assigned sports to the toy department of human affairs, deeming it unworthy of logical, professional inquiry. But this very lack of scientific inquiry into the social dynamics of sports has perhaps nurtured the mythology of egalitarianism planted by propagandists and sports-financed public-relations agencies. As a result many Americans not only believe the mythology but actively defend it.

Blacks are no less taken in by the propaganda, and all too frequently accept white definitions and perspectives of reality. I have long believed that the two major factors contributing to racial inequality in America are white racism on the one hand and a substantial lack of black expertise and serious black analytical perspectives on the other. The black citizen, like his white counterpart, has largely accepted integrated sports as a boon to the development and enfranchisement of black people. Likewise, he has viewed the success of a few black superstars as tangible proof that the American Dream is a reality for the masses of black people. But the acceptance of these perspectives on black involvement in sport has been an act of faith on the part of Afro-Americans.

Over the last two or three decades, black athletes have become increasingly visible on national television. In 1954, the year the National Basketball Association was reorganized, only five percent of the players were black. By 1970, that percentage had jumped to 56 percent. In the National Football League in 1957, the percentage of active black players was 14 percent, and 34 percent in a combined NFL-AFL Superleague by 1971. In professional baseball, the number of black players went from one in 1947 to 36 percent in 1970. By the narrow logic of numbers the gains look impressive. But let us look further. I view the participation of blacks in big-time sport from three perspectives. First, far from being a positive force in the development of the black masses, integrated big-time sport in its present form is perhaps a negative influence. Second, despite black domination of a few "superstar" categories, sport offers little or no opportunity to the masses of black people in terms of social advancement and economic opportunity. And finally, rather than indicating progress toward equality either in the larger society or in the sports world, black domination of some sports indicates a continuation of black oppression in America.

After almost 400 years, America still relegates blacks to the lower socioeconomic echelons. Despite the few highly publicized advances made by some blacks, the masses still live a life of poverty, squalor, and racist degradation. And it is to these blacks that sport tends to have its greatest appeal as a "way out" through participation as either athletes or as sports fans.

The Black Fan. Sports provide the black fan with the illusion of spiritual reinforcement in his own life struggles. This reinforcement comes from the common values that the general society and sports share. In accordance with these values, which place an exaggerated emphasis on individual achievement, each person is presumed to be accountable for his failures and to deserve rewards and status when he succeeds. Yet, in this highly complex society, no individual can hope to control all of the intricate and impersonal relationships that influence his life, even though he adheres to American ideals. Rewards often fall short of expectations, producing personal strain or dissatisfaction in the disappointed striver. If the individual perceives the forces impeding his achievement to be categorical, e.g., based on race rather than merely impersonal, then his dissatisfaction and resultant strain are likely to be even greater.

Social Balm. The circus of sport offers not only social stability but balm for individual stresses and anxieties. The sports fan, for example, finds that the success of his favorite team or athlete reinforces his faith in those values that define established and legitimate means of achievement. He returns from the game to his job or his community reassured that his efforts will eventually be successful. So when he is cheering for his team, he is actually cheering for himself. When he shouts "Kill the umpire!" he is calling for the destruction of all those impersonal forces that have so often hindered his own achievement.

In the case of the black fan, institutionalized racism and discrimination present additional obstacles to personal achievement. The black fan naturally identifies more directly with the black athlete. Given the functions of sport for the fan, the successful black athlete stimulates black people's individual hopes for eventually competing successfully as *equals* in society. A major consequence, however, is that young blacks are encouraged toward attempts at "making it" through athletic participation, rather than through pursuit of other occupations that hold greater potential for meeting the real political and material needs of both themselves and their people. Athletics, then, stifles the pursuit of rational alternatives by black people. For the black masses, struggling for political and social survival, the ideal of individual achievement must appear after 400 years of racist oppression, to be a treadmill and a "con game." So while sport *may* reinforce certain values in white fans, it is unlikely that it has anything more, finally, than a sedative effect on blacks, a soporific that keeps them from overcoming the impediments to black achievement.

There are black superstars in every major sports field who have supposedly "demonstrated" the viability of the American system, but racism and oppression are still the dominant facts of black life. This is as true today as it was when Jack Johnson became the first black heavyweight champion. Yet, this relatively insignificant number of blacks who have managed to achieve some degree of success in sport have also engendered a hope in the potentialities of athletic participation and in traditional American means and values that amounts to no more than spiritual masturbation. This false hope ignores our interests as a people. America is a society in which even the threat of black proximity causes whites to abandon schools and entire neighborhoods, engage in costly court battles, and conspire to circumvent Supreme Court decisions.

Given this attitude, it is perhaps the novocain effect of sport on the black masses that causes this society so often to encourage black participation in sport; it is common for example, to put swimming pools and other athletic facilities in "troubled" black communities before "long hot summers." But the real needs of course, are always jobs, adequate school systems, and political power. And, as the case of Henry Aaron illustrates so well, even black achievement in sport is often met with brutal white castigation when such achievement is seen as threatening some cherished white value, goal, or standard.

Despite its political and spiritual consequences for the black masses, some have argued that sport has the potential of freeing blacks from the ghettos. Indeed, in an article in the June 10, 1973 *Los Angeles Times* entitled "White Man's Games a Path to the Black Man's Salvation," this was precisely the thesis developed. Presented there was a highly exaggerated perspective of a tragic situation. It is true that a handful of blacks have achieved affluence and escaped from the ghettos through sports; but the escape of these few individuals has had a negligible impact on the plight of the black masses. Although such articles promote the illusion of a large number of professional black athletes, there are far fewer blacks playing on professional teams than there would be if racism were not rampant in sport.

Quotas and Stacking. Sports organizations are small societies with definite structures. First, each operates at every level under informal quotas for the number of blacks who will be allowed to make the roster. Second, *stacking* or positional segregation is common in sports that have fixed areas of responsibility, such as baseball and football. Limited at first by a "quota system," blacks as a group then face sharply limited opportunities because only one black athlete can man a "black position" at one time. Were it not for these racist practices, there is a strong likelihood that blacks would hold a majority of *all* positions from coach to rookies.

We must also consider that to the extent that sport provides an escape route from the ghetto at all, it does so only for black *males*. Black female athletes tend to be involved in track and field sports which offer no direct financial rewards. In tennis, golf, and other money-making sports for women, blacks are invisible. And the escape of a few black men does not mean that an equal number of black women will go with them as their wives or girlfriends; consequently there is no guarantee that even a few black women will benefit from the successes achieved by black male professional athletes. Indeed, one of black people's more persistent criticisms of black celebrities, athletes included, is that they often date, marry or associate primarily with whites once they "make it."

For those few athletes who are able to gain access to some financially rewarding sports activity, job security and lucrative "fringe benefits" such as endorsements are practically nonexistent. When Bob Cousy and Bill Russell played for the Boston Celtics, Cousy was requested to be a guest speaker at a social-club banquet for an honorarium of $1,500. Cousy was unable to come, so the club's officials requested Bill Russell—at $500, even though Russell, not Cousy, had been the NBA's most valuable player during the preceding season.

The reputation of sport as a "road of salvation" is based not on evidence but on a few highly publicized "breakthroughs": Jackie Robinson's entrance into baseball, Bill Russell's signing as an NBA player-coach, and the insignificant number of blacks who sign what *appear* to be multimillion dollar contracts are such examples. (Many of these contracts only appear to be multimillion dollar deals because in some cases it is impossible for an athlete to meet all the requirements necessary to obtain the full face value of the contract.)

Racial Superiority. There have been many attempts to explain the phenomenon of apparent black domination in certain sports. Martin Kane, senior editor for *Sports Illustrated* magazine, in a January 1971 article, "An Assessment of 'Black is Best,'" attempted to develop a logical, scientifically based theory that certain racial characteristics found in blacks, but not in whites, cause athletic superiority.

Kane suggests three major determinants of athletic superiority: (1) Race-linked physical and physiological characteristics, (2) Race-linked psychological traits, and (3) Racially specific historical occurrences. His theory suffers from two basic flaws, however; one is his method, and the other is his dependence upon the scientifically debatable assumption of "racial differences" in man and their impact on physical prowess.

Kane's data were not statistically valid. Instead of a random sample of the black American population, his data came from black athletes of proven excellence or from individual and unrelated studies of blacks around the country. To generalize these findings to the whole black population is scientifically dubious.

Kane's assumption of the biological and genetic validity of races of human population poses another problem. He apparently disregards the fact that cultural circumstances, social and political conditions, as well as opportunity, propinquity and convenience determine human breeding populations; similarity in physical characteristics are only one part of the equation. He implies that blacks have bred only among themselves, and that except for an occasional mutation brought on by natural selection, have maintained original genotypical and anatomical traits. This, of course, is nonsense. There are widespread disagreements among biologists and anthropologists concerning the definitions and identifications of the races of man. Virtually every attempt to define specific races or to pose problems within a context that assumes the genetic and biological validity of race has been difficult for the scientist involved to defend. "Race" does have a political and social reality. Racial definitions do constitute a fundamental basis of socioeconomic and political stratification in America and therefore influence the determination of who shall have access to valued goods and services.

Furthermore, scientists have never been successful in deriving consistent patterns or valid relationships between racial heritage and social, intellectual, or physical capabilities. Hence, from the moment Kane bases his theory on the assumption that we possess scientific definitions of race, he is on shaky ground.

Black Physical Traits. If blacks have certain innate physical characteristics that make them superior athletes, one might assume that most black athletes resemble one another. But while attempting to explain the "looseness" of black athletes, one of Kane's resource people inadvertently destroyed this assumption:

"[Lloyd C. 'Bud'] Winter [former coach of a long line of successful black track and field athletes] makes the quite obvious point that black athletes differ from each other physically quite as much as whites do. . . . He notes that Ray Norton, a sprinter, was tall and skinny with scarcely discernible hips, that Bobby Poynter, also a sprinter, was squat and dumpy with a swayback and a big butt, that Dennis Johnson was short and wiry, that

Tommie Smith was tall and wiry, and so on." Furthermore, in comparing the physical characteristics of Kareem Abdul-Jabbar with Elgin Baylor, or Wilt Chamberlain with Al Attles, one sees that Chamberlain and Jabbar have more in common physically with Mel Counts and Hank Finkel, two seven-foot white athletes than with most of their fellow black athletes. Hence, there exist more differences *between* individual members of any one racial group than between any two groups as a whole. Black athletes and the black population do not fit into any artificial racial "average"; but rather they show a wide range of anatomical, physiological and biological features.

Genetic Mix. An exception to his theory forced Kane to make an incredible qualification. A popular opinion among track coaches is that blacks dominate the sports requiring speed and strength (such as sprints), while whites excel at sports requiring endurance (for example, distance runners). In the 1968 Olympics, however, a black Kenyan, Kipchoge Keino, defeated a highly publicized white, Jim Ryun, in distance races, and black Americans John Carlos, Tommie Smith, Lee Evans, and others defeated both whites and black Africans in sprint and dash races in the games. Kane makes the ridiculous assertion that:

"The black Africans on the East Coast—the Ethiopians, Kenyans and others—have a *genetic mix*. Keino (a Kenyan) is a man with black skin and many white features. So is Bikila (an Ethiopian). It is a cliche in American track to say that black runners are good only in the sprints and the shorter runs. . . . This is not true of blacks from East Africa—but the American blacks' ancestors came mostly from the West Coast, where there was little genetic contact from outside. This area of Africa is pretty much isolated by ocean and desert. The American black athlete's breeding is different from that of the East Africans, who often excel at distance running." It is obvious from Kane's theory that West Africa is the wrong side of the track for distance runners.

Heat Dissipation. Kane bases his physiological evidence of black athletic superiority partly on the theory that blacks are more efficient heat dissipators because of body elongation, that is, they sweat more. He agrees with anthropologist Robert M. Malina of the University of Texas, who cites well-known findings which suggest that animals living in hot climates tend to have longer extremities and a lesser body mass in order to dissipate heat. "With their long legs and arms, blacks have a greater surface area from which to dissipate heat through the skin." There is no proof that efficient heat dissipation in humans is related to athletic performance.

Either tall or short individuals may have builds that enable them to function as relatively efficient heat dissipators. The efficiency with which one's body dissipates heat is only incidentally related to height. It is directly related, however, to the ratio of body surface to body mass.

The Pygmy, for example, simply by being small acquires the same surface-to-mass ratio as the Watusi who is elongated in shape. These two groups live less than two and one-half miles apart in the hottest part of equatorial Africa. This fact illustrates, then, that a small white athlete could be as efficient a heat dissipator as an elongated black athlete.

Kane's argument is invalid; it is clear that black athletes of a variety of shapes and sizes have dominated many sports events over white athletes who themselves embodied a variety of shapes and sizes. There are far too many variables that determine athletic excellence to rely upon observable differences in individuals for explanation.

The Happy-Go-Lucky Character. Kane's second explanation for black athletic superiority is based upon what he believes is the black athlete's innate ability to relax under pressure. This is perhaps the most ludicrous and degrading part of his theory. The academic belief in the existence of a racial "personality" was supposedly discarded by scholars decades ago. It appears to persist, however, among certain segments of the American population, coaches and sports reporters in particular. Kane, with some help, recreates a portrait of the black athlete as the happy-go-lucky, casual, what-me-worry Negro made so familiar to Americans by Stepin Fetchit movies. Kane again quotes Winter:

"A limber athlete has body control, and body control is part of skill. It is obvious that many black people have some sort of head-start motor in them, but for now I can only theorize that their great advantage is relaxation under stress. As a class, the black athletes that have trained with me are far ahead of the whites in that one factor—relaxation under pressure. It is their secret."

Two psychologists specializing in athletic research, Bruce C. Ogilvie and Thomas A. Tutko, found evidence that contradicts Winter's statement. Using the 16 Personality Factor Test, which has a high degree of reliability in both crosscultural and simple comparative research, they judged the psychological orientations of successful black and white athletes. The following results emerged.

1. On the IPAT, successful black athletes showed themselves to be considerably more serious, concerned, and "up tight" than their white counterparts as indicated by their relative scores on the item "sober—happy-go-lucky." Blacks had a mean score of 5.1 as compared to a mean score for whites of 5.5.
2. On the IPAT item of "casual—controlled" successful black athletes scored significantly higher than white athletes, indicating a more controlled orientation. Blacks had a mean score of 6.6 as compared with the whites' mean score of 6.2.

Black athletes compete against whites in highly pressurized situations. They realize that there are limited rewards available for everyone, especially for blacks in a racist white society. Furthermore, since many blacks often "go out for" sports to the neglect of their academic responsibilities, losing often means *total* personal

failure. The assertion that black athletes are more "relaxed" than white athletes not only falls by the standard of scientific proof, but is an affront to common sense.

Slavery and Natural Selection. Kane bases the final part of his theory upon racially specific historical occurrences—slavery in particular. Here he enlists the opinions of undoubtedly well-meaning but uninformed and unthinking black athletes to support his opinions. Calvin Hill, a Yale graduate who plays for the Dallas Cowboys:

"I have a theory about why so many pro stars are black. I think it boils down to the survival of the fittest. Think of what the African slaves were forced to endure in this country merely to survive. Well, black athletes are their descendants. They are the offspring of those who are physically and mentally tough enough to survive."

Lee Evans, black Olympian 400-meter and 500-yard dash world record holder:

"We were bred for it. Certainly the black people who survived in the slave ships must have contained a high proportion of the strongest. Then, on the plantations, a strong black man was mated with a strong black woman. We were simply bred for physical qualities."

It is apparent from their remarks that Kane's sources do not fully understand the process of natural selection. "Survival of the fittest," or natural selection, has been less dependent upon strength and physical attributes in mankind than in any other form of animal life. Man's survival has depended instead upon his tremendously developed mental capabilities. Records of life among black slaves on Southern plantations indicate that slaves survived as much because of their shrewdness and thinking abilities as their physical prowess. Since physical and mental abilities are not mutually exclusive, and indeed often go together, it is likely that the black slave population were individuals who had varying mixtures of both mental acuity and physical strength. These diverse traits were probably valuable in aiding slaves to survive the rigorous plantation life.

When speaking of natural selection, once again the issue of racial purity arises. Kane and his informants speak as if blacks in American society have somehow remained "pure" as a racial stock. Although that argument has already been refuted, I should add here that our best sociological and historical knowledge indicates that inbreeding between blacks and other so-called racial groupings in America has been extensive. This was, of course, especially true of blacks and whites during slavery, despite strong pressures against interracial sex between black men and white women. So survival had little to do with natural selection, and the genetic make-up or physical prowess of the original slaves has little to do with determining the athletic excellence of today's black athlete. Kane's theory of natural selection implies that blacks need only exercise their "innate" physical ability to become successful athletes. But there are a great number of psychological, political and racial hurdles to conquer before one becomes a Bill Russell, or a Henry Aaron. So what really determines black athletic superiority is not a genetic heritage but a grim determination to overcome arbitrary and deliberately contrived barriers to black success. Bill Russell once stated that he had to work as hard to achieve his status as the greatest basketball player of the last decade as the president of General Motors had to work to achieve his position. Given the racist character of both American society and American sport, Russell probably had to work *harder*.

Kane in effect tells blacks that they are "natural athletes," and ignores the lifetime of dedication and hard work exacted from them. Perhaps it is coincidental, but Kane's argument allows the racist segments of America to affirm the black athlete's superiority on one hand, and maintain their negative, racist images of black people and black athletes on the other.

Racist Justifications. The notion that blacks are physically superior also helps to justify the practice of stacking. If blacks are physically superior, then whites can monopolize key positions which ostensibly require greater thinking and organizational ability; for example, quarterback, and team captain.

If the black man is an effortless, natural athlete, but the white man must work at mastering the sport, then the white athlete would probably know the intricacies and dynamics of the sport better. This, of course, implies that the white athlete would make a better coach, manager, league commissioner, or even TV or radio sportscaster.

Kane's argument opens the door for the tacit acceptance of the idea that whites are intellectually superior to blacks. By being physically inferior whites lose nothing; *any number of animals are physically superior to whites*. On the other hand, technology has made intellectual capability the highest priced commodity on the market today. If one has the intellectual abilities, physical inferiority matters little. So, if in a fit of black identity or simple stupidity we accept Kane's argument of innate black physical superiority in any realm, we could be inadvertently accepting an ideology that has rationalized the existence of slavery, segregation and general racial oppression.

In conclusion, Kane states:

"Needless to say, not all success of the black man in boxing or in other sports is due to physical characteristics. Motivation is a vital factor . . . but in recent years sports has opened some very special doors. Every male black child, however he might be discouraged from a career with a Wall Street brokerage firm or other occupational choices, knows he has a sporting chance in baseball, football, boxing, basketball or track. The black youngster has something real to aspire to when he picks up a bat or dribbles a basketball. . . ."

A Meaningless Channel. It is unfortunate that in his concluding remarks Kane encourages millions of black America's most aspirant and capable male youth into a highly competitive arena where the odds are prohibitive. To suggest an area where there is room for just so many athletes and even fewer blacks is both ridiculous and shameful. The overwhelming majority are doomed to be shuttled back to the ghetto, either because they were not of black superstar potential, or because they either could not or would not "adjust" to the political and psychological oppression of organized sport.

The real determinant of black superiority in sports lies in this society, which implicitly demands that black youth strive first and foremost to be the world's greatest athletes. It is worthy of note that Kane does not question why black youths cannot join Wall Street brokerage firms, or make other occupational choices.

Black culture, as does the white culture, teaches its members to strive for the most desirable among *achievable* goals. TV has communicated all the ostensible influence, glamour and prosperity of the successful athlete to young, black males. Athletics then appears to be the most achievable goal. In contrast, black role models in high prestige positions outside of the sports realm are all but invisible to young blacks. And a lack of TV exposure is not the only reason; once successful, the black bourgeoisie rarely maintain contact with the black masses. Whites have more visible prestige role models and greater occupational alternatives, and thus can distribute their talents over a broader range of endeavors. Under these circumstances, black athletes naturally predominate.

I am not encouraging black society to completely abandon its involvement in American sport. Too many people have made too many sacrifices in order to open even partially that single avenue of black expression. Aspiring to achieve in sport is as legitimate as aspiring to achieve in medicine, law, or any other area of life. And since black athletes, among all blacks, have most visibly established the unequivocal potential of blacks for excellence, we should not deny the legitimacy of black participation in sport.

Ideally, I would advocate that blacks remain in sport but that *they use their participation to establish values more consistent with the interests of the masses of black people*. The inherent problem in this tactic, however, is arriving at a consensus as to *what* system of values and political perspectives would be most effective in contributing to the solution of black problems.

Stay Involved, but Alert. I advocate that black people strive to understand the political, social and economic realities engendered by black participation in sport. The logical extension of this position is to urge black people to gain whatever utility they can out of sport, once they fully understand its established function in maintaining the status quo. In all probability, an increasing number of blacks would come to applaud and support those black athletes who utilized their positions to protest the condition of blacks in this country. Not since the beginning of black involvement in big-time sport has there been any question as to whether or not blacks should *become* involved in the politics of sport. *Blacks are already involved and have been at least since 1936*. The only question now is whether blacks will choose to participate in a way favorable to their own interests.

Blacks must also initiate deliberate and well-planned steps to stem the black cultural tendency to channel millions of black youth into activities that provide only individual rewards at best, and these to only a few of the thousands who often squander their lives and expend tremendous efforts in pursuit of a tragically unrealistic goal—that of becoming successful 20th-century gladiators in the service of white America.

WHITEY'S SPORT

Jonathan J. Brower

Professional football is a tough game. It takes teamwork to win, and man is accorded status by how he performs rather than by what he is. But a sociologist, looking behind the scenes in National Football League, finds that status comes harder for some people. Especially if they happen to be black.

On a Sunday afternoon in autumn, the game is pure escape. The competition is tough, the rules are strict and a man is judged solely by how well he plays and not by his personal attributes. Sport, we can let ourselves believe, is blissfully immune to the social problems that plague our society. In particular, it's easy to think of it as a showcase of interracial harmony and understanding.

From the distance of the television screen or even the fifty-yard line, it seems to be so. There has been an increasing number of blacks entering professional sports in the past two decades and many have become superstars. Some knowledgeable fans may even argue that the prime mythology of sport and an important part of American folklore is integration and democratization. Sport should serve as a mirror, as it were, of American ideals.

However, I recently completed a two-and-a-half-year study of institutional racism in the National Football League and I found that such notions are a long way from objective reality. Sport is part of the large society; indeed, it is embedded in the society. And while it does reflect its ideals, or at least those of the dominant group, it also carries the stresses and strains of the society. What I discovered was a subtle but pervasive form of racism. It is called culture clash and involves the inappropriateness of the black subculture in the white world of professional football.

Fortunately for the sociologist, the world of professional football is relatively open to view. A wide range of publications is available for analysis. Over the period of the study, I read popular magazines, books, official football publications such as record books and programs and newspaper articles. Several months prior to the football season, each team publishes an annual media guide that gives information on the team's personnel—front office and players—and general team operations. I studied these media guides covering the twelve-year period of 1960-1971.

Interviews with participants in professional sports are usually easy since football people are used to and expect to be interviewed. This makes the sociological investigator a less obtrusive research instrument than he or she would be in many other types of social settings. In the course of the study, I talked to dozens of players, coaches, scouts and owners.

Finally, I was granted permission to study an NFL team during two successive summer training camps in 1970 and 1971. The team, fictitiously called the Jaguars here, had no idea I was studying racism. I felt the topic was too emotionally loaded.

My experiences later bore this out. At dinner one evening a high NFL team management official offered his views of social problems: "All Communists in America should be thrown out of the country," he said. "Any teacher *accused* of Communist affiliations should not be allowed to teach in our schools . . . America has gone downhill ever since World War II when we fought to save the Jews. . . . There are too many intellectuals around today. . . . People like Sirhan Sirhan and Angela Davis shouldn't have trials wasted on them; they're guilty and everybody knows it. . . . Communism and socialism are the same bullshit."

At several points our conversation turned toward blacks in general. Early in the talk he referred to them as "Negroes": as it progressed, and he became more relaxed, he used the term "nigger" several times. He appeared to feel no uneasiness using this derogatory term; apparently it was a natural part of his vocabulary.

I was allowed free range at camp with few restrictions. Although I did not stay overnight, I was a constant

Jonathan J. Brower, Ph.D., is an assistant professor in the sociology department at California State University, Fullerton. He is currently researching adult-child conflict in Little League baseball.

fixture there for much of every day, observing camp life and interviewing—formally and informally—trainers, players, coaches, management and sportswriters.

Racism is a term with many different meanings or focuses. But here I was concerned with certain patterns of behavior the consequences of which maintain and reinforce present inequalities among ethnic groups. It does not matter whether the consequences are intended or not. In fact, the disturbing aspect of institutional racism is that many racist consequences are entirely unintentional.

Football is dominated and controlled by whites. At the professional level, as well as in the high school and collegiate ranks, the game is infused with traditional white middle-class values. It is considered by many self-appointed guardians of the sport to be one of the few stable aspects of a society engulfed in turbulent change. I discovered, moreover, that the people who control professional football spend a great deal of effort seeing that football remains the last bastion of traditional American values.

But more than 30 percent of the professional players today are black and they, like other blacks in the United States, are questioning white ethnocentric assumptions that have racist overtones and implications. And assertive blacks who want equality don't always fit easily into a system of traditional values.

The clash starts early in the recruiting process. The scouting system in professional football is the principal vehicle by which potential players are spotted, evaluated and brought into the league. Once scouts were only interested in the playing ability of the candidates, but in recent years they have also developed a critical eye for the psychological or "adjustment" characteristics of athletes.

Supposedly, a player with the wrong attitude can't be an asset to the team, but determining just what that attitude is can be difficult. *Attitude* is a very general catch-all term meaning just about anything that helps or hinders the performance of the player and his team. And judgment of attitude is not only subjective but is measured against the norms of football and in the light of how a scout or a coach sees his own responsibilities.

One scouting report I saw on a black collegiate running back described in glowing terms his physical prowess. But then it went on to caution that he was "an individualist but worth the risk."

Why should an individualist be evaluated as a risk? The answer seems to be that any player, regardless of race, must be a team player, and in most team sports, individualists and team players are incompatible.

Scouts actually believe in the word *individualist* as they use it, although most of the people in the scouting system are white, with little or no knowledge of the black experience, and their prejudices can color their judgment. In their context, blacks can be either accommodating Negroes or individualists. Thus, the "black individualist" tends to be evaluated more harshly than whites. The black individualist is too uncertain a quantity—a package of unexpected problems, and because his standards are less likely to match those of the white middle class, he is more readily tagged as a "team dissenter."

The coaches, almost exclusively a white group, believe in the traditional social values of football as much if not more than the scouts. While they may not be necessarily antagonistic toward black players, they often work with outmoded definitions and expectations that apply to white players but that are considered racist today.

For example, coaches generally prefer "respectful" players who show the proper deference to their mentors. This rankles many black players who are loath to perform the subservient role and thus perpetuate behavior demanded of blacks throughout the history of the United States. This often causes misunderstandings between blacks, who do not defer in the expected manner, and the coaches.

The coaches' opposition to long-haired athletes is another rule that interferes with black pride. Sociologist Harry Edwards has argued that the long-haired white athlete is seen as a "hippie"—a role that embodies values opposed to the American sports creed of goal-oriented hard work—while the Afro or natural hairdo of blacks labels the wearer a "revolutionary." Whites can more easily slip out of the role of hippie, at least temporarily, than blacks can from the role of revolutionary, especially when a "revolutionary" is a black who is honestly expressing his identity and loyalty to his oppressed people.

The black ghetto subculture is generally misinterpreted, then found offensive to white football personnel. The everyday activities and most commonplace expressions of blacks, such as gait and speech patterns, are often read as both socially offensive and as rebellious behavior. One NFL scout told me that the coaches of the team for which he works interpret the characteristic walk of young men of the black ghetto, observable in many pro black players, as revealing "a chip on their shoulders." Black ghetto speech patterns, they also believe, are indicative of lazy people.

In the Jaguars' training camp, coaches would "over-explain" football techniques and assignments more often to blacks than to whites. In most cases, this was done without malice; the coaches just wanted to be sure all their players understood the assignments. Understandably, perhaps, it grew out of the coaches' own anxiety, since their tenure in the NFL is notoriously shaky.

But, at the same time, it was clear that they perceived the blacks to be intellectually hazy, and a vicious circle developed around the issue. The blacks who received this extra attention often would not respond to the explanations with the normal middle-class cues of head-nodding and "uh-huhs" to show that they understood. Instead, many of them would listen with expressionless face and no outward signs of response. Then the coaches, not certain they had been understood, would reexplain things. The blacks, who may have been stony-faced for other reasons than lack of understanding—such as anger and defiance directed at an all-white coaching staff, grievances against the club for some perceived injustices or the habit of maintaining a "cool" demeanor—became even more unresponsive, since they saw the coaches' overexplanation as a condescending gesture.

I could see subtle reactions to the biracial issue in the Jaguars' training camp. The white players, coaches and management feel liberal if not self-righteous. Coaches, maintaining that they only try to field the best team possible and run a well-disciplined unit, are sometimes quick to insist they are "color-blind."

Management likes to believe it is giving blacks a chance to "better themselves." One man from the front office said, "These guys are getting the chance of a lifetime. If it weren't for pro ball, they'd be poor." In addition to the direct benefits, management argues that the entire black community is gaining pride and a sense of commitment to the American system because blacks have made good in football and, moreover, that these blacks are living proof of the fact that opportunity and open competition flourish in America.

Black players, on the other hand, are becoming aware of the fallacy of this argument. They are conscious of the fact that the great majority of athletic hopefuls don't make the grade and so slip back into the oblivion of the ghetto. Many of the blacks who make it in the league are in a constant state of low-key anger. They feel that white players and management personnel are insensitive to their unique needs and problems. While many of the problems may at times be exaggerated, they are nonetheless real and immediate. And what is significant, of course, is that a group of blacks—well paid and well treated in relation to most blacks in the United States—*believes* these issues to be real.

Cultures clash off the field as well as on. A few sportswriters have noted the informal segregation that exists, but the issue has generally been ignored by the public and most social scientists who claim that sport is a vehicle for integration.

Social psychologists have maintained that when members of various racial groups are in prolonged contact in a variety of contexts and are working for a common goal, race relations will improve to the point where participants will see one another as unique individuals, not representatives of racial categories. I found little to confirm this in the training camp of the Jaguars.

I asked many players—black and white—if they felt that being in professional football had broadened their outlook in certain ways, helping them to get along with people from other regions and of other races and different political persuasions. A white Southerner, in the NFL for several years, expressed not untypical sentiments when he answered my question: "I don't believe that all people are created equal. It's just not possible. I may be wrong, but I don't think blacks are equal to whites. I've never been close with any blacks on the team, although I've been friendly with some. But I just don't think they're as good as whites. Maybe I'm wrong and maybe I'll change my mind some day, but I don't think so. It's the way I've been brought up and it's what I believe." This white player, while never rude to blacks at summer training camp, was always cool and reserved toward his black teammates, although quite the opposite toward his white ones.

The camp was conducted in a quiet college community. The college athletic facilities were used by the team while a privately owned dormitory, located about a mile from the football fields and locker room, housed all the team personnel (players, coaches, management, trainers and doctor) except the one female secretary.

I asked one of the management officials how roommates were assigned. He explained that they were paired up alphabetically, both rookies and veterans. There was, in fact, a good deal of integration in the rookie rooms, but a rookie's presence there is likely to be temporary. Only about five of 25 or 30 rookies will make the team. If a rookie makes it then he ceases to be a rookie after one season of play.

But the veterans, in spite of management's claims, were not assigned alphabetically. If they had been, there would have been nine integrated veteran pairs. In the 1970 and 1971 summer camps I observed, there were only three such pairs.

One of the sportswriters then told me that frequently many veteran players are assigned on the basis of playing position, i.e., complementary positions such as quarterback and receiver. Only six pairs could have been assigned according to position. Obviously, veterans must be assigned roommates on the basis of nonofficial criteria, one of which is race. And since veterans, who have been in the league for a number of years, are accustomed to, and expect, segregated rooms, management finds it more comfortable to go along with the way things are usually done.

These compromises are not made as a result of major policy decisions; rather, given the way organizations work and the way people work and need to get through the day, a pattern develops as the result of seemingly inconsequential daily decisions. But it adds up to the same thing.

In 1970, the veteran room assignments consisted of 12 white, seven black and three integrated pairs. Of the three integrated room assignments, one of the integrated pairs was cut from the team. The consensus around camp was that those two players were not expected to make the team anyway, so it was "safe" to room them together since they would be around for a short time and would help make the team look more integrated than it actually was. The other two pairs of integrated roommates were established stars, all of whom were likely to have publicized who their roommates were. No wonder several black players I talked to were convinced that integration was only a token gesture.

The players would have an hour or more to get ready for practice. Getting ready would not take any one player an hour, but it did take an hour to handle all the players. A team rule requires every player to have his ankles taped. Also, many players would have injuries that also needed taping or medication. Since there were only two trainers to administer to all the athletes, the arrival times at the locker room were staggered.

Most players don't like to wait around for an hour in the locker room. Therefore, those players with little or no seniority had to go first. The rookies were expected to be in the locker room an hour before practice. The veterans came later, reporting according to the length of time they had been playing professional football. Thus, reporting to the locker room fifteen minutes before practice was not only a luxury but also a badge of seniority.

But I saw that black and white veterans with equal seniority didn't report at the same time. Blacks came in earlier than required. I asked a black veteran why this was so. "We can't look too secure," he said. "It's just not expected of blacks to take all the privileges. If we appear too comfortable, the man will come down on us in one way or another."

Even on the field there was a kind of informal segregation. Between the players' arrival and the arrival of the coaches, visiting and talking among the players were, for the most part, on a segregated basis. Usually, players jogging or warming up before practice would do so either by themselves or with other players of the same race.

In the dining commons, there were two types of segregation. The rookies were separated from the veterans, a time-honored professional football tradition; then, within each group there was further segregation along racial lines.

The rookies sat farther from the food, which was served cafeteria style, than the veterans. But the black veterans, it turned out, sat farther from the food than the white veterans. Apart from the random integration of the rookies, there was also a small degree of mixing among the veterans when whites would sit in the black section.

The veterans most likely to be integrated were teammates of many years' standing. But veterans who had been recently acquired from other teams would not enter the few integrated circles. In any case, not too many whites were enthusiastic mixers. Of those who were, most belonged to the Fellowship of Christian Athletes. But even so, many blacks, including even a few who belonged to the FCA, felt that the white FCA members were intent only on demonstrating and proselytizing for their Christian ideology.

The blacks, on the other hand, seldom mixed voluntarily with the whites. For some this was a dilemma. In order to convince coaches and management that they could get along with all types of teammates, they felt obligated to eat with a wide variety of players, but they found it an uncomfortable experience.

One player told me, "After a hard day of practice, I'm tired. I don't feel like expending much energy at dinner. I want to have easy communication. I don't want to have to explain in detail to a white what I can say in a few words to a brother."

Others agreed with this justification, but still there were black players who had grown up in nonghetto middle-class environments where the traditional black-ghetto manner of speaking was seldom if ever used. They appeared articulate and comfortable when talking to whites, but more often than not I found them at mealtime rapping with their black brothers. Said one, "Sure, I can talk like a white guy. But we don't have all that much in common. We can use the same words but still not communicate worth shit."

Once again, a time-honored arrangement that had grown into a structured hierarchy had become institutionalized for some kind of biracial interaction. But on white peoples' terms.

Even during the two free nights each week, blacks and whites went their separate ways to bars, parties or other forms of entertainment. Time off from the training grind would find many more blacks than whites remaining at the dormitory because blacks often felt they had no place to go in a town with few entertainment spots that catered especially to them.

Much of the institutional racism in professional football starts and ends at the top with the owners. Most men who own football teams originally go into the venture to have fun. To mingle with the players and take an active part in dealing with the team's strategy help the owner to enjoy vicariously an identity as an athlete and thus fulfill a lifelong fantasy.

But fun and ego fulfillment, for many owners, cannot be realized by simply owning a team. They are also prudent financial investors, and football teams are expensive toys; the going price for an NFL franchise currently is $20 million and clearly these toys are for the exceedingly wealthy. Most professional athletic team owners are hard workers who also want to see results in terms of financial profit. Given these two factors—fun-and-games and financial profit—it is not hard to understand the impatience of owners with troublemakers.

The owners comprise a small and fairly exclusive sort of club. Not only do their sports endeavors afford them common outlooks and policy standpoints on club ownership matters, but these men usually share many of the same social values. Since they are tuned in on the same wave length, they can readily agree on collective action regarding the operation of the NFL.

In my interviews with professional athletic team owners, I always asked the same question: "What qualities do you like in your players besides actual playing ability?" The answer was always much like the one given by one team owner, who said, "I like good citizens, morally upstanding men." From the interviews, this could be translated to mean that these qualities insured cooperative players who readily accept the authority of the team as it is manifested through actions of the owner, front office and coaches.

One candid owner told me that he and others prefer players "with blond hair and blue eyes." He is by no means a hooded klansman or Southern red-neck; rather, he is a prudent businessman who views the white middle-class standards of America as the appropriate standards for human conduct.

When he admitted this, he paused a moment in the conversation and gave a nervous, quiet laugh, then went on to explain his reasons, implying that he was not personally negative towards black people. There were two points, he said. First, from an economic point of view, white players are desirable because white fans identify with them more readily than with blacks, and most paying customers are white.

Secondly, there are fewer problems with whites since blacks today have chips on their shoulders. He felt the mistreatment and discrimination by management that some blacks claim to exist were really imaginary. This incorrect perception, he maintained, disrupts the effective functioning of a team during athletic competition.

Owners, then, want cooperative players who conform to the accepted, dominant-group ideal standards of the white middle class. As a cohesive collective, they keep in touch about troublesome players. This is not to say that owners are seething with paranoia, obsessed with staying on top of the latest scuttlebutt concerning "coach baiters" or "locker-room menaces." They don't need to be. The front-office management, coaches and scouts are well aware of the potential power of the owners.

Why can't blacks do something about it within the system? One of the answers is that these forms of racism are usually apparent only to the blacks. The discrimination and relative deprivation of black players in comparison to their white counterparts are often so subtle they cannot even be articulated. And white players feel they are accommodating themselves to the needs of the blacks, and usually believe they are doing everything possible to create harmony within the team. When the occasional charge of racial discrimination is brought into the open, white owners, coaches and players are usually genuinely dumbfounded.

Procedures for redressing grievances or hearing appeals are rigged, and blacks are particularly affected. Players see no point in taking their complaints to the NFL commissioner, since he is paid by the owners; hence, in the player's eyes, he cannot be impartial.

Furthermore, football players have an average career span of only 4.6 years, so they cannot afford to wait out the several years it takes for a grievance to go through the channels of the National Labor Relations Board. Under this board's current rules, a player filing a grievance must win his case at several different levels before going to court. "If you want to play ball," said one player representative resignedly, "you can't go through all the rigamarole."

The channels—such as they are—discourage reform. The white world of professional football is fairly new to blacks, who are aware of and encounter in it the problems that are uniquely theirs in any white institution. What they find is that avenues of due process lead nowhere. The dead ends occur because the methods for rectifying blacks' grievances are under the control of the team owners—and their employee, the commissioner. Thus, the players, required to work through the power structure of professional football, have little hope for redressing wrongs, and redressing racist practices is even more difficult.

Equally significant is the fact that for the most part black players will not speak out publicly about such grievances. White players may complain about injustice, but a black player who may complain about the same injustice runs the risk of being labeled a "troublemaker." And the black player who steps out of his accepted role too often or too blatantly will either be traded to another team or blackballed from football completely.

More than that, the black football player wants to succeed; hence, he is concerned about himself as a professional athlete as well as a black man. Most blacks are willing to tolerate a good deal of racial unpleasantness since salaries in professional football are considerably higher than most players, black or white, could earn in any other work they are qualified to do. And when their playing careers are over, other lucrative occupations may be opened to them as a result of the status as a former professional athlete.

Meanwhile, the tensions continue. Many of the whites sense the resentment but they cannot understand the smoldering, poorly concealed anger of these "privileged" blacks. Blacks, on the other hand, are impatient with and frustrated by the white football establishment. Meanwhile, the patterns of institutional racism persist. And so do the myths and folklore of sport.

THE SEGREGATION BY PLAYING POSITION HYPOTHESIS IN SPORT:
AN ALTERNATIVE EXPLANATION[1]

Barry D. McPherson

In recent years social scientists and journalists have increasingly considered discrimination in sport to be a problem worthy of investigation.[2] As a result of this interest, unequal opportunity in the assignment to playing positions has been identified as one form of discrimination within the sport milieu. To date this discrimination has been attributed to subtle or overt discrimination by whites in decision-making roles, to stereotyping[3] or to the degree of relative outcome control or leadership responsibilities associated with the various sport roles.[4] That is, individuals are excluded from occupying specific roles on arbitrary grounds. This paper suggests that involvement in specific sport roles by members of minority groups may be self-induced, rather than due to overt or subtle discrimination by white leaders within the sport system.

Segregation by Playing Position

In addition to journalistic accounts which have documented the percentage of Afro-Americans occupying specific positions on sport teams, recent empirical studies have attempted to explain this phenomenon.

Rosenblatt[5] hypothesized that it is difficult for a black to be a pitcher because it is a decision-making position. He also suggested that by occupying the role of pitcher, a black is placed in a face-to-face confrontation (in which he has control) with whites, thus creating a situation wherein racial conflict could be initiated. Similarly, he stated that when a black occupies a position in the outfield he does not interact directly with white teammates or opponents. Rosenblatt concluded that blacks are forced to occupy follower rather than leadership roles within organized sport.

Loy and McElvogue,[6] drawing upon Grusky's[7] theory of the formal structure of organizations, generated the proposition that discrimination is positively related to centrality. In their investigation of baseball they classified outfield positions as non-central and found that blacks occupied these positions to a greater extent. Similar results were noted when the offensive and defensive positions in professional football were dichotomized into central and non-central roles.[8] Thus, they concluded that racial segregation in professional sport is positively related to centrality.

Based on a survey of the 1968 Baseball Register, Pascal and Rapping[9] found that a high percentage of blacks were outfielders (53 percent) and first basemen (40 percent), while a low percentage were pitchers (9 percent) and catchers (12 percent). They attributed this segregation by playing position to the fact that blacks are excluded from the key decision-making positions of pitcher and catcher because blacks cannot be trusted

with this responsibility.[10] A second explanation argued that pitchers and catchers require more coaching and minor league experience, and therefore, if managers and coaches prefer not to interact with blacks, players attempting to play these positions are at a disadvantage. A final explanation by Pascal and Rapping recognized the importance of role models. They suggested that segregation by position is reinforced as black youths concentrate on positions in which black stars are most visible. More recently, Edwards[11] argued that blacks are excluded from positions where leadership and outcome control role responsibilities are attached to a specific sport position, while Brower[12] reported that blacks are found in specific positions because of stereotypes held by themselves and white decision-makers.

In summary, although it appears that Afro-Americans are underrepresented in certain sport positions, a definitive explanation for this phenomenon has yet to be derived. In the following section it is argued that involvement in sport by members of minority groups may be accounted for by differential socialization experiences in early life, and that the learning and subsequent occupation of specific sport roles may result from self-induced imitative learning, rather than from overt or subtle discrimination by members of the majority group in the sport system.

Socialization of the Black into a Sport Role

The socialization process for individuals in minority groups appears to have a differential pattern and outcome. That is, differences in socializing agents, social structure, and group-influenced personal traits and expectations exist and should be considered in any attempt to describe and explain black involvement in white social institutions such as sport. With their entrance into amateur and professional athletics, blacks were extremely successful in a wide variety of sports, especially baseball, basketball, boxing, football, and track and field. In attempting to account for this supremacy, it was frequently argued that the black had a superior genetic and physiological make-up which suited him for hard physical work, and therefore sport. Anthropologists, physical educators, and psychologists, who compared blacks and whites on anthropometric and motor performance measures, generally concluded that there are few, if any, physical differences which could account for this supremacy. Alternatively, investigators have suggested that the success of the black in athletic competition is related to either environmental forces,[13] cultural

From *Social Science Quarterly*, 55 (March, 1975), pp. 960-966.

influences,[14] or sociological and psychological differences.[15] Therefore, in an attempt to explain how blacks become involved in specific sport roles, the following factors are utilized in a conceptual framework: the social situation, the personal attributes of the socializee, and the role of significant others.

Social Situation. The social environment in which the black is socialized exerts a profound influence on his life-style, including his recreational pursuits. Davis[16] suggested that the majority of blacks are forced to develop their athletic skill in a sports ghetto. Clift[17] reported that ghetto youth are being deprived of the opportunity to establish worthy leisure habits. In addition, he reported that limited economic resources prohibit certain types of leisure activities, that longer employment hours restrict their ability to engage in leisure-time pursuits because of physical fatigue, and that the ghetto schools are financially burdened to the extent that they are unable to provide for the formation of desirable leisure-time attitudes, interests, and behavioral patterns. Kraus[18] found that black neighborhoods possessed the oldest, most limited and least adequate facilities in the communities studied. He also reported that when blacks entered the school or park recreational programs, a substantial number of whites withdrew. Thus prejudice within the social situation appears to influence black involvement in sport. Despite being economically disadvantaged the black does learn to participate and attain success in a variety of sport roles. For example, Brown[19] drew a parallel between the elite Jewish basketball players of the 1920's and 1930's and the elite black basketball players of today—both came from a ghetto where basketball courts and nets were the most accessible sport facility. In summary, it appears that the availability of facilities, leadership, and organized programs in the social milieu influences the extent to which blacks become involved in sport.

Personal Attributes. The personal attributes of black youth also contribute to the learning of sport roles. Stoll, Inbar and Fennessey[20] investigated the role of play and games in the socialization process and found that sports are played by black students who hold attitudes conducive to achievement, yet who are uninterested in school; whereas white students who participate in sport are very interested in school. The investigators suggested that the frequent participation in sport and individual games exhibited by blacks is related to a feeling that one can learn and succeed in at least one domain. In an attempt to account for the differences between races, they suggested that there is a differential selection process into the same game by race. They found that blacks who frequently participated in sport had higher achievement scores than infrequent players. Similarly, Rosenblatt[21] found that compared to white adolescents, blacks assigned greater esteem to a sport career and thus a larger proportion had aspirations to become professional athletes. In addition, he suggested that the black considers success in sport more within his grasp than careers which require years of academic training.

Closely allied with achievement is the attainment of status. Henderson[22] stated that being an athlete gives black youth a status they might not otherwise attain. In a study of black involvement in voluntary associations, Babchuk and Thompson[23] noted that blacks were more active in voluntary associations because they were not permitted to be active in other facets of society. In summary, it appears that black youth may have different values and different achievement motivation with respect to involvement in sport. Thus, personal attributes may also account for differential socialization into sport involvement.

Significant Others. If a novice is to learn a sport role then significant others who enact these roles must be available. Thus, a socializee must have the opportunity to observe a member of the family, a peer, or a professional athlete enacting the role. For example, Loy[24] suggested that there is much identification or mimicry associated with sport by some economic or social classes, and that generally the lower economic groups tend to indulge in hero worship and ethnic identification with athletes from their own group. Similarly, Henderson[25] stated that blacks usually identify with entertainers and athletes. Frazier[26] reported that black athletes have become symbols of achievement and symbols of black participation in a white world. This has occurred to such an extent that black youths may be segregating themselves into specific sport roles because they concentrate on positions in which black stars are most notable.[27] Similarly, Davis[28] suggested that one reason, in addition to lack of facilities, that there have been few black golfers, tennis players or swimmers is that there has been no tradition of successful black role models.

Weinberg and Arond[29] also supported this view when they reported that successful amateur and professional boxers serve as highly visible role models for lower-class males, especially urban blacks. They found that most boxers seem to have been influenced by a boxer in the neighborhood or by a member of the family. On the other hand, Brown[30] suggested that teachers and coaches often discourage black youth from participating in such activities as golf, tennis and swimming in order to prevent later frustration and embarrassment. Finally, Boyle[31] reported that most major league teams have unofficial black leaders who socialize black rookies into the major leagues with respect to acceptable behavior on and off the field.

In summary, an individual's aspirations and behavior are greatly influenced by the achievements of visible role models. For the black male, the most visible black role models are successful professional athletes. Therefore, even though it is unrealistic to place such emphasis on the attainment of a professional sport role, the role attractiveness, plus the lack of black high-level achievers in other domains, leads to imitation of black professional athletes. More specifically, since success increases visibility, the greater the success achieved by an individual occupying a specific role (e.g., pitcher), the greater the exposure and the greater the imitation of this role by novices. Therefore, it is argued that black youth, who are in the early stages of sport socialization, will seek to enact the specific role played by blacks who currently have attained a high level of achievement. For example, it is hypothesized that the recent success of black pitchers and quarterbacks will result, within the next two decades, in an increasing number of blacks in these positions at all levels of competition.

The following system of propositions may be useful in explaining why blacks are overrepresented in specific sport roles:

1. The lower the socioeconomic status, the greater the identification with athletes from their own ethnic or racial group.
2. The greater the success achieved by the occupant of a sport role, the greater the exposure in the mass media.
3. The greater the exposure, the greater the role attractiveness.
4. The greater the role attractiveness, the greater the imitation of the role by novices.

Although empirical support for these hypotheses is not available at the present time, by way of retrospect it is noted that the first black baseball players to enter the major leagues played first base and in the outfield. At the present time, blacks are overrepresented at these positions. Similarly, in football the first positions to be occupied by blacks were offensive and defensive backs; today, blacks are overrepresented in these positions. Finally, until empirical support indicating the number of blacks who receive negative sanctions for attempting to play a specific sport role in sandlot, high school, or college leagues is available, there is little evidence to support the segregation by playing position hypothesis.

Socialization into the Role of Olympic Track and Field Athlete

In order to provide some support for the hypothesis that members of minority groups are differentially socialized into sport roles, interpretations based on an examination of the frequency distributions of data collected in 1968 are presented.[32] On August, 1968, questionnaires were completed by 96 white athletes and 17 black athletes who were competing in the Olympic Track and Field trials at Lake Tahoe.[33] The basic differences between the two groups with respect to the socialization process are presented below.

Significant Others. It was noted that compared to white athletes, the black athletes: (a) before high school, received more encouragement (positive sanctions) from the mother than the father, thereby suggesting that matriarchal domination is present; (b) before high school, considered their peers to be most influential as role models; (c) in high school, received the most encouragement to participate in sport from track coaches and peers; (d) more frequently reported that they had an

idol in high school; and that the idol was a successful track and field athlete (100 percent of the blacks indicated that their idol was an athlete, whereas only 81 percent of the whites indicated that their idol was an athlete); and, (e) in college, received the most encouragements from peers, track coaches, and the father.[34]

Thus, different role models may serve as significant others for blacks, and there may be variations in the amount of influence the models exert at various stages in the athlete's career.

Social Situation. An examination of the frequency distributions for the variables related to the social situation suggested that compared to white athletes, the black athletes: (a) came from larger families (4.5 children compared to 2.4 children for whites); (b) were from a lower socioeconomic background (none of the fathers had a college degree whereas 25 percent of the fathers of the white athletes did); (c) were raised in large cities to a greater extent (56 percent to 29 percent); (d) were more involved in other sports before specializing in track and field; (e) were involved in track events at an earlier age (75 percent of the blacks were competing by the end of elementary school whereas only 25 percent of the whites were competing at this time); and, (f) developed their first interest in track in the neighborhood and home, rather than in the school as the white athletes had.

Thus, it is suggested that a different opportunity structure and a different social milieu may account for an earlier involvement in sport, and for the learning of the specific role of track and field athlete.

Personal Attributes. An examination of the frequency distributions revealed only two major differences between the two groups. First, the black athletes experienced success at an earlier age and, second, they were less religious.

Summary and Conclusions

Although little empirical support is available at this time, it is argued that the opportunity set, the value orientations, and the type of role models present early in life may account for involvement in sport by members of a minority group. More specifically, it is hypothesized that members of a minority group may segregate themselves into specific sport positions due to imitation of members of the minority group who are highly successful in a specific sport role. Until further empirical evidence is presented which indicates that members of minority groups are required by whites to play specific positions in the youth, high school, college and minor professional leagues, the segregation by playing position hypothesis is open to alternative explanations.

NOTES

1. Based on a paper presented at the Third International Symposium on the Sociology of Sport, Waterloo, Ontario, Canada (Aug. 22-28, 1971).

2. See B.D. McPherson, "Minority Group Involvement In Sport: The Black Athlete," in J.H. Wilmore, ed., *Exercise and Sport Sciences Reviews* (New York: Academic Press, 1974), Vol. 2, pp. 71-101.

3. J. Brower, "The Racial Basis of the Division of Labor Among Players in The NFL as a Function of Stereotypes," Paper presented at the Pacific Sociological Association (April, 1972).

4. H. Edwards, *Sociology of Sport* (Homewood, Ill.: The Dorsey Press, 1973).

5. A. Rosenblatt, "Negroes in Baseball: The Failure of Success," *Transaction*, 5 (Sept., 1967), pp. 51-53.

6. J.W. Loy and J.F. McElvogue, "Racial Segregation in American Sport," *International Review of Sport Sociology*, 5 (1970), pp. 5-23.

7. O. Grusky, "The Effects of Formal Structure on Managerial Recruitment," *Sociometry*, 26 (Sept., 1963), pp. 345-353.

8. It should be noted that while there may be clusters of positions which are structurally central, these same positions may not be functionally central in terms of the purpose of the game, namely success. For example, some baseball managers would argue that the key to a team's success is the level of ability "down the middle"—that is, catcher, pitcher, second baseman, and centerfielder. Therefore, it might be worthwhile to re-analyze the data in terms of functionally central roles.

9. A.H. Pascal and L.A. Rapping, "The Economics of Racial Discrimination In Organized Baseball," in A.H. Pascal, ed., *Racial Discrimination in Economic Life* (Lexington, Mass.: D.C. Heath, 1972), pp. 119-156.

10. The validity of this argument is questionable in view of the many outstanding pitchers and catchers who have been highly instrumental in their team's success.

11. Edwards, *Sociology of Sport*.

12. Brower, "The Racial Basis."

13. J.R. Williams and R.B. Scott, "Growth and Development of Negro Infants: Motor Development and Its Relationship to Child Rearing Practices in Two Groups of Negro Infants," *Child Development*, 24 (June, 1953), pp. 103-121.

14. R. Malina, "An Anthropological Perspective of Man in Action," in R.C. Brown and B.J. Cratty, eds., *New Perspectives of Man in Action* (Englewood Cliffs, N.J.: Prentice-Hall, 1969), pp. 147-162.

15. E. Jokl, *Medical Sociology and Cultural Anthropology of Sport and Physical Education* (Springfield: C.C. Thomas, 1964), pp. 65-71.

16. J.P. Davis, "The Negro in American Sports," J.P. Davis, ed., *The American Negro Reference Book*, (Englewood Cliffs, N.J.: Prentice-Hall, 1966), pp. 775-825.

17. V.A. Clift, "Recreational and Leisure-Time Problems and Needs of Negro Children and Youth," *Journal of Negro Education*, 19 (1950), pp. 333-340.

18. R. Kraus, "Race and Sports: The Challenge To Recreation," *J.O.H.P.E.R.*, 40 (April, 1969), pp. 32-34.

19. R.C. Brown, "The Black Athlete in Perspective," Paper presented at the Annual Meeting of the American College of Sports Medicine, Atlanta, Georgia (May 1, 1969).

20. C.S. Stoll; M. Inbar; and J.S. Fennessey, "Socialization and Games: An Exploratory Study of Race Differences," Report No. 31 (Baltimore: Center For The Study of Social Organization of Schools, John Hopkins University, 1968).

21. Rosenblatt, "Negroes in Baseball."

22. E.G. Henderson, *The Black Athlete—Emergence and Arrival* (New York: Publishers Company Inc., 1968).

23. N. Babchuk and R.V. Thompson, "The Voluntary Associations of Negroes," *American Sociological Review*, 27 (Oct., 1962), pp. 647-655.

24. J.W. Loy, "Game Forms, Social Structure, and Anomie," in Brown and Cratty, eds., *New Perspectives of Man in Action*.

25. Henderson, *The Black Athlete—Emergence and Arrival*.

26. E.F. Frazier, *Black Bourgeoisie* (Glencoe, Ill.: The Free Press, 1957).

27. Pascal and Rapping, "The Economics of Racial Discrimination."

28. Davis, "The Negro in American Sports."

29. S.K. Weinberg and H. Arond, "The Occupational Culture of the Boxer," *American Journal of Sociology*, 57 (March, 1952), pp. 460-469.

30. Brown, "The Black Athlete in Perspective."

31. R.H. Boyle, "A Minority Group—The Negro Baseball Player," in *Sport—Mirror of American Life* (Boston: Little, Brown and Company), pp. 100-134.

32. The author is indebted to G.S. Kenyon for permitting access to the data.

33. Forty-seven percent of the black athletes and 27 percent of the white athletes were ultimately selected for the Olympic team.

34. The reinforcement by the father late in the athlete's career may reflect a desire by the father to identify with a successful individual.

DISCUSSION QUESTIONS

A. *Barry McPherson*

1. Briefly describe the history of black involvement in amateur and professional sport in America.

2. How do you explain the fact that the black female athlete is underrepresented in most sports?

3. Give some examples of how blacks have been discriminated against in social institutions other than sport.

4. Summarize, in your own words, what the popular and empirical literature has to say about black involvement in sport.

B. *Harry Edwards*

1. According to Edwards, which two major social factors have contributed to racial inequality in America?

2. In what ways can integrated, big-time sport have a negative influence on the black masses?

3. How does Edwards explain black superiority in certain sports?

4. Can you cite any recent examples in American sport which suggest that the prohibitive "color line" is not as relevant today as the author would lead us to believe?

5. Write a short paragraph comparing racial integration in at least three other American social institutions with racial integration in the sport institution.

C. *Jonathan Brower*

1. Which research methodologies did the author use in gathering the data presented in this paper?

2. What major conclusion did Brower's research suggest?

3. List some cultural values of the white establishment that clash with black cultural values.

4. Compare Brower's findings with the position that Edwards takes in "The Black Athletes 20th Century Gladiators for White America."

E. *Barry McPherson*

1. List at least three reasons why the black social milieu is conducive to socializing black youths into sport.

2. How does the author account for the overrepresentation of blacks in certain sport roles, e.g., defensive halfback?

3. Compare the segregation by playing position hypothesis with McPherson's socialization hypothesis.

4. Can you think of other reasons which may account for the overrepresentation of blacks in certain sports and sport roles?

Unit X

Sex-Role Stereotyping and Sport

Since the advent of the women's liberation movement, the American public has become more conscious of the social inequalities which exist between men and women. Partly as a result of this awareness, many social institutions have been forced to undergo structural change. Social inequalities within the sport institution have, within the past few years also come to the public's attention. The proliferation of writings by numerous sports critics, calling for fundamental changes in the institutional structure of American sport, is ample evidence of the growing awareness of the problem. In fact, there are clear indications from practically every sector of society that the public is no longer willing to accept sexism in sport. At the national level, the Federal Government, in response to mounting pressure passed legislation (Title IX) designed to secure equal rights for female participants in sport. The goal of this unit is to provide the reader with insight into the problem of discrimination in sport, and, to offer several explanations as to why sport, "the last bastion of manhood" is so steadfastly guarded against "infiltration" by the opposite sex.

In the first selection, authors Thomas Boslooper and Marcia Hayes explain why so many women appear nonassertive and submissive in their interaction with men. They suggest that most women play a life-long game, "the femininity game," deliberately underachieving in order to win the love of men. Furthermore, the authors argue that women are socialized into underachieving and noncompetitive behavior patterns which, in turn, makes it extremely difficult for them to compete successfully in sport; since the latter demands an achievement-oriented, competitive orientation, it explains why women until recently have been underrepresented in sport.

Physical educator Judith Zoble discusses, in the second reading, how the family and society play instrumental roles in the development of the female sex role stereotype. The author also explains how stereotyping can hinder the development of an achievement-oriented personality and argues that women can achieve in sport without losing their femininity.

In the next selection, psychiatrist Arnold Beisser examines the role of sport in relation to the male ego. The author argues that sport serves an important function for the male, given that technology has minimized his biological superiority (in terms of strength and endurance) over the female; furthermore, he suggests that sport has become, for males, a substitute for physical labor and a means by which they can continue to assert and reaffirm their "masculinity."

In the last reading, physical educator Marie Hart examines how individuals are stigmatized when they pursue activities which deviate from stereotypical sex roles. This point is made explicit in her discussion of women who choose physical education as a profession, and men who select careers in dance.

CINDERELLA WAS A WINNER

Thomas Boslooper and Marcia Hayes

Just about the most common complaint of talented women . . . is that they *can't finish things*. Partly because finishing implies being judged—but also because finishing things means being grown up. More important, it means possibly succeeding at something. And success, for women, is always partly failure.

Erica Long
Ms.
December 1972

The game women play is men, and perhaps that leaves them free to be less involved with this one.

"Adam Smith"
The Money Game [1]

Most women are losers. Sometimes they lose through lack of opportunity; more often, they lose by choice. Even those who have the odds in their favor in terms of education, money, and intelligence—and who are competing in the most favorable feminist climate the world has seen for some three thousand years—still end up throwing the game. Women don't know how to win or how to compete, and they're programed not to try.

These are meant to be fighting words. For if women are ever to get to a point where they can do something, *really* do something, to change their lives and society, they will have to learn to win and win big. Not in imitation of men, but in full realization of themselves.

A lot has been said and written recently about unreasonable sexual roles, about the arbitrary attitudes that divide masculine and feminine natures into polar opposites, like male and female electrical plugs and outlets. It's now generally acknowledged, in theory if not in practice, that women are men's intellectual equals and deserve the same career opportunities and pay.

But for all the new laws and policies, few women—even when they make it—can stand long in the winner's circle. Women have been conditioned to fear success, and to cop out when it gets too close. The cop-out can be as glamorous as living happily ever after with a prince or an oil tycoon, as sordid as an overdose of Seconal, as selfless as sacrificing personal ambitions to the cause of sisterhood. The first alternative will be applauded, the second pitied, the last scorned. But all are viewed as the natural outcome of feminine ambition—as, in a way, they are.

The big game is fixed. Women who don't take a dive become, in society's eyes, losers in a more basic sense: neuters who have broken the rules on their home playground—the rules of the femininity game.

All women know about this game. At one time or another most have played it. And with the possible exception of lesbians and the most dedicated women's liberationists, most still do. The goal is a man and, traditionally, marriage. The sporting equipment is charm, guile, social shrewdness, clothes, cosmetics—and, underneath it all, one's own physical apparatus (hopefully 36-24-36). No holds are barred. Deception, flattery, and manipulation are all respectable tactics. The competitors are all other eligible women, beginning, in preadolescence, with Mom.

The femininity game meets the two basic requirements of other destructive life games. It is essentially dishonest, having an ulterior motive, and it has a dramatic payoff. [2] But unlike other games classified by transactional analysts (the species of social psychiatrist who first defined life games and now referee them), the femininity game is not entirely voluntary. Women play it because the payoff—love—is too tempting to resist. For love, women are persuaded to smother their identities and their ambitions, channeling all their competitive and aggressive instincts into the game.

At some magical moment, usually determined by adolescent alterations in their bodies, girls are expected to trade in their tennis shoes for glass slippers. Like Cinderella's sisters, they struggle to fit oversized feet into tiny glass shoes. Usually they manage to squeeze them on and totter through a lifetime of discomfort, blaming themselves for the bad fit instead of the capricious cobbler, who had a passion for glass and triple-A size fours.

Only ladies can play the game, and ladies are supposed to be supportive, passive, unaggressive, even frail. The role and the game could be amusing as an occasional charade under soft candlelight. Unfortunately, it's taken very seriously by both sexes. Girls who don't play it will have a rough time with parents, friends, and teachers.

A basic rule of the femininity game is that its contestants must be prepared to lose all the other games. Men don't love women who win. This fact of life was illustrated recently in an episode of the family television series *My World and Welcome to It*. The juvenile star of the show has just finished a chess game with her father, who is accepting defeat less than graciously. Her mother calls her aside for a heart-to-heart chat. "There's a game all women play, dear," she says. "It's called getting married and living happily ever after."

"But I can beat Daddy at chess," says the girl. "You mean I have to let him win?"

"I think," says Mom, "that it would be the feminine thing to do."

Margaret Mead would call it negative reinforcement. Winning games against men elicits such a negative response that girls learn early to lose rather than face rejection—whether from boys and girls their own age, or from fathers.

"The bribe offered to the little girl by the father is love and tenderness," psychiatrist Helene Deutsch has written. "For its sake she renounces any further intensification of her activities, particularly of her aggressions."[3]

Social and parental bribes are not often subtle. At home a girl may be confronted, as was one Michigan girl, with a father who wants to exchange her baseball bat for an electric blender. Or she may beat her father at arm wrestling and be sent to a psychiatrist—which happened to the daughter of a New York YMCA executive. Or, if she goes to a Midwestern sorority-oriented school, she may find, as one student did, that "you can be a sorority girl or a track and field girl. You can't be both."

"When I was about fourteen, I was pressured into giving up sports," says Judy Mage, founder and former president of the New York Social Service Employees' Union and one-time vice-presidential candidate on the Peace and Freedom Party ticket. "I used to play street games with the boys on our block in the Bronx. But as I got older, people would just stop and stare at a girl playing, as if I were a freak. I was getting into liking boys, and wanted to be accepted. One night after a dance I got into a snowball fight with some boys. The girls took me aside later and said 'boys don't like that'. And that's when I gave up."

Betty Friedan has noted that at puberty girls drop special interests and pursue those that will appeal to boys. "Men compete for awards, and we compete for men," said a recent *MS.* editorial.

Having been taught that "winning" means losing love, girls usually find that achievement is accompanied by anxiety. In a study conducted by Matina Horner, now president of Radcliffe College, 65 per cent of a group of women at the University of Michigan expressed anxiety over feminine success figures, equating success with a loss of femininity. At Radcliffe, students were asked to describe a hypothetical student named Anne, who is at the top of her medical school class. Nearly 75 per cent of the group pictured her as unattractive and hard up for dates. When asked what would happen to Anne when she learned about her top standing in the class, one student replied: "Anne will deliberately lower her academic standing during the next term, while she does all she can to subtly help Carl. His grades come up, and Anne soon drops out of medical school. They marry, and he goes on in school while she raises their family."[4]

No comparable study has been done on reactions to successful sportswomen, but one can assume that the negative percentages would be considerably higher.

Physical prowess and the aggressive, competitive instincts that go with it are thought of as exclusively masculine qualities.

"I didn't take physical education in college, even though I love sports," says a girl who was named queen of the Drake Relays, an annual track event in the Midwest. "I was really afraid that I would be associated with the typical physical-education majors, who were definitely mannish."

The result of this kind of pressure is that "as age increases, sports prowess increases in boys but not in girls," says Dr. John Kane of St. Mary's College, London." A girl's performance level is deflected to other, more acceptable behavior during late adolescence." And he adds: "With society's expectations of women, it's not surprising we get the kind of women we're asking for."[5]

Women's attitudes toward competition and success are established early. Infant girls are handled differently from boys—more affectionately, more protectively. And as soon as they learn to walk, girls are *trained* differently. Socioiogists John Roberts and Brian Sutton-Smith confirmed this in a cross-cultural study of 1900 elementary-school children given a variety of psychological tests and interviews. "Boys . . . are given higher achievement training," they concluded, "while girls are given more consistent obedience-and-responsibility training. These differences in socialization correspond to the general differences between adult male and female roles over the world."[6]

It doesn't stop there. Anyone who has snoozed through introductory psych knows about Skinner's boxes and Pavlov's dogs. Behavioral training has to be reinforced to be effective. And in all cultures, games and sport serve this purpose. They are not idle play but life models—dress rehearsals, as it were, for the real thing.

Competitive team sports involving displays of power and physical skill, Roberts and Sutton-Smith found, were game models for youngsters—mostly boys—whose parents encouraged achievement and success.

Games of strategy were found to mirror childhood training in responsibility. For boys, who are trained in social responsibility, strategy games are preparation for gaining a responsible position in life; games like football, which combine strategy and physical skill, are models both for social responsibility and for power.

Finally, games of chance and fortune were the choice of two groups: those children who had been strictly disciplined in obedience (a preference shared in maturity by minority and low-income groups) and girls. Discouraged from initiative and achievement, these children could only dream that their ambitions might some day be realized by chance.

Roberts, Sutton-Smith, and Robert Kozelka followed up this research on children with polls of some 7000 adults who had a variety of occupations and income levels. (The polls were conducted by Minnesota, Gallup, and Roper.) The same game preferences were indicated.

Business executives, politicians, and other men in positions of power, for instance, overwhelmingly favored games that combined strategy and physical skill. Those in professional occupations—accountants, for instance—preferred games of strategy, like poker. Men in blue-collar jobs enjoyed games of pure physical skill, such as bowling, while women (and members of ghetto-ized minority groups) showed an overwhelming preference for games of pure chance, or those combining strategy and chance.

It would appear then that the battle really *was* won on the playing fields of Eton. Boys train for success and power through competitive games and sports. Feminine skills and wiles are honed at the bridge table, the bingo board, and the lottery ticket window, perfected in the femininity game.

This same group of sociologists found that real-life stituations have equivalents or parallels not only in games and sport but in myths. Fairy tales and other stories written to formula are really literary games which can be scored in terms of winners and losers. Ideally, they provide a way for children to experiment with winning and losing in symbolic situations.

"Desiring to beat opponents but frightened to lose," say Roberts, Sutton-Smith, and Kozelka, "the child is motivated . . . to deal with his conflict in more manageable fashion. He is attracted to a variety of expressive models. Some of these may be as vicarious as folk tales, comics, and television, and may suggest that the small participant can win . . . or that the central figure may have powers to overcome insuperable odds (Superman) . . . . Through these [play] models, society tries to provide a form of buffered learning, through which the child can make . . . step-by-step progress toward adult behavior."[7]

Boys have Superman and Jack the Giant Killer; girls have Cinderella—the beautiful, unassuming, supportive drudge whose lucky number is written on the prince's shoebox. Cinderella was obviously a winner and the wicked stepsisters losers in what is essentially a vicarious game of chance. This theme—a literary form of the femininity game—pits feminine woman against unfeminine shrew, bitch, or witch. The payoff is the prince, and usually princely sums of money as well. A well-known variation is the tomboy-turned-lady plot (*Annie Get Your Gun, The Taming of the Shrew*), a sort of double solitaire in which both women and men win by playing their respective roles to the hilt.

Because the femininity game combines strategy and chance, it is an attractive alternative to real life, one which mirrors early training and offers a strong incentive—love—as reward for conforming to a stereotype. The game is self-perpetuating because the payoff depends on masking real identity. Players know they are loved not for themselves but for their roles, and few have the self-confidence necessary to break away from the game.

Another sociologist, Roger Caillois, would classify the femininity game as mimicry. "Every game [involving mimicry] presupposes the temporary acceptance, if not of an illusion . . . at least of a closed, conventional and

in certain respects, ficitious, universe," he has written. "The subject plays at believing, at pretending to himself or at making others believe that he is someone other than he is; he temporarily forgets, disguises, strips his own personality in order to be another."[8]

Faced with a conflict between what she is and what she is expected to be, an ambitious, competitive, athletic girl often responds by becoming defensively aggressive and masculine in attitude. Resenting her restrictive role but lacking the self-confidence and initiative to create something else, she becomes a hostile mimic of the only success models around: men.

Occasionally, given parental support or outside encouragement, she may create a new, successful role for herself. Unfortunately, unless her mother has been an athlete or a career woman, she will find few feminine success models to imitate. At the 1972 Penn State Conference on Women and Sport, a study of elementary school students was cited in which boys listed 150 life roles they wanted to imitate. Girls could think of only 25.[9]

Most women, of course, neither rebel nor create. They play the game—sometimes pretending, sometimes even believing themselves to be something they're not. And for centuries, the game and the role requirements have been an effective way to keep women insulated from life.

Women, conditioned to the femininity game from infancy, are expected to play for a lifetime. Society thus dooms them to perpetual childhood, playing adult as they once played house as children, dependent on husbands as they were once dependent on parents, chastised for showing initiative and independence.

Full-time gameswomen will find all sorts of subsidiary contests to occupy them after the big prize has been won at the wedding: New House, Expectant Mother, Hostess—and, more and more often, Divorce and Remarry, when the original payoff palls.

The game also creates a masculinity trap for men, who feel threatened when their wives take over roles they are expected to perform. A man's independence often hinges on his wife's dependence. "When a man is thought superior because he is a man," Florida Scott-Maxwell has written, "then woman is crippled by the inferiority she sees in him."

A woman sufficiently attractive and talented may decide to play both sides of the fence, using the game as an entree to the career world. Women have often been criticized for this, for using feminine wiles to gain power. But these tactics are the only ones most women know. Their equipment is looks and charm, which tend to erode with age, so they play the game as hard as they can in the limited time available. Their power base is men. Their opponents, unfortunately, are other women.

Women who play the game successfully find, when the crow's feet begin to track the corners of their eyes, that it's a losing proposition. At forty-five or fifty, after decades of dedication to beauty and passivity, they suddenly find themselves out of the competition, with no identity or purpose to fall back on. As Freud once put it, "The difficult development which leads to femininity [seems to] exhaust all the possibilities of the individual."[10] Freud should know. He wrote part of the script.

The physical requirements of the femininity game encourage a neurotic preoccupation with physical appearance. Women are usually self-conscious rather than proud of their bodies, spending an excessive amount of time trying to improve their looks. Because men are the payoff, players tend to evaluate themselves and other women through a man's eyes. The seductively clad girls on the cover of *Cosmopolitan* and other women's magazines are models that women will presumably envy and try to emulate. When women meet for the first time, they size each other up in terms of attractiveness—not to each other, but to men.

This perspective also leads women to think of themselves and each other as objects, both to envy other women for qualities they lack and to despise them, as they often despise themselves, for the role they are playing. Because the financial and personal destiny of players so often rests on the payoff, one can expect to find jealousy and disloyalty affecting adult feminine friendships—attitudes often carried into the career world.

Women aren't *born* losers. They're brainwashed. They don't know how to win because they've been conned and coerced from infancy into believing they shouldn't try. Except for fashionable differences in dimension—from the Rubens model to Twiggy—the physical image of woman has remained the same for thousands of years. Women have succeeded in liberating their intellects, but their bodies are still in corsets. They still think of themselves as passive, nonaggressive, and supportive. And that's why, no matter how intellectually or sexually liberated they are, women continue to lose.

NOTES

1. "Adam Smith," *The Money Game*, New York, Dell, p. 106.
2. The criteria used to define life games by Eric Berne in *Games People Play*.
3. Helene Deutsch, *The Psychology of Women*, Vol. 1, p. 251.
4. "Radcliffe's President Matina Horner," *New York Times Magazine*, January 14, 1973. Also "Femininity and Successful Achievement," a research study conducted at the University of Michigan, quoted in *Parade*, July 9, 1972.
5. Dr. John Kane. From authors' notes at Penn State Conference on Women and Sport, August 1972.
6. John M. Roberts and Brian Sutton-Smith, "Child Training and Game Involvement," *Sport, Culture and Society*, p. 126.
7. Brian Sutton-Smith with John M. Roberts and Robert Kozelka, "Game Involvement in Adults," *Sport, Culture and Society*, p. 253.
8. Roger Caillois, "The Structure and Classification of Games," *Sport, Culture and Society*, p. 49.
9. From authors notes at Penn State Conference on Women and Sport, August 1972.
10. Sigmund Freud, *New Introductory Lectures in Psychoanalysis*, p. 184.

FEMININITY AND ACHIEVEMENT IN SPORTS

Judith E. Zoble

One day this summer, I turned on the radio in the middle of a Paul Harvey news report which I will never forget. A town was running the traditional soap box derby and at the start were scores of little boys and one little girl. They were off. At the finish, sliding in ahead of all the others, was the little girl. When presented with her trophy, she sobbed, "I didn't mean to win." Why?! How does one *race* without meaning to win? But, we must give her some credit; most of her sisters would not have entered the race in the first place.

The purpose of this paper is to review with you the general female non-achievement syndrome in sports which this incident represents. The final aim is to see how the factors in the female personality and feminine role might affect sports participation and achievement. There is not much that we physical educators and coaches can do about basic gender identity, except, perhaps, to understand it. For this identity has been developed long before the female would have the opportunity to achieve under us in sport. But, the way in which the female interprets her identity will affect her ability to achieve. Thus, I feel that there are definite concepts that we can gain about the roles a female can play which can help her integrate her different activities into a more enriching life. This understanding could aid us as coaches in developing our own philosophy of encouragement and interaction with our players.

Woman's achievement has been hampered in sports as it has been in other non-domestic endeavors: it is the female entrance into a culturally male activity. This has imposed barriers from without, as well as within, the female psyche itself.

Lardner (1972) notes that the area of sports has always been special to the male *machismo*. Playing sports, he notes, originally was a peacetime exercise to test courage and indifference to pain. Holliman (1969)

Judith Zoble, "Femininity and Achievement in Sports" in Harris, Dorothy V. (ed.), *Women and Sport: A National Research Conference*, The Pennsylvania State University, (Penn State HPER Series No. 2), pp. 203-224.

notes distinctly different recreational roles of men and women in Colonial America: men were the athletes and foxhunters; women were the seamstresses.

A separation of activities for men and for women has continued. Metheny (1965, p. 49-52) has classified sports according to their acceptability for women from data on attitudes expressed by American college women. Those which were acceptable involve projecting the body through space in aesthetically pleasing patterns, using force through a light implement, or overcoming the resistance of a light object with skill and manipulation. Unacceptable sports involve body contact, application of force to a heavy object, and projecting the body through space over long distances. Studies by Harres (1968), Park (1955), and Sherriff (1971) indicate that women prefer individual sports to team sports. About half of the teenage girls in the sample to which Sherriff refers felt that participation in intense competitive programs led to the development of "masculine" mannerisms and attitudes. However, half of the collegiate golfers and tennis players in Malumphy's study (1970) actually felt that their feminine image was enhanced by their participation.

That certain sports are considered more or less feminine than others, and that sports, in general, are considered less proper for females than for males in our culture, might on face value be accepted as the explanation why more women do not achieve in sports. However, when looked at in relationship to feminine achievement in other non-domestic areas, non-achievement in sport becomes a part of the whole spectrum of stereotyped female incompetence. In the next few sections, I will briefly discuss the feminine role as it develops in the setting of the family, society, and the individual female's physiology. Then I will review how the role stereotypes lead to what might be called non-achievement training. Finally, I will discuss how women might retain their femininity as well as achieve, with sports being one channel for achievement.

Theories of Sex-Role Development

One way or another, children learn what sex they are and what behaviors are a part of that sex. Many theories have been suggested and experimentally tested as to how this happens. A few will be briefly reviewed here.

Hartley (1966) looks at sex-role learning developmentally, in terms of what the child understands about her role in relation to what she does and how she is treated. Female infants may be gentled, while males may be roughhoused. The child learns to manipulate the sex-typed toys given to her. Bringing in Piaget's theories of cognitive development, Hartley notes that the familiarization and repetition with these toys brings mastery and preference for them. Parents also utter sex appropriate verbal appelations, such as "good girl," or "just like Mommy." Thus, what little girls are called and what they play with, becomes part of their sex-role definition.

Heilbrun (1965) showed data supporting his theory that the sexes differ in the way they learn to identify with parents as models of the male and female sexes. Males become more similar to their fathers, while females identify more equally with both parents. This may be because the female can remain dependent longer on both parents and has a greater chance to internalize the feelings of both. Also, the female has a greater cultural freedom to practice both roles.

Lynn (1966) hypothesizes that the initial parental identity of both sexes is with the mother, resulting from mother-infant interactions. The boys must then shift their identity to the masculine role, which at that stage is less defined to them, but is more rigorously enforced by society. Thus, as they get older, males show a firmer identification with the masculine role than do the females. Lynn notes that this, plus the greater prestige associated with the masculine role, may explain why more females show a preference for opposite sex activities.

Johnson (1963) discusses Parson's reciprocal-role hypothesis in terms of sex-role learning. The expressive role player is oriented toward sensitivity and responsiveness to the attitudes of others, while the instrumental role player is oriented toward success in the working world, viewing interaction as the means to an end. Johnson suggests that the main mechanism of the development of sex-role identity in both males and females is the internalizing of a reciprocal-role relationship with the father. Both sexes are nurtured by and identify with the expressive mother during infancy. The father differentiates his roles toward his male and female children. He encourages instrumentalism in his son by being more demanding of him. He is less demanding of his daughter, and praises her for such feminine things as looking pretty. Thus, he plays mentor to his son and husband to his daughter. The life task of the girl, then, is to shift her expressive attachment from her mother and father to a more mature expressive attachment to husband and family. The boy, in addition, must learn instrumentalism to cope with the non-familial environment.

Mischel (1966) looks at sex-role development from the viewpoint of social learning theory. He states, "In social learning theory, sex-typed behaviors may be defined as behaviors that typically elicit different rewards for one sex than for the other." (p. 56)

Thus, femininity is something developed in relation to father, patterned from father, and consistent with cultural training and expectations.

Antecedents of Individual Differences

While there is a cultural guide for females to develop along a type of passive, expressive role, and for males to develop an instrumental role, there are individual differences in developing and mature personalities. These differences are often the result of antecedent situations involving the relationship with mother, the learning situations, the sex of siblings, and the social class in which the girl may have been reared.

Bardwick (1971, p. 140) suggests that "feminization" of the daughter is the result of a warm relationship with a mother who holds herself in esteem and with a father who encourages and responds to the girl's emerging femininity.

Both Kagan and Moss (1962, p. 221) and Veroff, as reported by Bardwick (1971, p. 176), suggest that maternal hostility, exhibited in a critical or rejecting attitude of the mother toward the child, is a factor in the development of a need for achievement in the female. Perhaps the mother, being critical rather than expressive, pushes the girl into an instrumental orientation, as the father would normally do to the son.

Meier (1972), studying attitudes toward feminine social equality, found that the way the mother fills her role is important in shaping the sex-role attitudes of youth. More liberal attitudes toward feminine social equality were associated with the mother participating to a greater extent in the socialization of the child and the mother exhibiting more attributes of social achievement herself. These were in terms of a higher education level, work outside the home, and the prestige and ego-involvement of that work.

Minnuchin (1965) studied fourth graders from two traditional and two modern schools and found less sex typical reactions in the modern schools. Higher aggression in males and a stronger family orientation in females were associated with the traditional schools. Her study suggests that different philosophies of child rearing and education are influential in the formation of sex-role attitudes and reactions.

Another factor which affects the child's sex-role preference is the sex of his siblings. Koch (1956), studying "sissiness" and "tomboyishness" in children from two child families, found that boys with an older sister tended to be more "sissyish" than the other boys. Though not significant, there was a strong suggestion that girls with an older brother were more likely to be "tomboyish" than those with an older sister. Rosenberg and Sutton-Smith (1964) did a study which confirmed Koch's findings, and they suggested that the presence of opposite sex siblings tends to decrease self-sex preferences, while the presence of like-sex siblings tends to reinforce self-sex preferences. Sutton-Smith and Rosenberg also found this to be true in their study of college sophomores (1965). Leventhal's data (1970), however, does not reflect the opposite sex influence in this way for males. With boys having older sisters, he noted stronger masculine behavior, perhaps reflecting the stronger need of boys to be sure in their identity.

Bardwick (1971) mentions that sex-typing is more rigorous in the lower classes (p. 151). This agrees with the findings of Kagan and Moss (1962) which indicate that the higher the education level of the family (used as the socio-economic determinant), the less likely the individual will adhere to orthodox sex-role traits (p. 171).

Thus, the child's sex-role preferences which ac-company sex-role identity are modified by the social situation.

Effect of Puberty of the Female's Psyche

Before puberty, sex appropriate attitudes and play preferences are not emphasized for the female to the extent that they are for the male. However, Bardwick (1970) points out that after puberty, the societal view of success for females is interpersonal success, while for males it is academic and occupational success. After puberty, she notes that the female's sex identity, "which now has to be proven, will fuse interpersonal success and adolescent perceptions of sex and reproduction." (p. 6) Dating becomes the testing ground of desirability as a woman. Bardwick notes that there is a cultural emphasis on the cosmetic exterior of the sexual body, but she says that "adolescent girls can verbalize their concern about their competitive appearance, but not their fears about internal reproductive functions." (p. 6) These fears and defenses, she notes, appear in dreams and fantasies of being hurt and torn.

Douvan (1970) feels that the regular fluctuation of the female's body system "will result in a self-system that is more fluid and more vulnerable to environmental influences than the self-system developed by boys." (p. 32) Since these cues are less stable, she feels that the girl will rely more on external cues and the expectations of others as "anchors for her self-definition." (p. 33) Thus, she notes, in Witkin's studies, sex differences in field dependence are first obvious at about age ten or eleven, with females generally more field dependent than males.

Bardwick (1970) and her associates have done studies of females over the menstrual cycles. They have found that levels of anxiety and hostility are related to levels of estrogen and progesterone, even to the point of the females showing different personality profiles on projective tests at different times during the cycle. Anxiety and hostility themes were most prevalent premenstrually, while themes of success and ability to cope were predominant during ovulation.

Sex Differences in Temperament

Broom and Selznick (1968) state that the difference in masculine and feminine roles in Western society is associated with differences in temperament. The female is seen as naturally non-aggressive and passive, and the male is seen as naturally aggressive and active. What causes these differences revolving around passivity, dependence and aggressiveness? Some researchers feel that females are more generally prone to passivity than the males who have more muscled mesomorphs among their sex.

This average difference in body builds of the sexes is later reflected in the preferred body stereotype of the sexes. Studies by Sugarman and Haronian (1964), Caskey and Felker (1971), Kurtz, and Staffieri (as reported by Caskey and Felker), indicate that males view the mesomorphic body type most favorably, while females view the ectomorphic body type most favorably, beginning in about second grade.

Goldberg and Lewis (1969) found sex differences in 13 month old children's reactions to a frustration barrier placed between the child and the mother. The males were more likely to actively react and try to push down or get around the barrier. The girls were more likely to stand in the middle and cry. Using earlier data on the same children, they noted that very early differences in the handling of infants of the two sexes may have shaped the likelihood of these later different reactions to frustration.

Bardwick (1970) describes a developmental view of independence differences. Girls, less sexually active and physically active and aggressive than boys, may be less likely than boys to perceive parents as people who thwart impulses. Therefore, they are less likely to be separated from parents as sources of support and nurturance. Also, since society discourages dependence in boys, they are forced to develop internal sources, independent of others, for good feelings about the self. Since dependency is permitted in the female and her affectionate bond to the parents is less likely to be jeopardized, Bardwick notes that unless something intervenes, the girl and woman will continue to have a greater need for approval.

Another area in which this might occur is school work. Maccoby (1963) suggests that since girls mature slightly earlier than boys in fine motor and perceptual abilities (as well as the ability to sit still), they may be more likely to receive the teacher's praise for neat work, while the boys will have to look elsewhere for personal satisfaction. Thus, the girls will be more likely to work for praise at school.

One behavior which is more consistently punished in females than in males is aggressive behavior (Kagan and Moss, 1962). Thus, Bardwick (1971) feels that girls withdraw not from aggression, but from the more obvious direct physical aggression. She feels that girls are really more aggressive than the studies usually show, but that they are not overtly aggressive because their interpersonal dependence makes them feel guilty when ignoring society's negative feelings toward aggressive behavior for girls. Her hunch was supported in studies in which she used the prisoner's dilemma, and eliminated the interpersonal factor by not having the experimenter and the opponent visible to the subject. The women were found to be more aggressive toward each other than were the men toward each other. Bardwick suggests that the early verbal behavior of the girls enables them to develop more sophisticated (and less punishable) methods of coping with aggression. These include the withdrawal of friendship, verbal slams, the use of adult intercession, gossip, tears, and somatic complaints (p. 125). Perhaps, as the female sublimates her aggression into a less physical expression, it becomes less obvious to her that certain actions are, in fact, aggressive behavior, and she may link aggressiveness with overt, physical aggressiveness, and couple that with masculinity.

Sex Differences in Play Choices

Erikson (1963, p. 195) suggests that children's play reflects the situations which the child is trying to master. It is interesting then, that the emerging sexual role differences show in children's play. Cratty (1967) notes that males are more active and gain leadership through physical endeavor, while the females engage more in manipulative activity and gain status through verbal behavior. However, the girls seem to exhibit a wider range of games, as indicated in studies by Brown (1958), Ward (1968), and Rosenberg and Sutton-Smith (1960). Sutton-Smith, Rosenberg, and Morgan (1963), studying changes in play choices of children between grades three and six, found that at about the fourth grade level, girls began to choose a wider number of masculine and feminine games than did boys. They wondered if this phenomenon of a wider choice of games by pre-pubertal girls was not also a defense against sex-role anxiety which might be occurring at this time because of the lack of a definite prescribed role. Friedan (1963) notes that at puberty, girls tend to drop special interests, zeroing in on what they think will appeal to the boys.

Comparing the results of cross-cultural studies and child rearing practices, Roberts and Sutton-Smith (1962) suggest that anxiety over child rearing practices is reflected in involvement in expressive models, such as games. Building on an earlier study by Roberts, Arth, and Bush (1959), they found relationships between obedience training and games of strategy, between responsibility training and games of chance, and between achievement training and games of physical skill. Thus, one receiving more training in achievement, or in the instrumental role (i.e. boys over girls), may be more likely to seek out games of physical skill and express mastery and achievement in sport. One who receives more obedience and responsibility training (i.e. girls over boys in home chores) would seek out games of chance or strategy. A more instrumental or critical upbringing of a girl, as achievement training, might, using Roberts' and Sutton-Smith's model, make her more likely to engage in physical activity as an avenue to practice mastery and achievement.

Thus, we see that as biology and culture interact during the female's development, she is more likely than the male to become passive, dependent, and non-aggressive, to be less sure of her prescribed role, and to choose a wider range of play choices just before puberty, which she will probably narrow after puberty when she reaches an age where society offers a more definite stereotyped role for her. As we shall see, this later role has been fed to her by the media and society all her life, and has its greatest toll on her curtailed achievement.

Problems in Achievement

As the female becomes interested in being desired by males, she de-emphasizes competition in academics, and even more so, in sports. McCandless and Ali (1966) compared ninth grade girls from a coed school and two girls schools on fourteen relationships. While the test results from the three schools were similar in most respects, social acceptance was more highly correlated with physical skills for both sex segregated samples.

As girls become more interested in boys, competition itself is not eliminated, however. *Ms.* writer, Pogrebin (1972), states:

> Boys were praised for what they did and made. We were praised for what we looked like. Having the prettiest dress and best hairdo meant competing. Attracting compliments meant competing. . . . Men compete for rewards and achievements; we compete for men (p. 79).

She notes that it was not the actions of the parents, but the attitude. Girls were sent to piano lessons, dancing school, and college, not to develop competence, but to develop that intangible quality, charm, to give them an edge over the other girls on the husband market.

Few Role Models

Another area hampering the development of academic and sports achievement in women is the lack of reference groups, especially role models, of women who achieve in these areas. Kemper (1968), in a theory of achievement motivation, contends that achievement is

> . . .powerfully related to the types of reference groups available to an individual, and that lacking these groups, his achievement striving will be seriously hampered. Furthermore, achievement must be seen as the endpoint of a process beginning in ordinary socialization and role-learning, and proceeding through several stages of increasing competence in role performance (p. 31).

What type of female role model is available to the preadolescent? One key to this is a content analysis of children's readers. The organization, Women on Words and Images (1972), studied 2,760 stories from 134 readers now used in three suburban towns. They found that the readers definitely embody the female in the cultural stereotype. They state, "Typical girl in any reader is a frilly thing with a smile on her face and a passive attitude toward life." (p. 15) The boys are the doers; in one story, Tommy does not play house, he builds one. Sally puts on her bonnet and admires it. The males seek the readers' approval through achievement; the female seeks approval by being pleasing, docile, and defaulting, encouraging others to achieve. When a girl achieves or discovers, it is usually by luck, not by her own actions, such as the girl who discovers silk when a cocoon falls into her tea. The readers' message to the boys is that the goal of getting rich is desirable. What can a girl do? Marry well.

Competitiveness is, overall, a male trait. They state:

> Although girls win at least half as often as do boys, in the readers, it's often the result of a fluke, or after the boys have painstakingly taught the girls to play in the first place (p. 17).

They state some interesting statistics. The main characters are more often male than female, with a low of two to one for animal stories and a high of six to one for biographies. Women must not be interesting enough to write about! The main character in stories expressing the themes of ingenuity, creativity, bravery, perseverance, achievement, adventurousness, curiosity, sportsmanship, generativity, autonomy, and self respect were males, four to one. There were 147 different role possibilities for boys and 25 for girls.

Flora (1971) analyzed short stories from middle and working class United States and Latin American women's magazines. Here again, the female character was rewarded for passive behavior. Few models of females were shown actually controlling their lives. Passive behavior was stressed least by United States working class women's magazines. Very few females in the stories held careers with ego-commitment. Even when this occurred, the careers were usually viewed as a step to acquiring a husband. Very few stories showed the women continuing to work after marriage.

Ehrlich (1971) studied six college marriage and family texts published 1964 or later. She noted comments which seemed to be unsupported value judgments or statements of dubious scientific worth. She found stereotyping in the areas of sexual attitudes, sex-roles and socialization, mate selection, marriage and divorce, and working women. Alas, if the authors of marriage and family texts succumb to stereotyping, where else can we look?

Broverman et al. (1970) administered a sex-role stereotyped questionnaire to practicing psychiatrists, psychologists, and psychiatric social workers with one of three sets of instructions: to describe a healthy, mature, socially competent (a) adult, (b) man, or (c) woman. They found a high agreement in responses between clinicians and between males and females. Their results indicated that the clinicians had different concepts of health for men and women which paralleled the sex-role stereotypes! They were less likely to attribute the traits which characterize healthy adults to a healthy female than to a healthy male. Some traits given to females were that they were less independent, more emotional, and less objective. Broverman, et al. interpreted this as a double standard of health for men and women which they felt may have stemmed from the "adjustment" notion of mental health. Thus, to be healthy, a female must accept the behavioral norms of her sex, even though these are considered less healthy for the generalized competent and mature adult. Those women accepting the self-actualization or fulfillment concepts of mental health, must risk having their "femininity" questioned, as they are deviant in terms of being an average woman.

Weisstein (1971) points to the tremendous effect and importance of expectation of others in behavior, and suggests that this has had a greater effect on females than has generally been considered. She refers to research which has been done by Rosenthal and his co-workers, which shows that even in carefully controlled experiments, and even with no outward or conscious difference in behavior, the experimenter starting with a hypothesis can influence the behavior of a human or an animal. She states:

> . . . If students become intelligent because teachers expect them to be intelligent, and rats run mazes better because the experimenters are told the rats are bright, then it is obvious that a study of human behavior requires first and foremost, a study of the social contexts within which people move, and the expectations as to how they will behave. . . (p. 77).

One result of the expectation that healthy females are less objective and competent was explored by Goldberg (1968). College girls were given three articles written by men and three written by women in six different fields, supposedly as a test of their ability to critically evaluate professional articles. The only difference between the two groups was that the articles supposedly written by men in one group were attributed to women in the other group, and vise versa, by switching only the first names. For example, one was switched from John to Joan. The women were more critical toward the articles attributed to women in both groups, even the articles concerning traditionally feminine fields, such as home economics!

Megargee (1969) found that sex-role prescripts affect the manifestation of leadership in pairs working on a task in which one member of the pair must accept the role labelled "leader" and the other, the role labelled "follower." He placed the subjects in the pairs with reference to scores on the Dominance Scale of the CIP, and found that in the same sex groups, 70 to 75 percent of the high dominance subjects took the leadership role, as might be expected. In the group when the high dominant male was paired with a low dominant female, the male took the role of "leader" 90 percent of the time. However, when a high dominant female was paired with a low dominant male, the female took the leadership role only 20 percent of the time.

Lesser, Krawitz, and Packard (1963) did a study which gives a clue to individual differences in achievement behavior. They studied junior and senior high school girls from the first and fourth quartiles of the class rank at Hunter High School, a school for girls which places great emphasis on intellectual accomplishments. The girls were matched for I.Q., and there was no significant difference between the way the girls reacted to the neutral versus the achievement oriented cues as a whole. However, the achievement motivation scores of the higher grade achievers were higher with achievement cues containing pictures of females, but not males. In contrast the achievement motivation scores of underachievers were higher to achievement cues containing pictures of males, not females. The experimenters state:

> The results . . . suggest that these social conditions have different impacts upon different girls. It appears that the girl who retains a perception of the female role as including intellectual achievement goals succeeds intellec-

tually under conditions of strong academic competition with other girls; by comparison, the girl who accepts the social prescription that intellectual achievement strivings are relevant to the male role and not the female role does not succeed as well. . . (p. 64).

Fear of Success

The achievement orientation of the female seems to involve both a fear of failure and a fear of success. This lessens the motive to achieve and perpetuates passive dependence. Kagan and Moss (1962) found that the young male adolescent will continue striving despite the possibility of failure, whereas the girl will be more likely to withdraw. They attributed this to the fact that culturally, the girl has the option to withdraw, while the boy does not. According to Horner (1969, 1971) the girl may also withdraw to avoid success. In our society competitiveness is a valued trait for the male, but not for the female. Horner (1971) explains that positive motivation to do something is aroused by the expectancy that the behavior will be followed by positive consequences. Anticipation of negative consequences leads to anxiety, which tends to inhibit the individual from doing the activity. She notes that since in our society competition in achievement situations is generally associated with aggressive, masculine overtones, these would not be rewarded in the female, and anticipation of negative consequences might lead to anxiety and inhibition of actions. Horner refers to "the disposition to become anxious in competitive achievement situations as the motive to avoid success." (p. 105)

After separating a group of subjects into high and low fear of success imagery, using a projective test, Horner (1971) tested subjects in various competitive and noncompetitive situations and tasks. She found that females who scored high in fear-of-success imagery did better working alone than in competition, and that subjects low in fear-of-success imagery did better in competition. Also, subjects with a high fear-of-success imagery reported a lower level of importance for doing well than those with low fear-of-success imagery scores.

Horner indicated that fear-of-success imagery was greater in the subjects in the senior high school than that of those in junior high school, and was greater in college senior women than in college freshmen women. She referred to a study by Schwenn, in which the major factor in the arousal of the motive to avoid success was the girls' male peers. Those girls who scored high in fear-of-success imagery or had anxiety about social rejection either did not date or dated men who disapproved of career women. The girls who were not fearful to strive were more likely engaged or seriously dating men who were not threatened by the girls' success, and actively encouraged them to succeed.

The results of a study by Matthews and Tiedeman (1964) parallel the increase in fear of success imagery found by Horner. They found a drop in career commitment in females from junior to senior high school, perhaps, they suggest, because of the imminent possibility of marriage. They state:

> It appears that many girls and women structure their lives on the premise that males view the female's use of her intelligence with distaste and that it is therefore wise to accept this situation if one wishes to marry. . . . Parents usually state a wish for girls to be able to earn a living, and yet they are fully as concerned that their daughters be marriageable. This leads many parents to caution their daughters not to be overly competent in their careers and to seek a "suitable" marriage partner (p. 382-83).

Farmer and Bohn (1970) instructed a group of business women to pretend that men like intelligent women and that raising a family does not interfere with a career. The women then retook the Strong Vocational Interest Inventory. In this testing, the women scored higher on career related scales. In a sense, being told that men like smart career women either freed the women to respond in that direction, or it encouraged their interests to shift in the direction toward what men like.

Bardwick (1971) sees the ability of the thirty to forty year old woman to return to a career as an outgrowth of the stability that she has achieved in the accepted role of wife and mother, and that her affiliation need has been fulfilled.

Thus, the general lack of female role models for achievement, the expectation of society reflected in literature and in the social sciences that women are less competent than men, and the female's fear of success because being successful and competent may mean being unfeminine and unmarriageable, have traditionally put the female through what I will dub, "non-achievement training." This, further coupled with the even more negative social consequences which might be feared from success in the man's world of sports, has made competence and achievement in sport a desired goal for even a smaller segment of the population.

Changes in the '70s

But one need only look around to see that things are changing, labor saving devices, family planning, and the consciousness raising of the 1970s are allowing more and more women to break from tradition. The good health and nutrition movement is bringing a focus back to the natural body and is emphasizing the need for everyone to get exercise. As we can see by reading the newspapers, Women's Lib is opening up participation for women in many areas: economics, politics, and sports, also. The great success of Women's Lib in this year's Virginia Slims Tennis Tour (*Newsweek*, 1972) points to exciting possibilities for the future, as these dedicated women offer a publicized model of achievement for other female sports enthusiasts to follow.

We have seen that such factors as the relationship with parents, the age and sex status of siblings, and the social class can work to develop women who have interests which are less sex typical. However, Maccoby

(1963) has mentioned that girls who so deviate and are more independent than their stereotyped peers may pay the price in anxiety. The research by Lesser, Krawitz, and Packard (1963) indicates that a girl may be able to achieve more if she perceives that intellectual achievement can be relevant to the female role. Bardwick (1971) states that if a girl has a positive sense of esteem as a woman and is not fixated at less mature levels of development, she can learn techniques of achievement without rejecting her sex (p. 18). Thus, the deciding factor in achievement is the level of self esteem. If a woman is sure of herself as a woman, she is more likely to see her own interests as relevant to her own role as a woman. Bardwick states:

> The lower a person's self esteem the greater the anxiety and the greater the response to assume a role. . . . An exaggerated conformity to the stereotype of the sex roles in behaviors and personality traits is probably indicative of anxiety about one's core masculinity or femininity (pp. 155, 166).

Harris refers in this way to female sports participants.

> In general, females who take the risk and participate in such (competitive) sports are either secure in their role as a female so that participation does not strike them as a threat, or they do not care, and have 'nothing' to lose (1971, p. 2).

We have been emphasizing the cultural impact. Does biology have no effect on attitudes toward achievement? This, as Weisstein (1971) has pointed out, is hard to ascertain, when in the past so much of the feminine role development has been mixed with cultural expectations. Even if these expectations were erased, the research cited by Bardwick (1970) and Douvan (1970) indicates possibilities that the beginning of an internal biological cycle in females at puberty may have an effect on their psyche. I would like to suggest to you that these differences point to the need for the female to be able to understand her cyclic feelings related to her biological self, and also develop a feeling of competence in the different, but consistent roles which she can play. Perhaps, since some girls may be less sure of their own day to day consistency, they might be less confident to go out from themselves to be independent and achieve in relation to standards which are more constant, such as those in some sports. Thus, perhaps, even without cultural pressure, some women might prefer to compete in relation to themselves, working by themselves, as some girls in the study by Horner (1971) preferred to do. Also, if a girl had unresolved fears about her inner functions and fears about being hurt as Bardwick (1970) reported, even though the fears may be irrational, she might be less likely to engage in sports where she could get hurt.

However, a feminine cyclic versus a masculine linear sexual development need not dictate dependence or independence, and certainly not interests or roles which can be freely chosen. A healthy female (or male) should be able to display dependence or independence, depending on the situation. Bardwick states:

> In women, healthy dependence means a sensitivity to the needs of the persons who are important to them, which allows appropriate nurturant or supportive behaviors. . . . Independence in achievement behaviors results from learning that one can accomplish by oneself, can reply upon one's abilities, can trust one's own judgment, and can become invested in a task for its own sake (1971, p. 115).

The result of the feminine non-achievement training has traditionally been the virtue of displayed non-competence. The stereotype says that the housewife should not take the initiative when the husband is present, but as soon as he is at work, she is to suddenly turn into a coping, resourceful mother. That qualities of competence are so specific to the situation indicates that they are not necessarily determined by sex.

We have seen that interests and activities are not in themselves masculine or feminine, nor are they necessarily what the individual would inherently like to do because he is a male or female. Rather, they are more often things which one has been conditioned to do because one is masculine or feminine.

What about stable personality traits, such as passivity or aggressiveness? Brim (1960) looks at personality development in terms of learned roles specific to situations. Emphasizing adaptability and discrimination, rather than consistency and stereotyped responses, he notes that consistency across behavior, or traits, may indeed reflect incomplete socialization. This may result from inexperience in certain interaction situations which may lead to a limited repertoire of roles, or from limited training in discrimination between different roles.

This theory is important to include when talking about the role of achievement training, or sports competition, in the life of the female being socialized (or, growing up). Girls must be taught that careers and sports are life compartments, or roles, which society offers the individual to add to life fulfillment. Sports are interaction situations which involve certain responses, and define behavior in the situation. Sports actions are not necessarily masculine or feminine; the gender belongs to the doer, not the thing done. Sportsmanship and courtesies should be expected of all players, regardless of sex. It may be sensible that certain sports are best suited to certain body builds. But the role of "athlete" should be specific to that set of behaviors which we would expect of the best in all our youth as they participate in sport.

Before closing, I would like to note that time has prevented me from covering more fully all the variables involved in the antecedents to female behavior as it relates to later achievement. I have stressed the social input, but I also want to emphasize that although each individual is affected in a slightly different way by her personal social system (including social status, parental attitudes, siblings, school environment, and so on), other variables further individualize the effects of the social system. These include how the female's biology interacts with her psyche and how she herself has come to understand about herself, logically or not so logically, as a woman in a nuclear family and in society. Further research might take these variables into account as they relate to sport.

Also, I would like to suggest that further research include and vary the social contingencies of the experimental situation as well as keep track of past experiences with the situation. For example, studies show that, in general, females with older brothers have less feminine interests than other girls. Now, taking a sample of women, how do those with older brothers compare with those having older sisters in other situations, such as competing with men versus competing with women, or in seeing achievement in sport possibilities as part of the male or female role? Also, does seeing sport as part of the female versus male role separate champions from the other skilled athletes as it separated high academic achievers from the other bright girls in the Lesser, Krawitz, and Packard (1963) study?

Besides the ways females differ in their past experience with the multitudinal inputs labelled achievement training, other things may obscure factors on paper and pencil tests. If mature behavior is a set of flexible roles rather than rigid traits, a paper and pencil test may be limited to discovering the traits or reactions specific to the situation of taking a paper and pencil test of what you might do in a certain situation. Also, we have seen that the optimism versus anxiety swings accompanying the female cycle were enough to show different profiles on a projective test. This presents the possibility that a range of responses obtained by a one day testing of many females at different points in their own cycles may obscure the real results.

But, back from the research to the application and my original motivation for this area of study. What can the physical educator or coach, drawing on what research has shown to this point, do to help females make achieving in sports a part of the array of rolls open to them? It would seem that the route toward developing an independent, self-assured woman would involve her understanding of some of the types of things which I have discussed with you today. As the female begins to understand what is fact, what is cultural, and what is myth, she would have a basis from which to understand and select the roles she would like to play.

In addition, some factors might be built into the physical education program to increase the understanding and social desirability of women's sports for the women themselves. Sex-stereotyped movements might be discussed in basic movement units. For example, the question, "Is there such a thing as a male or female movement or sport?" might be discussed. Aggressiveness might be discussed in terms of its obvious (movement) or subtle (verbal, attitudinal) forms. Since the more popular sports, such as tennis, golf, and swimming, are often learned in a coed club situation, more attempts might be made to have coeducational classes where the activity permits it. However, this would be only after the skill level of the girls is brought to a point where they can learn on an equal level with the boys, and will be able to offer teamwork and competition to the situation. Otherwise, we would perpetuate the present problems associated with non-competence. Attempts should also be made to get the males interested as spectators of all-girl sports, to give them more understanding, and hopefully, to generate approval of sports for women from that sector to which they look for approval, the males.

Ultimately, girls must understand that achieving in sport is a thing to do, or an interaction situation to be experienced, which does not have to change the girl's being or femininity outside of that situation, except, perhaps to enrich it. Nor must girls be led to think that masculine behavior beyond the sport situation will improve chances of achievement in the situation. The important goal is total involvement in the sport situation and, then, the ability to enter into other and different interaction situations after the game is over.

The Woman's Dilemma

Thus, the woman's social dilemma: living in an achievement oriented society, she is discouraged from achieving. Her continued expressive and dependent roles orient her to external social motivations for her behavior. At the same time, she is allowed a large range of activity choices, stretching across the male-female social continuum, in which the "masculine" choices are more tempting in light of American values. If she chooses masculine activities, she may look "unfeminine" to society, and, since she is oriented toward the approval of others, the marriage orientation, and a vague idea of a real feminine role, she is more likely to conform to the stereotype of femininity, for that at least defines a role which society will accept.

Those women who are successful achievers, from the social standpoint, may have regressively thrown off concerns about being "feminine," or, more likely, have developed an independent and positive sense of self-esteem as women that makes them "able to elect their roles and enjoy their freedom of choice." (Bardwick, 1971, p. 205) One of the roles which they can elect is that of the sportswoman.

REFERENCES

1. Bardwick, Judith M. "Psychological Conflict and the Reproductive System." *Feminine Personality and Conflict.* Belmont, Calif.: Brooks/Cole Publishing Co., 1970.
2. ———. *Psychology of Women: A Study of Bio-Cultural Conflicts.* New York: Harper and Row, 1971.
3. Brim, Orville G. "Personality Development as Role-Learning." *Personality Development in Children.* Edited by Ira Iscoe and Harold W. Stevenson. Austin: University of Texas Press, 1960.
4. Broom, Leonard and Selznick, Philip. *Sociology.* New York: Harper and Row, 1968, p. 114.
5. Broverman, Inge *et al.* "Sex-Role Stereotypes and Clinical Judgments of Mental Health." *Journal of Consulting and Clinical Psychology.* 34:1:1-7, 1970.
6. Brown, Daniel G. "Sex-Role Development in a Changing Culture." *Psychological Bulletin.* 55:4:232-241, 1958.
7. Caskey, Sheila and Felker, Donald W. "Social Stereotyping of Female Body Image by Elementary School Girls." *The Research Quarterly.* 42:3:251-255, Oct., 1971.
8. Cratty, Bryant J. *Social Dimensions of Physical Activity.* Englewood Cliffs, New Jersey: Prentice-Hall, Inc., 1967, Chapter 6.
9. Douvan, Elizabeth. "New Sources of Conflict in Females at Adolescence and Early Adulthood." *Feminine Personality and Conflict.* By Bardwick, Douban, Horner, and Gutman. Belmont, Calif.: Brooks/Cole Publishing Co., 1960.
10. Ehrlich, Carol. "The Male Sociologist's Burden: The Place of Women in Marriage and Family Texts." *Journal of Marriage and the Family.* 33:3:421-30, Aug., 1971.
11. Erikson, Erik. *Childhood and Society.* New York: Norton, 1963.
12. Farmer, Helen S. and Bohn, Martin J., Jr. "Home-Career Conflict and the Development of Career Interest in Women." *Journal of Counseling Psychology.* 17:3:228-232, 1970.
13. Flora, Cornelia B. "The Passive Female: Her Comparative Image by Class and Culture in Women's Magazine Fiction." *Journal of Marriage and the Family.* 33:3:435-444, Aug., 1971.
14. Friedan, Betty. *The Feminine Mystique.* New York: Dell Publishing Co., 1963.
15. Goldberg, Philip. "Are Women Prejudiced Against Women?" *Transaction.* 5:5:28-30, April, 1968.
16. Goldberg, Susan and Lewis, Michael. "Play Behavior in the Year Old Infant: Early Sex Differences." *Child Development.* 40:1:21-31, March, 1969.
17. Harres, Bea. "Attitudes of Students Toward Women's Athletic Competition." *The Research Quarterly.* 39:2:278-284, May, 1968.
18. Harris, Dorothy V. "The Sportswoman in Our Society." *DGWS Research Reports: Women in Sports.* Wash.: AAHPER, 1971.
19. Hartley, Ruth E. "A Developmental View of Female Sex-Role Identification." *Role Theory: Concepts and Research.* Edited by Bruce J. Biddle and Edwin Thomas. New York: John Wiley and Sons, Inc., 1966.
20. Harvey, Paul. Newscast, June 16, 1972.
21. Heilbrun, Alfred B., Jr. "Sex Differences in Identification Learning." *The Journal of Genetic Psychology.* 106:185-193, 1965.
22. Holliman, Jeannie. *American Sports [1785-1835].* Cleveland: Micro Photo, 1969.
23. Horner, Matina S. "Fail: Bright Women." *Psychology Today.* 3:6:36-38, Nov., 1969.
24. ———. "Femininity and Successful Achievement: A Basic Inconsistency." *Roles Women Play: Readings Toward Women's Liberation.* Edited by Michele Garskoff. Belmont, Calif.: Brooks/Cole Publishing Co., 1971.
25. Johnson, Miriam M. "Sex-Role Learning in the Nuclear Family." *Child Development.* 34:319-333, 1963.
26. Kagan, Jerome and Moss, Howard A. *Birth to Maturity.* New York: John Wiley and Sons, Inc., 1962.
27. Kemper, Theodore D. "Reference Groups, Socialization, and Achievement." *American Sociological Review.* 33:1:31-45, Feb., 1968.
28. Koch, Helen. "Sissiness and Tomboyishness in Relation to Sibling Characteristics." *The Journal of Genetic Psychology.* 88:231-244, 1956.
29. Lardner, Rex. "Women Athletes: Tell Your Man to Watch Out—The Girls are Catching Up." *Cosmopolitan.* 172:4:206, 222. April, 1972.
30. Lesser, Gerald S.; Krawitz, Rhonda N.; and Packard, Rita. "Experimental Arousal of Achievement Motivation in Adolescent Girls." *Journal of Abnormal and Social Psychology.* 66:1:59-66, 1963.
31. Leventhal, Gerald S. "Influence of Brothers and Sisters on Sex Role Behavior." *Journal of Personality and Social Psychology.* 16:3:452-465, 1970.
32. Lynn, David B. "The Process of Learning Parental and Sex-Role Identification." *Journal of Marriage and the Family.* 28:4:466-470, Nov., 1966.
33. Maccoby, Eleanor E. "Woman's Intellect." *The Potential of*

Woman. Edited by Seymour Farber and Roger Wilson. New York: McGraw-Hill Book Co., Inc., 1963.

34. Malumphy, Theresa. "The College Woman Athlete—Questions and Tentative Answers." *Quest*. Mono. XIV, June, 1970, pp. 24-26.

35. ———. "The Personality and General Characteristics of Women Athletes in Intercollegiate Competition." Unpublished Doctoral Dissertation, The Ohio State University, Columbus, 1966.

36. Matthews, Esther and Tiedeman, David V. "Attitudes toward Career and Marriage and the Development of Life Style in Young Women." *Journal of Counseling Psychology*. 11:4:375-384, 1964.

37. McCandless, Boyd R. and Ali, Fahmida. "Relations Among Physical Skills and Personal and Social Variables in Three Cultures of Adolescent Girls." *Journal of Educational Psychology*. 57:6:366-372, 1966.

38. Megargee, Edwin. "Influence of Sex-Roles on the Manifestation of Leadership." *Journal of Applied Psychology*. 53:5:377-82, Oct., 1969.

39. Meier, Harold C. "Mother Centeredness and College Youths' Attitudes toward Social Equality for Women: Some Empirical Findings." *Journal of Marriage and the Family*. 34:1:115-121, Feb., 1972.

40. Metheny, Eleanor. *Connotations of Movement in Sport and Dance*. Dubuque, Iowa: Wm. C. Brown, Co., 1965.

41. Millan, Anne F. "Sex Differences: Do They Make any Difference?" *The Physical Educator*. 26:3:114-115, Oct., 1969.

42. Minnuchin, Patricia. "Sex-Role Concepts and Sex Typing in Children as a Function of School and Home Environments." *Child Development*. 36:1033-1049, 1965.

43. Mischel, Walter. "A Social Learning View of Sex Differences in Behavior." *The Development of Sex Differences*. Edited by Eleanor Maccoby. Stanford: Stanford Univ. Press, 1966.

44. *Newsweek*, June 26, 1972, pp. 56-63.

45. Park, Roberta Jewel. "Competitive Sports for Girls and Women: A Study of Attitudes Held by a Select Group of Ohio State Univer-sity Women Undergraduates." Unpublished Master's Theses, The Ohio State University, Columbus, 1955.

46. Pogrebin, Letty Cottin. "Competing With Women" *Ms*. 1:1:78-81, July, 1972.

47. Roberts, John M.; Arth, Malcolm J.; and Bush, Robert R. "Games in Culture." *American Anthropologist*. 61:2:97-605, Aug., 1959.

48. Roberts, John M. and Sutton-Smith, Brian. "Child Training and Game Involvement." *Ethnology*. 1:2:166-185, April, 1962.

49. Rosenberg, B.G. and Sutton-Smith, B. "A Revised Conception of Masculine-Feminine Differences in Play Activities." *The Journal of Genetic Psychology*. 96:165-170, March, 1960.

50. ———. "Family Interaction Effects on Masculinity-Femininity." *Journal of Personality and Social Psychology*. 8:2:117-120, 1968.

51. ———. "Ordinal Position and Sex-Role Identification." *Genetic Psychology Monographs*. 70:297-328, 1964.

52. Sherriff, Marie. "Girls Compete???" *DGWS Reports: Women in Sports*. Edited by Dorothy V. Harris. Wash.: AAHPER, 1971.

53. Sugarman, A. Arthur and Haronian, Frank. "Body Types and Sophistication of Body Concept." *Journal of Personality*. 32:380-394, 1964.

54. Sutton-Smith, B. and Rosenberg, B.G. "Age Changes in Effects of Ordinal Position on Sex-Role Identification." *Journal of Genetic Psychology*. 107:61-73, 1965.

55. Sutton-Smith, B.; Rosenberg, B.G.; and Morgan, E.F., Jr. "Development of Sex Differences on Play Choices During Preadolescence." *Child Development*. 34:119-126, 1963.

56. Ward, William D. "Variance of Sex-Role Preference Among Boys and Girls." *Psychological Reports*. 23:467-470, 1968.

57. Weisstein, Naomi. "Psychology Constructs the Female, or the Fantasy Life of the Male Psychologist." *Roles Women Play: Readings Toward Women's Liberation*. Belmont, Calif.: Brooks/Cole Publishing Co., 1971.

58. Women on Words and Images. "Look Jane Look. See Sex Stereotypes." *NJEA Review*. 45:7:14-19, March, 1972.

THE AMERICAN SEASONAL MASCULINITY RITES

Arnold R. Beisser

Not all of the characteristics which are attributed to being male or female are to the same degree biologically determined. Some, considered to be basic to masculinity or femininity, are determined by the culture in which one lives rather than by obvious physical differences. In our culture athletics are considered the most masculine of activities. Let us turn now to a consideration of what part sexual orientation plays in the intense interest in sports in America.

Before puberty, boys can be distinguished from girls mainly on the basis of primary sexual characteristics. When puberty is reached, biological distinctions become more apparent. At that time, with the differences in hormonal balance, the distinct secondary sexual characteristics begin to develop. Boys begin to have hair on their faces, and their bodies and become more muscular and angular. Girls become more curvaceous and develop breasts. Primary and secondary characteristics are predictable and universal: girls' hips broaden; boys' shoulders grow wider.

Beyond these physical characteristics are others which are largely, if not exclusively, determined by the society in which one lives. These can be termed tertiary characteristics and are transmitted from generation to generation by the examples of the men and women in the culture. To suggest, as Margaret Mead does, that the nature of maleness and femaleness, outside the physical characteristics, is culturally determined, may be an extreme point of view. For differences must develop just from living in a male body which has greater physical strength compared to living in a female body which experiences menstruation and pregnancy. Nevertheless, it is true that many of the male or female characteristics which are taken for granted in our society are determined by social custom rather than genetics. For example, up to very recently in this country, boys wore short hair and girls wore long hair, but in other parts of the world the

From Arnold R. Beisser, *The Madness in Sports*, New York: Appleton-Century-Crofts, 1967. Chapter 16, pp. 214-225.

reverse is true.[1] Similarly, an American boy would hide in shame if he had to wear a skirt, but in Greece it is the attire worn by a particularly virile and courageous group of soldiers.

There is a story which, although of doubtful validity, nevertheless illustrates the importance of these tertiary sexual characteristics: "Two children were playing outside a nudist camp. One of them discovered a hole through which he could look in the wall surrounding the camp. While he peeked through the hole, the other child excitedly inquired, 'What do you see, are they men or women'? The peeper responded in dismay, 'I don't know, they don't have any clothes on'!"

Tertiary sexual characteristics, such as dominance, mannerisms, dress, and speech, are often considered unalterable, yet studies of different cultures reveal quite different ideas about what constitutes male and female behavior. Each culture assumes that it "knows" how a man or woman should act. The folklore is justified by a self-fulfilling prophecy, as parents transmit to children their cultural expectations.

To be considered feminine in Victorian society women had to be frail, passive, and the potential victims of aggressive, lecherous males. Yet, according to the stories of Greek mythology, women were as urgently sexed as men. In our own age primitive tribes differ grossly in what we consider basic masculinity and femininity. Among the Arapesh tribes of New Guinea, for example, studies in the early twentieth century found that men as well as women showed such characteristics as concern, giving, protectiveness, which we in America associate with mothering. Their neighbors, the Mundugumor, living only a short distance away, had quite opposite attitudes, with both men and women being strong, tough, and aggressive, like the idealized pioneer male in the United States.[2]

Another tribe in New Guinea, the Tchambuli, showed a reversal of conceptions about masculinity-femininity in another way. The male job was head-hunting, war making, and war preparation. To carry out their plans the men congregated daily in the "men's house." The women on the other hand were charged with all of the economic responsibilities in the village, such as fishing, food preparation, pottery, basket weaving. When the British banned head-hunting and imposed a peace upon these people, the men became essentially unemployed, while the women continued their traditional activities. These women were temperamentally stable, secure, and cooperative with others, but the men, having lost their important function, became insecure, capricious, and aesthetic. Although men could no longer make war, the preparation rituals were continued. Their interest in the cosmetic arts and in creating suitable costumes, previously an important part of war, was now used instead to make themselves sexually attractive in competing through charm for the favors of the "important sex," the women. The women were tolerant of their men whom they viewed as gossipy, self-centered playthings.

Among the Manus it is the father who is endowed with what in America are considered maternal characteristics. While the women are occupied with the economy and have little time for children, the father cares for and raises them. When Dr. Mead brought dolls to the children of the Manus, she found that it was the boys who eagerly played with them, while the girls were disinterested. The boys in their play were emulating their fathers' activities.

Largely, then, the tertiary sexual characteristics of people, the ones which are most visible and apparent, are socially determined and subject to considerable change from one generation to another and from one culture to another. Sometimes, however, the roles assigned to certain members of a society are intolerable, and in order for such a society to survive and maintain stability there have to be safety valves through which those who are placed in ambiguous or deprecated positions can gain some satisfaction or status.

The Iatmul are a tribe of New Guinea natives who had such a culture. The men despised women, considered them unimportant, worthless, almost subhuman, allocating to them only the most menial and routine of tasks. Men, in contrast, were considered to be the "real human beings," strong, brave, and courageous; they, too, were head hunters. The men were expected to be proud, the women self-effacing. Everything in this culture was either all black or all white, all good or all bad. There were no shades of gray. To be a man was to approach perfection; women epitomized all that was to be avoided. If a man showed the slightest feminine interests or characteristics, he was considered to be sliding toward the subhuman. Such rigid standards of human behavior placed each man in constant jeopardy of losing his humanity. This dichotomy was hard on the women, but it was equally difficult for the men. Adjustment of the Iatmul society was precarious: men walked a tight rope and women were scorned.

A society like the Iatmul has doubtful durability, for the tensions and resentment engendered are at an explosive pitch. This tribe's "safety valve" was the ceremony of Naven,[3] an annual occasion in which bitterness and tensions were discharged in a convulsive reversal of the year's pressures. Naven was a ceremony of cultural transvestism, during which men and women exchanged not only their clothes but also their roles. Boys who had been rigorously taught the shamefulness of femininity were now contemptuously called "wife" by their maternal uncles. They were bullied in the same way that women had been bullied throughout the year. The women, during Naven, were given a vacation from their despised roles and identified themselves dramatically as men, wearing their clothes and assuming their actions, strutting and swaggering. They could enter the "men's house" and could even beat certain designated men. They could engage in a theatrical simulation of the war games that men played. The men, who had spent the year taking elaborate ritualized precautions to avoid anything feminine could relax during the ceremony. It was a great relief actually to assume, in deliberate fashion, the female role.

By the end of the ceremony the tensions and resentments accumulated during the year were dissipated. The women felt better about their position in the community and the men admired the women for having been able to assume the masculine position. For a short time the women had become human and the men could love them. Over the next year the tensions built up again and hatred prevaded community life until the next Naven.

The Naven ceremony of the Iatmul is not unique, for other cultures have similar festivals. Rome's ancient feast of Saturnalia served a related function in discharging the year's accumulated tensions between masters and slaves. In this ceremony, slaves were waited upon by their masters and enjoyed all the privileges which they were denied during the year. It is easy to understand the necessity for such rites and their vital function in preserving a culture. Beyond a certain point, tensions and resentment would destroy any community life.

The Iatmul looked forward throughout the year to their ceremony of Naven. The Romans, both slaves and masters, eagerly awaited the festival of Saturnalia. In fact, in these cultures and others with similar rites, the populace lived from festival to festival. These were the most important events in their lives. Similarly Americans, particularly many American males, mark time by their own seasonal rites: football season, basketball season, baseball season, and so on. Many men live from one sports season to the next, with sports representing the most vital part of their lives.

Iatmul men and women were in a precarious psychological position as a result of the extreme demands which their culture placed upon them. The Naven rite offered an opportunity for the expression of strong feelings which had to be disowned throughout the year preceding the ceremony. For the women it was denial of self-assertion and aggression; for the men it was denial of passivity, with no opportunities for relaxation of their facade of superstrength. Naven saved the Iatmul people from the otherwise impossible demands of their culture and thereby saved the culture from extinction.

American men, as we have seen, are also on shaky cultural ground. Their position is precarious as a result of the contradictions in their lives. To an ever-increasing degree, American male children early in their lives have close physical and emotional experiences with their fathers. Fathers share almost equally with mothers in the maternal activities; feeding, bathing, cuddling, and comforting, which were once the exclusive domain of the American female. American parents are apt to take turns in getting up with the baby when he cries at night. When either parent has a "night out" the other serves as baby sitter. If the egalitarianism is disrupted it is likely for bitterness to develop.

"Togetherness" has largely meant the diminution of the uniqueness of the female position as well as the male position in the family. Father is no longer the ultimate authority; he has become a "pal"; he is now not a teacher but a co-learner. He has an equal, but not a greater voice in the collective activities of the household than have the children and his wife. The wife, who may have a job outside the home and may make as much as or even more money than her husband, quite naturally expects him to share the housecleaning, dishwashing, and caring for the children. The roles are diffused and the differences between male and female, between adult and child are diminished.

Like the Tchambuli, American men have had a change in status. The Tchambuli men lost their principal function, head hunting; American men have had to share with their wives their economic productivity as bread winners. Tchambuli men became superfluous; the authority and uniqueness of the American man has diminished. Previously, the main way men were superior to women was in their physical strength. Now, development of machines has caused male strength to be less important, almost obsolete. Machines are stronger than men, and the sexes are equally competent in running most machines. Dexterity has become more important than power, and women are at least as competent as men in this respect. The serious consequence is, that in their work, the new breed of factory and office workers are essentially neuter in gender.

While these changes in technology and in the family have taken place, the cultural expectations of masculinity have remained fixed as they were in pioneer days. Physical strength and agility were the qualities by which a man was measured, for then only the strong were able to survive. Obviously, such values are more appropriate to the frontier than to the office. Now, in order to fit this already obsolete image, men and boys must engage in artificial, nonproductive displays of strength.

As the real demands for what was considered traditional male strength have decreased, the expectation of show of strength has grown. Parents have a special concern that their boys are not aggressively masculine enough. Mothers are more apt to be concerned about passive, compliant behavior in male children than about their destructiveness. Often they are even relieved by, and subtly encourage, overt displays of aggression, for in that way, they are reassured that their sons are not "sissies." This is quite different from the concept of several decades ago that the quiet child was the "good" child.

As fathers and sons have grown closer together, an obsessive cultural concern with homosexuality has grown. In a counter move to avoid such taint, as already noted, children are pushed earlier and earlier into heterosexual relationships. The tragedy of this parental encouragement is that it is self-defeating, since the child in latency has other more important business to learn than sex appeal. In addition, his premature explorations in heterosexuality promote a sense of inadequacy within him as he recognizes his inability to perform as expected. This inadequacy, in turn, is interpreted as the "taint" and the parental efforts and encouragement towards aggression and heterosexuality are redoubled, the situation becoming a vicious circle.

Just as Naven helps to relieve the Iatmul tensions, American sports have a similar function. The first man outside the home that a boy encounters is usually a coach. In school he meets a series of female teachers who are the purveyors of morality, knowledge, and competence. The coach is not only a man among men but, more important, a man among women teachers. Boys try to model themselves after the coach and find security in imitating him. Their roles are clearer on the diamond than in the classroom, for it is on the athletic field in those seasonal masculinity rites that males become the kind of men their grandfathers were and their mothers want them to be. Strength is king; men are separated from boys, and boys, in turn, from girls. In the best tradition of the frontier, an athlete overpowers his opponent, and the sexual roles are re-established to conform with the expectancies of the culture. Male and female are relieved of their discrepancy just as they are following the Naven ceremony. Fortunately, this can be accomplished, not only by participation, but by observation as a spectator who identifies with the players. They can both then return to the office and the home with renewed respect for the uniqueness of the sexes and the reestablishment of their own identities, until the distinction gradually diminishes and another masculinity rite is necessary.

In a subtle way, these supermasculine "frontier rites" also allow for the expression of warmth and closeness among men which society compels them to disown. In sports, players huddle together; they caress, pat "fannies," shout affectionate phrases, and engage in activities which are scorned elsewhere but condoned in sports. In a recent heavyweight boxing match, the victor was embraced and kissed by his manager before several thousand fans in the sports arena and perhaps several million more on television. Such behavior anywhere but in the context of sports would be highly suspect. But here, with full cultural approval and without detracting from the supermasculine atmosphere, men can satisfy either physically or vicariously their needs for close male companionship like that which they experienced in childhood. In this context, physical contact, either aggressive or friendly, is applauded rather than condemned, and in the frenzy of American sports, males are purged of their femininity, and at the same time provided with an outlet for close contact.

Among the Iatmul, Naven takes place annually, and a single festival appears to take care of a year's accumulated tensions between the sexes. Fifty years ago a single sports season, namely baseball, sufficed for Americans. Today each season of the year is occupied with a different sport. Sport seasons now fuse with one another into a continuous succession of ceremonial demonstrations. The fall rite, football, now overlaps with the spring rite of baseball and track. The vacant moments are filled with transitional rites: basketball, hockey, tennis, and golf, to mention a few.

Although the potential for wild celebration is always present, the pitch of these ceremonies is somewhat lower than the yearly Naven in New Guinea. This is consistent with the lower pitch of all activities in our sophisticated country. Very little can be termed a "special event," since we are bombarded daily with the spectacular and the overwhelming. Just as the differences between sexes have diminished, the difference between holiday and weekday has also. Activities converge into a more integrated (for the hopeful) or amorphous (for the pessimistic) mass of ongoing activities. The Fourth of July, once fraught with danger and excitement, is now closely controlled and tame. Similarly, other holidays such as Armistice Day, Flag Day, St. Patrick's Day have lost their appeal except to the most enthusiastic. Since the range of the pitch is lower, the exposure time must be increased. Thus, sports go on continuously from the beginning to the end of the year.

Among primitives, the transition from boyhood to manhood is accomplished in a single, brief ceremony—the puberty rite. A symbolic gesture, such as circumcision or knocking out a tooth, bears witness to the cliche, "Today I am a man." For American men the transition is quite different. Puberty, the time of traditional manhood when the secondary sexual characteristics appear, is now only the signal for the prolonged period of suspension between boyhood and manhood called adolescence. Biologically and sexually, manhood has been reached, but the technical complexity of our society requires an extension of many years of education and preparation before the productive work of life can begin. The preparation extends temporally toward mandatory early retirement, which advances from the other side, allowing only a relatively brief period for the adult work career.

The adolescent is thus in a state of moratorium, suspended in his choices of occupation and a wife, prohibited from sexual activity, prevented from making any firm commitment.[4] No true identity can be achieved in the face of such a moratorium. In the medical profession this problem is well exemplified. A boy who decides that he wants to be a doctor must make this decision at least a score of years before his goal is achieved. If, for example, he wishes to be a surgeon he may not complete his training until he is past thirty. Failure at any stage of this process would force him to seek a new occupation and a new direction for his life. With the endless series of what can be likened to initiation rites— high school, college for four years, medical school for four years, residency—it is as senescence approaches that the moratorium is over and the man can say with some degree of finality, "I have an identity, I am a doctor."

Because of the nature of this moratorium, adolescence is a period of turmoil. Rebellion and confusion can be expected from the man who has not yet found a place for himself, who is suspended, seemingly for an infinite length of time, between his family of origin and his family of procreation.

But as we have seen, a culture with contradictions

and ambiguities, if it is to survive, must have some way of relieving and integrating its tensions. Sports form an elongated bridge across childhood, adolescence, and adulthood for American males. Although the adolescent boy may have to suspend decision and commitment on most of his affairs until many years hence, he can enter athletics with full exuberance and play and work at sports with a dedication which satisfies his personality and his society.

Among my patients has been a successful attorney who came to treatment because his marriage was on the point of dissolution. The bone of contention between him and his wife was that in her eyes he was not "man enough." She was bitterly disappointed that he was not handy around the house, that he did not make the family decisions, and was not more assertive—all qualities she had admired in her father. Her husband's competence in a learned profession seemed unimportant, while her father's physical strength resulting from his being an unskilled laborer was important. She feared that their son would develop into a "passive man" like her husband. The husband, too, doubted his own masculinity, shared her fears, and so sought therapy in order to try to conform to her expectations of him. The bickering that went on between them always subsided when they engaged in sports or jointly watched sports events. This seemed to adjust the perspective and after such activity each respected the other for his or her distinctiveness.

This is not an unusual case. Wives are worried about their husbands not being aggressively masculine enough; mothers are worried about their sons being too passive; men fear that they will be dominated or thought to be effeminate.

In reality, men are larger and weigh more than women, they do have more powerful muscles, they do have bigger lung and heart capacities, and they do have a sexual organ which makes them different. They are built for physical combat, for hunting, as well as for a unique sexual role. In the work and social world, however, this combat strength is largely obsolete. A 200-pound man can easily lose a business encounter (symbolic combat) to a 130-pound man or to a 90-pound woman. Slender feminine fingers can push the buttons on a computer as well as can thick, strong, male fingers, perhaps better. Machines are stronger than either men or women, and to the machine it makes no difference if its buttons are pushed hard or lightly. Male strength has, at least in part, lost its function and its value in society.

In sports, male and female are placed in their historical biological roles. In sports, strength and speed do count, for they determine the winner. As in pre-mechanized combat, women can never be more than second place to men in sports. They can cheer their men on, but a quick review of the record books comparing achievements in sports of men and women confirms the distinctness of the sexes here.

It is small wonder that the American male has a strong affinity for sports. He has learned that this is one area where there is no doubt about sexual differences and where his biology is not obsolete. Athletics help assure his difference from women in a world where his functions have come to resemble theirs.

NOTES

1. Since the above comments were first written, a remarkable change has taken place in the dress and hair styles of American teenagers and young people. Boys often now wear long hair and bright attention-getting clothing making their dress more similar to the traditional feminine attire. Girls frequently wear trousers and male-style shirts. These changes are consistent with the reduction of difference between the sexes in our society as discussed in previous chapters. For the purposes of this chapter it is sufficient to note that standards of dress can change depending on taste and are not inherently either male or female.

2. The information in this paragraph and the following paragraphs about New Guinea is from Margaret Mead, *Sex and Temperament in Three Primitive Societies: Manus, Mundugumor, and Tchambuli* (New York: William Morrow & Co., Inc., 1939), 2, pp. 1-384, 3, pp. 164-244, 237-322; and from a lecture by the noted anthropologist, Weston LaBarre.

3. Gregory Bateson, "The Naven Ceremony in New Guinea," *Primitive Heritage: An Anthropological Anthology,* eds. Margaret Mead and Nicholas Calas (New York: Random House, 1953), pp. 186-202.

4. In the past decade young people have revolted against this state of suspension. They have adopted new and more permissive sexual mores and have often shown an unwillingness to delay gratification. They often choose not to wait the required period of time to achieve an occupational identity or traditionally defined marriage.

STIGMA OR PRESTIGE: THE ALL-AMERICAN CHOICE

Marie Hart

Ignorance about, and lack of investigation concerning human social relationships in physical activity is due largely to preoccupation with numbers. Many students and faculty members have become increasingly disenchanted with the recitations of statistical measures as a means of understanding social behavior. It has become a professional and personal requirement in America to view life through numerical abstractions. The impor-

Reprinted from *Issues in Physical Education and Sports* by George C. McGlynn (ed.) by Mayfield Publishing Company, formerly National Press Books. Copyright ©.

tance of facts as a basis for action, for knowledge about people in social relationships now and in the past, is undeniable. However, many researchers and scholars appear satisfied to stop when the statistics suggest that the hypothesis is, indeed, proven to be true.

However, we need to know more than correlations, standard deviations, insurance rate increases, and the statistics on incoming athletes. We need to know what social conditions, taboos, norms, superstitions, expected roles, and rewards make people behave as they do. In physical education, why do people group, regroup, divide, alienate, subdivide, collect and subcollect in such great diversity? The tension and conflict engendered by the archaic social rules and roles which govern physical education are no longer tenable, and furthermore, they are the cause of the divisions within physical education.

I propose that a social situation, heavy in prestige for some and laden with stigma for others, has been created and is perpetuated by the archaic male and female role expectations. Due to these role expectations, female athletes and male dancers live a stigmatized life much of the time. The male cultural environment of sport sets up this difficult social situation.

Beisser (1967) and Fiske (1972) have suggested that sport acts as a rite of passage into the male adult role in American society. The male is expected to be, or to act biologically superior, and sport is the only remaining testing ground. Sport gives the young male an opportunity to learn and practice the attributes still held and valued by his elders. Dance exposes the young female to accepted attributes of grace, poise, and beauty but dance is not nearly so pervasive and regulated as the sport system is for the male. Physical education is largely conducted according to male needs and expected role behavior, thereby creating the problems for female students and teachers.

Women's roles in society are in conflict with those perpetuated in physical education. In an investigation of women's roles, Griffin stated: "Being involved in sport and education, she combines the roles of woman athlete and woman professor and accordingly, is perceived as possessing all the "unsavory" characteristics of the active and potent woman. She is seen as intelligent, competitive, aggressive, strong, and experimental. These characteristics, while desirable for success in realms of sport and academia, appear to be of much less value to a woman in the social world. Physical educators must be aware of the conflict of the traits expected of women in the social world and women in athletics and the professions" (1973, 98). These traits may not only be of less value in the social world, they may, indeed, bring stigma to a woman.

Goffman's (1963) ideas on stigma and social identity may add insight to American social behavior in sport and dance. He defines stigma as "an attribute that is deeply discrediting, but it should be seen that a language of relationships, not attributes, is really needed. An attribute that stigmatizes one type of possessor can confirm the usualness of another, and therefore is neither

creditable nor discreditable as a thing in itself" (p.3). If this definition seems too harsh, he offers another: "the situation of the individual who is disqualified from full social acceptance" (preface). In Goffman's terms, attributes in certain situations and relationships create positive social identity (normalize an individual). Those same attributes in a different context may create negative social identity, and cause the individual to acquire stigma. In contrast with the stigmatized person, Goffman states: ". . . in an important sense there is only one complete unblushing male in America: a young, married, white, urban, northern, heterosexual Protestant father of college education, fully employed, of good complexion, weight, and height, and a recent record in sports." (p. 128) It is suggested here that the only one complete unblushing American female is married to this unblushing male.

If this is the definition of the most normal and accepted people in America, what is the result for those individuals who do not measure up to the list of all-American attributes? They are "disqualified from full social acceptance." The female athlete and the male dancer, in particular, do not measure up to this unblushing individual.

The model which follows may help to illustrate the relationships between female and male roles, and the cultural forms of sport and dance. It is suggested that these relationships can result in negative social identity, and cause the information of groups, based on stigma.

The acquisition of stigma appears to be the natural result, since women athletes are in male cultural territory and male dancers are in female cultural territory. Goffman (1963) suggests several behavior patterns engaged in by the stigmatized person. Three seem especially appropriate to physical education and sex roles: (1) the stigmatized individual may use his disadvantage as a basis for organizing his life; (2) he may control carefully the stigmatizing information; and (3) he may develop tension management activities.

Organizing life in terms of one's social disadvantage becomes apparent in the half-world of women's sport and dance, which largely take place in sexually segregated groups. Physical education and athletic organization for women are often organized around the recognition that women are not welcome in male sport groups. These groups were well established as all-male before women became involved in sport, and that tradition is often tenaciously maintained. Women are misrepresented, underrepresented, underbudgeted, and often not well trained as athletes because of the traditional male dominance of sport in American institutions. But organizing into a half-world is only a reaction; it does not answer the needs of the woman in sports.

Separatism in sport in contemporary American society is basically perpetuated by the middle class, which traditionally supports educational sport and dance. Such separatism does not provide for shared social experiences; it cannot form a basis for common interests, experiences, and conversation. Instead of providing a basis for interchange, sport tends to isolate and alienate people. In physical education male-designed architecture and separatist organizations contribute to isolation and alienation. Some sexual privacy may be necessary, but the present situation leads to exceedingly limited communication and little if any shared experience.

One important result of the stigmatizing process is how information is handled and controlled. When asked what he does, or what he teaches, a person may formulate the information carefully. Typical reactions from outsiders are often clumsy or, worse yet, insulting. Remarks like "I never would have guessed you were a dancer (to a male)"; or "I wish there were more women athletes with your looks" are loaded with double meaning. Consequently, they set up tension within the recipient.

Figure 1. The American Sport Experience and Social Identity.

I. *Through sport:*

  A. The Male Achieves, Derives, Pursues and Accepts:

    Prestige and Positive Social Identity

```
                                                    +
+                                                   +
_____
     least (aesthetic and              most (strength and
     noncontact)                                  contact)
```

  B. The Female Usually Acquires but Can Avoid:

    Stigma and Negative Social Identity

```
_                                                   _
                                                    _
     least (aesthetic and              most (strength and
     rhythmical)                                  contact)
```

II. *Through dance:*

  A. The Female Achieves, Derives, Pursues and Accepts:

    Prestige and Positive Social Identity

  B. The Male Acquires and Rarely Avoids:

    Stigma and Negative Social Identity

The media control information about women athletes in much the same way as individuals do. Either the media gives no information, or dresses up the message to be pretty, to be acceptable. Newspapers and magazines cover only selected sports for women, and most often show how attractive the woman is in her costume, rather than how skillful she is in action. *Women's Track and Field World Yearbook* (1968) is an extreme case in point. It emphasizes, through pictures and descriptions, the eyes, measurements, legs and figures of the athletes as much as it does their athletic achievement. The captions read: "a woman athlete doesn't have to look like a horse to run like a thoroughbred"; "the lady with the alluring lips," "Diamond Lil is a darned attractive bab," and "the two sweetest dimples we've ever seen." The oversell of the femininity of these world class athletes is demeaning. They are presented as "super attractive" females as if they were competing in a beauty contest rather than competing in world class track and field. It is a way of protesting the masculine image and promoting the feminine one. There is never a need to sell male athletes in this way.

Finally, much effort is directed toward diminishing the tension created by the masculine attributes associated with women in sport, and the feminine attributes associated with male dancers. As meaningless, futile, and unnecessary as such behavior may seem to outsiders, it nevertheless continues endlessly. Women coaches often ask or require sports teams to wear dresses when travelling. Orientation meetings are held in many institutions, for the sole purpose of instructing women physical education majors in a special dress code. College women in history, drama, or sociology would not tolerate such humiliation. Men taking courses in dance may find wearing a leotard personally difficult, if not impossible. The stigma is heavy.

One woman college student illustrates the intensity of the conflict in the following statement: "The female athlete feels very unfeminine when she enters the male-dominated sports world. If she shows any athletic ability or correct technique, she is not praised because of ability or technique but because she can "move like a man." Our student then asks, "What does this do to the woman in sport? I can only answer that from my own feelings and those of my friends. It makes me question my own femininity—the very roots of my being. If I am a woman, why do I enjoy sport? Why do I participate?"

Women have not been publishing or writing about their sport experiences long enough for educators and the public to realize what meaning the experiences carry for the woman athlete. Current writing is often eloquent in its expression of the inner struggle for identity. There is also a drive to resolve the conflict, a drive reflected in a group of verses from the poem "First Peace," by Barbara Lamblin:

> i was the all american girl, the winner, the champion,
> the swell kid, good gal, national swimmer,
> model of the prize daughter bringing it home for dad
> i even got the father's trophy
>
> i was also a jock, dyke, stupid dumb blond
> frigid, castrating, domineering bitch,
> called all these names in silence,
> the double standard wearing me down
> inside
>
> on the victory stand winning my medals
> for father and coach
> and perhaps a me deep down somewhere
> who couln't fail because of all the hours
> and training and tears
> wrapped into an identity of muscle and power
> and physical strength
> a champion,
>
> not softness and grace
>
> now at 31, still suffering from the overheard
> locker room talk, from the bragging and swaggering
> the stares past my tank suit
> insults about my muscles
> the fears, the nameless fears

about my undiscovered womanhood
disturbing unknown femininity,
femaleness

feminine power.

The masculine-feminine game as now played needs careful and expert study. It also needs to be called off in departments of physical education and athletics.

In the preface to their book, *Masculine/Feminine: Readings in Sexual Mythology and the Liberation of Women* (1969), the Roszaks state with eloquence and force:

> He is playing the kind of man that he thinks the kind of woman she is playing ought to admire. She is playing the kind of woman that he thinks the kind of man he is playing ought to desire.
>
> If he were not playing masculine, he might well be more feminine than she is—except when she is playing very feminine, she might well be more masculine than he is—except when he is playing very masculine.
>
> So he plays harder. And she plays . . . softer.

But the female athlete does not always play softer. She does not always lose on purpose. She may not always see it as a compliment to have her athletic endeavors compared with male records and then disregarded. The final result of role playing is emphasized by the Roszaks when they state: "He is becoming less and less what he wants to be. She is becoming less and less what she wants to be. But now he is more manly than ever, and she is more womanly than ever. Examples of this phenomenon in sport and dance populate gymnasiums and dance studios in American schools. The inflated male athlete, girl cheer leaders, song leaders, "major and minor" sports, women in approved sports and dance acting superior to women in "masculine" sports are only a few examples of the roles played. The Roszaks draw a conclusion and make a final plea to a society caught up in these social roles: "She is stifling under the triviality of her femininity. The world is groaning beneath the terrors of his masculinity. He is playing masculine. She is playing feminine. How do we call off the game?"

REFERENCES

1. Beisser, Arnold. *The Madness of Sport.* New York: Appleton-Century-Crofts, 1967.
2. Cevasco, Rose. "Femininity and the Woman Athlete." Unpublished student paper. California State University, Hayward, 1972.
3. Fiske, Shirley. "Pigskin Review: An American Initiation." In *Sport in the Socio-cultural Process,* edited by M.M. Hart. Dubuque, Iowa: Wm. C. Brown, 1972.
4. Goffman, Erving. *Stigma.* Englewood Cliffs, N.J.: Prentice-Hall, 1963.
5. Griffin, Patricia. "What's a Nice Girl Like You Doing in a Profession Like This?" *Quest* 14(1973):96-101.
6. Lamblin, Barbara. "First Peace." Unpublished poem. Hayward, California, 1973.
7. Roszak, Betty and Roszak, Theodore. *Masculine/Feminine: Readings in Sexual Mythology and the Liberation of Women.* New York: Harper Colophon, 1969.
8. *Women's Track and Field World Yearbook.* Claremont, Calif.: Women's Track and Field World, 1968.

DISCUSSION QUESTIONS

A. *Thomas Boslooper and Marcia Hayes*

1. According to Boslooper and Hayes, what is the main goal of the "femininity game" and who are the protagonists?
2. How do girls and boys differ with respect to game preference? How do these preferences relate to sex role socialization practices?
3. What happens to the middle aged woman who can no longer compete in the "femininity game"?
4. What is your personal reaction to Boslooper and Hayes' thesis that women try not to win or achieve too much for fear of ruining their chances of attracting men? Do you feel that professional female athletes are less concerned with the "femininity game" than other professional women?

B. *Judith Zoble*

1. Briefly discuss some theories of sex-role development.
2. How can one account for differences in "femininity" and "masculinity" among children?
3. How do girls and boys differ with respect to temperament?
4. What obstacles have thwarted women in their development of achievement-oriented personalities?
5. Describe some of the ways the mass media have contributed to maintaining sex role stereotypes in sport.

C. *Arnold R. Beisser*

1. Why is it difficult for men to feel secure of their masculinity in American society?
2. What is the function of initiation rites in primitive societies? Identify comparable rites in modern industrial society.
3. According to Beisser, what ritualistic measures do American men take in order to reaffirm their masculinity?
4. Do you feel that men are just as enslaved to their male roles as women are to their female roles? Explain.
5. What is your reaction to those who would argue that sport is male territory and women should keep out?

D. *M. Marie Hart*

1. What is meant by the term, "stigma"?
2. Why are male dancers and female athletes frequently stigmatized?
3. How can the American female who participates in sport avoid stigmatization?
4. What do you think motivates women to pursue an occupation which is negatively sanctioned by society?

Unit XI
Violence in Sport

There can be little argument that both crowd and player violence in sport are increasing at an alarming rate. The escalation of this phenomenon has prompted the formation of special commissions, at both local and national levels, to investigate its causes.

Two of the most popular types of violence studied by sport sociologists are crowd nonnormative behavior and individual normative behavior. Crowd violence is labelled *collective behavior* when it does not follow organized patterns of conventions and expectations. Such violence is typically unstructured, nontraditional and thus, nonnormative. Individual acts of violence (normative) are accounted for in terms of the *learning* and *enactment* of social roles within specific subcultural contexts. The selections in this unit reflect both of these types of violence as observed in sport.

In the first selection, sports writer Ron Fimrite documents the escalation of spectator violence in American sport and offers several explanations for its increase. The author accounts for this phenomenon in terms of the fan's frustration with society which manifests itself in hostile outbursts at sporting events.

In the second reading, sport sociologist Michael Smith uses Smelser's theory of collective behavior to analyze the causes of a number of soccer riots. Smith reports that the two most frequent causes of crowd violence were hostile acts committed by individual players (precipitating event) and unpopular referees' decisions (growth and spread of a generalized belief).

A second selection by Michael Smith offers a social psychological explanation of individual player violence. The author posits that individual aggression is *learned* in social contexts and reinforced by supportive reference groups.

In the last reading, sociologist Edmund Vaz's findings on the culture of young hockey players provide support for Smith's explanation of individual aggression in sport. Vaz points out that, interestingly enough, aggression in the form of illegal tactics was considered appropriate and legitimate behavior by both players and coaches. The author concluded that individual aggressive behavior in ice hockey is learned, normative, and positively sanctioned within the sport's subculture.

TAKE ME OUT TO THE BRAWL GAME
Ron Fimrite

Ugly incidents caused by rowdy fans are multiplying, and the reasons go far beyond the sale of cheap beer in the grandstand.

At first, they were merely capricious, fools clowning in the stands, spilling onto the playing field to gambol on the forbidden turf like rebellious children. There were streakers, naturally, and a woman who attempted to embrace Home Plate Umpire Larry McCoy, and teenagers sprinting across the outfield. They created irritating delays in the game between the Cleveland Indians and the visiting Texas Rangers but, in the beginning, at least, they seemed manageable.

Some difficulty had been anticipated, for beer at Cleveland's Municipal Stadium on the night of June 4 was selling at 10c a cup, and of the 25,134 "Beer Night" celebrants, a few would obviously be attending the ball game in quest of a cheap high. The stadium security force was, therefore, beefed up from a normal 32 men to 48, just in case.

As the night wore on and the beer took hold, more than a few fans turned ugly. They dropped firecrackers near the Rangers' bullpen and suspended others on strings into the Ranger dugout. They tossed cherry bombs onto the field and poured beer on the Rangers as they returned to their bench. In the ninth inning, after the Indians, who had been trailing by two runs, had rallied dramatically to tie the score at 5-5, dozens of rowdy fans jumped onto the outfield, belligerent, spoiling for trouble.

One group surrounded Ranger Right-fielder Jeff Burroughs. Somebody snatched his cap, and as he sought to retrieve it he was hit and jostled by the crowd. Burroughs fought back as scores of sodden spectators joined the battle. It was then that Ranger Manager Billy Martin, never one to avoid a fight, led his players in a rescue charge. Some were carrying bats. Still, they were outnumbered and outgunned by the chair-throwing, bottle-swinging fans. The Indians, Manager Ken Aspromonte in the forefront, rushed out to assist the Rangers, a gesture not without irony since the two teams had fought each other in a typical baseball brawl only a week earlier. Order was never fully restored, so Nestor Chylak, the senior umpire, forfeited the game to Texas. Still, the fans continued to swarm, scrapping now among themselves, until security guards and hastily summoned city police forcibly quieted them.

Nine persons were arrested and charged with disorderly conduct. Three Rangers, one Indian and Chylak himself were injured in the melee. "The fans were uncontrolled beasts," said Chylak, nursing a cut hand. "I've never seen anything like it except in a zoo."

"I've been in this game 25 years," said Billy Martin, "and I've never had an experience like this. . . . That was the closest I ever saw to someone getting killed in baseball. . . . People were acting like idiots. Was it the beer? I don't know."

The beer? More than 60,000 10-ounce cups were downed that night, clear indication that at least some of the tipplers were slightly crocked and that some of these could have been pugnacious drunks. Chylak called the rioters "punks," and it is true that the majority were young men. Just a bunch of drunken kids acting out their hostility, then? Possibly, but while the Cleveland riot was by all odds the worst and most dispiriting incident of the current sports year, it was not the only disturbing one.

There has been an alarming upsurge in fan violence in all sports these past months, to the point where unusual security measures are now taken for even the most benign events. Team owners and league commissioners, meanwhile, have been forced to take long soul-searching looks at what they have created. They must begin to wonder if it is even possible now, in an age of free expression and at a time when violent action and reaction are everyday facts of life, to assemble large numbers of people in one place, excite them, and expect them to behave themselves. The question seems wholly legitimate in light of some sorry recent occurrences.

Late last month in Cincinnati's Riverfront Stadium, Bob Watson, the Houston Astros' outfielder, lay stunned at the base of the left-field fence. The lenses of his sunglasses had shattered when he crashed into the fence in futile pursuit of a ball hit by the Reds' Merv Rettenmund, and he was bleeding from facial wounds inflicted by the broken glass.

A group of spectators, perhaps 10 or more, at least some of them drunk, leaned over the railing above the fence, presumably concerned about the injured player's condition. Then, as Watson's teammates, who had run out to help him, backed off in astonishment, the fans began to rain beer down on him and to pelt him with ice cubes and crushed paper cups. There was an angry, profane exchange between the players and Watson's assailants, during which the players were improbably invited to scale the 12-foot-high fence and give battle.

"This is a crazy world," commented Houston Manager Preston Gomez afterward in a monument of understatement. "I couldn't believe they felt nothing for an injured man lying on the ground."

That same afternoon in Cincinnati four persons were arrested for brawling, and only a week before, Umpire Satch Davidson had been struck in the small of the back by a full can of beer tossed from the grandstand.

The Reds' own Pete Rose, a superb athlete and a popular player even on the road before his fight with the Mets' Bud Harrelson in last year's National League playoff, is now a target of abuse not only in New York but in Los Angeles, San Diego and San Francisco. A game last month in Los Angeles was delayed for several minutes when Rose was subjected to a shower of ice cubes, food, flashlight batteries and other assorted debris by the normally good-natured fans in the left-field pavilion. In New York last week, Mets' officials took pains to ensure that Rose's first appearance there since the playoffs would be without incident. Seats within throwing range of the outfield were not put on sale and 45 extra security guards circulated through the stands. Fortunately, Rose endured nothing more injurious than boos, banners and a few shouted insults, some in dubious taste, but all fair enough in the eyes of experienced athletes.

"They can boo me," Rose has said, "but I can't get it in my head that a ballplayer should have to stand there and have bottles, ice and batteries thrown at him. I don't think a ticket gives anybody the right to throw garbage at a player."

Even Henry Aaron, honored wherever he plays in this, his showcase season, has been subjected to abuse from grandstand delinquents. At a recent game in San

Francisco a young spectator leaned into the Braves' dugout and hurled an orange, which struck Aaron on the side of the head.

In Boston a fan rolled a cherry bomb into the Minnesota dugout, the fragments causing slight injury to several players, including Pitcher Ray Corbin, who was hit perilously close to an eye.

In Arlington, Texas, Cleveland Catcher Dave Duncan was struck by a full can of beer and in Milwaukee, Detroit Outfielder Willie Horton was showered with beer as he stood in left field. Horton, who is one of an increasing number of players who wear batting helmets for protection on the field, was also hit with an orange in his home park, Tiger Stadium. Houston's Bob Gallagher summed up the players' growing concern when he said last week, "It seems like everybody in the outfield stands is either young kids or drunk old men. It's unbelievable what we put up with."

Baseball has no monopoly on outrageous fan behavior. Atlanta hockey Coach Bernie Geoffrion was hit on the arm by a full bottle of beer thrown at him from the first balcony of Chicago Stadium. Philadelphia Flyer Coach Fred Shero was barely missed by a liquor bottle thrown at him after the second play-off game with the Bruins in Boston. And in Houston, Minnesota Fighting Saints players were obliged to fight their way through a mob of truculent spectators to the visitors' dressing room.

The supposedly more sophisticated sports have also had their moments of disgraceful behavior. Fans at the U.S. Grand Prix auto race in Watkins Glen distinguished themselves by pitching both private cars and private citizens into a muddy pit along the race route enchantingly referred to as "The Bog." "The Bog wants the Porsche," the mostly young miscreants would howl before rolling an expensive foreign car into the ooze. Fans in the infield at Churchill Downs tossed bottles at passing horses in the race immediately following the Kentucky Derby. And World Team Tennis paid dearly for encouraging its spectators to violate the game's mores and express themselves vocally when seized by the mood. As it developed, the players' sensibilities were not entirely attuned to the verbal pyrotechnics considered routine in less-cultivated activities. Jimmy Connors, playing for the Baltimore Banners, climbed into the stands in search of one particularly abrasive spectator and Francoise Durr of the Denver Racquets angrily slammed a ball into the crowd, hitting a spectator on the head, after someone shattered her concentration during a serve by shouting, "Boo!"

These are only the more notable incidents. They do not include the routine fistfights, vandalism, profanity, theft and, for the moment at least, streaking, that seem so much a part of the contemporary sports scene. There are times, regrettably, when there is more action in the grandstand than on the field.

For all of this, Americans are still a long way from the hysterical behavior of soccer fans in other parts of the world. So far, we have not experienced a riot comparable to the one which took place a decade ago during a match in Lima, Peru, where 293 fans were killed and 500 injured. But by our own standards, we seem to be growing increasingly unruly.

Not that organized sport in this country has ever contributed significantly to public civility. The baseball fan at the beginning of the century—free of the possibly inhibiting influence of women spectators and close enough to the playing field in those tiny ball parks to take immediate action against erring players or umpires—was, by all accounts, an abysmal churl.

"Fans sometimes fought the players," reported David Quentin Voigt in Volume II of his *American Baseball.* "And their most lethal missiles were pop bottles."

But the ball parks grew larger and the players, seen from a greater distance, grew smaller, less familiar, less vulnerable. From afar, they looked like heroes, and for at least 30 years or more there was a general trend toward spectator conformity. The ball diamond was a sanctuary not to be broken into by Philistines. Then, too, there was no television to tantalize the show-offs.

There were incidents, of course. The Cardinals' Ducky Medwick had to be removed from the field by order of Commissioner Kenesaw Mountain Landis to restore order to the seventh game of the 1934 World Series in Detroit. Medwick had charged into Tiger Third Baseman Marv Owen in a close play at third, and when he returned to his position in the outfield the fans showered him with garbage. But for the most part, ballplayers were regarded with respect, even awe, and if the fans were not always orderly, they were at least cheerful. That can scarcely be said of the mob in Cleveland.

One of the more disturbing aspects of the recent assaults has been the apparent hostility the fan directs at friend and foe alike. Controversial players are no safer from abuse at home than they are on the road. To the athlete this is puzzling, frightening.

"If you hear what is hollered at us here and elsewhere," said the Reds' Johnny Bench in Cincinnati, "you would think they don't believe anybody is anything. It's dehumanizing."

"The old fan yelled, 'Kill the umpire'!" says Dr. Arnold Beisser, a Los Angeles psychiatrist who is a student of fan behavior. "The new fan tries to do it."

The recent nastiness is variously blamed on increased drinking in stadiums, on young persons accustomed to venting their emotions publicly and without restraint and to a general breakdown in manners throughout the country. But there has been beer in the ball parks for years and the owners themselves have long courted the young crowd. Can it simply be the national mood?

"That some incidents seem more outrageous and sometimes criminal now is probably little more than a reflection of the times," says Dick Beardsley, a longtime sports reporter now with the *Atlanta Journal.* "Anti-Establishment feelings have run strong in recent years, not so much in the number of people who feel them as in the expression their feelings take. Pranks have become less innocent. Now if you're going to exhibit displeasure, it seems fashionable to do so in a manner more shocking than in the past. It is no longer enough to run onto the field and try to shake hands with a player or to sit in your seat and be satisfied with a simple boo."

There is also the suggestion of something perhaps more ominous—an alienation of affections between fan and athlete. The modern fan does not take his rebuffs lightly. The athlete who pushes past an autograph-seeker is creating, to some degree, an enemy. The player who callously jumps leagues in quest of even richer rewards, can only disillusion the fan who might naively consider him beholden to the old hometown. And when a baseball player announces, as Chicago's Dick Allen has, that the game for him is merely a job, the fan begins to question whether his own loyalty has not been misplaced.

In his defense, the athlete-businessman is merely portraying himself as just another working stiff with the same problems, the same aspirations, the same capacity for greed as the next fellow. But it is just possible that though the athlete now sees himself, in his interminable financial haggling with the owners, as anti-Establishment, the fan sees him, with his huge salary, as only another member of the Establishment.

"Sports and the rest of society," says Dr. Beisser, "are mirrors of one another. The sports fan reflects society's dissatisfactions—a disillusionment, for example, with materialism."

And what, in the name of Mammon, is more rampant in sports today than materialism?

It is a dilemma, one that threatens the basis of spectator sports. The ball park was once a place to escape the pressures and violence of life outside. Now, it seems, there is no escape.

HOSTILE OUTBURSTS IN SPORT
Michael D. Smith

Collective violence appears increasingly to be plaguing sport. Hostile outbursts involving spectators, and sometimes players, have occurred during and following soccer matches in Great Britain, Italy, Pakistan, Turkey, and several Central and South American Countries; and have been associated with a variety of high school, college, and professional sports in Canada, the United States, and elsewhere. Despite the seriousness of the problem, however, and the handful of scholarly analysis, collective violence remains more shrouded in mystery than perhaps any other of the social manifestations of sport. The void in understanding is due in large part, needless to say, to the elusiveness of the subject matter.

What follows is a preliminary and cursory content analysis of reports (from the *New York Times* and assorted news magazines) of seventeen soccer "riots" dating from 1947. These represent but a sprinkling of like occurrences for which data are presently being collected and which eventually will be analyzed quantitatively. Neil Smelser's (1963) theory of collective behavior provides the framework for analysis here although, unfortunately, space does not permit doing full justice to the complexity of his formulations.

The fundamental determinants of any type of collective behavior, according to Smelser's scheme, are social structural; namely, structural conduciveness and structural strain. Given these conditions, the dynamics of a collective episode may take place: the growth of a generalized belief, the occurrence of precipitating factors, and the mobilization of participants for action. Finally, the operation of social control arches over all, in effect, serving as a counter-determinant which prevents or alters the accumulation of the other conditions. It is important to note that a single empirical event may represent more than one determinant and that although all the determinants must be present, each adding its value to the others in a temporal sequence, any determinant may have existed for an indefinite time before activation as a cause of a specific incident.

Social Structure

Structural conduciveness to hostile outbursts may take a variety of forms. First, and perhaps most important, is the presence of ethnic, religious, class, national, regional, or other cleavages. It is not surprising, for example, in hindsight, that collective violence marred the game in Vienna, September, 1947, between Hakoah, a Jewish Sports Club, and the Austrian Police Sports Club. Reportedly sparked by anti-semetic taunts, spectators fought with each other in the stands to be quelled eventually be a police riot squad. Exploiting existing antagonisms (sometimes euphemistically called "natural rivalries"), of course, is part of the very currency of sport.

A second type of structural conduciveness is the unavailability of alternate avenues of protest for grievances, or the unavailability of appropriate targets to which can be assigned responsibility for troubles. Smelser hypothesizes that the less modernized a country, the fewer the institutionalized channels for expressing grievances. This may be one of the intervening mechanisms contributing to the apparent positive cor-

This is a slightly revised version of an article that appeared in the *Sport Sociology Bulletin*, Vol. 2 No. 1, Spring 1973, pp. 6-10.

relation between sport riots and industrial under-development, Great Britain notwithstanding.

Third, conditions must be conducive to the rapid communication of hostile beliefs and to the organization of the outbursts themselves; thus, newspapers (and other mass media), which in many countries devote disproportionate space to sports, and which also serve as an instrument for the spread of rumor, ease the dissemination of hostile beliefs; and cheek-to-jowl congestion in the stadium facilitates rapid communication, a common definition of the situation, and the mobilization of the rioters for action.

Fourth, the accessibility of objects of attack determines whether or not an incident will occur and the form it takes. Referees, despite increasingly elaborate precautions, have been particularly vulnerable in this regard. In March, 1948, in Buenos Aires, a soccer official was beaten to death by players and fans who disagreed with his call. More fortunate was the referee of a 1954 Rio de Janeiro match beaten unconscious by spectators who then set his dressing-room afire. They had managed to ford a nine-foot wide moat to gain the field. Similarly, an iron paling-topped fence failed to stop Matias Rojas (who had a police record for previous attacks on referees) from reaching the field during the closing minutes of the 1964 Peru-Argentina game in Lima. Rojas was followed by others who tore holes in the "massive" fence and then raced to center field to battle a phalanx of police. (The Lima riot and ensuing panic left approximately 293 dead.) In seven of the outbursts studied, spectators were reported to have entered the playing field to assault officials or players. Frequently, bottles, stones, wooden seats torn from their moorings, and the like were thrown at persons on the field. Property was often selected for attack: British soccer fans, returning from games, periodically sacked railroad coaches during the 1960's; the railway station in Caserta, Italy, in September, 1969, was gutted in protest of a decision affecting the local team; widespread destruction of buildings and automobiles in areas adjacent to the stadiums took place during several of the outbursts.

Conditions of conduciveness merely make the hostile outburst possible. The existence of a strain, conflict, deprivation, or ambiguity, usually accompanied by stereotyped beliefs assigning responsibility for evils to other groups, is the second structural determinant. The 1969 Honduras-El Salvador "soccer war" is a case-in-point. The illegal immigration of an estimated 300,000 people, in a period of several years prior to 1969, from relatively industrialized and rich, but overpopulated, El Salvador to underdeveloped, rural Honduras had deepened already existing Honduran resentment of El Salvadorean prosperity. At one point, according to El Salvador officials, Honduran crowds had attacked El Salvadoreans forcing at least 10,000 back across the border. These events, together with frequent disputes over the ill-defined border between the countries, provide a backdrop for the riotous outbursts that accompanied all three World Cup soccer games between the two coun-

tries in June, 1969, and culminated in a severing of diplomatic relations following the third game and the mobilization of the El Salvadorean armed forces.

Ian Taylor (1969) has suggested that the collective violence associated with British soccer during the last decade is essentially a class conflict: "the last proletarian resistance movement" against the increasing takeover of a working-man's game. On the other hand, Catholic-Protestant antagonism reportedly underlay the violence associated with Glasgow Celtics versus Rangers contests during 1965 and 1966. Supporters of the Italian teams of Bari and Taranto—said to have a "longstanding rivalry from shipping to soccer"—clashed after a 1957 game in the former city, fighting with police and setting up roadblocks in the streets. Likewise, a game between rival Turkish cities Kayseri and Sivas, in 1967, erupted in violence which spread to both cities necessitating the ordering of troops to the border between the provinces in which each city is located. Existing strains presumably were partial determinants of the riots that interrupted a Liverpool-Glasgow match in April, 1966, resulting in more than one hundred injured spectators, and a 1957 Northern Ireland-Roma match, in Belfast, in which Irish fans ran onto the field and attacked the Italian players.

Other kinds of more specific and immediate strains may be created through ignorance or lack of information; for instance, in the Caserta episode, mentioned above, followers of the local team waited in apprehension for several days while officials vacillated over the decision to drop Caserta to a lower division because of an alleged bribery attempt by one of the players. When news finally came that the team was demoted, a general strike ensued featuring two days of clashes between police and protesters, thirty injured persons, seventy-five arrests, and much property damage.

Dynamics

Given structural conduciveness and strain, is set for the dynamics of the riotous outburst. Initially, the growth and spread of a generalized hostile belief gives meaning to the structural strain, attributing certain characteristics to the source and sometimes specifying certain responses as possible or appropriate. Prior to and during the three game Honduras-El Salvador series, for example, the press reported charges of "mistreatment" of Honduran fans at the hands of El Salvadoreans and accusations of "brutality" directed at players on both teams. Similarly, Taylor notes a belief in English soccer that hooliganism is the result of "contamination" by visiting "Latin" teams. Industrious research is required to ferret out the presence and nature of hostile beliefs linked with sport riots.

Precipitating factors narrow hostile beliefs into specific antipathies—as when rough games confirm beliefs about "they" being brutal or "dirty." Further research may reveal that many of the contests in which spectator violence has occurred were particularly rough. This seemed to be the case when Napoli met Rapid of

Vienna in Brooklyn, United States, in June, 1959; here, "players' tempers flared all afternoon." Indeed, in many of the soccer episodes, the events said to "touch-off" the collective violence were themselves violent: rough play, spectator aggression (such as stone throwing between groups of team supporters in Dacca Stadium, Karachi, August, 1966), police reaction to fan misbehavior (as when hoses were turned on the crowd after it objected to a last-minute penalty against a Naples player during the closing minutes of a Milan-Naples contest in January, 1955, thus prompting crowd members to hurl missiles at the police). The most frequently reported precipitants, however, were disputed referees' calls (many of which, interestingly, were responses to player fouls) during the final minutes of closely contested games. Disallowing a goal, ejecting a player from the game, an act of violence, and the like may be interpreted by team supporters as intolerable norm violations which demand redress. Often, a chain of escalating precipitating events appears to develop; what is more, one hostile outburst may precipitate another. Differentiating precipitants from the collective action proper presents a problem for the investigator.

When a widespread hostile belief has crystallized around a precipitating incident, or series of incidents, the mobilization of the participants for action begins. Leadership sometimes figures strongly at this stage; for example, the spectator who runs onto the field may deliberately or accidentally "model" that behavior for others, as in panics. In the 1964 Lima tragedy, Rojas, the first to scramble over the fence, showed the way for dozens of followers. Rojas was apprehended by police before he reached the referee. But the second man over the fence was tripped by an officer, then struck with a truncheon apparently diverting the crowd's anger from the referee to the police.

The nature of the crowd plays a part in the formation of collective episodes. Smelser notes that the greater the preexisting organization of the participants, the more organized their behavior: an ordinary stadium crowd may erupt in uncoordinated brawling, whereas hostile outbursts associated with organized social movements, such as the protests against apartheid that occurred during South Africa-Australia rugger matches in 1969 and 1971, and South Africa-England cricket in 1971, usually take somewhat different forms—at least initially.

The ecology of the stadium and surrounding area also shapes the outburst. When some objects of attack are inaccessible, others are substituted. Hence, the action may take place outside rather than inside the stadium and may focus on property as opposed to persons. The panic that accompanied the 1964 Lima riot seems to have been due, in part, to the population density in the stadium's north stands. On this occasion, police tear gas was blown by the wind into the north stands causing thousands to flee for the exits. But three of the five fourteen-foot wide steel doors had been left closed and unattended by their keepers (later accused of deserting their posts to watch the game). As a result, an estimated two hundred fleeing people were crushed by the press of the crowd behind them while futilely attempting to get through closed gates.

Social Control

Arching over the foregoing determinants, which together form a sufficient condition for the hostile outburst, is the exercise of social control: "counter-determinants which prevent, interrupt, deflect, or inhibit" the accumulation of the other determinants. Social control can prevent hostile episodes by minimizing structural conduciveness and strain; for instance, by providing orderly means of alleviating strains. More immediately, after an episode has begun to materialize, control agencies determine "how fast, how far, and in what directions the episode will develop."

Quick and unequivocal action by authorities tends to control collective violence effectively. On the other hand, when officials hesitate, are biased, actively support one side, or desert their posts, conditions are often made worse. Sometimes, too, officials may act prematurely or unwisely as in the police use of tear gas in the Lima riot and panic. Nor is a show of force always an effective means of control: five-hundred policemen assigned to Glasgow's Ibrox Stadium for a Ranger-Celtic game on January 1, 1965, failed to prevent a riot which resulted in more than forty injured.

Conclusion

Conclusions about collective violence in sport must be very tentative at this point: the representativeness of the present sample of incidents for the population of hostile outbursts in sport has not been determined; and the data, gleaned largely from the *New York Times,* is both incomplete and like most journalistic accounts of dramatic happenings, prone to unreliability.

These difficulties notwithstanding, one conclusion is inescapable; namely, that spectator-oriented sport serves as a catalyst for the ingredients that make up the hostile outburst. Added to this, and in the light of present knowledge regarding inter-group competition and conflict, sport probably often exacerbates the very strains that initially give rise to collective hostility.

REFERENCES

1. Smelser, Neil. *Theory of Collective Behavior.* New York: The Free Press, 1963.
2. Taylor, Ian. "Holligans: Soccer's Resistance Movement." *New Society.* August 7, 1969, pp. 204-207.

AGGRESSION* IN SPORT:
TOWARD A ROLE APPROACH

Michael D. Smith

Current theories of aggression, for the most part, are inadequate to deal with aggression in sport.[1] Moreover, some deliberately exclude "instrumental aggression" such as observed in violent crime, war, and sports. This fact does not, however, obviate the need for research on these aspects of human violence.

The pervasiveness of aggression in contemporary sport can be documented almost daily in the world press. What is unclear is why it occurs to such a marked degree? Three answers seem plausible. The first, and most frequently encountered, states that the nature of certain games is such (speed, body-contact, etc.) that undesirable violence is an inevitable by-product. While this notion, assuredly, is valid, it cannot account for the extensiveness of the violence. The fact that in some cultures sport is comparatively free of hostile content buttresses the claim that aggression is not necessarily inherent in the nature of athletic competition. A second explanation holds that athletes tend to be more aggressive than non-athletes. Although this may be so, research evidence for the personality trait approach is unconvincing owing to the severe methodological flaws which characterize most of the studies.[2] It is the intent of the present paper to focus on a third explanation; to develop the thesis that much of the aggression in sport is of concern to the sociologist; that it is a product of the values, norms, and role requirements of participants in the social systems that comprise the various sports. Simply stated, athletes—like the military—display aggression because it is expected.

A conceptual framework is herein proposed within which is developed the rudiments of a role approach to the study of aggression in sport. Specifically, the following questions are asked: What are the values that legitimize aggression in sport? What are the norms which coordinate and direct this behavior? What are the mechanisms by which individuals learn to fill aggressive roles? Since the above components may have different meanings at different levels of specificity, they are asked on four levels: societal, institutional, organizational, and role. This system, then, has two dimensions, each arranged hierarchically from general to specific; one dimension is concerned with the components of the system, the other with their levels of meanings.[3]

Values

The most general component in the system is values, ". . . conceptions of desirable states of affairs that are utilized in selective conduct as criteria for preference or choice or as justification for proposed or actual behavior" (Williams, 1969, p. 333). Thus, values act as broad guides for social action.

What are the societal values which legitimize aggressive behavior in sport? The twin themes of "violence" and "success" which often intermesh in the sporting context, may serve this end. There has been, in recent years, a spate of persuasive writings which argue that violence is an implicitly held value, particularly in North America (cf. Graham and Gurr, 1969). The fact that violence flourishes in some institutional sectors of society—such as war and sport—adds credence to these claims. Casual observation reveals an ambivalent attitude toward violence in society; on the one hand it is deplored (crime, child-beating, etc.), while on the other it is applauded (war, sports, etc.). In much the same way, apparently, people may simultaneously hold the values of "equality" and "racism," seeming polar opposites (see Williams, 1969). Unlike violence, the achievement—or success—value in modern industrial society has been empirically verified time and again and can hardly be disputed (Williams, 1969).

Moving from general to more specific: at the institutional level—that is, sport[4]—violence means aggression and success means winning. Teams, or possibly leagues, are found on the organizational plane. Here, the higher level values of winning and aggression sometimes intertwine; aggression may be valued both because it confers high status—as in a delinquent subculture[5]—and is a means to victory—it being widely held that physical intimidation of one's opponent enhances winning. At the role level is specified the appropriate kind of commitment for the actor. "Personal success" means commitment to the higher level values. To the degree this is accomplished, prestige accrues to the actor. Competing values such as "fairness," of course, act as brakes on aggression.

Norms

Closely related to (and sometimes indistinguishable from) values are norms, the second component in the system. Social norms are "rules for conduct . . . standards of reference to which behavior is judged and approved or disapproved" (Williams, 1968, p. 204). Norms are learned in the socialization process and may be particular to small groups, large collectivities, or whole civilizations.

Following Williams' advice that "a sound general principle in observing social behavior is to follow the dynamic course of sanctions wherever they may lead" (1968, p. 285), what type of sanctions are attached to aggression in sport? Hockey in the Canadian milieu offers trenchant illustration. Here, violation of official norms

Michael D. Smith, "Aggression in Sport: Toward a Role Approach," *Journal of the Canadian Association for Health, Physical Education and Recreation*, January-February, 1971, Volume 371, pp. 22-25.

*Aggression is defined loosely as behavior, the goal of which is to inflict injury on a person. It should not be confused with "aggressiveness," meaning assertiveness. Violence is used here as a synonym for aggression. Defining aggression precisely presents many difficulties. Lack of space does not warrant an excursion into the area at this time.

(rules) results in apparent negative sanctions (penalties) but in the same acts, unofficial norms such as "toughness" and "retaliation" are upheld and may be rewarded in the form of social approval of teammates, spectators, and even coaches. This approval may be tacit only, yet players gain prestige for acquitting themselves well in aggressive encounters. Thus, in hockey, a paradox exists; official norms are violated with impunity even though official negative sanctions are attached, while unofficial but apparently more obligatory aggressive norms are conformed to rather closely.

In middle-class society, both officially and unofficially, physical aggression is nonnormative behavior. Only where violence is institutionalized is aggression a norm. Merton (1957, p. 140) has observed that when a particular value is stressed, there may be little concern with the institutionalized means; instead illegitimate but technically efficient norms are followed.

The official norms at the institutional level are the rules of a particular sport. The unofficial norms might be called the "rules of the game"—widely held beliefs about how cateories of actors should behave. The "rules of the game" in some sports positively sanction aggression, albeit within certain confines.

At the organizational level, official rules vary somewhat according to culture, age division, etc., and, as well, a wide range of interpretation may be noted. The unofficial norms relating to aggression vary also from organization to organization.

At the level of role, compliance with aggression norms held by the organization is expected role behavior. These norms are specified further by auxilliary norms regarding the techniques of violence. For instance, the basketball player may learn to intimidate his opponent under the basket by discreet but vicious use of elbows.

Mobilization into Roles

Closely associated with social norms are sets of statuses and their roles. One's status is his position in a group, often defined by how others treat him. An individual has a status for each group in which he participates and for each status there is a corresponding role. Thus, a person's role is the dynamic aspect of his status. One reason why statuses, roles, and norms are so well accepted and why their behavioral dictates are so well conformed to is that most people are "trained by parents and peers to accept the existing local situation as normal, natural, and inevitable" (Thomlinson, 1965, p. 9). Although role theory has been criticized as containing no real theory but merely a set of constructs with little to tie the constructs together (Biddle and Thomas, 1966; Deutsch and Krauss, 1965), role, nevertheless, is very amenable to empirical investigation and thus serves as a useful vehicle for the study of social behavior.

While there are differentiated roles among athletes (forward, play-maker, captain, etc.) it is useful to think of the more generalized role of "athlete." Status associated with this position is achieved through superior playing ability and/or aggression. The role of athlete may be broken down into prescribed, subjective, and enacted segments. Part of the prescribed role may be to show aggression when required by the dictates of the role. Obviously, this will cause conflict if prescribed behavior does not coincide with the actor's conception of "self"—his subjective role. The resulting—or enacted—role is what is actually observed. Although roles are more or less structured, a wide range of deviation is normally possible. Thus, it is still possible to play the role of athlete without playing aggressively. How far in this direction the actor can move may be a function of his ability as a player; the "star" may be less constrained to be aggressive than the journeyman.

Reference groups. It is difficult to talk about role without also talking about reference groups. Moreover, like role theory, reference group theory is both popular and almost devoid of real theory. A reference group is "a group, collectivity, or person which the actor takes into account in some manner in the course of selecting a behavior from among a set of alternatives or in making a judgement about a problematic issue" (Kemper, 1969, p. 298). Although some writers distinguish between reference individual and role model, Kemper (1969) prefers to utilize the concept of role model as merely a type of reference group.

Kemper's (1969) taxonomy of reference groups—normative, comparison, and audience—appropriately modified, proves useful as a vehicle for depicting some of the mechanisms by which individuals are socialized into aggressive roles in sport. The normative group comprises "groups, collectivities, or persons that provide the actor with a guide to action by explicitly setting norms and espousing values." The athlete's normative reference group is his team. The identifying characteristic of a normative group is that the individual acts in reference to the norms or values the group promulgates. Generally, however, he conforms.

The comparison group comprises "groups, collectivities, or persons that provide the actor with a frame of reference which serves to facilitate judgements about any of several problematic issues." There are four types of comparison groups, two of which are relevant to the purpose at hand. The actor utilizes the "legitimator" group when a question arises as to the legitimacy of his behavior or opinions. For the young athlete, this function may be provided by the high status professional player. The second type of comparison group is the role model. "Usually an individual rather than a group, and possibly a fictional character or historical figure, the role model demonstrates for the individual how something is done in the technical sense."[6] In fact, the same individual may serve as both role model and legitimator. The young athlete learns by observation not only the techniques of aggression but uses the model, also to legitimize his actions.

The third type of reference group is the audience group. Theoretically, this is a group which demands neither normative nor value-validating behavior of the actor for whom it serves as referent. The actor, however, attributes certain values to an audience group and attempts to behave in accordance with these values. For the athlete, the "fans" comprise the audience group. Audience and normative groups differ in that the actor must attract the audience's attention whereas a normative group demands conformity to its norms or values. In addition, different sanctioning techniques are employed—the audience group dispenses reward; the normative group uses punishment. In sport, unlike Kemper's ideal types, the audience group has some of the characteristics, of the normative group and vice versa.

"Reference groups then serve to articulate individuals with significant social processes in society especially that of socialization" (Kemper, 1969, p. 300). The above groups, it should be stressed, although separate analytically, empirically, may reside in the same locus.

Individuals are mobilized into aggressive roles via socialization processes some of which have just been discussed. As with values and norms—the more general components of the conceptual scheme—socialization occurs on increasingly specified planes. Persons first acquire the basic capacity to enter roles of various sorts in society such as the male sex role. Although infancy and childhood may be the most crucial periods, socialization is a life-long process. At the institutional level the individual is socialized into sport, learning to play the generalized role of athlete with its prescriptions for aggression. The acquisition of attitudes and skills geared to specific sport roles takes place on the organizational level, the nature of these specific roles, of course, being contingent upon the nature of the team. Finally, at the level of role, the athlete—in most cases internalizing his role duties and obligations—becomes committed to play a specific aggressive role.

Conclusion

Aggression in sport has been viewed from what is essentially a sociological stance. Sports are seen as social systems consisting of, in part, values which legitimize aggression, norms which provide rules for the conduct of aggression, and mechanisms by which individuals are mobilized into aggressive roles. The techniques of violence may be socially learned, legitimized, and reinforced by various types of reference groups.

As in most of the social domains of sport, armchair theorizing on aggression abounds and empirical research data is conspicuously absent. A role approach to the study of aggression in sport could possibly yield data which would begin to fill this void.

REFERENCES

1. Bandura A. and Walters, R.H. *Social Learning and Personality Development.* New York: Holt, Rinehart and Winston, 1963.
2. Biddle, B.J. and Thomas, E.J. *Role Theory: Concepts and Research.* New York: Wiley, 1966.
3. Blau, P.M. *Exchange and Power in Social Life.* New York: Wiley, 1967.
4. Cloward R. and Ohlin, L.E. *Delinquency and Opportunity: A Theory of Delinquent Gangs.* New York: Free Press, 1960.
5. Deutsch, M. and Krauss, R.M. *Theories in Social Psychology.* New York: Basic Books, 1965.
6. Graham, H.D. and Gurr, T.R. *The History of Violence in America.* New York: Bantam, 1969.
7. Himmelweit, H.T. *et al. Television and the Child.* London: Oxford University Press, 1958.
8. Husman, B. "Sport and Personality Dynamics," Proceedings Annual NCPEAM, Jan. 8-11, 1969, Durham, N.C.
9. Kemper, T.D. "Reference Groups, Socialization and Achievement," in E.F. Borgatta (ed.) *Social Psychology: Readings and Perspective.* Chicago: Rand-McNally, 1969.
10. Merton, R.K. *Social Theory and Social Structure.* Glencoe, Ill.: The Free Press, 1957.
11. Parsons, T. and Shils, E.A. *Toward a General Theory of Action.* Cambridge: Harvard University Press, 1962.
12. Sears, R.; Maccoby, E.; and Levin, H. *Patterns of Child Rearing.* Evanston, Ill.: Row, Peterson, 1957.
13. Schachter, S. "The Interaction of Cognitive and Physiological Determinants of Emotional State," in L. Berkowitz (ed.) *Advances in Experimental Social Psychology.* Vol. 1. New York: Academic Press, 1964.
14. Schramm, W. *et al. Television in the Lives of Our Children.* Stanford: Stanford University Press, 1958.
15. Smelser, N.J. *Theory of Collective Behavior.* New York: The Free Press, 1962.
16. Smith, M.D. Aggression and Sport. Paper presented at the Wisconsin Sociological Association Annual Meetings, Waukesha, Wis., Nov. 10, 1969. (mimeographed.)
17. Thomlinson, R. *Sociological Concepts and Research.* New York: Random House, 1965.
18. Williams, R.D. "The Concept of Norms," in D.L. Sills (ed.) *International Encyclopedia of the Social Sciences.* Vol. 16, 1968, pp. 204-208.
19. Williams, R.M. "Individual and Group Values," in E.F. Borgatta (ed.) *Social Psychology: Readings and Perspective.* Chicago: Rand-McNally, 1969.
20. Wolfgang, M.E. and Ferracuti, F. *The Subculture of Violence.* London: Tavistock, 1967.

NOTES

1. The major theoretical positions are: the instinct theory of aggression with its Freudian, neo-Freudian, and ethology schools; the frustration-aggression hypothesis; restatements of the frustration-aggression hypothesis by Berkowitz and by Buss; and Bandura and Walter's social learning theory. For a review see Smith (1969). There are, as well, many theories on "mass" aggression such as riot, revolution, and war, most of which can be reduced to one of the above psychologically-oriented positions.
2. For a review of these studies see Husman (1969).
3. This scheme owes much to the work of Parsons and Shils (1962) and Smelser (1962).
4. Sport clearly meets the criteria for classification as a social institution as set forth by Blau (1967).
5. The similarity between delinquent subcultures and some sport, in terms of values, norms, and role expectations, is striking. See, for example, Cloward and Ohlin (1960) or Wolfgang and Ferracuti (1967).
6. The findings of Bandura and Walters (1963), and various co-workers, demonstrate, unequivocally, children learn aggression by imitating the aggressive behavior of role models, viewed in person or via film. The work of Sears, Maccoby, and Levin (1957), Himmelweit *et al.* (1958), Schramm *et al.* (1961), and Schachter (1964), among others, supports this social learning theory either directly or indirectly.

THE CULTURE OF YOUNG HOCKEY PLAYERS:
SOME INITIAL OBSERVATIONS
Edmund W. Vaz

Because young hockey players undergo a recurrent set of relatively common experiences there develops an occupational culture, a system of values, rules and attitudes that helps guide the behavior of players. Although the value system of the larger community tends to subsume the "official" rhetoric of the Minor Hockey League, the informal values attitudes and customs of the League fit more easily into the general value system of the lower socioeconomic strata. Moreover, boys who remain in Allstar Minor League Hockey likely come from lower socioeconomic levels; this facilitates their adaptation to the role of hockey player, and the acceptance of its values, attitudes and practices.

Older Allstar players (seventeen to nineteen years) often face a conflict between academic and hockey obligations. Problematic academic success, the improbability of a university education, the lack of clear occupational goals, plus the increasing likelihood of being selected for the Junior professional ranks make a professional hockey career appear meaningfully realistic for these boys.

We suggest that physically aggressive behavior is normative, institutionalized behavior, and is learned during the formal and informal socialization of young hockey players. This kind of behavior becomes an integral part of the role obligations of older Allstar players. Intense competition, the injunction to use increasingly aggressive means, and the strong motivation to be chosen for the Junior professional ranks are structural conditions which help generate, and differentially account for physical aggression in the league, i.e., among players on higher level teams. These conditions are less applicable to younger boys.

This is a working paper based on my first impressions of data collected during the first stage of a research project among boys aged 8 to 20 engaged in Minor League Hockey[1] in a medium-sized town in Ontario. Our interest is in the occupational culture of young players, their socioeconomic status, the process of their professionalization, with special consideration given the use of illegal tactics and physical aggression in their role as hockey player. This paper will touch on a few of these points.

Occupational Culture

Most groups that play together and work together develop a common set of norms (both formal and informal) that helps guide the behavior of their members. There emerges also a set of relatively common values and sentiments that underlies group norms, strengthens group solidarity, and often helps members overcome their everyday occupational anxieties and problems. This is the occupational culture—the group heritage that is transmitted to members. And research has revealed the occupational cultures of boxers, medical doctors, pickpockets, professors, even pot smokers. There is also the occupational culture of young hockey players.

Part of the culture of an occupation is its charter, the more or less formal statement of rhetoric of its objectives and ideals. This resembles an official version of meanings directed towards the representation of a specific image or impression of the group and what transpires within it, and is necessarily couched in abstract terms. It relates the group to the general values of the total community in which it operates, and in turn the group receives the blessings of the community.

In general the rhetoric of Minor League Hockey tends to emphasize the following objectives: to provide exercise, health and recreation for young people; to develop respect for the spirit and letter of the law, to develop sportsmanship and fair play; to develop the qualities of self-discipline and loyalty, and also to develop emotional maturity, social competence and moral character in young boys. This is an imposing list, and any community concerned about its young people would find it hard to reject a group that espouses and publicizes these virtues.

But we know that things are seldom what they seem. Good intentions and purposes are one thing, what transpires in the dressing rooms and on the ice is something else. In the course of reaching objectives and realizing goals social change occurs: original intentions are forgotten, meanings are transformed, short-term goals subvert long-term objectives, strategy replaces ideals. For example, the conceptions of sportsmanship and fair play have different meanings for different age groups. Youngsters think of it as shaking hands after the game and being a good loser. Among older experienced boys on the higher level teams the practice of shaking hands often leads to violence.[2] Similarly the qualities of sportsmanship and fair play are differentially emphasized in the system. Once boys reach the Bantam level (thirteen or fourteen years) these virtues are nearly dead letters.

Similarly, at the higher levels the value of success, i.e., winning the game, rapidly takes precedence over other considerations among coaches and managers as well as players. Little attention is paid to developing respect for the "spirit and letter" of the normative rules of the game. In fact, at an early age youngsters learn the institutionalized means of violating certain rules, and this becomes routine practice. They learn that there are

Edmund W. Vaz, "The Culture of Young Hockey Players: Some Initial Observations" in Taylor (ed.) *Training—Its Scientific Basis and Application*, 1972, pp. 222-234.

Note: This study was aided by a research grant from the Canada Council for which I am grateful. I am also indebted to Mr. Barry Boddy, my assistant, who helped collect much of the material.

"good" and "bad" penalties; the former are tolerated even encouraged, the latter are deplored.

Although the values of the larger community tend to subsume the purposes and ideals of Minor League Hockey, in fact what occurs in the dressing rooms and on the ice, and the informal codes and tactics by which players are controlled and the game conducted, reflect a narrower perspective. Many of the attitudes and values common to Minor League Hockey seem to fit neatly into the general value system of the *lower socioeconomic strata*. We know that there is a relationship between body-contact sports and socioeconomic levels; body-contact sports are correlated with the lower socio-economic strata.(1) Within Minor League Hockey body contact is a much proclaimed and highly cherished virtue of the sport; it is alleged that to eliminate or seriously reduce the amount of body contact would irreparably damage the sport of hockey.

One of the most closely guarded privileges of the professions is their right to determine the proper training and education for entry into a profession, i.e., before full professional status is granted. Whenever, and in whatever manner, the professional education and training is acquired it may be viewed also as part of the recruit's socialization. Learning the expectations and obligations of the role of hockey player is the process of socialization, and it is an integral part of learning the culture of the occupation. A major function of the socialization of Allstar hockey players in the Minor Hockey League is their preparation for the higher professional ranks. And the standards according to which this training takes place reflect the considerable influence of the higher professional groups on the socialization of young players.

An important subject matter of rules is establishing the criteria for recognizing a true fellow worker, or in this case, a true hockey player. Although technical skills and competence (especially skating and shooting) are necessary features of the role of hockey players they are not sufficient. Justification for the violation of formal rules, such as tripping, elbowing, fighting, use of one's stick in a fight, besides one's attitudes towards courage, toughness, the ability to endure pain, among others, are vital aspects in recognizing the developing professional hockey player. These are not technical skills, but qualities that mirror the internalization of cherished values and the success of the professionalization process.

If the middle-class ethic tends to value the cultivation of patience, the inhibition of spontaneity, self-control and the regulation of physical aggression, then the working class tends to emphasize the spontaneity of behavior; it praises courage, stamina, physical strength and resiliency, and rewards those who "never back down from a fight." Toughness is considered a virtue, and within the working class fighting is often recognized as a moral and legitimate activity in settling disputes. This suggests that the working class both supports the sport of hockey and is supported by it through the relatively common attitudes and general system of values that they

share. This overlap in values between the working class and hockey suggests that hockey is likely considered a prestigious occupation and is acceptable to both working-class boys and their fathers. This differential evaluation of occupations will likely influence some individuals to select hockey as a career.

Socioeconomic Status

All socioeconomic strata are likely represented among the youngest age groups that volunteer to play Minor League Hockey. Although the majority of boys will come from the lower socioeconomic levels, the sons of professionals will also be found. But I believe that the data will show that the majority of boys who *remain* in Allstar Minor League Hockey until seventeen or eighteen years come largely from the working and lower middle classes. Boys from the higher socioeconomic levels drop out of hockey. This implies that the National Hockey League is comprised largely of players from working-class levels.

We know that there exists a strong relationship between the years a boy remains in school and his family's socioeconomic status; sons of the most favored families stay in school longer and more often attend university. Children of less favored families drop out of school earlier, and fewer enroll in university.(2) It may be that as a career hockey becomes a meaningful occupational choice to those boys who contemplate dropping out of high school, or who are doing poorly in school and/or who do not envisage a university career—boys generally from the lower socioeconomic strata. Furthermore, as a career hockey will likely fall within the range of preferred occupational choices of working-class boys, but not those from the higher socioeconomic strata.

An area of particular interest is to study the variables that influence a boy's decision to select hockey as a career. Although a number of variables will operate, such as parental influence (which is apt to be encouraging), a boy's hockey "talent," family tradition, and available alternative work opportunities, there are a number of structural features that strongly corral working-class boys toward a professional hockey career.

By sixteen or seventeen years of age a boy who remains in Allstar hockey has reached the Midget level of the league where the competition becomes intense. It is precisely at this level that boys are scouted and evaluated for advancement to the Junior professional ranks. At this point they identify strongly with their team and are strongly motivated to play in the higher ranks, but the increasingly heavy emphasis on size, toughness, physical strength, aggressiveness and the ability to withstand pain makes conformity to role obligations especially difficult to achieve. Their efforts to conform to these expectations, the intense competition, the risk of being "dropped" from the team, and their desire to reach the Junior professional[3] ranks comprise a major structural source of anxiety.

At the same time these boys are still in high school

where the work is becoming difficult, and successful examination results critical for academic promotion. The conflict of academic expectations and increasingly stringent hockey obligations is a further structural source of strain.[4] Under these circumstances many boys will experience academic problems; in any case (and this is important) few boys will envisage a university education. Yet they have now reached a point where they must at least begin to consider their future careers. But academic success is problematic, a university education unlikely, and many will not have any clearcut occupational goal. Moreover, at this time they are continuously preoccupied with hockey and faced with the possibility of being chosen for Junior professional teams. It is at this juncture that hockey as an occupational career will appear more meaningful and attractive to them, precisely because it has become a realistic possibility. Once they are selected for the Junior professional teams their chances of playing in the higher professional ranks are greatly enhanced.[5]

Fighting and Physical Aggression

Where fighting is found to be a relatively recurrent activity,[6] differentially distributed in the system, and assumes much the same form, the sociologist will suspect that it is attributable to some structural condition of the system itself. Explanations that focus on personality defects, faulty control systems or the debilitating childhood experiences of individuals are apt to be bypassed.

Sports have traditionally been considered a means of controlling violence. Yet the "routinization of violence" has never been complete. Violence has persistently erupted in the form of rough play and dirty tactics. But this behavior is not necessarily an uncontrolled, spontaneous outburst of physical aggression. Fighting, rough play, and dirty tactics may be normative, expected forms of conduct. I suggest that the larger amount of physical aggression, especially fighting, that occurs at the Midget and Junior professional levels is normative, institutionalized behavior; it is learned during the socialization of the youngster, and it is part of the role expectations of the player. Under certain conditions failure to fight is variously sanctioned by coaches and players. The bulk of fighting can be accounted for according to structurally produced strains within the system itself.

If boys are to succeed in professional hockey they are expected to demonstrate hockey "potential" no later than the Bantam level (thirteen or fourteen years).[7] It is at this level that the criteria for player evaluation gradually undergo change. There is an increased emphasis on body contact ("hitting"); players must be continuously aggressive; physical size becomes a major factor in the selection of players ("a good big man is always better than a good small man"); there is the expectation that a boy "play with pain," and still greater emphasis is placed on winning the game. The ideals of sportsmanship and fair play are soon ignored.[8]

The influence of the mass media, the selection of professionals as role models, and the formal teaching of coaches are major sources of learning in the socialization of the developing player. As boys progress from the Bantam to Midget ranks (fifteen to seventeen years) the cultural value of winning increases even more. Less attention is paid to the legitimate rules of success. At the Midget level teaching concentrates on the technical aspects of "playing the man" and the subtler methods of "hitting" the opposing player and "taking him out." It is perhaps no exaggeration to say that the implicit objective is to put the opposing star player out of action without doing him serious injury. Illegal tactics and "tricks" of the game are both encouraged and taught; rough play and physically aggressive performance are strongly encouraged, and sometimes players are taught the techniques of fighting. Minimal[9] consideration is given the formal normative rules of the game, and the conceptions of sportsmanship and fair play are forgotten. Evaluation of individual performances (whether deviant or not) is according to their contribution to the ultimate success of the team. Of course certain rule violations are normative, expected. Under such conditions playing the game according to the "spirit and letter of the law" seems meaningless.[10] By the time boys reach the Midget and Junior professional levels dominant role expectations of the hockey player include toughness, aggressiveness, physical strength and size, and the ability to endure pain.[11] Gradually the team is molded into a tough fighting unit prepared for violence whose primary objective is to win hockey games.[12]

Simultaneously, competition intensifies for selection to the Junior professional ranks, and the boys are made patently aware of the spartan criteria for advancement. The obligation to "produce," i.e., to perform in an unrelentingly, physically aggressive manner becomes normative, routine, and substandard performance is not tolerated. The sanctions of being "dropped" from the team or "benched" become a reality. As competition intensifies so does the structurally generated pressure in attempting to meet these difficult standards.

The major structural conditions which generate the amount and differential distribution of fighting and violent behavior among players in the league, i.e., at the Midget and Junior professional levels, comprise (a) the strong motivation of these players to advance to higher level teams (and thereby improve their opportunities for a professional hockey career),[13] (b) the considerable competition for a limited number of positions on Junior professional teams, and (c) the informal injunction to employ increasingly aggressive and rough means in the performance of their role. Because these boys are highly motivated to learn and incorporate the appropriate attitudes, sentiments and behavior of the role, they are thereby constrained to conform to the demands of the role they admire and wish others to identify them with. These attitudes and sentiments, and their role performance coincide with those groups that comprise their reference groups and with others to whom they look for encouragement and validity for their conduct.

The violation of a rule depends as much on the occurrence of an act as on the existence of the rule. Any explanation of rule violation (which includes fighting) in the game of hockey must consider the particular set of rules that governs the contest. A change in the rules may not only discourage deviance (e.g., physical aggression), but indeed create it or, as in this instance, foster conditions especially conductive to physical violence. A change in rules in a contest will often transform the course of the game, and affect teams to adapt their game strategies and tactics.

Introduction of the red line which divides the ice surface into opposing zones has forced teams to employ new game tactics and strategies. This has led to an increase in physical aggression. The strategy of "shooting it in," i.e., shooting the puck from the red line into the corner of the opposing team's zone has rendered each of the corners of the ice a veritable "no man's land." This kind of game strategy has greatly increased violent body contact between opposing players and also contributed to violation of the rules. Some players participate in fear of having to engage in corner activity. Indeed, so crucial is the quality of toughness to the game that a player's ability in the corners is often a significant criterion in judging his determination, courage and professional potential. Coaching of younger players (eight to twelve years) usually focuses on the rudiments of hockey, and game strategies are less often employed among younger aged teams. Hence corner activity is less feared among younger players.

We can now ask the question, why is there much less fighting and physical aggression among players (aged eight to twelve) on the lower level teams? If we are correct the major variables that help account for fighting and violence among higher level teams should be less important to these youngsters.

As a career hockey has little real meaning for younger aged boys. Unlike older boys their futures do not yet require serious consideration nor decision making. Although they aspire to play hockey professionally their ambitions are "fantasy choices," rational considerations are not yet involved in their selections. They are not yet seriously oriented towards the Junior professional ranks and there is less competition for advancement.

At this age conflict between academic expectations and hockey obligations is minimal; school work is easier, examinations less important and hockey obligations less demanding. These boys are too young to be scouted and evaluated for their professional potential which eliminates another source of pressure. While they are strongly motivated to play Allstar hockey, conformity to role expectations does not as often require toughness, physical aggressiveness, nor courage. These are not yet major role obligations, which greatly reduces the amount and quality of violence in their performances. Youngsters receive little or no instruction in fighting, in fact fighting is strongly discouraged at the younger age levels. Although some illegal tactics are already institutionalized, these kids generally believe in the normative rules

of the game and in the "official" virtues of sportsmanship and fair play. This is reflected in the formal practice of shaking hands with opposing players at the end of each game—and these youngsters believe that this practice is an important sign of sportsmanship. Finally, fighting and physical aggression accomplish little for these youngsters; it gets them a bad name; it interferes with their performance since it is not expected of them and it jeopardizes the good name and ideology of the league. Briefly, there are few structured sources of pressure towards fighting and violence; their training strongly discourages violence and there is little common motivation for this kind of conduct. Fighters are not rewarded at this level.

Functions of Institutionalized Physical Aggression Among Young Hockey Players

If deviance is not contained it always becomes a threat to the organization of the system in which it occurs. At the same time under certain conditions institutionalized deviance may contribute to the vitality and operation of the system. At the higher levels of Minor League Hockey physical aggression becomes a criterion according to which rewards are distributed to those who uphold its values and attitudes, and who conform to role obligations. The player whose role performance personifies highly desired professional values and attitudes, and who conforms to behavioral expectations will rank high in the scale of evaluation.

Again physical aggressiveness reflects the success of the socialization process, i.e., the professionalization of young players for Junior professional and higher professional ranks. Players who "have guts," who "never back down from a fight," who never "give up," and who are otherwise consistently aggressive are breathing examples of the success of the prevailing system and its values and definitions of the game.

Given the accumulation of pressure, strain and discontent from daily participation in the legitimate order of the system, e.g., practices, games, (playoffs), the spartan requirements of training, school obligations, and other formal and informal controls, a certain amount of deviance (physical aggression) which is not rigorously repressed may serve to release tension. This acts as a safety valve and helps drain some of the strain and discontent off the legitimate order. The tactics used by referees in handling fights suggest this. Combatants are permitted to "fight it out." This helps insure that they will not wish to renew hostilities. In such instances the function of the referees is to prevent the interference of others and thereby control the spread of violence.

The collective meanings and definitions of young hockey players are reflected in the norms, attitudes and practices which govern their work performance. The "official" rhetoric of the Minor Hockey League does not always coincide with what transpires among its members. Although the value system of the larger community likely subsumes the official objectives and ideals of

Minor League Hockey, the everyday working values, attitudes and customs of the group coincide more closely with working-class values.

It was suggested that Allstar players who remain in Minor League Hockey come from the lower socio-economic levels of the community. This facilitates their adaptation to role obligations and their preparation for the Junior professional ranks. Once they reach a certain level in Minor League Hockey, structural conditions influence many of these boys to pursue a professional hockey career.

The principal conditions that generate fighting and physical aggression among players on higher level teams are (a) the strong motivation of players to be selected for Junior professional ranks, (b) the intense competition for a limited number of positions on Junior professional teams, and (c) the informal obligation to employ increasing aggressive, sometimes violent means in the performance of their roles. It was noted also that changes in the rules governing conduct of the game created conditions conducive to physical aggression.

REFERENCES

1. Loy, John W., Jr.: The study of sport and social mobility. In *Aspects of Contemporary Sport Sociology*, Gerald S. Kenyon (ed.). University of Wisconsin, The Athletic Institute, 1969.
2. Porter, John: *The Vertical Mosaic*. Ontario, University of Toronto Press, p. 165, 1965.

NOTES

1. Three methods were used to collect the data for this project. First, a portable tape recorder was used throughout one season to gather material in the dressing rooms of teams at all levels in the Minor Hockey League. This involved visiting teams in their dressing rooms before a game, between periods and after a game. Second, a series of partially structured interviews was conducted with players from the Minor and Junior professional leagues. Each interview lasted approximately 1 1/2 hours. Junior professional players were paid five dollars per interview. Third, a questionnaire was designed and data were collected from all players enrolled in the Minor Hockey League.
2. In more than one instance the practice of shaking hands after the game had to be discontinued because of the regular outbreaks of violence among players.
3. The term professional is used since players on Junior A and B teams are paid for their services.
4. When seemingly distinct although interrelated groups create conflicting demands on their joint members, sometimes tiny albeit deviant efforts are made by one group to help alleviate the strain. In this case coaches and managers sometimes attempt to get high school examinations postponed or special conditions arranged for their players. The status of athletics is so high and its influence so pervasive in the high schools that independent of outside pressure players are often given special treatment, consideration and privileges by teachers. This helps players remain in school, play on the team, and also helps reduce strain. In any case at this level few Allstar players are apt to sacrifice hockey for school obligations.
5. With the slowly increasing number of athletic scholarships a trickle of boys are able to play hockey while attending university. This provides another though longer route towards the professional ranks. One question is: to what extent does playing hockey subvert their desire to complete their education once in university? Is it the university dropout who pursues a professional hockey career? Any large increase in the number of players who proceed to the National Hockey League via the university route must ultimately mean a shorter career for them since they begin

later, the National Hockey League schedule is getting longer, and the game has become more physically demanding.
6. It is generally agreed throughout the league that there is more physical aggression at the Midget and Junior professional levels than among the lower level teams.
7. Some boys develop more slowly than others and scouts and coaches are alert for "late starters."
8. This reflects the influence of the higher professional leagues. These criteria are used by professional scouts and mirror the skills, attitudes and values desired by professional teams.
9. So common is fighting and rough play that the role of "policeman" is common knowledge in the league and is employed by coaches. A "policeman" on a team is a player who is recognized as being especially tough and able to "handle himself." The "policeman" is sometimes used by coaches to "get" an opposing player who is especially rough or "dirty."
10. The coaches themselves are notorious for violating at least the "spirit of the law." The seemingly innumerable methods they employ to prolong the game or otherwise interfere with the smooth conduct of the game in order to benefit their teams are hardly commendable, nor does it set a good example for youngsters.
11. This does not deny the considerable amount of body contact that occurs among the younger aged boys. Hard body contact is strongly encouraged at the very early stages of development throughout the league.
12. Coaches and managers of higher level teams pay lip service only to the value of education for their players. At game time hockey comes first. Players who opt for homework during examination time lose favor, and are sometimes "benched."
13. We have already noted that at this level boys will give greater consideration to pursuing hockey as a professional career.

DISCUSSION QUESTIONS

A. *Ron Fimrite*

1. Describe an incident of spectator violence in sport which you personally witnessed. What do you think caused the violence in this particular incident?
2. What possible reasons does the author give to explain the recent increase of spectator violence in sport?
3. Describe the history of spectator violence in American baseball from the early 1900s to the present.
4. According to psychiatrist Arnold Beisser, how are sport and society mirror reflections of one another?

B. *Michael D. Smith*

1. Refer to Neil Smelser's work and list and describe the fundamental determinants of any type of collective behavior.
2. Use Smelser's theory of collective behavior to analyze an incident of spectator violence which you personally witnessed.
3. Describe some athletic contests where crowd violence was expected by you or others but never materialized. Which of the fundamental determinants deterred the outbreak of violent behavior?
4. What is your response to the belief that crowd violence is unpredictable?

C. *Michael D. Smith*

1. Which two explanations of aggression (violence) in sport are discussed but rejected by the author?
2. How does the author explain aggression in sport?

3. According to the author, is aggression an innate human characteristic or is it learned? Explain your answer.

4. Assume that an extremely aggressive football player is traded by his team to another whereupon he becomes less aggressive. How would Smith explain this player's change in behavior?

D. *Edmund W. Vaz*

1. What are some of the values cherished by Minor League Hockey players? What is the relationship of some of these values to the working class?

2. Is Vaz's analysis of the aggressive tendencies of young hockey players in accordance with Smith's explanation of aggression in sport? Explain your answer.

3. According to Vaz, why does fighting increase as young hockey players advance into the Midget and Junior Professional levels of play?

4. What functions does violence or physical aggression serve among young hockey players?

5. How do you account for player violence in American football?

Unit XII

The Future
of American Sport

It is fitting that we conclude this book with a unit that looks at the future of sport in American society—the games we may be playing in the years to come and the value orientations we bring to those games. Futurists or "tomorrow-experts" have the dubious task of guessing the unguessable, of forecasting future trends and happenings oftentimes from scant or incomplete facts. Whether such guesswork, no matter how carefully and systematically done, can be raised to the level of a science is really not our concern. What is important is that the authors of the four selections which follow have each taken a serious and perceptive look at sport in the future. Whether the changes they foresee for sport are "good" or "bad," desirable or to be resisted is for the reader to decide. At the least, these provocative articles should stimulate our thinking and perhaps motivate us to take our *own* glimpse at what the future holds for sport.

Sociologist Harry Edwards contends in the first selection that "the crisis in sport today is only the initial manifestation of value changes that promise ultimately to alter the character of sport in America in significant ways." He believes that changing value orientations brought on by emerging changes in the main aspects of life in America are likely to render some of our most cherished current practices, including the games we play and the manner in which we play them, passé and irrelevant. Edwards mixes together some contemporary societal values, the conservatism of athletic coaches, the current economic crisis, and the growing drug problem in athletics and comes up with a far from optimistic forecast for the future of sport in American society, either in its present form or, in any form at all.

Author and lecturer George Leonard introduces us to the world of New Games in the next reading. Leonard believes that these games are an answer to his own rhetorical question, "How much more do we need to encourage aggression and territorial war (football), relentless fakery (basketball), and obsession with records and categories (baseball)?" Whether frisbees, hang gliders, kites, six-foot volleyballs, giant dice, and hula hoops are a viable alternative to footballs, basketballs, and baseballs is an interesting question for students of sport to ponder. Anyone for Infinity Volleyball?

Author and sportswriter William Johnson picks the minds of several scholars representing a variety of fields of interest in the next selection in order to gain a glimpse of what American sport will look like in the year 2000. Johnson also offers his own prediction that sport in the future will fit into two broad categories, namely, *Technosport*—sport which is the product of machines and technicians, and, *Ecosport*—sport which springs from the natural relationship between man and his environment.

In the last selection, physical educator Hal Lawson offers a scholarly critique of physical education and sport as they are presently embedded in the American sociocultural milieu; he identifies current trends and makes logical extrapolations to the future. *Influence pessimism* (a *negative* future alternative) and *influence optimism* (a *positive* future alternative) are then discussed in relation to society, physical education, and sport.

SPORT AND SOCIAL CHANGE
Harry Edwards

Today not only is there an increase in the amount of publicity or notoriety granted athletic dissenters but there are changes in the sources of dissent and in the character of dissent. In the past, the chief critics of sport's traditional functioning have been for the most part a few middle-aged journalists and social reformers, and faculty members and academic administrators, repulsed and dismayed over the corruption in sports and the perceived failure of coaches and others to operate organized sports in a way that was conducive to realizing the goals of the sports creed. But the critics of the 1930s and other eras on the whole did not criticize or dispute the claimed *potentialities* of sport (though there is at least one notable exception, namely, John Tunis). In one of the most thorough studies of intercollegiate athletics ever carried out—the work of Tunis notwithstanding—the question was never considered as to whether or not organized sport as then established should have been abolished or *radically* altered in form and function. The introduction to the massive two-volume study by the Carnegie Foundation for the Advancement of Teaching stated:

> . . . The competitions and contests, the delight in bodily activity, the loyalties, and the honor that form a part of that vast organism called athletics are the reflections in our college life of characteristics that are common to the youth of the world. In the pages that follow, these and other less pleasing phenomena of college athletics will be examined in the hope that those aspects which are good may in course of time achieve an unassailable predominance over those which are less worthy to survive. There can be no question of abolishing college athletics, nor should there be. What can be looked for is a gradual establishment through concrete action of a few general principles, to which all men would agree in the abstract. But even this slow change will be impossible without the sanction of an enlightened college and public opinion. . .1

Today the situation is quite different. For not only do dissenters receive greater public exposure, but they are younger people ("under thirty"), more numerous, and they are demanding changes in athletics at all levels that would effectively alter the institution of sport as we know it today.

That the very values emphasized and the orientation underlying the structure of sport are being questioned is significant because, "Only those orientations that are strongly invested with attention and effort escape the museum of [acknowledged] cultural fictions."2 The younger generation of today controls the society tomorrow. Their increasing tendency to perceive sports as irrelevant and, in many cases, as a malignancy in the social body provides little basis for the faith many older persons express in the future of sport.

The societal environment in which sports exist in America today is radically different from that of the 1930s or even a decade ago. Essentially what is happening in sport is only secondarily related to the agitation of a Jack Scott or a Harry Edwards or any other of the dissenters often attacked by the sports establishment as *responsible* for sports' troubles. What is happening in sports today results from the impact of the twentieth century, with its affluence, its speed, its mass communications—all of which have combined to create a much smaller world and new definitions of reality. As tradition has become less and less relevant to contemporary perceptions of reality, tremendous strains have resulted. These strains themselves are manifestations of social change—a change which is rapidly approaching "critical mass" wherein not only is an adjustment in institutional processes demanded, but an alteration in institutional foundations and structural relationships as well. As early as 1956, Sutton et al., noted:

> . . . [Present] institutional changes are the conspicuous and tangible results of deeply rooted and pervasive changes in American society: changes that involve important shifts in values. These shifts represent the working out of a set of values well grounded in our heritage—activism, universalism, and social responsibility. . . [In contrast to an all pervasive orientation toward individual achievement].3

To the extent that the current revolt in athletics is a manifestation of developmental trends cited by Sutton almost two decades ago, it would appear that the revolt is not a passing fad. The specific issues of the revolt may change (e.g., hair length, grooming practices, and so forth), but the fundamental conflict between those value emphases vested by societal tradition in the institution of sport and those value emphases dictated by the younger generation's perceptions of contemporary reality will in all likelihood remain. It would thus seem that, through token concessions, those attempting to save sport as we know it today may be able to buy time, but it would also appear that many of our most popular sports activities are likely to undergo substantial changes in character and some may even follow the path of another once widespread pastime—pitching horseshoes. In a general sense, the life style, technology, and other changes emergent during the course of the twentieth century are responsible for the demise of pitching horseshoes. The continually emerging changes in the main aspects of life in America will ultimately also affect our value orientations to the degree that even our most cherished current practices could become passe' and irrelevant.

Value Changes

Throughout this work, the persistence and stability of the value emphases within the institution of sport have been demonstrated. It has also been pointed out that

Abridged from Chapter 12, "Sport and Social Change," in *Sociology of Sport* by Harry Edwards (Homewood, Illinois: The Dorsey Press, 1973), pp. 348-364. Reprinted by permission of the author.

while the value emphases of sport constitute the primary source of sports' appeal, these value orientations are also key factors to be considered in understanding such recent phenomena as the perceived inflexibility of coaches, athlete rebellions, and so forth. It could very well be that these problems and conflicts are precursors of more far-reaching and fundamental altercations which lie in wait in the not too distant future.

By definition, an institution manifests some stability or continuity. To a greater extent than is the case with most institutions (excepting, perhaps, religion) the institution of sport has been obliged—because of its societal functions—to narrowly constrain both the structure of its component activities and the degree to which the values regulating human behavior within its sphere could legitimately vary from emphasized societal ideals. While these features have traditionally provided the institution of sport and its component activities and relationships with a stability of character, in times of incipient change such stabilizing influences could lead to inflexibility, or inability to alter internal structures and processes to accommodate external realities. In short, when an institution makes for itself a Procrustean bed, it is preparing the way for its own destruction by the on-moving and dynamic agents of social change. Such destruction may come about as a result of internal disruption or external neglect. The former is already underway in sport and the forerunners of the latter—though now quite minimal—have also emerged; for example, a wanning interest among student bodies in sports activities, or the difficulties some coaches are experiencing in recruiting athletes from high-school student populations. As objective conditions of social life in America undergo rapid change, traditional value orientations are bound to be affected, and opposing value orientations invariably come to the fore. If the institution is sufficiently inflexible, there ensues a period in which confusion reigns as to which value orientation—the new or the traditional—is more legitimate. If the forces opposing tradition continue to grow, those in control of established sport must either make concessions—that is attempt the readjustment of the institution themselves—or they must face conflict and confrontation with the parties of opposition. If only minor concessions are made (e.g., to longer hair styles, hiring *acceptable* black *assistant* coaches) conflict and confrontation is inevitable. This appears to be the course that the athletic establishment in America has chosen. Such occurrences as the defeat of the Curt Flood case against the reserse clause in baseball, the dismissal of dissenting and nonconforming athletes and coaches, and the labeling of those advocating change in sport as "agents of foreign revolutionary powers" may prolong the stability of the sports institution in the short run. But, in the long run, these actions in opposition to change could give rise to changes of a less gradual, deliberate sort and, in the process, result in even greater disruption and destruction than that presently feared by the sports establishment.

How much "adjustment" can be made in the struc-

ture and functioning of sport? That is, how incongruous can the actual operation of sport become in relation to the dominant creedal values emphasized before changes in the very character of sports are required? This question focuses on the scope of the institution of sport as a "value receptacle." In this regard, there are limits on the capacity of sport as now established to mirror values. Beyond these limits, change must occur in both the structure and functioning of the institution of sport and the activities which comprise its focal concerns. As a societal institution, sport in America not only reflects the values, but its character and the structure of its component activities are also determined by those values. Thus, for example, for interactions within an institution of sport to manifest an emphasis on individual "competitiveness," the social system of which that institution is a component must place high value upon a commitment to achievement through individual-centered competition. To the extent that activities carried out within the context of an institution are so far at variance with prevailing societal value "blueprints" as not to command personal commitment and involvement by large numbers of people, these activities and the institution itself must be either altered in character to more closely conform to prevailing values or become irrelevant and ultimately extinct.

All institutions are therefore vulnerable to the pervasive affects of value changes among significant segments of the society. For, by definition, institutions are based upon traditional values and norms. A conflict thus arises when current value trends conflict with those which have traditionally prevailed.

Now the institution of sport is particularly vulnerable to value changes. As an institution, sport is today caught on the margins of a value change situation wherein large numbers of people are clinging to traditional values and significant numbers are espousing values which often conflict with those traditionally prescribed. There is also a great segment of the population which seems to be increasingly questioning both the old and the new values.

Under these circumstances, the beliefs associated with sports involvement and scientifically definable as "cultural fictions" have been publically acknowledged by significant segments of the population as *cultural fictions in fact*. In this regard, Williams states:

> . . . [The widespread acknowledgements of] cultural fictions often represent more subtle processes of "loss of conviction," expressed in the language of psychology as withdrawal of affect or loss identification and involvement . . .[4]

It is at the point that this "loss of conviction" begins to manifest itself that one finds widespread sentiments holding that even such sports spectaculars as the Super Bowl in football and the World Series in baseball have become "dull," "lackluster," or "unexciting."

Now, "value orientations retain effective regulatory power only to the extent that they are defended when attacked, used as referents for concrete actions, and affirmed in social interaction. . ."[5] It follows then, that to the extent that significant numbers of people do not defend, refer to, or affirm the system of beliefs espoused in the institution of sport, these beliefs become irrelevant in terms of serving a function for such persons. To the extent that such perceptions of sport-related beliefs become prevalent in society, sports activities become irrelevant also, unless the values propagated are altered to conform to the values espoused by those who no longer view sports as relevant. Herein lies the crux of the chief dilemma faced by sport today. Though the economic situation poses the most immediate threat, the long-range threat is much less obvious. Sport in America is, in effect, being challenged to alter its structure and functioning. But this is not as simply and easily accomplished as many of the advocates of change in sport believe it to be. In fact, without some massive change in the value prescriptions of American society as a whole—and not merely among some significant segments thereof—the institution of sport cannot alter its structure and functioning and still survive. Even assuming that new values could be immediately substituted for the traditional ones, the "sports" which would emerge from such a fundamental change would in all likelihood manifest few of the characteristics we have come to associate with sports today. But, in point of fact, such fundamental changes are seldom immediate (excepting, of course, in situations, where revolution alters the structure and functioning of the entire social order), and it is doubtful that coaches could institute changes in the general structure and functioning of the institution of sport even if they were inclined to do so. Part of the reason underlying many athletic dissenters' assumption that coaches *can* alter the character of sports at will has to do with the misconception that coaches as a group are simply "bad men" who have deliberately structured sports to meet their own selfish ends. While such a conception of coaches has obvious ideological utility for athletic dissenters, the characterization is nonetheless naive, simplistic, and fallacious. As we have seen, coaches say what they say and behave as they do more as a result of their institutionalized role responsibilities and the relations between the institution of sport and the general society than as a result of any group—specific personality characteristics. Given these constraints which set limits upon the alternative choices open to coaches in terms of fulfilling their role functions in sport, to go beyond the limits set would undoubtedly result in the demise of the very activities that such action by coaches would be aimed at salvaging.

Whereas the present structure and functioning of sports antagonizes significant numbers of people adhering to and placing emphasis upon values which conflict with those emphasized in and espoused through sport, to the extent that any change toward accommodating the new values emphasis occurs, those individuals who concur with the traditional value emphasis and who presently identify with sport will be antagonized and alienated from sports activities. So even if they were inclined to initiate sweeping changes in sport, coaches have tremendous incentive *not* to do so: (1) the changes demanded would alter radically, if not totally destroy, the very activities which coaches' accommodating behavior would be geared to salvage; (2) those fans who now identify with athletic units would be alienated and would thus cease to support, financially and otherwise, these aggregations and sports in general; and (3) coaches' own internalized values, which affect every aspect of their functioning in society including their occupational achievement aspirations, would constitute monumental obstacles to fundamental changes in sport—even if such changes were acknowledged as necessary and "right." Most coaches would probably drop out of coaching if such changes could be and were forced. So if changes were immediately instituted, sports as we know them today would probably become extinct.

But on the other hand, the future of established sports also seems bleak if it continues to adhere to tradition, since the chief source of dissent from sport is found among the young, particularly the white, middle-class young. Here we have a category of people who have seldom, if ever, known material want, who have for the most part been insulated from the more mundane struggles of day-to-day existence, and many of whom have come to view the sphere of organized sport as crass, vulgar, and oppressive in its functioning. As part of the white youth culture, the perspectives and attitudes of this segment of the youth population carry tremendous influence and significance. It is the middle-class youth who for the most part populate the nation's college campuses. It is from among their ranks that most of the nation's athletes come. Under these circumstances, the perspectives of the middle-class nonathletes of the youth culture was bound to have impact upon the athletes given the relationship between the institutions of sport and education in American society. As the perception of sport as "irrelevant" pervaded the youth culture to a greater and greater extent, it was inevitable that athletes would eventually internalize the definitions of sport espoused by their nonathletic peers. Athletes then begin to question, rebel, and/or drop out of sports completely. If these definitions of the significance and character of sport persist among members of the youth culture into their adult years, sport as we know it today is likely to decline for want of attention and interest.

Two Problems

The speed at which sport is moving toward change could be further increased by two problems discussed earlier: the economic crisis in athletics and the drug problem. As yet, no real promise of a possible solution to the economic problem has appeared which would save any but a handful of sports aggregations. The eleven-game schedule in college football, more television exposure for all sports, expansion of athletic schedules in basketball and baseball, making freshmen eligible for varsity competition, and the formation of new conferences and leagues have failed to ameliorate the financial problems of most collegiate athletic departments. The only sure "solution" thus far has been to either de-emphasize sports or drop them completely. The tendency today for athletes, fans, and the United States Congress to balk at the idea of mergers in professional sports seems to portend an ominous future for these activities also.

Perhaps the most promising step for dealing with the economic crisis in sport is that which sport officialdom is most reluctant to take—off-track betting, or OTB. State-run off-track betting on all sports has been proposed numerous times, but has always been rejected. Those advocating OTB have generally based their arguments on the supposed economic advantages to be gained. If the state legalized off-track betting on all sports activities, it could cut substantially into the estimated billions of dollars gambled away by the American public each year illegally, and share the proceeds with sports bodies. If the winnings from legal sports gambling were ruled "tax-free" income, tremendous incentive to engage in legitimate sports gambling would be created thus destroying illegal gambling activities—or so the argument goes. It is further argued that, since sports gambling is extremely prevalent in America today, any question as to the morality of gambling on sports events is irrelevant. The only question is "Will the state control and share in the economic benefits of this gambling or will it continue to allow these benefits to be siphoned off by illegal bookmaking activities and small-time office pools?" In short, as one advocate of OTB has stated "Americans are going to bet anyway. If there were only two Americans left on the face of the earth, one would bet the other on who would die first."

The arguments posed against OTB have been several. First there is the fear that the legalization of OTB will encourage gambling and contribute to increasing its prevalence. Thus, few of the politicians who would have to vote in favor of state controlled gambling on sports events have been willing to take a strong affirmative public stand in this regard. Gambling is still considered sinful and immoral in many areas of the nation, so any elected official advocating legalized OTB runs the risk of courting political disaster despite the fact that the activity is thriving illegally.

Second, there is the question of controlling corruption. Memories of the "point-shaving" scandals which almost destroyed collegiate basketball in recent decades are still fresh. How would such potentialities as point shaving be controlled if gambling were legalized? In fact, would athletes be allowed to bet at all—either on other teams or for or against their own teams? The NFL Players Association has come out against OTB because of the heightened pressures that it would put on athletes. Even the best athletes occasionally drop well-thrown passes in the end-zone, muff "gut lay-ups" in basketball, get caught off base in baseball, and so forth. If OTB were legalized, there would always be the suspicion that an athlete, especially an exceptional one, had deliberately fouled up on such occasions. The legitimacy of the

expectation that even the greatest athletes will occasionally make a disastrous, but human, mistake would be severely curtailed. In short, legalized OTB on all sports would add the element of direct "economic interest" to fan involvement. The legalization of OTB could turn fan attention from consideration of strategies, hard work, character, discipline and so forth on the part of a sports aggregation to a more intense concern about luck and the likelihood of bad breaks—not to speak of the deliberate "throwing " of an athletic event. This change in the average fan's relationship to the sports aggregation from one predicated upon a belief in a rationalism and achievement toward one based upon fatalism and luck could transform the entire atmosphere of the sports realm and undermine the established relationship between the institution of sport and the larger society.

Nonetheless, it should be expected that coming decades will bring the legalization of OTB. The economic crises faced today by the nation's educational institutions and by the sports world, coupled with a growing dissatisfaction with sky-rocketing property and sales taxes will likely make OTB inevitable. And just as inevitably, there will emerge with legalized OTB increased allegations of corruption—especially in amateur sports where economic corruption is made all the more tempting by the demands placed upon the athlete who wishes to maintain his amateur status.

With regard to the drug problem in sport, it is only a matter of time before there is a case of an athlete dropping dead or of unsavory drug-induced behavior *on the athletic field*. Regardless of official denials, the drug problem is immense and it is growing. According to the president of the German Olympic Organizing Committee, the number-one problem faced by Olympic officials at the 1972 Summer Games was the drug problem. Aside from the likelihood of unfortunate incidents on the athletic field stemming from drug abuse among athletes, there is another way that this problem poses a direct health threat to sports participants. We have noted that injury is an accepted risk in many sports. The hazards of injury are increased immeasurably, however, when the physician treating a particular athlete does not know the athlete's drug-use history. It has long been recognized that combining drugs is dangerous. Unless the drug problem in sport is brought out into the open and steps are taken to deal with it effectively, sports participation is going to become even more dangerous then it presently is. It would be naive to lay the whole of the drug problem to the current emphasis on winning in sport. "We are a drug-oriented society" William Cambell, chairman of the California Subcommittee on Drug Abuse and Alcoholism, states.

In horse racing, when a horse is found to have been administered drugs, the owner and trainer of the animal are fined or suspended or both. It is unlikely that such a fining or suspending of owners, coaches, and team physicians when athletes are found to use drugs will work in sports in which the primary actors are human beings.

Drugs are simply too readily available to athletes via sources outside of sport. The only method of control that promises to be reasonably effective is that of regularly and irregularly administered tests for drug abuse. An effective system of monitoring and of imposing sanctions, however, remains to be devised and implemented.

Conclusion

This then is American sport. Whether the present structure and functioning of sport is "bad" or "good" or "right" or "wrong," or whether the changes that apparently await it in the future are desirable or to be regretted have concerned me, but have not been my central focus here. The effort has been to present an honest and comprehensive portrait of sport in America. As to further specific value judgments, the reader must decide.

If the reader has concluded that there *is* something "wrong" in sport, one further conclusion is inescapable: from its racial problems to drug abuse, from its economic crisis to female segregation, what is "wrong" with sport in America reflects America itself—particularly the relationships between contemporary social, political, and economic realities and this nation's value priorities, its attitudes and its perspectives. Sport, as one of the less flexible components of a dynamic social system, has been moved by imperceptible steps and under the influence of external factors beyond its control to the point where significant changes in its structure and functioning are demanded if it is to survive under any guise at all. The degree of flexibility of sport as an institution, then, will perhaps be the ultimate factor in determining its future.

The Future: Toward a Sociology of Sports

As to the future of the "Sociology of Sport" as a sub-discipline within the field of sociology, I believe that it promises to be extraordinarily productive. The institution of sport provides a "natural" laboratory for sociological inquiry of significance far beyond the realm of sport itself. In sport, the presence of the social scientist does not contaminate or interfere with the character of the phenomena being studied. The spectator is a natural part of the sporting event. Thus, for the price of a ticket, the sociologist who has done his homework and knows what to look for, can gain access to a mirror reflecting the past traditions, the present turmoil, and, to a great extent, the future destiny of society. Whether one's concern is with specific areas such as interracial relations or male-female role relationships, or with more general areas of scientific inquiry such as social organization and social change, sport offers a virtually unexplored avenue for generating new knowledge and gaining better insights into old problems. In the not-too-distant future, therefore, it would not be surprising if among sociologists there emerged a new appreciation for the old sports refrain "Take Me Out to the Ball Game."

NOTES

1. See Carnegie Foundation for the Advancement of Teaching, *Athletics In American Colleges and Universities*, Volumes 23 and 24, 1928-29.
2. Robin M. Williams, *American Society* (New York: Alfred A. Knopf, 1970), p. 436.
3. Sutton, Francis X. et al., *The American Business Creed* (Cambridge: Harvard University Press, 1956), p. 397.
4. Ibid., p. 395.
5. Ibid., p. 395.

...THE GAMES PEOPLE SHOULD PLAY
George B. Leonard

First rule: the side with the highest consciousness wins.

The seasons are subtle and often mischievous in my part of California. Spring is early but undependable; languorous January days may precede slashing winter storms. To know the change of seasons, I depend not on calendar or temperature but the ten-year-old next door. A day comes (never mind the weather) when he marches from his house carrying a baseball and glove rather than a football and helmet, and I am satisfied that a seasonal milestone has passed.

My amber-eyed, honey-haired neighbor is slight of build but large of heart. He has a voice for driving mules. During football season that voice takes on the clipped authority of a quarterback directing a two-minute drill. When the baseball is flying that same voice achieves a

Middle Eastern drone. Pepper talk. "Put-it-there-baby-now-let's-hear-it-attaboy-baby-come-on-come-on-let's-have-it-right-here-baby-'at's-the-way." My neighbor plays flag football (tight end) and Little League baseball (pitcher). After the games, he returns to our neighborhood, his face flushed with the heat of victory or salt-encrusted with the tears of defeat. Still, he has not had enough. On those afternoons, the ball flies up and falls back into his hands until it is a pale shadow against the trees. We have no way of knowing his particular dreams as he plays with gravity and darkness, but we do know that he has a tried-and-true portfolio from which to choose: the tie-breaking home run, locker-room jubilation, his name on bubble-gum wrappers.

The games he has taken for his own are rich ones, reaching wide and deep into the culture and the psyche. They have well-established heroes and traditions, a reliable vocabulary, thoroughly documented norms, and satisfyingly complex strategies. They connect with the larger world in a thousand known and unknown ways, yet they are worlds in themselves, complete with relationship, redundancy, difference—the pattern of certainty upon which men with confusing lives can practice making fine distinctions. No wonder disagreements concerning three points out of a thousand in a batting average can start a fight in a bar. And if all this were not enough, there are hidden dimensions, worlds within worlds, in even the most traditional games.

And yet the moment finally comes in every culture when the larger world itself begins to change in ways that confound the old games and the old rules. Our most cherished sports begin to parody themselves. One time too many the announcer reaches down into that bottomless bag of statistics to tell us that a new record for triples in one game by left-handed batters against left-handed pitchers on cloudy days has just been set. One time too many we leave the television set dispirited and dyspeptic after nine straight hours of pro action and God knows how much beer and peanuts. At last (the moment finally comes) we are sick of being pummeled and twisted and squeezed dry by every promoter who can sell another ticket, put together another league or push another underarm deodorant.

It all started back in school, when we began learning precisely those sports that are least likely to become lifelong pursuits. My ten-year-old neighbor may have vivid dreams, but the cold odds are long against his playing baseball or football into his thirties. Those and the other team sports taught in the typical high-school athletic program practically demand that we turn into adult spectators and gulls. They call for specialized, standardized players, officials, coaches, equipment salesmen. They are exclusive, hierarchical. They travel poorly and age not well at all. For the run-of-the-mill householder, a gridiron, diamond or court is a place to practice sitting down.

And what if we *could* play football, basketball, baseball all our lives? Would we really *want* to? Anthropologists, after decades of neglect, are beginning to study the significance of play. Their basic conclusion is obvious if overdue: a culture's sports and games mirror the culture's structure and values. That being the case and the world being as it is today, let's ask how much more we need to encourage aggression and territorial war (football), relentless fakery (basketball) and obsession with records and categories (baseball). It's a fundamental law of evolution that the final period in any line of development is marked by grotesqueries and extremes. The widespread glorification of winning at all costs reached its height during a war this nation did not win.

Hyped-up sports metaphor—"game plans," "enemy lists" and the like—came to preoccupy a national Administration just before that game was up. Even tennis, once a relatively gentle and somewhat stuffy game, began to go crazy as it went public. Net play more and more resembles World War II, with red-faced, tense-muscled, middle-aged men crouching at the front lines every Sunday, itching to fire their nylon howitzers down their opponents' throats. And golfers by the millions still idolize Arnold Palmer, even though he is past his prime, simply because he found a way to liken this game of contemplative strolls and shimmering distances to a cavalry charge. No wonder I began to find the sports section of my newspaper particularly unsatisfactory. The new games of a new culture should have their physical equivalents, but here were the same old pictures, the same old clichés, year after year. By the mid-Sixties the World Series had lost its charm for me. I watched the Super Bowl on television, but each year I swore I wouldn't watch it the next. The football I kept in the trunk of my car went flat. I turned to the more complex and aerodynamically pleasing flight of the Frisbee. I took up aikido, a martial art that completely dismantles the game of attack and defense as we know it.

I began to have my own dreams of sports glory. I envisaged a Super Bowl of the new culture. A mythic valley, sunstruck at noon, shrouded by mist in the setting sun. Tents and domes and multicolored banners. Thousands of people glowing with their own radiance—all players, no spectators. Men, women and children playing together, flowing in and out of games which themselves flow and change. The air filled with Frisbees, balls, kites and laughter. A scene both medieval and surreal. A picture by Brueghel, Salvador Dali and Hieronymus Bosch. A tournament of new games!

The dream did not wholly possess me; it seemed too unlikely. But I managed to get a piece of it into my 1968 book, *Education and Ecstasy.* I thought I was describing a playfield of the year 2001, where futuristic children could glide gracefully past the limiting boundaries of our present-day sports. But futurists are always wrong. The first New Games Tournament took place not in the twenty-first century, but in October, 1973. Over five thousand people attended, and it was held, yes, in a mythic valley in the Marin County headlands near the edge of the Pacific. In many ways, the event surpassed my dreams; the hang-gliders that soared over the valley—giant insects with human bodies—had been beyond my power to imagine in the mid-Sixties.

My first encounter with the particular train of events that led to the New Games Tournament, as a matter of fact, involved no arcadian play whatever, but participation in something called Slaughter, a game devised by *Whole Earth Catalog* publisher and counterculture organizer Steward Brand. In the Spring of 1973, Brand and I were billed as leaders in a sports symposium inaugurating an Esalen Sports Center devoted to a transformation of sports and physical education. (With uncharacteristic enthusiasm, The New York *Times* reported that "the occasion may be to a change in sports what the storming of the French Bastille was to the French Revolution.") After performing my various chores on the symposium's opening day, I hurried to Brand's afternoon session on New Games, eager to learn what I could of Brand's subject, and of Brand himself.

He was there on the main floor of a large gymnasium with his boffers, Styrofoam sabers with which you can whack your opponent with much sound and fury and no lasting damage. Brand was doing just that as television technicians circled and dodged to evade the widely flailing plastic swords. The duel finished, Brand began a short talk on the theory of New Games. Still breathing hard, he explained the rules of game-changing to about a hundred of us gathered around him on a gym mat.

"You can't change the game by winning it, losing it, refereeing it or spectating it. You can change the game by leaving it. Then you can start a new game. If it has its own strength and appeal, it may survive. Most likely it won't. In either case, you will have learned something about the process of game-changing and the particular limitations imposed on us by certain games."

He went on to tell us how all games are necessarily limited and thus made possible by rules, equipment and field of play. To make a new game from the stuff of an old game requires a significant shift in one or more of these. For instance, basketball played with two balls would be a new game. Old games, he said, have gone through a long evolution. All the obvious lines of play have been tried out. Strategic innovation is possible, but it probably will not be of a sweeping nature. In new games, on the other hand, everything is up for grabs. Nobody knows what lines of play will succeed. Strategists can have a field day.

We would now play a game, Brand said, that he had invented. Since it had been played on only four previous occasions, this would be a good chance to work out a winning strategy. None was currently known. The name of the game was Slaughter. It would be played on a large gym mat, about fifty by thirty feet. There would be two teams of indeterminate size; anyone who wanted to could play. Each team would be given a sturdy plastic basket with two balls in it, and would start the game at opposite ends of the mat. The object of the game would be to get one of your balls in your opponents' basket while keeping the other in your own basket. Each team's need to control two places at once, Brand explained, would tend to keep the game strung out rather than bunched up at one end of the mat. Players could force members of the opposing team off the mat. Anyone forced off would be dead, out of the game. Spectators would stand around the edges of the mat and serve as judges of the slaughter. To minimize injuries, no one would be allowed to stand up during the game. It would be played on hands and knees, shoes off.

Before Brand had finished his explanation, a winning strategy appeared, *tout ensemble*, like a cartoon light bulb over my head. Brand must have seen it, for he asked me to captain one of the teams. In spite of the game's

forbidding name, forty volunteers stayed on the mat; the others prudently took their positions as spectator-judges. The captains were given a few minutes to brief their teams.

Out of my twenty players, I asked for seven who were particularly dogged and persistent, who like to play defensively. These were to guard the two balls in our own basket. We would make no attempt to advance a ball until we had total control of the mat. I then put together four teams of Marauders, three in each team. I asked each threesome to hold hands during the briefing, to get to know each other, to become inseparable, to think and act as a unit. At the opening count, I explained, the four Marauder teams would move out as fast as they possibly could and start dragging people off the mat. Whenever possible, they would isolate members of the opposing team and create temporary favorable odds of three to one. After most or all of the opponents were thus eliminated, then and only then would we attempt to place one of our balls in their basket. I hoped the other team would try to advance their ball early in the game. This would only diffuse their energy. In any case, I said, our superior organization and purpose would undoubtedly prevail.

From the other end of the mat, the opposition let out an enthusiastic and threatening cheer. I glanced over and met the eyes of my wife, one of their players. Brand lined up the two teams and gave the signal to begin. There was a roar, a scramble and then a great melee— shouts, squeals, grunts, a contusion of bodies in awkward positions. I crawled from struggle to struggle, helping a Marauder team shove someone off myself.

The game was rougher than I had expected. At one point I had a vague sensation of being clobbered in the face, but was too interested in the game to pay any attention. About this time, I heard a happy shout. The opposition had tried to advance one of their balls and now our team had it. The player with the ball asked what to do with it. Not knowing the rules in this situation, I told him to throw it as far away as he could and continue our strategy. Brand retrieved the ball and returned it to the opposition, but now it was of little use to them; our strategy was beginning to pay off. Totally exhausted at this point, both teams pulled back and there was a pause in the battle. I noted there were now thirteen of us and only seven of them.

"Let's take a few moments to regroup," I said between gasps.

"They're more disorganized than we are," one of the younger men on my team said. "Let's go get 'em now."

"Okay. *Attack!*"

Again a mad scramble, grunts, cries of protest and pain. I released three of my seven defenders to go on the offensive. I saw my wife being shoved off the mat. She looked furious. There was another brief pause in the struggle. Now we were ten and they were four. We finished them off quickly and placed one of our balls in their basket.

Later that afternoon, I explained the whole strategy to Brand. He was as fascinated as I.

"Well," he mused, "as of now it's the strategy to beat."

As soon as he uttered these words, I found myself thinking up a counter-strategy. Now, if we could just be *sure* the opposition would use *this* strategy, *then* we could. . . . Stewart was right. A brand-new game offers an endless series of brand-new moves to play with.

My wife saw the matter in a different light. "I want you to know," she said as we were driving home, "that I really hated that game of Slaughter. I especially hated the way you played it—so cool, so inexorable. I want you to know that it was *no fun* for me or for anybody on my team—no fun at all." Along with many other people, she had left the New Games session after Slaughter. I told her that the games played later were entirely different. Egg Toss had two players throwing an uncooked egg back and forth while gradually increasing the distance between them. It was amazing, I said, how far apart they could get without the egg's breaking. Another game, Blind Basketball, had us all rolling hilariously on the lawn. It was a childlike game. It was fun.

"I hope so," she said, "because if all new games are like Slaughter, I'll stick with old games. Anyway, look at your eye."

It was already red and swollen, well on its way to becoming a classic shiner.

Early in September, 1973, just five months after the Esalen event, Brand phoned to tell me that his own **Point** Foundation, originally endowed with about a million dollars left over from the *Whole Earth Catalog*, was giving $12,500 for a New Games Tournament of large dimensions. They had their hands on a fabulous piece of land, 2200 acres of wild valley and rolling hills. The Tournament would be held as soon as possible, to beat the winter rains. He asked me to be there.

A month later, at noon on Friday, October 19, the first New Games Tournament officially opened. At that hour, some of the pavilions and winglike tensile structures were not quite completed; our aikido mat, a canvas tarp stretched out over straw, was still "on the way"; and there seemed to be more media people than game-players in attendance. But by the next afternoon there were some two thousand people playing Earth Ball, Le Mans Tug-O-War, Infinity Volleyball, Yogi Tag, New Frisbee, Boffing, Slaughter and other games too numerous or obscure to mention. The rains came that night, so the Sunday session was canceled and the Games were repeated the next weekend, on two gorgeous Indian summer days.

During that first Tournament, something about the nature of New Games began to come clear. We learned that the team games adapt themselves easily to groups of varying size. Earth Ball, for example, can be played by two people or by two hundred, the object of the most common version being simply to push the six-foot ball over one goal line or another. Players can wander in and out of the game at the end of each segment of play. A majority of the games require no specialized equipment whatever. No game is played against time as are football, soccer, basketball and the like; a leisured sense of informality generally prevails. And all the games are subject to further evolution. They are, in physical-education jargon, "low-organization games."

Regular teams, standings and statistics would be impossible in this setting. Sharp competition adds spice to the proceedings, but there is simply no way to build up the rigid machinery that supports the overblown, institutionalized, codified worship of winning that currently defaces our national sports scene.

Slaughter was played, with more laughter than strategy, at the Tournament, and there were other games offering hard physical contact for those who wanted it. But there were also gentle games and games of cooperation. In Infinity Volleyball, for instance, the object is to see how long the ball can be kept in the air. Just as in regular volleyball, each team must hit the ball no more than three times before sending it over the net. Both teams chant the number of times the ball has been hit, and both share the final score. This game was among the Tournament's most popular.

On the last day of the first New Games Tournament, everything came together to create a context for play surpassing perhaps even the hopes of its organizers.

A scene of constant flux and flow: near the entrance, the Mantra Sun Mountain Band, composed of members of a mountain-rescue squad, is playing good-time music. When it rests, a makeshift string band takes up the slack. A bright green hang-glider swoops overhead, then wheels to land in a meadow fifty yards farther down the slope. Beneath a red-and-white-striped pavilion men, women and children—players and kibitzers—are engrossed in board games, trying out new versions of chess, Monopoly, Parcheesi. Outside the pavilion, men are throwing giant dice, two feet square. I have no idea what game they are playing. Some thirty yards downhill, in the foundations of what must have been a large house, people are huddled around the consoles of computer games—Space Race, Pong, Gotcha. Nearby are two long tables laden with food—chili with large chunks of chopped pepper, bean salad, avocado and cheese sandwiches on brown bread, carrot cake with cream cheese.

Children are everywhere, making kites, playing with Frisbees and Hula Hoops, blowing wooden flutes and slide whistles given out at the equipment tent. Three mimes wander through the crowd. A juggler and a girl with a bird-face mask entertain a gathering of children. Boys and girls from three to thirteen wait to have their faces painted by volunteer makeup artists. And young artists are painting a mural of the Games on a long sheet of press paper.

A bullhorn blares. Stewart Brand is announcing the next Le Mans Tug-O-War. People run from all directions to a creek over which is stretched a hundred-yard-long ship's hawser. Men, women and children line up on either bank of the creek. When Stewart fires the starting gun, they run pell-mell to the other banks, grab the huge rope and start pulling. Children on the losing team have the most fun. They hold on to the rope and get a ride across the creek, from one bank to the other.

Nearly time for the New Frisbee Tournament. I head down toward the valley floor, a flat area larger than a football field, calling for players on a bullhorn. At the far end of the valley I can see two Infinity Volleyball games in progress. A chant floats to me on the still air: "Fifty-one! Fifty-two! Fifty-three!"

There is to be a game of Earth Ball before the Frisbee Tournament begins. I watch as two teams of about fifty players each line up at opposite ends of the field with the oversized globe resting halfway between them. Referee and Hog Farm minstrel Wavy Gravy, resplendent in cap and bells, raises the starting gun, fires. With a roar, the teams converge, two stampeding herds. My heart gives a jump. There is my nine-year-old daughter running along in the middle of the stampede. Surely she'll be trampled. Renouncing my tendency towards overprotection, I shrug and look the other way. **Play hard. Play fair. Nobody Hurt.** Nobody is.

Before long there are forty Frisbees in the air. And when that is finished, the center of action moves upslope again to a game of Scalp War and then another Le Mans Tug-O-War and then to the mat for an aikido demonstration, Energy Games and Yogi Tag.

The day passes swiftly. The sun drops behind a hill and a pennant of afternoon fog slips in to take its place. Deliciously exhausted, I return home.

That night I phone a friend who had turned down my invitation to come to the Tournament since he had tickets to a pro football game.

"How was the game?" I ask.

"Terrible. The Forty-niners lost."

"How was the traffic?"

"Terrible. It was awful."

I can't resist another question. "Did your children enjoy it?"

"Oh, they didn't go. I only had two tickets."

He asks about the Tournament and I begin telling him. But it's hard to explain. And anyway, he's not very interested. So we talk about the 49ers. It's not a very good year. There are some injuries at key positions. But maybe next week. The game will be on TV.

FROM HERE TO 2000

William O. Johnson

Umpires may be replaced by sensors, football scored like figure skating, tennis played in the nude and butterflies used as game balls.

Charles O. Finley is rarely, if ever, at a loss for words, but when asked what he thought American sport would be like in the year 2000, he was nearly dumbstruck. "All I know," he said, "is that the baseball will be bright orange by 1998." Others are less in awe of the great unknown. Lynn Stone, president of Churchill Downs and Hialeah Park, flatly declares that the $2 bet, for years the basic wager at U.S. tracks, will be replaced by a $3 or a $5 minimum. Bill Veeck predicts women will be playing on major league baseball teams and John Schapiro, president of Laurel Race Course, ventures that a majority of jockeys may be women.

Other experts hold that drugs will be sold openly at sporting-event concessions and that the hot dog of tomorrow will pack the same kick as the marijuana brownie of today; that there will be only one division in boxing, the heavyweight, all other classes having vanished because of boredom or bankruptcy; and that ski boots will have sensors that release the binding if the stress on a leg bone approaches the breaking point. Still other prophets foresee that non-contact sports will be played in the nude; that a round of golf will be played in

one spot, by means of a computer and TV screen; and that ice hockey will be played on Teflon.

Mike Palmer of the Institute for the Future in Menlo Park, Calif., contends that "it is irrational to attach pro teams to cities; no one has loyalty to a city in these days of suburbs and transiency. I wouldn't be surprised if owners began to organize teams based on ethnic or ideological loyalties to regenerate enthusiasm—games featuring the Steelworkers vs. the Executives, the Hippies vs. the Straights, Hunters vs. Animal Lovers."

Dr. Robert Kerlan, the Los Angeles orthopedic surgeon who is team doctor for the Lakers, the Kings and the Rams, says, "By the year 2000, athletes will compete much longer—for 25 years or more. We will probably live to be 150 or 200 and an athlete's career will be just like a businessman's." Joe Delouise, a Chicago psychic, foretells, "I see skydiving increasing in popularity, with many housewives participating." Because of domed roofs and artificial surfaces, the vagaries of weather will be a thing of the past for almost all sports participants (possibly including racehorses and skiers, but probably not skydiving housewives). Subjective decisions will also be obsolete, sensors having been installed in sidelines, baselines, home-plate zones, etc. Even the scoring of a boxing match will be electronic, with sensors in the gloves and a sensitized powder on the fighters' bodies so that telling blows can be registered on a scoreboard. Some people even predict that Taiwan will be readmitted to the Little League World Series, since in 15 years the major leagues will be international, having expanded to include teams from Japan, Venezuela, Mexico and Cuba.

And so it goes, as one chronicler of the future puts it.

In discussing the specific future of sport, one must assume that there *will* be a future and that it will not be all that bad. For the purposes of this article ignore the threats of nuclear lunacy, global famine, worldwide economic depression and poisoned skies. In searching out the future of sport, one has to guess the unguessable. Indeed, there is really only one point of certitude: As it always has, sport will continue to reflect the society in which it occurs.

During American colonial days 95 of every 100 people were involved in farming. Sport was rustic, family-oriented. In colonial America, as in medieval Europe, spectatorship was reserved for church and hangings. Then came the Industrial Revolution, and in the mid-19th century Americans began to leave the fields for the factories, exchanging farms for slums. Enormous crowds were crammed together: massive pools of athletic talent were suddenly gathered in one place. At the same time, family allegiances were being replaced by neighborhood loyalties or factory friendships and it was natural to hold athletic contests among these groups. Soon it became important that one group of factory workers prove it was better than another on the athletic field, so only the best players were used. The other workers retired to the sidelines to cheer and, later, to celebrate victories that demonstrated their team, factory, neighborhood or fraternal lodge was better. Thus, in a short period of social upheaval two phenomena were created—mass spectatorship and the win syndrome.

As C.P. Snow said, "Until this century social change was so slow that it would pass unnoticed in one person's lifetime. That is no longer so. The rate of change has increased so much that our imagination can't keep up." No one but a madman could have foreseen the technological, social, moral and economic revolutions of the American 20th century. As puritanism moved offstage, sport responded with Sunday games, beer sold openly at public stadiums and winning-justifies-the-means philosophies. As education became widespread, a superficially simple game like baseball was replaced in popularity by the apparently more complex strategies of football. As the American consumer society expanded—indeed, fairly exploded—and as the profit motive became more and more the national rationale, sport

followed by becoming a hard-sell consumer business, too. It expanded enormously, until, as Joel Spring, professor of education at Cleveland's Case Western Reserve University, puts it: "Athletics have become big business, a business dependent on a large body of consumers or spectators. It operates on the profit motive, and that means it has to have lots more people in the stands than there are on the field. Games have come to be played under scientific management with factorylike specialization and expertise. The resulting trends could be continual changes in rules and forms of major sports to make them more consumer-oriented."

Thus far, 75 years into the 20th century, the mirror of American sport reflects a society of hard sell and high production, of enormous growth and rocketing optimism. But times are changing. The signs of a cooling off have long been at hand. Gregory Schmid, an economist at the Institute for the Future, says, "I don't think we will take for granted the consistent optimism of the past. There is suddenly more uncertainty in our lives. Inflation is up and growth is down. We are coming into a period of moderation."

When futurists write of tomorrow, they speak in terms of "scenarios," meaning contrived situations and conditions extrapolated from known facts and trends of the past. This is complex stuff and the point of it all is to raise guesswork to the level of a science. A number of intelligent people are trying to see what is ahead so we can prepare for it, and we should be grateful for their efforts—right or wrong.

Futurists speak frequently of the "post-industrial society," an era which is probably already upon us and will likely continue through the year 2000. In short, this refers to a time (or scenario) when the American Way of Life will not be so intensely focused on the efficient production of goods and the mindless consumption of same. Harvard Sociologist Daniel Bell, in his book *The Coming of Post-Industrial Society*, explained it this way: "The first and simplest characteristic . . . is that the majority of the labor force is no longer engaged in agriculture or manufacturing but in services which are defined, residually, as trade, finance, transport, health, recreation, research, education, and government."

This means, wrote Bell, that the dominant worker in the U.S. labor force will be the "brain worker." This trend has been clear for many years: jobs that require some college education have been increasing at a rate double that of those filled by the rest of the U.S. work force, and the number of scientists and engineers, a group Bell calls "the key group in the post-industrial society," has been growing at a rate *triple* that of the rest of the work force.

Thus the U.S. is rapidly shifting toward a society which will be far more cerebral. And, obviously, the braininess of the nation will have a profound effect on sport. Brian Sutton-Smith, professor of psychology at Columbia's Teachers College, says, "As we become more cerebral, sport has to become better and better. The spectator becomes more and more critical. We are coming the other way around from the automated man. There are riots at soccer matches because people are not willing to sit and watch dull, routine matches. Spectators rebel and cause their own happening at a dull match. In a more cerebral future there will probably be a tendency away from massive followings of the monolithic spectator sports and toward more diversity. The popularity of football, basketball and baseball will become commensurate with things like orienteering, volleyball, bicycling. And the large sports of today will possibly become more like art, with a skilled critic commenting on slow-motion TV replays—someone like Howard Cosell to analyze and interpret the play.''

If one projects this cerebralness to a logical end, a football game of the future may consist of no more than four plays, each replayed over and over, dissected, analyzed and criticized from a dozen angles of slow-motion replays, with each player's performance judged and scored for its nearness to perfection (like figure skating). The winner of the game will not be the team that scores the most touchdowns, but the team that executes its four plays perfectly. Such might be the content of Monday Night Football for a nation of intellectuals in the year 2000 (although when The Old Intellectual himself was asked his opinion of such a prospect, Cosell rasped, ''That's an absurd extreme'').

If the general intelligence of the population improves, the appeal of violence in sport might be reduced. John W. Loy, a sociologist at the University of Massachusetts, says, ''I don't see any great demand for blood sport in the future. The growth of sport in the U.S. actually parallels increasing controls over violence. There are more rules than ever protecting players from injury, and better equipment—face masks in hockey, batting helmets in baseball.'' A colleague adds, ''If there is a split in society in the future—a wealthy middle class and a poor lower class—then there is a possibility of split sport forms, with the cerebral and gentler games for the upper class, the brutality for the prols.'' Sociologist Fred R. Crawford of Atlanta's Emory University also sees little chance for more violent games: ''We don't even support the death penalty for criminals. Our value system is actually moving in the opposite direction and in the future I think an Evel Knievel would have to prove that he is *not* going to be killed before they allow him to do it.''

Possibly. Yet perhaps the future was already with us last month when President Ford appeared at a U.S. Army camp in Korea and was ''entertained'' by the game of ''combat football''—an invention in which there are 42 men on each side, two balls in play at once and no limitation on blocking, tackling, kicking or piling-on. One fellow who thinks such brutality may even be desirable is Lee Walburn, an outspoken executive with Atlanta's Omni group, which owns the NHL Flames and the NBA Hawks. Walburn says, ''I think the sports that will claim the big on-site crowds are the violent sports, where there is the chance of injury. People who enjoy that kind of sport won't be able to get the true experience without being on the site to see the blood, hear the smack of the

fist on the head or witness the crash of an automobile. On the other hand, the 'beautiful' sports like basketball, tennis and baseball will be watched by esthetes at home on cable and pay TV where they can admire the grace and beauty, like they would a Peggy Fleming ice show. But I think hockey and football will be more violent in the year 2000 because we may be such a sedentary society that we need some release for our emotions. It'll be a matter of psychological therapy to have violent sport. We may not see men fighting to the death, but we could have animals killing each other—cockfights, pit bulldogs, maybe even piranhas eating each other to death on television.''

In the glowing '60s, when consumer-spectator interest seemed to have no limit, sport expanded as rapidly as the rest of the economy. But a 1974 Harris survey showed that only tennis and horse racing had gained in spectator interest in the past year. All other sports had declined. Pro football is still No. 1, but season-ticket sales dropped 6% and TV ratings are down. Even Pete Rozelle is slightly glum. ''There has been a dilution in football,'' he says, ''because of the new league. There has been a dilution in all sports. You turn on the radio and hear about teams you didn't even know existed. You ask, 'Where is that team? Is it hockey or what?' The days of simplistic identification are over. There are just too many teams.'' Whatever there may be too many of, Rozelle obviously doesn't think they are NFL teams. The league is *still* expanding as blithely as if it were 1965—to 28 teams in 1976, to 30 in 1977 or 1978, and, perhaps by next year, on to Europe for a mini-NFL: the Vienna Lipizzaners, the Istanbul Conquerors, the Rome Gladiators.

Rozelle sees the drop in football popularity as temporary and believes it has been caused by an invasion of bleak real life into the previously escapist ''oasis'' of pro football. ''We are a form of entertainment,'' he says. ''In the future, I hope we can keep our off-field problems removed from the game. The public doesn't want strikes and lawsuits, they want enjoyment. I hope we can make pro football an escape valve for the fan again, an oasis from a troubled world.'' At the moment, Rozelle still sees commerical television and the spectator-consumer as pro football's economic base, and he says the NFL is no longer even toying with the idea of starting its own independent network, an idea that was fairly close to reality five years ago. However, if mass spectator appeal takes a deeper nose dive and ratings drop further, the networks may be unwilling to support the NFL in the manner to which it has become accustomed, namely at a rate of $55 million a year. Cable and pay television will then become a very real possibility.

The payoff for pay television could be nearly astronomical. Jack Kent Cooke, principal owner of the Los Angeles Lakers and Kings, as well as largest single stockholder of the Washington Redskins and chairman of TelePromTer Corp., did some figuring about the Southern California basin where there are some 3.5 million homes. ''If just 20% want to watch the Rams, the

Dodgers, the Lakers, the Kings or whatever," says Cooke, "you have a total of 700,000 homes. Let's say it's $5 per home. You are playing a numbers game that knocks you for a loop—that's $3.5 million per *game*!"

But the most likely source of income for sport in the future will be gambling money. Few realists doubt it. Bill Veeck says, "There undoubtedly will be legalized gambling on all sports. There will be off-park betting, of course, and eventually there will be mutuels in our stadiums. There's not a thing wrong with it." University of Michigan Athletic Director Don Canham agrees: "The next step will be legalized gambling—state-controlled mutuel windows. Oh, maybe not at colleges, but certainly for the pros. That's not far out. Rozelle's against it now, but he's progressive as hell and he will probably be the first guy to put betting booths in the stadiums."

Assuming proper controls, which would be little different from the controls now in effect to keep illegal gambling from influencing game results, sport could be run almost entirely from gambling proceeds. Indeed, stadium seats now going for as much as $10 might be as cheap as general admission to racetracks, now averaging $1.50, or even be free. Not only could the economy of sports be revitalized, gambling might add enthusiasm to spectatorship in general. Lee Vander Velden, an assistant professor of physical education at the University of Maryland, says: "Team loyalties are fading out, I think, and more people are interested in a game like Atlanta vs. San Diego only because they want to see if they can beat the line. Putting a little money up is one guaranteed way to get an individual to work up some excitement over a game he might not ordinarily care about."

An even more logical projection that would hype spectator gambling interest would combine pay television of sorts with your friendly neighborhood bookmaker, or banker. Atlanta Sociologist Fred Crawford says, "We haven't really even started to explore the potential of betting on live games on television. It could work like an American Express Card—you could actually bet against your own bank, say, through your TV set. Something with an electronic key that's activated by a credit card, with computerized punch buttons to show how you want to bet, what point spread you like, etc. All the gambler would have to do is send in his chit to the bank and have his winnings transferred to his account—or losings deducted."

So, with electronic gambling to solve the economic problems of professional sports, what about the colleges? Michigan's Canham says flatly: "The economics of college sports are critical right now. If you're talking about 25 years, I think that by then—in fact, in a lot less time—we'll have nothing but a coast-to-coast super conference in football. No school will stay in the game except the super powers—maybe 20 teams, maybe 25. Everyone else will be in club sports. Right now Michigan happens to be one of the fortunate schools, but down the line there is deep trouble. I give us five years, at least I

think we can keep our head above water for five years, but certainly not 25 years. We generate $4.5 million here in revenue, and when *we* get to the point where *we* can't afford big-time football, what must be happening at other schools?"

Another change will be a substantial increase in leisure time. Herman Kahn and Anthony J. Wiener of the Hudson Institute concocted a scenario in their book *The Year 2000* in which working hours were cut from 1,900 to 1,100 a year. This resulted in a 7 1/2-hour workday, a four-day work week, based on 39 work weeks, including holidays, and added up to 147 workdays and 218 days off each year. But leisure may not be the blessing it seems. There will be huge adjustments to be made in terms of soothing the American sense of guilt over not working. Kahn and Wiener wrote: "Typically an American businessman or professional man apologizes for taking a vacation by explaining it is only 'in order to recharge his batteries'; he justifies rest or play mostly in terms of returning to do a better job. Thus if the average American had an opportunity to live on the beach for six months a year doing nothing, he might have severe guilt feelings in addition to a sunburn. . . . He usually must go through a preliminary justification such as the following: 'The system is corrupt, I reject it. . . . To hell with these puritanical, obsolete concepts.' Unless an American has taken an ideological and moralistic stance against the work-oriented value system, he cannot abandon work."

Despite the Kahn-Wiener scenario with almost a 2-to-1 ratio of leisure time over work time (which they say is a maximized possibility), the fact is that in the past 20 years leisure time in America has not changed much— nor has the habit of involvement in sport. Indeed, it has been argued by Staffan B. Linder in a book called *The Harried Leisure Class* that Americans use less time for relaxation than one would assume, for even though "non-work hours" have increased while work hours have gone down slightly, our advanced technology has actually caused us to expend a lot of "non-work time" at "non-leisure" pursuits such as commuting to and from work for an hour or two a day. Indeed, a clear-cut passivity has been built into American life over the past 20 years despite the so-called Sports Boom. The average amount of time spent participating in sports or vigorous exercise by Americans is only 5.5 minutes a day.

Whether the American society maintains its level of lassitude remains to be seen, but one thing that may change it is the attitude toward physical education in the public schools. For nearly all the years of the Sports Boom, the great majority of American children have had spectatorship thrust upon them from the moment they start school. The average child—and God knows, the inferior child—was neglected or ignored in physical education. The emphasis in high schools has been almost entirely upon the elite male athlete and on team games (the moneymakers). Psychologist Thomas Tutko of San Jose State University says, "It's very painful to think of all the youngsters who love sport but who are being eliminated at every stage just because they aren't going to be 'winners'—because they are too short or too weak. The genuine benefits of athletics—health, sociability and developing personal psychological growth, cooperation, loyalty and pride—are being undermined." Katherine Ley, president of the American Alliance for Health, Physical Education, and Recreation, says, "We should be offering all kinds of experiences to high school kids—orienteering, bicycling, camping, hiking. And in the future physical education should be located primarily in the elementary schools or even offered to preschool youngsters. We are too win-oriented, and in athletics we should stress the learning situation, not the *winning* situation. If competitive sport isn't an education tool, then it should be taken out of the public schools. A coach could sit in the stands and let the kids run the game—that's where the future of school sports could lie."

It is possible, however, that the very personality of the American population as it develops in the next 25 years will be more active than passive, more involved than inert. For the rest of the 20th century will be dominated by the energetic, hell-raising crowd of activist-skeptics born during the Baby Boom of the early '50s, plus the less obviously dynamic but perhaps equally dubious bunch who came a few years later. Some 80 million Americans were born between 1945 and 1965, a birth rate of 23.3 per thousand (an enormous increase compared to the 18.7 rate of 1935 and the slackening rate of 14.9 in 1973). This great bulge of people will affect American demographics right through the millennium. The average age in the U.S. will rise dramatically—from 28 in 1970 to 35.8 in 2000.

The numerical influence of this crowd will be impressive. The Department of the Interior, for example, predicts that whereas there were 14 million backpackers in 1970, by the year 2000 there will be 43 million. Last year no fewer than 21 national parks required campsite reservations. These large numbers work the other way, too: whereas American professional sports are now riding the crest of the Baby Boom and have the greatest pool of young athletic talent available in the history of the world, within a few more years, perhaps only five, that pool will be drying up and the level of excellence will fall as the lower birth rates of the late '60s begin to affect the number of excellent athletes available.

Beyond its numerical force, this crowd has a further influence. In his book *Sociology of Sport*, Berkeley Sociologist Harry Edwards wrote: "Here we have a category of people who have seldom, if ever, known material want, who have for the most part been insulated from the more mundane struggles of day-to-day existence, and many of whom have come to view the sphere of organized sport as crass, vulgar and oppressive. . . . If these definitions of the significance and character of sport persist among members of the youth culture into their adult years, sport as we know it today is likely to decline for want of attention and interest."

David N. Campbell, associate professor of education at the University of Pittsburgh, sees another, more specific shift in that generation's view of sport: "They

were a revolutionary generation who rejected competition. They had endured it to a degree that the rest of us never knew. They were ranked, graded and sorted in every effort they undertook. There were too many people for every possibility, every activity, every job, every class. That put most people into a losing status and now we have a society with a majority of losers. And as for competition, I don't think it's ever going to come back as strong as it used to be. These kids have just had too much of it. There's a myth in this country that's propagated by Ford and Nixon that America was made great by competition. If you read American history, you'll find that pioneers were not competitive people, they were a cooperative people. They wouldn't have survived otherwise, so competition is no more an intrinsic part of the American Way than these new generations see it—and they've rejected it."

Competition or non-competition, the future of American sport probably best fits into two broad scenarios: Technosport, that sport which is the product of machines and technicians, and Ecosport, that sport which springs from the natural relationship between man and his environment. They are opposites, yet they are in no way mutually exclusive for, as a number of tomorrow-experts have said, a dominant characteristic of our future will probably be "pluralism," that which allows nearly everything to exist with nearly everything else.

A Technosport scenario will bring a deluge of complexities. Dr. Edward Lawless of the Midwest Research Institute, a Kansas City think tank, says, "Technological developments are likely to get piled upon one another, which will decrease the role of the human being. There will be more 'technological fixes'; urine tests for athletes will be mandatory because drug stimulants will be so common. Football players will be so padded they will begin to look like grotesque robots."

There is talk today, still theoretical, of "genetic engineering," a kind of technological biology in which men can be specifically designed *before* birth to become nine-foot basketball centers with the hands of concert pianists or 375-pound, eight-foot running backs who do the 100 in eight flat. This kind of *Brave New World* concept fits the Technosport scenario, for fans of these games will be spectators supreme—pathological watchers who worship the specialist, adore the elite athlete.

Although jock-breeding might be desirable to Technosport fanatics, it seems unlikely it will be more than a theory by the year 2000. Says Dr. Laurence E. Karp, an obstetrician who does research in reproductive genetics at the University of Washington School of Medicine, "Breeding super athletes may be possible, but there is really no guarantee that mating an athletically inclined male with a similarly inclined female will produce an athletic offspring. Once the fertilization process begins, the genetic roulette wheel is spun. The two strong mates could produce a Milquetoast."

However, perhaps massive genetic engineering—nature's way—has already begun to give us supermen.

Dr. Robert Hamilton, a Chicago orthopedic surgeon who works with several high school teams, says, "We will see 360-pound, 7 1/2-foot tackles in football in 15 years. Take a high school roster 15 years ago, examine the heights and weights and you will find a 15% to 20% increase today—in some cases 50%."

Laurence E. Morehouse of the Department of Kinesiology at UCLA agrees. "There is no limit at the present time to the size people we will produce," he says. "Men eight feet tall, weighing 350 pounds, are possible in the future. The reasons are not genetic engineering, but random mating in an increasing population to bring together diversified genes, plus better nutrition and the absence of childhood diseases." Everyone agrees that one mandatory change in both football and basketball of the future will be larger playing areas to contain tomorrow's giants.

Technosport stadiums will be grand monuments—domed, air-conditioned, artificially turfed—vast Sybaritic arenas equipped with everything from push-button vending machines at each seat to individual TV replays that can be punched up at will. Architect Charles Luckman, whose firm designed the new Madison Square Garden, the L.A. Forum and the still incomplete Honolulu Multi-Sport Movable Stadium (which will have mobile sections on air cushions to change the stadium from a baseball to a football arena), predicts the day is not far off when people will be led to their seats by the sound of ocean waves, of wind, of singing birds, of gurgling brooks, a lovely addition to the cold artificial environs of a typical Technosport stadium.

Computers will be important in Technosport, and every dugout, every sideline bench will have one to pop out sheets of probability tables to help call each play, each pitch, each infield shift. Moreover, spectators will be able to punch up computerized odds and bet against management on every kind of trivial possibility.

Technosport spectators will also feel closer to the game. They will be able to listen in to press-box scouts giving advice to the bench, to miked-and-wired conversations at the pitching mound, to quarterback's calls in the huddle, to halftime pep talks.

Lee Walburn of Atlanta's Omni group has a wild, but possibly not too far-out, idea for bringing the fan even closer to the contest. "At least by early in the 21st century," he says, "we will have something called Feel-A-Vision—electronic sensory perceptors so the spectator who may lack the ability to take part in sport himself can experience the pain, the emotion, the physical actions of the athletes. You could go in a theater, sit down, have buttons on your seat which are hooked into a certain player—to his heartbeats, his brain waves, his pulmonary system. And you could get the transmissions from a quarterback when he throws a touchdown pass. You could feel how Ali felt when Foreman was trying to hit him on the ropes. You could even have been wired into Evel Knievel—but, for God's sake, what if he got killed? Think of the thrill you'd get."

Perhaps a more probable addition to Technosport spectating is something that might be called Democracy Football. It is a Monday night in November, 1999, and the Houston Oilers are about to play the Chicago Bears. In this scenario there are 556,191 homes in Houston with television sets, each equipped with a console containing rows of multicolored buttons. Each viewer has a playbook for the Oiler offense, a playbook for the defense. In Chicago there are 817,911 TV homes, each identically equipped, except, of course, the viewers have Bear playbooks. Now the official flips the coin. Heads for Houston. The Houston viewers vote by pushing a button—529,876 to receive, one (idiot!) to kick off. The vote is instantly counted, computerized, flashed into the helmets of the Houston team. The Democracy Football game is under way. A Houston back returns the kickoff to his 38-yard line. All over Houston viewers consult their playbooks (they have one minute) and then they press a combination of buttons to call a play. Instantaneously, the computer totals the Oiler fan-coaches' votes: 307,278 vote for a zig-out pass into the left flat to the tight end; 121,908 for an off-tackle slant to the right with the fullback carrying; 100,689 for a sweep to the right; one man votes for a quick kick (same idiot). Meanwhile, all of Chicago is voting on which defense to use and the plurality—315,924—pushes buttons calling for a four-three-four.

The wishes of the Oiler TV fans are relayed to the Houston quarterback's helmet. He cannot disobey, of course. He calls the pass to the flat. The Oilers move to the line of scrimmage. The Bears go into the defensive formation their fans have called. The Oilers try the prescribed pass to the left flat. It is knocked to the ground by a Bear linebacker. Houston moans, Chicago cheers. It is second and 10. The viewers vote. And so it goes. Houston plays Chicago, *literally* citizen against citizen. Thus would Technosport produce a technological miracle of something which might hitherto have been thought a contradiction in terms: Spectator-Participation.

Now Ecosport. Here we have the other extreme, for technology and artificiality are abhorred, disdained. Ecosport consists of natural play, unstructured, free-blown. Its games are open, flowing, perhaps without boundaries, often without rules, usually without scoreboards, sometimes without end or middle or measurable victory. Everyone participates and the overriding slogan might well be, "If a sport is worth playing, it is worth playing badly."

Many think there will be a massive new enthusiasm for natural sport. Michael Novak, author and philosopher, says, "A convulsion is coming, an attempt to throw off the corporation and professionalization—to shake off the cold hand of the 20th century—and return sports to their primitive vigor." The chairman of the Human Development program at the University of Chicago with the incredible name of Mihaly Csikszentmihalyi, says: "We have moved from spontaneity to point ratings, from individual talent to computerized cards. There are far more statistics than heroics in sports and I think there will be a reaction against all this, a change back to naturalness."

In the era of Ecosport men may not only begin to doubt the famed Vince Lombardi motto, "Winning isn't everything, it's the only thing," they may actually swing around to Author George Leonard's proclamation that, "Winning is not only not everything, winning is not *anything*." As John McMurtry, a philosopher from Canada's University of Guelph, said during a sports symposium last year: "Actually, the pursuit of victory works to reduce the chance for excellence in the true performance of the sport. It tends to distract our attention from excellence of performance by rendering it subservient to emerging victorious. I suspect that our conventional mistake of presuming the opposite—presuming that the contest-for-prize framework and excellence of performance are somehow related as a unique cause and effect—may be the deepest-lying prejudice of civilized thought. . . . Keeping score in any game—especially team games—is a substantial indication that the activity in question is not interesting enough in itself to those who keep score."

The forms of Ecosport will be enormously varied. Soccer, which may be one of the Big Four in America within a decade, is an offspring of Ecosport, for it is flowing, natural and played by men who are built on a human scale and need no sophisticated equipment. The fine and gentle pastimes will increase, such as orienteering, hiking, non-competitive swimming.

The emphasis in Ecosport is on *un*structured play. Perhaps the ultimate event in such a scenario is something one may call the Never Never Game, since it is a sport invented on the spot for a given afternoon, something that was never, never played before and will never, never be played again. The Never Never Game eliminates all specialists, all statistics. It demands the ordinary all-round person, the average man, since one can never know what skills will be demanded in the game of the day.

The Never Never Game: It is a soft sunny afternoon

and on a meadow somewhere in the U.S. about 100 people—men, women, children—have gathered. They separate into two groups, approximately equal, and a man carries a small container filled with beads of half a dozen different colors. Under his arm he has the Never Never Game Book. This book is filled with myriad possibilities for games—one section has different kinds of balls or stones or items to be used, another section has lists of field sizes and shapes, another the rules of play for many games. Each of the different items in each section is identified with a color combination. The man in the center of the meadow reaches into the Never Never bead jar and without looking takes out a handful of beads and throws them on the ground. The colors are two reds, a yellow, four blues, a white, two greens. In the Never Never Book section on "game balls" he finds "a disk the size of a pie plate" next to this color combination. He throws more beads on the ground, finds that the combination in the "field size" section calls for a circular area 300 yards in diameter. More beads: the game will last three hours. More beads: players will hop on one leg. They will use forked sticks to carry the disk to the perimeter of the field. When one player carries the disk through the other team he may hop on either leg but when two players share in carrying the disk with their forked sticks they may both use both legs—etc., etc.

After consultation to arrange tactics and review the rules, the Never Never Game begins. After three hours it is over. The score is inconsequential, no records are kept, and no specialists are discovered or developed. Everyone has played, some better in this Never Never Game than in another. This game will never be played again. The next Never Never Game may involve flocks of butterflies as the "game ball," perhaps a net across the field with which to catch them, perhaps balloons to fend off the other team's butterflies. Who knows? Who cares? The point of Ecosport—as of all sport—is to play, to enjoy, to exist.

PHYSICAL EDUCATION AND SPORT: ALTERNATIVES FOR THE FUTURE

Hal A. Lawson

Until recently, the study of the future was not considered to be a worthy topic for serious scholarly endeavor. Forces which impeded sophisticated forms of investigation in this area included the traditional, manifestly Western brand of millenarian Christian determinism and also what were deemed frivolous fantasies regarding the future as they were embodied in science fiction novels. On the other hand, the increasingly popular view that man may possess the potential to become the primary architect of his own destiny and its corollary, that an awareness of the future makes possible

a voluntary choice among foreseeable alternatives that can be depicted from the standpoint of the here and now, have been instrumental in promoting attempts to explore

Hal Lawson, "Physical Education and Sport: Alternatives for the Future, *Quest*, Monograph XXI, January 1974, pp. 19-29.

About the Author

Hal A. Lawson is Assistant Professor in Physical Education, the University of Washington. His primary interest is in the professional studies program in physical education.

the future. These belief systems in concert with what many believe to be impending ecological disaster have made the study of the future not only desirable but necessary.

The purpose of this paper is to explore future alternatives for physical education and sport, the one negative or pessimistic, the other positive or optimistic. Procedurally, the frameworks presented in Polak's *The Image of the Future* and in Kahn and Weiner's *The Year 2000: A Framework For Speculation on the Next Thirty-Three Years* will be employed both as explanatory and organizational mechanisms. Polak (1973) has noted that any study of the future must begin with a critique of the present, a process that will be accomplished with particular attention to physical education and sport as they are embedded in the sociocultural milieu. Such a critique effects what Marcuse (1964) has labeled the "estrangement effect" whereby a dispassionate, analytical view of the present may be accomplished. At the same time, such an analysis affords the basis for the identification of current trends in the phenomena under inspection to afford logical extrapolations to the future.

In a critique of physical education and sport, it is the resultant awareness that all is not perfect in comparison to stated goals that constitutes an additional stimulus for venturing beyond the present. The "push-pull" dynamic between the present as it has been influenced by the past and projections for the future prompts creative endeavor in the search for alternatives. The "split man" lifts one leg forward while the other drags back; this dividedness compels a struggle for resolution. Polak's (1973) explanation of this phenomenon is consistent with psychological dissonance theory.

> The image of the future lives in and on such a mental dividedness. It is these tortured split souls, tossed about by the currents of the age, seeking, liberating, binding, self-propelled and yet driven, who create the images. Split inwardly, it is they who generate the strength to split the outward world of space and time. Because of their own profound experience of the ambiguity and double meaning of life and their awareness of the split between this and the Other, they are uniquely equipped to create an image of the Other, to mirror the realm of the future [p. 86].

A Critique of the Present

James (1969) has noted the threefold cultural shift that has taken place during the course of the century in American society. These changes include an artistic change from value culture to pop culture, a psychological change in cultural orientation from elevation to escape, and a philosophical shift from concern with end products to a preoccupation with the means. Alterations in the sport and physical education programs have corresponded to these larger transitions in cultural orientations. The factors which were influential in these changes were essentially twofold.

Veblen (1912) observed in American society a process of class emulation in which lower socio-economic groups valued and hence aspired to adopt facets of the life style of what he labeled the leisure class. Consequently, when the technology of industrialization made leisure a time concept in lieu of a class concept, the formerly exclusive movement forms such as tennis and golf became increasingly accessible to people in lower social classes. Understanding, however, did not accompany this process of emulation. James demonstrated the extent to which the kind and style of participation in these activities changed as they became increasingly popular. The code of ethics which centered upon the ultimate purposes (ends) of these forms and which at the same time assured their elevation or social distance was sacrificed.

Secondly, the Protestant ethic, traditionally an obstacle to leisure, play, and bodily pleasures contributed to lower-class difficulties in adjusting to widespread leisure. Whereas the leisure class was accustomed to such pursuits and maintained a life style which included ludic forms within the context of reality, the work ethic was so heavily ingrained in the behavior of the larger fabric of society that it rendered all "unproductive" forms of human endeavor escapist. James (1969) stated that this flight from the perils of an ordinary life characterized by work to ludic forms portending security and joy presented the classical example of man's fragmentation, and if James' viewpoint might be extended, illustrates Marxian alienation as well.

These patterns persist into the present. Maheu (1962) delineates sociological, ethical, and aesthetic reasons for the exclusion of popular sport from value culture, reasons which are on the whole congruent with the explanation provided above. The ultimate irony of course concerns the alienation of the patrons of value culture from sport as it was vulgarized, this in spite of the fact that at one time the luxury of leisure kept many of these ludic forms within the sole purview of upper-class patrons. Sport, then, in its current form conforms to the notion of pop culture, available to all, yet excluded by those few people who continue to patronize value culture.

A number of writers have addressed themselves to the topic of sport as a social institution (Loy, 1968; Loy and Ingham, 1973). In the context of Social Darwinian thought which rationalizes the Protestant ethic, capitalism, and supposedly laissez-faire governmental action and inaction, physical education and sport in their contemporary institutionalized form become ultimately debased from their original essence of play. Leonard (1973) delineated the *conformity* which is the derivative of institutionalized and excessive forms of competition in lieu of the purported "rugged individualism." Competition is not inherently evil in physical education and sport; rather, its over-emphasis becomes suspect.

> There is nothing wrong with competition in its proper proportion. Like a little salt, it adds zest to the game and to life itself. But when the seasoning is mistaken for the substance, only sickness can follow. Similarly, when winning becomes the only thing, it can lead only to eventual emptiness and anomie [p. 47].

Instrinsic satisfactions, such as the search for identity through positive stress-seeking, are replaced by the rationale orientation of production technology, complete with industrial-like quality controls. Man the subject becomes man the object for physical fitness, nationalism, and conformity. Programs of physical education and sport become exclusionary by design, exemplified in Williams's classical pyramid with physical education at the base and athletics for the gifted few at the apex. All the while the supportive ideology contributes grandiose claims for athletics, while never posing basic questions about the ends of these programs. For example, if it can be documented that athletics produces some desirable outcomes, why should they be limited to a select few?

In an institutional network preoccupied with the *means* of production, however, questions such as this one not only go unanswered, they are rarely posed. Programs designed to prepare professionals working in such programs are the targets of undergraduate professional preparation. At least one writer (Morford, 1972) has underscored the importance of the body of knowledge emanating from the study of the various aspects of man's participation in ludic activities for the professional, emphasizing that the subject matter field is always the basis for professional authentication. Yet, the theoretical underpinnings of the practitioner which can be derived from an academic subject field are relegated to secondary or tertiary roles in Performance-Based Teacher Education (Houston, 1972) and similar programs. Likewise subordinate are the necessary understandings of man's quest for play, a form of knowledge which might spearhead an attack on the institutionalized forms of physical education and sport which undermine play's essence. Instead, the machine continues to produce carbon copies for the status quo in spite of its functional inadequacies, and its products perpetuate the obvious dissonances with the philanthropic goals of physical education and sport programs.

Albeit macro-sociologists and cultural anthropologists describe the functions of physical education and sport in American society in benign terms such as pattern maintenance, tensions management, and integration, these and other descriptions are reducible to the process of social control. In sport and physical education, the Hobbesian dilemma between the freedom of the individual and the sanctity of the state is resolved in favor of the latter. Man, already alienated from his work in many instances, likewise becomes alienated from his play. Survival is for the fittest, and so are the rewards (grades) in physical education as well as exclusive privileges and opportunities in sports programs.

The rhetoric which rationalizes the entire production, largely undocumented empirically, conforms to what Polak (1973) labels a social myth. These myths about physical education and sport have become absolute and sacred as a function of institutionalization. Edwards (1972), has noted that sport has all the characteristics of a thriving religion, including gods (superstar athletes), saints (high-status sports figures who have passed to the great beyond), scribes (sports writers and sports-casters whose object is to spread the word about deeds, glories, and miracles), houses of worship (exclusive stadia and halls of fame), and throngs of true believers who bestow unquestioned adulation and worship in mystical fashion. Those who pose a threat to the athletic establishment are dealt with accordingly, as reported by Scott (1972) in *The Athletic Revolution*. Thus, sport's institutionalization has produced an ideology of class dominance and control in which sport becomes an opiate for the masses.

> What we mean by an "opiate" is anything that tends to frustrate the solution of social problems by providing individuals with either (1) a temporary high (or as Bill Bradley put it, a "fix") which takes their minds off the problem for a while but does nothing to deal with it; or (2) a distorted frame of reference or identification which encourages them to look for salvation through patently false channels [Hoch, 1972, p. 20].

The above critique of the present status of physical education and sport serves as a basis for futuristic projections. Borrowing from Polak's (1973) categorizations, it becomes possible to speak of these forms in the contexts of influence pessimism and influence optimism.

Influence Pessimism: A Negative Alternative for the Future

Influence pessimism directly links man's actions or inactions to a precarious future. Whereas deterministic thought relegates man to the inevitable course of events in a world in which chaos overrules cosmos (Polak, 1973), this genus of pessimism treats man as culpable for the precarious or negative future which he will confront. Mesthene (1970) discusses technology, man's creation, in this light. Similarly, the M.I.T.-coordinated study, *The Limits to Growth*, depicts overpopulation and the increasing demands of the parent technology as primary factors in a shortened future: man is held responsible. Contrariwise, Betts' (1953) paper links the initial rise of sport to the technological revolution, depicting a potentially positive by-product of technology. Thus, the question might well be whether technology per se is inherently noxious, or if man's utilization of technology is open to criticism. In either instance, the course for the future in the framework of influence pessimism is identical.

In exploring the consequences of the pattern of decreased work and increased leisure via technology, Kahn and Weiner (1967) identify the need for additional systems of social control to preclude the possibility of chaos. Physical education and sport offer likely avenues for continued organizational controls of human behavior. In citing the insidious potential of athletic aids produced by technology, Kahn and Weiner present a negative by-product of participation in sport.

> If athletes begin to make use of prosthetic devices as well as drugs to improve their performance, we may gradually produce almost entirely artificial athletes, for whom bionic robots might eventually substitute. By the end of this

general process man's confidence in himself and his role in the world may be seriously undercut [p. 350-351].

The pervasiveness of control via technology is already visible in sport. Although the Orwellian norm has not yet been reached, the reversibility of the adverse effects of technology and its offspring control systems declines as a function of time. Schecter (1969) addresses himself to the propagandistic functions of the mass media in sport; the media in effect serve the entrees that are most palatable to the producers (entrepreneurs), not the consumer. Freedom of the press in this light becomes a delectable, yet meaningless aphorism as journalists in order to survive serve the vested interests of company men. Similarly, Hoch (1972) identifies a symbiotic relationship between sport and the mass media as an integral facet of their dual functions in the larger society.

> A symbiosis between sports and the news media was quickly established in which sports became *the* decisive promotional device for selling popular newspapers, and newspapers were *the* decisive promotional device for selling sports spectacles. (This symbiotic relationship between sports and the media, now including radio and television, is a central feature of the political economy of both sports and the media to this day.) [p. 36]

In clairvoyantly depicting the technical innovations most likely to gain utility during the last third of the twentieth century, Kahn and Weiner include the following: (1) new techniques for the surveillance, monitoring, and control of individuals and organizations, (2) new and more reliable "educational" and propaganda techniques for affecting human behavior, public and private, (3) design and extensive use of super-controlled environments, (4) new techniques and institutions for the education of children. When applied to physical education, sport, and other aspects of society, the possibilities for mass control systems in the future become alarming. The groundwork, already laid in sport, is also apparent in education and more recently in physical education.

Rushall and Siedentop (1972), for example, present oversimplified techniques for Skinnerian behavior modification in physical education and sport. Their bias, reflected in the title of their work, is to develop and *control* individuals in authoritarian, chauvinistic fashion. Not bothering to question the end products of their procedures like so many of their peers, they present the *means* for effective behavioral change, a continuation of education for the status quo, perpetuating the cultural lag. Indeed, Ulich (1964) and others have repeatedly underscored the need for the abolition of control techniques such as the ones described by these behaviorists. Enigmatically, Rushall and Siedentop continue to preach for the utilization of Skinnerian control technologies designed to insure the occurrence of simple paired responses, at a time, as Toffler (1970) notes, when a variegated battery of possible alternative responses is necessitated by our complex culture.

Ultimately, stagnation results from such effective control technologies. Albeit the potential for change remains possible structurally, the values and alternative ways of thinking necessary to initiate change are extinguished. Already Sarason (1972) in using the phrase "the more things change, the more they remain the same" sees man as a prisoner of his own socialization processes.

> . . . the social context from which a new setting emerges as well as the thinking of those who create new settings, reflects what seems "natural" in society. And what seems natural is almost always a function of the culture to a degree that usually renders us incapable of recognizing wherein we are prisoners of our culture. Those who create new settings always want to do something new, usually unaware that they are armed with and will be subsequently disarmed by, categories of thought which helped to produce the conditions the new setting hopes to remedy [p. 12, 13].

Polak's (1973) central thesis blends nicely with Sarason's observation; according to the former, the "push-pull" dynamic identified earlier has been severely crippled. In agreement with the James (1969) thesis, he sees man as preoccupied with the present and the means, a consequence of what Marcuse (1964) has deemed "institutional desublimation." The subsequent dearth of images of the future thus precedes the fall of cultures. Man falls prey to his own institutions as external conditions render life on earth more finite than heretofore imagined. This is the alternative provided by influence pessimism: a continuation of the trends identified earlier in the critique of the present status of physical education and ludic forms, exacerbated by man-made systems which control the creator to the point of increasing dehumanization and ultimate destruction.

Influence Optimism: A Positive Future Alternative

Classical Hellas provides the best example of influence optimism (Polak, 1973) with what Jaeger (1965) and others have called the *Paideia-creating man*. As Polak observed:

> The last stage in the evolution of Greek culture represents a coming of age in the discovery of highest human values, which in turn represent the Greek images of the future. They point to a coming *paideia*, the vision of the glorious civilization created by human effort [emphasis mine] [p. 33].

Hence influence optimism, which can be traced to Plato, could be extended from individual determination of one's own destiny to collective determination of mankind's destiny, all by the conscious deliberate actions of rational human beings. All elements of culture, including physical education and sport, are both educative and responsive to alteration by humans, signifying a dynamic process of interaction that moves toward perfection. In the context of influence optimism, the problems which confront social planners in the present, including those in physical education and sport, are capable of solution by mankind.

If man's inept utilization of technology is accepted as a major contributor to a negative alternative for the future, this same variable can be viewed conversely under the microscope of influence optimism. This latter view contends that man can harness his creations, in this instance using technology prudently and efficaciously. In lieu of being inherently negative, technology becomes vehicular for man's realization of a culture in which he is freed from the burdens of production, thereby allowing him to pursue a life in which leisure and eudaemonism are the most evident features.

Mesthene (1970) has stated that technology must be viewed in relation to the social setting in which it is introduced, for the setting will be instrumental in determining whether, to what extent, in what ways and ultimately how the innovation is utilized. Citing recent attempts at introducing the educational technology in the schools as exemplary, he noted that schools are apparently "ideally designed to resist change." The massive potential import of learning technology for physical education has been identified by a host of writers. Yet, the paucity of its utilization at the present time in physical education as well as in other subject matter areas lends credence to Mesthene's contentions.

> The study concludes that neither educational technology of the school establishment is ready to consummate the revolution in learning that will bring individualistic instruction to every child, systematic planning and uniform standards to 25,000 separate school districts and an answer to bad teachers and unmovable bureaucracies, and the implementation of national policy to educate every American to his full potential for a useful and satisfying life [p. 22].

Mesthene has therefore identified the central barrier to the implementation of widespread technological change. Anachronistic human values underlying institutional sluggishness must be altered if a positive future is to be realized. Earlier in the paper, it was concluded that at present physical education and certainly sport are conducted in ways that are congruent with and at the same time act to reinforce the ideology of an emerging capitalistic, industrial nation. In actuality, however, the economy of this country shifted in favor of a service orientation some sixteen years ago. Blatant discrepancies such as this one must be corrected if the optimistic aspirations for man's future are to be brought to fruition.

Attempts to modify the existing institutional forms such as physical education and sport have been greeted with extensive criticism. Spokesmen for the "counterculture" for youth (e.g., Roszak, 1969) have offered positions that have been deemed "pretheoretical" (Berger *et al.,* 1973), a criticism that can be extended to the "radical ethic" in sport (Scott, 1973). Yet, Scott remains the major spokesman for alternative models for sport, models that are directed toward a value system which contrasts sharply with the dominating counterpart

as it currently exists in physical education and sport. Such alternative proposals have gained national visibility with their freshness and concurrently have earned their originator and his few counterparts more than a modicum of professional notoriety.

It is impossible to ignore, however, the similarity of the ingredients in Scott's brand of "athletics for athletes" and those contained in alternative models for education which could drastically affect the conduct of school physical education programs. Characterized by what Parker and Rubin (1962) have labeled the "process orientation," the emphasis is placed upon democratic models of governance, explicitly recognizing the rights and privileges of individuals to make decisions about matters that will influence them, be it the selection of a coach or the advisability of pursuing certain subject matter. The process of participation is self-reinforcing; the search for gratification is continuous. Heightened awareness of individual goals likewise brings an emphasis upon intrinsic or qualitative variables in lieu of the overemphasis upon the outputs of production. Signalling the coming of a new era, such alternatives have students and athletes in the vanguard for change, consistent with influence optimism. Even in the case of professional football, the case has been made for an alternative model reflecting a more equitable and humane form of conduct in which athletes gain greater control over their participation (Parrish, 1971).

These nascent forms carry the promise of the return to the paideia-creating man of the future. Kahn and Weiner (1967) in identifying this alternative describe the resultant culture as "individualistic and sensate." The post-mass consumption society becomes characterized by novel ingredients, among them the following: (1) most economic activities are service-oriented, (2) there are effective floors on income and welfare, (3) efficiency is no longer a primary concern, (4) widespread cybernation exists, (5) work-oriented, achievement-oriented, and national interest values become eroded, (6) leisure is viewed as a blessing instead of a vice, (7) secular, humanist, self-indulgent criteria become paramount, (8) a learning society evolves (Kahn and Weiner, 1967).

This future society, made possible by man's effective utilization of technology and his successful alterations of present institutional inadequacies, brings its own maintenance problems. The first of these is constituted by a new form of alienation. For the masses, meaning in life in the society of mass-consumption was derived from work and its by-products, this in spite of increasing amounts of leisure time. Man must seek other realms of meaning in the post-consumption society. The quest for identity through vicarious realms of human endeavor becomes paramount, and physical education and sport, wisely conducted in accordance with this objective, become a primary avenue for the attainment of the highest in human self-realization. Such outcomes have been deemed integral facets of participation in such activities (Slusher, 1967; Morford, 1970; Harper, 1973), albeit advocates of this position have lamented that the modes of conduct for these activities at present interfere with and frequently negate the knowing of self.

Kahn and Weiner (1967), cognizant of the role of all ludic forms in a leisured society, explain the quest for meaningful realms of activity.

> One could imagine, for example, a very serious emphasis upon sports, on competitive partner games (chess, bridge), on music, art, languages, or serious travel, or on the study of science, philosophy, and so on. The crucial point here is that a large majority of the population may feel it important to develop skills, activities, arts, and knowledges to meet very high minimum absolute standards, and a large minority more or less compete to be an elite of elites . . . there are likely to be at least subtle pressures for self-development [p. 217].

The above quotation introduces social stratification ("elite of elites") as a second maintenance problem. Polak (1973) has said that the problem of human equality must be solved to allow the establishment of the ideal society. What have been labeled Utopian thought, Utopian socialism, and socialism proper are all directed toward the realization of human equality. Even in the supercontrolled environments possible in the future, however, the evidence at present is ample to question the extent to which genetic variability in I.Q. alone (Eysenck, 1973; Jencks, 1972) can be counterbalanced without genetic engineering. Consequently, variegated patterns of behavior can be expected to persist. Moreover, Kahn and Weiner (1967) reveal that people who behave in novel or different modes will simply look down on those who do not. Such is the dynamic by which social strata are formed; the adoption and repetition of unique behaviors are utilized to signal social distance. The mere presence of ludic forms, on the other hand, can insulate the society from internal isolationism in the extreme. All play forms require the individual, regardless of external social standing, to subjugate himself to the logic of the form, i.e., its rules, as Duncan (1970) has observed:

> In any play-form of sociation there will be differences of skill, energy, or will. Some will play harder than others, some will have positions which the rules themselves make more important than others. But this is not the same as differences in wealth, fame, social position, or education, which have been established by factors extrinsic to the rules and which must be subordinated to the rules if the game is to continue; whatever remains purely personal, or reflects moods or depression, despondency, or exhilaration, mitigates against play [p. 330].

Forms of play, by their essence, can provide a formalized avenue for genuine sociation in any society in which they exist.

Ironically enough, the establishment of elites coupled with the search for new forms of meaning in life, i.e., questioning the *ends*, promises to reverse the threefold cultural shift identified by James (1969). Service-oriented activity is pursued for the experience which can be derived from catering to the needs of others; the term "work" is given new meaning, no longer dichotomous with play. The individualistic, sensate culture reflects a cyclical view of history that is unpalatable to the majority of historians. While the return to elevation, the concern for ends, and the eventual re-establishment of value culture can be granted, the remainder of the leisure society as a function of technology differs markedly from earlier societies containing the same three elements. The essential question, however, remains whether sport will return to what some experts consider to be its nobler essence, predicated upon the individualistic quest of personal excellence and perfection (*Arete*) via the *agon* (struggle), or whether they would be utilized by man to achieve collectively designated social ends.

The question is further illuminated in the discussion of a third cultural maintenance problem, namely how to preclude the possibility of excessive fragmentation in a society directed toward individualism. Riesman's (1961) other-directed man has been altered; a society of people pursuing discrete paths is threatened by chaos. Education, including physical education, and of course sport, retain the potential for social control, but will this function continue in a novel culture?

Commenting on the role of education and implicitly physical education, Illich (1971) presents elaborate alternative mechanisms for learning in the "deschooled" society. Utilizing computer technology and local referral agencies, Illich obliterates out-dated distinctions among education, physical education, recreation, adult education, etc. Educational networks which provide people with essential goods and services necessary to function in the learning society help to provide the structure needed to maintain order. The alternative mechanisms of skill exchanges, peer matching, the accessibility of educational objects, and reference services provided by educators-at-large provide the basis for a "convivial" in lieu of "manipulative" institution, which stabilizes society while not unduly encroaching upon the rights and privileges of individuals. Thus, all elements in the culture are utilized for their educative potential, and unnecessary duplications of efforts are eliminated.

Sport by its very nature would seemingly continue to provide a measure of the necessary symmetry between individual and collective concerns, for numerous team sports require cooperative effort. More importantly, the rule structures and the amount and style of participation appear to be largely a function of cultural influences. Sport tends to be especially vulnerable to a tradeoff, becoming a mechanism to produce a healthy cosmos in which individual freedoms can be practiced. Ingham and Loy (1973) have addressed themselves to this facet of sport in the socio-cultural milieu in some detail. Cognizant of the various levels at which sport may operate simultaneously, it is possible to foresee the continuance of habitualization and legitimation while allowing the realization of humanistic objectives as by-products of the deliberate social planning identified by one author (Bell, 1973).

Industrial society is the coordination of machines and men for the production of goods. Post-industrial society is organized around knowledge, for the purpose of social control and the directing of innovation and change; and this in turn gives rise to new social relationships and new structures which have to be managed politically.

This commitment to social control introduces the need for planning and forecasting into society [p. 105].

Large numbers of professionals will be required for physical education and participatory sport. In *The New Professionals* Postman (1971) characterizes professional educators as those who can take a variety of roles and who, at the same time, utilize the educative potential of both peers and varied environments. In the case of those professionals involved with physical education and sport, the demands are considerably greater than those of the present. With reference to this future society, the need exists for skilled performers who understand the hows, whys, and wherefores of both human behavior in a socio-cultural context and the idiosyncratic behaviors mani-fested in the forms under their management. Comment-ing upon the import of theoretical knowledge in all professions, Bell (1973) reveals:

. . . the advances in a field become increasingly dependent on the primacy of theoretical work, which codifies what is known and points the way to empirical confirmation. In effect, theoretical knowledge increasingly becomes the strategic resource of a society [p. 107].

Bell continues by asserting that those institutions in which theoretical knowledge is codified and enriched therefore become "the axial structures of the emergent society."

The gratification derived from effective interpersonal relations, as stated before, remains a primary motive for such professional activity. Quite obviously, then, the cur-rent practice of preparing professionals would have to be modified to avoid the shortage of qualified personnel Sarason (1971) attributes to "the myth of unending resources." At the same time, knowledge gleaned from the study of man's participation in physical and ludic ac-tivities will be pivotal in determining professional effec-tiveness.

In the context of influence optimism, such obstacles are temporal barriers to man. The society characterized by mass leisure and affluence is within man's grasp, awaiting only the necessary effort. Physical education and ludic forms in the context of cultural eudaemonism may thrive as never before, reaching a higher ethical plane. Certainly prognosticators are still deemed idealistic, and changes such as these may appear to be remote and distant. Yet, in Polak's words, "the imag-ined tomorrow is today's idea." The alternatives for the future are already visible.

REFERENCES

1. Bell, D. Five dimensions of post-industrial society. *Social Policy*, 1973, 4(1), 103-111.

2. Berger, P.L. *et al*. Demodernizing consciousness. *Social Policy*, 1973, 3(6), 3-10.

3. Betts, J.R. The technological revolution and the rise of sport, 1850-1900. *The Mississippi Valley Historical Review*, 1953, 40, 231-256.

4. Duncan, H.D. *Communication and social order*. New York: Ox-ford University Press, 1970.

5. Edwards, H. Desegregating sexist sport. *Intellectual Digest*, November 1972, 82-83.

6. Eysenck, H.J. IQ, social class, and educational policy. *Change*, 1973, 5(7), 38-42.

7. Freire, P. *Pedagogy of the oppressed*. New York: Seabury, 1973.

8. Harper, W. Movement and measurement: the case of the in-compatible marriage. *Quest*, 1973, 20, 92-98.

9. Hoch, P. *Rip-off the big game*. Garden City: Anchor, 1972.

10. Illich, I. *Deschooling society*. New York: Harper & Row, 1971.

11. Jaeger, W. *Paideia*. New York: Oxford University Press, 1965.

12. James, D. An investigation of values held for the play element in sport: in 19th century England and 20th century America. Un-published master's thesis, California State College at Hayward, 1969.

13. Jencks, C. *et al*. *Inequality: a reassessment of the effect of family and schooling in America*. New York: Basic Books, 1972.

14. Kahn, H. and Weiner, A. *The year 2000: a framework for specula-tion on the next twenty-three years*. New York: Macmillan, 1967.

15. Ingham, A. and Loy, J.W. The social system of sport: a humanistic perspective. *Quest*, 1973, 19, 3-23.

16. Loy, J.W. The nature of sport: a definitional effort. *Quest*, 1968, 10, 1-15.

17. Loy, J.W. and Ingham, A. Play, games, and sport in the socio-psychological development of children and youth. In G.L. Rarick (ed.), *Physical activity: human growth and development*. New York: Academic Press, 1973.

18. Leonard, G.B. Winning isn't everything its nothing. *Intellectual Digest*, 1973, 4(2), 45-47.

19. Maheu, R. Sport and culture. *International Journal of Adult and Youth Education*, 1962, 14, 169-178.

20. Marcuse, H. *One-dimensional man*. Boston: Beacon Press, 1964.

21. Meadows, D.H. *et al*. *The limits to growth*. New York: Signet, 1972.

22. Mesthene, E.G. *Technological change: its impact on man and society*. Cambridge: Harvard University Press, 1970.

23. Morford, W.R. Physical education and the betrayal of sport. Paper presented at the Southern Association for Physical Educa-tion of College Women, Biloxi, October 1971.

24. ———. Toward a profession, not a craft. *Quest*, 1971, 18, 88-93.

25. Parker, J.C. and Rubin, L.J. *Process as content: curriculum design and the application of knowledge*. New York: Rand McNally, 1966.

26. Parrish, B. *They call it a game*. New York: Signet, 1971.

27. Polak, F. *The image of the future*. (Translated by E. Boulding) San Francisco: Jossey-Bass/Elsevier, 1973.

28. Postman, N.S. *The new teacher*. In R. Gross & P. Osterman (eds.), *The new professionals*. New York: Simon and Schuster, 1971.

29. Riesman, D. *et al*. *The lonely crowd*. New Haven: Yale University Press, 1961.

30. Roszak, T. *The making of a counter culture*. Garden City: Anchor, 1969.

31. Rushall, B. and Siedentop, D. *The development and control of behavior in sport and physical education*. Philadelphia: Lea and Febiger, 1972.

32. Sarason, S.B. *The creation of settings and the future societies*. San Francisco: Jossey-Bass, 1972.

33. Schecter, L. *The jocks*. New York: Warner, 1972.

34. Scott, J. *Athletics for athletes*. Oakland: Other Ways Books, 1969.

35. ———. Sport and the radical ethic. *Quest*, 1973, 19, 71-76.

36. ———. *The athletic revolution*. New York: The Free Press, 1971.

37. Slusher, H.S. *Man, sport, and existence: a critical analysis*. Philadelphia: Lea and Febiger, 1967.

38. Tannenbaum, A. *Social psychology of the work organization*. Belmont: Wadsworth, 1966.
39. Toffler, A. *Future shock*. New York: Bantam, 1970.
40. Ulich, R. (ed.) *Education and the idea of mankind*. New York: Harcourt, Brace, and World, 1964.
41. Veblen, T. *The theory of the leisure class*. New York: Macmillan, 1912.

DISCUSSION QUESTIONS

A. *Harry Edwards*

1. In what ways has the nature of athletic dissent in the United States changed over the last 40 years?

2. List and briefly discuss some of the developmental trends and value shifts that have taken place over the past 25 years which are calling for an adjustment and alteration in our basic institutional processes, institutional foundations, and structural relationships?

3. In what ways are the values vested by societal tradition in the sport institution in conflict with the value emphases of the younger generation?

4. How does the stability and continuity which characterizes the sport institution help prepare the way for its eventual *destruction*? More broadly speaking, in what way are *all* social institutions vulnerable to the affects of value change?

5. Why do white, middle class youth have such an important role to play in deciding the future of sport in the United States?

6. According to Edwards, in the last analysis, what will be the ultimate factor which determines the future of American sport?

B. *George B. Leonard*

1. Why is Leonard so critical of America's traditional games?

2. Do you think we are approaching the moment that Leonard speaks of when the American culture, because of fundamental social changes, will no longer be interested in maintaining and sustaining our traditional games?

3. In what ways is the game *Slaughter* similar to, and, different from, traditional games?

4. What major obstacles stand in the way of such games as New Frisbee, Infinity Volleyball, and Yogi Tag before they can gain large followings and become popular game forms in the American culture?

5. Do you think that you would enjoy playing one of the New Games? Explain your answer.

C. *William O. Johnson*

1. To what socio-historical factors does Johnson attribute American sport's conversion from a rustic, family-oriented activity during the colonial days to the mass spectatorship and win-at-all-cost sport which made its first appearance in the mid-1800s?

2. What are the implications for sport if, as some futurists claim, there is going to be a shift in post-industrial society toward the "cerebral" with the "brain worker" coming to dominate the United States labor force?

3. According to some "tomorrow-experts," what does the future hold for sports gambling in the United States?

4. Describe a *Technosport* scenario as it is envisioned by some futurists.

5. According to Johnson, in what ways does *Ecosport* differ from *Technosport?*

D. *Hal A. Lawson*

1. According to Lawson, why is the study of the future worthy of serious scholarly attention?

2. What effect, if any, has American society's change from a "value culture" to a "pop culture" had on sport?

3. What effect, if any, has the philosophical shift from "a concern with end products to a preoccupation with the means" had on sport?

4. From an "influence pessimism" point of view, what does the future hold for physical education and sport?

5. In the context of "influence optimism," what does the future hold for physical education and sport?

6. What are some "maintenance problems" that American society will face even if technology is used effectively in the future and certain institutional inadequacies are corrected? What role can physical education and sport play in solving these problems?

7. Do you think "influence pessimism" or "influence optimism" is the most realistic alternative for the future of physical education and sport? Explain your answer.

8. Wherein lies the value of studying in a scientific way social change and its implications for the future of physical education and sport in the United States? In other words, why should students of sport concern themselves with anything more than understanding the *present*?

9. Personally speaking, do you believe that you will have any effect on the future of American sport? Explain your answer.